MW01617176

PRINCIPLES OF MICROECONOMICS

FOURTH EDITION

Eugene Silberberg
University of Washington

PEARSON Custom Publishing

PEARSON Prentice Hall

Cover photograph by Bev Corwin and Gene Silberberg.

Printed in the United States of America

10 9 8 7 6 5 4 3 2

ISBN 0-536-83169-6

2004160102

AK

Please visit our web site at *www.pearsoncustom.com*

PEARSON
Custom Publishing

PEARSON CUSTOM PUBLISHING
75 Arlington Street, Suite 300, Boston, MA 02116
A Pearson Education Company

To Thomas Jefferson and his friends
who devised the system of
laws and institutions from which,
hand-in-hand, our freedom
and prosperity derive.

"Good ideals are cheap.
It's easy to have good ideals.
What's difficult are
good ideas."

—Eric Hoffer, Interview with CBS NEWS
correspondent Eric Sevareid, Tuesday,
Janury 28, 1969.

Marginal Machine Works. Photo by George Stigler, ca. 1935. Courtesy of Stephen M. Stigler

Stigler, who passed away in 1992, was a distinguished professor of economics at the University of Chicago and a 1982 winner of the Nobel prize. The firm depicted in the picture was located on East Marginal Way in Seattle, Washington, where Stigler grew up. Noted for his wit, Stigler took this photo to highlight what he found an amusing play on the concept of the marginal firm.

Preface to Fourth Edition

My friend Doug Allen remarked that this text would be used mainly by people who wanted a book that complemented their teaching, rather than by instructors who see textbooks as a substitute for their teaching effort. I tend to agree with the thrust of this proposition, though all textbooks of course provide a mechanism for students to learn the material on their own if they choose. I have certainly striven to write enough in the way of explanations so that a student could do that. However, I have also written about provocative and sometimes oddball topics, such as women's liberation, sex and fertility and religion, which I hope will stimulate classroom discussion. In my own classes I try to provoke students into thinking rigorously about topics like these, because I think that economics has something to say about them, and because students are usually surprised that economists dwell on such issues. One reviewer was shocked and outraged at my use of adoption as an example of economic markets. He or she will never use this text.

This is a text for people who enjoy seeing how far they can stretch the paradigm. That takes some effort. It is much easier to talk about how the demand curve for steel changes when the price of aluminum increases, but it is also pretty boring. I'd rather be criticized for stretching the paradigm too far than for not taking any chances. So I hope you like the offbeat nature of the examples and I hope they stimulate interesting classroom discussion. Every now and then I get a class that rises to the occasion, and I remember those classes as my fondest teaching experiences.

Many propositions, like the law of demand, are easy enough to state. But it is only by working through example after example that we come to appreciate the significance of such propositions. In economics, true appreciation of the law of demand comes after we apply it to everyday problems like marriage and divorce, participation in religion, suicide, smoking, crime and punishment, diamonds and water, consumption over time, in addition to the more mundane "meat and potatoes" applications.

Examples, however, must be examined within a consistent, unifying framework. Without theory, examples are nothing but a series of unrelated or special cases. In this text, therefore, I have continually stressed the unifying propositions that underlay the analyses of the examples we discuss. Without theory, we cannot generalize from these examples and explain other events. As we analyze additional problems, we discover the subtleties that are often encountered in scientific endeavors, and we improve our skills at applying the theory.

In this text, I have not relegated the illustrations and examples to "boxes" or "sidebars." The examples are precisely the central concern of economics; they are the whole point of the theory. They are the only reason for developing a systematic framework. What purpose is there for developing the laws of demand and diminishing marginal product other than to analyze real, observable issues? The "story problems" are economics, not "illustrations" of economic theory.

We don't have the luxury, in economics, of being able to set up laboratory conditions in which to conduct some experiment; we have to wait for the world to produce conditions which allow empirical testing. However, armed with some elementary propositions, economists are able to explain a wide variety of important issues. The lingering importance of most of our Nobel Laureates' work, for example, is their creative and insightful applications of elementary ideas. It is therefore with real-world applications of a simple, consistent framework that this text is concerned.

Arrangement of the Text

I have written this text in a "straight ahead" fashion. I have striven to minimize clutter and other distractions. There are no dazzling special effects or attempts at a multimedia presentation. I have moved the Shortages and Surpluses section to chapter 5, where I always liked it best. Up through Chapter 8, the material builds on preceding chapters. Starting with Chapter 9, Transactions Costs and Property Rights, the chapters could be covered in most any order, except that Monopoly, Chapter 11, necessarily comes before Imperfect Competition, Chapter 12. When I teach this material in a ten week quarter, I cover Chapters 1 through 10, in order, though I leave out some sections. Depending on the class, I usually include some material from Chapter 13, Labor Economics, particularly the discussion of households, and some mention of misallocation due to monopoly. I dwell heavily on the common property problem discussed in chapter 7. With a simple numerical illustration, students are able to understand why common property causes excess use of resources. Moreover, I find the Knight highway problem in Chapter 9 reinforces students' understanding of the common property problem, and I always leave time for that topic. I usually spend two weeks on Chapter 10, Interest Rates and Capital Values, but that is an emphasis all may not share.

I give Comparative Advantage front row treatment, in Chapter 6, the first chapter on cost and production. I have always considered this topic to be a fundamental idea in economics, particularly, about opportunity cost and cost minimization. It is the source of rising long run marginal costs and the appearance of rents. Moreover, it is easy to present, especially when you omit the unnecessary additional step of invoking coefficients of production, and students seem to genuinely understand the idea.

My goal is that by the end of the term, students understand that explanations based on assertions about tastes are not acceptable, that they understand the diamond water paradox, comparative advantage, the difference between shortages and scarcity, diminishing marginal product and its relation to the problem of common property, and the idea that capital values incorporate all anticipated future incomes. These are easily attainable goals for a reasonably conscientious student. What's more, these tools are the fundamental building blocks of almost all important policy applications of economics.

Lastly, I again cannot exaggerate the importance of my wife Jane's love and encouragement, and her good humor about letting me make her an occasional classroom and text example.

Contents

CHAPTER 1

But Will It Work in Theory?

Do you ever wonder about how things are different for you than they were for your parents and their parents? For example, nowadays almost three quarters of young married women work outside the home, whereas a generation ago less than a quarter did so. Moreover, women are working in career type jobs their parent's generation only rarely participated in. Cohabitation outside of marriage, once about as scandalous as any activity could be, is now shrugged off by most young people. It is easy to simply explain these changes in society by making up some statement about how people are different now. In this chapter, and in this text, we apply some more systematic, or scientific theory about how human beings behave to these kinds of issues, so that we can gain a greater appreciation of their causes and consequences.

1.1 Introduction

My own introduction to the field of economics came in the seventh grade. My social studies teacher, a nice guy, asked the class which was better for a country: to import more goods than it exported, or to export more than it imported. I remember the class's reaction clearly: we agreed unanimously that it was better to import more than we exported. Importing more than we exported meant our country received more goods than it gave up. It was obvious enough, as seventh graders, that having more goods was the better idea. Well, our teacher disagreed and proceeded to convince us we were wrong. If a country imports more than it exports, we were told, it has to pay the difference with gold. A country loses gold if this policy is pursued. We certainly didn't want to lose gold, so it was better to export more than we imported. This analysis has in fact been conventional wisdom for many people throughout history. It is so ingrained that a country that imports more than it exports is said to have a "deficit" (which we all know is bad) in its international balance of payments.[1]

What are we to make of this? Economics is no more difficult a subject to master than most academic or professional subjects, yet many people go astray over the simplest propositions. Why do so many otherwise reasonable people worry about importing too much? It's like worrying about being too rich. More goods are better than less goods. If only other countries would continually send us more goods than we send in return! A country that continually sends abroad more than it receives will be poorer for it.[2]

One of the more cynical definitions of economics is "common sense made difficult." Common sense should never be difficult. However, we often need explanations to make some proposition become common sense. In fact, that is

1. If some foreigners come to this country with cash, buy our goods and take them back to their country, which effectively prevents *us* from consuming those items, this is "good," according to the national income accounts: it lowers our "deficit" in international trade, or increases our "surplus." If these same foreigners use their money to build a new automobile plant in this country, this is "bad:" it increases our deficit or lowers our surplus. Why is it that when foreigners eat our food this is a good thing, and we should encourage it, whereas when they create wealth in this country, by adding new factories, building new machinery, etc. (we say, increasing our *capital*), it's bad, and we should discourage it?

2. Some people advocate restricting imports because they compete with a product they are producing, thus perhaps lowering wages or employment opportunities and business profits. This is really just another argument to restrict consumers' choices so as to benefit the special interests of a particular industry, rather than an argument against imports per se.

the primary goal of this text: to offer explanations of various social events (i.e., having to do with people), in order that the reasons why certain things occur in the economic system may become clear. There is much we can explain with the aid of just a few elementary assumptions about the behavior of people and their relationship with their environment. By drawing on a few basic principles, we can see the forest instead of a bunch of trees.

The Economy: Prices and Markets

One of the most extraordinary aspects of our modern economy is that when we go to the supermarket to buy milk or bread, or to a hardware store for some device to repair leaky plumbing or a faulty electrical circuit, we almost always find that the store indeed has the good we desire. Moreover, the prices we are charged for these items are generally stable: they don't fluctuate wildly from day to day, or week to week. But this is truly remarkable! Think of what had to take place before any of these items actually reached the shelves. How did these suppliers come to possess these goods in the first place? What decisions did they make in anticipation of consumers' desires for these goods?

As I sit and type these words, I'm wearing pretty ordinary clothes—jeans and a shirt, and so forth. Yet I notice that my shoes were in fact made in Hungary, my shirt contains cotton grown in the United States, but it was sewn together in Singapore. My socks were manufactured in England; the jeans are an American fabric but were manufactured in the Dominican Republic. Yet all these clothes appeared in stores in Seattle, Washington, where, on various occasions, I voluntarily purchased them with money I earned teaching economics. Consumers rarely know or care about the race, sex or national origin of the producers; our concern is whether it's a good pair of jeans for the money. The prices of these items today are similar to the prices I paid some months or years in the past. At some time in the past, the material in these clothes was growing on a plant in some cotton field, or being manufactured out of petroleum in some chemical plant. Its production at that time was guided by people knowledgeable in, for example, growing cotton. Soon after, it fell to transport workers to ship the raw goods to factories where they were converted into fabrics and thread. Later, people skilled in operating industrial sewing machines applied designs created by other individuals in an office on seventh avenue in New York to create the finished goods. But these goods still had to be shipped to stores where consumers could conveniently make purchases; all this had to take place before any of us were able to buy our ordinary clothes.

This feat of coordination of effort to produce a useful end is truly astonishing. No single person directed any more than a tiny part of the production of any of these goods. Moreover, no single individual could on their own produce any of these goods. Their knowledge is confined to only a small facet of the finished good. The person sewing clothes knows nothing about growing cotton; the cotton grower similarly knows nothing about transforming the raw cotton into fabric. Each worker or manager, acting in their own interest on very narrowly defined projects such as designing or sewing create useful goods for consumers. How does it all happen? No single person gives "marching orders" for all these producers. There is no "central planner;" the decision process is highly **decentralized**. At all points along the production process, individuals decide voluntarily to engage in some specified effort in return for wages or other remuneration. Amazingly, useful finished goods appear in the stores.

In **unplanned**, market economies, these activities are based on **mutual benefits** coordinated by **prices** determined in the market. These prices are determined both by the actions of consumers, which we designate as **demand**, and by the actions of producers, which we call **supply**. At any moment in time, the prices of goods indicate the willingness of consumers to forgo other goods in order to obtain that particular good. If a consumer voluntarily purchases a pair of jeans for $30, she reveals that she would rather have the jeans than $30 worth of other goods. These prices thereby convey valuable information to producers: with this knowledge, producers can determine if it is in their interest to produce jeans. If they can do it for less than $30, they stand to gain. In fact, anyone who could produce some jeans at less than or equal to that price will try to get in on the action. Eventually, the market price will reflect not only consumers' valuations of additional jeans, but producers' costs of manufacturing some more jeans. It is this information, and the incentives they provide, that directs the production of goods in market economies. It is a remarkable system, allowing for great economy in the amount of information and resources used to produce useful goods for consumers. In this book we will study how the forces of supply and demand interact in order to coordinate and direct output.

What Economics Is *Not* About

Many people harbor strange ideas of what economics is all about. Economics is not about how to balance your checkbook, or how to shop wisely. Economists are no better at these useful tasks than others. Neither is it concerned with how to make a lot of money, especially in the stock market. I am frequently asked (mainly by strangers) whether the stock market will rise or fall in the near future. My stock reply (to make a bad, but inevitable pun) is that if I knew all that, I wouldn't be teaching economics. I'd be busy getting rich in the stock market. Although I dearly wish it were true, economics is *not* about how to get rich. Becoming rich (properly known as the accumulation of wealth) is a subject economists study. Economics can identify reasons why some individuals rather than others, or, more importantly, why some nations accumulate wealth. However, individuals who become rich usually acquired their skills in places other than economics textbooks.[3]

Economics: Part of Social Science

Economics, above all, is a science. It is scientific in that it seeks explanations of events which take place in the real world. An important aspect of science is the ability to predict that when certain situations arise, certain other events will occur. A theory that can predict events successfully is a powerful tool for understanding the world. Prediction is probably the truest test of a theory's explanatory powers. Economics uses a set of principles, or propositions, to analyze human behavior. Analyzing human behavior is what makes economics part of *social* science. Social science is the study of human behavior. There are several

3. In fact, stock market investing is one of those few activities for which the adage, "If you're so smart, why aren't you rich?" is really true. Being smart about investments *means* being rich. Moral: Don't take stock market advice from brokers whose principal source of income is selling stocks for others (as opposed to actually acting on their own advice), or who are teaching a class on investing (in order to pick up some extra cash)!

disciplines within social science, principally, anthropology, economics, political science, psychology and sociology. All are concerned with explaining some aspect of human behavior; they differ in the problems they pose and the frameworks within which each discipline analyzes those problems.

Economists believe that it is important to separate one's own beliefs about what is desirable from what we believe to be true or false. We say that economic science should consist of **positive** statements, not **normative** statements. Positive statements are statements that can be classified as either true or false. They are statements about what *is,* as opposed to what an observer feels *ought* to be. Statements about the desirability of some policy are value judgments, and no matter how widely shared, they are not a part of science. We recognize that we all make some important decisions, e.g., that certain topics and issues are more important than others, which are normative statements of our own values. The decision to exclude value judgments is itself a value judgment. Nevertheless, in the analysis of economic problems, we try to maintain the separation of our normative opinions from the positive analysis of what is true.

As an example, consider the two statements:

1. Capital punishment (the death penalty) reduces crime.
2. Capital punishment should be imposed for certain crimes.

The first proposition is a positive statement: it is either true or false. It is a hypothesis that we can at least in principle test empirically. Indeed, there have been many investigations into the deterrent power of the death penalty. Some recent articles in economics find, for example, after controlling for population and sociological influences, a lower murder rate in states with more frequent application of the death penalty. The second proposition, however, is a different story. It is a statement about one's own values. It is not something that is subject to scientific testing because it is not a proposition that is objectively true or false. Even if we were to accept the first (positive) statement as true, i.e., that capital punishment truly reduces crime, it does not follow that we should therefore impose it. It is not a logical implication of the deterrent effect, but rather an ethical judgment. Even if we accept as true that the death penalty reduces the incidence of crime for which that penalty is imposed, would we therefore necessarily impose the death penalty for exceeding the speed limit or for petty thievery? Suppose that we enacted a law calling for the public hanging of all drivers who exceed posted speed limits, and really carried it out. I would be willing to bet heavily that speeding would drastically diminish, and, what's more, highway deaths would decrease as well. However, very few of us (and certainly the author) would be in favor of adopting such draconian laws, even though they would have the intended effect. Likewise, many countries have very severe laws against the personal use of illegal drugs, including caning, imprisonment and even death. These policies do in fact reduce the incidence of drug use—a positive proposition—but it is a value judgment, i.e., a normative proposition, to advocate whether or not we should impose such laws. Economics, as a part of social science, is concerned with enunciating positive statements that could be false, but which survive empirical testing, so that we believe them to be objectively true. We regard value judgments as to what policies individuals or the government ought to pursue (normative statements) as outside the field of economics.

Other examples are the many bills that are introduced in Congress to reduce the quantity of various goods that can be imported into the United States, especially textiles, shoes, automobiles and computer chips, and the bills proposing restrictions in the outsourcing of production to foreign firms. Some of these bills call for actual quotas, or limits on the total number of such goods imported; some call for punitive taxes (tariffs). Others require that a certain fraction of the final product must be constructed out of American-made parts (Domestic content).

The common element in all these schemes is to discourage Americans from buying these foreign goods by making those goods more expensive, and thereby to encourage Americans to purchase more American-made goods. The net effect (which is easy to accept, though its proof will have to wait for a later chapter), is to raise the price of these goods—foreign and domestic—to Americans. Consumers are clearly *worse off* since the prices of the goods they purchase are raised. (Other losers will be workers in the foreign companies.) The beneficiaries of these policies are domestic workers who produce competing products, for whom there will be more jobs at higher pay, and of course the owners of those firms.

Analyzing the effects of laws and policies such as trade restrictions is part of the positive science of economics. We make predictions about the effects of changes in various "rules" governing people's actions, and, in the process, offer explanations of why the events we predict are likely to occur. The scientific analysis ends, however, with the discussion of the effects of some action. Scientific analysis doesn't provide recommendations, e.g., that we should enact laws restricting foreign automobile sales. These opinions are normative statements, based on one's value judgments.[4] Normative statements cannot be tested because they cannot be classified as either true or false. They are just opinions about the ethical desirability of some policy. Although these decisions are important in any society, such value judgments are outside the field of economics.

Changes in government policies or new laws have effects. Economics identifies those effects and analyzes the consequences for individuals. However, new laws or policies always benefit some people and harm others. There is no law that is universally beneficial. If there ever were, it has long since been enacted. The desirability of laws and policies will therefore always be a value judgment for individuals, and not science. One hopes, however, that the scientific aspect of economics, i.e., predicting what is likely to occur, will affect how a person feels about some issue (and about perhaps its ethical aspects).

Social and Physical Sciences: Some Differences The social and physical sciences share the common thread of seeking explanations of real events. Economics and other social sciences, however, analyze human behavior, i.e., relationships of people to one another and to the environment. The physical sciences generally analyze objects not having conscious thought—atoms, molecules, mechanical and electronic devices, living cells. This forces some differences in approach between the various fields. One practical difference is that economists can rarely set up a laboratory experiment to test some idea or theory. We have to wait until the world produces a situation that provides an empirical test. For economics, the world is the laboratory.

On a more fundamental basis, however, the physical sciences are generally based on conservation laws, e.g., conservation of energy and momentum. In classical physics, energy may be transformed in some situation, but it is not lost,

4. People's *professed* value judgments on issues such as the above trade restrictions are, however, often correlated, in an obvious way, with the pecuniary effects of these laws on those individuals. Predicting the protestations of individuals affected by laws is therefore part of positive social science.

nor is there some net gain in energy (save nuclear reactions in which matter is converted to energy).

The situation in economics is fundamentally different. In economics, production and exchanges occur because of the mutual benefit of the persons involved. When we go to the store and make a purchase, both we and the store derive benefits. When we agree to work for some employer, we gain from the pay we receive and the employer also gains from the useful output we produce. With voluntary systems (we exclude slavery and involuntary military service, for example) when humans interact, they do so for their *mutual interest,* else someone would back out of the arrangement. By contrast, in poker, for example, what one person gains, another loses. Economists refer to that type of interaction as a *zero-sum game.* Economic transactions are "positive sum" games in that all parties stand to gain. There is no conservation of net benefits law. The mutual benefits we derive by production and exchange are what drives the economy.

One last difference that bears mentioning is that since it is *people* who are ultimately the object of economics, it is sometimes hard for us to be unbiased in our analyses. It frequently arises that economic analysis conflicts with our long-held value-judgments about some issue. There is a natural tendency to reject the scientific evidence in favor of maintaining our own biases. For this reason, it is often more difficult to be objective in economics than in the physical sciences. In fact, economics can sometimes be dangerous to your social health.

Explanations and Refutable Propositions

Being a part of science, economics is therefore interested in explanations and predictions. By explanation we mean an interpretation of events in terms of some more general proposition or law. Physicists explain the phenomena of falling objects in terms of Newton's laws of gravitational attraction and motion, rather than reporting an isolated incident of a given object approaching the ground. We explain the appearance of salty water, when hydrochloric acid and sodium hydroxide are mixed together, in terms of general laws of chemical attraction. By so doing, we unify previously unrelated events under a common framework and further implications and predictions often become apparent.

A major problem in learning is the way we come to believe that certain propositions are true. Many people believe that the road to knowledge is to "let the facts speak for themselves." The problem with this approach is that there are too many facts in the world. A visit to the government documents section of your University library will quickly convince you of this. A good place to start is *The Statistical Abstract of the United States,* published by the U.S. Commerce Department every year. It is a compendium of statistics from various agencies of the U.S. government and from private sources as well. Among the data published each year in just this one volume are the following exciting facts.

- There were 4,026,000 live births in the U.S. in 2001, up from 3,137,000 in 1973, but down from 4,258,000 in 1960.
- There were 69,456,000 children enrolled in school in 2003.
- In 2001, 229.2 million tons of solid waste were generated in the U.S.
- 7,291,000 persons held two or more jobs in 2002.
- 5,417,034 firms were owned by women in 1997, up from 411,800 in 1987.

- 1,023 people were killed by railroads in 1996, down from 2,255 in 1970.
- 10,227 million lbs. of apples were produced in 1997.
- Mt. St. Helens erupted violently on May 18, 1980.
- The years 1980 and 1981 were marked by unusual solar activity (sunspots).

The list of facts goes on and on. There are an infinite number of facts. How are we to decide which ones are relevant? The appearance of sunspots was seriously proposed in times past as a cause of business fluctuations (but then again so were witchcraft and insanity). Volcanic eruptions have sometimes caused disruptions in weather severe enough to reduce harvests. Can we reject these explanations just because we regard them as implausible?

The only way we can reject some facts and accept others as having some bearing on any particular problem, is to have some *conceptual framework* in which we think. A framework in which, for example, we reject sunspots while perhaps we consider changes in prices is the start of a *theory.* Economists use theories because the facts rarely, if ever, speak for themselves. The number of potential facts is overwhelming, mind-boggling, stupefying. The only way we can make sense of all these facts is to be selective. The only way we can choose the relevant facts is to have some notion, or *theory,* as to what is important to observe and what is unimportant. We can then test the assertions of the theory against specific facts. This is the way all sciences progress.

A **theory**, therefore, consists of assertions or propositions we consider to be universally true. Perhaps the most famous of all theories are Newton's laws of motion, which describe the movement of mechanical systems. That theory is enormously useful, in part because of its *simplicity.*[5] With just three simple laws Newton was able to describe the orbits of planets around the sun and to solve otherwise intractable problems of motion. The postulates of modern economics are less well known than Newton's laws; most people in fact are surprised economists believe such axioms exist. Economics *does* have a theory—postulates economists believe to be universally true. We summarize these postulates by the familiar terms supply and demand. We discuss these postulates in detail in this and the next few chapters. This theory (the laws of supply and demand) is useful both because it provides a set of unifying ideas with which we can analyze certain problems, and because it consists of only a few simple ideas. Both *simplicity* and *generality* are useful qualities of theories, but increasing either one of these attributes often decreases the other (we say, for example, the *cost* of greater simplicity is a loss of generality). In this book we will apply these principles consistently to analyze important problems about economic behavior.[6]

---

5. An example of carrying simplicity too far is provided by the Indiana legislature, which, in 1906 passed a bill requiring that the ratio of the circumference to the diameter of a circle, π, be equal to 3, exactly. The bill was vetoed by the governor.

6. The word *model* sometimes is used synonymously with theory. Often, it means "simplified theory," i.e., some first approximation to a more general and elaborate framework, though this use is now less frequent. A theory, in fact, must always contain some simplifications of reality in order to be tractable, i.e., capable of being understood and analyzed by mere humans. Lastly, the word "model" sometimes is used to represent just the logical or mathematical framework of a theory, before it is tied to real world objects and events. There is a useful degree of *specialization,* a topic we shall return to later, in most academic fields, into "theory" and "applications." This partitioning allows individuals with a special gift for logic and mathematics to pursue the logical implications of theories,

It is always easy to conjure up a theory to explain a single event, but such explanations are useless. Theories that explain only one event are called *ad hoc*. They provide no basis for generalizations to other events; they are little better than just saying that some event happened because it happened, or because someone simply enjoyed it. For decades, the tendency of Americans to drive relatively large cars has been attributed to a "love affair with big cars." This "explains" the phenomenon by saying that Americans drive big cars because Americans like to drive big cars. Economics insists on explanations in terms of an accepted framework that provides explanations for more than just one event.

The explanations that are most interesting and useful are those that *could* be wrong and turn out correct. It is not very useful to predict that it will be either sunny or cloudy tomorrow. Whatever happens, the prediction will come true. Weather forecasters perform a useful service only if they make predictions like: "It will be sunny tomorrow" or "It will be warm tomorrow"—predictions that could be wrong, but which turn out to be correct. Statements or propositions that could in principle be wrong, are called **refutable propositions**. These are the most interesting and useful statements in science. For example, economics attempts to explain why some prices rise while others fall, why we once waited in line for gasoline but not at other times, and why it is much harder to find an apartment in New York City than elsewhere. We try to predict when these events will occur, or under what circumstances these events will be observed. Like other sciences, economics seeks to make statements and propositions that could, in principle at least, be wrong but turn out to be consistent with the facts.

Sometimes people say that an explanation is "good in theory" but lousy "in practice." What they are really saying is that it is a lousy theory. A group of propositions can't really be a good theory if it predicts poorly, because one of the truest tests of a good theory is that it predicts well. However, only very rarely does some experiment truly convince the overwhelming majority of a profession that some proposition is true. People tend to evaluate results differently; what seems compelling to some is often unconvincing to others. Usually, people decide to believe some proposition only after researchers have completed many independent investigations.[7]

We use the term "refutable," as opposed to "provable" because it is in fact logically impossible to prove theories. A theory says that some postulate *A* implies some event *B*. If we observe *B*, we unfortunately cannot validly infer that *A* is true. This is such a famous fallacy it even has a name: it is called **affirming the consequent**. Something else entirely could have caused *B* to be true. A theorem does not imply its converse.[8] A common terminology is to say that when we find evidence that supports a theory, the theory is *confirmed*. "Confirmed" does not mean "proven;" it just means "consistent with the theory." Usually, our confidence in a theory grows only after it is confirmed in repeated tests.

---

while others specialize in testing theories against actual events in the real world (a very imposing and difficult endeavor, to anyone who has ever tried it).

7. The famous Michelson-Morley experiment of 1887, designed to measure the velocity of the "ether" stream relative to the Earth, is often cited as one of those rare critical tests which utterly refuted an earlier theory (though that was not its intent). This experiment, which implied that the velocity of light was independent of the velocity of its source led Einstein to the development of the theory of relativity.

8. If two triangles are congruent then they are similar; if they are similar, they are not necessarily congruent. If one is intelligent, one can obtain a Ph.D.; if one has a Ph.D. . . .

Figure 1-1 *Two Theories of the Shape of the Earth*

The observation that ships approaching the shore appear from the top down is compelling evidence that the earth is round, for the reasons shown in panel (a). However, panel (b) shows that we observe the same thing if the earth is flat and light waves travel convex to the surface of the earth. Therefore, seeing the ships from the top down as they approach the shore does not *prove* the earth is round!

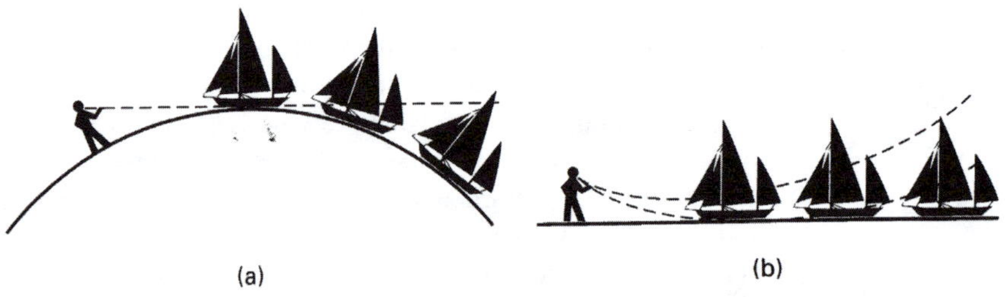

Figure 1-1 provides a marvelous example of this logic. It had long been argued that the earth is round because as ships approached port, at first only the top of the ship was visible, and then more and more of the ship became visible, moving from the top down. The left panel shows why we expect this with a round earth. However, this explanation assumes also that light waves travel in straight lines. The same observation is implied by a flat earth with light waves that travel convex to the surface (as they in fact do when the air just above the surface is heated by sunlight and is thinner than the air above it.) This explanation is shown in the right panel. This observation, therefore, is inconclusive as to the earth being round![9]

Many times, when the occurrence of two different events seem to be *correlated,* that is, when one occurs more frequently, the other is more likely (or less likely) to occur, it is tempting to assign some sort of causality to the events. We are tempted to say that one event (or its absence) is *causing* the other. Almost every day we read that some food is hazardous to our health. Most of these reports are based on a statistical correlation between consumption of that good and the incidence of some condition. Most often, the researchers have no idea as to what agent could actually be causing the condition or disease. They draw their conclusions solely on the basis of statistics.

In the absence of a theory, that is, some general axioms which would lead a reasonable person to attach some plausibility to the events, the conclusion of causality from mere correlation is fraught with danger. Often we wind up merely confirming our own biases. For generations, for example, parents insisted that their children would catch colds if they went out without a coat. Indeed, most people catch more colds in the winter, when it is cold out, than in the summer. Colds are correlated (inversely) with the temperature outside. But does cold weather actually cause infectious diseases? Recent research seems to indicate that people catch colds (and the flu, etc.) from other people. We pass our viruses on to others by close contact. The reason we catch more colds in the winter than in the summer apparently is that we are more frequently indoors, around other people, in the winter. The correlation between outside temperature and the appearance of the common cold is apparently *spurious,* i.e., it does not indicate a causality between the two.

9. Taken from Irving M. Copi, *Introduction to Logic,* 4th ed. Macmillan, New York, 1972.

When my house is cold, my furnace is more frequently on. If we use the correlation between house temperatures and furnaces operating, the inescapable conclusion is that furnaces *cool* houses. Jerzy Neymen, one of the architects of modern statistics, recounts the experience of a friend who studied birth rates in 54 counties in New York State. He found that births were positively correlated with the number of storks present in each county—more storks, more babies. Someone soon pointed out that this correlation was spurious, because in larger counties there were naturally more storks *and* more people and therefore more babies. His friend pressed on, and decided to compare birth *rates*—babies (B) per women of child-bearing age (W), or B/W—with the number of storks (S) per women, S/W. He again found a correlation—more storks per women, more babies per women. Maybe storks actually *do* cause babies. Or maybe, as Neymen pointed out, in counties with many women, both ratios B/W and S/W fell, because the denominators of these expressions became larger, and the statistical correlation was still spurious, though now more subtle. Statistics in the absence of theory can be hazardous to your intellectual health!

"It Was Obvious"

(An old illustration of the power of theory.)

A Talmudic Scholar from Marmaresch was on his way home from a visit to Budapest. Opposite him in the railway carriage sat another Jew, dressed in modern fashion and smoking a cigar. When the conductor came around to collect the tickets the scholar noticed that his neighbor opposite was also on his way to Marmaresch.

This seemed odd to him.

"Who can it be, and why is he going to Marmaresch," he wondered.

As it would not be polite to ask outright he tried to figure it out for himself.

"Now, let me see," he mused. "He is a modern Jew, well dressed, and he smokes a cigar. Whom could a man of this type be visiting in Marmaresch? Possibly he's on his way to our town doctor's wedding. But no, that can't be! That's two weeks off. Certainly this kind of man wouldn't twiddle his thumbs in our town for two weeks!

"Why then is he on his way to Marmaresch? Perhaps he's courting a woman there? But who could it be? Now let me see. Moses Goldman's daughter Esther? Yes, definitely, it's she and nobody else . . . ! But now that I think of it—that couldn't be! She's too old—he wouldn't have her under any circumstances! Maybe it's Haikeh Wasservogel? Phooey! She's so ugly! Who then? Could it be Leah, the moneylender's daughter? N-no! What a match for such a nice man! Who then? There aren't any more marriageable girls in Marmaresch. That's settled then, he's not going courting.

"What then brings him?

"Wait, I've got it! It's about Mottel Kohn's bankruptcy case! But what connection could he have with that? Could it be that he is one of his creditors? Hardly! Just look at him sitting there so calmly, reading his newspaper and smiling to himself. Anybody can see nothing worries him! No, he's not a creditor. But I'll bet it has something to do with the bankruptcy! Now what could it be?

"Wait a minute, I think I've got it. Mottel Kohn must have corresponded with a lawyer from Budapest about his bankruptcy. But that swindler Mottel certainly wouldn't confide his business secrets to a stranger! So it stands to reason that the lawyer must be a member of the family.

"Now who could it be? Could it be his sister Shprinzah's son? No, that's impossible. She got married twenty-six years ago—I remember it very well because the wedding took place in the green synagogue. And this man here looks at least thirty-five.

"A funny thing! Who could it be, after all . . . ? Wait a minute! It's clear as day! This is his nephew, his brother Hayyim's son, because Hayyim Kohn got married thirty-seven years and two months ago in the stone synagogue near the market place. Yes, that's who he is!

"In a nutshell—he is lawyer Kohn from Budapest. But a lawyer from Budapest surely must have the title 'Doctor'! So, he is Doctor Kohn from Budapest, no? But wait a minute! A lawyer from Budapest who calls himself 'Doctor' won't call himself 'Kohn'! Anybody knows that. It's certain that he has changed his name into Hungarian. Now what kind of a name could he have made out of Kohn? Kovacs! Yes, that's it—Kovacs! In short, this is Doctor Kovacs from Budapest!"

Eager to start a conversation the scholar turned to his traveling companion and asked, "Doctor Kovacs, do you mind if I open the window?"

"Not at all," answered the other. "But tell me, how do you know that I am Doctor Kovacs?"

"It was obvious," replied the scholar.[10]

1.2 The Economic Paradigm

The occasion for studying economics, or, for that matter, all of the social sciences, is **scarcity** of goods and resources. The term scarce means that there are not enough of the items humans find desirable to satisfy everyone's wants. If goods were handed out free to all who wanted them in unrestricted quantities, there would simply not be enough to go around. We would, in short order, run out.

Scarce is not the same thing as limited. In order for something to be scarce it must actually be a *good,* i.e., useful to humans, at least in some quantities. Cockroaches and garbage are limited, but not scarce. (For some reason, no generally accepted word has ever been coined to mean the opposite of a good, e.g., a "bad," to represent garbage, cockroaches and such things.) Although something must be a good in order for it to be scarce, some goods may not be scarce. There

10. From *A Treasury of Jewish Folklore,* by Nathan Ausubel, (New York: Crown Publishers, 1948.) Ausubel attributes this story to *Royte Pomeransten,* by Immanuel Olsvanger, (New York: Schocken Books, 1947). The story apparently was intended to poke gentle fun at Talmudic scholars who drew fantastical implications out of skimpy assumptions.

are, for example, air (but not *fresh* air, since resources must be used either to clean the air or to keep it clean), the sun in the morning and the moon at night.

Contrary to the lyrics of various songs and poems, for most people, the best things in life are *not* free. Essentially all goods are scarce. As a consequence, a fundamental problem arises with which all societies have to grapple. How are these scarce goods to be distributed among members of society? What rules will be used to make those decisions? Furthermore, since resources (land, labor, equipment or capital) can be used to produce many different things, all of which at least some people desire, how shall society decide to what uses, and to what extent it will utilize a country's resources?

Economics is concerned with this central issue. *Economics is the study of how scarce resources, that have alternative uses, are allocated amongst competing ends.* This problem can be separated into two parts: **prodution**, i.e., deciding *what* to produce and *how much;* and **allocation**, i.e., deciding *who* gets the goods society produces. All societies—capitalist, socialist, communist, fascist, everything in between or more extreme—must somehow come to grips with the production and allocation of resources and goods. The outcomes depend on such matters as the skills of the population, the degree of industrialization of the country, and the laws and customs of the country. The laws of economics are relevant to all these types of societies. Application of economic theory to different societies must, however, take into account the particular constraints the laws and customs of the country impose on its people, as well as the technology and resources available.

Scarcity and Competition

Although the laws and customs of a society affect the production and allocation of goods and resources, it is impossible to enact laws that eliminate the underlying scarcity of goods and resources. The horrible truth is that scarcity is a pervasive empirical fact about the world. It is caused by the demands on the world's resources by consumers of those resources—mainly humans—in amounts greater than the earth would produce on its own. We cannot legislate scarcity out of existence any more than we can abolish the law of gravity. What laws can and do change are the means by which people compete for the scarce goods and resources. The verb *compete,* or the noun *competition,* have various meanings (we will discuss a technical meaning in economics in a later chapter on the organization of markets). To some it connotes aggression, as, for example, its use in sports. Competition also describes the process of getting admitted to college; we use the term in business when we speak of maintaining or increasing one's market share relative to others who provide a similar service or good. To some, competition is a benign concept, while to others it is a concern for alarm. We use it here merely to articulate that in the face of scarcity, with whatever rules society imposes on individual behavior, some people will get goods that others also desire. Inevitably, therefore, people compete with each other in order to acquire more goods. This doesn't mean that we are condemned to a dog-eat-dog world. Competition can be polite and civilized. It can also be cruel and warlike. An important issue in economics, in fact, is what rules (laws) will make competition less warlike and more benign. However, as long as human beings are so constituted as to prefer more goods for themselves and their children, scarcity, and therefore competition, will exist. The two are inextricably intertwined.

Cost

Because of scarcity, every human action has a **cost** associated with it. The word cost is a term that has many different meanings and connotations. Economists have occasion to dwell seriously and precisely on cost, for it is part and parcel of scarcity. In economics, cost always means a forgone alternative (more precisely, the highest valued alternative, but more on that later) resulting from some action or decision. For this reason economists frequently use the terms *"opportunity cost"* or *"alternative cost"* instead of just *"cost."* The adjectives alternative and opportunity are really redundant; we use them to emphasize the meaning of cost as a forgone opportunity or alternative. When resources are scarce, a decision to do one thing necessarily means that something else doesn't get done. That something else is at least part of the cost. For example, the cost of attending college, in addition to the tuition, is the income a person would have been able to enjoy had he or she decided to get a job or go into business rather than going to school. These earnings represent the value of the additional output the student could be producing by working instead of going to college. This lost production, plus an appropriate fraction of the alternative production that the professors and resources now engaged in education could have produced elsewhere that is the true cost of a person's education.

All this being said, the correct computation of cost is a sometimes slippery affair. Suppose you are digging around in your back yard one day, and you come upon a glass-like rock. You take it to a jeweler who informs you it is a diamond; he estimates its worth at about $4,000.00—he is prepared to write you a check. You decide instead to have the diamond cut into a gem and set in a ring, for an additional $1,000. If you went to buy the ring, it would cost $5,000; but since you found the raw diamond, the ring only "cost" you $1,000. Or did it?

You've purchased a ticket for a concert for $20. At the gate, a "scalper" offers you $50 for the ticket. You decide to go to the concert; it's worth $20, although you do wonder whether it's worth $50. How much did that concert cost you anyway?

You own a small grocery store and you regularly purchase fresh produce for resale. You have just stocked a shipment of fresh Florida oranges at a wholesale cost of 25¢ per lb., with the intention of reselling them for 50¢ per lb. You suddenly hear on the news that a freeze has wiped out a substantial part of the current citrus crop, and you notice that supermarkets are raising the retail price of oranges to $1.00 per lb. At 50¢ per lb., you'll be out of oranges in less than a day (consumers know a bargain when they see one). What is the true wholesale cost of oranges to you? That is, would you simply proceed on the basis of the historical cost of 25¢ per lb., or do you act as though the oranges are now more expensive, even though you in actuality paid 25¢ per lb. for the oranges?

These examples reveal the need to be clear about the definition of cost. Is the cost of something simply what a person paid historically, e.g., $1,000 for the diamond ring, or $20 for the concert, 25¢ per lb. for oranges? To economists, cost is always defined by what a person must give up, or forgo, in order to consume something, or pursue some activity. The cost of any activity is the highest valued opportunity that is foregone when that activity is pursued. Cost *means* alternative, or opportunity cost. We use those modifiers for emphasis, because the concept of cost as a foregone alternative is so central to economics.

What do you give up when you consume the diamond ring? What does it cost you in terms of opportunities foregone for you (or your person of all persons) to be able to show off this ring to friends? Clearly, the ring cost you \$5,000, not \$1,000. The jeweler was prepared to give you a check for \$4,000; this amount plus the extra \$1,000 spent converting the stone into a ring totals \$5,000 worth of other goods that were available to you, which you gave up, in order to consume the ring. It is this amount, not the historical cost of \$1,000, that measures your sacrifice in behalf of this particular diamond consumption. The same analysis applies to gifts. Suppose your grandmother gives you her \$5,000 diamond ring for your engagement. Is it free, because you didn't pay your grandmother for it? Clearly, either you or your grandmother could sell the diamond (though maybe not for the full retail price). The cost of consuming the diamond is the foregone opportunity to consume some amount (perhaps the wholesale price of \$2,500) of other goods generated from the sale of the diamond. The diamond is not free, even if it is a gift.

In the same way, the cost of attending the concert is not the historical ticket price of \$20; it is the \$50 of other goods you could have consumed by accepting the scalper's offer. Just before entering you are in possession of *either* of two assets: a right to enter the concert (the ticket) *or* \$50 of other goods. Either is available, but not both, since to receive one means forgoing the other. The opportunity cost of going to the concert is therefore \$50 because that is what you give up by the decision to attend. Neither the historic cost of \$20 nor the windfall profit of \$30 received on sale of the ticket to the scalper measures what is actually foregone by going to the concert. Thus they do not measure the true cost to you of that decision. The historical cost of \$20 plus the windfall gain of \$30 together add up to the true alternative cost of attending the concert. Similarly, the Florida oranges cost you their current wholesale price, as you'll find out when you reorder. *Cost means alternative cost.*

If your parents bought a bottle of fine wine to celebrate your birth, stored it in a wine cellar so that it could age in order to serve it at your graduation from college, the cost of the wine, even ignoring changes in the over all price level, is not its historical cost. The wine may now be worth several times the original outlay, in terms of what other wine fanciers would pay to be able to drink a vintage, aged wine.

When military reservists are called up for duty, as happened in 1990 and most recently to fight in Iraq, the cost of those operations is greater than the military pay received by those personnel. The cost of the armed services, though usually evaluated in terms of how much it costs to procure the personnel and equipment, is more accurately measured by the decrease in private production that takes place because these workers have to leave their regular jobs in order to produce military output.

When the military procured personnel through the draft, salaries were less than would have been necessary to attract volunteers into the armed services. The pay scales then in effect, therefore understated the true opportunity cost of maintaining the military. If a person who could make \$20,000 per year in private life is inducted into the army and paid \$1,000, the cost of having that person in the army is \$20,000, not \$1,000. When this person is drafted, \$20,000 worth of output disappears which he or she could have enjoyed. That is the true opportunity cost of maintaining this person in the army.

In the case of a volunteer army, military pay must reflect the true opportunity cost of military personnel. In order to attract people into the armed services, the pay will have to be comparable to soldiers' next best alternatives. The cost to taxpayers of maintaining the military establishment will therefore be accurately measured by the cost of personnel and the cost of purchasing military equipment. With the advent of the volunteer military, the cost of maintaining an armed services has been shifted to the general taxpayers and away from the individual inductees.

1.3 Demand and Supply

Human beings possess conscious thought. When presented with competing opportunities, humans *choose.* Choice is unfortunately foisted upon us. The necessity of choosing is a consequence of scarcity. If goods (and time) were not scarce, we would never have to choose among competing alternatives. However, saying that people choose is not saying very much. In order to qualify as a science, economics must be able to characterize choices in a systematic way, so that these choices are, to some extent, predictable. We seek *regularities of behavior* so that refutable propositions about human actions are possible.

Economists have found it convenient to separate choices about *consumption* from those concerning *production.* The theory of consumer behavior is an analysis of the choices individuals make with regard to the goods and services they consume directly for their enjoyment. Economists refer to this as the theory of demand. The theory of supply refers to the choices we make with regard to the goods that we produced or contemplate for production. In each of these analyses, we seek to characterize these choices as part of a general framework, so that we can treat those decisions as more than just isolated events.

Demand

The theory of consumer behavior begins by separating the influences on our choices into two distinct classes:

- Constraints, or opportunities
- Tastes, or preferences

By constraints, we mean all the things that impinge on our behavior and which we could in principle measure. For example, our incomes are a major constraint on our choices. Most of us spend little time wondering which yacht to buy, because they are all beyond our means.[11] People choose hamburger instead of steak, used cars instead of new ones, because of the constraint of income. In a similar way, the prices of goods affect our choices. The price of petroleum has varied by as much as 50% in the past twenty-five years. When it became expensive, people changed the way they consumed oil and oil-related goods so as to enhance their ability to purchase other goods. What other constraints might we imagine? A list of constraints might reasonably include:

- Income
- Prices of goods
- Time
- Technology (the "state of the arts")

11. J.P Morgan is reported to have said to an acquaintance, "If you have to ask about the price, you can't afford it."

- Laws and customs
- The state of our health
- Our education, skills, etc.

We shall later delve into these constraints in more detail. For now, however, suppose we made up a list of *all* the constraints we could possibly imagine, that affect human behavior. The items above are, at least in principle, *measurable.* Incomes can be estimated with tax returns, prices of goods are generally posted or available, individual ages are identifiable, technology is describable in some way (though this is not easy), laws are stated on the books and their applicability is documented in the courts. Suppose now we were in possession of detailed measurements of all of these constraints, with regard to certain individuals. Would we then be able to predict the choices those individuals would make? Could we predict whether a person would attend rock versus classical concerts? Buy expensive stereo equipment and cheap clothes, versus expensive duds and a Sony Walkman? Buy a Porsche and eat peanut butter rather than indulge in French restaurant cuisine and drive a Ford Escort?

Common sense tells us that such predictions about behavior would still not be possible even with a complete list of measurable constraints. There will still be other variables that influence our choices. We call these other, essentially unmeasurable influences **tastes** or **preferences**. Some people love opera, others simply detest it; some people love chopped liver, others love squid. The variety of human preferences is enormous, and everyday experience tells us that tastes vary greatly from individual to individual. Here then is the central puzzle that the paradigm of economics addresses. How can we discover regularities in behavior, in the face of admittedly large variability in unmeasurable tastes among humans? To a large extent, the answer to this important question defines the conceptual framework of economics.

Since we cannot measure tastes, we must make some simplifying assumptions. We assume that however tastes are defined or measured, *they do not change during the course of investigation.* Any *changes* in observable events can then be attributed to *changes* in observable constraints. Moreover, if tastes are such that humans display regularities of behavior, then by asserting appropriate postulates about the structure of tastes, we may be able to predict how these choices *change* when the constraints people face *change,* even though we may not be able to predict the original choices made by individuals. In particular, we assert that *all individuals strive to mitigate, or reduce the adverse consequences of the constraints they face; if any constraint changes, people will respond so as to reduce rather than reinforce these adverse effects.* If some constraint is relaxed, i.e., impinges less on our choices, we assert that people will respond so as to exploit, that is, to take advantage of the greater opportunities now available, rather than to ignore or reduce the new advantages. Using this postulate of behavior, and the simplifying assumption of constant tastes, we assert refutable hypotheses about how individuals *respond* to changes in the constraints they face.

The behavior we just described is conveniently summarized by the graph in Fig. 1-2. On the horizontal axis units of some good are plotted. On the vertical axis, various hypothetical prices of this good are indicated. The curve is *negatively sloped;* higher prices are associated with smaller quantities. This curve is called a **demand curve**. It says, for example, that at price p_1, consumers will

Figure 1-2 *The Demand Curve*

A demand curve shows the amount of a good consumers wish to purchase at specified prices. Its outstanding characteristic is that it is downward sloping. This means that when the price is raised, say, from p_1 to p_2, consumers reduce the amount purchased, from quantity q_1 to q_2, and vice versa.

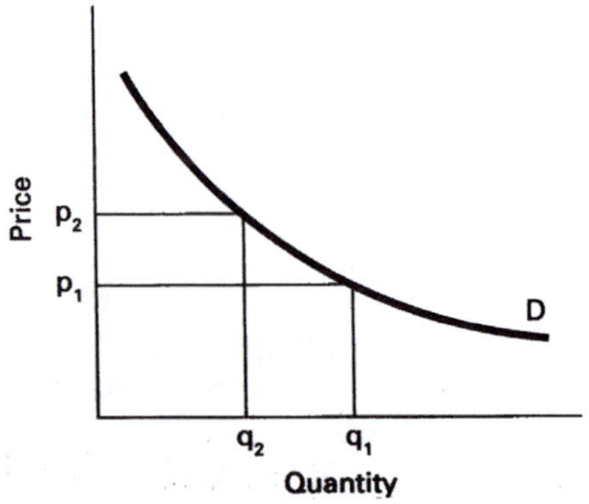

purchase some amount q_1. If, however, (other things remaining the same), the price of this good were to rise to p_2, consumers would respond to this increased constraint on their consumption by purchasing a lower amount, q_2. That is, consumers mitigate the damages of the higher price by decreasing the level of their consumption. This fundamental regularity is known as the **law of demand**. It is one of the central postulates of economics. The basis for this law and its application are the subject of the next several chapters.

Supply

The theory of supply seeks to organize and explain the decisions individuals make with regard to production and offering of goods for sale. We noted at the beginning of the chapter that production is characterized by extensive specialization, or division of labor. This specialization allows greater production to take place with the same resources. Chances are you are taking this course from a person who has specialized in economics in college, graduate school, and as a professor. Your classes in chemistry, literature and mathematics are similarly staffed by persons specializing in those disciplines. You'd be wise to avoid taking literature from economics professors or economics from chemists. It's hard enough to become competent in one field. We know from common experience that the generalist cannot compete with the specialist. This process of specialization is an important part of production, and we devote considerable space to it in later chapters.

Although we derive benefits from specialization, this process has its limits. Not everyone can be proficient at, say, engineering, or play in the National Football League. As interest in professional football has expanded in recent years (we say, the demand has increased), teams have endeavored to hire more quarterbacks. But this is a difficult position to play, and finding additional players becomes increasingly difficult. As a result, those who are most proficient earn extremely high salaries. We notice that at a given moment, as economies produce greater and greater amounts of any good, certain costs of production tend to rise. That is, as output expands, the cost of producing additional units tends to increase, due to the inability to replicate the most efficient resources.

The relationship between the price of a good and the willingness of individuals to offer the good for sale is called a **supply curve**. We depict it in Fig. 1-3. As in Fig. 1-2, the price of a good is plotted on the vertical axis, and quantities of

Figure 1-3 *The Supply Curve*

A supply curve shows the amount of some good sellers are willing to offer at various prices. For example, at price p_1, sellers offer some amount q_1 for sale. If the price were to increase, say to p_2, sellers would increase the amount offered to q_2. Supply curves are generally upward sloping.

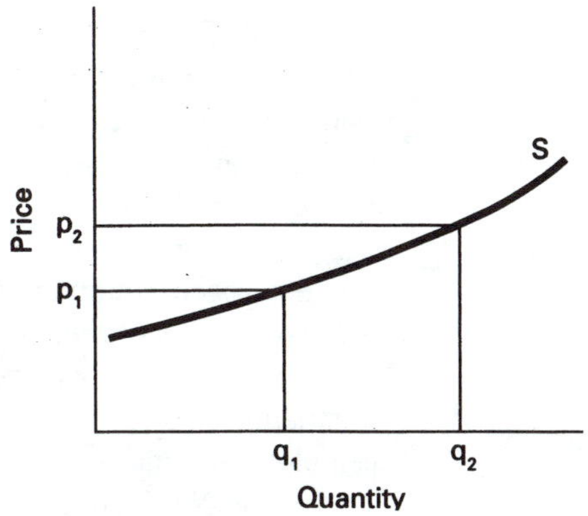

the good are plotted horizontally. In this case, the curve is *positively sloped;* higher prices are associated with higher quantities offered for sale. The behavior this supply curve describes is that higher prices induce greater amounts of goods supplied. For example, at price p_1, some quantity q_1 is offered for sale. At the higher price p_2, the greater amount q_2 is forthcoming.

Putting It Together

We use demand and supply curves to depict the activities of buying and selling in the market. In Fig. 1-4 a supply and demand curve for some good is depicted. These two curves are shown intersecting at some point *E*. This intersection occurs at price p_E. At that price, the quantity of this good that consumers wish to buy equals the amount suppliers want to sell, q_E. This important **market equilibrium** is the subject of most of economics. How it comes about and how it changes when some external constraint changes is the subject of economics.

This then is the conceptual framework, or paradigm of economics. In fact, the very definition of an economic explanation is an explanation using the above methodology. We devote the rest of the book to elucidating this framework and showing its application to real events.

Figure 1-4 *Supply and Demand Curves*

The intersection of supply and demand curves determines the price of goods and the amount sold in organized markets. We will have much to say about this important market equilibrium throughout this text.

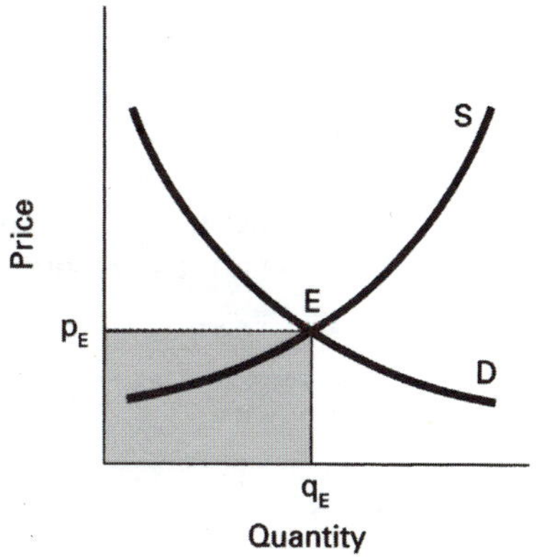

Microeconomics and Macroeconomics

In this text we deal with the formation of markets and how these markets respond when certain outside forces change. We analyze individual decision makers and inquire how they respond to changes in laws, the invention of new technologies, changes in the availability of resources and the like. Because the focus is on the responses of *individual* decision makers to changes in their environment, even though it is invariably their combined effects that interest us, we refer to these topics as part of **microeconomics** (micro meaning small.) By contrast, **macroecoeconomics** (macro meaning large), which we leave to other texts, is concerned with these changes aggregated over the entire economy. Macroeconomics is concerned with what determines, for example, changes in the inflation rate (the average increase in the overall price level), the level of unemployment and the level of income produced in the whole economy. The effect of the North American Free Trade Agreement (NAFTA) on a particular industry, say, the automobile industry, would be part of microeconomics; its effect on national income and aggregate employment would be part of macroeconomics.

1.4 Examples

1. *The American Love Affair with Automobiles* For the past two generations, numerous commentators have expressed considerable moral concern that Americans have generally driven much larger cars than drivers in others other countries. They attribute this to a peculiar American love affair with big cars. Economics rejects such explanations out of hand. This so-called explanation is *ad hoc*—made up to suit the facts, after the fact. It is an assertion about unmeasurable taste variables and is thus completely untestable. It is incapable of generalization to other phenomena. There is no hint as to why Americans, among all the peoples of the world, should have a peculiar preference along these lines.[12] Anything at all can be "explained" on the basis that people somehow like to do whatever they are doing, and that's why they do it.[13] In order to qualify as an explanation, the tendency of Americans to drive relatively large cars must be interpreted in terms of some general principle, or postulates of behavior, based on observable differences in the constraints faced by American versus foreign drivers. It is not too difficult to find these differences in constraints. Throughout most of the twentieth century, the price of gasoline in America has been only one-third to one-half the price in Europe and Asia. (Most of the price differential is due to much higher taxes imposed on gasoline by foreign governments.) It is much more costly for Europeans to operate an automobile for this reason. Europeans therefore respond so as to mitigate the damage caused by relatively high gas prices. The obvious way to do this is to drive cars that get better mileage, e.g., smaller cars. Additional responses are greater carpooling and use of mass transit. This is an economic explanation. First, it is not based on an ad hoc asser-

---

12. It is especially peculiar in light of the fact that Americans are descended from people from the rest of the world.

13. (An old joke) When asked why he was hitting himself over the head with a hammer, it was explained that "it feels good when I stop." *Anything* can be explained by asserting a peculiar taste for that activity.

tion about differences in tastes, and second, it predicts an observable response to a higher gasoline price on the basis of lessening of damages imposed by an observable change in constraints.

We can further test the explanation, because it carries implications any time the price of gasoline changes relative to other goods. The price of gasoline moved up and down by up to 50% during the past thirty years. In 1973, after the breakout of war in the Middle East, the Islamic countries boycotted the sale of oil to the United States. Prices rose, in early 1974, by approximately 50%, from about 40 cents to around 60 cents.[14] After the original price increase, prices at the pump (nominal, or money prices unadjusted for inflation), rose only slightly, but by 1979 general price inflation in the economy had raised other prices and incomes by approximately 50%. As a result, the price of gasoline relative to other goods and people's incomes was close to its original pre-embargo price. If the American pattern of car usage was just some peculiar taste, no changes would be predicted in Americans' automobile consumption. In fact, right after the initial price increase, energy conservation became a prominent activity. People drove less and carpooled more. Small cars became the rage, and Volkswagen beetles sold at substantial premiums over their sticker price. As the 1970s drew on, many commentators noted that people were going back to their old driving habits, a clear response to the falling relative price of oil. In 1979, the Shah of Iran was deposed and replaced by the Ayatollah Khomeini. Prices again rose sharply. Small cars again became popular. In the mid 1980s, the price of oil fell dramatically—when adjusted for inflation, the price was well below the price prior to the 1973 embargo—and larger, higher performance cars became popular again. Gasoline prices remained low through 2002, but prices at the pump rose in 2003 and at this writing in 2004 they are hovering around $2.00 per gallon. We predict that SUV sales will decline if this higher gasoline price persists.

These changes in behavior are all clear efforts to reduce the impact of changing constraints. To explain these changes otherwise would require one to believe that the American love affair with big cars just happened to go through these erratic changes, coincident with the opposite changes in the price of gasoline. We prefer the general theory based on response to changes in constraints, over the ad hoc theory based on unpredictable, and unfounded changes in tastes.

When U.S. Air Force Colonel Douglas Nelson (retired) was a student at the Air Force Academy in Colorado Springs, he noticed that people who lived in base housing the Air Force provided typically left their sprinklers running all night, whereas townspeople rarely did this. By obtaining records from the utility companies, he compared water, gas and electricity usage for base families and townspeople whose houses were comparable (in an attempt to compare families of like incomes.) The families who lived on base used two to three times as much of these basic commodities as did the civilians. It could be, of course, that the military families "loved" gas, water and electricity more than civilian families. More likely, however, these differences in behavior were attributable to not charging families living in base housing for these goods. The Air Force contracted with the utility companies for a total amount of these goods, but they did not meter individual families' consumption. As far as families living on base

14. For a few months after the embargo, government mandated price controls were in effect, preventing actual price hikes. The ensuing waiting lines and other forms of "nonprice rationing' will be analyzed later.

were concerned, these were free goods; the townspeople faced more severe constraints in the use of these goods and mitigated the effects in an obvious way.

2. *You Can't Teach an Old Dog New Tricks* Many young people consider their parents and their parents' cohorts impossibly conservative, un-hip, unreceptive to new ideas or new music, unteachable about new technology. This could in fact be a feature of the aging process, although biology lends scant support to the degree of brain rot attributed to middle-aged adults by their children. Yet this perception seems to exist in every generation. (Warning to the present readers of this passage: it'll happen to you too. You'll know you've hit middle age when you start hating the music teenagers listen to.) Can we replace an *ad hoc* assertion about changing tastes, as one ages, with an explanation based on changing constraints?

Learning anything new is rarely easy. Learning how to operate new cell phones, new computer software, or a remote control device for televisions and DVDs requires some set-up costs before a person derives any benefits. After considerable experimentation, middle-aged adults will have developed various survival skills and general behaviors which they have found enhance their ability to succeed in society. These procedures work for those using them. When some new course of action is proposed, the costs might very well be the same for the old as for the young. However, the young will have more years to enjoy the benefits and will not have yet developed other procedures for the same task. It is therefore relatively more advantageous for the young to be receptive to new ideas. We expect the young to more readily learn new tricks and the old to perfect the old tried and true tricks for this simple reason.

3. *The World War II Baby Boom and Its Consequences: Stretching the Paradigm* As a last example, we apply the economic paradigm to some nontraditional areas for economics—topics usually reserved for sociology and political science—and perhaps "stick our necks out" a bit in the process. Consider that many profound changes have taken place in the past generation. In the late 1960s and early 1970s (usually referred to as the "sixties"), women's liberation, always present to some degree but never a major issue, suddenly burst upon the scene. The traditional "Leave it to Beaver" family, where the husband worked and the wife devoted herself to raising the kids and smiling gamely when her husband unexpectedly brought his boss home for dinner, became for many an object of humor and ridicule. Mary Tyler Moore, who portrayed such a wife on the Dick Van Dyke show in the early sixties, became a single, career newswomen in her 1970s show.[15] Sexual activity and cohabitation outside of marriage, once major scandals, have now become commonplace. Women much more frequently participate in the labor market, and enter nontraditional careers, such as engineering, medicine (as physicians), law, and the like. Economics classes, once almost exclusively male, are now filled with women, most of whom aspire to the same careers as their male counterparts. What caused these trends to suddenly accelerate the way they did? One could simply conclude that the sixties generation was just a different and wild bunch of kids, but economics rejects such *ad hoc* theorizing. Why should that generation have been different from the ones that came to maturity in the fifties, eighties or nineties?

15. Ironically, the previous generations regarded the "liberation" of women to mean freeing women from the necessity of working outside the home so that more time could be devoted to motherly activities.

At least some part of these changes can be traced to one of the most significant peace-time events of the twentieth century. It is still affecting our lives and will continue to do so for many years to come. This event is known as the post-World War II baby-boom. Two hundred years of steadily declining birth rates bottomed out during the great depression of the 1930s and remained low during the war years. Birthrates then climbed to levels unprecedented in recent history. By 1945, as World War II was drawing to a close, birth rates were 85.9 per 1,000 women of child-bearing age, and actual births were 2,858,000. Then, in 1946 and 1947, births simply went through the roof. In 1946, 553,000 *more* children were born than in 1945, and in 1947, 406,000 more children were born than in 1946. The number of births was 33% higher in 1947 than in 1945. Altogether, there were over three and a half million more children born from 1946 through 1950 than were born from 1941 through 1945, a 24% increase.

The result of this increase in fertility was an unusually large group of people (usually referred to as a cohort) within, say, a ten-year age-span of each other. Taking 1950 as the middle year of birth for these war babies or boomers, as they were commonly called, this cohort reached high school in the mid-1960s and entered the labor force or were attending college in the late 1960s and early 1970s, plus or minus a few years.

Consider first the effects of this increase in birthrates on the wages and incomes this cohort received when all these people reached their late teens and early twenties and entered the labor force. Although we will later develop the specific tools of supply and demand with which we analyze such questions, it is easy to accept that this increase in the supply of young workers depressed the wages for jobs available to those workers (typically, entry-level jobs requiring little training and experience, such as jobs at fast-food chains, assembly-line work, janitorial work, and the like). One consequence of the low entry level wages, was that the two-earner family, where both husband and wife are employed became much more prevalent.

In addition to an increase in the number of women working, the type of participation in the labor force by women changed. When women worked principally as wives and mothers, it was common for women to enter the labor force during their early twenties, and drop out of the labor force a few years later to raise children. Only when those women were middle-aged, after the kids were much older, say teenagers, or out of the house entirely, did those women return to the labor force. The result of this pattern of participation was that women typically took non-career jobs, such as secretarial, clerical, sales, or waitressing jobs, for which entrance into the labor market was fairly easy, and for which long periods of training were not required. These jobs were also relatively easy to regain when the women reentered the labor force later on.

Men, on the other hand, who believed that they would always be the principal breadwinners of their families, took a longer-term view of their jobs and careers. A person who was fairly certain of lifetime employment would be prudent in many cases to endure extended training, such as a college education, or apprenticeship in blue-collar crafts, at low or no pay, for the prospect of much higher income later. Thus it was principally men who showed up in such career-oriented college programs as engineering, accounting and business, or in craft-apprentice programs. If one expected to leave the labor force in a few years anyway, and to remain out of the labor force for ten to twenty years, then these training programs, and the investments in time and finances that they required, would be far less attractive. Women stayed away from them in droves. When those women finally re-entered the labor force, they went back to their old, lower-paying jobs, whereas men of the same age had accumulated many years of experience and on-the-job training. Not surprisingly, a comparison of women's and men's earnings reveals striking differences.

This generation of workers, which had formed expectations similar to their older siblings and relatives on the basis of their past experiences, were met with disappointing opportunities in the labor market. The attractive entry-level jobs that people five or ten years older had faced simply were not available to the baby-boomers. It is therefore not surprising that the 1960s generation of young people were a disenchanted lot. Society dealt them an unpopular war to fight in Vietnam, and economic opportunities noticeably less attractive than those experienced by their older peers.[16] These lower income levels have continued to plague this cohort, albeit at reduced rates, as they have gotten older. The Vietnam veterans, belonging to this age-group, have fared relatively worse than veterans of World War II and Korea; they are victims not only of the effects of the war but of the baby boom.[17]

College students in the 1990s, i.e., those born in the 1970s, faced the opposite situation. This was a period of very low birth rates. By the late 1980s and early 1990s, McDonalds and other employers providing entry level, minimum wage jobs were finding that too few workers applied for work at those wages. As a result, wages for those jobs were typically well above the legal minimum wage. This cohort will probably enjoy better than average prospects than their parents. Currently, however, the baby boomers' children—a large cohort, since the number of baby-boomers was large—are reaching adulthood, and most of the readers of this text are likely in this group. We can expect the people reaching adulthood in the first decade of the twenty-first century to have many experiences in common with their parents. Getting into college and professional school will be more difficult, and we can expect the incomes this cohort earns to be less than that of the cohort which preceded it by a decade.

The "Marriage Squeeze" In the traditional marriage, women typically married men a few years older than themselves. Although there is more than one reason for this, a contributing factor would be that older men have higher earning capacity than younger men. The earnings of young men right out of high school are unpredictable, not very high, and thus generally insufficient for sharing in marriage. The low earning potential for women right out of school was of less importance in the traditional marriage situation since most women did not work outside the home. However, whatever the reasons, by the time of the late 1960s it had become arithmetically impossible for this traditional situation to continue for many women. By 1970, there were many more young women in their early twenties than men in their later twenties. The women born in the late 1940s were

16. The experience of the 1930s provides confirming evidence that depressed economic conditions produce radicalism. In that decade there was world-wide depression, with unemployment levels in the United States reaching 25% of the labor force in 1932. This decade was clearly the most radical in U.S. history. The socialist candidate for president, Norman Thomas, received 881,951 votes in 1932, up from 267,835 votes in 1928. The 1950s, by contrast, when the small cohort born in the 1930s entered the labor force, was a conservative decade, under Republican president Eisenhower.

17. See, e.g., "Effects of Cohort Size on Earnings: The Baby Boom Babies' Financial Bust," *Journal of Political Economy,* October 1979, by Finis Welch for an empirical investigation of the effects of the baby boom on the wage rates of the baby boom generation.

seeking mates born in the early 1940s when births were some 25% lower. There were simply not enough males to go around.

During the late 1940s, 3.5 million *more* babies were born than in the first half of that decade. Approximately half of those post-war babies, 1.75 million, were female, the other half male. In 1970, these females were all 20–24 years old, and perhaps interested in somewhat older men. But this means, for example, that there were approximately 1.75 million fewer men aged 25–29 than there were women aged 20–24. This difference in the male-female population amounted to over 20% of that female cohort. Is there any wonder, therefore, that the traditional marriage model broke down at that time? For perhaps 20% of the young female population, it was simply impossible, as a matter of arithmetic, for it to continue.

The result of this change in population structure, therefore, was that many young women in those years had to change their plans, by, for example, entering the labor force. By 1970, there was considerable "consciousness raising," to use the then-popular term, among young women about alternatives to dependency on men for support. However, to a large extent these were people who had not expected to be in the labor force as young adults, and had not studied marketable course work, such as engineering, the sciences, and business. Thus the women's liberation movement was reborn—not as a random event in history, but as a response to a major change in the opportunities and constraints faced by the young women of that period.

At the same time, the traditional values that stressed sexual abstinence until marriage began to look hopelessly old-fashioned to many of the baby-boomers. This new morality is consistent with the events described above. The average age of first marriage in 1960 was around 21 among females, and somewhat older for males. By about 1970, it appeared to many young people that they would not get married at that tender age, and perhaps not at all. (At present [2002], the age of first marriage is 25.3 for women and 26.9 for men.) In addition, a more convenient and reliable contraceptive technique—the pill—became available. The cost of chastity therefore seemed to be increasing for many people. The sexual revolution (complete with an epidemic of the sexually transmitted disease Herpes and later, AIDS) took hold of the baby-boom population. American society will never be quite the same. However, we are now into the baby *bust* years, where the young adult population is composed of those born during the years of extremely low birth rates. Men in their late thirties now vastly outnumber women in their early thirties. Young women are now especially scarce, to an unprecedented extent. We expect therefore a return, at least in part, to more traditional values.

CHAPTER SUMMARY

- Market economies are characterized by highly decentralized decision-making. Actions of individuals are coordinated by *prices* in the market. Prices provide information and incentives to produce goods that people want.
- Economics is a *science:* it seeks explanations of real events. It is part of social science because it studies the behavior of humans.
- Scientific statements must be free of value-judgments. That is, explanations must consist of *positive* statements which are either true or false, and not

normative statements which only reflect the observer's opinion as to what *ought* to be.

- Theories are necessary in order to organize our thoughts. Otherwise, we are confronted with a sea of unrelated facts.
- We reject *ad hoc* theories made up just to suit some particular facts. In particular, theories based on *ad hoc* assertions about individual preferences are never acceptable.
- *Scarcity* of goods is the fundamental reason for the study of economics and the other social sciences. Because of scarcity, we are forced to compete with each other and to choose how to allocate resources which have alternative uses.
- We never explain changes in behavior on the basis that tastes somehow changed or that one group of people is somehow "different" from others. These are *ad hoc*. We look for changes in the severity of constraints people face, and assume people act to mitigate the damages caused by those constraints.
- The *cost* of any action is the highest valued thing that doesn't occur because that action was taken. If some goods are produced, the costs of those goods are the other goods that we might have had if we hadn't produced these goods.
- *Demand* is the analysis of how consumers choose. Economics asserts a fundamental regularity of behavior, known as the *law of demand:* other things remaining the same, if the price of some activity is increased, individuals reduce their pursuit of that activity (and *vice versa* for price decreases).
- *Supply* is the analysis of how individuals choose goods to produce. We most frequently assert a law of supply: higher prices induce suppliers to increase the amount of goods offered for sale.
- In unrestricted markets, prices are established for which the quantity demanded equals the quantity supplied.

REVIEW QUESTIONS

1. What are the general mechanisms for determining and coordinating in a decentralized economy?
2. Why do we restrict science to positive rather than normative statements?
3. Why do we use the term refutable proposition as opposed to provable proposition?
4. What is the true cost of attending college for four years?
5. Why do economists not use explanations based on tastes, or preferences?
6. What are the laws of demand and supply?

PROBLEMS

1. How is it that unplanned, "market" economies operate at all? What aspect of human behavior puts bread and meat on the shelves of groceries?

2. It is apparent that most of the time, goods are not wasted, or thrown away because no one wants to buy them. How is it that approximately the "correct" amount of goods get produced in each market, and what mechanisms are there for correcting erroneous decisions about production levels?

3. Why is economics considered a science? What types of statements are to be avoided if the subject is to be scientific?

4. Is "scientific" the same thing as "true?"

5. What is it that makes some proposition scientifically interesting and useful?

6. Can theories be "proven?" Explain what it means to have "confirmed" a theory, or theoretical explanation of some event.

7. Can propositions be "good in theory but lousy in practice?"

8. Make up some examples of events which seem to happen together, but for which neither event *causes* the other.

9. Make sure you understand the concept of positive and negative slopes. Explain the meaning of supply and demand curves and the meaning of the slopes of these curves.

10. People in the Pacific Northwest consume more water per person than people in the southwest. Does this mean that Northwesterners like water more, or are in general thirstier than Southwesterners?

11. Distinguish "scarce" and "limited" (they are not the same).

12. "If only people learned to love other people more and to respect differences of opinions, we wouldn't have to live in such a competitive, unpleasant world." Do you agree? What is the fundamental reason why competition for goods exists?

13. "As a matter of public policy, the government should promote a more equitable distribution of income." How would you define "equitable distribution of income?" Is it capable of scientific determination?

14. What is the cost to you of going to college? Is it just the tuition, or is there something else involved?

15. In some countries, a test that can determine the sex of a fetus (amniocentesus) is being used to abort female fetuses. As a result, 60% or more of the babies born in some of these areas are male. What do you suppose will be the long-term effects of this on traditional gender and marriage roles?

16. A survey once showed that 70 percent of married men are bald. Does this mean that marriage leads to baldness? What general principle does this illustrate about the problem of inferring causality from correlation?

17. Can a good be scarce for some people and not for others? If you think so, give some examples.

18. The rules for competing differ in different contexts. What types of competition are allowed, for example, in business that are not allowed for getting high grades? Can politicians compete for your vote the same way retailers compete for your dollars?

19. What does free enterprise mean? Does it mean we are free to do anything we want?

20. Some define economics as the study of the proposition, "there's no such thing as a free lunch." Do you think this is a good definition?

21. (An exercise in logic and global thinking.) A man goes on a bear hunt. He starts out from his camp and hikes five miles south, but he doesn't see any bears, so he hikes five miles east, where he shoots a bear. He then hikes five miles back to camp. What was the color of the bear?

QUESTIONS FOR DISCUSSION

1. What kinds of social science questions (give some examples) are outside the paradigm of economics?

2. Given the low birth rates in the late 1970s and 1980s, do you think we will ever go back to traditional morality in this country?

CHAPTER 2

The Theory of Consumer Behavior

Every year, Americans spend more on pet food than they do on milk for their children. Does this mean we care more about our pets than our children? Have you ever wondered why diamonds, which are pretty, but let's face it, we can live happy lives without them, are expensive, whereas water, which is essential to life, is generally cheap? This ancient puzzle, known as the diamond-water paradox, and which is the same as the pet food-milk puzzle, stymied economists and other thinkers for centuries. It was only with the advent of modern economic reasoning that we finally cracked this puzzle. In this chapter, we introduce this framework, called marginal analysis, and we resolve this and other puzzles about the way people choose.

2.1 Economic Behavior

Most people use the phrase "behaving economically" to mean that a person is acting prudently where money is concerned. For example, we might apply the phrase when we shop at a discount store rather than a more expensive retail outlet, or when we carefully save for future expenses such as college costs and the like. Purchasing an expensive wardrobe and then wondering how we'll finance the next week's meals is sometimes regarded as not behaving economically. Although economists use this phraseology in ordinary speech as do others, in scientific discussions we mean something else entirely.

Economics asserts that people engage in some sort of purposeful behavior. Sometimes this is called rational behavior or maximizing behavior, but these terms are loaded with connotations we don't mean to include. We don't mean to assert that people are selfish, or shrewdly calculating, or always purchasing goods at the lowest possible price, or maximizing one's pecuniary, or monetary wealth at all times. Nobody works around the clock, allowing only the biologically minimum time for sleep. Almost all people give some income to others, either as charity, or to family members, asking little or nothing in return. We take jobs that pay less than other available jobs, but which have nicer working conditions, are more conveniently located. In this chapter, we explore more fully the kind of behavior economics assumes. The reason why we feel we must assert *something* about human behavior is that without a theory of human behavior, it is impossible to state scientifically interesting propositions. Our propositions would be *ad hoc,* i.e., made up to suit the facts in a particular case. We seek always to develop statements that could be wrong but which withstand repeated testing. That is the goal of all science and it is the goal of economics as well.

So, we now state our fundamental beliefs about human behavior. In order to be useful, the economic postulates have to be stated in terms of actions that can be observed. We are not able to read people's minds. It also bears mentioning that although we state these postulates as universal propositions, that is, we assert that certain behaviors are true for all individuals at all times, these propositions are in fact just postulates—assertions about behavior. It may turn out that certain anomalies exist which are contrary to these axioms. We would then judge the postulates as to how useful they were in analyzing problems, even though they might in some instances give wrong answers. If the wrong answers were to become significant, the theory would at that point have to be revised.[1]

1. The elementary chemistry that was taught to many of us in college implied that the inert gases, neon, argon, etc., could not combine with other elements. Yet it was discovered that xenon some-

Individual, not Group Preferences

We pause to note that the proposed postulates of behavior are all about *individual* preferences, not group preferences. Although economics rarely focuses on only what single individuals do, being more concerned with the consequences of the combined actions of individuals, the behavioral postulates themselves are all about individual behavior, not about what groups do. The reason, simply put, is that we have reason to believe that we cannot accurately describe the preferences of a group.

Consider a situation where there are three individuals, *I, II* and *III,* about to vote on three proposals, or candidates, *A, B* and *C*. Each person ranks the candidates as follows, where the greater than symbol, >, means preferred to. Suppose, for example, person *I* prefers *A* to *B,* and *B* to *C* (and therefore, *A* to *C*). We write this, and the preferences of *II* and *III* as

$$I\text{: } A > B > C$$
$$II\text{: } B > C > A$$
$$III\text{: } C > A > B$$

All the individual preferences are clear enough, but suppose we wished to define the preferences of this group, i.e., to assign in a meaningful way the decision most preferred by this group. Consider candidate *A*. A majority of this group in fact finds *A* a less attractive alternative than *C:* persons *II* and *III* both prefer *C* to *A*. Likewise, persons *I* and *III* both prefer *A* to *B*. And, to round things out, persons *I* and *II* both prefer *B* to *C*. No matter which candidate is chosen, a (changing) *majority* would rather have someone else!

This voting paradox was first noted over two centuries ago by a French political economist, Condercet. An American Nobel Laureate in economics, Kenneth Arrow, highlighted it in the early 1950s in a famous monograph about the impossibility of choosing aggregate, or social preferences. It shows clearly the futility of such an endeavor. It is not implied that such cyclic preferences will always occur. However, the possibility that it *might* occur means that no systematic structure can be imposed on the preferences of a group which would reliably predict the behavior of that group.

It is, of course, the case that in many instances large numbers of people will have a common interest in some policy. We prefer to regard that, however, as commonality of individuals' private interests, rather than asserting that the group has such a preference. It is generally unreliable to predict the preferences of individuals on the basis of whether, for example, they are workers, whether they own assets (capitalists?) or are white collar professionals, etc. On issues restricting the imports of textiles, workers and owners in the textile industry speak with one voice in support, for the incomes of all those individuals will likely increase as a result. On the other hand, when wage negotiations are under way, these two groups have divergent interests. Thus, while the actions of a single individual are rarely the focus of economics, the postulates of behavior are stated in terms of individual preferences because that is likely to be more fruitful for deriving refutable propositions about the actions of large numbers of people.

---

times combined with fluorine to make xenon fluoride. The older chemistry, which produced such products as penicillin and polyester, was technically wrong. Yet we continue to largely use it because it still reliably predicts outcomes for the empirically significant part of the science. Anomalies, however, often lead to greater understanding of the underlying processes.

2.2 The Postulates of Behavior

Postulate 1. *People have preferences.* So that we know what we're talking about, it's useful to set this out first. Economics asserts that people exercise tastes, or preferences about the things they choose. In particular, suppose a person is confronted with two alternative baskets of goods, say, one with 5 lbs. of potatoes and 1 steak, and another with only 2 lbs. of potatoes but with 2 steaks. Then we say that people can distinguish these (or any) bundles of goods in the following sense: the consumer either prefers the first to the second, the second to the first, or is indifferent between the two. If a person prefers some bundle *A* to bundle *B,* it means only that if given a free choice between the two, so that he or she can have either one (but not both) just for the asking, the person chooses *A.* If the person is indifferent between *A* and *B,* it means the person would be happy to let someone else choose for him or her. Economics does not go on to quantify the psychological degree to which these preferences are felt. We do not make assertions such as "This bundle of goods gives me twice the pleasure of that bundle." We simply assert that people can and do *rank* various alternatives and act on those preferences. Economists typically express this by saying that we can measure the utility or pleasure we get from consuming goods only as an ordinal number, not as a cardinal number. The ordinal numbers are the rankings first, second, third, etc.; the cardinal numbers refer to the measurable amounts one, two, three. In elections and in most sports, only the ordinal measure counts: the person or team that get the most votes or points wins. On the other hand, your grade in this course and your cumulative GPA are cardinal measures of your success.

Postulate 2. *More is preferred to less.* Around the beginning of the twentieth century, Samuel Gompers, the first president of the American Federation of Labor, was asked what it was he wanted for his union workers. His reply was simple and to the point: "More." Human wants are insatiable. No matter how rich we become, there will always be better houses, bigger yachts, fancier airplanes, and fancier food to consume. The list of potential goods to be enjoyed is endless. Most of us don't think much about really big-ticket items, since we are not likely to be able to consume them. They are wholly beyond our wealth. But there is no limit to even commonplace goods such as stereo equipment, high-performance cars, computers, homes and home furnishings, etc., on which we can easily imagine spending our income. Occasionally we read that in this modern age, we have finally overcome the ravages of scarcity, that our standard of living is adequate for any reasonable person, and that any further increases in consumption would be extravagantly wasteful. Such value judgments do not accurately predict actual behavior. If this were true, the rich would give away their wealth beyond some point. We do not observe charity on the scale implied by such statements.

Although the statement "more is preferred to less" conveys the gist of this aspect of human behavior, we prefer greater precision. A person might not really want a third milkshake, and we certainly don't want more cockroaches and garbage. The items must at the very least be desirable to humans in some amount, that is to say, they must be *goods.* The postulate refers to greater *access to goods.* Sometimes, for example when people realize a sudden large increase in wealth, it takes time for them to discover the goods now within their means. They rationally would have spent little time acquiring information on Lear jets and the like. However, with the passage of time, people adjust their expenditures to the new goods available with the higher incomes.

Postulate 3. *People are willing to substitute one good for another.* This substitution postulate is a fundamental aspect of behavior. It says people are willing to make *trade-offs.* People are willing to give up some beef, say, if they can obtain some chicken in exchange; people will trade off a more luxurious car for a better home, eating out for better clothes, and so forth. It extends even to bribes. We decided to eat our broccoli when our parents offered us more ice cream—trading off one good, less broccoli, for additional dessert.

Though somewhat innocent sounding, the implications of this postulate are profound. It denies, in the first place, the concept of needs. People desire many goods simultaneously. If one is willing to trade off even small amounts of one good in order to have more of another, then one cannot say that we need all of that good. Of course, we do require minimal amounts of food, water, etc., for survival. In ordinary speech, when life and death choices are concerned, we all say we need food, water, air, etc. However, the actions to obtain those minimal amounts of air and water then are really non-choices. We must have these things to survive; there is nothing we can do about them. If there is truly nothing to decide, there is nothing really worth studying.[2] Such actions fall outside of economics and the rest of social science.

Beyond subsistence levels of income, we observe that people consume food, clothing, shelter, recreation, etc. in varying amounts. The specific goods within these categories also vary from individual to individual. The substitution postulate denies priorities of wants. We cannot say that food is more important than clothing, or vice-versa. If even very poor people suffer a loss in income, they will likely contract their consumption of all the general categories of goods they presently consume; not simply decrease consumption of goods somehow lower on the list of priorities. We do not expect to see a person consuming, literally, no food or no clothing. People make a great variety of trade-offs, from simple, mundane choices of, say, choosing steak over hamburgers, to trading security for excitement, e.g., by joining the marines, or becoming astronauts and test pilots rather than civil servants. People choose amongst occupations that present differing prospects of wealth versus intellectual stimulation. Some careers are well-paid but boring. Teaching is often psychologically rewarding but often not well paying.

It is often argued that safety is a good with high (or perhaps highest) priority, but daily we observe individuals trading off safety for enjoyment of other goods. We sometimes drive excessively fast, increasing our chances of death or injury, just to get to a movie or dinner on time. Automobile safety became a big issue in the 1960s after the publication of *Unsafe at Any Speed,* by Ralph Nader, who argued that the General Motors Corvair was, among other things, highly prone to roll over.[3] Certain things are obvious: big cars are safer than small cars (this follows from the law of conservation of momentum), new cars are safer

---

2. We do in fact observe people making life and death choices. Many terminally ill persons choose, through living wills, to forgo expensive medical procedures that would prolong their lives (at sometimes great expense) so that their families can retain that income for themselves.

3. Actually, the book bombed until it was discovered that G.M. had apparently hired some young women to trail Mr. Nader, hoping to get him into a compromising situation. Nader caught on, however, Congressional hearings were held, and then people decided that maybe he had something worth reading. It's still an open question.

than old cars (less chance of mechanical failure), new tires are safer than old tires (better traction, handling, stopping ability), seat belts save many lives (though with rear lap belts only, the chance of death is lowered, but serious injury to the spine and lower organs raised), driving fast is more dangerous than driving slow (also from the law of conservation of momentum), and alcohol and cars are very dangerous to consume together. Yet it is a commonplace observation that many of us drive small, old cars with balding tires, sometimes at breakneck speed, and sometimes after consumption of alcohol or other drugs. People everyday trade safety, the probability of life itself, for other goods. Big new cars are expensive; in order to consume them, one might have to give up movies, compact disks, eating out, and maybe eating anything beyond beans and rice. People choose to take the risks of driving small, older cars in order to be able to enjoy other things. We occasionally drive faster than we should because we are late for something, or because of the thrill of it, even though we know it increases the risk of death or injury. Every year in the United States about 35,000 people are killed in automobile accidents. We could cut this rate practically to zero by enacting, and hiring enough police to enforce, a 25 mph national speed limit. But this policy would be so unpopular, it will never be proposed.

Another important trade-off involving safety occurs in the area of testing and approving new prescription drugs. It is very expensive to bring new drugs onto the market. The Food and Drug Administration (FDA) requires drug manufacturers to prove, using animal and then human studies, that the drugs are not only effective, but are also safe. In the 1950s, Thalidomide, a British drug that helped control nausea in pregnant women, was found to sometimes cause severe birth defects in the form of shortened arms or legs. Partly in reaction to this event, the FDA placed very substantial conditions on safety before it would approve new drugs. As a result, the cost of bringing new drugs to market can take many years and cost upwards of $100 million.

When the AIDS epidemic hit in the 1980s, people began to question whether these FDA rules caused *too much safety*. How can goods be too safe? In the case of full-blown AIDS, if left untreated, the disease is shortly fatal. Although a rush was on to develop drugs that would slow or reverse the disease, even after a drug was shown to be effective, it typically took years to prove that a drug was safe. In the meantime, the current AIDS victims would all die. For the first time, the FDA had to confront the idea that its rules for approving drugs for diseases like AIDS and cancer might reasonably be different than for approving drugs for less lethal conditions. As a result, the FDA relaxed the rules and allowed more use of unproven drugs on patients with otherwise terminal conditions. Some of these procedures were unsuccessful, and some new drugs turn out to actually be harmful, but the cost of not allowing the new drugs to be used on a more widespread basis was even greater—more people would die without the drugs than with them.

The Wall Street Journal carried an interesting story about Lupus, an autoimmune disease affecting approximately 250,000 to 1,000,000 people in the United States.[4] The disease causes the body's immune system to attack healthy tissue; young women are its most common victims. The wide variation in the estimated number of cases is due partly to the difficulty in diagnosing the disease, which causes painful symptoms ranging from rashes to arthritis and kidney disease. The FDA has not approved a new drug for Lupus in forty years. One of the problems is

4. April 15, 2004, Page 1, Col. 1.

that because of the variety of symptoms and their ebb and flow even if untreated, it is difficult to prove to the FDA that a drug is actually working. Some doctors believe the chemotherapy drug cyclophosphamide used for cancer patients is effective for lupus patients and prescribe it, even though it is not approved by the FDA for lupus. But because doctors do in fact use it, any new drug must be proven to be even more effective than cyclophosphamide in order to gain approval. The FDA is currently working to provide new markers for showing that a drug is working, but its guidelines are often vague and subject to review. As a result, drug manufacturers are not willing to commit large amounts of money to research new drugs for this disease.

At this writing, corporate executive and media personality Martha Stewart is appealing her conviction of lying to federal agents about her sales of Imclone stock shortly before the FDA rejected the company's new drug Erbitux, in 2002. Her friend Sam Waskal, the owner of Imclone, was convicted of insider trading and is now in jail. (Waskel sold his stock just prior to the FDA's rejection of Erbitux. He had *inside knowledge* of this ruling, and knew that it would cause the price of Imclone to drop. Such sales (or purchases) by corporate executives of their company's stocks are illegal.) Ironically, two years later, the FDA approved Erbitux, finding that it safely and effectively treats late-stage colon cancer. It is probable that thousands of Americans died or died sooner because this drug was not approved earlier.

Thus drug safety is not free—it reduces the available number of drugs. People often are willing to substitute less safety for the prospect of an improved or longer life, but the problem of constructing a proper public health policy is obviously very difficult.

Marriage—forsaking all others—is one of the most important trade-offs any of us are likely to make in our lifetimes. When we marry, we agree, among other things, not to lead ourselves into temptation regarding persons of the opposite sex. But it is a common occurrence in the course of a lifetime to be attracted to new acquaintances, and to contemplate cheating on one's spouse. The postulate "more is preferred to less" makes us want the affair *and* the security and companionship of our spouse, but the likely outcome of an affair is to have only one or the other. Thus we have to choose which we prefer. Monogamy has its costs, but its longevity in history is testimony to its benefits.

Safety from criminals is an important good of which we prefer more. Incarceration of individuals who intend to harm our property or person is a widely shared preference. Nonetheless, it seems that many individuals roam the streets despite what many people consider strong evidence they are criminals. An important reason is that there is another good, protection of the innocent, of which we also desire more. It is not easy to have more of *both* convictions of criminals and protection of the innocent. We could convict more criminals and have less crime by the simple expedient of jailing all persons accused by the police. However, this would certainly result in the incarceration of innocent persons as well. Likewise, we could insure against false conviction of the innocent by never convicting anyone, but this would result in more crime. The meaningful debate on this important issue revolves around the degree of protection that should be afforded the accused, e.g., whether a confession in the absence of an attorney is admissible in court, whether evidence obtained with a faulty, though well-intentioned search warrant is admissible, and the like. These are debates about the value of extra public safety versus protection of the innocent. It is one of the more important trade-offs faced by free societies.

Check your understanding: Current medical evidence is quite compelling that fatty foods—ice cream, hot dogs, French fries—are bad for us. Yet we see many people eating these foods on a regular basis. Is this a sign of irrationality? What behavior would you expect to see if the news about these foods became even worse?

The Meaning of Value

The willingness of individuals to trade off one good for another is a fundamental observation of economics. Moreover, it provides the only operational, i.e., *observable* definition of the concept of value. People often say that they like this or that thing a lot or that they strongly support some cause, yet it is sometimes difficult to verify their protestations. Absent the ability to read minds, how are we to truly know that a person has strongly held preferences or beliefs about some good or issue? Benjamin Franklin (or someone) once said, "Talk is cheap." It really *is* cheap, because nothing has to be sacrificed, save a little time, in order to talk. We know a person is serious when they do something that entails a personal cost to them. That is why actions speak louder than words.

In economics, we measure value by what we are willing to give up in order to obtain something. When a person purchases a hamburger at $3.00, he or she is giving up $3.00 of other goods by making that choice. In that way, the person *reveals* a preference for hamburger over these other goods. We feel comfortable saying this person values the hamburger by at least $3.00. Talk-show guests sometimes seem embarrassed that they don't like opera. The host asks them if they like opera, and they eagerly affirm this proper, becoming taste. They admit they don't get to the opera as much as they'd like to, and when pressed, admit that not only have they never gone, they don't even own a single recording of any opera or opera star. We are duly skeptical. It is not backed up by any observable action that would lead a sensible person to conclude that the individual really likes opera at all.

The value of a good is determined solely by the willingness of human beings to give up other goods in order to get that particular good. One sometimes hears that certain goods have intrinsic value, for example, a fine work of art, an exceptional quality diamond, a unique property. This is an assertion that these goods have a value determined without regard to the actions of individuals. But this cannot be. An object cannot have value beyond what people are willing to pay for. If no person will pay anything to secure the right to some item, then at least at that particular time and place that item has no value.

The process by which people decide the value they place on consumption goods is largely beyond economics. For the most part, we leave that investigation to psychologists. Sometimes it seems mysterious why some goods are cheap and others are so expensive. A painting by Vincent Van Gogh, who never sold a painting in his own lifetime, might now sell for $25 million; however, if museum curators suddenly discovered by spectroscopic and chemical analysis of the paint that the painting was done in 1955 by Vinny Vangozzi of the Bronx, its price will likely fall to perhaps $5,000, even though nobody will have changed their opinion as to its artistic merits. Why should people place such a large value just on the signature, as opposed to the art itself? And why should Van Gogh's art sell for so much now when formerly, people thought they were junk and wouldn't buy them? Why should Jennifer Lopez and other entertainers make tens of millions of dollars per year ("Heck, my daughter sings almost as well.")? Why should a diamond, which is visually indistinguishable from cubic zirconia (CZs) even by most experts, sell for 1,000 or more times the price of CZs? Economists take no position on these questions. They are statements about people's tastes and are beyond our expertise.[5] Obviously, *some* people believe there is a difference between these goods. The prices of some goods are relatively high only because enough people are willing to put their money where their mouths are and pay those amounts. These goods or services can have no value independent of that disposition to trade. There is no such thing as intrinsic value.

Measuring the Value of Life

Over two hundred years ago, Adam Smith observed in *The Wealth of Nations* (1776) that wages in the marketplace reflected the pleasant or unpleasant aspects of a job. He noted that garbage men would receive pay comparable to teachers, because many people find garbage collection distasteful. This feature of the job market enables economists to evaluate the market price of unpleasant amenities, and in particular, the increased probability of dying on the job. Suppose two jobs are comparable in the sense of requiring workers with the same skills and from the same pool of workers. Then if the two jobs differ only in that one entails a higher risk of injury or death than the other, the wage premium in the riskier job measures how much employers have to pay in the market in order to get workers to *voluntarily* accept the higher risk. Measuring the wage differential that accompanies the additional probability of death in a certain job establishes an economic, or market price of accepting that additional risk of death.

According to statistics compiled by the U.S. Department of Labor, the average annual fatality rate in blue collar occupations is approximately 1/10,000. That is, every year, approximately 1 in 10,000 workers in these occupations dies from a job-related injury. Suppose, for illustration, blue collar workers on average earn $30,000 per year. If the fatality risk were to increase to 2/10,000 and the other job characteristics remained the same, the market wage of these workers would have to rise to compensate for this unpleasant aspect. Assume the market wage rises to $31,000. That is, in order to induce enough workers to voluntarily accept the higher risk of death of .0002 instead of .0001 per year, an additional $1,000 per year must be paid by employers. Formerly, out of 10,000 people on the old job, 1 could be expected to die from an on the job injury; now, fatalities rise to 2. In the market, this extra life lost requires paying 10,000 workers an extra $1,000 each, a total payment of 10,000 x $1,000 = $10,000,000. Equivalently, since each of 10,000 workers would accept $1,000 *less* for a safer job, a total savings of $10,000,000 in aggregate wage payments would be realized by reducing the fatality rate from .0002 to .0001. A market, or revealed value of life is thus established; with these numbers, it would be $10,000,000.

The concept of an economic or market value of life is offensive to many people. Part of this reaction is based on a misunderstanding of the term. The numerical value one might derive is *not* an ethical judgment. Rather, it is simply an observation from the marketplace based on actual human behavior. The

5. The sentiment is sometimes expressed with the Latin phrase, *"De gustibus non est disputandum,"* or, "There's no accounting for tastes."

market premium for risk of death is what human beings in fact accept, at the margin, in payment for added risk of death on the job. It does not indicate that a particular person "should" or would be willing to give up their life for such an amount. Suppose a house which would normally sell for $200,000 sells for only $150,000 because it is located under an airport flight path. The $50,000 differential measures the going market price of contending with airplane noise. It does not mean that a person "ought" to be willing to live near the airport and save the $50,000. It just means that enough people indicate their willingness to accept that amount so that this price appears in the market.

Although the theory of compensating differentials is straightforward, empirical implementation of the theory is difficult and has only recently begun. It is not easy to find good data on the riskiness of actual jobs and to relate those risks to wages and the other associated job characteristics, so that the wage differential created by risk and other job aspects can be estimated. With the invention of modern econometric analysis and powerful new computers, economists have made successful inroads on this issue. Harvard Professor Kip Viscusi has estimated the value of life at approximately $5 million to $10 million.[6] Although economists are interested in these estimates as a matter of intellectual curiosity, these are not mere academic exercises. Important policy questions depend on how much people are willing to pay to preserve life. Consider, for example, that with recent advances in modern medicine, it is now often possible to prolong human life to an extent not dreamed of in earlier generations. Although most would agree that the invention of life-saving or life-extending technology is a good thing for the human race, a major ethical debate has arisen because these techniques are often very expensive, and society, rather than the individual patient, is often being asked to pay for the service. Suppose some taxpayer funded program would save one life by spending an extra $200,000. Is it worth it? Would you vote to impose this tax on yourself and others? Suppose it cost $2,000,000 to save one life in this way. Would that affect your vote? How about $20 billion?

Because of the involvement of the government in the provision of medical services such as this, this important ethical question is forced upon us. Whereas economics can provide no objective answer to the normative question of evaluating life, the theory tells us that a relevant question is, "What is the opportunity cost of these sums?" Suppose the money was instead spent on purchasing prescription medicines such as penicillin, etc., for the indigent. It might be the case that the same sum of money would save even more lives when spent on some other program, perhaps, not even in medicine. Ultimately, the trade-offs made in the marketplace and public policy for life-extending activities reveal the extent to which humans actually go in order to reduce the probability of death.

The value of life also enters public policy in assessing a manufacturer's liability for damages in the case of defective products. For example, cars have been made safer by the addition of reinforced doors to lessen the effects of side impacts, collapsible steering columns, ABS breaking systems and front and side panel airbags. There are always more improvements that could be made. It is always possible to improve the safety of products, but it almost always raises the cost of the product. Sometimes when a person is injured or killed in, say, an auto accident, the injured parties sue the manufacturer for having produced a defective

6. "The Value of Life: Estimates With Risks by Occupation and Industry," *Economic Inquiry,* 42 (January 2004): 29–48.

product. If the plaintiffs (the party suing) can prove that the defendants could have avoided one death per year at some low cost, say, $100,000, they will almost certainly prevail, and be in a position to collect damages. If, however, the company can show that it would have cost over $10,000,000 to avoid one death per year, the law would probably regard this as an unreasonable burden to impose on the manufacturer, and the plaintiff would not be able to collect damages. Thus, the market value of life plays an important role in safety legislation and case law.

Marginal versus Total Values

Economics makes an important distinction between the amount a person would be willing to pay (forgo of other goods) in order to consume *an additional unit* of some good, versus what a person would pay in order to consume *all units* presently consumed of some good, rather than none at all. In fact, it is one of the more important contributions to the theory of choice. We use the adjective marginal to mean incremental. The **marginal value** of a good is the amount of other goods we would be willing to give up in order to obtain an *incremental* amount of that good. The marginal value of a hamburger is the amount an individual would be willing to pay to get *another* hamburger. The **total value** of hamburgers, on the other hand, is the amount a person would be willing to pay to have all of his or her hamburgers rather than have no hamburgers at all. When we use the term pay as in the above phrase, willing to pay, we think in terms of paying money, because we almost never engage in actual barter of goods for goods. However, paying money ultimately means giving up other goods. Throughout this discussion of human preferences, the trade-offs all involve goods for goods. Even though money is used to facilitate transactions, the value of a good is measured by the amount of other goods a person is willing to give up.

There are, of course, many things we might give up to obtain another hamburger, for example, one kernel of popcorn, two raisins, a weekend listening to Barry Manilow. Among the things we might forgo in order to consume something, some are more highly valued to us than others. The value of something we desire is measured by the *maximum* amount of other goods we would be willing to give up in order to obtain the good. This maximum value is most conveniently measured by using money as the good being given up. We ask, what is the maximum amount of money a consumer will give up in order to consume another hamburger? This amount of money is the amount that leaves the consumer no better or worse off after the trade-off is made. This maximum amount is the value of any good or any contemplated activity. The value of a good therefore becomes the *highest valued* of all the alternative goods that might have been consumed.

With this firmly in mind, we now come to the postulate that imposes the fundamental structure on preferences that allows for the derivation of refutable hypotheses.

Postulate 4. *For all individuals and all goods, the marginal value of goods decreases, as more of that good is consumed, holding other things constant.*[7]

7. More advanced texts specify that the level of satisfaction, or utility must be held constant; we shall not be concerned with this here. See Eugene Silberberg, *The Structure of Economics,* 2nd ed., (McGraw-Hill, 1990) for a complete mathematical discussion of this issue. It is not to be confused with an older proposition of diminishing marginal "utility," a now archaic, and for the most part abandoned assertion, though it appears, with suitable caveats, in the modern theory of risk.

This postulate says that the amount of other goods we are willing to forgo in order to consume additional units of a good, becomes continually less. Think about it. Suppose we are willing to pay a dollar for a milkshake. How much would we be willing to pay to consume the second, and maybe the third? We might pay a few cents for the second; for the third, some one would surely have to pay us to get us to consume it, as we would soon become ill. The marginal value will not only fall, it will become negative in this case, though that extreme outcome is not a central issue.

An old proverb says, "Variety is the spice of life." Why is variety, rather than monotony, the spice of life? It is because as people consume additional units of some good, say hamburgers, we eventually value the first unit of some other good, say, french fries, by more than, say, the third hamburger. Suppose the marginal values of goods increased. In that case, as we consumed more and more of any good, we would be willing to trade off ever increasing amounts of other goods to get additional amounts of the original good. If it paid to buy one hamburger, the gain from buying another would be even greater. In this case we would observe that people would spend their entire income on only one good. Monotony would in fact be the spice of life. But we do not observe this behavior; it is refuted by common experience. The only postulate consistent with actual behavior is diminishing marginal values. The veracity of this postulate is so highly regarded, it is commonly referred to as the law of diminishing marginal values.[8]

Check your understanding: Have you ever noticed that people whose birthdays fall right around Christmas often feel cheated, because they get both gifts at the same time? How does the postulate of diminishing marginal values explain this?

2.3 Marginal Values and Demand Curves

In Table 2-1, we list some hypothetical marginal and total values. Assume this table refers to the rate per month at which some person is willing to consume steaks. The first column is self-explanatory; it simply indicates the level of consumption of steaks per month. The second column, Marginal Value, indicates the amount of other goods, measured in money, this consumer would be willing to give up in order to consume one more steak. The consumer is willing to pay \$10, i.e., forgo the consumption of \$10 of other goods, in order to consume the first steak each month.

Consider now the prospect of consuming a second steak. Since the consumer is already consuming one steak (per month), the law of diminishing marginal values implies the consumer will forgo something *less* than \$10 of other goods in order to obtain a second steak. We arbitrarily choose \$9 to represent this new marginal value. Proceeding down the marginal value column, the marginal value of each succeeding steak must be less than the one just before it. The table shows a linear decline down to zero dollars at the 11th steak. This last entry indicates that this consumer would pay nothing to consume an eleventh steak per month. After consuming 10 steaks, this person is so sick of steaks he or she wouldn't divert any resources to additional steaks. It is of course of no importance that the marginal value of steaks decreases by exactly \$1 for each succeeding steak; these numbers

8. Many texts refer to this law as diminishing marginal rate of substitution.

are chosen for arithmetic ease. The crucial property is that the marginal values decline, as more steaks are consumed per month.

The actual marginal values of some good such as steak for a particular consumer depends on that person's tastes for the good in question, his or her income and the amounts of other goods, such as pork and chicken that are also consumed per month. If pork and chicken are not available, the marginal values of steak at any consumption level might be larger than the values listed in Table 2-1. Our only assertion about the actual magnitudes of these marginal values is that whatever they are at some level of consumption, those marginal values *decrease* as additional units are consumed.

Turn now to the next column, Total Value. Total value means the amount a consumer would be willing to pay (in terms of other goods forgone) in order to have all units of this good rather than none at all. It is an all-or-nothing choice—take it all or leave it all. For the first steak, the total value is simply the $10 for that steak. Since the consumer now values the second steak at $9 of other goods, he or she would be willing to pay up to $19 ($10 + $9) to consume both steaks, rather than none. The total value is simply the sum of the respective marginal values. In like fashion, the total value of three steaks to this consumer is $10 + $9 + $8 = $27, and so on down the table. The consumer would be willing to forgo $27 of other goods in order to consume three steaks per month, rather than have no steaks; he or she would be willing to pay $45 to have 6 steaks rather than none, etc.

Notice that the total values increase successively, with increased consumption. Although the marginal values of steak are declining as more steaks are consumed, up through the tenth steak, steaks are still a *good,* because the consumer is willing to pay *something* to get one more. Thus total value increases, albeit at a decreasing rate. If we continued the table beyond the eleventh unit, and forced the consumer to consume steaks to the point where their marginal value was negative, then total value would decrease; we would be foisting a "bad" on someone.

Total Value versus Total Expenditure

Fortunately, we almost never actually have to pay the entire total value of our purchases. Don't forget—these total values are the *maximum* we would be willing to pay for certain amounts of goods rather than go without any. These

Table 2-1

Quantity	Marginal Value	Total Value
1	$10	$10
2	9	19
3	8	27
4	7	34
5	6	40
6	5	45
7	4	49
8	3	52
9	2	54
10	1	55
11	0	55

all-or-nothing choices do not occur very often, because sellers rarely have that much information about our preferences, and are not usually in a position to exploit that information even if they had it. The typical contract with sellers is that they offer goods for sale in identifiable units, at some stated constant price per unit, *and we then get to choose how much we wish to purchase,* such as supermarket purchases or gasoline at the pump. The choice of what quantity to purchase is almost always the consumer's, and it is that aspect of purchase that causes us to pay *less* than the maximum we would be willing to pay. (Some contracts exist in which the choice of quantity is restricted for the consumer, such as package deals for automobile accessories, commitments by movie theaters to show all movies produced by a film producer; we shall defer discussion of these very interesting issues to a later chapter.)

What happens when we are offered the usual supermarket contract of a fixed price, with the quantity decision left up to us? Suppose we are the consumer of Table 2-1, and the price of steaks is $5.00. Since we are willing to give up $10 per month of other goods in order to consume the first steak, and we can obtain this steak at only $5, it is implied, by the postulate of more is preferred to less that we will make this purchase. We get a $10 value for only $5, a net gain to us of $5. In like fashion, we would be willing to pay $9 for the second steak, and we can get it, too, at $5, so we receive a net gain of $4 when we make this purchase. As long as our marginal value of a good exceeds the price we have to pay for it in the market, we gain the difference between our marginal value of the good and its market price by making the purchase. We continue to purchase the good until its marginal value to us falls to its market price. In the present example, with a price of $5 for steaks, a consumer with the preferences indicated in the table would purchase up to 6 steaks, although with these numbers, the last purchase is a tie, with no net gain received. We arbitrarily assume the consumer always makes this last purchase. If we extended the analysis to allow for purchases of fractional units, the marginal value of the 5½th unit would be $5.50; with a continuous scale of prices and quantities, 6 units would in fact be purchased. This behavior is summarized in the first two columns of Table 2-2.

This example illustrates a fundamental aspect of choice. Although it does not show up on any accountant's balance sheet, or any ledger anywhere, consumers *gain* by making these purchases. Consider the numbers in Table 2-2. In addition to the various prices charged and resulting quantities of goods purchased shown in the first two columns, the table displays for each price the

Table 2-2

Price	Quantity Purchased	Total Expenditure	Total Value	Consumer's Surplus
$10	1	$10	$10	$0
9	2	18	19	1
8	3	24	27	3
7	4	28	34	6
6	5	30	40	10
5	6	30	45	15
4	7	28	49	21
3	8	24	52	28
2	9	18	54	36
1	10	10	55	45

resulting total expenditure made by the consumer, the total value, taken from Table 2-1, and a last column, denoted Consumer's Surplus. If the price is, say $5 per steak, this consumer purchases 6 steaks, for a total expenditure of $5 × 6 = $30. However, the *total value* of 6 steaks to this consumer is $45. The consumer is willing to pay $45 for those 6 steaks, rather than have none at all, and yet pays only $30. There is therefore a net gain of $15 to the consumer from this purchase. This gain is the differences between what the consumer *would be willing to pay* for a given quantity of a good (total value), and what he or she *actually does pay* (the total expenditure). These values, for the various prices and amounts purchased, are shown in the last column of Table 2-2. We call this net gain *consumer's surplus.* The term simply means gains from trade. It is a monetary evaluation of the benefits received when we purchase goods at some given market price.[9]

The reason why we *voluntarily* make purchases is that we receive these gains from exchange. No one has to force us to shop. We purchase goods on our own, because we derive net benefits from so doing. We pay less than the maximum we would be willing to pay to receive a given number of units of a good. Consumer's surplus is the difference between what we *would* pay and what we actually *do* pay when we make a purchase. This difference cannot be negative, and is generally positive if the transaction is voluntary.

These benefits (consumer's surplus) exist because of diminishing marginal values, and our ability to purchase all units of a good at the same price. They would not exist if there were only one seller, and he or she somehow knew how much we would be willing to pay for each steak. A single seller, known as a monopolist, with this information, could charge us $10 for the first steak, $9 for the second, and so on, extracting the full total value from us. Or, equivalently, the seller could offer us 6 steaks for a bit less than $45, take it or leave it. We would take it, since $45 is our total value of 6 steaks. In so doing, the monopolist would extract all the gains from us. Fortunately, we rarely face such sellers. They not only would need to have no competitors (who would immediately undercut each other's price), but they also would have to really know how much we would pay for all those steaks. The infrequency of such sales is testimony to the difficulty of arranging these circumstances.

Check your understanding: Consider Table 2-2. When the price is $10, this consumer purchases 1 unit, for a total expenditure of $10. When the price is lowered to $9, she chooses 2 units for $18 instead of 1 unit for $10; her gain is therefore $8. When the price is lowered to $8, she gets 3 units for $24; her gain must therefore be $6 (= $24–$18). If the price were lowered to $5, she would get no gain, and she would actually *lose* $2 if the price were lowered further. . . . HELP! What's going on here?

2.4 The Law of Demand

The law of diminishing marginal values provides the central prediction of behavioral economics: the response to a change in the price. Suppose the price of steaks falls from $5 to $3. Now, the seventh steak, which has a marginal value of $4, becomes a worthwhile purchase. The consumer will now purchase this

9. A vast literature exists (including some pieces by the author) concerning the multitude of possible measures of gains from trade. We use this well-defined measure here for its clarity and simplicity.

unit, and, under our standard assumption, purchase the eighth unit also, which has a marginal value equal to the price. In like manner, if the price had *risen* to, say, $7, the consumer would have cut back on purchases, to 4 units, for now, the fifth and sixth units would be worth less in terms of other goods forgone than the marginal value of the steaks. Therefore, we see that as long as the values in the table remain stable, the quantity of a good a person will choose to purchase varies *inversely* with the price. If the price increases, the quantity chosen, or demanded, falls; if the price decreases, the quantity demanded rises. This proposition is of such central importance in economics we refer to it as a law; it is known as the law of demand. The formal statement of the law is:

> The quantity demanded of any good, or the level of any activity pursued varies inversely with the price of that good or activity, holding other things constant.[10]

The other things that must be held constant are the other variables, or constraints, which, in addition to the price of the good, could reasonably affect an individual's consumption of that good. Prominent examples of such variables are the consumer's income, the prices of closely related goods, and of course, tastes. Suppose, for example, the price of steaks increased, but the consumer's income also rose, coincidentally. Then we would have two influences on steak consumption that would likely oppose one another: the higher price would cause the individual to cut back on steak consumption, whereas the higher income would likely tend to increase his or her consumption of this particular good. A refutable prediction would not be forthcoming, unless we could independently measure the quantitative effects separately. Likewise, suppose the price of steak fell, leading the individual to consume more, but suppose at the same time, the price of pork also fell. In this case, the consumer might switch mainly to pork for meat consumption, and consume less steak, even though its price has fallen. When two relevant prices change simultaneously, there is a danger that the implications will be confounded by opposing influences. Thus, the implication of the law of demand is restricted to those cases in which all other relevant influences on the demand for that commodity remain constant.

In Fig. 2-1 we plot the quantity of some good along the horizontal axis, and its marginal value to some consumer along the vertical axis, using the numbers in Table 2-1, and connect these points with a smooth curve. The height of the curve DD', (a straight line because the marginal values decreased at a constant rate in this example), represents the marginal values of steaks for each quantity. (We ignore for the moment the unshaded little triangles where the curve exceeds the marginal values.) The line is *negatively sloped* because of the postulate of diminishing marginal values. The thin rectangular areas for each unit represent the marginal value of that unit. Since the total value of some number of units, say, six, is the sum of the marginal values up to six units, the total value is represented by the area *under* the marginal value curve, ignoring, again, the little triangles. For six units, this total area is $45, as derived from Table 2-1.

The marginal value curve indicates how much of a good a consumer will purchase, at given prices. As long as the marginal value exceeds the market price of a good, a consumer will find it to his or her advantage to purchase the good. If the price of, say, steaks, is $5, the graph shows that six units will be bought.

10. The "other things constant" part, is often referred to by a Latin phrase, *ceteris paribus*.

Figure 2-1 *Diminishing Marginal Values*

As individuals consume additional units of any good, the amount of other goods that consumers will give up (measured in dollars) in order to acquire still another unit diminishes. In this example the marginal value of the first unit is $10; the marginal value of the sixth unit is $5.

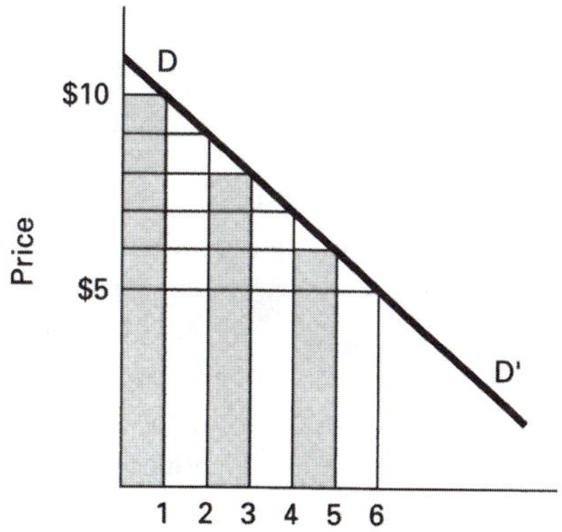

Moreover, the area between the marginal value of the good and the price, being the difference between those two values, represents the net consumer's gain, or consumer's surplus, from the purchase of six units at a price of $5 each.

In Fig. 2-2 we smooth out the curve, and treat the good as something that can be bought in continuous amounts. For example, gasoline, water, and many other liquids are in fact purchased essentially in any real amount, not just in discrete units. We consider the consumption of goods as an *average rate* per unit time, rather than focus in on the discreteness of the units of purchase. If we purchase a loaf of bread on Monday, another on Friday, and another the following Tuesday, this is a rate of consumption of 1 loaf every 4 days (4/7th of a week), or 7/4 loaves per week. We can imagine increasing or decreasing this rate by any continuous amount, large or small.

In Fig. 2-2, quantities are plotted horizontally, and the marginal values are plotted vertically. The height of the curve at any arbitrary quantity represents the marginal value of the good at that level of consumption. At a price above $11, the consumer chooses not to consume this good at all; this value is called the reservation price. The curve falls continuously as quantity increases. Alternatively, we can interpret this curve as showing the amount of this good a consumer will

Figure 2-2 *The Demand Curve, Responding to Decrease in Price*

Initially, the price of this good is $6; the consumer purchases 5 units. If the price decreases to $4, the consumer purchases additional units until his or her marginal value of the goods falls to $4. The *law of demand* says that other things constant, as the price of a good falls, the quantity demanded increases (and vice versa).

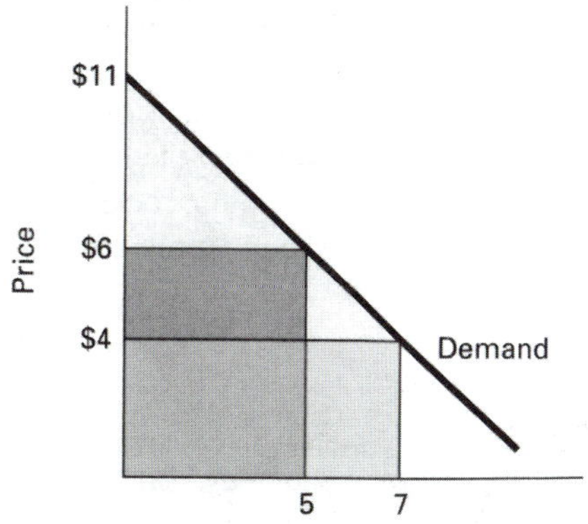

purchase, at given prices. For example, if the market price is $6, the consumer will purchase the good until the marginal value falls to this level. This quantity is 5 units. If the price falls to $4, the consumer extends his or her purchases to 7 units. In this interpretation, we treat the causality as going from price to quantity, or the vertical axis to the horizontal axis. Price is the independent variable, quantity the dependent variable.

With this interpretation, we call this a demand curve. It shows, again, the amount of a good an individual will choose to consume at the various prices indicated along the vertical axis. Along this demand curve, other things must be held constant, such as income and the prices of closely related goods. The negative slope indicates that as the price decreases, the quantity demanded increases, and vice versa. If the price decreases to some smaller value, the consumer will choose to purchase some larger amount indicated by the demand curve. *The law of demand is the statement that this curve is negatively sloped.* The law of demand is the central behavioral proposition in economics. Its veracity is not really open to debate; to deny this proposition is to deny economics. The phrase economic explanation to a large extent *means* an explanation based on the law of demand.

Electricity is one of those goods, along with water and other utilities that many people regard as essentials. We tend to think we need certain amounts of these goods to survive. The data, however, show that the amount of these utilities people use depends on the price charged for its use, and their use is in conformance with the law of demand. Table 2-3 shows electricity rates and average household consumption of electricity in 1975. Electricity in the Pacific Northwest was heavily subsidized by the Bonneville Power Authority, created in the 1930s to administer electricity distribution from the dams newly built along the Columbia and other rivers. As a result, cities such as Seattle had much lower rates than cities in the East. For example, the cost per kilowatt hour (kwh) in Seattle was 1¢ and 1.9¢ in Portland Oregon. Midwestern cities paid a higher rate, e.g., 3.6¢ per kwh in Milwaukee. By contrast, customers in New York city paid 8.4¢ per kwh. (These rate differences have narrowed in recent years.) The results of these differing prices are shown dramatically in Fig. 2-3.[11] The price of electricity, in cents per kwh are plotted vertically; average consumption of electricity, kwh's per month, is plotted on the horizontal axis. The cities with the lowest price, such as Seattle, Tacoma and Portland, had the highest per household use of electricity. Households in Seattle used, on average, 1,069 kwh's per month. In Eastern cities such as New York, where the price of electricity was about eight times as expensive as in the west, electricity consumption was much less. Household consumption in New York, for example, was only 243 kwh's per month, roughly one fifth of Seattle.

These differences come about by adjusting the use of electricity, and also by utilizing other fuels. In Seattle, electricity was more commonly used for heating and cooking than in the Northeast. Cities in the Northeast were more likely to economize on the high priced electricity by switching to relatively lower price natural gas for cooking and oil for heating. Beyond these substitutions, people for example turned the lights out more frequently in the East than in the West.

11. The demand for electricity also depends on the price of alternative fuels, such as oil and natural gas. Strict application of the law of demand requires that these other prices be held constant. If these other prices were substantially different in these cities, the results are less clear. The graph, however, is quite compelling.

Table 2-3 *Electricity Rates and Consumption, 1975*

Household Consumption (kwhs)	Price of Electricity (Cents per kwh)	City
1,347	1.02	Tacoma,WA
1,069	1	Seattle, WA
958	1.9	Portland, OR
802	2.9	Birmingham, AL
727	2.5	Indianapolis, IN
560	3.3	Kansas City, MO
518	2.7	Louisville, KY
464	4.2	Pittsburgh, PA
425	3.6	Milwaukee, WI
383	4.3	Los Angeles, CA
314	6.3	Jersey City, NJ
284	5.8	Newark, NJ
243	8.4	New York, NY

Figure 2-3 *The Demand for Electricity*

As evident from the scatter of points, cities in which the price of electricity is relatively high use less electricity per household than cities such as those in the Pacific Northwest, where electricity is relatively cheap. There is no absolute need for electricity; its use depends inversely on the price the utility charges.

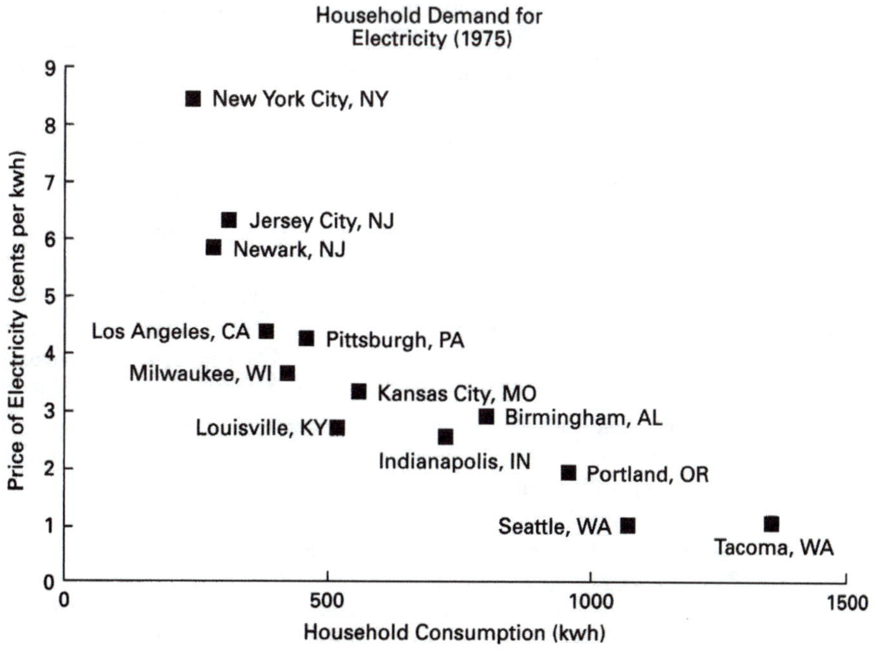

Charity: Noneconomic Behavior?

Many people regard the phenomenon of gifts to charities as an example of noneconomic behavior, or behavior contrary to self-interest, and take this as a refutation of economics. That conclusion represents a misunderstanding of what the economic postulates assert.

The phrase economic behavior is often taken to mean maximizing pecuniary wealth, or squeezing every last dollar out of some opportunity. It is obvious from common experience that nobody actually does that. Such a theory would rule out the enjoyment of leisure time. It would be difficult to find, among ourselves and our acquaintances, people who, for example, took the highest paying job, irrespective of location, working conditions, or who worked every day until the necessity of sleep demanded otherwise. Having children is one of the great wealth-reducing activities in modern society, yet births still occur. A theory based on maximization of pecuniary wealth would fail miserably.

The economic postulates do *not* imply such behavior. Pecuniary wealth is a good which, *other things equal,* we prefer more of to less. Wealth allows us to purchase goods in the marketplace. This does not imply that no substitution can take place between pecuniary wealth and other goods. The substitution postulate states that individuals are willing to substitute one good for another. Many of the things we enjoy are nonpecuniary in nature, e.g., enjoying the affection of friends, taking satisfaction in knowing we have helped some other person, and elementary things such as taking walks. Charity is one of these activities that humans engage in. We really have no explanation for it, but neither do we have an explanation of why people like hamburgers. The analysis of tastes is not, at present, a part of economics; we take tastes as given, and then seek regularities of behavior as constraints *change.*

Economic analysis of charity consists of examining how charitable activities *change* when the price of giving to charity *changes.* For example, in the United States and other countries, donations to charity are deductible from income, to one degree or another, when income taxes are calculated. If a person is in the 33% marginal tax bracket, for every additional dollar earned, the government takes \$.33. Giving a dollar to charity means reducing income by one dollar, but also saving \$.33 in taxes. For such an individual, the net cost of giving a dollar to charity is only \$.67. Not long ago, the top tax bracket in the United States was 70%: a person kept only \$.30 of every dollar earned after some point. In that case, giving \$1,000 to charity cost the person only \$300. In the 1980s, tax reform in the United States lowered marginal tax rates (though these were raised somewhat in the early 1990s), and made it more advantageous to take the standard deduction, which excludes the itemizations of charitable expenses. As a result, the price of charity has *increased* for many taxpayers, because the attendant reduction in tax liabilities is now less. We expect to see a decrease in charitable donations on that account. Nowhere, however, is it implied by the postulates that charitable giving should be zero.

Economist William C. Randolph investigated the effects of changes in marginal tax rates on charitable giving in the U.S.[12] He (and others) found that lowering these rates has two effects: the resulting higher disposable income increases charitable giving, while the resulting higher tax "price" lowers charitable giving. Randolph

12. Randolph, William C., "Dynamic Income, Progressive Taxes and the Timing of Charitable Contributions," *Journal of Political Economy,* 1995, vol. 103, no. 4, 709–738.

found that the two almost offset one another, but the income effect is very small if a household had only a temporary income increase in a given year, whereas the tax price effect is large in that instance and small when households move permanently to higher incomes. When income is transitorily high, a 1 percent decrease in all marginal tax rates decreases charitable giving by 54 percent when the marginal tax rate is 40 percent and the average tax rate is 27 percent.

2.5 Market Demand Curves

The demand curves of primary interest to economists are the aggregates of individuals' demands rather than an isolated individual's demand. The transition from an individual's demand curve to the market demand curve is elementary. If, say, one person would purchase 2 units of a good at some price, and another would purchase 3 at that same price, then together they will purchase 5 units. The combined, or market demand curve is simply the sum of the amounts each consumer wants to purchase (demand) at each price.

In Fig. 2-4, the demand curves of two individuals, *A* and *B,* are plotted. As shown, person *A*'s reservation price is $10, *B*'s is $6. Above these respective prices, these consumers choose not to make any purchases of this good. At prices between $6 and $10, the market demand is simply *A*'s demand, since *B* chooses not to purchase the good at prices exceeding $6. When the price falls below $6, *A* and *B* both purchase positive amounts; the combined demand is therefore the sum of the two demand curves. Since quantity is plotted on the horizontal axis, the market demand curve is the "lateral" sum of *A*'s and *B*'s demand curves. The market demand curve therefore appears flatter than either *A*'s or *B*'s demand curves, but this flatter slope really indicates that as the price falls, the change in the quantity demanded is *greater* than would take place on the part of either *A* or *B* alone. The procedure generalizes in an obvious way for more than two consumers. The combined, *market* demand curve is the lateral sum of all the individual demand curves, representing the sum of the amounts each consumer is willing to purchase at each price.[13]

The law of demand extends to market demand curves for two distinct reasons. As the price falls, those currently consuming the good individually consume

Figure 2-4 *Market Demand Curves*

The market demand curve is the *lateral* sum of individual demand curves. At prices above $6, only person *A* has a positive demand for this good. At $4, *A* wants 7 units and *B* wants 3 units. The total market demand is the sum, 10 units.

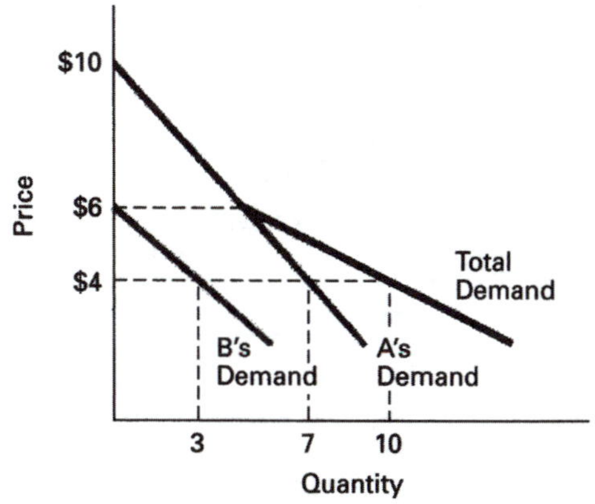

13. A similar procedure is used for summing supply curves. We deal with this in the next two chapters.

greater amounts, thus leading to greater market demand. In addition, however, as the price falls, new consumers, who chose not to purchase the good at the higher price, begin to consume the good in positive amounts. This new demand contributes to greater consumption at lower prices. When electronic calculators were first introduced, in the early 1970s, they sold for a few hundred dollars, (and they only performed the four basic arithmetic functions). The only people who purchased them were businesses and individuals, e.g., accountants, who had great occasion for calculating. As the price fell, some of these high-intensity users purchased additional machines (e.g., one for the office, one for the house, etc.) while other individuals who had only a more occasional use for these devices started purchasing them. Eventually, the price of "basic" calculators came down to virtually the price of the plastic case and retail costs. At that point, families bought calculators for doing checkbooks and other routine household tasks, and people commonly own more than one. The lower price led to greater consumption among current users, and also induced new consumers to purchase the machines.

The interpretations of the various areas under individual demand curves extend to market demands. These areas all have the units of dollars. The sum of total expenditures of each consumer is the total expenditure of all consumers; the amount that all consumers combined would pay in order to consume a given quantity, is the sum of what each consumer individually would pay for that quantity rather than have none at all. Thus, we can interpret the area under the market demand curve as total value, in the sense of an all-or-nothing choice, in the same manner as we interpret that area for individual demands: what all consumers together would be willing to pay to receive the given level of the good rather than all go without. Lastly, at a given quantity, the *height* of the market demand curve represents the marginal value of the good for each consumer who is currently purchasing the good, because each consumer demands the good until the marginal value falls to the market price.

2.6 The Diamond-Water Paradox

We now show how the concepts of marginal and total values enable us to resolve one of the age-old paradoxes of economics: why is it that diamonds, which are mere frivolities, are expensive, whereas water, which is essential to life, is generally cheap? How can the prices at which these commodities trade in the market be so opposite to their apparent usefulness to humans? The puzzle was first stated in this fashion by Adam Smith, in *The Wealth of Nations,* (published in an otherwise famous year, 1776). His answer (also given almost a century later by Karl Marx) was that diamonds have high exchange value but low use value, and for water, it is the reverse. But this is not much of an explanation at all; it is merely a tautological labeling of the phenomenon. It does not explain why such commodities could exist.[14]

14. Technically, it is incorrect to say that diamonds are more expensive than water, unless a common unit is used to measure the two. It is certainly true that a bucket of diamonds is more expensive than a bucket of water, but diamonds are not sold for their bulk. Diamonds very effectively separate out light into the colors of the rainbow (dispersion), and internally reflect light well because of their high index of refraction. In these units, diamonds are cheaper than water, which is why diamonds are used for jewelry rather than water. A nice diamond ring might cost $2,000, but it would take vastly more money to fashion a pretty ring out of water.

The paradox is resolved if we note that market prices of goods, in this case diamonds and water, reflect consumers' *marginal values* of these goods, not their total values. The prices of water and diamonds do not take into account the consumer's surplus we receive when we consume these goods. Moreover, it is obvious that the consumer's surplus associated with water consumption is far greater than that of diamonds. The total value of water is the amount we would pay for all the water we now consume, rather than have none at all. This is surely a very large amount, since we cannot live without water. Although the amount we would pay for all our diamonds rather than have none might be some large figure, it clearly must be far smaller than an amount that relates to our very survival.

We depict the situation in Fig. 2-5. In panel (a), the demand for water is drawn, along with a vertical supply curve. In panel (b), the demand curve for diamonds is drawn, with a vertical supply curve. Because we have a great deal of water, the marginal value of water is low; the amount any of us would pay for an extra gallon of water is only a few cents, because we already have so much. The total expenditure on water, the rectangular area up to the price of $1 and out to the total quantity supplied, is also probably not too great, although we are dealing with the product of a large quantity and a small price. Note, however, the large area of consumer's surplus. The marginal value of the first units of water are very high (off the page), since survival is at stake. We sometimes observe these very high intramarginal values when water becomes very scarce, such as during wartime, or on a desert. People in those circumstances very often trade their diamonds for some water. The *total value* of water is therefore high, indicated by the area under the demand curve producing the large amount of consumer's surplus. Diamonds, on the other hand, are relatively scarce; their marginal value is high at the quantities now available. The corresponding total value of diamonds, however, is not as large as that for water, nor is the consumer's surplus. The consumer's surplus is relatively small because the quantity of diamonds itself is small, and the price high.

Figure 2-5 *The Diamond-Water Paradox*

Although the *marginal value* of diamonds is relatively high, their *total value*, measured by what a person would pay to have all rather than none, is low relative to water. The consumer's surplus we receive from water is far greater than the consumer's surplus we receive from diamonds.

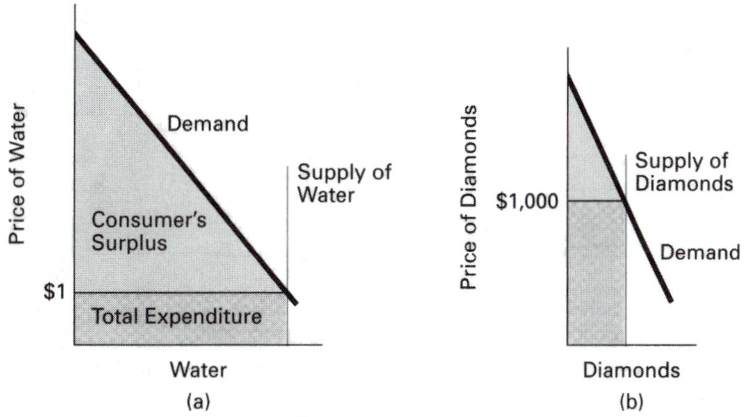

The diamond-water paradox has many applications to modern problems. Many times when some commonly used good suddenly becomes more scarce, someone proposes to share the burden equally by reducing all consumers' consumption of the good in the same proportion. That is, if, say, 10 percent less gasoline became available, it is alleged that having each consumer reduce his or her consumption of gasoline by 10 percent would in some sense equitably share the burden of this added scarcity. Equity is of course a value judgement, and economists are not qualified to make pronouncements about it. Consider, however, the impact of such an arrangement on consumers with differing demands for the product in question. Fig. 2-6 shows the demand curves for two consumers of gasoline. Both consumers face the same price of gasoline, and, to keep the analysis free of any distractions, we can assume the quantities they consume are equal as well. The consumer depicted in panel (a), however, has a demand curve that is quite flat. This consumer gets very little consumer's surplus from consuming gasoline. Perhaps she lives in the city, on a convenient transit line, so that if the price of gasoline were to rise slightly, she could easily economize on gasoline with little inconvenience. The consumer depicted in panel (b), has a very different demand for gasoline. This person might live in a rural area where public transportation is largely unavailable. This person cannot easily avoid using her car. If these two consumers are each forced to give up the same amount of gasoline, the impacts will be very different. The loss of consumer's surplus is depicted by the triangular area *ABC* in each diagram, but this loss is much greater for the rural versus the urban dweller. These two people will not likely feel the same way about the fairness of such an arrangement.

When government budgets have to be cut, it is sometimes proposed to cut all agencies across the board. That is, if the entire budget must be cut by 10 percent, all agencies of the government are to be cut by 10 percent. These proposals are never enacted. There are some agencies whose work is very popular, while

Figure 2-6 *The Impact of Equal Quantity Reductions on Consumers with Different Demands*

In Panel (a), we depict a consumer who can easily avoid this good. Panel (b) depicts a consumer who cannot easily avoid using some good, e.g., the demand for gasoline for an outside sales representative who has to make numerous trips to widely dispersed retail establishments. If these two consumers must give up the same amount of this good, e.g., gasoline, the loss of consumer's surplus, *ABC*, will be much greater for the consumer in Panel (b) than the one depicted in Panel (a).

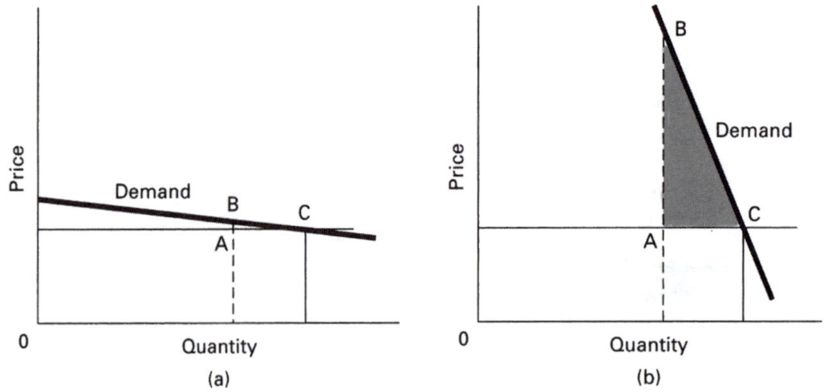

others could be cut with little public outcry. The populace does not regard all agencies as equal candidates for cutting, because the demands for the services of these agencies differs in ways depicted for the two consumers in Fig. 2-6. Thus even when the overall budget is cut, some agencies may actually be granted increases in budgets. Governments do this because to do otherwise would result in relatively greater losses of consumer's surplus.

Many important public policy issues in fact hinge on a correct understanding of the diamond-water paradox. For example, it is sometimes remarked that Americans love their pets more than their children, because they spend more on pet food than on baby food and milk. Also, mechanics (a male dominated profession), often earn more than nurses (a female dominated profession), demonstrating perhaps that Americans consider fixing machines more important than fixing people and maybe that these wages are an example of discrimination against female workers. These assertions are based on a lack of understanding of the diamond-water paradox.

The total expenditures by Americans (or anyone else) on milk, or pet food, etc., do not represent the *total value* of these items, in the sense of what people would be willing to pay for these goods rather than have none at all. The amount consumers spend on goods is the rectangular area of price times quantity, and omits the triangular area of consumer's surplus. The usefulness of milk and pet food is not reliably measured by total expenditure, and therefore, comparing these areas is not a valid comparison.

Comparable Worth

In like manner the wages of mechanics, nurses, and workers in general are the *prices* of the services they provide. They represent the *marginal* value of these services to consumers, through the goods they produce. These marginal values, as the marginal values of diamonds versus the marginal value of water, do not reflect the total usefulness of mechanics versus nurses to humans. They measure what consumers would be willing to pay in order to get the services of *one more nurse* or *one more mechanic,* a value dependent upon the amount of those services already available. It seems that there are sufficient numbers of people capable and inclined to be nurses so that the marginal value of this service often turns out to be less than that of mechanics. No one should seriously conclude that these marginal values in some way meaningfully reflect society's total values of these two professions.

These types of comparisons underlie the recently emerging idea of comparable worth—the policy of comparing the wages paid in occupations that appear similar to some observer. In fact, it is a very difficult endeavor to in some way explain wages on the basis of various kinds of job characteristics, such as educational requirements, duration on the job, numbers of workers supervised, etc. In academia, for example, the wages of professors vary widely across the different fields. On average, salaries of professors in the humanities are the lowest, and salaries of professors in engineering, computer science, and in business schools, such as finance and accounting are highest. These professors have similar, or comparable training and responsibilities, regarding teaching and research, etc., yet salaries often differ by a factor of two or more.

These professions are in fact only superficially similar, or comparable. The talents useful for achieving expertise in these various fields are widely divergent.

The mathematical skills required for the scientific disciplines seem less prevalent than the verbal and language skills needed for the humanities. In addition, faculty in the scientific disciplines often have opportunities for employment outside of academia. In order to attract them to academia, universities must bid these faculty away from their next highest alternative employment. The *marginal* values of workers can therefore differ greatly between fields, even if they are all professors doing equally arduous work with the same responsibilities.[15] The marketplace in fact produces many instances of goods that appear comparable but which trade at divergent prices. Most jewelers cannot tell, on the basis of visual inspection, a diamond from a well-cut cubic zirconia. The optical properties of these stones are virtually identical, yet they differ in price by a thousandfold. Many people cannot distinguish instant from brewed coffee; butter from margarine, or cheap versus expensive wine. The prices of these goods are determined by what some individuals are willing to pay for these items (or some person's labor), that is, the *demand* for these items, and the availability of those goods or labor, their *supply.*

Professional Sports Stadiums

Many cities across North America have been faced with threats by the owners of professional sports teams that their teams will move to some other city unless the city or county contributes heavily to building a new sports facility. At this writing, George Steinbrenner, owner of the New York Yankees, is threatening to take the team to New Jersey, unless the city of New York spends upward of a billion dollars building a new stadium. The public debates sometimes get quite heated. Sports fans are often happy to oblige, but others question why the general public should subsidize the likes of millionaire owners and players who earn ten or a hundred times the amounts earned by ordinary citizens. The history of these franchise moves is that most often, the public authorities largely accede to the owners wishes and spend the public's money on new stadiums. But this raises a question: why is this the generally politically popular thing to do?

The first thing to recognize is that owners of these major sports franchises are in a position few sellers enjoy: they have the ability to withhold the services of something consumers value. The owners of supermarkets, for example, have no such power. Supermarkets have many competitors selling similar or identical merchandise. If some particular chain closes shop and leaves a city, there will be others remaining, and new supermarkets will be ready to take their place. Only providers who have some *monopoly* power, i.e., sellers who provide essentially

---

15. In the 1970s, a comparable worth lawsuit was filed in the State of Washington by the Washington Federation of State Employees, contending that certain female dominated jobs were underpaid. In a Comparable Worth Study ordered by the governor and published in September 1974, employees were asked to rate their own jobs on the basis of four factors: "Knowledge & Skills," Mental Demands," "Accountability" and "Working Conditions." Their responses were sometimes modified after interviews. These factors were scaled differently: the highest value ("points") given to "Knowledge & Skills" was 280; the highest value given to "Working Conditions" was 20. No explanations were offered for the differences. The individual ratings were then arithmetically totaled. Separate graphs for male and female dominated job classifications were created with these point totals on the horizontal axis and salaries on the vertical axis. A line with a "dogleg" was eyeballed through the resulting scatter of points and compared for the "male" and "female" jobs. On the basis of this evidence, the trial judge ruled in favor of the plaintiffs. The State appealed, but the process was stopped after the legislature adjusted salaries in some degree of accordance with these findings.

the entire output in some industry, have this kind of power. The water, electricity and natural gas utilities, and the companies providing local telephone service have this kind of monopoly power, but it is exactly for that reason that the state regulates these companies. What seems apparent is that the owners of sports teams not only have this power to withhold services, but in addition, the services they provide seem to generate considerable consumers' surplus. Measuring consumers' surplus is a tricky affair, but consider the amount of newspaper space and (expensive) television time devoted to covering these sports. It is plausible that the total value of professional sports to consumers considerably exceeds the total expenditures on professional sports activities by consumers. Therefore, if consumers were faced with an all-or-nothing choice about their local team, they would in many instances be willing to sacrifice some of their consumers' surplus to keep the local team in town. If someone could withhold the city's water, consumers would be willing to bribe them to not do it. It is less likely they would be willing to bribe the diamond merchants to not withhold sales of diamonds.

2.7 Consumption Over Time

The previous analysis concerned choices among contemporaneous commodities, i.e., goods chosen during the same time frame. An important choice made by consumers, however, relates to consumption *over time,* in particular, how one allocates income earned in different time periods to consumption. We notice, for example, that college students are in general poor, that earnings are highest during a person's middle age, and earnings fall after retirement; the typical response to this pattern of income is to borrow when one is young, and lend (e.g. in the form of investing in a retirement fund) during middle age. It seems that when income is earned in an erratic pattern, individuals attempt to smooth out their consumption through borrowing and lending. In this way, people's consumption varies less than their income. What produces this behavior?

In Fig. 2-7 a demand curve for *present consumption* is drawn. The *price* of present consumption is the amount of *future* consumption a person has to give up in order to consume a unit of present consumption. This curve, or schedule indicates that when a person's present consumption is very low, their willingness to give up future consumption in order to eat a little better now, is relatively high. In the extreme case, if present consumption is so low that starvation is a concern, a person might be willing to trade a considerable amount of future consumption in order to gain even a small extra amount of present consumption. On the other hand, a person who had a great deal of income available in the present, but anticipated lower income in the future might very well be willing to exchange $1,000 now for something less, say, $900, in the future, when his or her fortunes might be less attractive. In Fig. 2-8, the price 1 indicates one unit of future consumption is traded for one unit of present consumption. We allow, at least theoretically, the demand or marginal value curve to fall below the price of 1, at some relatively high income, though trading some amount of income now for a *smaller* amount in the future is a contract that is rarely observed.[16]

16. The conditions under which a person might enter into such a contract are discussed in chap. 10.

Figure 2-7 *The Demand for Present Consumption*

In addition to choosing amongst goods in the same time period, individuals makes choices concerning the levels of total consumption in different time periods. The marginal value of consuming goods today is the amount of future consumption a person would be willing to give up in order to get an additional unit of present consumption. This marginal value or demand schedule is downward sloping like all other marginal value schedules.

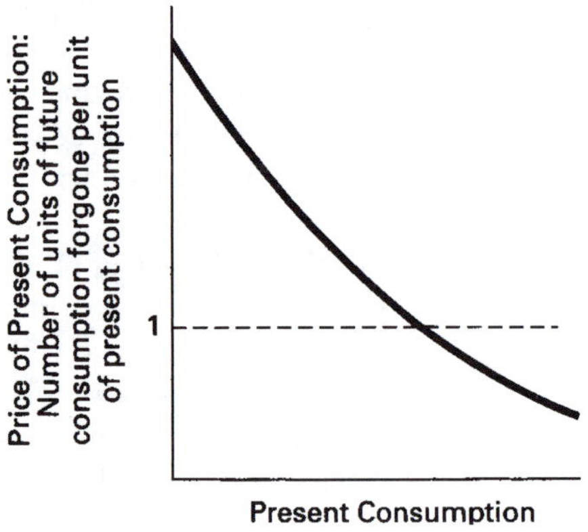

The tendency to even out the flow of consumption is a consequence of the law of demand. The height of the demand curve for present consumption is the marginal value of present consumption in terms of future consumption forgone. That is, the subjective price of present consumption along the demand curve represents the amount of future consumption the individual is willing to trade in order to acquire an additional increment of present consumption. Suppose an individual has the option of consuming some amount, say, $20,000 in each of two consecutive time periods, versus consuming $10,000 in the first time period, and then $30,000 in the second period. That is, compare the relative merits of steady consumption versus varying consumption (feast and famine), where the steady consumption level is equal to the average of the low and high levels. These options are shown in Fig. 2-8. During the time of feast, the marginal value of present consumption is some relatively low value, *c;* during famine, the marginal value of present consumption is relatively high, *a.* If the consumer can transfer a unit of income from the time of feast to the time of famine, he or she will experience a net gain of *a–c,* by converting relatively low-valued consumption into higher-valued consumption. As such transfers of consumption continue, the respective marginal values converge to *b,* the marginal value of present consumption when consumption is steady. Thus by either borrowing or lending so as to equalize the flow of consumption, a person achieves a more preferred consumption plan than when consumption varies over time.[17]

Alternatively, consider the *total* values of consuming various levels of present consumption. These total benefits are measured by the area under the demand curve. These areas represent the amounts of future income an individual would be willing to pay to consume the specified level of present consumption rather than none at all. Denote the areas under the demand curve up to $10,000,

17. The analysis must be modified slightly if individuals are *impatient,* i.e., they have a time preference for consumption in the present, or, if interest payments are available between the present and the future. Then, instead of constant consumption, consumption will either rise steadily or fall steadily at some rate. It is still the case that consumption will not be erratic, in the sense of varying up and down over time, but it will not be literally constant. These more advanced topics are addressed in Chapter 10.

Figure 2-8 *Maximizing Total Value by Smoothing Out the Flow of Consumption*

When a person consumes the same amount of income each year, say, \$20,000, the total value of that consumption is $2(A + B)$. This is greater than consuming the same total income, \$40,000 in uneven amounts, of \$10,000 and then \$30,000. In that case, the total value of this consumption is only $A + (A + B + C) = 2A + B + C$. This is less than the previous amount because $C < B$ due to the law of demand.

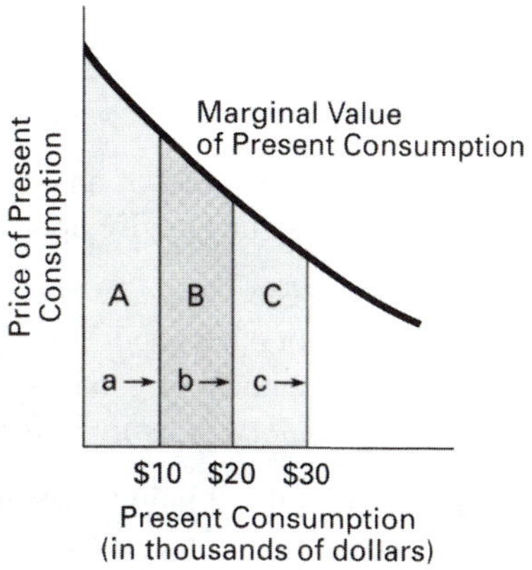

between \$10,000 and \$20,000, and between \$20,000 and \$30,000 as *A, B* and *C*, respectively. Then the total value of consuming \$20,000 for two years is $2(A + B) = 2A + 2B$. On the other hand, the total value of the feast/famine pattern is $(A + B + C) + A = 2A + B + C$. This is less than the total value of the steady consumption since $C < B$ due to the negative slope of the demand curve. Thus income is more highly valued if it is consumed at an even rather than uneven rate.

This result is the basis of the *permanent income hypothesis,* due to Milton Friedman,[18] and the *life cycle hypothesis* developed by Franco Modigliani and others.[19] These hypotheses state that an individual's consumption in a given time period is related mainly to his or her *permanent* level of income, or to *lifetime earnings,* rather than to income in that particular time period. These hypotheses are important parts of modern macroeconomic analyses of consumption. Suppose, for example, in a given year, two individuals each have an income of \$30,000, but individual *A* has this income every year, whereas individual *B* usually earns \$20,000, but had unusually good fortune this year. Which individual is likely to save more (or dissave less)? Individual *B* has had a temporary increase in wealth; his or her marginal value of present consumption is therefore low relative to future income. Assuming capital markets are available in which individuals borrow and lend, this person will therefore transfer some income to the future. This increase in wealth will then be spread out over many time periods. The individual will do this by saving. Saving can take many forms, e.g. purchasing bonds, or, perhaps purchasing consumer durables, such as a house or car, or investing in one's education. Thus we would expect persons with temporary increases in income to have greater savings rates than those consuming near their permanent or normal income.

---

18. Milton Friedman, *A Theory of the Consumption Function,* National Bureau of Economic Research, Princeton: Princeton University Press, 1957.

19. See, in particular, Franco Modigliani and R. Blumberg, "Utility Analysis and the Consumption Function: An interpretation of Cross Section Data," in *Post Keynesian Economics,* K. Kurihara, ed., New Brunswick, NJ: Rutgers University Press, 1954, and Menahem Yaari, "On the Consumer's Lifetime allocation Process, " *International Economic Review,* 5, 1964, 304–317.

CHAPTER SUMMARY

- Economics asserts that people's behavior can be characterized by postulates of behavior. People prefer more goods to less, and are willing to substitute one good for another.
- The *value* of any good to an individual is measured by what he or she is willing to give up in order to obtain that good.
- The *marginal value* of a good is what an individual is willing to pay (give up of other goods) to acquire *one more unit* of the good; the *total value* of some amount of goods is what the individual would be willing to pay to have *all units presently consumed,* rather than none at all.
- For all individuals and goods, the marginal value of a good falls as additional units are consumed, holding other things constant.
- The *law of demand* follows from the postulate of diminishing marginal values: other things remaining the same, as the price of any good decreases, more of that good is consumed; as the price increases, less is consumed.
- Although the postulates of behavior are stated in terms of *individual* preferences, the demand curves of interest are the aggregate of all consumers in a market. These market demand curves are simply the sum of each individual's demand curve. Graphically, market demand curves are the *lateral sum* of the individual curves.
- Market demands are downward sloping for two distinct reasons. First, as the price of some good decreases, the individuals already consuming the good increase their consumption. In addition, however, new consumers enter the market and commence consumption of the good, adding their demand to the others already in the market.
- On a diagram with price on the vertical axis and quantity on the horizontal axis, the *demand curve* indicates the amount a consumer wishes to purchase at given prices. The law of demand is the statement that demand curves are negatively sloped.
- When we purchase goods in the marketplace, we do so until our marginal value of the good falls to the price we have to pay. Because we were willing to pay *more* for the first units purchased, we gain from these purchases.
- The difference between what we would be *willing* to pay for the units purchased (our total value of the goods), and what we actually *do* pay (our total *expenditure* on the good) is called *consumer's surplus.* It is simply another term for the gains from exchange.
- The *diamond–water paradox* is one of the oldest puzzles in economics. Why are diamonds (mere frivolities) expensive, while water, a good necessary for survival, is cheap? The paradox is resolved by understanding that the prices of these goods represent their *marginal* values, not the total values of diamonds versus water.

REVIEW QUESTIONS

1. Explain the voting paradox and why it makes defining preferences of groups difficult.
2. Explain the substitution postulate and give additional examples of it.
3. Why does economics insist on basing value on trade-offs rather than on the statement people make about how intensely they desire something?
4. Explain the difference between marginal, average and total values. Which one of these values does a market price reflect?
5. Why is variety rather than monotony the spice of life?
6. Explain why it is better to speak of the demand for electricity and water than our "need" for those goods.
7. Is charity an example of non-economic behavior? If not, what does economics have to say about it, if anything?
8. Explain what the diamond-water paradox is and how marginal analysis resolves it.

PROBLEMS

1. "I don't know anyone who sits around and calculates marginal values, and then makes choices on that basis. The postulates of behavior can't be relevant to social science." Comment.
2. "Recently, the price of shoes decreased. Nobody rushed out and bought another pair of shoes. The law of demand obviously doesn't apply to durable goods like shoes." Comment.
3. Are addictive drugs, like crack cocaine "goods?" Can the behavioral postulates be used to analyze drug use? Suppose a friend treats you to a weekend of skiing, and you decide you really like it. In fact, in the next months and years, as you ski more and more, you get better at it and enjoy it even more, and you devote increasing amounts of your income to this activity. In what way, if any, does this differ from drug addiction, and does the law of demand apply to skiing?
4. Safety of automobiles would be greater if it was against the law to drive older vehicles, e.g., cars more than 5 years old. Would you be in favor of such a law? What makes people drive these more dangerous vehicles?
5. Many people choose to work "graveyard" shifts, for example midnight to 8 a.m., because the work during those hours usually pays more than the usual "9 to 5" shifts. How does this illustrate the postulates?
6. Wages are higher in the Midwest region of the United States than on either coast. For example, a particular job in St. Louis pays, on average, more than the same job in San Francisco or New York. Explain this in terms of the postulates.

7. Why is it that when a husband gives his wife a food processor for her birthday, we regard it as insincere? What characteristics of gifts are truly statements of affection? Why is, for example, jewelry often given as a gift?

8. On "Super Sunday," when the Super Bowl is played, some corpulent gentlemen hurl themselves at an ovoid of pigskin. For these exertions, they earn more than most people make in a year, even those who provide a vital service, such as nurses, teachers of economics etc. Does this mean society values football players more than nurses or teachers?

9. "The law of demand wouldn't hold for diamonds, because if the price of diamonds fell, they would no longer be a prestige item, and people would therefore buy fewer diamonds." Evaluate.

10. Mean old mom forces her child to eat broccoli. The child does it on condition of getting more dessert. Explain this in terms of the postulates of behavior.

11. Diamonds and cubic zirconia (CZs) have virtually identical optical properties, though diamonds are much harder (however, CZs are harder than all other gemstones except ruby and sapphire). Jewelers can only tell them apart by the absence of flaws in CZs, or by testing their specific gravity or heat conductivity. Yet diamonds sell for a thousand times the price of a "comparable" CZ.

    a. How can it be that the market sets such disparate prices for such similar goods?
    b. If the prices of goods are very similar, does that mean the goods are "comparable?"
    c. If two workers do "comparable" work, should we expect them to be paid similar wages?

12. Many people get paid only once a month. Yet they do not consume their income only on that day; they smooth their consumption over the entire month. Explain why the postulates imply this behavior.

13. Canada and many states in the U.S. have enacted so-called "comparable worth" laws, which require wages paid in occupations legislatures (or the courts) deem comparable to be approximately equal. Consider that in academia, wages differ considerably across fields. Salaries of professors in economics and other social sciences are much higher than salaries in the humanities, such as literature. Do you think economics professors are "comparable" to literature professors? What would the effects be if salaries were equalized between these and all other academic fields?

14. (A Totally Marginal Question) The National Income accounts of the United States add up the "value" of all goods produced in the U.S. economy. The government multiplies the quantity of each (final) good produced by its price and adds all of these numbers together, obtaining what it calls the "total value of all (final) goods produced." [The word final refers to avoiding double counting, by not adding the value of, say, flour, to the value of the bread produced by that flour. Ignore this issue in this question.] It turns out that the value thus computed of pet food produced exceeds the value of milk (mostly consumed by children) produced. Does this mean that Americans place greater importance on feeding their pets than feeding their children? Explain.

15. Jane is willing to pay $9 for 1 steak per month, $8 for the 2nd, $7 for the 3rd, etc. The market price of steaks is $5. This same consumer is willing to pay $25 for 1 pizza per month, $20 for a 2nd, $15 for a 3rd, etc. The market price of pizzas is also $5.

    a. Explain why the consumer will purchase the same number of steaks as pizzas, and spend the same total amount on each.
    b. Does this equality of price and total expenditure mean that the consumer "values" steaks and pizzas equally? Explain clearly.
    c. How much would this consumer be willing to pay, per month, for the right to purchase steaks at $3, rather than at the market price of $5?

16. Aron's marginal values of hamburgers and French fries, per week, are as follows:

Quantity	**Hamburgers**	**French Fries**
1	$10	$6
2	8	5
3	6	4
		etc.

    Joe's Eats charges $4 for hamburgers and $1 for fries. Jake's Eats charges $2 and $3 respectively for the same quality burgers and fries.

    a. Where does Aron eat, assuming he can't buy burgers in one place and fries in the other? How many burgers and fries does he eat per week?
    b. Joe's decides to institute a new pricing policy: 1 burger and 1 order of fries must be purchased together. How much would Aron be willing to tip the waitperson per week in order to be able to buy burgers and fries separately, if he eats at Joe's?

17. Recently, a local Commission on Women's Affairs noted that automobile mechanics have a higher salary than nurses. This means, the commission concluded, that in this city, "fixing cars is more important than fixing people." Do you agree that the wage examples the Commission cites imply that?

18. A student spends weekday evenings socializing and crams for the Monday morning exam on Sunday night. How do these actions illustrate the behavioral postulates?

19. In 1999, pizzas cost $ 10; Rachel bought 40 during the year. In 2000, when the price fell to $8, she bought 50. Analyze the following statements:

    a. Since Rachel spent the same amount in both years, she was no better off, pizzawise, in 1999 than in 2000.
    b. Since she now buys 50 pizzas at $2 less than in the previous year, she is $100 better off in 2000 than in 1999.
    c. Rachel would pay about $90 to be able to purchase pizzas at $8 rather than $10.

20. The classical economists (Adam Smith and Karl Marx, to name just two) explained the diamond-water paradox by saying that whereas water had high "use value," diamonds had high "exchange value," and diamonds had low "use value." Why is this explanation unsatisfactory, Just from the

viewpoint of scientific methodology? How does marginal analysis explain the paradox?

21. Between 1974 and the late 1990s, the federal government imposed a 55 mph speed limit. This reduction in maximum speed probably saved, perhaps, thousands of lives per year. Why not, therefore, reduce the speed limit even further? (It is probably the case that if the government imposed and rigidly enforced a 10 mph speed limit, highway deaths might literally become zero.) Why is there so little support for such legislation?)

22. In 1890, "basic human needs" were generally thought to be food, clothing, and shelter. In 1990, Senator Ted Kennedy added medical care, affordable transportation, and day care to the above list. Have humans become more "needy" in the past 100 years? Is it possible to define scientifically "basic human needs?"

23. According to the law of demand, if vacations become cheaper, people should take more vacations. However, most people take exactly one vacation per year, whatever the cost. Does the law of demand not apply here?

24. Charlotte's demand for food is

Price	$10	9	8	7	6	5	4	3	2
Quantity demanded	1	2	3	4	5	6	7	8	9

The price of food is $6. Food stamps are available. People can purchase $1 of food stamps for $.50. Charlotte can buy, at most, $60 worth of food stamps (for $30).

a. Assuming Charlotte can't trade food and food stamps, how much food will Charlotte buy and at what total expenditure?
b. What is the gain (consumer's surplus) to Charlotte of being able to purchase food stamps?
c. Answer the same questions if Charlotte can only purchase $10 worth of food stamps (for $5).
d. Assume, once again, that Charlotte can purchase up to $60 worth of food stamps. If Charlotte can resell food and food stamps, how much food will Charlotte buy? How much food will Charlotte consume?
e. Which system does Charlotte prefer? Why do welfare agencies prevent resale of food stamps?

25. Sam is willing to pay $12 per month for 1 green egg per month, $10, for the 2nd, $8 for the 3rd, etc. The market price of green eggs is $8. He is willing to pay $20 per month for 1 slice of ham per month, $16 for a 2nd, $12 for a 3rd, etc. The market price of ham slices is $12.

a. How many green eggs and ham slices does Sam purchase per month, and how much does he spend on each?
b. Which good provides Sam with the greatest net benefits? Would your answer be the same if green eggs cost $6?
c. How much would Sam be willing to pay to be able to purchase ham slices at $8 rather than $12?

26. The local baseball team faces the following demand curve. At a ticket price of $50, nobody will show up for any games. At a price of $45, 1,000,000

tickets will be sold over the season, at $40, 2,000,000 tickets will be sold, at $35, 3,000,000 will be sold, and so forth. It costs the team $10 per fan, on average to put on the games, and assume they will charge this price. The team owner threatens to move the team unless the city subsidizes a new stadium. How much would the fans be willing to pay to keep the team in town? How much would they pay if the team owner charged $30 per ticket? Which price would make more money for the owner in the first year of operation, including profits on the tickets?

QUESTIONS FOR DISCUSSION

1. Do you think our government allocates the proper amount of resources to things like education, airline and automobile safety, fighting crime, medical research and the like? Why do we have to make these choices, and how would you justify spending more, or perhaps less on some social program?
2. Do you think universities should force students to take certain courses, or would it be better to simply let "the market" operate? Should students have to major in a specific field? What are the benefits and costs of these requirements?
3. Should we pass laws requiring comparable goods to sell at comparable prices? Who will we appoint to determine what goods and services are comparable? If we say that English professors are comparable to computer science professors, what changes will likely occur in university English and computer science departments?
4. Recent studies have shown that automobile air bags can be dangerous or even fatal to children and fully grown adults of small stature. Yet, over all, these devices seem to save lives. Should we continue to require these devices, and should we allow people to disconnect them if they so chose?

CHAPTER 3

Aspects of Demand Theory

3.1 Relative versus Absolute Prices
- The Law of Demand and Inflation

3.2 Elasticity of Demand
- Elasticity and Total Expenditure
- Drug-Related Crime
- Elasticity and Monopolistic Industries

3.3 The Second Law of Demand

3.4 Shipping the Good Apples Out

3.5 Further Applications of the Law of Demand
- Sex
- Fertility
- Religion
- Suicide
- Smoking
- Obesity
- Crime and Punishment
- Discrimination

Two eighty-year old men were chatting about life. One of them said to the other, "You know, if I'd known I was going to live this long, I would have taken better care of myself." Many dramatic improvements in medicine have taken place in the past generation. We now expect to live much longer than did our grandparents, and even our parents. What changes in behavior might this induce? Could it be that one reason why people smoke less than they used to is that there is now a larger payoff for not smoking? Along the same lines, could it be that the decline in unprotected sexual activity is nothing more than a simple consequence of the law of demand?

In this chapter, we investigate some of the nuts and bolts aspects of demand theory. Economists developed the theoretical framework we described in the previous chapter because they felt it was the most useful way to interpret certain aspects of human behavior. However, the actual application of the law of demand to real world problems is usually no easy matter. In the physical sciences, it is sometimes possible to set up a laboratory condition which isolates the effects of some experimental variable. In economics, there is no laboratory—the world is the laboratory. Unfortunately, in the real world, many things change at the same time, so isolating the effects of one change is often difficult. We begin with one of the most famous of these problems, the distinction between real, or relative prices, and absolute prices.

3.1 Relative versus Absolute Prices

The law of demand is a statement about the response to a change in some given price, *holding other things constant.* Unfortunately, as we have just said, it is difficult to fully control for other variables. At any given time, some prices are rising and others are falling. In modern economies, it has most often been the case that *on average,* prices have increased. An increase in the general price level is called *inflation;* a decrease in the average price of goods is called, similarly, *deflation.* In order to apply the law of demand, an over-all increase in prices (inflation) must be separated from the change in the price of one good *relative* to prices of other goods. Suppose, for example, the price of hamburgers had doubled in the past fifteen years, but the price of everything else had also doubled, as had family incomes. In that case, we would expect no change in the demand for hamburgers. We would have simply experienced a 100 percent inflation that affected all prices and incomes exactly proportionately; no price, including the price of labor (the wage rate) would have changed relative to any other price, and thus we would expect no changes in any choices consumers would make.

The measurement of inflation in the United States is done by the Bureau of Labor Statistics (universally referred to as the BLS), the research arm of the United States Department of Labor. The original purpose was to determine fair wages for shipyard workers when the United States entered World War I in 1917, because prices seemed to be rising rapidly. The BLS now conducts yearly surveys of some 20,000 households around the country. Families keep diaries of expenditures and the BLS also interviews some of them directly. From these surveys, the BLS periodically determines an average bundle of goods consumed by a typical family. This market basket of goods comprises several hundred actual individual items, in various groupings such as food, clothing, housing, entertainment, medical care and the like. The BLS also conducts regular monthly surveys of prices paid by consumers for these goods. The measure of inflation (or deflation) is the percent change in the cost of purchasing the same bundle of goods from one year to the next.

Suppose for simplicity the market basket consists of only two goods, steak, and potatoes.[1] Suppose also the average consumer as measured by the BLS consumed in an average week in 1998 2 lbs. of steak and 4 lbs. of potatoes, at prices $3.00 and $.50 per lb. respectively. The total budgetary expenditure would therefore be 2 × $3 + 4 × $.50 = $8.00. Suppose in 1999, the price of steak rose to $3.50 and the price of potatoes fell to $.40. Then the cost of purchasing the same 2 lbs. of steak and 4 lbs. of potatoes would have risen to 2 × $3.50 + 4 × $.40 = $8.60. The percent increase in the cost of purchasing the bundle of goods is ($8.60 – $8.00) ÷ $8.00 = .075 = 7.5%. If these two goods represented the entire bundle of goods purchased by consumers, the reported measure of inflation in the economy would be 7.5%.

In actuality, the BLS reports an *index* of the cost of purchasing the average bundle of goods, called the **Consumer Price Index** (*CPI*). In recent years, the cost of the standard market basket of goods has been stated as a ratio to the average cost in 1982–1984. The *CPI* for 1982–1984 is set arbitrarily at 100. If, for example, the average over those three years of the monthly cost of the bundle was $10,000, and in 1985 the cost was $10,760, the *CPI* in 1985 would then be (10,760 ÷ 10,000) × 100 = 107.6. The number 107.6 means that the expenditure required for this standard consumption bundle is 7.6% higher in 1985 than the average over the previous three years. This is in fact the *CPI* for 1985; for 1986 it was 109.6. That figure means on average, prices (as measured by the standard basket of goods) were 9.6% higher in 1986 than in 1982–1984. The increase in prices from 1985 to 1986 is measured by the ratio of the 1986 index to the 1985 index: 109.6 ÷ 107.6 = 1.0186, a 1.86% increase in the average price level.[2]

A change in the general price level, as measured, for example, by the *CPI,* is called a change in **absolute** prices. Application of the law of demand requires a change in one price relative to another, in other words, a change in **relative** prices. If all prices in the economy rose by 10% from one year to the next, and everyone's incomes rose equally by 10% *we would expect no change in behavior:* no constraint has changed for any person. There has been no change in any price relative to another. Suppose, however, some good's price rises by 4% from one year to the next, but the *CPI* increases by 10% in that same time period. Then although the money, or nominal price, as it is called, has increased, the *real,* or relative price of this good has actually *decreased,* by about 6%. Other things equal, we therefore expect, on the basis of the law of demand, an *increase* in the quantity of this good demanded, not a decrease, as focussing on only the increase in the good's nominal price might suggest.

Because most economies have experienced long term inflation, comparison of prices over extended time periods is often difficult. If we want to know whether some item is cheaper or more expensive than it was some time in the past, we have to compare the change in its price with the changes in all other prices and with the change in people's incomes. A particularly important example is the case of gasoline prices. The relevant data are shown in Table 3-1. In the 1960s and

---

1. I once had a roommate from Kansas for whom this would have been a pretty good approximation.

2. Another measure of price changes, the implicit price deflator for the gross domestic product measures the average change in price for all goods produced in the domestic economy. This measure includes items such as tractors and airplane parts that are not part of consumers' choices, and therefore may not necessarily reflect the change in the cost of living for consumers.

early 1970s, the price of regular gasoline was slightly less than \$.30 per gallon; in April 2004, the average price of regular unleaded was \$1.79. Has the price of gasoline increased or decreased in the past 30 years?

Table 3-1 shows, in column (2) the *CPI* for "all items" (1982–'84 = 100) for 1950, 1955, 1960 and all years following. Alongside those numbers, in column

Table 3-1

	Consumer Price Index		Gasoline Prices	
(1) Year	(2) All Items	(3) Annual % Change in Prices	(4) Price/ Gallon (Current $)	(5) Price/ Gallon (2004 $)
1950	24.1		$0.21	
1955	26.8	2.15%	$0.25	$1.74
1960	29.6	2.01%	$0.27	$1.71
1965	31.5	1.25%	$0.28	$1.66
1970	38.8	4.26%	$0.31	$1.49
1971	40.5	4.38%	$0.31	$1.43
1972	41.8	3.21%	$0.32	$1.43
1973	44.4	6.22%	$0.39	$1.64
1974	49.3	11.04%	$0.53	$2.01
1975	53.8	9.13%	$0.57	$1.98
1976	56.9	5.76%	$0.61	$2.00
1977	60.6	6.50%	$0.66	$2.04
1978	65.2	7.59%	$0.67	$1.92
1979	72.6	11.35%	$0.90	$2.32
1980	82.4	13.50%	$1.25	$2.84
1981	90.9	10.32%	$1.38	$2.84
1982	96.5	6.16%	$1.26	$2.44
1983	99.6	3.21%	$1.20	$2.25
1984	103.9	4.32%	$1.17	$2.11
1985	107.6	3.56%	$1.17	$2.03
1986	109.6	1.86%	$0.84	$1.43
1987	113.6	3.65%	$0.91	$1.50
1988	118.3	4.14%	$0.91	$1.44
1989	124.0	4.82%	$0.99	$1.49
1990	130.7	5.40%	$1.13	$1.62
1991	136.2	4.21%	$1.10	$1.51
1992	140.0	2.79%	$1.09	$1.46
1993	144.5	3.21%	$1.07	$1.38
1994	148.2	2.56%	$1.08	$1.36
1995	152.4	2.83%	$1.11	$1.36
1996	156.9	2.95%	$1.20	$1.43
1997	160.5	2.29%	$1.20	$1.40
1998	163.0	1.56%	$1.03	$1.18
1999	166.6	2.21%	$1.14	$1.28
2000	172.2	3.36%	$1.19	$1.29
2001	177.5	3.08%	$1.43	$1.51
2002	179.0	0.85%	$1.34	$1.40
2003	184.0	2.79%	$1.56	$1.59
2004 (April)	187.0	1.63%	$1.79	$1.79

(3), are the percent changes in the *CPI* from the previous year. For example, in 2002, the *CPI* was 179.0; in 2003 it had risen to 184.0, a 2.79% increase. The numbers in column (3) are the most commonly cited figures for the rate of inflation. Notice that historically, inflation was generally at a low level until the early 1970s. Inflation reached a peak of 13.5% in 1980. In recent years, the rate of inflation has slowed to practically zero. These figures tell the story of the inflation in the United States in the second half of the twentieth century. Notice that in the last twenty years of the twentieth century, the average price of consumer goods and services approximately more than doubled: the *CPI* rose from 82.4 in 1980 to 172.2 in 2000. If a person's income in 1999 was two times what it was in 1980, the person's *real* income, adjusted for inflation, would be unchanged.

In the past twenty-five years, the *CPI* has more than tripled: the *CPI* rose from 60.6 in 1977 to 187.0 in 2004, a factor of 187.0 ÷ 60.6 = 3.09. An average basket of goods that cost $100 in 1977 cost the consumer $309 in 2004. Between 1950 and 2000, the last half of the twentieth century, the price level increased by a factor of 172.2 ÷ 24.1 = 7.15. One-dollar bills in the 1950s had a purchasing power of more than five-dollar bills today; that generation used quarters and dimes the way we use dollar bills now. Whether a household's pecuniary standard of living increased or decreased during these various time periods depended on whether its income went up faster or slower than these average price increases.[3]

Column (4) shows the current price of gasoline for the years indicated. In early 1999, the price dropped to around $1 per gallon. The term "current price" means the price that consumers actually faced in that current year. For example, in 1972, the year prior to the Middle East war that established OPEC (the Organization of Petroleum Exporting Countries) as a major influence on world oil markets, consumers paid $.32 per gallon for regular gasoline. In 1984 we paid $1.17, and in early 2004, $1.79. The current price, however, reflects the level of absolute prices at the time. Using the *CPI,* we can analyze how the price of gasoline has moved *relative to other prices.* The answer is reached by converting all past current prices of gasoline to prices in a given year, say 2004. This is done by multiplying the actual (current) price in the past by the ratio of the 2004 *CPI* to the *CPI* in that year. The *real* (2004 equivalent) price of gasoline in 1972 is (187.0 ÷ 41.8) $.32 = $1.43. That is, if gasoline had increased in price from its 1972 price of $.32 per gallon in the same proportion as all other prices had increased, it would have sold in 2004 for $1.43 per gallon. This is approximately the same as its 2002 selling price, but less than the early 2004 price of $1.79. The figures in column (5) show these *real* prices of gasoline, all stated in terms of constant other prices, in this case, in terms of 2002 price levels. These figures show that gasoline actually has been *cheaper* in many recent years than it was in the 1950s and 1960s.

Certain episodes are important in understanding the real prices of gasoline shown in column (5). In the 1920s and 1930s, huge deposits of petroleum were

3. Comparisons such as these which take place over extended time periods have inherent measurement problems. Some commonplace goods available now didn't even exist in the 1950s, such as DVDs, calculators and desktop computers. Other products have changed drastically in quality, such as stereos, televisions, etc. There was no unleaded gas in the 1960s and our air was dirtier because of that. New additives have affected octane ratings and reduced unwanted emissions. The BLS attempts to control for these quality changes by not including price increases caused by an increase in quality. However, according to today's procedures, if an altogether new drug came out that cured AIDS, and it increased in price in the following year, this would be computed as an *increase* in the price of pharmaceuticals!

discovered in Texas and Oklahoma, and the United States became a major producer of world petroleum. In the second half of the twentieth century, the newly discovered deposits in the Middle East became increasingly prominent. Those countries formed an association, OPEC (the Organization of Petroleum Exporting Countries), that sought to raise world petroleum prices by acting in concert to reduce supply. By the early 1970s, these countries together accounted for approximately one half of world oil production, though it is now less. In late 1973, following the Arab-Israeli war, the OPEC countries reduced or halted altogether oil shipments to the United States for several months.[4] More importantly, since much mideast oil arrived circuitously in the United States through other countries, OPEC successfully reduced their total production through collusive effort. The price of gasoline soon rose by approximately 35%, from $.39 to $.53 per gallon, as shown in column (4), and energy conservation became an issue of national policy.[5] The United States government enacted the 55 miles per hour speed limit (now rescinded) and other energy conservation laws that are with us to this day.

The impact on consumers was similarly dramatic. Volkswagen Beetles, the leading economy car of the times, then selling for approximately $5,000, increased in price by approximately $1,000, well over its sticker price. The larger gas hogs stayed on dealers' lots until deep cuts in prices were made. Carpooling, never too popular amongst commuters, became more common. People became much more conscious about energy usage; they moved up along their demand curves for energy and in ways small and large, consumed less. For the next few years, however, OPEC increased its exports and gasoline prices rose only slightly at the pump. Other prices, however, increased at an even greater rate. Commentators in the late 1970s bemoaned the resurgence of Americans' old evil ways of preferring the larger, less fuel efficient cars. But this was exactly in accordance with the law of demand. Although the nominal price of gasoline increased from $.53 per gallon in 1974 to $.67 per gallon in 1978, its *real* price *fell*—in 2004 dollars, from $2.01 to $1.92 per gallon. Throughout the late 1970s, the price of gasoline fell relative to incomes and the prices of other goods, and that is why Americans reverted back to larger cars.

The next major episode began in 1979: the Shah of Iran was overthrown and the anti-western regime of the Ayatollah Khomeini took power in his place. The Khomeini regime sharply decreased exports as a matter of policy. Shortly thereafter, the Iraq-Iran war started, and eventually, due to the war, Iraq was forced to curtail petroleum exports. Gasoline prices reached their highest level ever in 1981: $2.84 per gallon in 2004 prices. Once again Americans and others switched to smaller cars. Although American car manufacturers had already engaged in some downsizing of their automobiles, American cars were still large relative to those produced in Europe and Japan. Various Japanese companies, notably Honda, Toyota and Mazda, had developed smaller cars in the 1970s and were ready with them when gasoline prices jumped. The events in the Middle

---

4. At that time, government price controls were in effect for petroleum products; in chapter 5 we shall discuss the effects of that policy, and in particular, its relation to the waiting lines at filling stations.

5. The initial change in the real price of gasoline was probably greater than this amount because it occurred rapidly, while other prices increased slowly throughout the year.

East were, for them, a fortuitous turn of events. They had the right product at the right time. Imports of Japanese made cars surged in the early 1980s.

As the 1980s proceeded, older cars were gradually replaced by the newer, smaller cars that got much better mileage. Average miles per gallon approximately doubled in that decade from earlier levels, from approximately 13 to 26 mpg. As a result, the price of gasoline started to fall. In 1986, the price dropped from $1.17 to $.84 per gallon, even though the average of other prices was still increasing. The real price fell, in 2004 dollars, from its high of $2.84 in 1981, to $1.40 in 2002, a decrease of 50%! Once again, as the twentieth century rolled to a close, performance cars such as the SUVs (Sports Utility Vehicles) have became more popular, and each succeeding year's models became larger than the cars they replaced. These heavy new cars in fact comprise about half of all new car sales.

The prices of gasoline and other energy sources were lower, until 2002, than when the whole energy episode began in 1973. It is not surprising, therefore, that the driving habits of Americans have been similar to what they were in the 1960s and earlier. Inflation has obscured the true picture. Only when the effects of inflation on other prices has been taken into account can the law of demand be applied. The law of demand is a statement about consumers' responses to changes in *relative,* or *real* prices, not responses to changes in nominal or money prices, which may reflect irrelevant changes in *all* prices due to inflation.[6]

Check your understanding: Since 1950, the price of modest sedans has gone from $2,000 to over $13,000, for, say, a Ford Focus or Chevrolet Cavalier. Yet the number of cars purchased by Americans has substantially increased. What accounts for this? By the way, are there additional quality issues that should be considered? Are today's cars the same as cars of the 1950s?

The Law of Demand and Inflation

We have spoken of inflation without explaining why it occurs. The fundamental explanation of at least the qualitative phenomenon of rising price levels is the law of demand. More precise quantitative explanations of the degree to which inflation occurs and the speed of its appearance, however, is the subject of considerable research by macro economists.

Consider why it would not be a successful strategy to eliminate poverty by having the government simply print $100 bills and mail everyone, say, 100 of them every month. People's nominal, or money incomes would rise by $10,000 per month, or $120,000 per year—sounds pretty good. It has in fact looked good to many governments in the past. During the U.S. civil war, the confederate government found it lacked the money to pay its soldiers, so it simply printed the money and gave it to them. It worked for a short time, but as everyone went to purchase goods with their new (confederate) dollars, merchants soon found that they would run out of goods at the old prices, and quickly raised prices. When future pay periods came along, the government needed successively larger

6. An additional factor in this picture is that cars now get approximately twice the miles per gallon compared with the cars of the sixties and early seventies. This change in technology is equivalent to halving the price of gasoline.

amounts of dollars to compensate the soldiers for the depreciation in the purchasing power of the currency, and so the policy was accelerated. Before the war ended, baskets full of currency, all in very large denominations, were needed even for purchases of ordinary goods and services. The German government (among others) pursued such a policy after World War I. By 1923, prices were rising so fast that workers were paid twice a *day* so that they could rush out and make purchases before the currency depreciated even more. Earlier, the price of a loaf of bread was about 1 Mark; by 1923 it was approximately 100,000,000,000,000 Marks.[7] In Belgrade in the former Yugoslavia in the summer of 1993, prices were increasing by 10% *daily.* The price of a Snickers candy bar in early August was some 6 million *dinars,* and a VCR went for 20,391,560,223 dinars.[8] Dinar bills with merely 6 zeros (millions) were small change, used like pennies in the United States. Apparently, due to the embargo of goods from elsewhere in Europe and the U.S., the prices of goods rose. In order to offset this loss, the government simply took to the printing presses and printed money. The Serbian government was printing dinars 24 hours per day, and even contracted with private printers to print money for them to keep up with the price increases. Why did these and like events happen?

There have always been three popular explanations for inflation:

- Greedy corporations, in their lust for profits, raise prices to unconscionable levels, lowering the standard of living of consumers.
- Greedy unions, in their lust for higher wages, raise wages to unconscionable levels, forcing corporations to raise prices to stay in business.
- Greedy consumers periodically go on buying binges, bidding up prices on scarce goods.

These "explanations" all fail for the same reason: they are all based on *ad hoc,* unexplained changes in tastes. The data in Table 3-1 show that inflation has varied in the past five decades from approximately zero to 13.5 % per year. (In the early 1930s, the price level *decreased* by almost 25% in three years.) In order to explain why something is *varying,* one has to come up with a cause that is itself varying, at least in some degree. Corporations are now and have always been interested in higher profits, unions are now and have always been interested in higher wages for their members. The puzzle is, therefore, why, in the greedy pursuit of maximum profits, was a 2% price increase the successful strategy in the 1950s, whereas the successful strategy became a 13% increase in 1980? Why were unions able to obtain double-digit pay increases around 1980, instead of the much lower percent increases of earlier years? The fraction of the labor force that belongs to unions in fact decreased throughout past decades; increased union power could hardly be an explanation. Lastly, why should consumers suddenly and inexplicably go on periodic buying binges, only to stop inexplicably at some later time? Changes in the average price level (the rate of inflation) must be explained in terms of responses to changes in constraints, based on a consistent, universal regularity of behavior. This universal postulate is, as always, the law of demand.

---

7. These episodes of extreme inflation are called *hyperinflation.* They are interesting and useful to study because the dramatic nature of the events makes it easier to sort out its causes.

8. *Wall Street Journal,* August 4, 1993, page 1.

The law of demand is a statement that the marginal value of any good falls as its quantity increases relative to other goods. The law applies to the good "money" as well. Money is a useful good: it lowers the cost of transacting. All societies have used money for this purpose because of the advantages it yields over direct barter. The *price* of money is the amount of other goods a person would give up in order to hold onto, say, one dollar of currency. We ordinarily state the price of goods in terms of money, but we can just as well state the price of money in terms of goods. If the price of a steak is $4.00, the price of money (1 dollar) in terms of steaks is 1/4 steak. If the supply of steaks were to increase, the dollar price of steaks might fall to $2.00; in that case we could equivalently say that the price of a dollar has risen to 1/2 steak. In the same fashion, if the quantity of *money* increases relative to the amount of goods available, the price of money will fall. When the government prints money in much greater amounts than increases in the amounts of goods available, the inevitable consequence is a decrease in the marginal value of money, or, equivalently, an *increase* in the price of goods in terms of money. This is the fundamental reason for inflation—there is no other. Inflation occurs because, and only because of increases in the amount of money in circulation relative to the goods available. In all modern societies, the central government issues money. Inflation, therefore, occurs or abates in response to how the government regulates the supply of money. It is not a phenomenon created or controlled by the private sector.[9]

This being said, quantitative measurement and control of the amount of money (the money supply) is not routine. In the first place, many items are used as money in today's society—cash, checks, money market accounts and credit cards. Various measures of the total supply of money exist, and none are regarded as perfect. Secondly, the *velocity* of money—the number of times a given dollar turns over, or is used in a year, that is, the number of transactions a given supply of money can support in a year—is not necessarily constant. There are some important costs associated with holding wealth in the form of cash, or in a non-interest bearing checking account. Suppose the rate of inflation is 10% per year. Then $100 cash will be able to purchase only $90 worth of goods in one year. The inflation rate thus taxes cash or non-interest accounts by the rate of inflation.[10] Therefore, by the law of demand, as inflation increases, individuals will reduce their cash holdings, and the number of transactions undertaken with the same stock of money will increase. This explains why, in the cases of hyperinflation cited above, people rushed out to buy goods almost as soon as they were paid, so as to avoid the losses attendant upon holding cash for even a few hours or days. Because effects such as this determine in part household demand for money, the relationship between small changes in the amount of money generated by the government and changes in the price level is not easy to predict. Over the long term, and especially for the types of large changes that produce hyperinflation, the relationship and causality is clear.

9. In World War II prisoner of war camps, cigarettes were the medium of exchange. These camps experienced hyperinflation in terms of cigarette prices when Red Cross parcels containing hundreds of thousands of cigarettes arrived at various times.

10. In chap. 10 we will discuss how interest rates are affected by anticipated inflation. Since the value of cash depreciates at the rate of inflation, the interest banks pay must reflect this anticipated cost. In times of inflation, therefore, market rates of interest are relatively high, to offset the decrease in purchasing power of currency.

3.2 Elasticity of Demand

The law of demand says nothing about the actual quantitative measure of the slope of demand curves. If a demand curve appears very steep in the ordinary sense of slope, as pictured in Fig. 3-1(a), then relatively large price changes will be associated with only small changes in the quantity demanded. If the demand curve is approximately flat, as in Fig. 3-1(b), then changes in the price will lead to relatively large absolute changes in the quantity demanded. The only restriction placed on the slopes of demand curves by the law of demand is the *qualitative* restriction of being negative. However, the actual *quantitative* relationship between changes in price and changes in the quantity demanded—the degree to which changes in price cause changes in the quantity demanded—is often useful data, and economists have occasion to measure these values.

The slope of a curve, as typically measured in the applied sciences, is the change in the variable plotted vertically (price) divided by the change in the variable plotted horizontally (quantity). These changes in the variables p and q are designated, respectively, Δp and Δq. We call the curve in Fig. 3-1(a) steep in the sense of interpreting the slope as $\Delta p/\Delta q$. However, demand curves are understood to mean the quantity demanded at a given price. The dependent variable, quantity q, (which depends on the price p), is measured along the *horizontal* axis, contrary to custom. Thus the slope of the demand curve should really be $\Delta q/\Delta p$, the change in the variable plotted horizontally divided by the change in the variable plotted vertically, not $\Delta p/\Delta q$. The reasons for this peculiar placement of the dependent variable are shrouded in mystery.[11] It has persisted, however, and the slope of a demand (or supply) curve is really the reciprocal of the slope as ordinarily defined. (In spite of this, economists still speak of the demand curves in Fig. 3-1(a) and (b) as steep and flat, respectively.)

If one tried to measure the responsiveness of the quantity demanded of gasoline as the price of gasoline changed, it would take the form of a statement such as, "when the price of gasoline fell by $.10, the market quantity of gasoline demanded

Figure 3-1 *Inelastic and Elastic Demands*

Although these words are casually used to mean steep and flat, *inelastic* means a small *percentage* response in quantity demanded to a given *percent* change in price. *Elastic* means a relatively large percentage response in quantity demanded per percent change in the price.

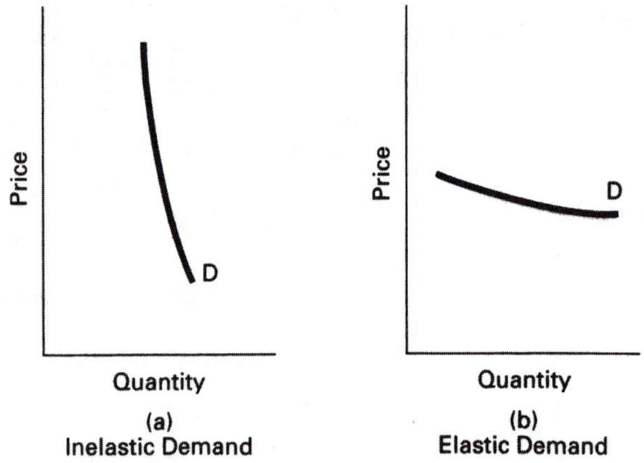

11. Rumor has it that it started as a typographical error in Afred Marshall's *Principles,* first published in 1890 in England.

rose by 1,000,000 gallons per week," yielding a slope of the demand curve $\Delta q/\Delta p = 10{,}000{,}000$ gallons per dollar. One problem with such a measure is that it would not really convey whether this was a large or a small change in consumption.

We really have to know first whether 1,000,000 gallons is large or small relative to total consumption. Also, it matters whether this \$.10 change in the price of gasoline lowered the price from \$.50 to \$.40, or from \$1.50 to \$1.40, or from \$3.50 to \$3.40. To make matters worse, the value of this slope would change if the units of measurement changed. In Canada, a gallon means an imperial gallon, equal to 5 rather than 4 quarts, and the dollars would be Canadian dollars. In that case, even if Canadian consumers were identical to U.S. consumers in their responsiveness to changes in the price of gasoline, the slope of the Canadian demand curve for gasoline would be a different number than the corresponding slope of the U.S. demand curve, making comparisons very difficult. (In fact Canada is now on the metric system and quantities are quoted in liters, further complicating the comparison.)

This sensitivity to the units of measurement can be eliminated by measuring the changes in price and quantity demanded as *percentage* changes. If the change in the price of a good is 10%, it doesn't matter whether the price is quoted in U.S. dollars, Canadian dollars, Euros, or any other currency. A 10% change is a 10% change. Likewise, a given percent change in quantity is independent of the units of measurement. A measure of responsiveness to price changes based on percent changes would therefore allow comparisons when different units were used, and also would better communicate the degree of response. For these reasons, the most common measure of demand response is the *elasticity of demand,* ϵ, defined as:

$$\epsilon = \frac{\textit{percent change in quantity}}{\textit{percent change in price}} = \frac{\frac{\Delta q}{q}}{\frac{\Delta p}{p}} \qquad (3\text{-}1)$$

The elasticity of demand is a *dimensionless* number. The units used to measure price and quantity all cancel in the above expression; there is nothing left but the numerical value. It is this feature that makes this type of measurement useful.

For demand curves, the value of elasticity must be negative, because price and quantity demanded move in opposite directions. If a 10% reduction in price were to produce a 50% increase in the quantity demanded, this would indicate a rather large response. We call such a portion of a demand curve *elastic,* meaning a small percent price change induced a large or elastic change in quantity demanded. More precisely, if the (absolute) percent change in quantity is greater than the (absolute) percent change in price, the demand is *elastic;* if the (absolute) percent change in quantity is smaller than the (absolute) percent change in price, we call the demand *inelastic.* If the two percent changes are equal in absolute value, we say the demand is *unitary* elastic. Summarizing,

Elastic demand: $-\infty < \epsilon < -1$

Inelastic demand: $-1 < \epsilon < 0$

Unitary elastic demand: $\epsilon = -1$

A linear (straight line) demand curve is depicted in Fig. 3-2. Three points are labeled, *A, B,* and *C* with the coordinates indicated. At price $p = 10$, the quantity demanded is $q = 2$. If the price is lowered by 1 to $p = 9$, the quantity demanded increases by 2 units, to $q = 4$. The midpoint of the demand curve, *B,* is where price = 5.50 and quantity = 11. Towards the horizontal axis, when $p = 2$, the quantity demanded $q = 18$, and when the price is further lowered to 1, $q = 20$. What are the values of the elasticities of demand at points *A, B* and *C*?

Although the formula in equation (3-1) defines elasticity, computation is easier if the compound fraction is simplified. In that case, elasticity becomes

$$\epsilon = \frac{p}{q} \cdot \frac{\Delta q}{\Delta p} \tag{3-2}$$

This formula says that elasticity equals the slope, $\Delta q/\Delta p$, times price over quantity, p/q. Since this particular demand curve is linear, its slope is constant. The slope as we are defining it, using points *A* and the point adjacent to it is $\Delta q/\Delta p = (4 - 2) \div (9 - 10) = -2$. At point *A*, therefore, the elasticity is $(10/2) \times (-2) = -10$. The demand curve is highly *elastic* at point *A*. The decrease in price of \$1 is a 10 percent change, yet it results in a 100 percent increase in the quantity demanded, from 2 to 4. The percent change in quantity approaches infinity as the quantity becomes smaller and smaller, i.e., as the price approaches the reservation price. Thus the value of ϵ approaches minus infinity as the demand curve nears the vertical axis. By contrast, the demand curve is highly *inelastic* at point *C*. The slope is again –2; thus $\epsilon = (1/20) \times (-2) = -.10$. At point *C,* a 100 percent increase in price, from \$1 to \$2 results in only a 10 percent decrease in quantity, from 20 units to 18. As the horizontal axis is approached, the value of ϵ approaches zero. Lastly, at the midpoint of the demand curve, point *B,* $\epsilon = (5.50/11) \times (-2) = -1$. At the midpoint, the percent change in quantity is exactly equal to the percent change in price, yielding unitary elasticity.[12]

As is evident from its definition and the preceding calculations, elasticity is not the same as slope. The elasticity can vary along a demand curve in ways that are not always apparent to the naked eye. For linear demand curves, the slope is constant, but the elasticity equals zero at the point where the demand curve intercepts the horizontal (quantity) axis, decreases to minus 1 at the midpoint of the curve, and approaches minus infinity as the vertical (price) axis is approached.

Some examples of price elasticities are shown in Table 3-2.

Elasticity and Total Expenditure

There is a very important relation between the elasticity of demand and consumers' total expenditure on a good. Starting near the reservation price, i.e., \$11 in Fig. 3-2, total expenditure *TE,* (or total revenue) is very small, since so few units (almost zero) are purchased. As the price is lowered, the quantity demanded increases, and total expenditure represented by the rectangle bounded

12. There is a certain ambiguity in calculating percents for elasticity. If the price goes down from \$2 to \$1, this is a 50% decrease. However, if the price then increases back to \$2, this is a 100% increase! We can avoid this confusion by using the formula (3-2) instead of the compound fraction, at a specific point on the demand curve.

Figure 3-2 *Calculation of Elasticity at Various Points Along a Demand Curve*

At point *A*, the demand is highly elastic. The slope is $\Delta q/\Delta p = (4 - 2) \div (9 - 10) = -2$. Multiplying by $p/q = 5$ yields an elasticity of -10. Similarly, the elasticity at point *C* is $-2 \times (1/20) = -0.10$.

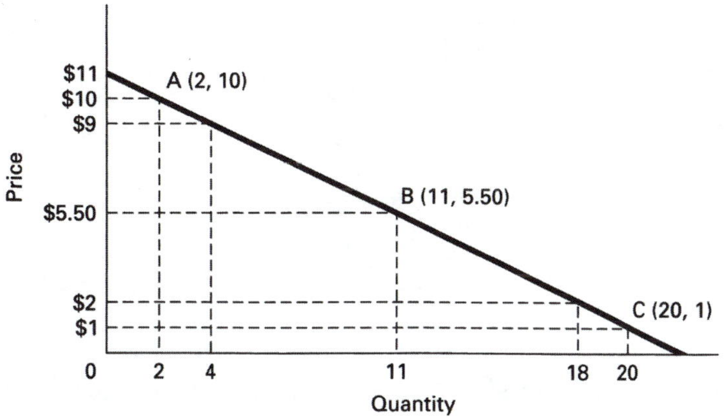

by the price charged and the quantity consumed increases. For example, in Fig. 3-2, at point *A*, total expenditure is $10 × 2 = $20. When the price decreases to $9, total expenditure = $9 × 4 = $36. In this elastic portion of the demand curve, as price decreases (and thus quantity increases), the rectangles of total expenditure on the good increases. With linear demand curves, as the price is lowered further, the point of maximum total expenditure occurs at the midpoint, where the demand is unitary elastic (*TE* = $5.50 × 11 = $60.50). Geometrically, the largest rectangle of total expenditure that can be inscribed under the demand curve is located at the midpoint of the curve. As the horizontal axis is approached, where the price approaches zero, total expenditure will again approach zero. This is the inelastic part of the demand curve. Thus starting at the reservation price, as price decreases and quantity increases, total expenditure *TE* at first increases, reaches a maximum at the point of unitary elasticity, and then decreases to zero. These changes in expenditure are dependent on the elasticity

Figure 3-3 *Elasticities Along a Straight Line Demand Curve*

The demand is elastic near the vertical (price) axis, unitary at the midpoint, and inelastic near the quantity axis.

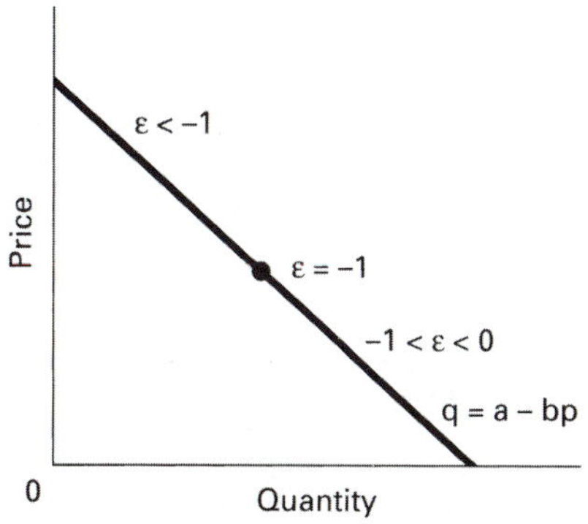

TABLE 3-2 *Representative Price Elasticities*

Item	Price Elasticity
Food	–0.21
Purchased Meals	–2.27
Beverages	–0.78
Clothing	–0.49
Medical Services	–0.20
Automobiles	–1.20
Housing	
Rental	–0.18
Owner Occ.	–1.20
Gasoline	–0.54
Electricity	–1.14
Books, Newspapers and Magazines	–0.34
Coffee	–0.16
Beer	–1.13
Tobacco	–0.61
Marijuana	–1.50
Gambling	–1.60

Sources: Food: H. Wold and L. Jureen, *Demand Analysis* (New York: John Wiley & Sons, Inc., 1953), p. 203. Books, Beverages and Tobacco: A. Mansur and J. Whalley, "Numerical Specification of Applied General Equilibrium Models: Estimation, Calibration and Data," in Applied General Equilibrium Analysis, H.E. Scarf and J. Shoven, eds., New York: Cambidge University Press, 1984. Medical Services: G. Rosenthal, "Price Elasticity of Demand for Short-Term General Hospital Services"; in *Empirical Studies in Health Economics,* Herbert Klarman, ed. (Baltimore: Johns Hopkins Press, 1970). Automobiles: Gregory C. Chow, *Demand for Automobiles in the United States* (Amsterdam: North Holland Publishing Company, 1957). Purchased Meals, Housing: H.S. Houthakker and L.D. Taylor, *Consumer Demand in the United States* (Cambridge, Mass.: Harvard University Press, 1970), pp. 166–167. Gasoline: Data Resources, Inc., "A Study of the Quarterly Demand for Gasoline," a study prepared for the Council on Environmental Quality, December 1973. Electricity: R.F. Halvorsen, "Residential Demand for Electricity," unpublished Ph.D. dissertation, Harvard University, December 1972. Coffee: J. Huang, J.J. Siegfried, and F. Zardoshty "The Demand for Coffee in the United States, 1963–77," *Quarterly Journal of Business and Economics* (Summer 1980): 36–50. Beer: T.F. Hogarty and K.G. Elsinger, "The Demand for Beer," *Review of Economics and Statistics* (May 1972): 195–198. Marijuana: T.C. Misket and F. Vakil, "Some Estimates of Price and Expenditure Elasticities among UCLA Students," *Review of Economics and Statistics* (November 1972): 474–475. Gambling: D.B. Suits, "The Elasticity of Demand for Gambling," *Quarterly Journal of Economics* (February 1979): 155–162.

of demand at each point along the demand curve. In the upper part of the demand curve, where demand is elastic, the percent increase in quantity is *greater* than the percent decrease in price. As a result, the increase in quantity purchased more than offsets the decrease in per unit price, and total expenditure increases as price falls and quantity increases. Likewise, in the lower part of the demand curve, where demand is inelastic, the percent increase in quantity is *less* than the percent decrease in price, thus total expenditure decreases.[13]

---

13. These results can be shown using calculus. Defining the demand curve in terms of quantity for mathematical convenience, as $p = p(q)$, total revenue (expenditure) $R = p(q)q$. Using the product rule for differentiation, the change in revenue as quantity changes, called *marginal revenue,* is $R' = p + q(dp/dq) = p[1 + (q/p)(dp/dq)] = p[1 + 1/\epsilon]$. Note that when $\epsilon = -1$, $R' = 0$. At this point, R is at a maximum. When $\epsilon = -2$, say, $R' = p/2 > 0$, so R increases as q increases (p decreases). With the demand curve $q = a - bp$, $\epsilon = -p/[(a/b) - p]$; $\epsilon = -1$ when $p = a/2b$, the midpoint of the demand curve.

Some demand curves have constant elasticity throughout: demand curves defined as $q = k/p$, where k is any positive constant, are the rectangular hyperbolas $pq = k$. This expression says literally that total expenditure is a constant, k, no matter what price is charged. If the price increases, consumers decrease their purchases by the exact amount so that total expenditure remains constant. This demand curve is everywhere unitary elastic, though its slope varies between zero to minus infinity. It is an easy exercise in elementary calculus to show that demand curves defined as $q = kp^{\epsilon}$, $\epsilon < 0$ have constant elasticity equal to ϵ over the whole demand curve.

Check your understanding: Sometimes when the citrus crop freezes in California or Florida, the media report that even though there are fewer fruit available for consumers, "the total value of the crop has increased," or words to that effect. How can this be? What does this say about the demand for citrus?

A demand curve that is elastic is indicative of a good or service for which individuals can relatively easily find alternative goods to consume as its price rises. For example, if the price of steak rises, but the prices of chicken and pork products remain the same, people substitute away from steak, towards those other meat products. The availability of good substitutes tends to increase the elasticity of demand. In part, the elasticity depends on how narrowly the commodity is defined. For example, we expect very high elasticity of sirloin steak, since most people easily substitute other cuts of beef (T-bone, porterhouse, etc.,) for sirloin if the price of sirloin changed relative to those other cuts. Various cuts of meat are often put on sale at local supermarkets. Consumers typically take advantage of these temporary price reductions and substitute towards those goods. The elasticity of beef would not be as great as the elasticity of a particular cut, say sirloin, since substitution would now be between different types of meat. Most consumers probably find it a more substantial change to switch between different kinds of meat versus different types of the same meat. Continuing, the elasticity of meat would be less than the elasticity of beef or pork, since now substitution would be between meat and non-meat foods. In general, the more narrowly a commodity is defined, the higher will be its elasticity of demand.[14] The elasticity of demand for a specific brand of a good, for example, is more elastic than the demand for the good as a whole.

The limiting case of highly elastic demand is when the demand curve is horizontal at some price. In this case we say the demand is infinitely, or perfectly elastic. This is the situation that confronts individual firms producing a very small part of the total output of an industry. For example, a single wheat farmer has no influence on the price of wheat. The world's production of wheat is so huge that no matter what level of production this one farmer engages in, the world price will not be affected. The world's demand for wheat is not perfectly elastic; changes in the price of wheat relative to other grains induce consumers to substitute towards the relatively lower priced grain. From the standpoint of one farmer, however, the demand curve looks like a horizontal line, at the world price. Firms that face this type of demand curve are called **price takers**. An industry composed of price takers is considered perfectly competitive. We shall return to this in a later chapter on market structure. Individual consumers are invariably price takers—we rarely can affect the market price by declining to make a purchase.

14. The price of some aggregate commodity such as meat means an average of the prices of the various kinds of meat, weighted by their relative quantities sold.

The demand for goods for which few substitutes are available is likely inelastic. For example, food as a whole category would have an inelastic demand. It would not be perfectly inelastic, i.e., vertical, since people can and do alter their food habits (including eating less) as the price of food changes. As we saw earlier in this chapter, in 1973–'74, during the first oil embargo by the OPEC countries, the price of gasoline increased by about 25% in two years. During that time, the quantity of gasoline demanded decreased about 5%, indicating a demand elasticity of about –.2 (highly inelastic). It is difficult for most consumers to substitute away from petroleum, especially gasoline, at least in the short run. People still had to get to work, and travel arrangements are not easily rearranged. Over time, carpooling becomes more prevalent and cars have become more fuel efficient, and thus the quantity of gasoline demanded fell further, indicating a more elastic response as time passed.

Drug-Related Crime

It is a major part of U.S. policy to reduce the availability of addictive drugs. The federal government spends billions of dollars each year in drug interdiction, and state and local governments spend billions more pursuing addicts and maintaining them in jails when they are incarcerated. A related but considerable part of the illegal drug problem has been the incidence of drug-related criminality. A major fraction of thefts are performed by addicts seeking funds to purchase their drugs. Some economists have raised the issue that drug interdiction may be doing more harm than good in regard to this drug-related crime.

The demand for drugs on the part of addicts is surely highly inelastic—the very concept of addiction means that a person is desperate for the good, and is thus unlikely to vary greatly the quantity consumed as the price increases. Drug interdiction—capturing or destroying drugs before they enter the U.S. market—reduces the amount available to be consumed, and so raises the street price of addictive drugs. But for goods with inelastic demands, total expenditure increases when the price increases. As a result, addicts now spend more on their drugs than previously. This increases their incentive to commit crimes. Thus drug interdiction may in fact lead to increases in crime, even though, with the higher prices, the quantity of drugs consumed decreases. This presents policy managers with a difficult choice: if we let more drugs into the country, we may be encouraging their use, but we may also be lowering drug-related crime. It's not an easy thing to decide.

Elasticity and Monopolistic Industries

When a business firm is large relative to the market it faces, its decisions about how much to produce can affect the price at which the good ultimately sells. If some firm is the sole vendor of some good, we typically refer to it as a monopoly (from the Greek, one seller). As we shall see, the ease with which other firms could enter the market and compete is very important. In 1998, the U.S. Government accused the Microsoft Corporation of engaging in monopolistic practices and filed an anti-trust suit against the firm. The government (and competitor Novell) pointed out that 95 percent of PCs used Microsoft's operating system, Windows. The government alleged that consumers were being hurt by this concentration of market power.

The reason consumers might worry about monopolists is that if they reduce their output, the price of their product will rise. This is in sharp contrast to, say, the situation of a wheat farmer. Even if the largest U.S. farmer decided to quit farming, the world price of wheat would not change—any one farmer is too small a part of that industry to affect prices. We can gain some insight into the question of whether a firm is acting like a monopolist by investigating the elasticity of demand it faces.

The profits any company makes equals its total revenue (its total receipts from the sales of its output) *minus* it total costs of production. Revenues and costs each depend on how much output is produced. Symbolically,

$$\text{Profits} = R(q) - C(q)$$

Consider the effect on profit if a firm decides to reduce output. With lower output, total cost $C(q)$ unambiguously decreases; it costs less to produce less. What, however, is the effect on revenues? If the demand facing the firm is inelastic, then reducing output *increases* revenue. Therefore, if the demand curve is inelastic, the firm can always derive larger profits by reducing output. Total cost decreases because less is produced, and total revenue increases because the demand curve is inelastic. It therefore follows that if a firm is a monopolist, meaning it affects the price when it chooses the quantity, then maximization of profits implies *the firm will never choose to sell its output at a price where the demand is inelastic.* It can make larger profits by contracting output. The profit maximizing output must therefore lie somewhere in the *elastic* portion of the demand curve. In the elastic portion, as output is contracted, total cost decreases and so does total revenue. The quantity at which profits are maximized is where revenue starts to decrease faster than cost, that is, at the point where the change in total revenue equals the change in total cost.[15] Contemplate now the likely elasticity of demand for Microsoft's Windows. Suppose the firm decided to raise its price by 10%. Is it likely that we would see a greater than 10% decrease in the use of this product? Casual empiricism suggests not—this is a very popular system. But if this is the case, Microsoft is certainly not exploiting its monopoly position to the fullest extent possible. It is charging a price lower than what a profit-maximizing monopolist would charge. One important reason why a firm would not charge the full monopoly price is to forestall the entry of new competitors. This threat always exists to some extent; it seems likely to have had a sobering effect on Microsoft's pricing policies.

Another important application of elasticity to monopolistic pricing is the long-standing suspicion on the part of government and consumers to the oil industry. In the past generation, there have been important episodes in which the price of oil has risen or fallen sharply: 1973–'74, 1979, 1985, 1991, 1999–2000. In each instance, the quantity demanded has moved in much smaller proportion than the price change. Relatively small percent changes in the quantity of petroleum available (around 5%) caused substantial increases, sometimes by as much as 25% in the prices of petroleum products, such as gasolinc. The demand was clearly inelastic. It seems, therefore, the oil companies had not been effectively

---

15. Maximizing the preceding profit function by setting the first derivative equal to zero yields $R'(q) - C'(q) = 0$. Since $C'(q)$, the cost of additional output (marginal cost) is positive, $R'(q)$ is positive. Applying formula in footnote 13 implies elasticity $\epsilon < -1$.

charging a monopoly price. If they had, they would not have chosen to sell in the inelastic portion of the demand curve. They were evidently precluded from selling in the elastic portion of the demand curve by the competitive pricing of other firms. The common perception of monopoly power, always appealing when the price of some good rises sharply, has not been borne out by the facts in the case of big oil.

3.3 The Second Law of Demand

The law of demand states that, holding other things constant, the quantity demanded of any good or activity varies inversely with its price. A second law is also commonly asserted: with the passage of time, the response to a change in price becomes absolutely greater. An alternative way of stating this second law is that at any given price, long-run demand curves are more elastic than short-run demand curves. The extent to which people respond to a change in price depends in part on how long they expect the price change to persist. The changes in consumption are greater if the price change is expected to be long-lived.

There are several reasons why this effect would occur. Consider the response to, say, an increase in the price of gasoline. The first response of consumers is simply to drive a little less, or more slowly, in order to conserve on the now more expensive gas. This is an elementary response that individuals can and do carry out on their own; it takes little planning or coordination. If the price increase is perceived to be long-lasting, it will pay for people to invest greater resources in order to reduce the damages imposed by the higher price. Greater planning and coordination of activities will take place so as to reduce the number of trips. Efforts to carpool will be stepped up, and perhaps work schedules will be adjusted to accommodate shared rides. These are activities that usually do not occur right away; they are costly and only worthwhile if the price increase is persistent.

If the price increase is perceived as essentially permanent, the automobiles driven will change over time. People who drive a great deal, such as suburban commuters, have an incentive to replace their cars with cars that get better mileage. They will bid up the prices of fuel-efficient cars, and some consumers who own such cars and who do not drive very much, will find it in their interest to sell their cars and purchase (at a lower price) the gas hogs. By reallocating the existing cars in this manner, the *average* miles per gallon for all drivers can increase, even though the same cars are being driven. Finally, as cars wear out, they will be replaced by new cars getting better mileage. A car that gets better mileage will sell at a greater price than a car with the same characteristics that gets inferior mileage, since consumers know they will save money on gasoline in the future. Investing in technology to build cars that get more miles per gallon will therefore take place voluntarily if price increases are perceived to be long lasting. In the long-run, therefore, for a given increase in price, the reduction in the quantity of gasoline consumed will be greater than in the short run, as less gasoline is used in the new cars. The strategies for mitigating the damages imposed by higher prices varies with the anticipated duration of the price increase. In the long-run, the incentives to alter behavior are relatively greater, and the difficulty with which we rearrange our patterns of consumption relatively less; thus we adjust behavior in ways we would not consider if the price increase was perceived to be short-lived.

Of course the same holds true for price decreases. In recent years, the price of gasoline has decreased to historically low levels. In the longer run, we develop better ways to take advantage of a lower priced resource. Consider, for example, the response to the decrease in the price of computer chips, i.e., in the price of computing. At first, only some well-known applications in number-crunching were explored. As time went on, new ideas sprang up, e.g., word processing, graphics, voice recognition, new statistical routines, etc., that formerly no one had any incentive to explore, since the cost of the final product would have made application of the new ideas prohibitively expensive. As prices of computing decreased, the incentives to produce new information increased. As that new information becomes available, people further adapt their behavior so as to mitigate the damages of the constraints they face.

3.4 Shipping the Good Apples Out[16]

An irate consumer once wrote to the editor of a Seattle newspaper wondering why it was, in a state known for its apple production, that she had trouble finding high-quality apples in the supermarkets. This complaint, though a casual empiricism at best, is in fact symptomatic of a pervasive phenomenon: higher qualities of goods tend to be shipped farther distances from their point of origin or manufacture than the lower quality items of the same good. Here are some examples.

- The French drink inexpensive, low-quality wine which is often sold in cans. These wines are never exported. Only the higher quality wines are exported to the U.S. and elsewhere. There are undoubtedly irate French consumers wondering why all the good wine is exported. The average quality of French wines consumed in North America is higher than that consumed in France.
- Clothing manufacturers wind up with many seconds, clothes that have minor faults due to errors in production. These lower-quality clothes are typically sold in factory outlet stores located close to the factory. Only the high quality clothes are shipped out to distant locations.
- Most of the high-grade beef (USDA Prime) winds up in restaurants, not in supermarkets for home use. Restaurants sell almost all of this high-grade beef.

The preceding seemingly disparate phenomena are in fact all consequences of the law of demand. Suppose there is some cost, for example, transportation, that increases the price of two varieties of a good by the same amount, irrespective of the quality or other attribute of the good. Transportation costs must be incurred before most goods are consumed; these costs often depend only on attributes of weight and volume that are unrelated to the quality or price of the good itself. Individuals seek ways to mitigate the damages to their incomes because of transportation and like costs. One way to do this is to pack as much of the desirable attributes of a good into the good as practical. For example, people enjoy various aspects of apples—taste, crunchiness, tartness, etc. Good apples

16. I find this application so intriguing, I give it its own section number. The argument following was first presented in 1964 by UCLA professors Armen Alchian and William Allen in their "principles" text, *Exchange and Production* (Wadsworth) and in later editions.

have more of these pleasing attributes than poor apples. It costs the same to transport a mediocre apple of a given weight as a good apple. By shipping only good apples, more good attributes are transported for the same cost than would be if only bad apples were shipped. Thus in a real sense the cost of transportation (of attributes of apples) is lowered, if the high-quality apples rather than the low-quality apples are transported. Thus shipping good apples reduces the severity of the constraint on consumption imposed by transportation costs and is thus the behavior which is most commonly observed. The same logic applies to the wine and clothing examples mentioned above. It costs the same amount to ship a poor-grade bottle of wine as a high-grade bottle from France to North America. However, more of what people want in a bottle of wine gets shipped per bottle if the good rather than the poor wine is shipped. Thus only the relatively better grades wind up in the U.S. and elsewhere.

A more formal way of looking at this phenomenon is as follows. Suppose a good apple costs forty cents at locations close to the orchards (e.g., in Washington State, Michigan, New York State, etc.) and a mediocre apple sells for only twenty cents there (see Table 3-3). Then the act of eating a good apple means that *two* mediocre apples are forgone. The *alternative cost* of a good apple is two mediocre apples; eating two good apples means forgoing *four* mediocre ones. We say the relative price of a good apple is two mediocre apples. Suppose it costs the same amount (and this is a critical assumption), say twenty cents, to ship either type of apple to a distant location, say, New Orleans. In New Orleans these apples would cost sixty and forty cents respectively. Since apples are more expensive in New Orleans than in the producing areas, the law of demand implies that fewer apples will be consumed in New Orleans. More intriguing, however, is the effect on the *mix* of apples consumed. Although both types of apples are more expensive, the good apples are no longer *twice* as expensive as the mediocre apples. They are now only 1.5 times as expensive. Eating two good apples in New Orleans means forgoing only *three,* not four, mediocre apples. In the distant location, the high-quality item has become *relatively cheaper,* i.e., cheaper relative to the lower-priced item. With a lower relative price, the law of demand predicts that proportionally more high-quality apples will be consumed, although the total amount of apples consumed will still be lower in distant locations than at locations closer to the orchards.[17]

Table 3-3

	Close to Orchard	Transportation Cost	Distant Location
Good Apple	40¢	20¢	60¢
Mediocre Apple	20¢	20¢	40¢
Price Ratio	2:1		3:2

17. However, when more than two goods are involved, a fixed cost added to both not only changes the relative prices of these two goods, but also their prices relative to other goods. Since more than one relative price changes, the law of demand cannot be applied in a straightforward manner. However, Professors Borcherding and Silberberg showed that the result would in general hold unless the goods had highly asymmetric relationships with the remaining goods. See Thomas Borcherding and Eugene Silberberg, "Shipping the Good Apples Out: The Alchian and Allen theorem Reconsidered," *Journal of Political Economy,* 86, No.1, February, 1978, 131–38.

A really fine steak might cost \$4 at home vs. \$2 for a so-so steak, but in a restaurant, with perhaps \$20 worth of service added (other food, waiters, dishwashers, fine decor, etc.), the prices become \$24 vs. \$22. At home, with the price ratio of 2:1 (\$4:\$2) most people will eat the less exotic steak, for eating the prime steak costs *two* of the others. At the restaurant price ratio of 12:11 (\$24:\$22), the law of demand predicts that relatively more prime steak will be consumed. Since steak in restaurants is more expensive than steak at home, more steak will be consumed in the home than in restaurants. However, the *proportion* of excellent to mediocre steak will not be the same in those locations. More of the high-grade steak will be consumed in restaurants because it is relatively cheaper there. For the same reasons, hamburgers never are on the menu in finer restaurants.

Taxes can have a similar effect as transportation costs, depending on how they are levied. In the 1920's, there were two prevalent grades of cigarettes: premium, which cost about ten cents per pack—this was a long time ago—and non-premium, which sold for approximately five cents per pack. With those prices, each premium cigarette smoked meant forgoing two of the lesser quality cigarettes. Many people found that too expensive and smoked the inferior grades. Then, a tax was imposed on cigarettes *by the pack,* raising the prices to twenty and fifteen cents, respectively. At the new prices, smoking three premium cigarettes meant forgoing only four of the others, not six, as would have been the case at the old price ratio. As a result, the lower grades of tobacco virtually disappeared from the market, and the premium grade of tobacco became the standard grade.

In some states, wine is taxed *by the bottle.* This type of taxing scheme will lead to greater relative consumption of higher grades of wine. It is exactly analogous to the transportation cost argument and the above cigarette tax analysis. The impact of the tax on consumption is lessened if one can cram more wine into a bottle. This can be done by increasing the quality of the wine, giving it more desirable attributes per bottle.

It is interesting to note that at the supermarket, produce is sometimes sold by the *piece,* and sometimes by weight. What would account for this? Standard-sized items such as cans of tuna fish, boxes of cereal, cans of coffee, etc., are easily identifiable by weight. There really is no distinction to be made as to whether it is \$1.00 for a 7.5-ounce can of tuna or 13.33 cents per ounce. Tuna fish, cereal, coffee, canned fruits and vegetables, etc., are items which are inexpensive to package in standard sizes. This lowers the cost to the consumer of discovering how much of the item is being offered for sale. With produce, however, the story is sometimes different.

Fresh fruits and vegetables never come in standard sizes. Moreover, weighing each individual item is a time-consuming (and therefore costly) activity, and ultimately one the consumer must share. *Counting* heads of lettuce or bunches of carrots is quickly and cheaply done. However, this kind of imprecise measurement can be costly to the supermarket if the variation in the size of the bundles of carrots or heads of lettuce is great, *and* if the produce itself is valuable. We would therefore expect selling produce by the imprecise measure of by the piece to be more prevalent when, other things being equal, the produce is not very expensive. This occurs when the vegetables are in season. During the summer, lettuce will be cheaper than in the winter, because more lettuce is available during the summer than in the winter. We are more apt in the summer to see stores reducing the cost of measurement of lettuce by selling it by the piece rather than weighing each head, than in the winter. The cost of weighing produce stays the same throughout the year. But when the produce is in season, and its price low, the measurement cost is *relatively* high, and so less measuring is done. The produce is sold by the piece. When the gains from precise measurement are less, less measuring will take place, by substituting cruder but cheaper measurements for the goods.

The above principle extends to goods other than produce. Consider that rhinestones and other costume jewelry are measured very crudely. This is because the good itself is not very valuable and precise measurements of weight, angles of cut, etc., would add enormously to the cost. On the other hand, diamonds and other precious gems are extensively measured: their weight is precisely determined, their color is analyzed with a spectrometer, etc. For these gems the costs of measurement are relatively *low,* since the gem is so valuable, and thus much more measurement takes place.

Eric Bertonazzi, Michael Maloney and Robert McCormick investigated the pattern of football tickets purchased for Clemson University's home games. They found that ticket-holders who came to see the games from relatively farther distances from Clemson bought the better, more expensive seats (nearer to the 50 yard line). This case is especially interesting since here, the consumers are being shipped to the goods, rather than the other way around. The reasoning is still valid, if the transportation cost is linked to the good being consumed.

It can be observed that relatively higher quality houses are built on relatively expensive lots, such as those located with a view. Many people in fact substitute consumption of one fancy house in the city for two lower priced houses, one located in a rural locale.[18] A \$100,000 house located on a lot of negligible value costs two \$50,000 houses. If the same houses are on view lots selling for \$50,000, the relative price of the better house falls from 2:1 to 1.5:1. Better houses are relatively cheaper on expensive lots. We expect to see relatively more higher quality houses located on expensive lots for this reason.[19]

The reasoning extends to the case where the fixed cost (the transportation cost, cost of service in the restaurant, etc.) is not in fact a cost, but a *subsidy.* Here's an example. When professors are recruited and visit the economics department at the University of Washington, the department contributes some fixed amount, say, \$10, to offset the cost of going out to dinner. How does this affect the quantity and quality of the meals consumed? Since the subsidy lowers the cost of eating out, the law of demand obviously implies a greater number of restaurant meals. More interestingly, the subsidy lowers the relative price of *cheap* meals. If the price of a good meal is \$30 and a lesser meal is \$15, eating one good meal out entails the sacrifice of two lesser meals. With the \$10 subsidy, however, the prices change to \$20 vs. \$5; now, eating the good meal costs the consumer *four* cheaper meals! Thus subsidies of fixed amounts lead to greater consumption over all, and relatively greater consumption of the lower quality items offered in the market.

---

18. The author, who springs from New York City, finds it mildly surprising that Seattle natives do this, because Seattle was the type of place we went *to* in the summer.

19. It should be mentioned that the effect on income of purchasing an expensive lot is an offsetting influence on this result. Such "income effects," if substantial, can sometimes negate the implications of the law of demand.

3.5 Further Applications of the Law of Demand

We conclude this chapter with some off-beat, but pertinent applications of the law of demand. It is my hope that these examples will reveal the power of this simple but important proposition.

Sex: The desire to have sex and to reproduce is one of the strongest human emotions. These activities, however, are not without some attendant costs. Although economics has little to say about the origins of sexual desire, and nothing at all to say about the issues of morality that inevitably accompany discussions of this subject, it can be used for objective analysis of how sexual and reproductive behavior *change* when the costs and benefits of sexual activity *change.*

We have already discussed, in Chapter 1, some of the effects brought on by the baby boom generation of the late 1960s and early 1970s. This large cohort of young adults faced a "marriage squeeze," because there were many more marriageable females (in their early twenties, born after World War II) than males of marrying age (mid to late twenties, born during or before the war). The prospects of getting married at the traditional age (early twenties) seemed vanishingly small to many women in the baby boom generation. As a result, the cost to these women of being a virgin at marriage, almost always regarded as a valued attribute, increased, perhaps dramatically for some. Morality is often costly, and with this increase in the price of (traditional) morality, this particular form of it became less widely pursued, and sexual activity outside of marriage became more commonplace. This is not meant to justify, excuse, celebrate or in any other way comment on the normative aspects of this choice. We seek to explain why these changes occurred when they did, not to approve or disapprove.

At the same time this major demographic event was taking place, a revolution in birth control, oral contraceptives, also occurred. The pill greatly reduced the chance of unwanted pregnancy, and reduced the planning required for non-reproductive sex. This was another important reduction in the cost or price of sexual activity, and as a result, the quantity demanded increased. Less than a generation later, we discovered that the sexual revolution, and in particular the abandonment of condoms led to an increase in sexually transmitted diseases, both, at this writing, incurable: genital Herpes, very annoying and contagious, and AIDS, inevitably fatal. These diseases represent an increase in the price of sex, especially casual sex between strangers. As a result, promiscuous sex has apparently decreased, and the older virtues are newly resurgent. The human desire for sex doesn't change; our willingness to *act* on that desire moves in opposite direction to its cost.

For reasons not completely understood, sexual reproduction is the biologically most efficient means of reproduction. Only the most primitive organisms reproduce asexually. However, the reproductive act impinges differently on men and women. A man's participation in reproduction is the sex act, during which time enough sperm are released to fertilize all the women in North America. Sperm are cheap, and no further participation by the male is necessary once conception has occurred. Women, on the other hand, must endure nine months of pregnancy, and, historically had to nurture infants during infancy. Reproduction is a much more costly activity for women than for men. These cost considerations help explain some stereotypical behaviors of men and women with regard to sex and marriage. In general, men have been more promiscuous, more willing to engage in casual sex than women. In fact, this behavior is reinforced by evolution: the male genes most likely to survive are those producing the trait of successfully fertilizing the largest number of women. Women, on the other hand, have an incentive to choose sexual partners more carefully, since they are likely to be at least partly dependent on the father during pregnancy and the child's infancy. A woman therefore is likely to attempt to select men who can be good providers, and therefore to not engage in activities leading possibly to reproduction in as casual a manner as men. These price considerations explain, at least in part, why the traditional marriage pattern was for women to marry men older than themselves. Being a good provider is a trait usually less evident during a man's teenage or young adult years. Thus these pervasive behaviors are all implications of the law of demand. Of course, with improved contraception, less sexually transmitted disease, and the conveniences of modern technology, these differential behaviors have already abated and will continue to do so as these cost differences between men and women narrow further. The law of demand provides a powerful explanation of the historical patterns.[20]

Fertility: Humans have long exercised some control over reproduction, though in the modern era, with greater availability of mechanical and pharmaceutical birth control devices, the ability to regulate conception has improved. As a result, birth rates are much lower than their historical levels, and are lower in urban rather than in rural areas. The *ability* to regulate births, however, doesn't mean that couples will in fact do so. What, for example, would account for the differences in urban versus rural birth rates? One could, of course, simply assert that rural parents are more fond of children than urban parents. Economics rejects such *ad hoc* explanations based on arbitrary differences in tastes. Such assertions are nonrefutable and therefore empty. We search instead for an explanation based on the law of demand.

There are in fact at least two outstanding reasons why the cost of having children in urban areas is higher than in rural areas. First, in urban areas, space is more expensive. The number of people occupying an acre of city land is much greater than the number occupying a rural acre. As a result, land rents are much higher in the city than in the country. Consequently, the cost of providing shelter to children is higher in the city than in the country; put another way, the cost of a large family is relatively greater in the city than in the country. The law of demand predicts therefore, that other things equal, fewer children will be consumed in the city than in the country. The second cost consideration, which reinforces the preceding reason for this pattern of birth rates derives from the value of children as assets. In rural areas, particularly on farms, even young children are capable of producing income for their parents. On farms, meaningful chores exist which children have done throughout the ages, from simple cleaning to laborious tasks as they became older. Although no money necessarily changes hands between the parents and the children, the performance of useful chores is real production of income. The income produced by children offsets the cost of caring and nurturing the children by their parents. In urban areas, the ability of

---

20. This analysis is associated with a field called sociobiology. Economists have recently begun to recognize its close relationship with their own field. For some fascinating further reading , see, e.g., *Whisperings Within,* by David Barash, a zoologist at the University of Washington (Harper & Row, 1979).

children, even young teenagers, to produce income is much more limited. The useful simple tasks done by farm children usually don't exist for apartment dwellers. Consequently, the cost of raising children in rural areas is relatively less, because of the offsetting income they produce. For both reasons, therefore, the law of demand predicts higher birth rates in rural than in urban areas. This income production in fact is the main reason why attempts on the part of western countries to limit births in the underdeveloped world have been so unsuccessful in the past. In those societies, children are productive assets.

The law of demand does not predict that *all* rural parents will have more children than all urban parents. In applying the law, we must hold other things constant. Potential parents do have different incomes and tastes with regard to having children, and some are biologically more fertile than others. The law can be applied to groups of rural and urban parents on the assumption that on average, large groups have these same characteristics. If it turns out that one group systematically is wealthier, or faces some different price of a related good, say, milk, then the law could not be validly applied.

Interestingly enough, the above cost considerations provide a basis for concluding that rural parents really will, on average, be more fond of children than urban parents, an assertion we previously rejected as *ad hoc*. Since parents can choose where to live, those with special fondness for children can reduce the cost of having children by moving to locations where the cost of raising children is relatively cheap. This explanation is not *ad hoc,* since it is based on the universal postulates of behavior.[21]

Religion: Religious beliefs are perhaps the most personal and strongly held convictions people maintain. These beliefs and values have been taught to children over the millennia. The extent to which people actually participate in religion, however, depends not only on the strength of their convictions (*tastes*), i.e., how religious they are, but also on the *constraints* imposed by religious participation. Various sociological studies have pointed to several regularities in religious activity:

- Women tend to participate in church-related activities more than men.
- Church attendance tends to increase with age, though some investigators note a decline in religious activity until age 30–35.
- A weak though usually positive relationship exists between social class and church attendance.
- Church attendance is higher in rural than in urban areas.
- Black Americans attend church more frequently than whites.

It is possible, of course, to "explain" these observations by simply asserting, for example, that women are more religious than men, that people become more religious as they age (except, perhaps, in their wild youth) and that the genteel wealthy are more religious than others. However, economists reject such explanations as *ad hoc*. They are clearly made up out of thin air just to agree with the facts. They offer no explanation for these mysterious differences in tastes between women and men, the old and the young, etc.

21. Econometricians refer to the resulting differences in rural versus urban parents as "selection bias."

In a fascinating article, economists Ron Ehrenberg and Corry Azzi analyzed survey data on the annual frequency of church attendance for approximately 1,500 adults.[22] They noted that the opportunity cost of participating in religion included such things as participation in the labor market, i.e., working for wages. When a person decides to leave work, they give up a certain amount of income, based on their hourly wage: the higher their wage, the higher the price of not working. Azzi and Ehrenberg noted that since men historically had higher wages than women, the greater participation in religious activities by women was a simple consequence of the law of demand. Women's alternative cost for participation has been lower than for men. This argument seems to imply that we should observe less participation as a family's income increases. This would be correct if all income came from wages. However, some income, and particularly the income of the very wealthy derives from *nonwage* sources, such as property and investments. If a person's income is solely from interest on inherited family wealth, their opportunity cost of participating in religion is very low. Thus we get ambiguous conclusions about the relation between income and participation in religion.

Azzi and Ehrenberg noted further that earnings rise rapidly for young adults, particularly males in the older data, In these years, a breadwinner is investing heavily in the development of skills useful for higher future earnings. Religious participation is therefore particularly costly for young adults. Thus it is not surprising to see participation fall during these years. As people get older, the prospect of death becomes closer in time. We show in Chapter 10 that events more distant in time have relatively less value than the same event in the present. Treating salvation as one of the motives for participating in religion, the cost of nonparticipation therefore rises with age. Also, after a person retires from the labor force, the cost of participating falls. Thus on both these accounts, the law of demand predicts an increase in religious participation with age.[23]

Lastly, consider the urban/rural differential in participation. In rural areas, churches serve more than a religious function. They are centers of social and even business activities. Participation in church is one important way in which individuals signal that they are honest, upstanding citizens. In urban areas, where people are more anonymous, this aspect of religious participation is less important. Thus the cost of nonparticipation is lower in urban areas and the law of demand implies less participation would be observed there. Azzi and Ehrenberg also noted that because racial discrimination may have restricted the range of consumption activities for blacks, the law of demand also explained the observed relatively higher religious participation rates for blacks.

Suicide: The voluntarily termination of life is a topic traditionally studied by sociologists and psychologists. Sociologists, for example, have looked for patterns of suicide in terms of a person's age, their literacy, their feelings of frustration and aggression and various other sociological variables. Economists Daniel Hamermesh and Neal Soss considered how some important economic variables,

---

22. Corry Azzi and Ronald Ehrenberg, "Household Allocation of Time and Church Attendance," *Journal of Political Economy,* 83, No. 1, February, 1975, 27–56. In this discussion, I use the word "church" generically to mean any house of religious worship.

23. Regarding the time dimension, a famous saying in World War II was "There are no atheists in foxholes."

24. Daniel Hamermesh and Neal Soss, "An Economic Theory of Suicide," *Journal of Political Economy,* 82, January/February 1974, 83–98.

particularly age and income, affected the rate of suicide.[24] Hamermesh and Soss reasoned that persons with higher incomes give up more than persons with low incomes when they terminate their lives. The law of demand therefore predicts that other things equal, suicide rates will fall as incomes rise. Similarly, the younger a person is, the more life they have left to enjoy and thus the more they have to lose by suicide. As people age, the quantity of natural life remaining decreases, so suicide is relatively less costly. Therefore, we expect increasing suicides with age, again, by implication of the law of demand. Hamermesh and Soss also postulated that although additional income was always desirable for an individual, the amount of the *additional* pleasure, or the *marginal utility* a person derived from income declined as income increased (a postulate we have not maintained in this text). They reasoned from this that although the suicide rate would decline with increases in income, it would decline at a decreasing rate as income increased.

Hamermesh and Soss analyzed data from the United States and several other countries. They first looked at suicide rates by ten-year age groupings, from 15–24 to 65–74, in 21 developed countries. In all but two cases suicide rates either rose with age, or reached a peak at age 55–64 and then leveled off. (In the remaining two cases, suicide rates peaked at the highest age, but did not rise steadily.) They also investigated how increases in inflation-adjusted (real) incomes in the post World War II American economy affected suicide rates. They again found that as incomes rose over time, from 1947 to 1967, suicide rates fell. Moreover, the suicide rate rose during spells of unemployment (which reduce incomes). Also, the data confirmed that although suicides decreased as incomes rose, the amount of the decrease became smaller at higher incomes. Finally, they studied suicide rates at a moment in time, across income levels. They again found that persons with higher incomes had lower suicide rates. For example, managers and professional workers, whose incomes were high relative to service workers and laborers, had suicide rates of approximately one third to one quarter of the lower paid occupations.

Hamermesh and Soss are the first to state that suicide is not determined only by pecuniary interests such as income. The psychological state that leads to termination of life is a multidimensional issue. These authors showed, however, that the law of demand is nonetheless a powerful tool in this analysis: holding constant the psychological taste variables describing a person's state of mind, suicides decrease as its alternative cost to a person increases.

Smoking: One of the most dramatic changes in behavior over the past generation has been with regard to smoking, especially in public places. Cigarette consumption has fallen from 4,000 per person per year (less than a pack a day on average, but this includes all the nonsmokers) in 1970 to 2,515 in 1995. Watching just one old movie from the 1940s will convince you of the pervasiveness of this practice a couple of generations ago. Smoking was regarded as sexy and cool, and Hollywood's biggest stars were often posed smoking, to increase their appeal. Nowadays, most restaurants now feature "no smoking" sections and many are entirely nonsmoking. Although some localities now enforce these no smoking practices by law, the fact that many public establishments now find it in their own self interest to maintain a nonsmoking policy on their own, even in the absence of laws to that effect, shows that consumers value their establishment more highly when such a policy is in place. What could account for such a dramatic shift in behavior? Have consumers suddenly changed their preferences, now despising something that was once enjoyed?

We can in fact identify two important constraints relative to smoking that have changed in the past generation. A great deal of medical research has taken place, producing new information about the adverse effects of smoking. In contrast with various other health claims, there seems to be universal agreement among researchers that smoking greatly increases one's chances of contracting heart disease and lung cancer, two debilitating and nearly always fatal diseases. Secondly, the antibiotics invented and introduced in the past two generations have substantially increased the chances of living into old age. Before the invention of penicillin and other pharmaceuticals, most deaths occurred because people succumbed to some bacterial infection. When common scrapes and sores became infected, it was often a life-threatening condition. We don't worry much about colds and the flu nowadays, but these sometimes minor viral infections sometimes lead to major bacterial infections which in previous times were often fatal. As a result, people did not expect to live to a truly old age; when it happened, it was considered more of a lucky accident. In earlier centuries, cancer was a rare disease because few people lived long enough to contract it.

This has now all changed. There are still many fatal dread diseases such as cancer, AIDS and the like, but if one is fortunate to avoid them (and most do), the likelihood is that we will live well into our seventies and eighties. There is now a greater payoff for adopting life-extending behavior than there was in previous generations. The payoff for not smoking, or for quitting smoking was much less substantial fifty years ago, because there was not much chance one would live to old age anyway. At present, not smoking (and some other modifications in behavior, such as wearing seat belts when riding in a car) can increase the likelihood of having substantially more life. We say *the cost of smoking has increased,* because we now know it to be injurious to one's health, and because of the availability of antibiotics, we stand to lose a greater number of years of life than in previous generations by smoking. Moreover, some research seems to indicate that just being around others who are smoking (second hand smoke) is also injurious. The reduction in smoking and the institution of "no smoking" rules are therefore implications of the law of demand. It could also be that by becoming less common, smoking is now perceived as less attractive than previously, but this is secondary to the response to the increase in the price of smoking.

The same analysis explains the current heightened interest in vitamins and health foods, keeping physically fit through jogging or aerobics, following a low-cholesterol diet and the like. These activities seem to be useful in increasing the probability of a longer life. Moreover, they are more likely than in previous generations to actually have a positive payoff. The cost of following these regimens is the sacrifice of some tasty food and loss of leisure or working time. However, the expected payoff has now increased: they may add several years of life. Modern medicine has thus effectively raised the cost of ice cream, hot dogs, French fries, pepperoni pizza and the like, and being a couch potato.

These various healthy life styles seem to be pursued mostly by relatively better educated, higher income adults. This is in accordance with the previous discussion of suicide. Other things equal, a person with a higher income has more to lose by a shorter life. Thus we see more attention paid to life-extending activities by people for whom a shorter life is relatively more costly, in accordance with the law of demand.

Obesity: In recent years there have been many alarms raised by public health officials over the expansion of the waistlines of Americans, and, indeed, children and adults all around the world. The rate of obesity in children has increased by factors of two to three in the United States, Europe and Asia in the past few decades. The National Institute of Health (NIH) estimates that approximately two-thirds of Americans are overweight and one-third of American adults are clinically obese. The growth in obesity is startling: according to the NIH, between 1960 and 2000, the percent of Americans who are obese rose from 13.3% to 30.9%, with slightly higher figures for women than for men. Also, most of the rise occurred in the last twenty years. Approximately 13% of children are currently overweight or obese, up from single digits not long ago.

The reason why public health officials are concerned with obesity is that it carries with it significant health problems. Obesity leads to higher incidences of several dangerous medical conditions, particularly diabetes, hypertension (high blood pressure) and, according to some new research, though it is not conclusive yet, cancer. The annual cost of this increase in obesity, measured in terms of additional expenditures on health care, diet products and physician and hospital visits is more than $100 billion. In addition, by causing loss of time at work, the economy produces less than it would with a healthier population.

Obesity is related in obvious ways to diet and exercise: more exercise, less obesity, more calories ingested, more obesity. Economists are interested in many aspects of obesity and other health problems. For example, we might inquire as to what constraints have changed in recent decades that would have led to changes in behavior that produce greater obesity. We note, for example, that starting in the nineteenth century, but accelerating during the twentieth century and up to the present, humans became much more efficient at harnessing mechanical and electrical power, reducing the amount of human strength required for many manufacturing and construction tasks. In addition, such strenuous occupations such as farming, manufacturing and construction have become a much smaller part of the U.S. economy. Today, approximately eighty percent of all jobs are in the service sector, where physical strength is not a job requirement. This accelerated rapidly in the past two decades with the widespread replacement of mechanical devices with computers and other electronic devices. Only ten to fifteen percent of all jobs have a significant physical component to them. Thus we can safely conclude that the amount of physical effort Americans expend at work has been declining for a long time, but probably declining most rapidly in recent decades. We can therefore reasonably attribute part of the increasing incidence of obesity to this long-term trend.

With regard to caloric intake, is there any case to be made that calories have become cheaper in recent decades? Many people argue that the invention of high fructose corn syrup (HFCS) in the 1970s did exactly that. (HFCS is manufactured by applying various enzymes to corn starch, producing a syrup that is about 55% fructose and the rest mostly glucose. Common table sugar is mostly sucrose, which is made up of combined glucose and sucrose polymers.) Manufacturers use HFCS because it is cheaper to transport and use than refined sugar. It shows up prominently in fruit drinks and soda, and many other processed foods. This innovation, by lowering the price of sweetness, could therefore be a cause of the obesity problem. In addition, there seems to be a plausible case that the rapid expansion of fast food enterprises has lowered the cost of caloric consumption, thereby, by the law of demand, increasing the amount of calories we consume. Fast food restaurants can produce French fries, for example, at much less expense than we can at home. It apparently would require a full marathon to burn off the calories in a large fast food meal consisting of a double cheeseburger, fries, soft drink and dessert. This is all the subject of ongoing research. It will be interesting to see what particular cost factors have been most influential in contributing to the overweight/obesity problem.

Crime and Punishment: Crime and criminal activity are topics studied in many disciplines. Economic analyses typically do not focus on the underlying psychological reasons why some individuals engage in crime while others, in the same circumstances, do not. Economists take tastes for criminal activity as given, and, using the law of demand, attempt to predict the *changes* in criminal activity that result from changes in identifiable constraints which individuals encounter when they choose to engage in crime.

It is obvious from common experience that crime is at least partially explainable on the basis of the law of demand. We typically lock the door when we leave our houses, especially when valuable items such as computers, stereo equipment and jewelry are about. We rarely leave bicycles lying around unlocked, or leave our keys in the car, etc. The cost of committing a crime is lowered when doors are left unlocked or keys are left in a car. We expect higher crime rates as a result; those expectations are virtually always confirmed. The sight of a police car on the highway makes drivers slow down; a ticket raises the cost of exceeding the speed limit, and so we do less speeding the more we fear that outcome.

What about "serious" crime, such as murder, armed robbery, etc.? Are crime rates for these categories subject to the law of demand, or is all such behavior impulsive and out of control? Consider that in the past generation, up until the mid 1990s, serious crime had been increasing, and probability of punishment and the severity of punishment had been falling. This seems to be a confirmation of the law of demand. However, some researchers have noted that an increase in crime due to, say, increasingly unstable families tends to place additional burdens on the police, producing lower arrest and prosecution rates. It is not easy to statistically identify the proper causality. As in most serious research, careful empirical testing is difficult. One of the first modern studies was by economist Isaac Erhlich, who compared murder rates in states with varying levels of enforcement of capital punishment (the death penalty).[25] He found greater incidence of murder in states with lower application rates of capital punishment. However, other researchers have failed to find the deterrent effect implied by the law of demand. In recent years, however, states and localities have legislated tougher penalties for crimes, such as the "three strikes, you're out" laws, where conviction of three felonies leads to extended prison sentences. Crime rates seem to have decreased in late 1990s, perhaps in response to these added costs we impose on criminal behavior. The subject is the object of current research.

Discrimination: Discrimination by race, sex, national origin and other criteria not related to merit is a prominent policy issue. Federal and many state laws require affirmative action in hiring, meaning employers must actively pursue the hiring of minority applicants. If an employer's work force is statistically different from the available labor pool (in terms of ethnic composition), that employer may be required to demonstrate that this pattern came about because of compelling business considerations, lest they face substantial civil (monetary) penalties. Recently, some states have passed, by voter initiative, laws banning state agen-

25. Isaac Erlich, "Participation in Illegal Activities: A Theoretical and Empirical Investigation," *Journal of Political Economy, 81,* 1973, 521–64. See also his "Capital Punishment and Deterrence: Some Thoughts and Additional Evidence," *Journal of Political Economy, 85,* 1977, 741–88.

cies, such as universities, from using race-based criteria in admissions and hiring. Many discussions of discrimination center on whether people are biased or prejudiced, as opposed to unprejudiced, and ask how we can reduce the extent of these biases. Economists generally reject these either-or categorizations. Prejudice, like other aspects of human preferences, affects our choices, but our actions are modified by the constraints we face. Economic analyses of discrimination assume that individuals to some degree have a taste for prejudice, the amount varying between individuals. Rather than asking how we can change people's tastes, economists typically study how behavior *varies* as the cost of acting in a discriminatory manner *changes*. We predict that capricious discrimination will be relatively less when the cost of discriminatory behavior is relatively high.

A useful starting point with regard to labor market discrimination is to ask why a business firm would engage in discriminatory hiring practices. Suppose some one was soliciting investments for a new factory to produce a new computer which seemed to you like a hot prospect. The firm expects to hire a few hundred workers. The owner suddenly announces that since he is especially fond of blue-eyed blonde women, the entire workforce is to be female blue-eyed blondes (young ones at that). How does this announcement affect your willingness to invest in this company? This arbitrary requirement, unrelated to worker productivity, can only reduce the profitability of this company. The company will make the most money if it hires the best workers it can find at the wages offered. By imposing this additional restriction, the cost of labor will be higher, and profits lower. The owner can, within limits imposed by possible bankruptcy, indulge his or her own tastes in this manner, but it is important to note that such discrimination is costly. The costs are especially high in highly competitive industries, with many other companies manufacturing similar items. Given the prospect of costly bankruptcy, involving loss of company goodwill, selling existing assets for relatively low salvage value, etc., firms have an incentive *not* to discriminate on bases other than merit.

Some firms, however, are, or have been government protected monopolies, i.e., competition has been reduced or eliminated by regulation. Until recently, the railroads and airlines were prominent examples of such firms. The regulated utilities, such as the gas and electric companies still largely are. Such firms are in a position to make large profits by virtue of their position as sole providers of some important service. However, their profitability is restricted by regulation. In cases like this, firms can exercise capricious discrimination in hiring with very little cost. The prospect of bankruptcy is nil, and prices can be raised to cover the increased labor costs with very little effect on the incomes of management or shareholders. In a seminal study of labor market discrimination, economist Gary Becker found much higher rates of discrimination by race in utilities and railroads than in the labor market in general.[26] For example, in railroads, African Americans historically were excluded from all jobs except that of Pullman porter. When the cost of discrimination was relatively low, more discrimination appeared.

Historically, blacks were excluded from the major professional sports leagues.[27] These leagues were specifically allowed to collude in their hiring

26. See Gary S. Becker, *The Economics of Discrimination,* 2nd ed. (Chicago: University of Chicago Press, 1971)

27. Baseball players who were black played on teams in the "Negro League."

practices, and to prevent other teams from competing for players, through a "reserve clause" in players' contracts. This clause prevented players from negotiating with any other team in the major leagues. This protection from the anti-trust laws derived from a U.S. Supreme Court decision, by Oliver Wendell Holmes (of all people), which ruled in 1922 that "baseball was a sport, not a business." A reason why any one team could deny itself the pool of black talent, and not go out of business, is that the other team owners also agreed to do the same thing. The agreement came to an abrupt end in 1946 when the owner of the Brooklyn Dodgers, Branch Rickey, hired Jackie Robinson. The rest, as they say, is history. It seems evident that this type of discrimination continued longer in professional sports than it otherwise would have because the peculiar legally sanctioned anti-competitive structure of the leagues lowered the cost to any one team owner of pursuing this policy.

Although the owners of firms have an incentive to hire on the basis of merit, managers and coworkers often do not have these same incentives. In large firms especially, the impact of any one worker may be small and difficult to measure; managers might very well personally benefit from hiring friends and relatives, and otherwise discriminate on the basis of characteristics not related to productivity. This phenomenon is known as the "principal-agent" or "agency" problem. A principal, e.g., the owner of a firm, hires a manager (the principal's agent) to benefit (increase the wealth of) the business; the manager, however has his own objectives, not all of which are consistent with the aims of the principal. The agent therefore, depending on the degree of control exercised by the owner, sometimes pursues policies not consistent with the firm's, i.e., the owner's, interests. The law of demand predicts that non productivity-related discrimination (including, e.g., nepotism—hiring one's relatives) will be observed least in industries not protected by government regulation, and in companies where the management pay is structured so that the income of management is closely tied to the firm's profits Additional analysis of this important issue appears in Chapter 13, Labor Markets.

CHAPTER SUMMARY

- *Absolute* price refers to the average price of goods consumed. *Relative* price means the price of one good in relation to another. If apples cost \$.25 and pears cost \$.50, the (relative) price of a pear is 2 apples. If inflation causes the prices of apples and pears to become \$.50 and \$1.00 respectively, then although absolute prices have increased, relative prices have remained the same.

- Economic theory predicts that only changes in relative prices causes behavior to change. If literally *all* prices were to change in the same proportion, no relative prices would have changed and therefore no choices would change. Such a perfectly neutral inflation would have no effects, being a change in absolute prices only. However, it is not likely to have this type of strictly proportional change in prices.

- The *elasticity* of demand, denoted ϵ, is a dimensionless measure of the responsiveness of the quantity demanded to changes in price. The slope of a demand curve is sensitive to the units of quantity and price. Elasticity of demand is defined as the percent change in quantity demanded per percent change in price. Elasticity is necessarily negative, since price and quantity move in opposite directions along a demand curve.

- Demand is called *elastic* if the percent change in quantity is absolutely greater than the percent change in price. In this case, $\epsilon < -1$, so that $|\epsilon| > 1$. Demand is *inelastic* if the percent change in quantity is absolutely smaller than the percent change in price. In this case, $-1 < \epsilon < 0$. When $\epsilon = -1$, demand is called *unitary elastic.*
- When demand is elastic, as the price decreases and quantity therefore increases, the *total expenditure* consumers make on the good increases, since quantity increases in greater proportion than the price decrease. Similarly, when demand is inelastic, as the price decreases, total expenditure decreases because the expansion in quantity purchased is proportionately less than the price decrease.
- If a fixed cost is added to the prices of two different qualities of some good, the premium good the one originally higher priced becomes *relatively cheaper.* As a result, such charges increase the consumption of premium goods relative to lower qualities.
- The law of demand applies to all behavior that can be characterized as choice subject to constraints. This applies to choices concerning basic human activities such as sex and marriage, fertility, crime and discrimination by race and gender. If any quantifiable cost associated with these activities increases, the law of demand predicts a decrease in the extent to which that activity is pursued.

REVIEW QUESTIONS

1. Housing prices have increased in many urban areas. How would you tell if this is an increase in the real (relative) price of houses? Could it be a decrease in real housing prices?
2. Define elasticity algebraically. How does it differ from the slope of the demand curve? If the slope is constant, does this mean the elasticity is constant?
3. Explain intuitively why with an elastic demand curve, total expenditure increases when the price falls (and vice versa for inelastic demand curves).
4. Explain why the demand curve for apples will likely be more elastic than the demand curve for fruit.
5. Why do apple growers ship the good apples out?
6. Are higher birth rates in rural areas evidence that rural parents are more fond of children than urban parents? What cost considerations apply to this question?
7. Why do retired people go to church more than younger people? Is it just that they are more religious?
8. Why do rich people commit suicide less frequently than poor people?

9. What additional costs does a business face if it discriminates on a basis other than merit in its hiring and promotion policies?

PROBLEMS

1. When IBM introduced the first PC in 1982, with 256,000 bytes of RAM and a 5 meg hard drive, it sold for $5,000. Fully loaded top of the line PCs now sell for about $2,500. Has the price of a PC halved in the past twenty or so years? What factors other than the nominal price would you have to consider?

2. Consult the *Statistical Abstract of the United States* and determine whether the prices of the following items have increased or decreased relative to the general price level in the past twenty years:

   a. Appliances
   b. Cars
   c. Physician services
   d. Medicine
   e. Food

3. Suppose some price in the bundle of goods used in computing the *CPI* increases in price, resulting in a computed increase in the price level of 5%. This calculation, however, assumes consumers keep consuming the same bundle of goods.

   a. How do consumers respond to this price increase?
   b. Explain why the calculated increase in the *CPI* therefore *overstates* the true impact of this price increase on consumers.

4. The price of gasoline is almost 4 times what it was a generation ago, and consumers seem to be consuming it the same as before, opting for big, performance cars, etc. How can the law of demand be operating?

5. Using the demand schedule summarized in Table 2-2, calculate the elasticity of demand at prices $8, $5 and $3.

6. Changes in immigration law have placed significant penalties on the hiring of illegal aliens. As a result, the cost of harvesting crops in California has increased. It has been noted in similar instances in the past that the "total value of crops increased" and therefore there was no harm to consumers. Evaluate this claim.

7. Explain why a firm that can choose whatever price it wishes will always set a price where the demand is elastic.

8. Find data on the actual amount of gasoline consumed by Americans in years when the real price changed substantially and calculate the implied elasticity of demand.

9. In the past two centuries, incomes in America have risen and the number of children families have chosen to have has decreased. Does this mean that rich people are less fond of children than poor people? If not, what might explain this phenomenon? (Hint: consider the change in American society from predominantly rural to predominantly urban.)

10. Historically, women entered the labor force in their early twenties and then dropped out for 10 to 20 years to raise children. It was frequently the case that employers discriminated against young women in hiring. Does this indicate a belief by employers that women were incapable in the jobs from which they were restricted?

11. Where are you more likely to find fine Italian leather goods, Rome or New York? Why?

12. Many universities charge the same tuition for any amount of credits over 12 per semester or quarter. How would this pricing structure affect the number of credits taken by students each term versus one which was strictly proportional to the number of credits?

13. Beginning in the 1980s, the Japanese have placed a "voluntary" (i.e. under threat of U.S. retaliation) quota on the number of cars exported to the United States. Until very recently, the number of cars exported to the U.S. from Japan has been less than what otherwise would have been exported, but for the quotas. In the early 1980s, the quotas raised the prices of Japanese cars by approximately $1,000 per car. The quotas are therefore equivalent to a tax of $1,000 per Japanese car, with the proceeds kept by the Japanese manufacturers.

    What effects have the quotas had on the average *quality* of Japanese cars sold in the U.S., e.g. durability, or the number of options (power steering and the like) included? Explain.

14. Suppose that in 1989, the prices of steak and potatoes were, respectively, $3.00 and $.50 per pound. In 1999, after some inflation, the prices became $4.00 and $.60, respectively. Other things equal (including a person's inflation-adjusted, or "real" income), how would you expect this person's consumption of steak and potatoes to have changed?

15. Answer the previous question assuming that the price of chicken changed from $1.50 to $3.00 per pound in the same time period.

16. Many young people regard their elders as rigid and conservative; young people are more frequently idealistic or radical (in the political, not the valley girl sense), and less inclined to follow traditional norms of behavior, etc. This could be a biological phenomena, or changing tastes or acquisition of wisdom with advancing age.

    a. Does changing behavior imply changes in taste, such as mentioned above?
    b. Assume changing one's behavior patterns is difficult (costly) to individuals. Who stands to gain the most from adopting new ways, young or old people, and what does this imply regarding the above observation about differences in behavior by age?
    c. How would the wages a person could earn in the labor market affect participation in political or idealistic activities?
    d. How, then, would a person's participation in those activities vary with age?
    e. What effect did the post World War II baby boom have on entry level wages when that cohort reached young adulthood?
    f. What relation, therefore, did the above baby boom have on the political climate of the late 1960s and early 1970s?

17. When the citrus crop was damaged in recent cold weather, the price of citrus fruits increased in greater proportion than the quantity of fruit destroyed, increasing the value of the remaining crop. This shows how irrational economic value is: a smaller real stock of goods has higher value than a larger stock! Evaluate.

18. Vegetables are sometimes sold by the piece, e.g. per head of lettuce, or per grapefruit, and sometimes by the pound, which is a slower process. Explain how the type of measuring (which is not free—it slows down the line) would be affected by whether the produce was in or out of season (when is it cheaper?) and by the quality of the produce, i.e. good vs. mediocre potatoes.

19. The elasticity of demand for coffee is estimated to be –.16. If the quantity demanded was 4 billion lbs. per year when the price is \$3.60 per lb., how much coffee would be demanded at \$2.40 per lb.?

20. Would you expect the demand for the following to be elastic or inelastic? Also, rank the goods in order of *increasing* elasticity:

    a. a Starbuck's brand double-tall skinny latte
    b. a cup of regular coffee
    c. a latte
    d. a cup of decaf coffee

21. Would you expect the demand for the following to be elastic or inelastic? Also, rank the goods in order of *increasing* elasticity:

    a. the demand for gasoline in Los Angeles
    b. the demand for gasoline in New York City
    c. the demand for premium gasoline in New York City
    d. the demand for gasoline in New Mexico

22. Can the demand for a good be everywhere inelastic? (Consider what would happen at high prices.)

23. Can the demand for a good be everywhere elastic?

24. In many poor countries, birth rates are very high. Western "experts" often advise the authorities in these countries to take steps to limit population growth, so as to reduce (relatively) the number of mouths to feed. Yet this advice is almost never taken. What would account for this policy failure?

25. Aron spends his entire income on hamburgers and pizza. His demand for hamburgers is inelastic. If the price of hamburgers increases, what happens to the amount of pizzas he buys? When there are only two goods, can you state a rule about the effect of a change in the price of one good on the amount of the other good purchased? (Hint: You must consider the elasticity of demand of the good whose price has changed.)

26. In 1998, apparently partially due to the effects of warming in the Pacific Ocean (*el nino*), Washington State apple growers produced substantially more apples than in previous years. However, the farmers complained because prices fell as well as their incomes (which are tied directly to apple sales). Many of them wondered if they would survive financially.

a. Some commentators have noted how peculiar economics is: consumers apparently value the larger crop of apples less than a smaller crop. Analyze this proposition, and explain what is happening in this market.
b. Many farmers indicated that because of the low prices, they would let the smaller and poorer grade apples simply rot in the field, and only ship the premium apples. Why would they do this? Why isn't it more profitable for them to ship the poorer grade apples and let the premium ones rot?

27. Suppose you are a consultant to the local city-owned bus company. They indicate their revenues are falling short of their costs. They wonder if they should increase fares. What advice, or perhaps research, would you suggest?

QUESTIONS FOR DISCUSSION

1. Do you think politicians pay attention to the law of demand when they take stands on issues? What perhaps explains their general reluctance to take a stand on almost anything?
2. For perhaps two thousand years people have been debating whether it is "nature" or "nurture" that determines most of human behavior. From your own experience, how do you rate the influence of your parents and peers in determining your personality? Your intelligence? How can we apply the economic methodology to this debate? (Hint: Which of the above two influences would come under the heading of tastes, and which would comprise our constraints?)
3. Suppose some employers discriminate against some ethnic or gender group. Explain how this creates a profit opportunity for other employers.
4. Do you think the amount of medical care people choose depends on its price? What evidence do you have for your position?

CHAPTER 4

Exchange and Supply

"The making of these bricks taught me an important lesson in regard to the relations of the two races in the South. Many white people who had no contact with the school [Tuskegee], and perhaps no sympathy with it, came to us to buy bricks because they found that ours were good bricks. . . . As the people of the neighborhood came to us to buy bricks, we got acquainted with them; they traded with us and we with them. Our business interests became intermingled. We had something they wanted; they had something we wanted. . . . In this way pleasant relations between the races have been stimulated.

My experience is that there is something in human nature which always makes an individual recognize and reward merit. . . . [T]he man who learns at Tuskegee to build and repair wagons and carts is regarded as a benefactor by both races in the community where he goes. The people with whom he lives and works are going to think twice before they part with such a man."*

4.1 The Gains from Exchange

Voluntary exchange is based on **mutual benefits**. This simple proposition is the basis for all trade. No one has to force people to do what is in their self-interest. In a truly voluntary setting, when two or more persons agree to a contract in which goods or money will be exchanged, it must be the case that all parties perceive net benefits, or else one or more would simply refuse to participate. If a contract is coercive, it necessarily is not based on mutual benefits, for no coercion would be necessary in such cases.

Although economists regard the proposition that voluntary exchange must be based on mutual benefits as true almost by definition, this concept is often roundly denied in political debates. A fierce current debate is raging on the outsourcing of production to third-world countries, where wages are often extremely low. The Nike shoe company, for example, has been severely criticized in this country for "exploiting" workers in Asia by paying them wages that are only a fraction of minimum wages in America. One has to ask why workers in these countries flock to jobs paying 50¢ per hour; in the U.S., one would starve at that wage. If these foreign workers are *voluntarily* accepting these jobs (in fact lining up for the chance to get them), it must be the case that those workers prefer those jobs to their next best alternative. Nike and other companies that hire these workers are just one of many potential employers; they have no coercive power over the workers. It is impossible that those foreign workers are made worse off when they voluntarily choose to work for American firms such as Nike. The real reason for the protests in this country (usually organized by labor unions) is that some American workers hope that by preventing firms like Nike from hiring foreign workers, these firms might otherwise employ Americans at our wage levels. This may be true (see the second theorem on trade, coming up), but the charge that those foreign workers are somehow exploited by these employers simply violates the commonsense proposition that voluntary exchange must be based on mutual benefits.

Consumers receive a net benefit from goods they purchase in the marketplace. We call these net gains, which we measure by the difference between the

* Booker T. Washington, *Up From Slavery* (1901; Reprint, New York: Penguin Books, 1986), 153–155. Page citations are to the reprint edition.

amount a person would be willing to spend for a given quantity of a good, and what that person actually does pay for them, consumer's surplus. These are the gains received by a consumer when he or she exchanges money for goods. The person or store receiving the money in exchange for the goods must also perceive some gains, evidenced by their willingness to voluntarily enter into this contract. This net benefit to *sellers* is the basis for supply. No one has to force supermarkets to stock their shelves with bread and milk; they find it in their self-interest to do so. We noted in Chap. 2 that the consumer's surplus derived from the purchase of goods in the market is not something that ever shows up on any accounting ledger. For similar though not identical reasons, the accounting data associated with the operation of a firm, may not fully measure the benefits that induce firms to voluntarily give up their goods in return for money and the prospect of acquisition of other goods.

Consider first the case of two individuals that each possess some goods, and who might consider trading with one another. What would lead them to do that? Suppose one lover of oysters[1] would value an oyster at \$6, not having had any recently, while another has just returned from an oyster-eating contest, having won first prize—consisting of a pail of fresh oysters. The second person's marginal value of oysters is, at the moment, zero. Under these circumstances, mutual benefits are available through exchange. The first person, call him *A,* would derive some net benefit if he could obtain an oyster for anything less than \$6. Person *B,* the contest winner, would derive net benefits if some one would pay her anything more than zero for an oyster. Negotiations would ensue, and some price between zero and \$6 would be agreed upon, say, \$4, and *A* would purchase an oyster from *B* at that price. *A* gains \$2 since he received something for \$2 less than he was actually willing to pay, and *B* gains \$4, because she received \$4 for something she was willing to give away free. The combined benefits total \$6, the difference between *A's* and *B's* marginal values of the oyster. Moreover, the combined benefits would total \$6 no matter what price *A* and *B* agreed on for the trade. If they had agreed to trade at \$1, then *A* would have gained \$5 and *B* only \$1, but the total is still \$6. This total is the difference between *A's* and *B's* marginal values of the good.

Check your understanding: Suppose *B* makes *A* "an offer he can't refuse," and sells *A* the first oyster for \$8. Are the gains from trade still \$6?

The source of the mutual benefits from exchange is the difference in the marginal evaluations of a good by different people. Anytime one person values an additional unit of a good more highly than does another person, mutually advantageous trade can take place. The person with the greater marginal value can always offer to buy a unit at some price below his or her marginal value and above the other person's marginal value. The second person will always agree to trade since he or she will gain. The trade will then take place, absent some legal or other barrier, leading to mutual benefits. Although these individuals' hypothetical balance sheets would just show an exchange of assets, they are in fact better off than prior to the trade. This creation of wealth through exchange, though often not understood, is the engine that drives self-regulating economies, and is the impetus for economic growth that is lacking in economies based on central command.

1. A peculiar, but widespread taste (author's value judgment).

Table 4-1

Quantity	A's Marginal Value	B's Marginal Value
1	$6	$10
2	5	9
3	4	8
4	3	7
5	2	6
6	1	5
7	0	4
8	0	3
9	0	2
10	0	1
11	0	0

Returning to the oyster lovers, after the first exchange, *A* has one oyster, and *B* now has one less. The marginal value schedules of oysters for *A* and *B* are shown in Table 4-1. Person *A* would pay $6 for the first oyster, $5 for the second, and so on down to $0 for the 7th. Person *B,* the contest winner, would pay $10 for the first, $9 for the second, and so on, down to $0 for the 11th. Assume the pail of oysters she won in the contest contained 11 oysters originally. She sold one to *A*, and now has only 10. She values that 10th oyster at $1, meaning that she would be willing to part with it if some one paid her anything more than $1 for it. At this point, there still are mutual benefits to be derived, since *A* would be willing to pay more than $1 for another oyster. The combined benefits will total $4, the current difference ($5 – $1) between *A's* and *B's* marginal values. Therefore, another exchange is implied, after which *A* has 2 oysters and *B* has 9. Their marginal values still differ, and so a third oyster will be exchanged, for combined mutual benefits of $4 – $2 = $2. At this point, however, *A* would be willing to pay only $3 for another oyster, while *B* will not sell one unless she receives at least $3. There are no further gains from exchange, and so voluntary trading ceases. (Because we eventually allow fractional units, assume that the fourth unit, for which the gains from trade are zero, is in fact exchanged.) We say *the gains from trade are exhausted.* The combined benefits to *A* and *B* from trading 4 oysters is $6 + $4 + $2 + $0 = $12. In the case of direct bilateral trading, the distribution of these gains depends on the exact prices negotiated for each unit. However, the total benefits would still be $12 for any other set of mutually agreeable prices.[2]

Two Theorems Concerning Trade

It is important to note that the individuals in the above example cannot be made worse off by allowing voluntary trade to take place. The reason is that they can

2. Even if trade took place at a coercive price, say, $8, the benefits would still total $12, but now *A* would be losing $2 + $3 + $4 = $9, while *B* would be gaining $8 + $7 + $6 = $21, for the same combined net gain of $21 – $9 = $12. Person *B* made person *A* an offer he couldn't refuse.

simply refuse to trade, and keep their original endowment. The *possibility* of trade cannot make them worse off; they can always go home with what they brought. If they decide to trade, it must be that each sees a benefit. Therefore,

Theorem 1. Some trade is preferred to no trade.

When we say preferred, we mean it in the scientific sense that no individuals will be worse off according to their own preferences when trade is allowed, versus when all trade is forbidden. We imply no normative proposition or value judgment.

If two individuals decide to trade further, it must be that they both perceive additional gains. However, when more than two traders are involved, it is possible for some individuals to arrange a trade that makes *them* better off, but leaves others (third parties, i.e., individuals not party to the contract) worse off. When individuals engage in trade, the *terms of trade,* i.e., the prices at which the goods are exchanged, in general change as trade intensifies. Suppose Bix is currently purchasing some goods from Louis at $10, and then Fletcher decides to expand his own purchases, bidding up the price to $20. Louis and Fletcher are better off for their trade, since they voluntarily entered into it, but Bix is worse off. He was formerly making purchases at $10, and now the price has risen to $20. If, for example, more foreign cars are allowed into this country, the price of cars will decrease, benefiting consumers, but wages in the domestic auto industry may also decrease, leading to net losses to those workers. Therefore,

Theorem 2. More trade is not necessarily preferred by all to less trade.

When there are no third parties, then more trade, since it takes place on a consensual basis, will always be preferred by all to less trade. This idea does not extend, however, to expansion of trade with more than two parties.

Economists, as a rule, tend to favor free trade, because of the mutual benefits that are available. We usually favor lowering tariffs on imported goods, removing state and federal regulations that impede commerce, such as the many rules imposed on the transportation industry, etc. However, these are ultimately value judgments. Freer trade generally helps some people and harms others. Removing restrictions on textile imports helps consumers, but harms workers in that industry. Even though the gains may outweigh the losses (because mutual benefits are being generated), the losers in these situations are rarely compensated. Still, we maintain a belief that individuals in a society full of trade restrictions eventually suffer from them, becaause of the decrease in long term economic growth these restrictions cause.

4.2 Supply Curves

Demand curves indicate how much of some good a person would like to purchase at given prices. To complete the analysis of actual exchange we need a corresponding concept of how many units of some good a person is willing to *give up,* that is, *supply* to interested buyers at those same prices. The great British economist Alfred Marshall, of the late 19th and early 20th centuries, likened the concepts of supply and demand to the two blades of a scissors: the analysis of markets cannot be completed without both tools.

In actuality, supply is intimately connected with costs of production. If it costs $100 to produce some good, then clearly, under normal circumstances none will be offered to the market at a price less than that amount. We defer discussion of this important aspect of supply until Chapters 6 and 7. For now, return to our oyster lovers. When person *B* owned the whole bucket of 11 oysters, she was faced with the decision of how many to actually consume. Although her marginal value of the 11th oyster was zero, others in the market were willing to make her an attractive offer for some of them. The *cost* to her of actually consuming an oyster is the maximum amount of other goods she could get by foregoing consumption of that oyster. It does not follow that if one owns something, one will necessarily consume it. Opportunities for exchange raise the cost of consuming the good to what the highest bidder would be willing to pay for it.[3]

In the absence of production, the supply of a good at specified prices is the amount some person who currently owns the good is willing to give up, at those prices. In an economy consisting only of persons engaging in trade (as opposed to production also), the resulting **supply curve** is the total amount of the good currently in existence minus the quantity demanded by the present owners. Since as the price rises, the owners choose less for their own good for personal consumption, they are willing to offer more for sale to others. Thus the supply curves of goods are in general *upward* or *positively sloping*. When we consider the impact of production on supply, we will derive a similar result: at higher prices, more people will be willing to go further out of their way in some fashion to increase production.

In Table 4-2, person *B*'s marginal value (demand) schedule is displayed, along with the amount she is willing to sell at prices between $0 and $10. This

Table 4-2

Market Price	B's Quantity Demanded	B's Supply Schedule (Initial Stock = 11)
$10	1	10
9	2	9
8	3	8
7	4	7
6	5	6
5	6	5
4	7	4
3	8	3
2	9	2
1	10	1
0	11	0

3. In the early 1980s, the Hunt family of Texas decided to corner the silver market, which they did do for awhile, and the price of silver rose approximately tenfold. Suddenly, silver place settings, for example, rose in value to several thousand dollars. Many people at the time took advantage of this opportunity to consume more of other goods, by trading in their now costly silver place settings for stainless, plus, e.g., a new stereo system. The event was short-lived; when the Hunts finally owned all that silver, their marginal value for it was small, and when they went to sell it, the price fell like the proverbial rock. They lost most of their fortunes (a few billion dollars) in the process.

Figure 4-1 *Upward Sloping Supply Curves*

The supply curve in a pure trading economy equals a person's endowment minus the quantity demanded. In Table 4-2, Ms. *B* owns 11 units initially; if the market price is $3, she consumes 8 herself and ofers 3 for sale. If the price were to rise to $5, she would reduce her own consumption (in accordance with the law of demand) to 6 units and offer a greater amount, 5 units, for sale.

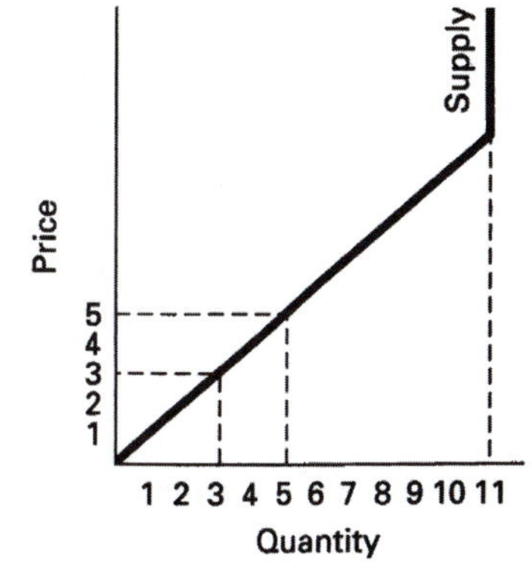

amount always equals her endowment, 11, minus her demand when her marginal value falls to the price. At a price of $3, she consumes 8 and offers 3 for sale; if the price were to rise to $5, she would consume 6 and offer 5 for sale. This supply curve is depicted in Fig. 4-1, with noninteger values included, so that the curve is a smooth line. (We imagine, for convenience, that she could sell 3.14159 oysters, remembering that these numbers are really average *rates* of consumption or supply.) The positive slope indicates increases in the quantity available as the price increases, and, of course, vice versa. Lastly, individual supply curves can be aggregated in the same manner as discussed in Chap. 2 for demand curves. Summing (laterally) the amounts offered for sale for each of several sellers yields the market supply curve.

Check your understanding: Suppose the government takes pity on oyster buyers and subsidizes oyster purchases by paying $1 per oyster towards all purchases. How many oysters will *A* now purchase from *B* and how much money will the government transfer to *A* from taxpayer funds?

4.3 Seller's Rents

For the same reasons that the area under the demand curve up to some quantity represents consumers' total value of a good, that is, the maximum amount consumers would pay for that quantity rather than have none at all, the area *under* the preceding supply curve up to some quantity represents the *minimum* total amount the suppliers *must be paid* in order for those individuals to voluntarily offer that quantity for sale. Using the numbers in Table 4-2, at a price of $1, Ms. *B* offers 1 oyster for sale. At $2, she consumes 9 herself and offers 2 for sale. On an all or nothing basis, she must be offered at least $3 ($1 for the first oyster relinquished plus $2 for the second) in order for her voluntarily to give up 2 oysters. In like fashion, since she offers a third oyster for sale only if the price rises to $3, she would have to be paid at least $6 ($1 + $2 + $3) in order for her voluntarily to give up 3 oysters. These prices are simply the height of the supply curve at the various quantities. Adding these heights in the same manner as adding consumer's marginal values yields the area under the supply curve.

If the market price is \$3, Ms. *B* sells 3 oysters. However, she receives \$9 (\$3 × 3) in total revenue for these 3 units sold. This amount exceeds the minimum amount she would have been willing to accept for the 3 units; which is \$6, as indicated above. She therefore receives a seller's surplus of \$3 (\$9 – \$6) on these 3 units sold. In like fashion, if the market price of oysters was \$5, *B* would be willing to sell 5 units, consuming 6 for herself. According to her marginal value schedule, she would have to be paid \$1 + \$2 + \$3 +\$4 + \$5 = \$15 for these 5 units relinquished. However, at a price of \$5 apiece, she would receive \$25 in revenue, thereby reaping a net gain of \$10.

The benefits received by this seller are derived from the same source as the benefits received by consumers. When consumers purchase multiple units of a good at some market price *p,* they benefit because the intramarginal units are valued at greater than *p*. That is, consumers would be willing to pay more than *p* for the first unit, somewhat less for the second, etc., until the marginal value falls to *p*. The difference between what the consumer would be willing to pay and what he or she actually does pay for each unit constitutes the consumer's surplus. For sellers, the surplus occurs because the market price is higher than the price she would accept for the intramarginal units.

Although the net benefits received by sellers from sales of units of some good in excess of the minimum amount they would actually have to be paid is aptly called seller's surplus (in complete analogy, in this example of pure trade, with consumer's surplus), the more accepted and widely used term is ***rent.*** In ordinary speech we typically use the term rent to mean the payment we make to property owners for the use of land, apartments, and so forth. In economics, this term has the specialized meaning of payments in excess of the minimum amount that is necessary to induce a person to relinquish their rights to some good. The term derives from the original perception that all payments for the use of land had this characteristic. But rents to sellers can appear for the same reason as rents to consumers: the pervasive phenomena of diminishing marginal values.

Check your understanding: Suppose the government subsidizes oyster sellers by paying them a dollar for each oyster they sell. How many oysters will *B* sell to *A,* and what will the total gains from trade (less the government transfer) increase or decrease?

In Fig. 4-2, we depict a smooth supply schedule, i.e., allowing fractional units. In the same way we laterally sum individual demand curves to get the market demand curve, we laterally sum individual supply curves to get a **market supply curve**. As the price rises, the supply increases for two reasons. First, any existing seller finds consumption more costly and therefore cuts back on his or her own consumption, thereby offering more for sale. Second, some sellers might not have been willing to sell any units until the price exceeded some minimum amount. As the price rises, new sellers enter the market and offer their goods to buyers.

The area under the supply curve consists of many narrow rectangles, the initial few of which are shown. The areas of these rectangles (their height times their width) represent the amounts sellers must be paid in order to relinquish successive units. At prices close to 0, very little is offered for sale; when the price reaches \$10, 20 units are offered. The minimum total amount it would take to induce suppliers to sell 20 units is the sum of all those rectangular areas under the supply curve, i.e., the area under the supply curve. This area, denoted cost in Fig. 4-2, equals (approximately—this supply curve is not depicted as linear)

Figure 4-2 *Costs and Rents*

The area under a supply curve up to some arbitrary quantity, e.g., 20 units, equals the minimum amount the person must be paid in order to voluntarily sell that amount to others. This is the sellers' alternative cost of those units. The area between the price, $10, and the supply curve represents the amounts sellers receive in excess of the minimum they would accept. This area is therefore a rent to sellers. The sum of costs plus rents is the rectangular area of total revenue or expenditure.

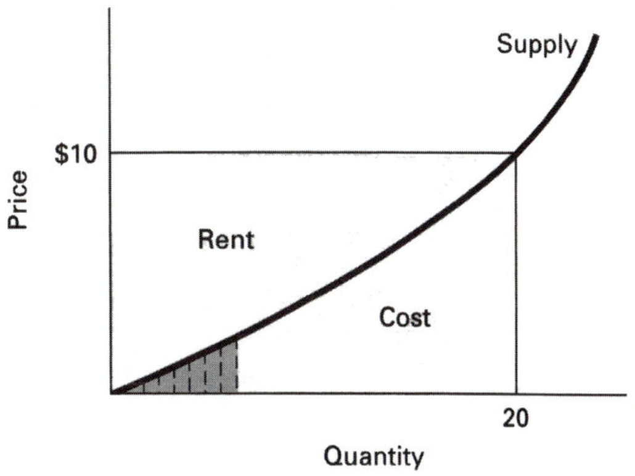

$100 (one-half the base, 20, times the height, $10). This area under the supply curve represents the *cost* to the sellers of providing this good. The reason why cost is a proper term is that the sellers would themselves like to consume this good, in varying amounts according to the price. Selling the good means giving up the right to consume the good. The value of this right is a seller's marginal value of each unit. Cost always means the value of foregone alternatives. The cost to person *B* in the previous example of selling, say, 5 oysters, is the sum of the marginal values of the 5 oysters relinquished, $15. These amounts are the areas under the supply curve up to the quantity sold.

In Fig. 4-2, at price $10, 20 units are sold by sellers. The total revenue received by the sellers is the rectangular area defined by the price of $10 and the quantity of 20 units. This area equals $200. Since the cost of providing the 20 units is the area under the supply curve, the remaining area *above* the supply curve represents the rents received by the sellers. The rent received on any particular unit sold is the difference between the price received and the cost of each unit, measured by the height of the supply curve. Summing these differences between the origin and quantity 20 produces the area of rent shown. If the price were to increase above $10, the rents to sellers would increase, as units sellers were previously willing to sell for $10 or less would command a still larger price.

4.4 Economic Efficiency

"As every individual direct[s] [his] industry that its produce may be of the greatest value, every individual necessarily labors to render the annual revenue of the society as great as he can. He generally, indeed neither intends to promote the public welfare nor knows how much he is promoting it . . . and he is in this, as in many other cases, led by an invisible hand to promote an end which was no part of his intention."[4]

Fig. 4-3 depicts market supply and demand curves, intersecting when the quantity of the good is 25 units. The demand curve shows consumers marginal

4. Adam Smith, *The Wealth of Nations,* 1776.

Figure 4-3 *Maximum Gains from Trade*

The largest mutual benefits occur when 25 units of this good are exchanged. Initially, $18 of mutual benefits are unavailable. As trading increases, these gains diminish. If 25 units are costlessly traded, no further gains are available.

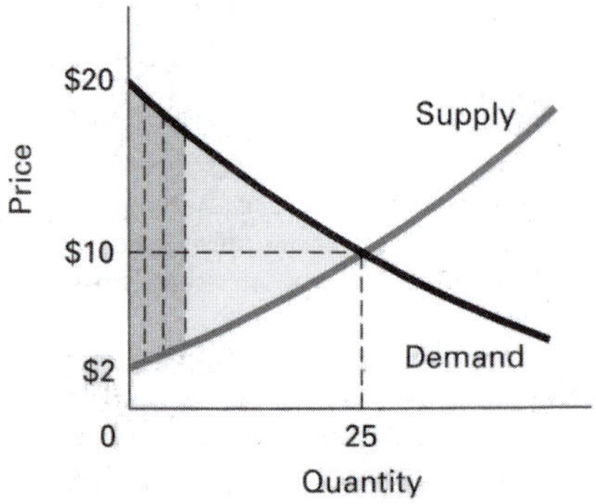

values of this good. Consumers purchase no units at any price greater than $20, the reservation price. Their marginal values decrease as more of the good is consumed. At 25 units, the marginal value of the good has fallen to $10. The supply curve shows the marginal willingness of other individuals to relinquish the good. As more is given up, the marginal values of the suppliers rise. What quantity will actually be transacted, and at what terms?

Initially, before any trade takes place, consumers are willing to pay $20 to get that first unit; suppliers are willing to relinquish it for only $2. Therefore $18 mutual benefits are available if this unit is exchanged. The gain is shown as the narrow rectangular area between the supply and the demand curve. If some units are exchanged, consumers' marginal values fall a bit since they have more of the good, and suppliers' marginal values increase, since they have less. As more and more units are exchanged, the area of mutual benefits decreases. Eventually, when 25 units are reached, buyers' and sellers' marginal values are all equal to $10. At that point, there are no further mutual benefits, and trading ceases. The gains from trade are exhausted at that point.

The exhaustion of mutual benefits through trade is an important concept in economics. An economy that achieves this situation is called **Pareto efficient**, or **Pareto optimal**, after a famous Italian economist Vilfredo Pareto, who developed the concept in the early twentieth century. The term efficient, or optimal in this context is not meant to be synonymous with desirable. A Pareto efficient economy is one in which the gains from trade are exhausted. This means, importantly, that it is not possible to improve any one person's situation without harming another in the process. If some rearrangement of goods or income could leave some people better off and no one worse off, (a situation we call *Pareto superior*), then in the absence of barriers to trade or some cost of transacting, the individuals would proceed to derive those benefits on their own, through trade. When the gains from trade are exhausted, the only way one person can gain is at some one else's expense, else the situation could not have been Pareto efficient in the first place.

The term efficient has a very different meaning in economics than its meaning in the physical sciences. When we say one machine is more efficient than another, we mean the first machine produces a higher percentage of useful output for, say, given energy inputs, than the second. A fluorescent light bulb is more efficient in this sense than an incandescent bulb: a forty watt fluorescent bulb yields more light than a forty watt incandescent bulb. If thermodynamic efficiency was the same as economic efficiency, it would be hard to explain why anyone would voluntarily purchase incandescent bulbs. The answer has to do with the quality of light produced and how consumers value those quality differences, and the relative costs of these bulbs. Consumers obviously prefer the higher priced incandescents to the fluorescents in some instances. It would not be the case that consumers would perceive themselves better off if the government mandated that only fluorescent bulbs could be used, even though the price of light would probably decrease. The steam locomotives that provided the cheapest transportation of goods and people over long distances in the 100 years prior to the 1940s, had thermodynamic efficiencies of only two to three percent: upwards of 98% of the energy input was dissipated as waste heat, rather than being converted to the useful product of locomotion. Yet, these machines were the most *economically* efficient means of transportation, as evidenced by their wide use.

However, to say that an economy is efficient in this sense is not to say it is desirable. Desirability is ultimately one's own value judgment, not a scientific evaluation. An economy in which certain individuals have no income and are starving may nonetheless be exhausting the available gains from exchange. Few would probably agree to the goodness of that allocation of resources. However, we shall show that certain institutions and laws better enable an economy to exhaust mutual gains than others. It is therefore prudent to investigate what those institutions are, since when gains from trade are exhausted, any given distribution of income could in principle, at least, be revised so as to make everyone better off by their own judgments, and leave no one worse off. In order to avoid value-laden terms, we use the term efficient in only this technical sense that mutual benefits are exhausted.

Check your understanding: The government requires appliance manufacturers to post the "energy efficiency" of the refrigerators and ranges they sell. These ratings show how much electricity is used per hour of service. Would consumers be better off with appliances with higher energy efficiency, and would you advocate laws requiring more energy efficiency in such appliances?

4.5 The Formation of Organized Markets

In a two-person trading economy, the price at which a good changes hands is not very well specified. In the Fig. 4-3, any price between \$2 and \$20 for the first unit exchanged leads to mutual benefits, and therefore no unique price is implied for this trade. Moreover, the price at which the second unit is exchanged is not necessarily the same as the first. The skill of bargaining, generally taken to mean the ability of one person to conceal their eagerness for the transaction will in part determine transaction prices.

In modern economies involving markets with many buyers and many sellers, individual haggling over the price is uncommon. Negotiation over price is never seen at supermarkets, discount houses, restaurants, sports venues and most other retail outlets, though it is common when purchasing a car. It is apparent that when repeated purchases are made, with many buyers and sellers present, a single price becomes established at which all transactions take place. This is sometimes called the **law of one price**. But why and how does this come about? No one mandates this kind of market structure. Its near universal appearance suggests it serves some function that is highly useful to both buyers and sellers. Therefore, in order to derive this outcome, we look for an explanation based on mutual benefits of buyers and sellers.

Imagine the scene of dozens or hundreds of people all trying to negotiate with each other. Fig. 4-4 reproduces Fig. 4-3, but the various points are given labels. The reservation price of $20 is point *A,* and the supply and demand curves intersect at price p_E at point *B*, etc. The mutual benefits available through trade is area *ACE.* Part or all of these gains would soon be wasted, or *dissipated,* if individuals had to use their time and other resources to negotiate with their trading partners. These losses are reduced if low-cost mechanisms are used to facilitate trade. The most common mechanism, one we are all familiar with from our daily purchases, is where all units are transacted at a single price. The particular price that appears is the price that equates the aggregate quantity that buyers, or consumers wish to purchase, to the quantity the sellers, or suppliers are inclined to sell.

The price that accomplishes this, in Fig. 4-4, is p_E, (distance *OB* along the vertical axis). If this price is established in the market, consumers will on their own choose to purchase the total quantity q_E, since at lesser quantities, their marginal values exceed this price, leading to net benefits. For the same reason, at this price, sellers will voluntarily supply q_E, since at lesser quantities, the price offered exceeds their marginal values, leading them to offer additional units for sale. If price p_E is established in the market, the quantity of this good demanded equals the quantity supplied. The situation is generally referred to as **market equilibrium**.

How is it that such an equilibrium can come about? After all, markets have no directors arranging trades, or setting prices. In fact, this is one of the most remarkable and efficient aspects of economies based on voluntary production and exchange. Each individual seller, perhaps experimentally, sets a price and waits to see how many consumers show up. If the goods are eagerly snapped up, then it will be obvious enough to that seller that the price quoted was too low (in terms of his or her self-interest). The seller will likely quote a higher price after goods have

Figure 4-4 *Maximum Gains from Trade*

Maximum gains from trade occur when individuals exchange quantity q_E. If all units are costlessly traded at price p_E, consumers' surplus is *ABE* and sellers' surplus rents are *CBE.*

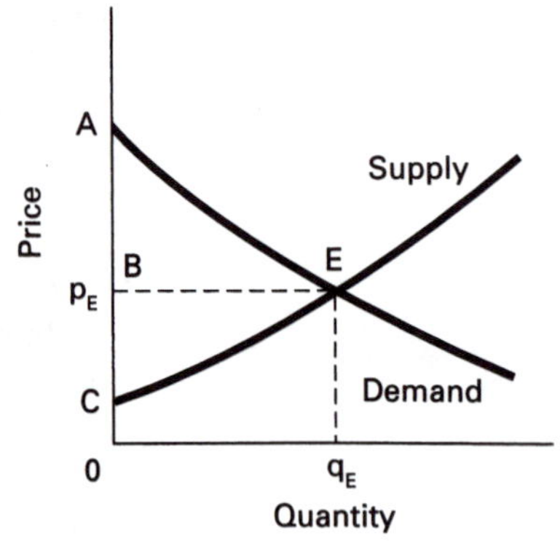

been reordered. Similarly, it will become obvious if the quoted price is too high: consumers will stay away in droves. Rather than consume all units themselves, at which point the marginal value would be very low, sellers will make the offers to buyers more attractive, by lowering prices. Eventually, each seller will find that price, very likely in the absence of knowledge of what any other seller is charging, at which the quantity *they* wish to sell equals the amount consumers would like to purchase *from them.* When all sellers have found such a price, it will soon all be the same price. If one seller was selling at a lower price than another, some third person would quickly purchase as many units of the good as possible from the low-priced seller, and retrade them to the high-priced seller. This activity is known as **arbitrage**. In so doing these arbitrageurs will raise the price of the low-priced seller and lower the price of the high-priced seller, driving this difference to zero and themselves out of business in the process.

In a fascinating article, a British soldier, R. A. Radford, described the formation of markets in the simple, pure-trade economy of the prisoner of war camp in which he was interred during World War II.

> We reached a transit camp in Italy about a fortnight after capture and received ¼ of a Red Cross parcel each a week later. At once exchanges, already established, multiplied in volume. Starting with simple direct barter, such as a non-smoker giving a smoker friend his cigarette issue in exchange for a chocolate ration, more complex exchanges soon became an accepted custom. Stories circulated of a padre who started off round the camp with a tin of cheese and five cigarettes and returned to his bed with a complete parcel in addition to his original cheese and cigarettes; the market was not yet perfect. Within a week or two, as the volume of trade grew, rough scales of exchange values came into existence. Sikhs, who had at first exchanged tinned beef for practically any other foodstuff, began to insist on jam and margarine. It was realised that a tin of jam was worth ½ lb. of margarine plus something else; that a cigarette issue was worth several chocolates issues, and a tin of diced carrots worth practically nothing.
>
> In this camp we did not visit other bungalows very much and prices varied from place to place; hence the germ of truth in the story of the itinerant priest. By the end of a month, when we reached our permanent camp, there was a lively trade in all commodities and their relative values were all well known, and not expressed in terms of one another—one didn't quote bully [canned beef] in terms of sugar—but in terms of cigarettes. The cigarette became the standard of value. . . . The unity of the market and the prevalence of a single price varied directly with the general level of organisation and comfort in the camp. A transit camp was always chaotic and uncomfortable . . . a transit camp was not one market but many. The price of a tin of salmon is known to have varied by two cigarettes in twenty between one end of a hut and the other. . . .
>
> The permanent camps in Germany saw the highest level of commercial organisation. In addition to the Exchange and Mart notice boards, a shop was organised as a public utility, controlled by representatives of the Senior British Officer, on a no profit basis. People left their surplus clothing toilet requisites and food there until they sold at a

> fixed price in cigarettes. Only sales in cigarettes were accepted—there was no barter—and there was no higgling. . . .
>
> . . . An influx of new prisoners, proverbially hungry, raised [the general price level]. Heavy air raids in the vicinity of the camp probably increased the non-monetary demand for cigarettes and accentuated deflation. . . .[5]

The fundamental reason why one price appears in most markets is that this is generally the cheapest method of arranging for mutual benefits through trade. Moreover, this market price provides buyers and sellers with the maximum possible mutual benefits from trade. At price p_E in Fig. 4-4, the quantity buyers wish to purchase, i.e., the quantity demanded, equals the quantity sellers would like to sell, the quantity supplied. The gains from trade received by consumers, consumer's surplus, is the area *ABE* below the demand curve and above price p_E. This area represents the accumulated differences between what consumers are willing to pay for this good, their marginal values, and what they actually do pay, p_E. The area below p_E and above the supply curve, *CBE,* represents the net gains or rents to sellers. They receive p_E even though they were willing to sell the various units at prices represented by the height of the supply curve. (Again, we use the term rents, rather than the analogous phrase producer's surplus to refer to this area.) These rents comprise the accumulated excess received by sellers over the minimum they would have required to offer q_E to the market. The resulting total net benefits to buyers and sellers from engaging in trade is the maximum available, sum of these two areas, *AEC.*

Consumers purchase goods until the marginal value of each good falls to the point where that person has to give up more, in terms of the value of goods foregone, than he or she receives by purchasing this good. With organized markets such as described above, this value of alternative goods foregone is the unique market price of that good. Moreover, consumers all face the same market price. *It follows, therefore, that consumers who do choose to purchase any given good all have the same marginal value of that good, its market price.* This does *not* mean that all consumers purchase the same quantity of the good. Buyers differ in terms of incomes and preferences for the good. But, whether a buyer wishes many units of a good or only a few, purchases continue until the marginal value of the good for each individual falls to the unique price in the market. Consumers who do not value the first unit as high as the market price choose, of course, not to purchase any units at all.

This aspect of competitive markets has a very important consequence in terms of economic efficiency. Recall that the gains from exchange are exhausted when the marginal values of the individual traders are all equal. Organized markets provide this efficiency because all traders face the same price and adjust their purchases or sales so that their marginal values equal this common value. We may all feel differently about, say, hamburgers, but if we all face the common price of $2 per pound of hamburgers, we all consume hamburgers until our marginal value of hamburgers falls to $2, the market price. Because everyone who consumes hamburgers all value hamburgers equally, at the margin, consumers have no further incentive to trade hamburgers amongst themselves.

5. R.A. Radford, The Economic Organisation of a P.O.W. Camp, Economica Volume XII, 1945

There are no further gains. Whereas we cannot be sure that markets will lead to a distribution of income that will please our normative values, we can at least be confident that no mutual gains are left on the table. This is the theoretical underpinning of Adam Smith's invisible hand, that leads individuals, through their own self-interest, to produce a result that is not of their intentions: the exhaustion of mutual benefits in society. We shall have more to say about the conditions for this in a while. It is safe to say that it is this aspect of free markets that has led to the growth in the general standard of living in countries employing this system.

The preceding analysis describes a decentralized process of exchange, based on self-interest. Such a mechanism can only occur if each participant has the right to make the decisions inherent in the process. In particular, each person must be legally free to sell or buy these goods at a mutually agreed upon price. The current owners and those to whom the goods ultimately are transferred must, for example, be secure in their ownership, meaning that the power of the state will be used to prevent theft. This condition is what we commonly call *private property.* If these conditions are lacking to some degree, gains from trade will be diminished. Instead of pursuing mutually advantageous gains, individuals will spend resources attempting to better secure ownership rights in the goods. We shall return to these important issues in later chapters. The effects of property rights on economic activity is a new and important field of economics, and we shall later analyze those effects in various contexts.

Property rights are the rules of the game. If these rights are well-defined, it means that people understand who is entitled to benefit from goods produced or exchanged. In that case, people have a mutual incentive to prevent those gains from being wasted, or dissipated. One of the simplest such mechanisms is the posting of a price, and letting buyers decide for themselves how much they wish to purchase. Haggling over the price, though possibly beneficial to one of the traders, is a time consuming and therefore costly device. Moreover, if the sellers have employed others to transact for them, designating discretion to those employees can be risky: the employees will not usually have the same interest as the owner. The employer will have to spend some resources monitoring the employees. If the good is familiar to consumers, e.g., one which they purchase frequently, then the gains from adopting these more costly selling techniques will likely be small. In that case, the resources saved by not allowing those activities can outweigh those gains, and the simple market mechanism we see at, say, supermarkets and discount houses will be predominant. Prices will be posted and nonnegotiable, with buyers choosing how much they wish to purchase. Although each seller is free to set prices, it is the combined impersonal actions of all traders that determines prices. We call markets in which many buyers and sellers transact with each other at unique prices that are beyond the direct control of any one trader **competitive markets**. The self-interests of each buyer and seller produces the unique market equilibrium depicted in Fig. 4-4, at which quantity q_E is transacted at price p_E.

Check your understanding: With organized markets, all consumers have the same marginal value (why?). Does this mean they all purchase the same number of units of the good?

4.6 The Role of Middlemen

When we exchange goods with others, we incur certain costs. There are usually some obvious, direct costs associated with a sale or purchase, such as simply getting to the market, selecting the goods desired, and waiting for checkout. More importantly, there are costs associated with determining exactly what it is that is being transacted, and guarding against dishonesty. In our two person exchange of oysters, neither party could be sure of the price at which the other would really be willing to transact. The seller of the oysters might have more information on the quality of the oysters (because she currently owns them) than does the buyer. In this case it would pay for both parties to invest some resources in order to better determine these unknown variables. Common examples of this behavior are inspecting produce at the supermarket, taking a used car to a mechanic for inspection before purchase, a bank inspecting a house before extending a mortgage. All of these costs which are associated with determining exactly what it is that is being transacted, and, including resources used to insure against bad outcomes, are called, appropriately enough, **transactions costs**. These are costs that would never be incurred in a one person economy, such as Robinson Crusoe living by himself on a deserted island. They are the costs associated with exchange.

The preceding paragraphs describe a highly stylized market consisting of individuals engaging only in exchange. Actual markets, of course, are more complicated, and involve original producers of goods. Most often, more than one layer of traders, called **middlemen**, exist between the producer of a good and the final consumer. A farmer or manufacturer will typically sell his or her output to some distributor, who may in turn resell it to wholesalers, who resell it to retailers, who finally, sell it to the end-user, the consumer. Each one of these intermediaries gets paid for their efforts. How can we explain the existence of these intermediaries? Could consumers benefit from eliminating the profits of these middlemen?[6]

In a voluntary exchange economy, efforts are directed at securing mutual benefits. If middlemen were in some way a more costly way to bring buyer and seller together, incentives would be present to eliminate such waste. It is more likely, therefore, that the persistence of these multiple layers of sellers is indicative of some useful function, i.e., *lowering* rather than raising transactions costs. It is not very difficult to see the gains these intermediaries provide.

Consider the case of agricultural goods. A farmer produces say, tomatoes, and sells the ripe or nearly ripe fruit to some distributor. Farmers don't sell their foodstuffs directly to consumers because most consumers live in urban areas, typically not located close to farms. It would be extremely costly and duplicative of effort if each consumer made his or her own trip to the farm to purchase a particular food. Moreover, farmers typically specialize in only one, or at most a few foods, so that trips to many different farms would be necessary before a complete meal was assembled. This would clearly be a very expensive and time-consuming way to distribute food to consumers. It is much less expensive for the farmer to sell his or her entire output to centralized wholesalers who pick up the crop in large trucks, transport this and other produce to centralized urban locations, and

6. I have tried, throughout this text, to use gender-neutral terms. I have found no adequate substitute for middlemen, which is still widely used, and have declined to replace it with middlepersons. Perhaps intermediary will eventually become the common term for these individuals.

then resell the goods to retailers located near residential neighborhoods. By shipping in bulk, transportation costs are greatly reduced. Moreover, by not having to engage in retail trade, farmers can concentrate on what they do best, i.e., growing crops, raising meat, etc., rather than having to devote their time to running a retail business alongside.[7] These gains from specialization are a very important aspect of production; we shall discuss them in more detail in Chapter 6.

The exact number of intermediaries that will be involved with a given final good is an interesting question, not admitting of an easy answer. Such factors as the geographical size of the market, the number and location of producers actively involved in each market, how specialized the good is and whether it is most beneficially sold alongside other goods would be important influences in determining the number of middlemen present. In modern economies, where production is highly specialized and where consumers do not live near producers, middlemen will be present. They make a living because they produce something of value to humans: they lower the transactions costs of the goods we desire. Eliminating the profits of the middleman in markets unrestricted by legal barriers against trade, would therefore result in *more* costly goods to consumers, as more expensive means are employed to bring buyer and seller together.

Middlemen and the Costs of Transacting

The consumers of goods and services are rarely the same people as the producers of those goods. Whereas farmers may actually eat a small portion of their produce directly, automobile mechanics may occasionally repair their own cars, and lawyers sometimes represent themselves in court (they have a fool for a client), these are very minor and empirically insignificant instances in developed economies. The typical situation is that consumers do not buy their food directly from farmers, but rather make their purchases at a supermarket, which purchased its inventory from wholesalers, who obtained their goods from distributors, who purchased their items from farmers, manufacturers, etc. These wholesale and distributor firms (middlemen) exist in order to *lower* the costs of bringing buyers and sellers together.

Supermarkets and discount houses are prominent examples of marketing techniques that have been devised to lower costs of transacting. In the 1930s and earlier, food was typically purchased from mom and pop grocery stores—small outlets where goods were gathered by the owners for the customers. As markets and urban density increased, the practice of letting buyers select items for themselves took hold. The first supermarkets, those run by the Great Atlantic and Pacific Tea Company (A & P), and the Kroger company were able to sell goods cheaper than the mom and pop stores, because their costs per unit sold were clearly lower. The result is that the older style food merchandising has all but disappeared. Large discount houses, begun mainly after World War II, have followed the same idea. Lately, this idea has been pushed even further by the large warehouse stores, such as Costco and Price Club, which sell items in bulk, and by catalogue houses (an idea developed over one hundred years ago with great

7. Farmers who bring their output directly to consumers, frequently by truck, are called truck farmers. The phrase actually derives from the French verb *troquer,* to exchange, as in the expression, I'll have no truck with you. These are generally local farmers with seasonal crops, whose farms are near urban areas. They apparently find it economical to bypass wholesalers and do their own retailing.

success, by Sears Roebuck, when transport costs for consumers were much higher than they are now) which dispense with retail outlets altogether.

The warehouse stores charge an annual fee for just the privilege of shopping in their stores. In part, this may just be a way of making up for the low prices. However, this annual license fee for the right to use the store alters the set of potential customers. Those consumers who just wish to purchase small amounts of the goods offered probably decline to join these warehouse clubs, because the annual savings in price is less than the cost of the membership. Only consumers who intend substantial purchases will find it in their interest to pay the annual license fee. By this means, the warehouses can save on the costs of processing people through the checkout lines. Some time is lost collecting money from each customer, and in particular, verifying checks. By adopting a pricing structure that discourages people with few purchases from shopping, the economies of bulk buying can be even further realized, lowering transactions costs still further. This gain is shared by the store and its customers on the basis as depicted in Fig. 5-10.

Supermarkets and discount stores sell items with which consumers are familiar, and which need essentially no explanation. Noticeably absent from discount chains are, say, intricate or advanced computers, custom-made clothes or furniture and generally high-end merchandise for which explanation by sales people is actually a benefit to the buyers. Hiring sales people to explain the intricacies of potatoes, lettuce or tuna fish is likely to be a waste of money. Even if consumers don't have all the information they want about these items, buying the item and trying it out will be a cheaper method of producing that information than hiring sales people. Although certain expenses are required to make all this work—for example, compact discs have been packaged in outsized containers partially to deter shoplifting, ordinary screws and nails are put into paper and plastic containers to facilitate measurement at the checkout counter—it is clear that these devices have lowered transacting costs for standard items. In a voluntary exchange economy, these innovations occur out of the self-interest of both buyers and sellers. The gains from lowering these costs are shared by both buyer and seller.

An important function middlemen provide is to lower the cost of information about the goods we buy. Many, and perhaps most consumers cannot reliably distinguish say, good quality suits from less expensive imitations, the freshness of fish or meat at the supermarket, the quality of diamonds. We solve this problem by shopping at stores whose reputation for selling a certain quality of good is known to us. Stores have specialists who can better determine these sometimes subtle quality variations than we can ourselves, because they deal in that merchandise all the time. We know that Nordstrom's generally carries clothing more attuned to people with greater concern for current fashion and fabric quality than does J.C. Penneys or Sears, but also that the clothes at Nordstrom's will likely be more expensive. We rely on the reputations of these stores to save us the cost of deciding which clothes are more likely of high quality when we decide to splurge a bit on clothes.

An interesting case where middlemen *raise* the cost of transacting is provided by the beer industry, but this is due to government regulation. In this instance, the federal government *forces* retailers to deal with middlemen they might otherwise choose to avoid. After the repeal of Prohibition in the 1930s, beer manufacturers were forbidden to own their own retail outlets. The law requires breweries to sell only to middlemen, or *distributors* as they are called.

Beer must be unloaded off the brewery's trucks and then reloaded onto the distributor's trucks. The beer companies can own distributors, and some do, but distributors cannot own retail outlets. Most small stores would choose to buy beer from wholesalers rather than directly from breweries, as they do with other commodities. However, some retailers such as Safeway, Walmart and the like operate on such a large volume that they and the breweries could profitably deal directly with each other. These retailers can easily purchase beer by the truckload, eliminating the intermediate unloading and loading step. Recently, therefore, the breweries have been selling to retailers through special (i.e., discount) distributors, bypassing their regular distributors. In some states, however, regulations forbid volume discounts to large retailers. Some retailers are therefore buying store brands from the breweries through these discount distributors. At this writing, these practices are being challenged in court by the regular distributors.

Check your understanding: Go back to Table 4-2 and suppose that *A*'s supply schedule included $1 for bringing the oysters to market. Suppose that cost is now eliminated through some market innovation. What will happen to the gains to *A*, to *B*, and to the total mutual benefits from trade?

4.7 The Use of Money for Exchange

In the preceding sections we have discussed various ways individuals have found to reduce the costs of transacting. One very important such device, so commonplace we tend to overlook it, is the use of **money**. The alternative to using money for exchange is to literally exchange goods for goods, a process known as **barter**. There have been times when small debts were paid in chickens or whatever else was handy, but this is not common nowadays. The problem with barter is that in order for it to be successful, not only must one person offer what another desires, the second person must also offer a good that the first person desires. I might wish to purchase your chickens, but if all I have to offer in exchange is broccoli, and you hate broccoli, the exchange will fail. The people who work for the Boeing airplane company don't want to be paid in airplane parts. The use of money avoids this problem, known as the **double coincidence of wants**. If we pay for our goods in money, we don't have to worry about what the other people want to do with their proceeds from the sale.

Money is such an important device for lowering transactions costs, its use is virtually universal, in societies past and present. We now associate money with coins and bills printed by governments, but before modern institutions of government existed, other items were used by private individuals to arrange exchange. The aboriginal peoples of North America used beads of various sorts, commonly known as wampum,[8] and ancient societies used gold and other precious items for this purpose. During World War II, in prisoner of war camps, and after the war in Germany, American cigarettes were used as money. What are the properties of these goods that are commonly used as money? That is, what attributes make certain goods useful as money?

8. Originally an Algonquian word for shell money, literally a string of white shells.

In the first place, money must be *easily recognizable* by ordinary people. To facilitate this, coins have milling around their edges to reveal whether they have been shaved. Money must also be handy, or *portable* so that people can take it with them when they go to purchase something. Also, it must be possible to carry large values of money in a convenient fashion. *Counterfeiting* must be difficult, lest money lose all value through extensive reproduction. Lastly, money must have *stable value relative to other goods.* If money varies wildly in purchasing power from day to day, its usefulness will be diminished.

In modern societies, money is almost always created by governments or government chartered banks. The common forms of money are coin, currency and checks, because those items have the above useful characteristics. Diamonds would not make good money, even though they are portable, because most people cannot distinguish diamonds from lesser gems and imitations such as cubic zirconia, and their value can vary tremendously on the basis of subtle and hard to detect flaws and coloration. Standard American cigarettes have many of these useful properties, but it would be difficult to make a major purchase with them. Gold has always been used as money, but it has occasionally been counterfeited by adding lead which weighs almost the same. In the United States and elsewhere, it seems to be legal to print your own money, as long as it is clear that you are not trying to counterfeit U.S. currency. Many banks sell traveler's checks, which are purely private sector creations. The Disney corporation sells Disney Dollars, exchangeable at Disney stores. There seems to be little to prevent people from accepting these coins or store gift certificates in payment of debts and using them as a medium of exchange.

Lastly, because of lower costs and increased speed of modern computers, electronic transfers of funds via credit and debit cards are now becoming more common. At most supermarkets, shoppers can make purchases by sliding their debit card through an electronic scanner. A computer reads information on the location and size of the buyer's bank account. If the funds exceed the purchase amount, the funds are immediately transferred into the store's bank account. (The same machines frequently also accept credit cards.) As this system becomes more widespread, this will likely become a very low-cost means of transacting, and probably will replace cash and especially personal checks (which have uncertain reliability to stores) to a substantial degree. The extent to which all this will occur is unknown at this writing, though it is certain to become a prominent means of transacting.

Gifts

Gift giving is sort of a barter transaction, in that frequently it is goods that are given rather than money. Indeed, a common idea when contemplating a gift for some friend or relative, is to try to buy him something he wouldn't buy for himself. But this is really odd. If we give someone a gift of cash, the recipient can spend the money on those goods that yield him or her the greatest satisfaction. When we give noncash gifts, we increase the likelihood that we are purchasing goods other than what the recipient values most highly. Indeed, specifically setting out to purchase goods the recipient would not himself or herself purchase increases further the likelihood that the gift will be valued *less* than its cost to the donor. Yale economist Joel Waldfogel has shown recently that the losses from

Christmas gift giving are substantial.[9] Waldfogel surveyed undergraduates, asking (among other things) how much they would have been willing to pay for the gifts they received. He found that the recipients valued their gifts at 10% to 33% less than the market value of the goods. Since in 1992 holiday gift-giving totaled some $38 billion, resources of approximately $4 billion to $13 billion were wasted in that one season alone.

Why is this pattern of gift-giving so prevalent, in the face of these losses? Economists have no really satisfying answer. We presume that giving gifts provides the donor with some satisfaction. The act itself of giving gifts is not the question; it is the particular way gifts are given, i.e., in kind, as opposed to cash, that is the puzzle. A person might give an in kind gift if he or she were truly better informed than the recipient about what that recipient might desire. Giving cash is sometimes regarded as crass. However, these are rather *ad hoc* explanations of the pattern. They imply that we would regularly assign someone else to shop for us, and make decisions with our own money as to what we should consume. We do not frequently observe this behavior. The law of demand provides some help: Waldfogel found that noncash gifts given by more socially distant acquaintances such as grandparents tended to have the lowest value (relative to market price), and therefore these donors tended relatively more often to give cash. Thus when information about the recipient's preferences is likely least available, noncash gifts tend to be least efficient, and such donors economize on these costs by giving cash.

Waldfogel points out that these issues may be significant in a larger sense, since federal and state (or provincial) governments often give out services *in kind,* e.g., housing, to welfare recipients, etc. It may be that cash is the more efficient medium of some public as well as private charity. Consider the case of food stamps, which are dispensed to low income persons in the United States and elsewhere. These stamps are legal tender for purchases of food items, but specifically not for tobacco, alcohol and other nonfood items. If the food stamps force a person to consume more food than they would if cash were given, then from the recipient's point of view, this is an inefficient gift. (The donor may be wishing to accomplish exactly that result, i.e. forcing the recipient to consume more food.) However, it is unlikely that this ever occurs. If the food stamps total less per month than the recipient would spend anyway for food, there is no difference between giving cash and giving food stamps. The recipient simply uses the food stamps for food, and cash for other goods. Also, since identities of food stamp recipients are rarely checked at stores, these coupons are readily traded illegally for cash at only a small discount. Thus the food stamp program is probably little different from a straight cash system, increasing its efficiency, but possibly undermining its intended effects.

4.8 Political Exchange

Market exchange is sometimes referred to as voting with dollars. The analogy with political choice is not really very apt. When we purchase goods, we can choose how many units to buy. We can spend a lot or a little on a good according to our

9. Joel Waldfogel, The Deadweight Loss of Christmas, *American Economic Review,* 83, No. 5, December 1993, 1328–36.

tastes and income. Political choice, in the form of voting, is different in this regard. We do not get to vote, as the old comic strip character Pogo once said, early and often. We vote only once, whether we feel strongly about a candidate or issue, or whether we barely care at all about the outcome. Additionally, when we purchase goods in the market, we do so because we expect to consume them. With political choice, whether we vote for the winner or the loser in an election, we all get to consume the winner. It is something of an all-or-nothing choice. Even if the actual vote was approximately 50–50, we don't get half of one candidate and half of the other. Lastly, political exchange is likely to affect the *endowments* of many people, e.g., through changes in the tax laws, laws granting specific property rights to engage in certain activities like logging, deep-sea fishing, land development, and the like. Political exchange deals not only with trade, but with redistribution of wealth as well.

Yet, as in the case of ordinary goods in the market, individuals have occasion to trade in political goods. The process, in legislatures, is called logrolling in America. It is the act of trading political goods for mutual benefit. It takes the form of one or more legislators agreeing to vote for another legislator's bill, if the second legislator will vote for the first one's bill. In recent years, this process has been analyzed by economists and political scientists using the principles of exchange discussed earlier.

Mutually advantageous trade takes place because individuals value goods differently at the margin. In the case of ordinary goods and services, trade takes place in organized markets. If a person values a commodity a great deal, he or she will continue to purchase the good until its marginal value falls to the market price. With ordinary goods, we get to adjust our level of consumption according to our preferences and income. Suppose, however, we favor a law subsidizing tuition for college students. Even if we feel strongly about our point of view, we cannot readily purchase additional units of tuition subsidies; we must pass legislation that will enact some specific subsidy. Not all citizens, however, will agree with our point of view; they will have to be coaxed in some way into voting for this legislation, if it is to pass. The way we induce people to voluntarily do something in our interest is to trade with them, i.e., to do something in their interest in exchange. We can explain various aspects of political choice, e.g., the types of bills enacted into law, by analyzing how the constraints imposed by democratic voting and voting by legislators affect the ability of citizens to overcome the transactions costs of political trade.

In the United States and other democracies, laws are most frequently enacted by elected representatives through votes in legislatures at the various levels of government (what our founding fathers called a republican form of government). However, many states also allow direct voting by the people, in referenda, or initiatives. This is the method of Athenian (from ancient Athens) democracy. The people themselves vote on legislation, rather than have elected representatives vote. A question that is to the point, and to which this chapter is generally addressed, is what accounts for the development of legislatures, i.e., representative government? Why not just have everyone of voting age vote on all issues? The answer lies in our attempts to secure mutual gains from trade by lowering transactions costs. Athenian democracy requires citizens to divert much of their time, and perhaps money, to political activity. In order to have any chance of enacting a law, supporters of some referendum must spend considerable time convincing the populace that the proposal is worthwhile, what its effects will be, etc. At the same time, opponents of the bill will likewise run expensive advertising campaigns showing the alleged bad effects of the bill. Since many people have to be persuaded one way or another, these campaigns are apt to be quite costly, and the truthfulness in advertising will probably not be very high. Athenian democracy clearly entails large transactions costs.

A very important issue faced by democracies is the problem of the tyranny of the majority, where the majority runs roughshod over the rights of the minority. An important distinction between laws and market goods is that when a bill passes into law, we all get the law, not just those who voted for it. It may be that the majority would like to deprive some minority of some valuable right or privilege. With straight majority voting, such an outcome is easily imaginable. One way to empower the minority is to give to them the opportunity to trade votes on this and other issues, so that through trade, enough majority legislators will find it in their own self-interest not to vote against the minority in given instances.

The opportunity for ordinary citizens to engage in mutually beneficial political trade is virtually nil. Suppose there are two types of voters. Voters *A* strongly favor some proposed law *X,* so much so that they would be willing to pay $100 each to a campaign fund in order to secure passage of *X*. However, voters *A* comprise only 40% of the electorate. Voters *B,* the remaining 60%, oppose *X,* but only mildly so. It would be no big catastrophe to them if *X* passed; they would only pay $10 each to prevent it. In such a case, which is in fact typical, in that many proposed laws are strongly favored by a minority and only weakly opposed by the majority, mutual gains could take place if the minority could in some way compensate the majority for voting for *X*. If the *A* voters, for example, simply *paid* all the *B* voters $15, in return for which the *B* voters voted for *X,* then a more efficient allocation would take place, since everyone would be better off than without the trade.

However, even if legally sanctioned, such an exchange could not likely take place. Identifying the *B* voters will be very difficult, partly because of their number, and also because if people discover that $15 is to be given to all citizens who intend to vote against *X,* everyone will declare themselves to be a *B* voter. There is no way to check if people are telling the truth. In addition, in virtually all democracies, people vote by secret ballot. There is no way to prevent voters from double crossing the proponents of *X* by voting against it once they are in the voting booth. As a result, exchanges of votes, meaning you vote for my candidate, or bill, and I'll vote for yours, can never take place among the voting public. The transactions costs are simply too high, both in terms of identifying the correct voters with whom to exchange votes, and in policing the agreement.

In order to reduce these costs, we elect representatives, who propose bills and vote for us in city councils, state and national legislatures, the congress or a parliament. By so doing, we relieve ourselves of the cost of being informed on all political issues, leaving us more time to pursue what we do best—earning a living in some field of endeavor. Unlike the citizenry, legislators can and do trade votes. Their transactions costs are much lower for several important reasons. The group of individuals elected representatives have to deal with is fairly small. Moreover, they vote on many issues, so it is possible for them to swap votes. Lastly, their votes are purposely *not* secret. They are usually posted as they vote, or votes are taken by a show of hands. They impose this nonsecret ballot rule on themselves precisely so that they can enforce political trades.

Legislators trade votes for the same reasons individuals trade goods: they have differing marginal values of goods, or, in the case of legislators, political issues, or proposed laws. Suppose a legislator from an urban area wants more money from the state to fight the drug problem. She feels really strongly about this issue. There aren't enough other urban representatives with the same interests, so she has to scrounge additional votes somewhere. It may turn out that a rural legislator is looking for some more money to improve irrigation in his district. It's a big deal for him, because farmers can then produce more crops and have higher incomes. He favors lowering urban crime, too, but it's not his primary goal; he was elected to improve rural services in his district. If these issues are put to a general ballot to the voters in a statewide referendum, both issues will likely fail. Only a minority of the voters are affected by either issue, and thus a majority will likely vote to keep more money for themselves. In a legislative setting, however, the outcome is likely to be different. The urban and rural legislators will strike a trade. When the urban crime bill comes up, the rural legislator will vote for it, and in return, the urban legislator will vote for the irrigation project when it is brought up. They can successfully effect this trade, because unlike ordinary citizenry, their transactions costs are relatively low.

Whether such logrolling leads to a more efficient allocation of resources is not easy to answer. If it were the case that, in this example, all urban voters have identical preferences regarding these bills, and all rural voters are also identical in that regard (but different from the urban voters), so that the legislators' preferences exactly matched those of their constituents, then if voters prefer having both bills to neither, this trade by their elected representatives is clearly mutually beneficial to all citizens, and by definition, Pareto superior. However, constituents' preferences are obviously not all identical, and some voters might very well prefer neither bill to both. Since all constituents get the law, whether they like it or not, some are likely to be made worse off. However, most, if not all people might very well opt for a legislative system even though we know laws will be passed which we do not favor, because the alternative, Athenian democracy, would lead to an even worse outcome. Thus a given system might be Pareto efficient even though at any given moment, there are disaffected voters.

Legislators also trade votes with the executive branches of government, although the manner differs between the state and federal levels. At the federal level, suppose the president favors increases in the defense budget while a majority in Congress is inclined to lower it, and the Congress would vote to liberalize abortion laws while the president would like to toughen them, the president favors less gun control legislation than does a majority of the congress, etc., etc. What Congress often does in these circumstances (which are typical) is to pass a bill with many riders attached to it. Thus, for example, attached to a defense expenditure bill may be an amendment to increase funding for school lunches. Congress tries to find a bill the president eagerly seeks, and then add as many provisions they favor but the president opposes so that when the entire package is presented as an all-or-nothing choice, the president will still sign rather than veto the multifaceted bill. This kind of tie-in sale is a self-enforcing method of trading votes on bills in Congress. The system reached extreme proportions in recent years when congress presented an omnibus expenditure bill to President Reagan consisting of essentially the entire year's legislation in one bill. Amidst much public gnashing of teeth, he signed it.

The process is somewhat different in state legislatures: virtually all states have provisions in their constitutions that bills can pertain to only one issue. A bill authorizing expenditures on both education and welfare is automatically unconstitutional. In this situation, the congressional practice of attaching riders cannot be used. Political deals, that is, agreements as to what the governor will sign, must be worked out beforehand. In addition, many state constitutions allow line-item vetoes, whereby the governor can literally cross out words and sentences in a bill, in some cases substantially altering the intent of the original legislation. This option gives the executive branch relatively greater ability to affect outcomes. The actual use of line-item vetoes depends on the degree to which the governor and the state legislature contract with each other on the nature of the bills to be passed. If it is known that the governor will change a bill in certain ways, the legislature will usually avoid wasting its time and fashion a bill that the governor will sign. Likewise, the governor has an incentive to avoid conflict by seeking mutually acceptable bills. Recently, Congress enacted the line-item veto for the president, but this was overturned in a court decision.

CHAPTER SUMMARY

- Voluntary exchange is based on *mutual benefits.* If both parties to a trade stand to benefit, they will gladly engage in the trade. If one stands to lose, he or she can simply refuse to trade.
- Mutually beneficial trade can occur whenever individuals have different marginal values of some good. If one person will pay only $2 for an additional unit of some good and another is willing to pay $6, mutual benefits equalling the difference between these two values, $4, will be created if the first person trades 1 unit to the second. The share of benefits received depends on the price, but the total must always be the difference between the persons' marginal values.
- As trade proceeds, the marginal values of the buyers fall, while the marginal values of the sellers, who now have less of the good, rise. In the absence of costs of trading, these marginal values are eventually brought into equality. At that point, the gains from trade are exhausted. We call such a situation *Pareto efficient,* or *Pareto optimal,* after the early 20th century Italian economist of that name.
- Individuals who own some units of a good will supply some of that good to others if the price is initially higher than their marginal value of the good. They will consume the good until their marginal value of it equals the price. The quantity they are willing to supply is the difference between what they own and what they would like to consume. If the price were to increase, they would choose to consume less for themselves and therefore supply more to others. For this reason, the supply curve in exchange markets is *upward,* or *positively sloping.*
- In large markets, negotiation between buyers and sellers is a very costly activity. These costs are typically lowered or eliminated by the mechanism of posting a price for the goods and letting consumers choose how much they wish to buy. In this fashion, market prices are formed, at which all transactions take place.

- When all persons transact at the same price, everyone's marginal values of any particular good are all equal. Therefore, such an economy is Pareto efficient, since no further gains from trade are available. It is for this reason that markets exist: they provide the greatest possible mutual benefits from exchange.
- Typically, costs must be incurred in order to bring buyer and seller together. These costs, called transactions costs, are *lowered* by the existence of middlemen, who are specialists in arranging for goods to be moved from the original suppliers to consumers. By lowering the cost of transacting, greater mutual benefits are derived. The profits of these middlemen are derived from the greater mutual benefits they can provide.
- The use of *money* is another means by which the cost of transacting is lowered, so that further mutual benefits can be derived.
- Markets of a sort also exist in the political arena. Politicians trade votes on issues when their marginal values of proposed laws differ from other politicians. They facilitate this process by having open, roll-call votes, so they can be sure others are living up to their agreements. Vote trading by ordinary citizens is difficult because secret ballots make it impossible to verify the trades, and there are too many citizens with which to arrange trades. Political vote trading may result in some mutually advantageous legislation, but it also enhances the power of special interests.

REVIEW QUESTIONS

1. Why is some trade always preferred by everyone to no trade, and why is more trade not always preferred by all to less trade?
2. Why are the marginal values of all consumers in a given market identical? Why does this lead to efficient markets?
3. Why are markets where buyers and sellers take the market price as given the norm? What efficiencies does this lead to?
4. Why is the height of a supply curve at a given quantity properly considered the cost of providing that last increment of the good (i.e., its marginal cost)?
5. Why is the area under the supply curve up to a given quantity properly considered the total cost of providing that quantity of good to the market?
6. What is the double coincidence of wants problem in barter transactions? Why is money so universally used in exchange?
7. Are gifts examples of noneconomic behavior? Why do people give gifts in kind rather than in cash?
8. Why does a reduction in middleman costs benefit both sellers and buyers?
9. What is political logrolling and why does it occur? Does it lead to further gains from trade?
10. Why don't legislators use a secret ballot?

PROBLEMS

1. "Trade occurs because some people have too much of some good." Do you agree? Does this mean that if a person's marginal value of some good is positive, she will never sell any?

2. Suppose an individual has the following marginal value schedule for hamburgers.

Quantity	Marginal value
1	$7
2	6
3	5
4	4
5	3
6	2
7	1
8	0

   a. Suppose this consumer is endowed with 7 hamburgers. What is this person's *supply* schedule of hamburgers?
   b. How would this supply curve change if the person started with only 5 hamburgers?

3. Suppose another person appears with the following marginal value schedule:

Quantity	Marginal value
1	$12
2	11
3	10
4	9
5	8
6	7
7	6
8	5
etc.	

   a. Suppose this person initially owns 4 hamburgers. What trade will take place, if any, between this person and the person in question 2?
   b. Suppose this person owns 13 hamburgers. Will this person be a net supplier or a net demander? What exchange will take place?

4. Does exchange pit buyer against seller, or buyer against buyer and seller against seller?

5. "The new large warehouse stores have lowered prices by allowing consumers to purchase directly from wholesalers, thus saving the costs of retailing." Evaluate. Is the retailer being bypassed or omitted, and does that affect any dimension of the good or service purchased?

6. How is the total amount of sellers' rents and consumers' surplus affected by the price at which goods are transacted?

7. Why is it that organized markets are characterized by sales at uniform prices, as opposed to individual negotiations between buyers and sellers?

8. In markets with many buyers and many sellers, the marginal values of all people trading will become equal. Why? Does this mean that everyone buys or sells the same amount?
9. The Commerce Clause of the U.S. Constitution prohibits states from restricting the free flow of people or goods across state lines. Do you think this is a good idea? Do your arguments extend to trade between the United States, Canada and Mexico?
10. "Prices to consumers could be reduced if the profits of the middlemen could be eliminated." Do you agree? What explains the general absence of truck farmers, who bring their produce to urban centers for direct sale to consumers?
11. In the former Soviet Union, it was common for farmers to bring their goods directly to urban centers and sell directly to consumers. What might explain this phenomenon?
12. Some urban communities have enacted ordinances that restrict the damage deposits on rental housing to some amount, e.g., $100 per apartment. What effects do such laws have on the following groups:

    a. apartment owners
    b. college students
    c. people with alternative lifestyles
    d. yuppie couples with neither children nor pets
    e. working couples with children and pets

    What effects do these restrictions have on the rentals charged tenants and the net amounts received by property owners?
13. What are some major differences between "voting" in the market and political voting? How able are we to express the intensity of our feelings about political issues versus market goods? Why is it that legislators do not use secret ballots, even though we regard that as a cherished right?
14. One famous problem with systems in which all citizens vote is the "tyranny of the majority," where the majority runs roughshod over the rights of some minority. How does the ability to trade votes in legislatures affect the majority's ability to do this?
15. The purchase of ordinary goods and services in the market is often referred to as "voting with dollars." The analogy is not, in fact, terribly good. To begin with, our endowments of income are different, whereas our political endowments are equal—one vote each (except, it is occasionally rumored, in Chicago.) Also, we all get the winner of an election, or the effects of some legislation, whether or not we voted for the winner or favored that bill. Lastly, citizens vote infrequently (as opposed to legislators.)

    a. What opportunities do individuals have for expressing the intensity of their preferences, in market versus political choices?
    b. How frequently do exchanges of votes ("You vote for my person/issue and I'll vote for yours.") take place among ordinary citizens relative to such trades among legislators?
    c. Why do legislators, in particular, engage in vote trading (the process is referred to as "logrolling" in America). What enables them to do this more than ordinary citizens?

d. Consider an issue that is mildly favored by a majority of voters, but strongly opposed by some minority. How would such an issue fare in the legislature versus in a referendum to the voters? Give an example of such an issue.
e. Suppose some law is contemplated. Why is this something of an all-or-nothing choice for consumers, as opposed to ordinary market purchases? How does this affect the amount of legislation that is passed relative to what we would purchase in the market on our own, if that were possible?

16. Individuals A, B and C constitute the entire electorate of a small town. They are debating whether to pave a road out to C's house, C being the only voter who doesn't live directly in town.

    a. With straight majority voting, what will be the likely outcome of the vote?
    b. Consider now that this electorate votes on many issues in a given year. Explain how this might affect the outcome of the road vote.
    c. Suppose there are in fact 1,000 voters each of type A, B and C. How would this affect your answers to parts a. and b.?
    d. What does the above analysis suggest regarding the incentives to replace Athenian town democracy with representative government, i.e., to use James Madison's terminology (Federalist Paper No. 10) to replace pure democracy with a republican form of government?

17. It is commonly argued that the only reason citizens vote is to satisfy their own desire to be a responsible citizen. After all, the probability of being a swing vote seems so negligible.

    a. Is the fraction of the electorate a voter represents an average or a marginal concept?
    b. Is the probability of being a swing vote an average or a marginal concept?
    c. Of these two measures, therefore, which should be more useful in economic analysis?
    d. Voter participation in U. S. elections varies from year to year and place to place. For example, in gubernatorial elections, participation has ranged from a high of 76% (Utah, 1964) to 17% (Georgia, 1962). Can citizen's duty or social responsibility explain this variation in voter participation?
    e. How would the following affect voter turnout in gubernatorial elections: a) the anticipated closeness of the election, b) the size of the voting age population of the state, c) the presence of other issues on the ballot, such as presidential or senatorial races. (For some empirical evidence, see Yoram Barzel and Eugene Silberberg, "Is the Act of Voting Rational," *Public Choice,* Fall, 1973.

QUESTIONS FOR DISCUSSION

1. Some states, e.g., California and other states mainly in the west allow voters to propose referenda, sometimes called voters' initiatives for public vote. Proponents argue this allows greater citizen participation in the political process; opponents argue these laws are often badly written and produce bad laws. What do you think of this institution?

2. The United States government is about to mint new one dollar coins, the first since the ill-fated Susan B. Anthony dollars of twenty years ago. Why did the Susan B.s fail, and why are the Canadian one dollar coins (loonies) and the new two dollar coins (toonies) widely accepted? What role has inflation played in the likelihood of success of these new coins?

3. Congress has been debating lessening restrictions on trade with China. Opponents cite China's poor civil rights record, and organized labor worries about cheap foreign imports. What do you think of freer trade with China and with other countries with whom we have serious disagreements?

CHAPTER 5

Supply and Demand

Markets are wondrous things when they work smoothly. We go to the store for something, and most often they have what we want, and we are out of there pretty quickly. Other times, though, things don't go so smoothly. Renting an apartment in New York City, San Francisco or Berkeley is a very different experience than renting an apartment in most cities. It can take weeks or months, and often one has to use an agent to help in the search. Many apartments that were formerly for rent are now for sale as condominiums. The reason for these differences has to do with the controls on rent these municipalities impose on property owners. In this chapter we investigate how unfettered markets work, and how things change when the government imposes restrictions on markets.

5.1 Change in Demand vs. Change in the Quantity Demanded

The law of demand is a statement only about the *slope* of demand curves. The postulates of behavior carry no implication regarding the *placement* of the demand curve, i.e., its location on a price-quantity graph, or the degree of its slope, save that is negative. The location of a demand curve is a statement of how intensely consumers wish to consume a given good. The quantity consumers wish to purchase at given prices depends, in addition to the price of the good itself, on the prices of closely related goods, the incomes of consumers, and of course tastes. These other influences, or variables must be held constant along a demand curve. If the price of a good changes, and some other price changes right along with it, then it will be impossible to isolate the effect of any single price change.

Consider the demand for gasoline. Gasoline is a useful commodity to humans, enabling us to travel considerable distances with little physical effort. At any moment, there is a demand curve for gasoline representing the amounts consumers would like to purchase at various prices. In conformance with the law of demand, it is downward sloping. Such a demand curve is depicted in Fig. 5-1. If the price of gasoline changes, holding other things constant, the change in gasoline consumption is represented by a movement along the demand curve. If the price falls from p_1 to p_2, gasoline consumption increases from q_1 to q_2. We call this response a **change in the quantity demanded**.

If any variable other than the price of this good changes, the demand curve itself *shifts,* i.e., the whole demand curve moves. For example, in the past two

Figure 5-1 *A Hypothetical Demand Curve for Gasoline*

Initially, consumers consume q_1 at price p_1. If the price falls from p_1 to p_2, consumers increase the amount they consume to q_2. This is a change in the quantity demanded since it is a movement along a demand curve.

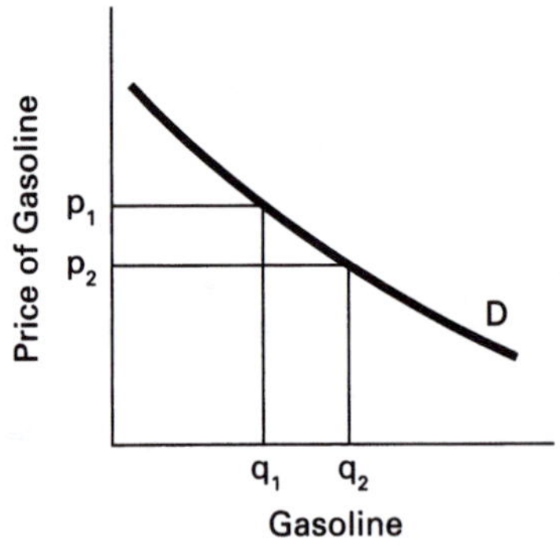

generations, influences other than the price of gasoline have affected demand for this handy good. Since the end of World War II in 1945, incomes have risen dramatically. As incomes rose, many people for the first time decided to purchase cars, and, as incomes rose further, many decided to own two or more cars per family. The effect of income on demand is not a movement *along* a demand curve, but rather a shift in the entire curve itself. At higher incomes, individuals want to consume more gasoline *at the old prices.* That is, at p_1 for example, consumers would now want to consume more than q_1, since the income constraint has been relaxed. This is shown on Fig. 5-2: a new demand curve, D' shows the (increased) demand for gasoline at the higher incomes. This shift is described as a shift *to the right,* meaning, at the old prices, a greater quantity is desired. It is also described as a shift *up,* meaning, at the old quantity, consumers' marginal values of the good have now increased. Both interpretations are valid, and both are useful to keep in mind when analyzing these changes.

A shift in the demand curve itself is called a **change in demand**. It must never be confused with a change in the quantity demanded. Never say "the demand increased," unless you mean the demand curve shifted to the right. That phrase should never mean that consumers decided to buy more because the price fell. Confusing a change in demand with a change in the quantity demanded invites disastrous confusion.

It is not in fact an implication of economics that demand curves shift to the right (or up) when incomes increase. There may be some goods whose consumption becomes less desirable as incomes increase. Certain foods, e.g., various kinds of beans, mustard greens, collards and the like, are nutritious but not appetizing to many people. Poor people tend to eat more of these foods than do the rich, because they provide relatively low-cost nutrition. As income increases, the demand curve for these goods, called **inferior goods**, shifts to the left, or down. Goods that are not inferior are usually called noninferior, or **normal**. For broad categories of goods, e.g., vegetables, clothes, etc., inferiority is rare. Also, starting at zero income, goods cannot be inferior: the consumer would never begin to consume the good in the first place. All goods, if they are truly goods, meaning at least some humans find them desirable, must be normal, or noninferior at some income levels for some people.

As incomes change, the manner in which consumers arrange for their consumption of desirable attributes changes. For example, as incomes increase, a consumer's consumption of meat will likely increase, but the particular type of

Figure 5-2 *A Change in Demand*

A shift in the entire demand curve, which we call *change in demand,* results from a change in some variable, other than the price of this good.

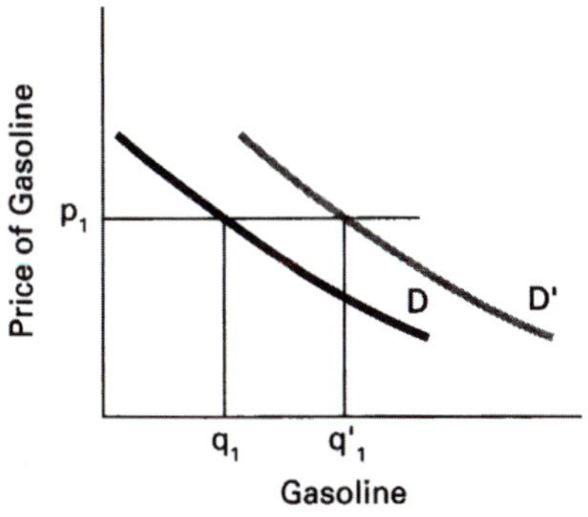

meat purchased to satisfy that desire may change. At low incomes, perhaps chuck roast, a tasty but somewhat tough cut, good for pot roasts only, will be consumed. This kind of very narrowly defined good, chuck roast, will eventually become inferior. As incomes increase, consumers substitute better cuts of meat, say, sirloin or porterhouse. However, even those higher quality goods are eventually apt to be replaced by still fancier cuts. The whole category, meat, however, does not seem to be inferior, nor would we expect similarly broad categories, such as food, clothing, shelter to be inferior. As incomes increase, consumption of the attributes of meat that are desired by humans will increase, though the particular meat will change. Although they are hard to measure, the real desires that people try to satisfy when they consume goods are such things as the desire to be warm, not to be hungry, the desire to be entertained, and so on. People process the commodities purchased in the market into the goods that actually satisfy those desires. It is the processing part, rather than the desirable properties of a good, that cause consumers to purchase less of some goods and more of others, as incomes rise. Thus as incomes rise, people satisfy their desire for protein by purchasing tastier and more enjoyable foods, e.g., fancier cuts of beef. Less enjoyable market goods are slowly replaced, i.e., they become inferior, as income rises. However, when goods are aggregated into broad categories, such as meat, vegetables, or even more broadly, for example into food, clothing, shelter, inferiority in the sense of consuming less as income increases is not a likely observation.

The other major influences on the location of a demand curve are the prices of closely related goods. The demand for coffee depends on the price of tea, and vice versa; the demand for bread depends on the price of butter, the demand for cars depends on the price of gasoline, and so forth. The impact on the demand for some good of changes in these other prices depends on whether these other goods are used together with this good, or as a replacement. We classify goods as **complements** if they are used together and **substitutes** if one good is generally used in place of the other.

Tea and coffee, for example, are substitutes; they are used in a similar manner by consumers. An increase in the price of coffee causes people to move up along their demand curve and consume less coffee. This contraction in coffee consumption causes an increase in the demand for tea, which has similar attributes to coffee. This is a *change in the demand* for tea. The entire demand curve for tea shifts out, or to the right. Because coffee has increased in price, consumers substitute towards the now relatively lower priced tea. Likewise, an increase in the price of tea causes a change in the demand for coffee—the demand curve for coffee shifts to the right. Of course, a decrease in the price of one of these goods has the opposite effect on the demand curve for the other good. A decrease in the price of tea shifts the demand curve for coffee to the left, or down.

By contrast, bread and butter are complementary goods, as are cars and gasoline, and computers and printers; they are used together in consumption.[1] An increase in the price of bread causes consumers to move up along their demand curve for bread—a change in the quantity of bread demanded—and consume less bread. As a result, consumers want to consume less butter, even at the old price of butter. Therefore, the demand curve for butter shifts down, or to

1. Extreme examples of complementarity are shoes and shoelaces, staples and staplers, etc., where one good is virtually useless without the other.

the left. Likewise, an increase in the price of gasoline causes a decrease in the demand for cars (though the effects on the demand for small versus large cars may be different). Lastly, to show that life is never easy, some goods are difficult to classify, and, to make matters worse, the answer may not always be the same. At low levels of income, ham and eggs may be substitute goods for many individuals, being alternative sources of protein. At higher incomes, many people like to consume these two goods together; they are more likely to be complementary goods for those individuals. As a person's income changes, or as the prices of still other goods change, it is possible for some goods to switch from being substitutes to complements, or vice versa.

Check your understanding: The price of DVD disks and disk players has been decreasing rapidly. Does this produce a change in demand or a change in the quantity demanded for DVD players and DVD disks? Likewise, how do we characterize the resulting changes in desired consumption of videotapes?

Income and Cross Elasticities

Recall that the elasticity of demand measures, in terms of percent changes, the response in the quantity demanded of some good to a change in the price of that good. We have noted that when a person's income changes, or when the price of some closely related good changes, the demand curve shifts, indicating a response to a change in those variables as well. It is convenient to measure the degree of these shifts in terms of percent changes in the incomes, prices and quantities involved. In a manner analogous to that as used in Chapter 3 for ordinary demand elasticities, we define the *income* elasticity η of some good as the *percent change in consumption due to a percent change in income.* Algebraically,

$$\eta = \frac{\textit{percent change in quantity}}{\textit{percent change in income}} = \frac{\frac{\Delta q}{q}}{\frac{\Delta M}{M}} = \frac{M}{q} \cdot \frac{\Delta q}{\Delta M}$$

where q denotes the quantity of the good consumed and Δq a change in that quantity, and where M denotes the consumer's income and ΔM a change in that income. The resulting number, η, measures the percent change in consumption of the good per percent change in income M.

Similarly, the *cross elasticity of demand* for some good x with respect to a change in the price of some other good y, is defined as the percent change in consumption x per the percent change in the price of y, p_y.

$$\epsilon_{xy} = \frac{\textit{percent of change in quantity of } x}{\textit{percent change in price of } y} = \frac{\frac{\Delta x}{x}}{\frac{\Delta p_y}{p_y}} = \frac{p_y}{x} \cdot \frac{\Delta x}{\Delta p_y}$$

This number measures the percent increase or decrease in the consumption of good x per percent change in the price of good y. This elasticity measure is also sometimes positive and sometimes negative, since goods can either be substitutes or complements. We expect the cross elasticities of substitutes, such as butter and margarine, to be positive, because if the price of margarine increases, consumers shift to butter. For substitutes, the price of one good and consumption of the other move in the same direction. The cross elasticity of complementary goods, such as cars and gasoline is negative. For these goods, the price of one good and the quantity consumed of the other move in opposite directions. Examples of these elasticities are presented in Tables 5-1 and 5-2. (Only sources not already cited in Table 3-1 in chapter 3 are listed.)

Income elasticities can in general be positive or negative. For normal, that is to say, noninferior goods, the income elasticity is positive. For such goods, the amount consumed moves in the same direction as income. The income elasticity of inferior goods is negative: less is consumed as income increases. Lastly, if a good increases in consumption in greater proportion than the increase in income, we call the good **income elastic**. If a good increases in smaller proportion than the increase in income, we call the good **income inelastic**. Luxury-type items, such as jewelry, high-end computers and stereo equipment are likely income elastic for most people. At relatively low incomes, little of such goods are consumed, but as income increases, a much greater proportion of income seems to be devoted to such purchases. As the table indicates, owner-occupied houses and cars are income elastic. These are goods for which people often defer consumption until some moderate income is attained, and then increase consumption rapidly with further increases in income.

On the other hand, basic survival goods tend to be **income inelastic**. On average, if income doubles (a 100% increase), food consumption increases by only 28%. Also, as one might expect, the demand for medical services changes much more slowly than changes in income. Ernst Engel, a German economist of

TABLE 5-1 *Representative Income Elasticities*

Item	Income Elasticity
Food	0.28
Medical Services	0.22
Automobiles	3.00
Housing	
Rental	1.00
Owner Occ.	1.20
Gasoline	1.06
Electricity	0.61
Coffee	0.51
Beer	0.93
Marijuana	0.00
Gambling	1.00

Sources: Medical Services: R. Andersen and L. Benham, "Factors Affecting the Relationship between Family Income and Medical Care Consumption"; in *Empirical Studies in Health Economics,* Herbert Klarman, ed. (Baltimore: Johns Hopkins Press, 1970). Housing: F. deLeeuw, "The Demand for Housing," *Review of Economics and Statistics* (February 1971);

Table 5-2 *Representative Cross-Price Elasticities of Demand*

Effect of Demand for First Good, per Price of Second	Elasticity Estimate
Butter/Margarine	1.53
Electricity/Natural Gas	0.50
Coffee/Tea	0.15

Sources: Butter: Dale M. Heien, "The Structure of Food Demand: Interrelatedness and Duality," *American Journal of Agricultural Economics* (May 1982): 214–221. Electricity: G.R. Lakshmanan and W. Anderson, "Residential Energy Demand in the United States," *Regional Science and Urban Economics* (August 1980): 371–386.

the 19th century, propounded a regularity about this behavior: As incomes increase, the consumption of what Engel described as primary goods (food, especially) becomes a smaller part of a family's total budget, while secondary and tertiary goods become a larger part. This observation is in fact a statement about the income elasticities of these goods. If a good is income inelastic, then when income increases by a certain percent, consumption increases by a smaller percent. Therefore, the amount spent on that good will fall as income increases.[2] Although not directly implied by the behavioral postulates stated above, the law has considerable empirical appeal. It agrees with common observation, though one must be careful to avoid circular reasoning in evaluating its predictions.

Change in Supply vs. Changes in the Quantity Supplied

The preceding remarks about movements along a demand curve versus shifts in the entire demand curve itself apply to supply curves as well. If the price of a good currently being sold increases, then firms respond by moving up their supply curve, supplying a higher quantity at the new higher price. This is a **change in the quantity supplied**. Farmers, for example, adjust their acreage and other inputs for the crop they produce on the basis of the price they expect to receive. If the anticipated price is relatively high, they plant more of that crop. When wheat prices increase, land that might be used for production of, say, sugar beets or alfalfa is converted to wheat production. These represent movements along a supply curve in response to changes in the price of the good in question.

Contrast the above with the effects of, say, developing a new hybrid of corn for which the yield of usable grain is 25 percent greater than with the previous strains. This is a **change in supply**, in particular, a shift of the entire supply curve to the right (or down). At any given market price, a greater amount of corn, say, will be forthcoming from sellers. Recently, a genetically engineered hormone, bovine somatotropin (BST), has been developed for cows and approved by the Food and Drug Administration. The hormone increases the cow's milk

2. The share of income M spent on good x_i is $= \kappa = p_i x_i/M$. Using the quotient rule of calculus, the rate of change of this quantity with respect to M is $\partial(p_i x_i/M)\partial M = (1/M)(\kappa\eta - \eta) = (\kappa/M)(\eta - 1)$, where η is the income elasticity as defined above. From this relationship, it can be seen that if $\eta < 1$ (income inelastic), the share of income spent on this good falls as income rises; if $\eta > 1$, the share of income spent on this good rises as income rises.

production. At virtually the same cost, dairy farmers can, by adding this compound to feed, increase the output of milk by some 10 to 15 percent. If adopted, the supply curve of milk will shift to the right, by the amount of the increase in production at each price. Similarly, a frost which destroys part of the citrus crop is a leftward shift in the supply curve. After the frost, the quantity supplied is less than previously. In the sections below, we analyze the market effects of changes in supply and changes in demand.

5.2 Analysis of Interrelated Markets

In Fig. 5-3, the supply and demand for oil are depicted, with a market price established of $20, and 80 billion barrels (bbls) of oil consumed. The total supply of oil consists of oil from domestic and from foreign sources. The domestic supply curve is the supply curve for oil from domestic wells; that is it shows the amount of oil that would be offered for sale at various prices, by domestic producers alone. The foreign supply curve likewise indicates the amount that would be offered for sale from foreign sources. The total supply curve is the (lateral) sum of the supplies of foreign oil and domestic oil. This aggregate supply function intersects the domestic demand curve for oil when the price is $20, leading to total consumption and production of 80 billion barrels. At the market price of $20, 30 billion barrels comes from foreign sources and 50 billion comes from domestic sources. Consumers' total expenditure on oil is the rectangular area bounded by the $20 price and 80 billion barrel quantity; it amounts to $20 × 80 billion barrels = $1,600 billion. This sum consists of the amount spent on foreign oil, $600 billion, determined by the supply curve of foreign oil, plus the amount spent on domestic oil, $1,000 billion, determined by the domestic supply curve. Suppose now the supply of foreign oil is restricted. To make things simpler analytically, assume it is cut off entirely, perhaps because of political instability abroad or a domestic policy to ban all foreign supply. In this case, the domestic supply curve now becomes the total supply curve. In effect, the supply curve has shifted to the left from the old total supply curve to the domestic supply curve.

After the supply shift—a change in supply—the equilibrium moves from point *E* to *E*′. Oil now trades at a higher price, $30. As a result, the quantity of oil demanded falls to 60 billion barrels. Consumers move up along the demand

Figure 5-3 *The Effects of Eliminating Foreign Oil*

If we prohibited foreign sources of oil, the domestic supply would be the total supply curve of oil. This would have the effect of moving the equilibrium from E to E'. the price would rise and the quantity consumed would fall. Domestic production would rise in response to the higher market price.

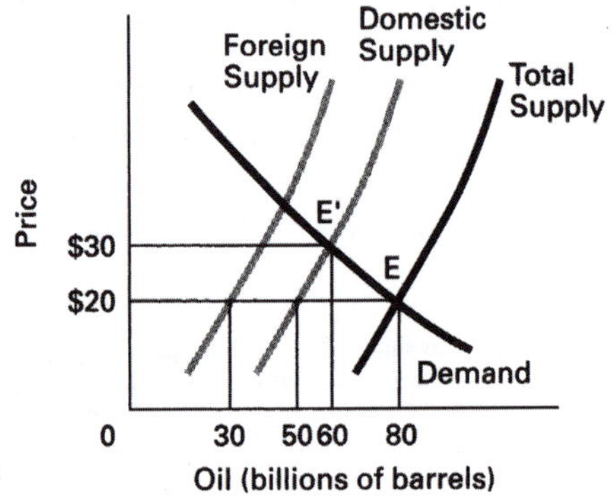

curve in response to a change in the price of this commodity; this is a *change in the quantity demanded.* Notice that at the higher price, the quantity of domestically supplied oil rises from 50 billion to 60 billion barrels, partially offsetting the change in supply due to the cutoff of foreign oil. At the higher price, aggregate consumer's surplus, the amount consumers would be willing to pay for this oil over and above the amount they are actually paying shrinks by the trapezoidal area to the left of the demand curve between the old and new price.

For the past quarter of a century, policy makers have worried about American dependence on foreign produced oil. Fig. 5-3 shows why the achievement of energy independence is so politically difficult. It is sometimes argued, for example, that the amount Americans spend on foreign produced oil is small relative to the entire economy, and, in particular, the economy grows by a like amount each year anyway. For example, in 1990, Americans spent $60.5 billion on foreign oil; the economy grew in total output by about $150 billion. Therefore, it is supposed, if foreign oil were banned it would only reduce standards of living to that of a half year ago—not a major calamity. This reasoning ignores the attendant loss of consumer's surplus. In the short-run, especially, the price increase is apt to be substantial. In 2000–'01, a very small decrease in quantity raised prices by almost 25% for a year or two. Thus the impact of energy independence will be much greater than what is shown by the rectangle of current expenditures on foreign oil. Moreover, it would provide a tremendous windfall to domestic oil companies, not a politically pretty picture.

Consider now the market for cars and coal, and how they respond to changes in the oil market. In Fig. 5-4, the supply and demand for cars is indicated. If the price of oil increases, driving becomes more expensive. Consumers mitigate the damages of higher-priced oil by driving less, carpooling, tuning cars so as to make them run more efficiently, etc. These actions cause cars to wear out less quickly, resulting in a shift to the left of the demand curve for new cars of a similar type. This is a *change in demand for new cars.* The immediate impact in the car market, therefore, is a lower price for new cars and a smaller quantity supplied.

However, not all cars are alike. Some get very good mileage, whilst others are "gas hogs." When the price of gasoline rose in the 1970s and 1980s, small cars became relatively more valuable than big cars. The demand for small, high-mileage cars shifted to the right, since these cars reduced the impact of the

Figure 5-4 *Effects of an Increase in the Price of Oil on the Market for Cars*

If the price of oil increases, the demand for cars shifts down or to the left, because cars are complementary goods to gasoline. Since people will consume less gasoline because of the increase in its price, they will also use fewer cars.

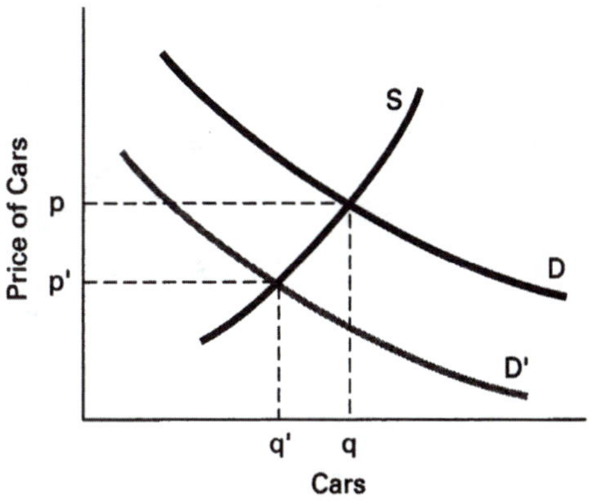

now expensive gasoline. Small cars are complementary to "high-priced" gasoline. On the other hand, the demand for low-mileage cars shifted to the left, producing large decreases in the price of those cars, with many fewer sold in later years. Thus as the price of gasoline rises, the mix of new cars produced shifts towards more fuel-efficient cars. Good mileage (a car that gets relatively many miles per gallon) is a substitute for gasoline. That is why high mileage cars became popular in the 1970s and early 1980s, and why high performance, relatively lower mileage cars have recently become more popular again. Since 1973, when the so-called energy crisis began, the average mileage of cars has approximately doubled, from 13 mpg to 26 mpg. This is roughly equivalent to halving the price of gasoline. If the price of gasoline were to decrease by half, consumers would move down their demand curves for gasoline and increase the quantity demanded. The low price of gas at the end of the twentieth century has led to the popularity of sports utility vehicles (SUVs), whose mileage is much worse than ordinary sedans. In fact, in recent years, SUVs and related vehicles make up about one-half of all new vehicle sales. The change in the fuel efficiency of cars produces a shift in the demand for gasoline that increases consumption at the old prices to what the equivalent lower price of gasoline would produce. Recently, the price of gasoline has increased dramatically, and new gas-saving hybrid cars such as the Toyota Prius, which gets up to 60 mpg, have become popular. It remains to be seen how this develops. If the price of gasoline remains high, we expect these hybrid cars will become much more popular and SUVs less popular.

Consider now the market for coal. Coal is a substitute for oil. Both fuels are used to generate electricity, and both can be used for heating homes and factories. When the price of oil rises, the demand curve for coal shifts to the right, as shown in Fig. 5-5. As a result, the price of coal and quantity transacted increase. The effect is a change (increase) in the demand for coal, and a change (increase) in the quantity supplied.

Whether goods are complements or substitutes is an empirical matter, that is, one not determined by economic postulates. Either case is possible. Many times the issue seems clear, as in the case of bread and butter, butter and margarine, oil and coal, etc. Sometimes the determination beforehand may not be easy, as in the previously mentioned case of ham and eggs. Goods are not intrin-

Figure 5-5 *Effects of an Increase in the Price of Oil on the Market for Coal*

If the price of oil increases, the demand curve for substitute goods, such as coal, shifts to the right. This has the effect of increasing both the price and the quantity of coal that people consume.

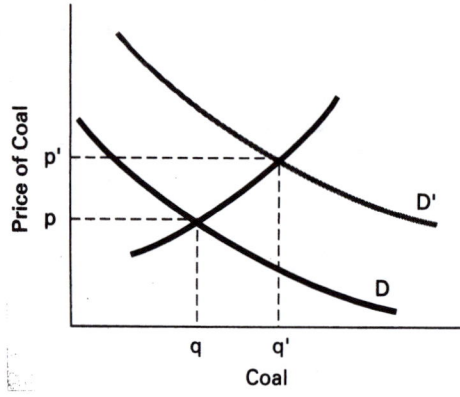

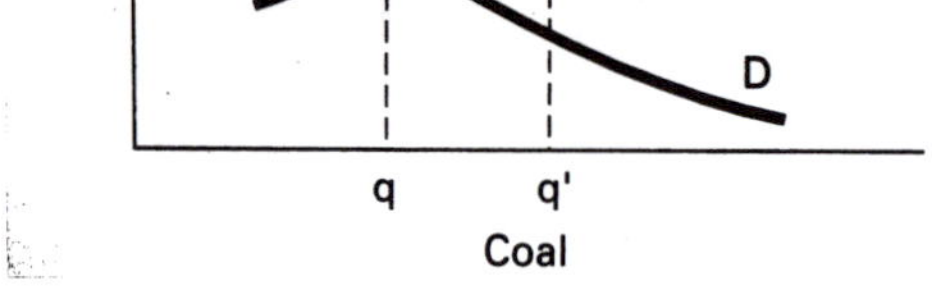

sically complements or substitutes; how individuals respond to a change in the price of another good can depend on income, for example, and perhaps also the availability and prices of other goods.

In recent years the U.S. government has promoted the development of "alternative" fuels for automobiles. California passed a law in the late 1990s mandating that 10 percent of the cars sold had to be nonpolluting, though its implementation is being delayed. The inability to store adequate energy in a compact battery is the main deterrent to developing a competitive electric car, though recently automobile manufacturers have made promising gains with so-called fuel cells powered by hydrogen or methane. Suppose that obstacle was overcome. How would that affect the markets for coal, petroleum and cars? The invention of efficient batteries would allow cars to be powered by coal, through the generation of electricity. This new use for coal would shift the demand for coal to the right, raising the price and quantity sold. The demand for gasoline powered cars would shift to the left, resulting in a lower price and lower quantity sold. The demand for petroleum for use as gasoline would fall (shift to the left), but increase for use in power generation. However, the combined net effect of these two shifts must be negative, since coal would now be substituted for petroleum in part for use in automobiles. Gradually, automobile manufacturers will switch over to production of electric cars. The ease with which they can do this will determine the slope of the supply curve of new electric cars. If the technology is largely transferable from petroleum to electric automobiles, the costs of the changeover to the new cars will be less.

Check your understanding: In an amusing but interesting article entitled "Coffee That's Good To the Last Twig," the Wall Street Journal reported in 2002 that Vietnam had now become tied with Columbia as the world's second largest producer of coffee, with 12% of the world's market each. Vietnam produced virtually no coffee a decade or more ago. (Brazil, the number one producer, sells 30% of the world's coffee.) Vietnam produces the low-quality *robusta* beans, used mainly in instant coffee and the cheaper brands, and the Journal reports that the level of impurities, such as twigs, is high. Columbia produces the high quality *arabica* beans. What do you suppose the effect of Vietnam's production has been on both the high quality and low quality coffee markets? Even more interestingly, in recent years, some coffee roasters such as Starbucks have entered into "fair-trade" purchases, where they pay coffee growers a premium over the market price for quality beans. Why do you think they do this, and do you suppose this recent movement has anything to do with the upsurge in Vietnamese production?

The Economics of Adoption

Being modern adults, my wife and I resolved never to be embarrassed, or to obfuscate about the facts of life to our children. We swore never to tell them that "we bought you at the store," or any such nonsense. Alas, when the time actually came, we had to tell them we bought them at the store—they were all adopted. Economists analyze the process of adoption with the use of supply and demand diagrams. Here, the item being exchanged is a human child, and that fact makes cold economic analysis offensive to some people. It smacks of slavery—buying and selling children. In fact adoption means that one person (or a couple) is voluntarily giving up something of value—a child—and may be receiving some sort of payment for that action, and the adoptive parents in general pay some amount of money to some middleman, perhaps to an adoption agency or to a lawyer, and receive something of value in exchange. Adoption is not the typical exchange of money for goods, but it surely is an exchange. As such, it should be amenable to analysis by the standard tools of supply and demand. The answers we derive should be independent of our normative judgments about the issues related to this subject.

Each year in the United States, Canada, and other countries, children (mostly infants and small children) are given up for adoption by young women who feel they are unable to provide the proper level of support and care for their children. These children are eagerly awaited by adoptive parents, who, in the main, are couples unable to have their own children. The numbers of people involved are significant. About 10% of all married couples are infertile, and the number who experience some problems with fertility is much higher. The number of children adopted in the United States by nonrelatives was 42,000 in 1952, rising to 89,000 in 1970, but then falling dramatically during the 1970s and later.

There are some important aspects of adoption which differentiate it from ordinary trade. Adoption is a distinctive type of exchange because it is everywhere illegal to call it an exchange, or sale. Adoptions are covered by state rather than national law in the U.S., and the laws vary from one state to another. However, certain features are common to all states' laws. Direct payment of money to the biological parent as compensation for giving up a child is illegal, except, in some states, payments for legitimate pregnancy costs (pre-natal care, medical checkups, etc.). Adoptions don't become final until some period of time has passed, in some states, up to a year. Adoptions usually take place through intermediaries, i.e., middlemen, in the form of adoption agencies, doctors and lawyers. These middlemen, under guidance of the law, usually keep the identities of the adoptive parents and biological parents unknown to each other, though this has been changing in recent years.[3]

Adoption, then, is basically an exchange which is illegal under all but very specific circumstances. It is not possible for ordinary citizens to arrange some mutually agreeable trade. If some childless couple (or person) offers their sports car for a woman's child, and the offer is accepted, then even if it can be conclusively shown that the child would be better off with the new set of parents, this transaction will be voided by the state, and the child returned to its biological parent. In the late 1980s, in the famous "Baby M" case, a couple in New Jersey hired a woman to give birth to a child with the husband's sperm. After the baby was born and transferred to the couple, the biological mother had second thoughts, and sued to have the baby returned to her. The law on such "surrogate motherhood" barely exists. In a case such as this, there is no universally accepted rule as to who "owns" the right to the good. The right of contract conflicted with the right of a woman to keep a child she birthed. Ironically, if the biological mother can show that she received a cash payment for the child, the hallmark of a voluntary exchange in economics, it is evidence in her favor that the baby was taken away from her "under duress" and that the baby is therefore rightfully hers. In the Baby "M" case, the courts upheld the contract and ruled for the adoptive parents.

---

3. [Source: U.S. National Center for Social Statistics. Adoption in 1970. Adoption in 1975. NCSS Report E-6]

Figure 5-6 *The Supply and Demand for Adoptable Children*

Economists assert that the tools of supply and demand are relevant for this unusual market. We expect birth mothers and adoptive parents to respond to changes in prices and other constraints in the usual manner.

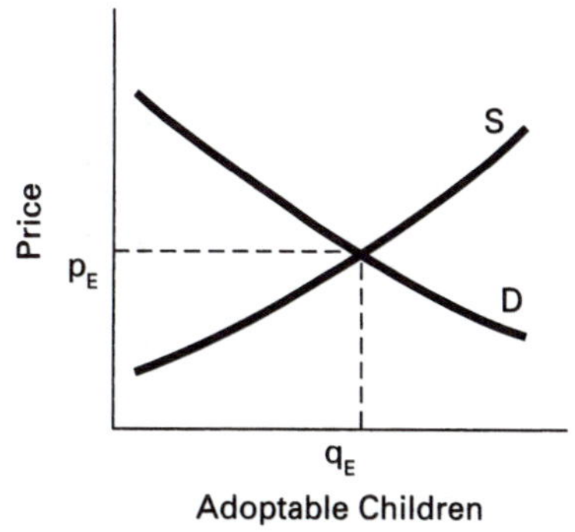

For the moment, subsume all the above transactions costs and nonprice rationing schemes into a stylized supply curve of adoptive children, displayed in Fig. 5-6 as the curve *S,* with a demand for these children by adoptive parents indicated by the demand curve *D.* Note the implications of this analysis. The desire to have children is considered in the context of a demand curve, which means that the actual number of children a couple might have (either naturally or by adoption) depends on the price of children, i.e., how costly it is to acquire (and then to raise) the children. Also, the rising supply curve of adoptive children means the number of children offered for adoption depends on price, i.e., on the level of compensation received by the biological parents for relinquishing their child for adoption. This curve postulates that, for example, a pregnant woman might choose to carry a baby to term and then give it up for adoption rather than obtain an abortion, if she for example receives payment for medical care plus some additional bonus.

The number of children placed for adoption rose throughout the 1950s and 1960s, then plummeted sharply in the early 1970s. Along with the sudden drop in placements was a sharp increase in the reported prices that adoptive parents were paying to receive the children. (Data on this issue is very difficult to document since these are largely private transactions and, as previously mentioned, direct payment to the biological parents is generally illegal; consequently, the parties involved are reluctant to discuss truthfully the terms of these arrangements.) Although historically the cost of adoption was in the $500 to $2,000 range, in the early 1970s these prices rose to over $10,000, with some undocumented newspaper accounts reporting figures twice that high. What was it that caused these changes?

Perhaps the first major influence on these events was the World War II baby boom. Birth rates jumped sharply (by more than 25%) in the U.S., and remained high throughout the 1950s and into the early 1960s. As a result, there were many more teenage girls in the 1960s than there were in earlier decades. Since this is the primary group that becomes pregnant out of wedlock and the group least capable of raising children on their own, there were more babies available for adoption in the 1960s than in earlier decades. In terms of economic analysis, this was a shift to the right of the supply curve of adoptable children, shown in Fig. 5-7, from *S* to *S′*. The supply curve *S′* represents the supply of adoptable children in the years of the increased teenage population resulting from the "baby boom." As a result of this supply shift, the price of babies fell and adoptions became easier for adoptive parents. Unfortunately, because of the large supply of healthy babies, children

Figure 5-7 *The Effects of the World War II Baby Boom on the Adoption Market*

Because of the baby boom, the supply of adoptable babies shifted to the right in the 1960s and early 1970s, when baby boomers became teenagers and young adults.

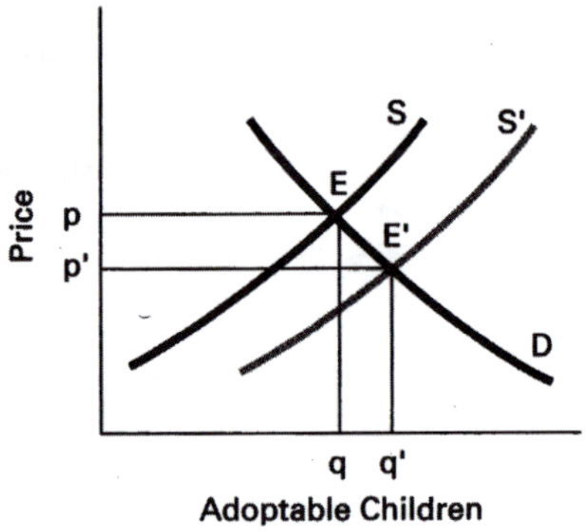

with unusual characteristics (such as being of mixed race, or having physical or mental disabilities) were usually not adopted. That is, the market-clearing price of some of these children was negative, meaning parents would have to be paid to accept them. Since no mechanism was available for this, these "different" children spent many (or all) of their childhood years in foundling homes.

In 1972, the major event that dominates this analysis occurred. In the case known as Roe vs. Wade, the U.S. Supreme Court declared that during the first six months of pregnancy a decision to abort the fetus was essentially the private decision of the pregnant woman and her doctor. Suddenly, a fairly inexpensive ($100 to $200) alternative to carrying a baby to term existed. (Also, birth control pills had recently become widely available.) As a result, the supply of adoptable babies plummeted. The number of legal abortions performed in the U.S. rose from 744,600 in 1973 to 1,409,600 in 1978. The supply curve of adoptable children shifted greatly to the left, shown in Fig. 5-8 as S'', the supply curve after the Supreme Court's abortion ruling.[4]

Figure 5-8 *The Effects of Roe v. Wade on the Adoption Market*

When the Supreme Court legalized abortions, the supply curve of adoptable children shifted to the left. This resulted in fewer babies placed in adoption and a higher price for those babies.

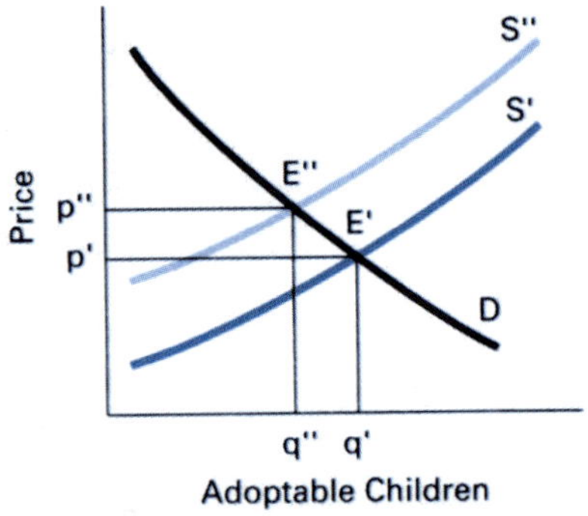

4. Births out of wedlock have continued to rise, but the social stigma is gone for most of these young women. Roe v. Wade continues to reduce the number of *unwanted* pregnancies.

Figure 5-9 *Increase in Demand for Hard-to-Place Babies*

When the price of healthy Caucasian babies increased, the demand for other children, that is, substitutes, increased.

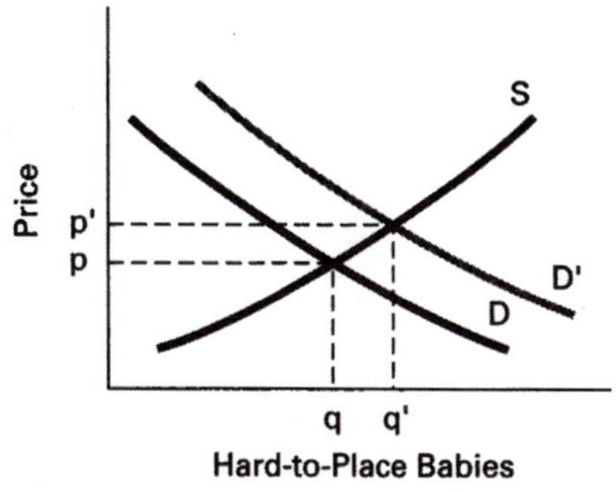

As a result, the quantity of babies adopted fell, and the price of adoptions to adoptive parents rose sharply. This is shown in Fig. 5-8 as moving from equilibrium E' to E''. An additional result, shown in Fig. 5-9, was the effect on "hard to adopt" children. Although the supply of these children dropped along with the supply of all adoptive children, with the sharp increase in the price of "healthy Caucasian" children, many parents chose to substitute away from their prior choice, towards the more available and often much lower-priced "special needs" children. This is shown as an outward shift of the demand for hard-to-place children, to D', in Fig. 5-9. As a result, virtually all of these children were placed in adoptive homes during the 1970s, even children with severe mental and physical handicaps. Families with children of a different race, once extremely rare, became much more common. It was not a matter necessarily of becoming more understanding, but rather a response to a change in constraints.

At the same time these supply shifts were taking place, the demand for adoptable children was shifting to the right. Toward the end of the 1970s, after some delay due to low entry level wages, the baby boomers started having families. Assuming these couples experienced the same degree of problems with infertility as previous generations, a somewhat greater demand for adoptive children would result, further raising the price of adoptive children.[5]

Economists have also studied other variables which affect the supply and demand curves for adoption. Marshall Medoff investigated the effects on adoptions of single vs. married status of the birth mother, the incomes of females and males, unemployment, education and some other variables such as affiliation with religions which prohibit abortions.[6] He argues that if the birth mother's income is relatively high, it raises the cost to her of bringing up the child herself and thus shifts the supply curve to the right. For the same reasons, being more educated, and being employed (vs. being unemployed or out of the labor market entirely) would tend to shift the supply curve to the right. However, having higher income also makes it easier to raise a child, e.g., by employing housekeepers,

5. Since many of these couples were starting their families in their 30s or older, infertility problems were likely even more prevalent.

6. Marshall H. Medoff, "An Empirical Analysis of Adoption," *Economic Inquiry, 31* No. 1, January, 1993, 59–70.

which would tend to shift the supply curve to the left. If the woman is married, she is more likely to have had another child already, and thus the cost of raising an additional one may be less, since many child-related items will have already been purchased. Thus we would expect "being married" to decrease the supply of adoptable babies.

Unfortunately, no data on the actual individuals involved in adoptions exists. Medoff instead investigated these questions using statewide data. He found that in states where female unemployment was low, and female participation in the labor force was high, adoptions were greater, in accordance with the theory. Also, states with a higher percentage of women completing high school had higher adoption rates, as expected. He got weak results for the effects of income, perhaps because there are two countervailing effects, as previously described. Lastly, fundamentalist women were found to be more likely than others to place a child for adoption. Medoff did not find evidence in the data that states which allow greater discretion to pay expenses for birth mothers, or which allowed private adoptions or ensured confidentiality had different adoption rates than states which were more restrictive on those issues. This runs counter to the theory developed in this section, which suggests such practices would induce more women to choose adoption over abortion. It may be that these influences are lost in the data because of the need to use statewide aggregates.

The adoption market is much more complicated than most markets because the good being transferred, the adoptive child itself, has rights guaranteed by the state. Before the process is finalized, rights to the child may not be clear. In the early 1990s, the poignant case of "Baby Jessica" occurred. The birth father had been misidentified by the birth mother, and "Jessica" was given to an adoptive family. The true birth father was identified when the child was only six weeks old, but after she had been placed with her new family. The birth parents married, and after a two-year custody battle in the courts, the child was returned to its birth parents. Because the law is not well developed, transactions costs are high, and mutual benefits may be dissipated through lengthy legal disputes.

Adoption markets provide an interesting example of how the cost of transacting affects markets. When we make purchases at the supermarket, the transactions costs are very low. For the most part, we purchase products whose characteristics are well known, and we require little sales help. Sometimes transactions costs are high, particularly when laws restrict trading, such as adopting children, or, more extremely, in the case of illegal goods such as marijuana. We can adapt our supply and demand analysis to display this activity. Consider Fig. 5-10 with a demand curve and supply curve S intersecting at point E. Let us now interpret S as the supply curve incorporating all the costs of production *except those associated with the act of bringing buyer and seller together*. Thus, S would exclude all the normal wholesale and retail activities and their costs. If, somehow, there were no transactions costs, quantity q_E would be transacted at price p_E, producing mutual gains from exchange represented by the area AEC. The supply curve which includes all the transactions costs in addition to the other costs of production is labeled S'; it lies above the curve S by the amount of those transactions costs. Since S' is in fact the true supply curve when all costs are correctly included, the market equilibrium, where the gains from exchange are maximized, must be at point E', at the intersection of the demand curve and S', producing net mutual gains of $A'C'E'$.

Figure 5-10 *The Costs of Bringing Buyer and Seller Together*

Costs of transacting shifts the supply curve up from S to S', by the amount of the per-unit transactions cost. These costs reduce the available mutual benefits from exchange to both buyer and seller. The equilibrium moves from *E* to *E'*, reducing total benefits from *AEC* to *AE'C'*. Consumers' surplus goes from *ABE* to *AB'E'* and sellers' rents (surplus) move from *CBE* to *C'B'E'*. Therefore, both consumers and sellers always have an incentive to find less expensive means of transacting.

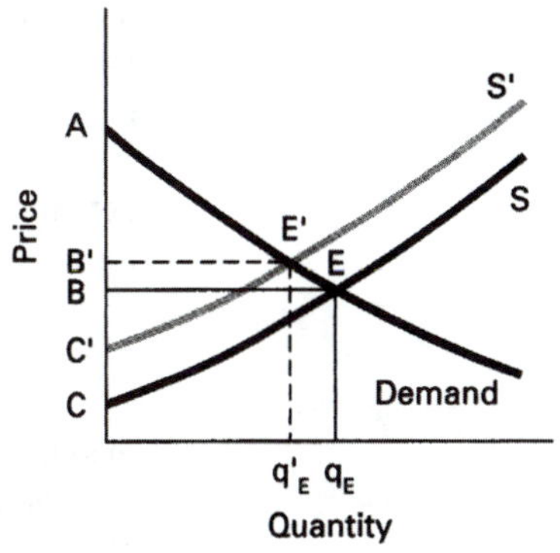

It is apparent from Fig. 5-10 that these mutual gains are smaller due to the positive costs of bringing buyer and seller together. Moreover, the benefits from exchange are reduced *to both buyers and sellers*. Consumers' surplus is reduced from *AEB* to *AE'B'*, and sellers' rents are reduced from *CBE* to *C'B'E'*. It follows that if transactions costs can be reduced, both buyers and sellers will capture greater gains from exchange. Lowering of transactions costs would shift *S'* down towards *S*. In so doing, *buyers and sellers both stand to gain*. Mutual benefits from the greater production and consumption expand from *A'C'E'* towards the theoretical maximum *ACE*. These enhanced benefits provide an incentive for people to explore ways of lowering transactions costs. If someone discovers a way of getting goods to consumers at a cost less than the amount that currently prevails, they will be able to keep at least part of that difference. As these cost-cutting methods become duplicated, competition forces the price lower, to the level of the supply price and the new lower transactions costs. When this occurs, consumers and producers will each capture greater rents—consumers' and producers' surplus—and receive the benefits from greater exchange.

Check your understanding: Explain why with a clearer and simpler set of laws, the resources spent on middlemen, e.g., lawyers, the courts, would be less, the cost to adoptive parents would be less, the amount received by the birth mother (either in prenatal care or other pregnancy support) would be larger, and the number of babies adopted would be greater.

5.3 Who Pays the Tax?

In 1978, voters in California passed the now-famous "Proposition 13," which lowered the tax on real property by over fifty percent. The measure, interpreted as a harbinger of the "tax revolt" of the 1980s, was hailed by its proponents as a boon to renters as well as home-owners, because the tax savings were going to be "passed on to the renter in the form of lower rents," or words to that effect.

The idea that taxes (or tax reductions) are automatically passed on to consumers is a questionable proposition that merits further study. Although taxes are usually *collected* by the seller, as with retail sales taxes, it does not follow that the actual tax money is coming out of the sellers' pockets. For example, if it turned out that the price of the commodity was raised by the full amount of the tax, then the consumer would be paying the tax, even though the seller would be the one actually sending the tax money to the government. In this case, it would really be the consumers' money that was being sent to the tax authorities. What determines who actually pays the tax? Sellers, of course, always prefer to pass the tax on to consumers, and consumers always resist this, hoping the tax will be "eaten" by the sellers. But what determines the actual outcome? The question can be answered using the tools of supply and demand curves.

The impact of a sales tax has to do not with what people *prefer,* but what market constraints *impose* on buyers and sellers. In Fig. 5-11, the supply and demand curves for gasoline for some period of time are drawn. The original supply curve is labeled *S*. Before imposition of the tax, the retail price of gasoline is \$1.00, and 100 million gallons are consumed. Suppose now a nationwide 20¢ sales tax is levied on gasoline. (There already is such a federal excise tax on this product.) The tax on gasoline in no way affects how people feel about using gasoline—the usefulness of gasoline to consumers is not changed, nor have consumers' incomes. Since this is a tax on gasoline only, other prices in the economy are not directly affected. In short, all the factors that go into determining the demand for gasoline are unaffected. The imposition of the sales tax therefore leaves the demand curve in Fig. 5-11 unchanged.

Assume for the moment that the sellers have to mail the tax receipts to the government. In that case, the original supply curve represents the supply of gasoline only when the price on the vertical axis means *net* price to the sellers, i.e., the money actually received by the sellers. The supply curve of gasoline in terms of the before-tax price, *S'*, must therefore lie above *S,* with the vertical distance between *S'* and *S* being everywhere equal to the per unit tax. If, for example, the tax on gasoline is 20¢ per gallon, then since the sellers will receive 20¢ per gallon less than the price at the pump, their decision on how much to supply will be based on the net price received after paying the sales tax. The supply curve, plotted against the gross price (before the tax is paid) is therefore everywhere 20¢ above the original supply curve. In Fig. 5-11, *S* and *S'* are drawn with this "parallel shift" of 20¢.[7]

Figure 5-11 *Effects of a Sales Tax*

A sales tax shifts the supply curve up by the amount of the tax. The price does not in general rise by the full amount of the tax. Consumers and sellers share the tax burden.

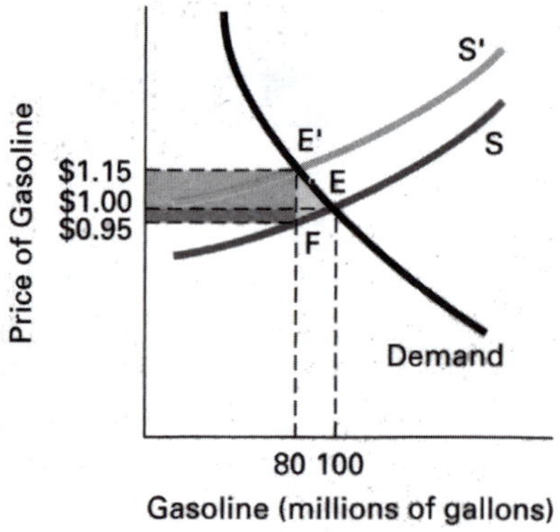

We can see in Fig. 5-11 the effects of the tax on the price and quantity of gasoline traded in the market. The original amount of gasoline sold, 100 million gallons, is determined by the intersection of the supply of gasoline, *S*, and the demand for gasoline, at point *E*. The price paid by buyers and received by sellers is $1.00. With the imposition of a sales tax, the supply curve shifts up by 20¢, the amount of the per unit tax, to *S′*. The new equilibrium occurs at point *E′*, at which the smaller quantity 80 million gallons is sold. Notice the effect on price. The price to consumers rises to $1.15, and the sellers receive only $.95, that is, $1.15 minus the tax. *The price to consumers does not in general go up by the full amount of the tax.* The price that sellers will accept is lower because the supply curve is upward sloping and a smaller quantity is sold. The entire tax is the shaded rectangular area in Fig. 5-11, amounting to 20¢ × 80 million = $16 million.

The tax is in fact shared by both consumers and sellers (producers). The portion of the tax consumers effectively pay is the top part of the rectangle, ($1.15 – $1.00) × 80 million = $12 million; the tax the producers pay is the bottom part of the rectangle, ($1.00 – $.95) × 80 million = $4 million. The share consumers pay comes out of their consumers' surplus, i.e., their net gains from trade; the share sellers pay derives from their net gains from trade, sellers', or producers' *rents.*

Lastly, notice that the tax drives a "wedge" between the price paid by consumers and the price received by sellers. Since the participants in this market no longer all face the same price, their marginal values of the good must differ. In particular, consumers' marginal values of this good all equal $1.15, whereas sellers' marginal values all equal the lower amount $.95. Any time individuals have different marginal values of some good, lost mutual benefits from exchange must exist. In Fig. 5-11, these nonrealized mutual benefits are represented by the triangular area *FE′E,* in this example, equal to approximately $2 million, using the formula for the area of a triangle, ½ base (20¢) × height ($20 million). This area, called **deadweight loss**, represents the lost gains from trade because output is reduced from the efficient level, 100 million gallons, to the lower amount 80 million gallons. The contraction in output accompanying a tax on some market thus causes a loss of mutual gains for the participants in that market.

What determines the relative impact of such a tax on consumers versus producers? Consider panels (a) and (b) of Fig. 5-12. In panel (a), the supply curve is fairly flat, i.e., nearly horizontal, while the demand curve has a steep slope. In panel (b), the situation is reversed—the demand curve is nearly horizontal while the supply curve is very steep. It is apparent from the illustration that in the first situation, the consumers bear most of the tax, while in the second situation, the producers pay most of the tax. The reason is that in panel (a), the marginal willingness of sellers to part with this good, or, the marginal cost of producing this item does not change very much over the relevant range of production. On the demand side, consumers' marginal value of this good rises rapidly with decreased quantity. Thus at a lower quantity, consumers are willing to pay much higher prices, while producers' marginal costs are not highly affected. Thus most

7. Most sales taxes are *ad valorem:* they are levied as a percent of the *value* of the item sold. An "8% sales tax" means 8% of the total amount purchased is added to the bill, rather than some fixed amount per physical unit of output. In that case, as the price of the good increases, the dollar amount of the tax also increases. The resulting supply curve *S′* is then not parallel to *S*, but rather its vertical distance above *S* increases at higher prices. The analysis following is not affected by this detail.

Figure 5-12 *Sharing of the Tax Burden*

When the demand curve is steep relative to the supply curve, consumers pay most of the tax, as we see in panel (a). When the demand curve is relatively flat, sellers pay most of the tax, as we see in panel (b).

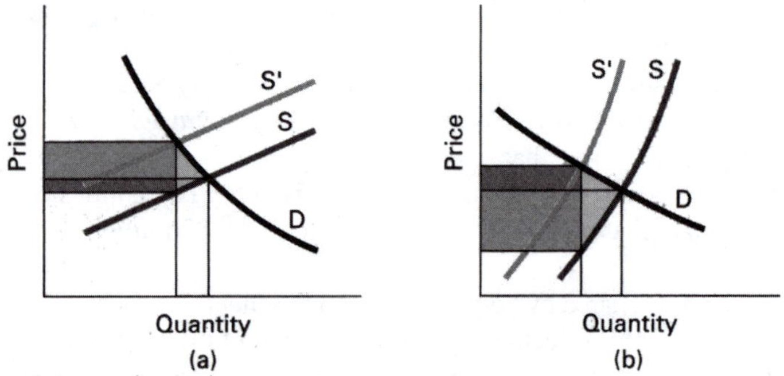

of the tax in this situation is paid by consumers. In panel (b), consumers' marginal value of the good does not change very much with decreased quantity. Also, the marginal willingness to part with the good, or the marginal cost of production falls rapidly with decreased quantity. In this case, therefore, most of the tax is paid by the producers.

Subsidies

The opposite of a tax is a *subsidy.* This is essentially a negative tax. It occurs when the government shares the cost of production. In this case, the supply curve shifts *down* by the amount of the subsidy, as shown in Fig. 5-13. The difference between the old supply curve *S* and the new supply curve *S′* is the amount of the subsidy. As with taxes, if the subsidy is paid per unit of output, the supply curve shifts parallel to itself, in this case, downward. (If the subsidy is *ad valorem,* i.e., in proportion to value, the distance between the two curves widens as the price (and quantity) increases).

Figure 5-13 *The Effects of a Subsidy*

A subsidy is like a negative tax. It shifts the supply curve down. Consumers pay a lower price as a result, but not by the full amount of the subsidy.

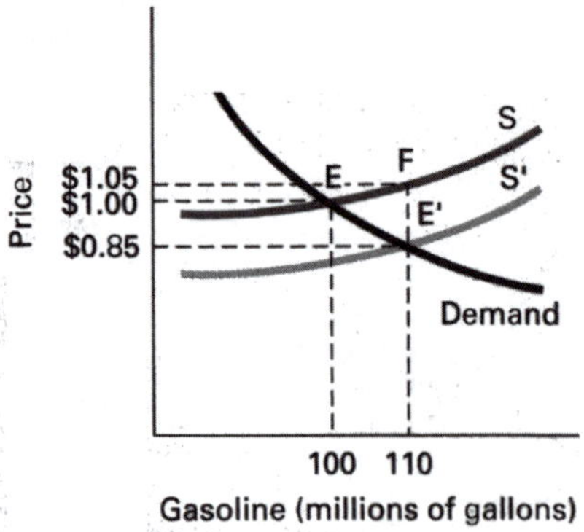

The original supply curve is shown as *S*, producing the market equilibrium indicated by point *E*. The price charged consumers is $1.00 and the quantity produced and traded is 100 million gallons. Suppose the subsidy is 20¢ per gallon. When the subsidy is instituted, the supply curve shifts *down* parallel to itself by 20¢, to *S′*, producing a new equilibrium at *E′*. The price to consumers does not decrease by the entire amount of the subsidy, but rather, in this example, to $.85. Since the price to consumers does in fact decrease, even if not by 20¢, the subsidy increases the quantity produced, to, say, 110 million gallons. As in the case of taxes, however, the subsidy is shared by buyers and sellers. The total subsidy that must be paid by taxpayers is the rectangular area $.20 × 110 million = $22 million. This cost is partially offset by the 15¢ decrease in price paid by consumers, which saves consumers $.15 × 110 million = $16.5 million. The net cost to taxpayers is thus the difference between the tax bill for the subsidies and the benefits of the lower price, or $5.5 million.

As in the case of taxes, however, a triangular area of deadweight loss is created. In this case, however, the losses come from too much production rather than too little. The area *EFE′* represents lost gains from trade. Production is carried beyond the point where the marginal value of this good to consumers equals its marginal value to producers. Beyond point *E*, consumers value resources more highly in some other use, indicated by the height of the original supply curve *S*. The sum of these excesses of the opportunity costs of using resources in the production of this good over consumers' marginal values of this good is measured by the triangular area *EFE′*, amounting to approximately $1 million in this example.

Check your understanding: How did we get $1 million for this deadweight loss?

Taxes on Immobile Resources

Return now to the case of taxes, and consider now a tax levied on some relatively immobile resource such as land, such as the tax that was reduced in California's famous "Proposition 13." The proponents of this legislation argued that renters would benefit as well as property owners, since the tax savings would be passed along to renters in the form of lower rents. The measure passed and property taxes were indeed lowered, but rents did not decline. It is easy to see why.

It is not possible to change the quantity of housing units very much in the short run. That is, in the space of a few months or even a few years, the supply of housing is fairly fixed. In terms of our supply and demand diagrams, the supply curve of housing is essentially vertical in the short run. We depict this in Fig. 5-14. We plot the quantity of housing on the horizontal axis, and the price of housing, the rental rate, on the vertical axis. The supply is essentially fixed at some amount, say, 100 units, resulting in some rental rate, say, $500 per month. The shaded rectangle represents all payments to landlords (price × quantity), $50,000. The government keeps some part of this rent in the form of taxes, shown as the lighter shaded part near the bottom of the expenditure rectangle.

Suppose now the tax on property is reduced. The demand for housing does not change. Nothing about people's desire to have a roof over their heads is affected by this legislation. Also, since the supply of housing is essentially fixed, nothing changes with regard to the number of housing units offered for rent.

Figure 5-14 *The Supply and Demand for Housing*

The supply of housing is relatively fixed in the short run. Therefore, property owners keep tax decreases in the short run.

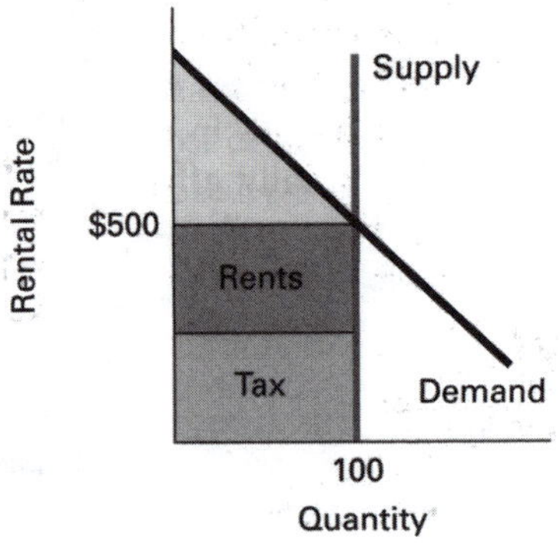

Since neither the supply nor the demand for housing changes, the market price, i.e., rental rates, cannot change. The equilibrium remains just where it always was. Any lowering of rents by the property owners would be pure altruism, a trait not commonly attributed to landlords. The only result of the tax decrease in the short run is to increase the share of the total expenditure on housing that landlords receive, and to decrease the share going to the government.

In the longer run, over the course of several years, say, rental rates will in fact go down. Lower property taxes raise the profitability of owning rental property. As a result, a relatively greater amount of new units will be built over time, and the supply curve will begin to shift to the right. With a greater supply of housing in the long run, rental rates must come down, according to the law of demand. The extent to which rentals fall in the future depends on the ease, i.e., the cost with which new housing can be built. If the new units are more expensive than the old units, due, say, to less available land, then rents will not fall, even in the long run, by the full amount of the tax decrease. In the case of California's Proposition 13, however, taxes were lowered only on *existing* real estate, and moreover, the tax benefit disappears when the property is transferred. Thus, this particular law reduced the incentive to replace existing real estate with newer housing units. As a result, the number of housing units might actually be less in the long run than they would have been without Prop. 13. In that case, the law may actually have *raised* rents in the long run.

In 1879, in *Progress and Poverty,* a self-taught American economist named Henry George proposed that all tax revenues be collected from taxes on the site value of land. Henry George's idea was that land which is valuable because of special attributes, such as having a good view, having a particularly convenient location, etc., is a fixed or immobile resource. He argued, essentially, that the supply of such resources is vertical, as in Fig. 5-14. In that case taxation of such resources would produce no output effect and thus no loss of economic efficiency in the form of deadweight loss, though George's argument was based mostly on distributional equity.[8]

8. Henry George spent the rest of his life campaigning for implementation of this single tax. Although the book is really quite exceptional for its time, his quixotic crusade caused him to acquire the reputation among serious scholars as something of a crackpot.

Who Pays a New Sales Tax on Food?

All but a handful of states levy a sales tax on consumer goods, but many states exclude food (and some other items) from the list of taxable goods. Suppose one of these states, which formerly had no sales tax on food, were to impose such a tax of 10 percent. Who would likely pay most of the tax: consumers, the producers of food, or supermarket owners?

Let us engage in some informed speculation as to the slope of the supply curve of food to one particular state in the United States, or to one province of Canada. Food production and distribution is nationwide, indeed international, in scope. Much produce we consume in the U.S. and Canada comes from Mexico, and when out of season, from South America; citrus fruits, grown mainly in Florida, Texas, and California, are shipped all over North America; meat originates largely in the plains states and goes to all points on the continent; wheat from the plains of Nebraska ends up as bread on tables from Los Angeles to Maine. The examples are too numerous to list. Although a certain amount of food, particularly produce, is home grown, i.e., produced near urban centers, whose consumers might account for a sizable proportion of that local area's production, in general the production and distribution system for food in North America is virtually continent-wide. In other words, the consumers in any one state are only a very small part of a large market.

Changes in the buying habits of the consumers of one state therefore cannot substantially affect the price of most food items. Even if consumers in one state or Canadian province were to stop eating altogether, the world price of food items would hardly change at all. The supply curve of food to any one state is thus nearly horizontal, as depicted in Fig. 5-15. The supply curve of food to the whole economy, of course, is not approximately horizontal, but here we are talking about the supply to one small segment of an entire international market. A small reduction in total production of food will not substantially change the marginal cost of producing food, even though such a reduction might loom large in any one locale's total consumption.

It is apparent from Fig. 5-15, with its rather flat supply curve, that most of the sales tax on food will be passed on to consumers in the form of higher prices for food. Supermarkets, which operate on a high-volume, low-markup basis (the

Figure 5-15 *Effects of a Sales Tax on Food*

The supply of food to any one region or state is highly elastic. Therefore, consumers will be the ones who pay a sales tax on food.

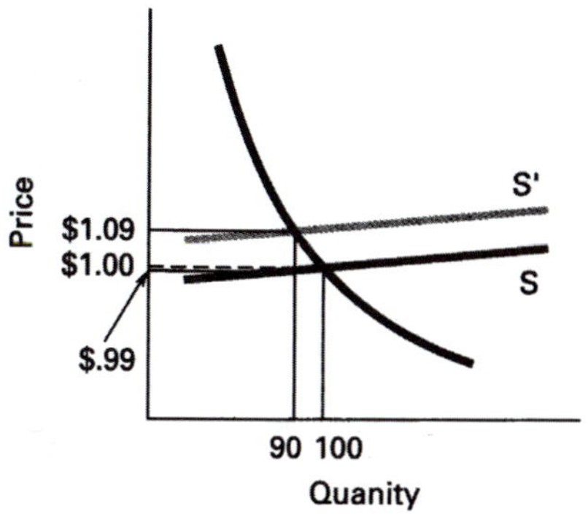

usual supermarket profits run one to two cents per dollar of sales) cannot absorb any of the sales tax—the marginal cost of supermarket services is essentially constant. With little or no adjustment possible on the cost side, the sales tax must be absorbed by consumers, on the demand side of the market. Thus consumers, not producers or sellers, will ultimately pay most of the sales tax.

The above analysis is for the imposition by one state of a sales tax on food. The story would be different if one were talking about the imposition of a nationwide tax of this sort. In that case, the relevant supply curve is the supply of food to the whole nation, and there can be no presumption that the aggregate supply curve to the whole of the United States, for example, is approximately horizontal. If such a nationwide tax were imposed, the additional cost of the sales tax would be shared more evenly between consumers and producers than in the above example, but the exact shares of the tax paid by each cannot be known without further empirical knowledge of the exact slopes of the aggregate supply and demand curves for food.

Payroll Taxes

In the preceding analysis, the tax receipts are mailed to the government by the sellers. For that reason, we shifted the supply curve up by the amount of the tax. At the new equilibrium (E' in Fig. 5-11), the price charged consumers rises to \$1.15, but the price received by the sellers is that amount net of the tax, \$.95. Some taxes, however, are collected on both buyers *and* sellers. Does it matter who actually sends the tax receipts to the government? Suppose the buyers paid the tax. Would that affect the share of the tax paid by buyers versus sellers?[9] For example, in the market for human labor, individuals supply labor to firms, and firms have a demand for that labor derived from the abilities of workers to generate profits to the employer. The labor market establishes an equilibrium price of labor of a given type. In the United States and most other countries, the government levies a tax on this market to pay for the social security system. The law says that the employer (the *buyer* of labor) must pay half the tax (7.65% at this writing) and an additional 7.65% is to be deducted from the paycheck of the *seller* of labor, the employee. The Clinton Administration once proposed a payroll tax whereby employers would pay 80% and employees would pay 20% of wages to pay for universal medical coverage. Does this 50–50 sharing of the social security tax, or 80–20 sharing of the medical insurance tax really mean that each party pays those exact shares?

How would we modify Fig. 5-11 if the buyer rather than the seller paid the entire tax? Instead of shifting the supply curve up by the amount of the tax, we would shift the demand curve *down* by the amount of the tax, shown as D' in Fig. 5-16. Since the amount of the shift is the same whether the supply curve shifts or the demand curve shifts, in either case, being equal to the entire tax, the net price received by the sellers, \$.95, must be the same as when the sellers pay the tax. Here, the buyers pay \$1.15 and hold out the tax from the sellers, who receive \$.95. The buyers mail the tax receipts (which total \$16 million as before).

9. It is an interesting question as to why having the seller collect and send in the tax receipts is the common mechanism for collecting taxes. Why do you suppose the state chooses this procedure rather than having consumers mail in the taxes on their purchases?

Figure 5-16 *The Effects of a Tax When the Buyers Collect the Tax*

In this case, the demand curve shifts down by the amount of the tax. Since the amount that the demand curve shifts is the same as the amount the supply curve would shift if the sellers paid the tax, the net effect on the burden of the tax is the same.

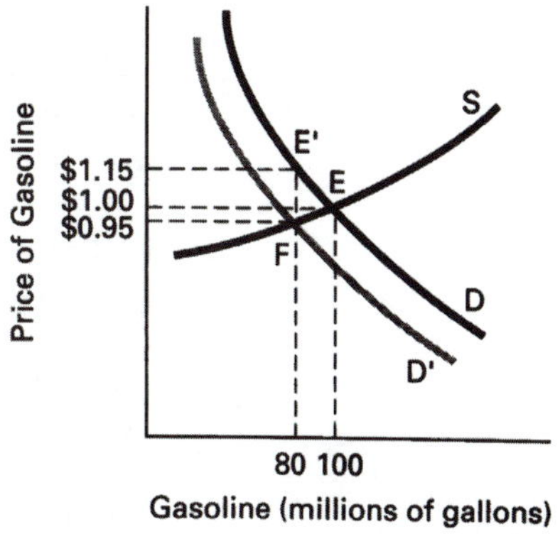

There is no change in who pays the tax. It is all a matter of which is the most convenient way of collecting the tax.

In the case of payroll taxes such as social security and the proposed medical care taxes, the tax comes from the receipts of both buyer and seller. In that case we thus have to shift the supply curve up by the amount the seller (the workers) pay, and shift the demand curve down by the amount the buyers (the employers) pay. But we have already seen that the prices received by buyer and seller net of the taxes is the same regardless of who sends the taxes to the government, as long as the same tax rate applies in both cases. Thus if some total amount is to be collected in labor markets, currently 12.40% of payroll for social security and another 2.9% for medical coverage, the amounts paid by workers versus their employers depends on the relative slopes of the supply and demand curves for that labor, and not on the legally specified shares. The shares of the total tax the sellers of labor (the employees) pay versus what the buyers of labor (the employers) pay depends on the slopes of the supply and demand curves for each particular kind of labor. It is an empirical matter, depending on supply and demand conditions in each individual labor market.

The application of this analysis to payroll taxes that are used to purchase services employees would on their own purchase may not, however, be so straightforward. Assume employees on their own would purchase a medical plan for $200 per month. Suppose instead, the employer will pay for it as a fringe benefit. Then, ignoring the federal income tax consequences of the two arrangements, in this case, the employee will pay the whole "tax" no matter what the slopes of the supply and demand curves are. To see this, suppose the fringe benefit is plain old cash, $200 per month. Then employees would be indifferent between their gross wage without the fringe benefit and their net wage of $200 less per month plus the fringe benefit. If the fringe benefit is valued equally with its cash value, the tax sharing argument is irrelevant. It is relevant only when the benefits come in a "lump sum" form, i.e., not directly related to the cost to the payers of the tax. This argument suggests that if the government forces employers to pay the full cost of employees' medical plans, wages will decrease by the full amount of those plans.

Other Effects of Taxes

The preceding analysis assumes that taxes induce changes only in the quantity of goods produced, but not other aspects of these goods, such as their quality, and also that taxes do not alter the mix of goods produced. In reality, taxes have these other, more extensive effects as well. In Chap.3, we mentioned that when cigarettes were taxed by the pack, the lower grade tobacco disappeared entirely from cigarette manufacture. When cigarettes are taxed in terms only of the number of cigarettes, and not on their quality or value, the effect was to increase the relative price of the poorer grades of tobacco. In a similar way, taxing wine by the bottle as opposed to price or quality of the wine induces a shift towards higher quality wine. In these types of cases, the taxes change the mix of goods from what consumers would want in their absence. This is a more subtle and more difficult to quantify welfare loss than the area of "deadweight loss" described earlier, but it exists none-the-less.

In the first half of the 1980s, the United States pressured the Japanese government to restrict exports of cars to America. This action was equivalent to a tariff (tax) on Japanese cars on the basis of the physical quantity of cars exported (except that in this case, the proceeds of the resulting increase in price were kept by the Japanese auto manufacturers instead of the U.S. Treasury). The Japanese car manufacturers avoided the tax in part by increasing the quality of the good. In those years, it was essentially impossible to purchase a Japanese car that was not loaded with virtually every option typically offered. In this way the Japanese manufacturers lowered the implied tariff as a percent of value, sharing some of these gains with American consumers. However, the quotas (or their equivalent tariffs) changed the mix of goods consumed because of the peculiar way they were defined. These distortions cause a welfare loss because consumers' marginal values of these goods relative to each other become unequal to the relative marginal values (costs) of these goods to producers.

Lastly, the United States and Canada formerly insisted that beer be first barreled before it could be sold. In 1984, the U.S. and Canada started to remove these laws, which had been on the books since Prohibition was repealed in 1933. As a result, a new type of business, the "brew pub," came into existence. These are small breweries which have a retail establishment, usually a small restaurant or tavern, on the same premises. They sell their beer directly from the vat, avoiding the cost of kegging the beer. This is a service that formerly did not exist, due in part to tax laws. These examples illustrate the power of taxation in determining the goods that get produced as well as the levels and qualities of the goods consumed.

The Tobacco Settlement

In 1998, the Attorneys General of many states sued the major tobacco firms for failing to disclose the extent of health problems associated with cigarette smoking. The plaintiffs (the people suing) in the case claimed, not unlike Claude Rains' character Captain Louis Renault in the 1943 Humphrey Bogart film, *Casablanca*, that they were "shocked, shocked" that cigarette smoking was dangerous. The four major tobacco companies, Philip Morris, R. J. Reynolds Tobacco, Lorillard Tobacco and Brown & Williamson Tobacco, agreed to pay approximately $250 billion to the states' treasuries over twenty-five years (less the $1.25 billion paid to the attorneys representing the states). What has been less well publicized is that the actual amount of the payments is to be proportional to the amount of cigarettes each company sells. A payment to the government that is proportional to the quantity of some good sold is a tax. The tobacco settlement is thus a new sales tax on certain tobacco companies except that it was imposed by the courts rather than by state legislatures. Since it is a sales tax, we know that payment is shared by the sellers (the tobacco companies) and consumers (smokers). The question of who pays the sales tax turns on the relative slopes of the supply and demand curves.

There is a compelling reason to believe the demand for tobacco is relatively steep and inelastic. Everyone agrees that quitting smoking is one of the most difficult things to accomplish. That is why the plaintiffs in this lawsuit used the word "addictive" in describing cigarettes. The supply curve of tobacco is probably not very steep. American cigarette manufacturers purchase tobacco grown all over the world. Thus it is reasonable to presume that the demand curve is relatively more steep, and perhaps much more steeply sloped than the supply curve, given the addictive nature of cigarettes. In that case, we know from the previous analysis that most of the tobacco settlement will be paid by smokers rather than by the tobacco companies, which is probably why the tobacco firms agreed to the settlement. Moreover, some part, perhaps most of the upward slope of the supply curve is based on the supply of tobacco, as opposed to the manufacture of cigarettes. Thus the tax paid by suppliers likely falls mostly on the farmers who produce tobacco, who are different people than the cigarette manufacturers.

It would be quite another matter if the government imposed some "lump-sum" tax on the tobacco companies, say, that they had to each pay $50 billion dollars over some time period, without regard to sales or anything else. In this case, this would be a straight transfer of wealth from the owners of cigarette companies to taxpayers. It is not surprising why this did not happen. In an even more ironic twist, the smaller cigarette manufacturers such as Liggett actually benefited from this settlement. Since the tax raised the price of a pack of cigarettes (by approximately 50 cents) the companies that were not sued have nonetheless seen the price of their product rise by 50 cents, and they don't have to make any payments at all!

5.4 Shortages and Surpluses

It is common to hear about an energy shortage, a housing shortage for the poor, and a shortage of good medical care. The fact that the United States imports some of its petroleum is taken as evidence of wasteful driving habits; the shortage would disappear if Americans built more rapid transit, drove slower, carpooled more, etc. Similarly, the existence of dilapidated housing and outright homelessness for some is described as a housing shortage. What does this term shortage mean, if anything, and, in particular, how is it different from scarcity? All goods—energy, housing and medical care certainly included—are scarce. Do the above statements signify anything other than the obvious fact that we would all prefer energy and housing somehow to be less scarce? When does scarcity become a shortage?

A similar puzzle concerns the term surplus. The United States seems to produce and export huge surpluses of agricultural goods, e.g., wheat, soybeans, etc. Yet wheat is obviously scarce, as evidenced by its positive price in the marketplace. How can there be a surplus of a good that is still scarce, meaning that even at current production levels, people would prefer to have more? These questions point out a need to have more precise terminology than is used by lay writers on economics. There is, in fact, an important distinction to be made between shortage and scarcity of goods, and likewise between surplus and non scarce.

Competition by Price

Before we address the above issues, let us review how unrestricted markets work. Consider Fig. 5-17, where we depict the market for gasoline where 100 units of gasoline transact an equilibrium price of $1.25 per gallon. Sellers are never sure what price is best for them. Prices of goods come about through a certain amount of trial and error. Sellers would like to sell all their goods at the highest possible prices, but if they charge more than their competitors, they will lose all their customers. Suppose sellers in the above example all chose to sell gasoline at $1.50 per gallon. We see from Fig. 5-17 that at this price, sellers offer 150 units for sale, but consumers wish to purchase only 80 units. We call the difference between these amounts, 70 units, excess supply. Sellers will in due time discover that they are engaging in costly excess production and will soon try to reduce their unsold inventories. They can do this only by dropping the price, and each individual seller will find it in his or her own self interest to do this.

In like manner, suppose the sellers had decided on a price of $1.00 per gallon. At this price, consumers wish to purchase 120 units, while sellers offer only 50 units. The difference, 70 units, is excess demand for this commodity. Again, the private actions of sellers will eliminate this excess demand. Sellers will quickly discover they can sell all their gasoline at a price higher than $1.00 and will each find it in their interest to raise their price.

We thus see that there is an automatic mechanism which produces the equilibrium price of $1.25. If the price is higher than that, the self interest of sellers competing against each other causes them to lower their price; if the price is below $1.25, buyers compete with each other for the bargain priced gasoline and soon bid up prices. The only stationary equilibrium is at $1.25, where the quantity supplied equals the quantity demanded. Moreover, at this price, mutual benefits are large as possible in this market.

Figure 5-17

At the price $1.25 per gallon, the quantity demanded equals the quantity supplied. At prices above $1.25, for example, $1.50, there is excess supply and sellers will try to unload this excess by lowering the price. If the price is $1.00, there is excess demand and buyers will bid the price up to $1.25.

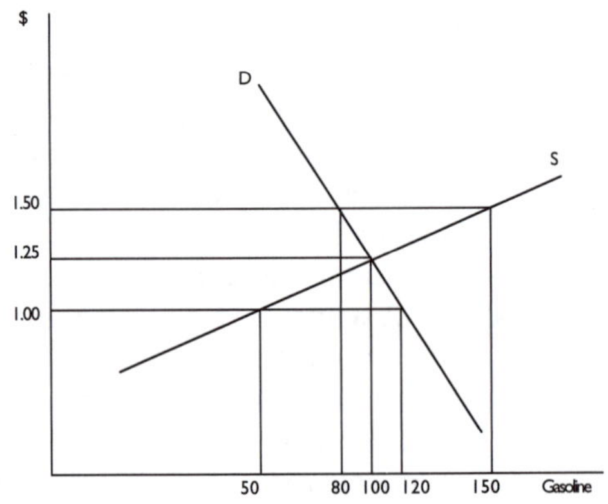

Shortages

There have been many instances of interruptions in supply. The OPEC countries perenially try to restrict petroleum output. Petroleum supplies were reduced in 1991 around the time of the Gulf War. The citrus crop froze in Florida a few years ago, and other weather related reductions in output have occurred in the recent past. These episodes quickly fade into memory, and for good reason: they are temporary and the market responds to the resulting higher prices with greater production. What has not happened during any of these episodes is that we have waited in line or physically fought over the gasoline or food items. Competition has taken the relatively benign form of **competition by price**, as opposed to other means, which we lump together as **nonprice competition**. In most important instances, we resort to nonprice competition only when competition by price is restricted or forbidden.

In each of the above mentioned episodes where the supply curve shifted to the left, the price rose accordingly. What would happen if instead the government had issued a ruling that sellers were forbidden to raise prices? Such a law is called a **price control**. Its effect, to use the example depicted in Fig. 5-17, is to make the excess demand a permanent feature of the market. If the price of gasoline is maintained by law at $1.00 in the above example, suppliers will every day run short of gasoline to sell. Consumers will then resort to other means of competition, such as waiting in line or perhaps violence. We call this enduring excess demand a **shortage**. It can occur only when some sort of price ceiling is imposed on the market.

Price controls have been infrequently used in the United States, with some outstanding exceptions. Rent controls exist in a number of cities, particularly New York, Berkeley and Santa Monica, CA. The Clinton Administration contemplated price controls on pharmaceuticals, physicians' and hospital fees and other medical services. We can gain an understanding of the consequences of such a policy by studying past episodes of price controls. The most famous such episode in recent history in the United States was the price controls on petroleum products in 1973 and 1974, though during World War II, much more extensive price controls were in effect.

In 2001, California citizens were treated to "rolling blackouts," where the electricity was turned off for hours at a time in many areas of the state. The state authorities had deregulated the wholesale price of electricity, but had maintained a price control on the retail price. When energy became very expensive that year, the wholesale price became larger than the retail price, and shortages appeared. Without the mechanism of letting prices allocate resources (electricity, in this case), non-price rationing in the form of simply turning off the power was used instead.

Fig. 5-18 depicts again the supply and demand for gasoline. A market clearing price of $1.25 per gallon is indicated, at which the amount 100 units would be transacted. Suppose, however, sellers are forbidden to charge more than $1.00 per gallon. This is what occurred during the winter of 1973–74, when the OPEC countries reduced shipments and during World War II, when prices were controlled on most consumer goods. At price $1.00, the quantity of gasoline consumers wish to purchase, 120 units, exceeds the quantity supplied, 50. This excess demand, the difference between what is demanded and what is offered, 120 – 50 = 70 units, is a *shortage.* Because of the price control, it doesn't disappear. The shortage persists because the mechanism by which such excess demands go away—raising the price—is forbidden by law.

Figure 5-18 *Shortages*

With price controls, the quantity demanded continually exceeds the quantity supplied. This excess demand, which is permanent as long as the price control is maintained, is a shortage. In the diagram, at the controlled price of $1.00, a (permanent) shortage of 70 units of gasoline exists.

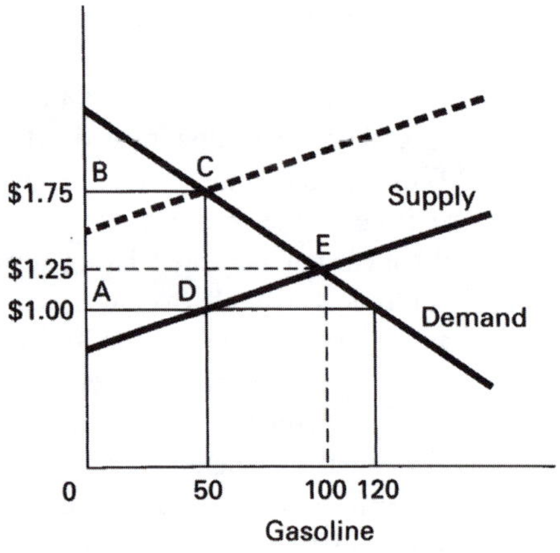

Under the price control, the quantity supplied is less than it would be without the price ceiling. This is an inefficient allocation of resources: too little gasoline, 50 units, is produced, instead of 100, where consumers' marginal value of gasoline equals the marginal opportunity cost of providing that good. Mutually beneficial gains are being lost, equal to the area under the demand curve and above the supply curve, between 50 and 100, *DCE.* This area measures consumers' willingness to pay more for a gallon of gas than other consumers are willing to pay in order that these resources be used in their next best alternative, as measured by the height of the supply curve. Area *DCE* is a deadweight loss; it is a similar loss of mutual benefits that occurs with taxes on specific goods.

At the quantity of gasoline brought to market, 50 units, consumers' marginal value of gasoline, determined by the height of the demand curve at that quantity, is not only higher than the controlled price, it is higher than the market clearing price, because the quantity supplied is reduced with the price ceiling. Consumers' marginal value is shown as $1.75 per gallon, $.75 more than the controlled price. What this means is that a person lucky enough to purchase gasoline at $1.00 per gallon receives a gift of $.75 for each gallon. If the average fill-up is 10 gallons, then consumers stand to receive a transfer of $7.50 from the oil companies when they fill their tanks.

The $.75 difference between consumers' marginal value of gasoline and the legal price of gasoline is what we refer to as income with no exclusive ownership. Oil companies (or their retail outlets) own the gasoline, but their right to transfer their gasoline to others is restricted by the price control. They do not have the right to sell gasoline at more than $1.00 per gallon, even though consumers would willingly enter into such a contract. Most importantly, no one owns the right to the $.75 difference between what consumers value the gasoline at and its legal price. Consequently, with price competition illegal, nonprice competition for that right ensues between potential consumers eager to receive the $.75 gift per gallon. Price controls cannot eliminate competition for scarce goods; competition is a result of scarcity. Controls only alter the means by which individuals compete.

In the case of price controls on gasoline during the 1973–74 episode, the major type of nonprice competition that appeared was waiting in line. It is still indelibly etched in the memories of everyone who was there, and it is the reason why the cabinet-level Department of Energy exists in the United States. Buying gasoline was no longer the simple act of pulling up to the pump. It became a major ordeal. Gasoline stations would announce the hours at which they would sell gasoline, and one or two hours prior to that time, cars would start queuing up, waiting for the opportunity to make a purchase. The lines were attributed by the authorities to everything other than their real cause—the price controls. The lines were said to be caused by our rapacious, wasteful overuse of petroleum, our love affair with big cars, etc. It was never explained why Canada and other western countries which were also subject to the same supply decrease, but which did not have price controls, did not have these waiting lines. The waiting lines were a constant and pervasive feature of the gasoline market at the time. This was not some fleeting happenstance because some seller underestimated demand. The shortage persisted over weeks and months, for as long as the price controls were in effect. The waiting lines gradually shortened as the controlled price ceiling was raised. When price controls were finally eliminated, the waiting lines disappeared.

It is obvious from Fig. 5-18 why nonprice rationing must occur with price controls, and equally clear why, in the absence of such restrictions, the price will adjust so as to eliminate these other forms of competition. The exact form of nonprice competition that will emerge under price controls depends to some extent on what price is being controlled and its severity. If price control results in large gifts to consumers, say, if the price of gasoline was restricted to $.25 per gallon, a scene out of the "Mad Max" movies would likely ensue. With gains that large from acquiring gasoline, people would likely resort to violence as a principal means of competition. Waiting in line and violence represent competition for the right to purchase the good. They are activities which take place only when rights to use goods are not clearly delineated. They represent unnecessary expenditures of resources, because costs can be reduced or eliminated by the proverbial "stroke of the pen" by the assignment of rights to goods. It is a waste of the mutual benefits from exchange, and appears only when less costly exchange is prevented. Nonprice rationing causes a **dissipation of rents**. The mutual benefits buyers and sellers might have received are wasted in nonproductive activities such as waiting in line. This dissipation of mutual gains occurs because of the lack of clearly delineated property rights in a valuable good.

As the waiting lines persisted in 1973–74, **political competition** for gasoline started to appear. Police and fire departments convinced the authorities that the public could ill-afford police cars and fire trucks waiting in line for gas while some emergency ensued, and so they were accorded rights to the cheap gasoline. Next, doctors and then farmers were given rights to purchase gasoline at the controlled price at any hour, and since some farmers use considerable quantities of fuel, they were allowed to fill up storage tanks with fuel. What followed was a boomlet in repairing and welding old storage tanks—anything that could hold fuel. The more organized and more powerful interest groups began lobbying Congress for the valuable right to purchase fuel below its opportunity cost, expending resources in the process that would have been unnecessary in the absence of price controls. All of the resources spent in the effort to secure rights to the low-priced gasoline, including the cost of political lobbying, represented dissipation of rents, i.e., lost mutual benefits from exchange.

An interesting and important aspect of price controls is that it suddenly becomes an important asset to know the seller. In our daily purchases in unregulated markets, sellers rarely care who we consumers are or what race or gender we are, neither do we consumers care about such characteristics of the sellers. If we have the money, retailers are happy to sell their goods to us; if they have what we want at an agreeable price, we are happy to buy it. With price controls, who you are and who you know becomes much more important. During World War II it was apparently helpful to be a beautiful young woman when controlled goods, such as meat and dairy products were purchased. People help their friends more than they help strangers, and knowing the owner of a gas station was particularly valuable in 1973–74. The owner took care of you, perhaps for an implicit promise for some return favor, a contract they could hardly enter into with strangers.

Some politicians and the media soon suggested schemes to alleviate the shortages because of the obvious waste of time and money incurred waiting in line. A fill-up could be had with an oil change and lube, and gasoline purchases were allowed on only even or odd numbered days, depending on the last digit of your license plate. It was even proposed that no one be allowed to drive a car without a passenger, a potential bonanza for unemployed teenagers getting into the "passenger" business. Most prominent, however, was the proposal to issue "ration coupons" for gasoline. Coupon rationing has been a prominent allocation device in the former Soviet Union, Cuba, China and the former communist countries of Eastern Europe. Coupons are issued to consumers entitling them to purchase one unit of a given good per coupon at a controlled money price. During World War II, most countries (including the United States) had extensive coupon rationing of most important consumer goods. The topic comes up in policy debates every time the price of some prominent good (particularly oil) increases sharply. It will almost certainly appear in the coming proposals regarding medical care.

A ration coupon is the right to purchase a unit of a good, say, a gallon of gasoline, at a given price. Examine Fig. 5-18 again, and consider the problem of trying to allocate gasoline by this method. The first question is to figure out how many coupons to issue. In 1973, the federal government suddenly found it had no idea how much gasoline and other petroleum products were actually consumed. Formerly, there had been no particular reason for anyone to know such a number. Moreover, it is not such an easy thing to find out. The United States is a big country, and at any given time, much oil is in transit or in partially filled storage tanks. Collecting data and accurately totaling gasoline availability is a prodigious effort—all unnecessary in the absence of price controls. A closely related problem is the ethical question of exactly who is to get the coupons. During the 1973–'74 episode, a lively debate ensued regarding whether some amount would be given out per family, or per adult, or per licensed driver; whether persons in the West, who typically drive to work rather than take mass transit, or who drive across vast distances in some states should get more coupons than urban commuters in the East, and like issues. These questions were never resolved due to the lifting of the price controls, but these are difficult, highly political and emotional issues. Price controls on important goods such as petroleum or medical care produce considerable expenditures of resources by various interest groups trying to direct the allocation in ways favorable to themselves, because even small changes in the allocation rules can have a large impact on the wealth of certain individuals or groups.

Ration coupons are an attempt to establish property rights in the nonexclusive income produced by the price control, and thereby to avoid the dissipation of rents associated with nonprice competition. In Fig. 5-18, continuing the gasoline framework, this nonexclusive income is the rectangular area *ABCD,* the difference between consumers' marginal value of gasoline ($1.75), and the price the sellers are allowed to receive ($1.00), times the quantity of gasoline transacted, 50 units. The stated purpose of rationing is to redistribute income, by equalizing the endowments of rights to purchase gasoline (or other goods). Without price controls, if 50 units are supplied, the price charged will be $1.75 instead of $1.00 with the controls. The ration coupons are an attempt to transfer the rents *ABCD* from sellers to consumers by establishing exclusive rights to what in their absence would otherwise be nonexclusive income.

Suppose the government has issued coupons equivalent to 50 units of gasoline, and distributed them equally to all licensed drivers. Gasoline purchases are allowed for $1.00 plus one coupon per gallon. In this situation, a surplus of gasoline will almost certainly ensue: gasoline will go begging at the pump. In all likelihood, some licensed drivers drive little, e.g., many urban dwellers, or many persons in families with more drivers than cars, or the elderly. Even at $1.00 per gallon, their demand for gasoline is less than the ration amount. The excess coupons are worthless to these consumers. The total of these unused coupons represents excess supply of gasoline at $1.00 per gallon; unless some reallocation is allowed, such as trading of coupons by consumers, this surplus will persist indefinitely.

Assume now that the government actually figures out how many coupons to issue, say, 10 per driver per week, and at the controlled price of $1.00, all coupons are used. Is this an efficient allocation of gasoline? The gains from trade are exhausted when all consumers' marginal values of gasoline are the same. In the absence of rationing, some individuals, e.g., traveling salespeople, consume many more gallons per week than the average for all consumers (10, in this example), while others, like those fabled previous owners of used cars who just drove to church on Sundays, consume much less. If each driver is allowed only the average amount of gasoline, the marginal value of gasoline for the heavy users will greatly exceed the marginal values of the light users. These consumers would therefore like to trade these coupons among themselves.

Rationing with untradable coupons therefore must lead to an inefficient allocation of resources: gains from trade amongst consumers are left on the table. These gains can be realized by the simple device of allowing consumers to trade the coupons. Literally no one can be made worse off by lifting this restriction. This is an application of the first proposition on trade: some trade is always better (more preferred) than no trade. A person still has the option of consuming or not consuming the ration allotment, say, 10 gallons. With trading, however, consumers now have additional options. If they wish to consume less than the allotment, meaning their marginal value of gasoline is less than the controlled price at the ration allotment, they can sell their coupons to consumers who value them more, and share the gains from that exchange. If their marginal value of gasoline is greater than the controlled price at the ration allotment, they can purchase coupons from some of the aforementioned consumers who value the good less highly.[10]

If the coupons are freely tradable, at what price will they trade? The price will be bid up until all consumers' marginal values of gasoline are equal.

10. Curiously enough, in virtually all instances where coupon rationing exists or has been proposed, such retrading has been forbidden by law. In 1973, when rationing was proposed for gasoline in the United States, the Energy Department (then, the Federal Energy Office) proposed, perhaps for the first time, that if coupon rationing were implemented, the coupons would be tradable. It is probably

The cost of consuming a gallon of gas will be equal to the direct money cost, the controlled price (in this example, \$1.00), plus the value of the coupon. The supply of gasoline is vertical at the quantity 50 units; when the full price to consumers is \$1.75, the quantity demanded equals the quantity supplied. The price of the coupons will therefore become \$.75. Even for a consumer who received 10 coupons and who wanted to consume only ten gallons of gas, so that he or she had no desire to either buy or sell coupons, the price of gasoline to that consumer would be \$1.75, not \$1.00. Choosing to consume a gallon of gas means foregoing \$.75 of other goods by selling a coupon.

The tradable ration system accomplishes the efficient allocation of 50 units of gasoline among consumers, because consumers face the true cost of consuming the product and are free to engage in mutually beneficial trade. The rectangular area *ABCD* of formerly nonexclusive income is in fact transferred to consumers, by assigning exclusive, transferable property rights to this income to consumers, through the mechanism of ration coupons. On the negative side is the cost of establishing and running such a system. The estimated cost of instituting such a system during the 1973–74 energy shortage in the United States was, in today's dollars, about 10 billion dollars.

Tradable coupons are in fact equivalent to a tax on gasoline, with the receipts of the tax rebated to consumers in a lump sum manner, that is, not related to a consumers' actual purchases. Suppose a sales tax of \$.75 is levied on gasoline. This would effectively shift the supply curve of gasoline up, parallel to itself, by \$.75. This new supply curve is shown as the dashed curve through point *C* in Fig. 5-18. With this tax in place, the price to consumers would rise to \$1.75, sellers would receive \$1.00, and the government would collect tax revenue in the amount represented by the rectangle $ABCD = \$.75 \times 50$. If the government now rebates this revenue to consumers, by simply mailing to each driver a check for his or her share of the proceeds (which would necessarily amount to \$7.50, the coupon price of \$.75 times the 10 gallon per driver allotment), the same allocation and income distribution as the tradable coupon scheme will result. Without instituting the complicated ration coupon system, with its attendant bureaucratic superstructure and political costs, the same outcome is achieved through the tax system. The individual rebate has to be unrelated to a driver's consumption of gasoline. If consuming a gallon at \$1.75 meant you would receive a rebate of \$.75 for that gallon, the price would effectively be lowered to \$1.00, and the lines would reappear. The rebate must be what economists refer to as a lump sum payment: independent of the actions and beyond the control of individual consumers.

We may get to test all this again. The state of Hawaii has just passed a gasoline price control measure to go into effect in the near future.

---

because two of the primary actors, George Schultz and Herb Stein were "Chicago Economists" familiar with this issue. The concept of tradable coupons appears in a problem in Nobel Prize winner Milton Friedman's famous text, *Price Theory,* used for many years in the graduate economics program at the University of Chicago, where Friedman was a major influence. Organized "consumers groups" were uniformly opposed to the idea of tradable coupons.

Rent Control[11]

Regulations of rental rates on residential property are perhaps the most prevalent instances of price controls in market economies. In the United States, price controls on many goods including rentals were imposed at the beginning of World War II on a nationwide basis. These controls were phased out after the war, but New York City maintained the controls on apartment rentals under separate city and state legislation. During the inflationary years following the Vietnam War, other communities imposed rent controls, so that approximately 200 communities now maintain them. Rent controls vary in scope and severity. Most exempt small units. Almost all ordinances exempt new construction, but these exemptions are sometimes rescinded in the future. New York City has twice imposed controls on buildings that were previously exempt. Many ordinances exempt units that have been voluntarily vacated by their tenants. Some ordinances allow price increases based on increases in prices in the economy, measured, for example, by the consumer price index (*CPI*), or if certain costs such as heating costs have increased. Lastly, some ordinances allow rent increases after remodeling or reconstruction of the units has taken place.

Rent controls are an attempt to transfer rents on land from property owners to tenants. This strategy for transferring income can succeed only if the rights to an apartment can be specified clearly. This is most practical in the short run when the supply curve of housing is essentially vertical. In that case, the income received by property owners is a pure rent, and transfer of those rents to tenants produces no short run losses of mutual benefits in the economy. At the beginning of World War II, increases in war production drew many people to the cities and increased the demand for urban housing. In addition, the government actively sought to limit resources in the civilian economy in order to free up resources for war production. The supply of housing was thus essentially fixed in the short run. As a result, rents would have increased, as shown in Fig. 5-19.

Assume that 100 units of housing are available initially and the market rental rate is $500 per month. (We use today's prices to keep the numbers current.) In the short run, and especially if it is difficult to build new housing because of wartime exigencies, the supply curve is essentially fixed, say, at 100 units. In that case, all income received by property owners is a pure rent. Assume now that the demand curve shifts from D to D' because of migration of people to cities. With no price controls, rentals would rise to $750, producing a net gain to property owners of $25,000. This increase in income is something of a windfall to property owners, since it occurs for reasons outside their control. Since there are many more renters than property owners, it is often politically popular to attempt to transfer these rents to consumers by maintaining the price at $500. This is essentially a tax on housing units of $250 per unit, with the proceeds immediately rebated back to renters. With rent controls, the tenants keep the $25,000 increase in the value of their housing. In the case where supply is fixed, so that the supply curve is vertical, no deadweight losses of mutual benefits occurs because of this tax.

11. The literature on this subject is vast. For a very readable account of the theory and a useful survey of empirical investigations, see Anthony Downs, *Residential Rent Controls: An Evaluation,* Washington, D.C.: The Urban Land Institute, 1988. Unless otherwise noted, all empirical results cited in this section are from research cited in this source.

Figure 5-19 *Rent Controls When the Supply of Housing Is Fixed*

Initially, with a fixed supply of 100 units, the market rental rate is $500 per month. When the demand increases from D to D', rentals would rise to $750. If a rent control law maintains the rental rate at $500 and the rights to the apartment are clearly delineated, the $25,000 windfall income increase that would have gone to property owners instead accrues to tenants. Since supply is fixed, no deadweight losses occur because of this tax on property owners.

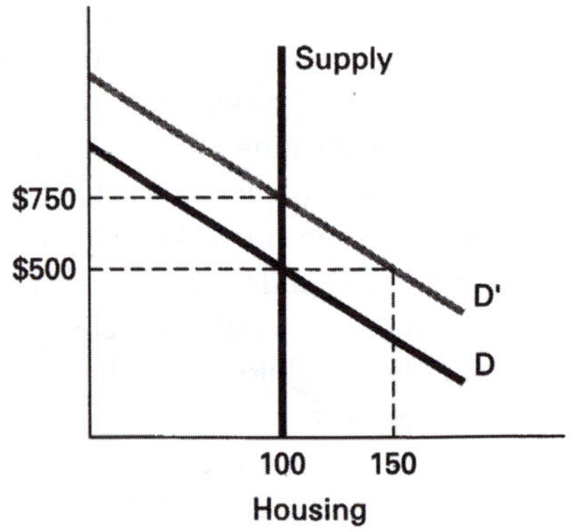

Although no deadweight losses occur in the short run, it is still the case that with the rent control in place, a housing shortage occurs. At the price of $500 per unit, consumers want to rent, say, 150 apartments, not 100. Moreover, since people often lose their rights to the controlled rent when they move, apartment turnover falls, so that vacancies decline. Some mechanism has to be created to allocate the existing apartments to consumers. Typically, existing tenants are given the right to stay in their current apartments. This essentially transfers part of the ownership rights to tenants. If the current tenants leave, however, it is often not clear what rent may be charged. In time, with actual rent control ordinances, whole bureaucracies have arisen to determine the rents that may be charged, dissipating part of the rents in the housing market. In Santa Monica, for example, $4.2 million is spent administering rent control on 30,000 units, or $140 per unit. Another mechanism for deciding these rights is the institution of "key money," where existing tenants sell the rights to an apartment to new tenants by supposedly selling the keys, or some of the furnishings. These transactions occur because under some of these ordinances, the tenant effectively becomes the owner of the right to reside in the apartment. They are thus able to sell this right when they move.

Rent controls can lead to greater discrimination against unpopular minorities. Suppose an apartment owner could easily rent all of his units for $750 per month, but is constrained by law to a maximum rent of $500. Many more qualified people eagerly apply for a lease than the owner can satisfy. The limitation of competition by price leads to competition by other means. Potential renters may offer bribes to the manager or owner for information that vacancies exist, or to actually secure an apartment. Suppose, however, a property owner has a prejudice against Walrasians. Without rent controls, every now and then the high bidder for an apartment might very well be a member of this group, which he despises. *Acting* on this prejudice requires owner to forego this attractive rent payment from the prospective tenant. With rent controls, however, the owner has no such worry. He or she already has more than enough tenants beating down the door to secure an apartment. As a result, persons who might otherwise be considered by the property owner may be turned away on more capricious grounds such as race, gender, or presence of small children. Rent controls lower the cost of discrimination on bases other than ability to pay, and thus foster decisions based on other criteria. The law of demand predicts more capricious discrimination will occur as a result.

In the long run however, resources become more available, and the supply curve of housing is not fixed. Rent controls affect the supply of housing in important ways. Unlike commodities such as gasoline, the supply of housing cannot be adjusted quickly. However, an apartment house owner faced with excess demand for his units can adjust the amount of service provided by the physical units in other ways. The rentals that can be charged depend in part on the level of maintenance of a building. If the building becomes rundown, the rents that can be charged become less. Without controls, an apartment owner has an incentive to maintain the complex at some level. When rent controls are imposed, there is excess demand for the apartments. The owner realizes he or she can save money on repairs and maintenance, let the apartments deteriorate, and there will still be excess demand (for a while, at least) for the units. With rent controls, the incentives to maintain the buildings are reduced and the rents begin to be dissipated. A U. S. Census Bureau study found in 1987 that in New York City, buildings under the strict rent control ordinance were in worse condition than buildings that were exempt or partially exempt. Rent controls thus produce deterioration of the housing stock.

Rent controls can have varying effects on reconstruction, depending on the way the ordinance is constructed. In some instances, rentals in a reconstructed building can be set at market rates. Steven Cheung reported that because of this Hong Kong once experienced a reconstruction craze. Buildings constructed in 1921 when controls went into effect were torn down in 1923.[12] When the ordinances have this feature, too much reconstruction may take place. Opposing this influence, however, are the disincentives rent controls create for investment in new housing. Individuals contemplating construction of new housing must always anticipate that rent controls will be someday applied to their new units by a new administration, even if they are currently declared exempt. In England, where stringent controls have been in place since World War I, the share of housing provided by private sources has plummeted from 53 percent in 1950 to 10 percent at present. Some cities set a maximum dividend yield on real estate investments. In the inflationary period of the late 1970s and early 1980s, it was possible to loan money to the federal government by purchasing U.S. Treasury Bonds at rates higher than those allowed by these municipal authorities. Given that loaning money to the U. S. government is much safer than investments in real estate, it is not surprising to find disinvestment in housing. In some areas of major cities in the U.S., buildings have been abandoned. The value of the rentals that can be collected are less than the cost of upkeep and taxes.

Once in place, rent controls are politically difficult to remove. These controls transfer valuable rights to tenants. In cities such as New York, a large part of the population owns these rights, and removing the controls would create many more losers than gainers in the short run. Citizens in these cities are not likely to vote to impose these losses upon themselves. As a result, the combined effects of deterioration of the existing housing stock and disincentives to produce new housing continually raise the effective cost of housing to individuals and families.

---

12. Steven N.S. Cheung, "Roofs or Stars: The Stated Intents and Actual Effects of a Rents Ordinance," *Economic Inquiry, 13,* March 1975, 1–21.

Medical Rationing

The provision of medical services is an important sector of the economy where allocation proceeds largely on a nonprice basis. This was not always true. Fifty years ago, when you went to the doctor, you paid cash at the time of your visit. If you needed an appendectomy, you paid for it, unless you qualified as a charity case. Perhaps you convinced your doctor to lower the fee, but it was still a cash transaction. Nowadays, this has all changed, both in the private and public sectors. In the private sector, most Americans have some sort of private health insurance, typically arranged through one's employer (or one's parent's or spouse's employer). In these plans, you prepay a certain monthly amount for medical coverage, and if you go to a doctor or hospital, the insurance company pays the bulk of your medical costs. Health Maintenance Organizations (HMOs) are prepaid group plans; you pay a certain monthly amount, and you are never sent a bill for any service they provide. In the United States, Medicare covers all persons over the age of 65. Although some supplemental plans exist, the federal government pays essentially for all medical costs (but, importantly, not for prescription drugs) for seniors. Poor people in the United States are covered by State Medicaid programs, which pick up the entire cost of care. Canada operates a universal coverage system: all Canadians are covered by the government plan and pay no fees for doctors or hospital care. The costs are paid through general revenue collected via payroll taxes. Canadians do, however, pay for their own prescription drugs.

The attribute common to all these medical systems is that patients, i.e., the consumers, pay less than the market price for medical services. Because of the law of demand and upward sloping supply curves, at these administered prices (zero in the case of Medicaid, Medicare and Canada), the quantity of medical services demanded exceeds the quantity supplied. Inevitably, therefore, nonprice rationing must be used to allocate the excess demand. This sometimes takes the form of insurance companies rejecting treatment recommended by doctors. HMOs often place restrictions on the amount of tests and referrals their doctors can prescribe. Plans differ, but they all must ration services by some device other than price, which is held below the market price. In Canada, referrals to specialists are reported to take much longer than in the United States. According to a study by the Fraser Institute in British Columbia in 1992, patients waited on average fifteen to twenty weeks for a referral to an orthopedist (bone and joint problems), ten to twenty-five weeks for a visit to a cardiologist (heart problems), and similar waits for other specialists. Access to heart bypass surgery is considerably greater in the U.S. than in Canada, and many Canadians travel to the U.S. at their own expense to get treatment for some of these ailments. The Wall Street Journal reports the case of a Vancouver B.C. man traveling to India (!) for a hip transplant rather than waiting a year or more for free treatment in Canada.[13] (At the same time, many Americans are now traveling to Canada to purchase prescription drugs at lower Canadian prices.)

The rising cost of medical services is perennially debated in Congress and in our presidential elections. Much of the political debate is the search for the elusive free lunch. It is clear from our elementary supply and demand analysis that the choice is between price and nonprice rationing; if price is held down

13. Wall Street Journal, April 26, 2004, Page 1, col. 1.

below the market price, someone other than the consumer will be making decisions on how much care consumer can have.

Surpluses

When the government sets a price below what the market would set, the quantity demanded by consumers exceeds the quantity supplied, producing a shortage of that good. There are many important instances, particularly in agriculture, where the government maintains a price *above* the free market level. In this case, the quantity demanded is less than the quantity supplied. This situation is referred to as a **surplus**, and is depicted in Fig. 5-20. The government could simply mandate that no product be sold below the controlled price; most typically, however, the government maintains that price by agreeing to purchase any amount of the good offered at that price.[14]

Assume that with a free market, 100 units of some good, say, wheat will be sold at a price of $3 per bushel. This is where consumers' marginal evaluations of wheat just equals the cost of providing an additional unit. At this level of production, the gains from trade, measured by the area between the demand and supply curves from the vertical axis to point *E*, are as large as possible. Suppose now the government imposes a price *floor* of $4 on wheat. That is, the government agrees to purchase any unsold wheat at $4 per bushel. With the price floor in effect, farmers will find it profitable to produce 120 units, where their marginal costs of production equal the government price. Also, since consumers face the higher price, their consumption is only 80 units. The difference between

Figure 5-20 *Surpluses*

With price floors, the quantity supplied exceeds the quantity demanded. With an imposed minimum price of $4 instead of the free market price of $3, producers produce 120 units instead of 100, and consumers cut back consumption to 80 units. The government has to purchase the surplus of 40 units produced but not consumed.

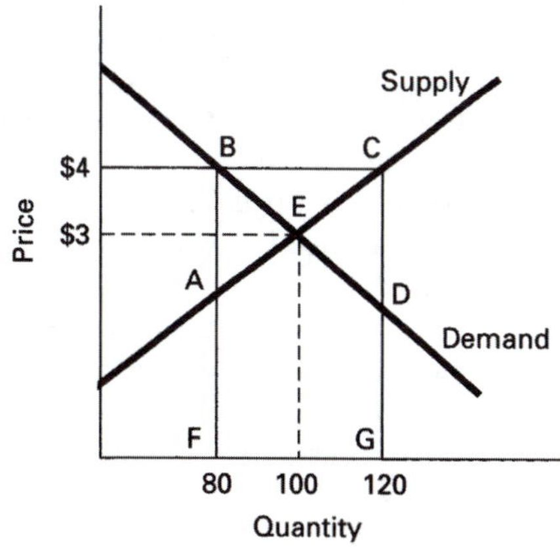

14. Without the guarantee of government purchases, the arrangement would quickly break down. Competition between sellers trying to unload their goods would produce schemes such as those encountered in private retail price maintenance. When stereo equipment, for example, was "fair-traded," meaning retailers could not sell the item below the retail price fixed by the manufacturer, it was common for retailers to "sell" phonograph cartridges for a dollar, or to sell package deals including other, non fair-traded goods, for example speakers (which were then heavily discounted), so as to produce the competitive price for the entire package.

the quantity demanded and the quantity supplied, 120 – 80 = 40, is a surplus. This excess supply perists over time as long as the government maintains the price floor.

Price floors such as in agriculture and depicted in Fig. 5-20 lead to two separate inefficiencies in production. In the first place, the same deadweight loss associated with price controls occurs because consumers wind up consuming too little of the good. In this case, this comes about not because suppliers are induced to produce too little, but because consumers are induced to purchase less than the efficient level of 100 units because the price is maintained above the market clearing price of $3. The scientific meaning of too little, once again, is that mutual benefits are available if consumers' marginal value of a good exceeds the sellers' marginal cost of providing the good. With the price support, consumers purchase only 80 units, even though producers would be happy to supply additional units at a mutually agreeable price. The area *ABE* of mutual benefits is lost because trade does not take place out to the efficient level, 100 units.

In addition to these deadweight losses which occur because consumers value the good at more than what they would value the next best alternative production, a certain amount of the good is being produced and not consumed at all. Recall that the opportunity cost of providing a good is measured by the area under the supply curve. In the case of a price floor such as depicted here, the area *FACG* represents the cost of producing 120 units of wheat instead of 80 units. This amount of resources is used by farmers to produce wheat which is going into government silos for storage, rather than for consumption. If the wheat in these silos is never consumed, perhaps because of spoilage, it is like spending resources that have alternative uses to hire farmers to dig holes in the ground and then fill them up again. Thus the area *FACG* represents additional costs to consumers of these types of programs. The total cost to consumers of farm price supports is the sum of the two areas just described. This total cost is thus *FBECG.*

One of the more curious price support programs is the one for dairy products. Using procedures known mainly to themselves, a committee first decides what the price of fresh milk should be in Eau Claire, Wisconsin. Then, the prices of fresh milk elsewhere in the country are determined by adding to that price the amount it would cost to ship milk from Eau Claire to that location. This rule applies even if no milk is actually shipped. Thus the price of milk in Miami, Florida is the Eau Claire price plus the shipping cost to Miami. It turns out that cows do not give very much milk in hot climates. Absent the price supports, milk would be shipped to the southern states from areas more suitable for dairy production. The price supports induce farmers to use relatively less efficient resources, e.g., land in hot climates to produce milk, instead of producing goods that consumers would find more valuable. In 1993, approximately twice as much milk was produced as consumed because of the price supports. These farm price supports are slowly being phased out under recent legislation, but their total elimination is still a long way off.

With the price support programs, the government purchases the excess production that is not consumed, and pays the farmers the support price of $4. The total expenditure on the farm price support programs is the area *FBCG,* $4 × 40 units, for each supported commodity. This is a cost to taxpayers in addition to the lost mutual benefits and wasted resources described previously. In the case of goods such as wheat, which is storable, the government simply stores the wheat. Eventually, they look for ways of disposing of these surpluses. In times past the

United States gave wheat away in foreign aid programs, but this had the effect of reducing the incentives for those countries to develop their own agriculture. More recently, the U.S. and European governments have been paying farmers to take farmland out production to reduce the surpluses. This reduces the wasted resources since the labor and other non-land resources that would have been used for producing goods for storage are now freed up for their next best alternative. However, it means that land which could be used to produce useful goods (e.g., food) lies fallow instead. In the case of milk, which is not storable, the government, (at taxpayer expense, of course) converts the fresh milk to powdered milk and cheese. These items are sometimes given away to the poor. If they were dumped on the market, it would lower the price and discombobulate the very groups the supports were intended to benefit.

As a result of these farm price support programs, each year in the United States, tremendous quantities of agricultural goods are produced and stored in government silos and warehouses. In 1999, for example, the total federal expenditure on all such agricultural price supports was $17.6 billion. Although many people ascribe these surpluses to the productive efficiency of American agriculture, Fig. 5-20 makes clear that surpluses occur only because the price is maintained above the market clearing price. The *size* of the surplus might have something to do with productivity in agriculture, but surpluses can and do occur with any good whatsoever, when the price is maintained above the market price. In fact, in 2002, Congress doubled the amount of farm subsidies due to price supports.

CHAPTER SUMMARY

- The response consumers make to a change in the price of some good is called a *change in the quantity demanded.* Similarly, the response of sellers to a change in the price they receive is called a *change in the quantity supplied.* A *change in demand* or a *change in supply* means that the entire demand or supply curve *shifts,* in response to a change in something *other* than the price of the good in question.

- If the price of some good, say, coffee increases, consumers choose less of that good; they reduce the quantity demanded. The demand curve for *substitute goods,* that is, goods that are used in place of coffee, such as tea, shifts out, or up, in response, because at the same price of tea, a greater amount is demanded. The demand curve for *complementary goods,* those used with coffee, such as cream and sugar, shifts *in* or to the left in response, since with less coffee consumed, the amount of cream demanded is less at the same price of cream.

- The income elasticity of a good is the percentage change in consumption caused per percentage change in income. For normal, or noninferior goods, this elasticity is positive. Similarly, the cross-elasticity of demand for one good with respect to a change in the price of another good is the percent change in consumption per percent change in the price of the other good. Cross elasticities are positive for substitute goods and negative for complements.

- If some good experiences a decrease in supply, the market price of that good will increase. The demand for substitutes will increase, increasing the market price in those markets. Likewise, the demand for complements will decrease, causing lower market prices for those goods.
- If a sales tax is imposed on some good, the market price will in general increase by less than the full amount of the tax. The flatter the slope of the supply curve relative to the demand curve, the more will be passed on to consumers. If the supply curve is vertical, the entire tax is paid by the sellers.
- Lowering middleman costs increases the mutually advantageous trade that can occur. With lower transactions costs, the sellers receive a higher price, and consumers pay a lower price.
- A shortage is a permanent excess of quantity demanded over the quantity supplied. It occurs only when the government imposes a price ceiling below the existing market price. Consumers then compete for the good via non-price competition such as waiting in line, or possibly violence.
- A surplus is a permanent excess of the quantity supplied over the quantity demanded. This occurs when the government imposes a price floor on some good, usually agricultural goods.

REVIEW QUESTIONS

1. What is the difference between a change in demand and a change in the quantity demanded? Which is it when we buy more gasoline because it has gotten cheaper? Which is it when Americans buy more SUVs because the price of gasoline has decreased?
2. What is income elasticity? Can it be a negative number?
3. If the middleman's cost decreases, what happens to the price the buyer pays and the price the seller receives?
4. Why can't sellers simply pass on any sales tax the government levies on them?
5. Why is there a housing shortage in New York city but not in Chicago?
6. "America has tremendous agricultural surpluses. That's why America exports so much grains and produce to the rest of the world." Do you agree?

PROBLEMS

1. "A decrease in supply will lead to an increase in the price, which will decrease demand, thus lowering price. Thus, a decrease in supply will have little effect on the price of a good." Do you agree? What confusion is present here?
2. How is it that the quantity demanded of some good can change even though there has been no change in demand? Can the quantity supplied change even though there has been no change in supply?

3. If some good x is a substitute for good y and good y is a substitute for good z, what relation do you suppose x has to z ? Answer the same question assuming x and y are complements, and give examples of goods that might fit these descriptions.

4. Why is it that *all* goods presently consumed by a consumer must initially be *normal,* i.e., noninferior in consumption? That is, why is it that goods can be inferior *only at the margin?*

5. Are CD players and tape decks complements or substitutes? What about TVs and VCRs, hot dogs and beans?

6. Suppose the government engages in a large scale transfer of income from the rich to the poor. What effect would this have on the prices and quantities sold of such items as porterhouse steaks, peanut butter, video games, small and large screen TVs? What economic characteristic of these goods determines whether the demand increases or decreases?

7. "Luxury" goods are sometimes defined as goods which are highly *income elastic,* i.e., the income elasticity exceeds unity. What does this mean for consumption, and do you think this is a good definition of luxury items?

8. What do you suppose is the effect of an increase in income on the demand for hamburgers? Explain why you feel the demand curve shifts, if at all.

9. Various studies of urban mass transit indicate that this service is an inferior good for most consumers. How does this affect plans to overcome congestion through use of mass transit? Is the problem hopeless?

10. When the stock market falls, analysts invariably report a "wave of selling." Yet all the stocks that are sold are purchased by someone else. Why don't they report a "wave of buying?" What is really going on?

11. In recent years women have participated in the labor force in much higher numbers than in previous generations. Moreover, when married, they typically work in locations different from their husbands. What is the effect of this on highway congestion?

12. Consider the market for coffee beans. For each of the following cases, give an example of some real world events that would lead to that outcome, and explain your reasoning:

    a. the quantity of coffee demanded decreases
    b. the demand for coffee decreases
    c. the quantity of coffee demanded decreases and the price of coffee increases
    d. the price of coffee increases with no change in the quantity of coffee sold
    e. the quantity of coffee supplied decreases

13. In recent years, there have been demonstrations (both for and against) the U.S. Supreme Court ruling *Roe v. Wade,* which for all intents and purposes legalized abortions in the United States. Prior to that ruling, abortions were illegal in most states, and doctors performing them could and did lose their licenses to practice medicine. Using appropriate supply and demand diagrams,

    a. What effect did this ruling have on the quantity of abortions performed and their price?

b. Suppose some one was to criticize your answer to part a., saying that it was really the other curve that shifted, or that you shifted the curve the wrong way, or that nothing changed at all. What *empirical* data would you look to in order to defend your conclusions and reject your critic's claims?
c. All licensed doctors can perform abortions. What effect did *Roe v. Wade* have on the quantity and price of other medical services doctors perform?

The abortion ruling also had an impact on another market, infant adoptions. Adoption is sort of a sale, in that a biological mother supplies a valuable item to people (the adoptive parents) who have a demand for that item. However, the transaction is much more complicated than an ordinary sale of a good. For example, the biological mother is not allowed to be paid for the child, except for pre-natal care and other costs of the pregnancy. In the famous case of "Baby M," the biological mother changed her mind some time after she had relinquished the child. The law (or lack of it) was unclear as to who had rights to the child.

d. What effect did *Roe v. Wade* have on the market for adoptions?
e. Suppose the laws regarding adoptions were made much clearer, e.g., they became uniform across states, adoptions became permanent upon transfer of the child, payments to the mother were allowed, etc. What effect would this have on the amount of adoptions, the price received by the biological mother and the amount paid by the adoptive parents?

14. Many people are concerned with the problem of consumption of alcoholic beverages by teenagers.

    a. What do you think of the legal minimum drinking age of 21? Apart from your own views of its merits or demerits, what effect do you think it has on drinking by underage individuals?
    b. Suppose the legal minimum age was eliminated (as is the case in much of Europe). What effect would this have on the market for alcoholic beverages?
    c. Explain the effects on the market for alcoholic beverages of the following policies:

        i. raising the price (through taxation) of alcoholic beverages
        ii. raising the minimum drinking age
        iii. increasing the penalties for underage drinking
        iv. restricting sales of alcoholic beverages to certain times, e.g., no late night sales.

15. "When a firm pays fringe benefits to its employees over and above the actual take-home pay, employees' incomes are effectively increased by the full amount of those benefits." Do you agree? What determines the extent to which these benefits come out of the employer's pockets, as opposed to the employee's?

16. Many states do not levy a sales tax on *professional services,* e.g., the services of lawyers, doctors, accountants and the like. If you visit one of these professionals, they do not add a sales tax to their fee for services.

    a. Draw a supply and demand diagram that reasonably represents the market for, say, lawyers' services *in the short-run,* and explain why you have drawn the curves as you have. Pay particular attention to the slopes of the demand and supply curves, in particular, whether they appear flat or steep, and justify why you have drawn them as you have.

b. If a sales tax is levied on these services, who will pay most of the tax *in the short run*—clients or the lawyers?

c. How does the market for lawyers' services and the shares of tax paid by the lawyers versus their clients respond *in the long run* to this imposition of taxes?

17. With the recent crisis in the Persian Gulf, there have been renewed calls to develop cars using alternative (non-petroleum) fuels, e.g., electric cars. Suppose a battery is developed making electric cars competitive with those powered with gasoline.

a. Using separate supply and demand diagrams, analyze the effects of this development on the prices charged and the quantities sold of:
   i. petroleum
   ii. other fuels, e.g., coal

Do *not* assume that the electricity used to charge the batteries will be "free."

b. Suppose, to further reduce American imports of Persian Gulf oil, environmental laws regarding the burning of coal are relaxed. Analyze the effects of this on the prices charged and the quantities sold of petroleum and coal.

18. Consider that social security taxes have been raised substantially in recent years. One half of this tax on labor is paid by the employers directly, and the other half is withheld from employees' paychecks. Does this mean that the employer and the employee in fact each share half the burden of the tax? What would determine their respective shares, and would it be the same for all workers, e.g., farm workers, skilled mechanics?

19. How is it possible to have a surplus of scarce goods. Isn't that a contradiction?

20. Currently, price supports are in effect for wheat and other agricultural goods, which effectively raise the prices of these goods above what they would be in the absence of these price floors. Suppose these price supports were eliminated. What effect would this have on the prices and quantities of these goods produced, rents on agricultural land, and the wages of farm workers?

21. The United States government maintains price supports on many agricultural goods, including wheat and corn. The resulting prices are higher than what would prevail in a free market.

a. Explain clearly why we have surpluses in these goods.

b. Suppose the price supports for corn were eliminated, but maintained for wheat. What would happen to the prices of these goods, the quantities consumed by consumers of each good, and the size of the wheat surplus?

22. In late 1990 and early 1991, after the Iraqi invasion of Kuwait, the price of petroleum increased on world markets, as traders anticipated possible supply interruptions. Noticeably absent during that crisis were waiting lines for gasoline and other petroleum products, unlike the experience of 1973–'74. The whole price episode in 1990 is now largely forgotten, whereas the earlier

episode lives on in people's memories and in new bureaucracies. What accounts for these different outcomes?

23. Many areas of the country, but particularly New York City have rent controls, i.e., legal maximums (below what would otherwise prevail) on the amount of rent that can be collected on rental housing. Vacancy rates there for apartments are very low, with very long waiting lists of eager prospective tenants. These characteristics seem largely absent in, say, Seattle.

    a. What explains the above phenomena? Is housing somehow more scarce in New York than, say, in Chicago or Seattle?
    b. What effect do rent controls have on the frequency of discrimination by landlords on the basis of such things as race, sexual preference etc.?
    c. Consider a locale such as Seattle, with many single-family houses, some of which are rented, and some of which are owner-occupied, and where houses can easily be converted from one form of contract to another. Suppose rent controls are imposed in Seattle. Explain the likely effects, if possible, on the price of rental housing, owner-occupied housing, and the amount of each type available on the market.

24. Because of the effects of *El Nino*—warming of the Pacific Ocean off the coast of South America—the winter of 1991–'92 in the Pacific Northwest was extremely mild, and the mountain snow pack from which cities such as Seattle get their water was virtually gone by the summer of 1992. In response to this, the City of Seattle announced emergency restrictions in water usage to avoid a water shortage the following summer. Consumers were asked to voluntarily restrict water use, and were forbidden to water lawns, wash cars and use sprinkler systems for shrubs.

    a. Is a water shortage a necessary consequence of reduced water supply? In the technical sense of the word, what caused the shortage? Explain your terms and definitions precisely.
    b. Suppose water was supplied to this area by many private water suppliers. What effect would *El Nino* have had on the market for water, and, in particular, would the above government actions have been required?
    c. Using a suitable supply and demand diagram, explain the effect of *El Nino* on the market for garden plants in 1992, under either of the above scenarios of water supply.

25. The wage for unskilled labor is presently about \$5 per hour. Suppose a law is passed raising the legal minimum wage to \$6 per hour. Treating labor as a commodity traded in the economy at some price (wage), determined by the supply and demand for various types of labor, answer the following:

    a. Price floors create surpluses. What do we call the surplus created in this market?
    b. What types of workers are likely to be most affected by this law, e.g., teenagers, skilled craftspersons, handicapped workers, etc.?
    c. Consider that unionized workers generally earn much more than the minimum wage (skilled construction workers earn approximately \$20.00 per hour, on average). Unions, however, have always strongly advocated increases in the minimum wage. What self-interest might the unions have in this regard?

26. In late 1973, the legal maximum retail price of gasoline was about $.40 (somewhat higher than where it is at this writing, relative to other prices). Drivers lined up for two hours to purchase gasoline, although the wait varied according to the capricious distribution of the fuel. What does a two hour wait signify with regard to what the price would have been without the price controls?

[*Hint:* The value of one's time, as an approximation, at least, is the income foregone during the wait. It is the amount one could have earned in that time interval. Consider that the wage paid by fast food outlets was about $1.50 per hour, and the average wage in the economy then was about $4.00 per hour. Assume a fill-up is 10 gallons. How long would a person earning these amounts be willing to wait in line, and what does this imply about the size of the transfer consumers gain?]

QUESTIONS FOR DISCUSSION

1. How do you feel about rent controls? They might, for example, provide you with lower rents while you are a student with not very much money. Do you think this is good public policy?
2. Agricultural price supports were first enacted to help poor farmers survive the vagaries of the market. Do you think this is a worthy goal? Should we similarly support other business people, for example, dry cleaners, car dealerships, bread makers? How has the composition of farmers changed since the 1930s, when this legislation was passed?
3. Current adoption law in every state forbids the use of direct monetary payments to a women as payment for giving up her child for adoption. Do you think this is good policy? Should prospective adoptive parents be allowed to pay for prenatal care for the mother?

CHAPTER 6

Cost and Production

The North American Free Trade Act (NAFTA) continues to be in the news. This legislation reduces restrictions on trade between the United States, Mexico and Canada. Similarly, Congress is debating whether to lower trade barriers with China. Legislators from some districts argue that these measures make Americans worse off by causing jobs to flee south to lower wage countries. Consumers, however, seem to choose many of these goods over domestically produced goods. Would we be better off if we restricted American presence in the global economy? Read on.

6.1 The Gains from Specialization

We now begin our more detailed discussion of the concepts of cost and production. We take a more detailed look at the supply curve and the factors that determine it. The first topics we investigate are the reasons why specialization of resources occurs, and what its effects on supply are. This theory, known as comparative advantage, is one of the most important concepts economists have developed. It helps us to understand many important issues of trade. It is the foundation of modern international trade theory, but its application is not limited to cross border issues only. We study it here as in the context of its effects on marginal cost and supply. In the next chapter, we study the famous (but famously misquoted) "law of diminishing returns" and the effects of that law on production and supply.

One of the outstanding features of the economy of the United States is the very high degree of **specialization of resources**. The United States Labor Department's *Dictionary of Occupational Titles* lists thousands of separate job classifications, and many subclassifications beyond those. No one planned this degree of specialization. It occurred apparently because of mutual self-interest of the individuals in the economy. In colleges and universities, there are separate academic departments, e.g., economics, mathematics, history, etc. It seems that scholars have found it useful to specialize in only one discipline, rather than to attempt to be a renaissance man, who knows something about many fields. In industry as well, people specialize in one occupation, in fact, one narrow part of one occupation, rather than attempting to be a jack of all trades. Computer programmers typically know little or nothing about the actual construction of the integrated circuits they program; the engineers and scientists who develop the techniques for constructing the actual chips used by programmers probably have only a scant knowledge of the software languages that are used with their hardware. Examples of specialized individuals and machines are easy to come by; what is difficult is to find examples of nonspecialized resources in modern economies. What accounts for this, that is, what are the sources of benefits for specialized production, and why do we see specialization increase as economies develop?

One of the first discussions of specialization appeared in 1776, in *The Wealth of Nations,* by Adam Smith. His reasoning is so lucid, we quote it at length.

> To take an example, . . . the trade of the pin maker; a worker not educated to this business, . . . could scarce, perhaps with his utmost industry, make one pin in a day, and certainly could not make twenty. But in the way in which this business is now carried on, not only the whole work is a peculiar trade, but it is divided into a number of branches, of

> which the greater part are likewise peculiar trades. One man draws out the wire, another straightens it, a third cuts it, a fourth points it, a fifth grinds it at the top for receiving the head; to make the head requires two or three distinct operations; to put it on is a peculiar business, to whiten the pins is another; it is even a trade by itself to put them into the paper; and the important business of making a pin is, in this manner, divided into about eighteen distinct operations. . . . I have seen a small manufactory of this kind where ten men only were employed, and where some of them consequently performed two or three distinct operations. But though they were very poor, and therefore but indifferently accommodated with the necessary machinery, they could, when they exerted themselves, make among them . . . upward of forty-eight thousand pins in a day. . . .
>
> This great increase of the quantity work which, in consequence of the division of labor, the same number of people are capable of performing is owing to three circumstances; first, to the increase of dexterity in every particular workman; secondly, to the saving of the time which is commonly lost in passing from one species of work to another; and lastly, to the invention of a great number of machines which facilitate and abridge labor and enable one man to do the work of many.
>
> First, the improvement of the dexterity of the workman necessarily increases the quantity of work he can perform; and the division of labor, by reducing every man's business to some one simple operation, and by making this operation the sole employment of his life, necessarily increases very much the dexterity of the workman. . . . Secondly, the advantage which is gained by saving the time which is commonly lost in passing from one sort of work to another is much greater than we should imagine it. It is impossible to pass very quickly from one kind of work to another that is carried on in a different place and with quite different tools. . . . A man commonly saunters a little in turning his hand from one sort of employment to another. When he first begins the new work, he is seldom keen and hearty. . . . Thirdly, and lastly, everybody must be sensible how much labor is facilitated and abridged by the application of proper machinery. . . . [T]he invention of all those machines by which labor is facilitated and abridged seems to have been originally owing to the division of labor. Men are much more likely to discover easier and readier methods of attaining any object when the whole attention of their minds is directed towards that single object than when it is dissipated among a great variety of things. But, in consequence of the division of labor, the whole of every man's attention comes naturally to be directed towards one simple object. . . .

It is no accident that university professors specialize in only one field. Becoming competent in even one small aspect of one of the traditional disciplines is a monumental task for most people.[1] Most microeconomists admit to only scant knowledge about what their colleagues in macroeconomics study, and

1. A tourist in midtown Manhattan encountered a street musician and asked, "Can you tell me how to get to Carnegie Hall?" *"Practice, practice,"* the musician emphasized.

vice versa. Historians of 20th century America usually politely refrain from answering questions about European history, to say nothing of ancient history; the examples go on and on. The traditional academic disciplines did not arise through some random process. People found that certain frameworks, or theories were useful for solving some particular problem. As people concentrated on those problems, certain puzzles were solved and others were discarded as not amenable to the present framework. In economics, for example, the study of the development of individual tastes has been largely abandoned. The tools that emerge from taking tastes as given and analyzing how people then respond to changes in constraints has been found to be very fruitful in a wide variety of problems, but it has not been found to be useful in analyzing how tastes emerge in the first place. Economists therefore leave that study to others, perhaps psychologists or sociologists. As individual scholars have concentrated on narrower and narrower problems, they developed specialized analytical tools that could not have been even conceived of by generalists.[2]

The modern study of statistics began in the biological sciences as researchers grappled with assessing the significance of their results.[3] As this tool became more sophisticated, it developed into its own field. The biologists who first posed the problems and perhaps made initial attempts at solutions had to choose whether to pursue mainly biology or mainly statistics, for to do both successfully is beyond the capabilities of the human mind. In all of modern commerce as well, people who attempt to be generalists are inevitably surpassed by those who specialize in only a narrow set of problems. Top managers cannot micro-manage individual departments, production workers have different skills than the sales force, and so on. Learning the details of the production process for computers will not likely make one a better computer salesperson. Learning the details of photo-engraving circuits will likely cost a salesperson money by distracting them from what they really need to know.

6.2 Comparative Advantage

We now turn to the analysis of production and its relation to cost, by considering the simplest economy imaginable: a one-person economy, such as faced by Daniel Defoe's character, Robinson Crusoe. Crusoe becomes stranded on a Caribbean island and must produce in order to survive. For some time, Crusoe lives alone; he can eat only what he produces. In time, another person, Friday comes to the island; at this point, the possibility of trade emerges. We investigate these separate issues of production and exchange in turn. By examining these fundamental problems in their simplest form, we can gain a clearer understanding of how a modern economy copes with these same issues.

2. Moral: It is generally wise to take courses from those who specialize in the subject taught. Take your microeconomics from microeconomists, your macro from macroeconomists, take history from historians, sociology from sociologists, and beware of those who claim to have gained competence in more than one field.

3. Modern statistical analysis began with questions such as the following. If 10 sick rats are given some medicine, and another 10 are not, and 5 of the medicated rats recover compared with 3 who received no medicine, is the medicine working, or is the favorable result just a chance occurrence?

The Robinson Crusoe Economy

Crusoe's economy is the simplest of all economies. It consists of one producer, Crusoe, who is also the sole consumer. Although vastly removed in scope from a modern industrial society, Crusoe's island economy illuminates some of the fundamental choices with which all societies must cope. Crusoe must decide *what* he can produce, and then *how much* of those goods he actually will produce. He must also decide whether to produce goods only for his current consumption or whether to divert part of his efforts into producing tools which will make him more productive in the future. By decreasing his consumption in the present in order to build capital goods—tools and machines to help him improve his efficiency at various tasks—he might be able to enjoy greater consumption in the future. This fundamental investment problem, a key feature of modern economies, is present even in Crusoe's isolated world. We deal with this investment and capital issue in Chap. 10.

Crusoe does not face, in his one-person economy, any issues having to do with exchange. There are no transaction costs because there is no one with whom to transact. When Friday arrives, Crusoe's island economy suddenly takes on new problems and opportunities. Crusoe and Friday must decide if cooperative effort might lead to mutual gain. In addition to the preceding *what* and *how much* problems, the distribution problem, *for whom and by whom*—the allocation of effort and total output of Crusoe and Friday—will be present, as it is in all modern economies.

For simplicity's sake, we initially restrict Crusoe's production to exactly two activities: gathering coconuts and fishing. Assume he has found some natural shelter on the island for which no expenditure of time and effort is required. In any one day Crusoe can either catch three fish or gather three coconuts; this is the maximum of each good he can produce. We assume also that Crusoe can divide his time between fishing and gathering coconuts, gathering, say one coconut and catching two fish. We represent his daily production on a graph (Fig. 6-1) with fish on the vertical axis and coconuts on the horizontal axis:

The various points on the graph show the combinations of fish and coconuts that Crusoe might produce in a day. He might decide to gather only coconuts—in a single day he will collect three (point *D*)—or he might spend the whole day fishing and end up with three fish and no coconuts (*A*). Alternatively, he might gather a single coconut and catch two fish (*B*) or gather two coconuts and catch only one fish (*C*). The extreme upper left-hand point, *A,* represents the maximum output of fish Crusoe can produce in a day, while the lower right-hand point, *D,* represents his maximum daily output of coconuts. Assume also that Crusoe could gather 1½ coconuts and 1½ fish (*E*), 2½ fish and ½ coconut, or any other combination lying along the straight line connecting these points. He could do this, for example, by producing at *C,* 2 coconuts and 1 fish one day, and at *B,* 1 coconut and 2 fish the next day, averaging 1½ of each item per day, point *E.* More realistically, if Crusoe were to shift tasks during the day, he would likely lose time getting from, say, the coconut trees to the shore for fishing, and he would likely have to spend some time closing down one job and setting up for the other. For these types of reasons, his production frontier might actually be bowed in, or convex to the origin. That is, with these costs of changing tasks, he would likely be able to produce somewhat less of both coconuts and fish than what is indicated by points *B* and *C* in Fig. 6-1. For simplicity, however, we disregard these economies of scale at this juncture.

The line in Fig. 6-1 connecting all the various combinations of coconuts and fish which Crusoe can gather in a single day, that is, his locus of production possibilities, describes graphically Crusoe's **production possibilities frontier**. This line, or frontier indicates, for a given level of one good, the maximum amount of the other good Crusoe can produce. It is possible, of course, that Crusoe might instead decide to sleep until noon and laze about the lagoon, and thereby choose to gather only one coconut and catch just one fish per day. We ignore this labor-leisure choice at this juncture, even though it is an important aspect of production. For the moment, we assume that Crusoe works full time, that is, he chooses some point on his production frontier.

In this simple economy, Crusoe works steadily each day and eats what he produces. He has no use for money since there is no one with whom to trade. Because there are no irrelevant distractions such as money or other people, Crusoe observes directly the concept of opportunity cost. There is little room for delusion or hidden costs on this island. If Crusoe wants an additional coconut he will have to give up a fish in order to get it. To have an additional fish, Crusoe must give up a coconut. That is the price he must pay for the fish even though he isn't using money. The **marginal cost** of some good is what one must give up to achieve an additional unit of that good. Crusoe understands explicitly that the marginal (or incremental) cost of one coconut is one fish and that the marginal cost of one fish is one coconut. In Crusoe's economy, therefore, the price of a fish is one coconut and the price of a coconut is one fish.

The story is now almost complete with regard to Crusoe. It remains only to determine exactly what combination of fish and coconuts he actually decides to consume, that is, at what point along his production frontier he decides to produce. This decision ultimately depends on his preferences for fish and coconuts. We can probably rule out two points, however—the corners *A* and *D*. Because of diminishing marginal values, variety is the spice of life; Crusoe will wind up at some point on the interior of line *AD*. At point *A*, Crusoe would ask himself, "How many fish would I be *willing* to give up in order to get one coconut?" At this consumption point he's probably saturated with fish, so he probably would readily give up 2 fish in order to get 1 coconut. However, Crusoe knows he need give up only 1 fish to gain a coconut. This is a bargain: he doesn't have to give up as many fish as he would be willing to in order to acquire a coconut. When Cru-

Figure 6-1 *Crusoe's Production Possibilities Frontier*

Crusoe can produce either 3 fish or 3 coconuts per day or any mixture of outputs along the straight line joining the two endpoints. His marginal cost of coconuts is 1 fish, his marginal cost of fish is 1 coconut.

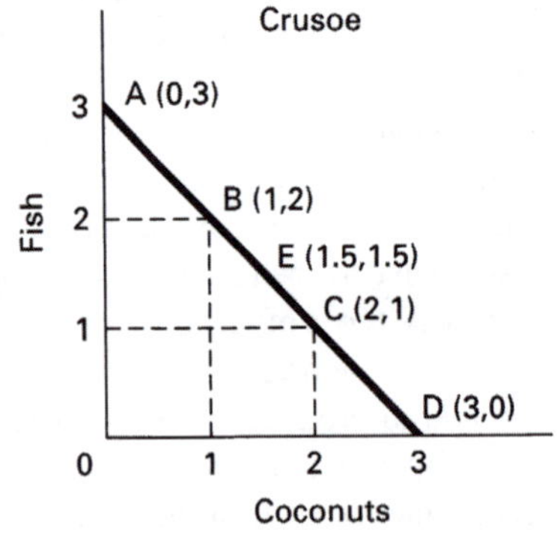

soe feels that he has more fish than he wants, he is saying that the marginal value of coconuts is greater than the marginal cost of coconuts, measured in terms of the only other good available, fish. We arbitrarily decide that Crusoe's most preferred consumption bundle is 2 coconuts and 1 fish, point *C* in Fig. 6-1. At this point, Crusoe's marginal value of coconuts equals his marginal cost of one fish; equivalently, his marginal value of fish equals his marginal cost of fish, one coconut.

Check your understanding: Suppose Crusoe could catch 6 fish, not 3, but still only gather 3 coconuts per day. What would be his marginal cost of fishing and coconut gathering?

The Arrival of Friday

We move now to the next stage in the analysis—the workings of a two-person economy. Crusoe's rescue of Friday brings in an important new economic element—the possibility of *exchange.* This activity makes the economy much more interesting to study and, as we shall see, gives Crusoe and Friday a more productive environment in which to live. In Defoe's novel, the original Robinson Crusoe was quite afraid when he saw an alien footprint on the beach, thinking he had had a visitation from the devil. He soon found out that the presence of another human being afforded both of them greater opportunities than either could have separately.

Let us rewrite the novel and assume that Friday, like Crusoe, is also busy fishing and gathering coconuts. Suppose that Friday is more successful as a producer under these conditions than is Crusoe. In a day, Friday can gather either eight coconuts or four fish, or any combination of the two along the straight line joining those two extremes. The resulting production possibilities frontier for Friday is shown in Fig. 6-2. The diagram indicates that Friday, in one day, can gather 8 coconuts and 0 fish (point *E*), or catch 4 fish only (point *A*). Alternatively, he can spend time at each task and, for example, gather two coconuts and catch three fish (*B*), gather four coconuts and catch two fish (C), or gather six coconuts and catch one fish (*D*). Because of diminishing marginal values, Friday, like Crusoe, will probably not choose points *A* or *E.* As with Crusoe, we

Figure 6-2 *Friday's Production Possibilities Frontier*

Friday can produce either 4 fish or 8 coconuts per day, or any mixture of outputs along the straight line joining the two endpoints. His marginal cost of coconuts is ½ fish, his marginal cost of fish is 2 coconuts.

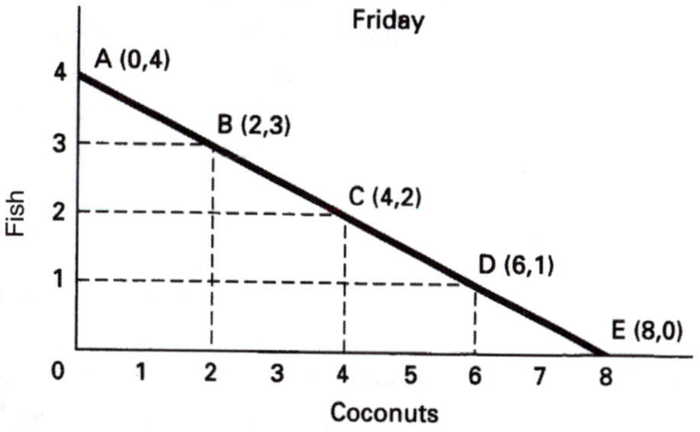

allow Friday to produce food at any point along this production possibilities line, such as 5 coconuts and 1½ fish, 3½ fish and 1 coconut, etc. The exact combination of coconuts and fish Friday chooses along this frontier depends on his preferences, just as in the case of Crusoe. We arbitrarily assume that Friday, acting alone, chooses to consume 4 coconuts and 2 fish, i.e., at point *C* along his production frontier.

Crusoe's and Friday's production frontiers differ in two important respects. First, in an absolute sense, Friday is the more productive worker. He can produce more of either coconuts or fish than can Crusoe. Crusoe's production frontier would fit entirely within Friday's. This means that acting on his own, Friday can enjoy a higher standard of living than Crusoe. Friday has greater opportunities for consumption because he is able to produce more in a given day. However, a second difference in these production frontiers is even more significant. These individuals differ in what they have to give up of one good in order to acquire an additional unit of the other good. Friday's marginal costs of producing coconuts and fish are different from Crusoe's.

Recall that Crusoe must give up one fish to acquire an additional coconut. This is determined by the slope of his production frontier. Notice, however, in Fig. 6-2, that if Friday gives up one fish, he can consume two additional coconuts. Or, allowing fractional units, to acquire an additional coconut, Friday must give up only ½ fish. Thus Friday's marginal cost of coconuts is only ½ fish, in contrast with Crusoe's marginal cost of coconuts, which is 1 fish. Friday can produce coconuts at one-half the cost (in terms of fish forgone) than Crusoe.

However, just because he is, overall, a more productive worker, it is not the case that Friday has lower marginal costs of producing coconuts. Crusoe must give up 1 coconut in order to gain an additional fish; his marginal cost of fish is 1 coconut. If we move up and to the left on Friday's production frontier, however, say from *D* to *C*, we notice that to gain an additional fish, Friday must give up two coconuts. Friday's marginal cost of fish is 2 coconuts, twice Crusoe's marginal cost for the same good! Friday's and Crusoe's marginal costs of production are determined by the slopes of their respective production frontiers, not by the location of those frontiers. It is of no consequence for determining marginal costs that Friday is absolutely more productive than Crusoe. Moreover, the fact that their marginal costs of production differ will lead Crusoe and Friday to organize production in a fashion different from that which they pursued when they were isolated from each other. In particular, they will exploit, for their mutual benefit, their respective cost advantages in producing these goods.

It is an obvious observation that we gain anytime we can purchase a good at a lower price. Acting alone, Crusoe and Friday each face prices of coconuts and fish based on what it costs each of them to produce these goods. However, with two people present, they can also consider at what price the other person might be willing to trade each good. It costs Crusoe 1 fish to get a coconut; it only costs Friday ½ fish. Maybe Friday will be willing to trade (sell) coconuts to Crusoe for ½ fish each. In a similar fashion, Friday realizes it costs him 2 coconuts to get a fish, while it only costs Crusoe 1 coconut. Maybe Crusoe would be willing to sell fish to Friday at only 1 coconut each. Even though Friday has an absolute advantage over Crusoe, in terms of the total amount of each good he can produce, each person has a **comparative advantage** in one good. Crusoe is the low cost producer of fish (1 coconut, versus 2 for Friday), and Friday is the low cost producer of coconuts (½ fish, versus 1 for Crusoe). Most importantly, both Crusoe and Friday can benefit by producing the good they do relatively cheapest, and then exchanging that good for some of the other. It is simply a matter of cost reduction.

Fig. 6-3 displays the combined production possibilities frontier for the Crusoe-Friday joint economy. If Crusoe and Friday both spent all their time fishing, they would wind up, each day, with zero coconuts and 7 fish: 3 caught by Crusoe and 4 by Friday. This is point *A* on the vertical axis. Similarly, if they devote their whole day to gathering coconuts, they will harvest a total of 11 coconuts, 3 by Crusoe's efforts and 8 by Friday's, and have no fish. This is point *C* on the horizontal axis. If, on the other hand, Friday only gathers coconuts and harvests his 8 per day, and Crusoe catches his 3 fish per day, they realize production point *B* (8,3).

Recall Crusoe's and Friday's original consumption levels, when each worked alone. Crusoe consumed 2 coconuts and 1 fish; Friday consumed 4 coconuts and 2 fish. Their combined consumption would be 6 coconuts and 3 fish, which is point *D,* with coordinates (6,3) in Fig. 6-3. Point *D* is in the interior of the production possibilities set, indicating that it represents less than the maximum total income this society can produce. Consider what is available to Crusoe and Friday if they specialize in what they do relatively best, and then engage in trade. In that case point *B* is available, which yields, along with 3 fish, 8 coconuts rather than the 6 they get by acting alone. They can each have an extra coconut, if they agree to specialize in the good for which they have a comparative advantage. Alternatively, if Crusoe specializes in fishing, and Friday produces 6 coconuts and 1 fish, (point *D* in Fig. 6-2), then each day, total production will be 6 coconuts and 4 fish (point *B′* in Fig. 6-3), rather than 6 coconuts and 3 fish. They can then share the fish they have caught in addition to what they would have caught acting alone.

This elementary example illustrates a phenomenon of great importance to modern as well as simple economies. Specialization and trade allows both Crusoe and Friday to consume more goods than they could by producing separately. In this example, they can together consume either two extra coconuts or one extra fish (or a combination of the two). If they split these evenly, each increases his income by one coconut or ½ fish over what previously was the maximum they could produce. This occurs because each person engages in only that activity for which they are the low-cost producer. We say they are pursuing their

Figure 6-3 *Production Possibilities Frontier of the Crusoe-Friday Economy*

When Crusoe and Friday cooperate in production, each specializing in the task for which he has a comparative advantage, the production possibilities curve becomes bowed outward. This allows each to consume a greater amount of goods than either could when acting alone.

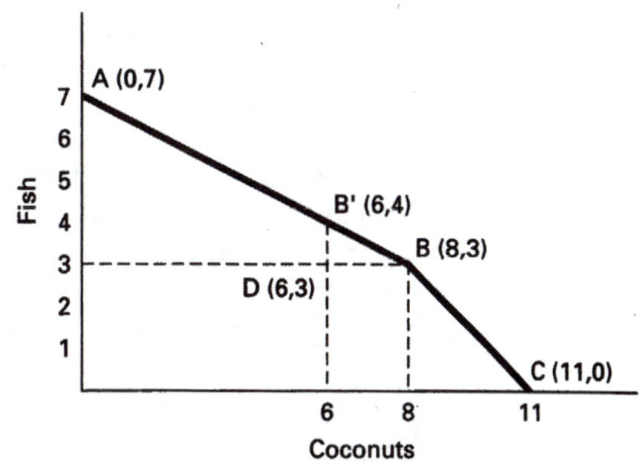

comparative advantage. It is common sense that individuals can gain by not producing something that someone else can produce cheaper; better to produce what you do best and purchase the other good from the low cost producer.

It is interesting and important that it is the differences in Friday's and Crusoe's talents that allow these mutual gains to occur. If Crusoe could clone himself he wouldn't be as well off as he is when working in partnership with Friday (and likewise for Friday). With clones, the comparative advantage one person has over another in one good is eliminated, and with it, the gains from specialization. Further, as Crusoe and Friday specialize, their talents at the task for which they are relatively most suited should improve. Because he is spending all of his time fishing, and directing all of his thoughts to that end rather than also worrying about how to efficiently spot and climb trees for coconuts, Crusoe's fishing skills will likely improve over time. His production frontier will likely expand beyond 3 fish, but possibly contract below 3 coconuts per day, as his skills in that endeavor become rusty. His production frontier will likely become steeper over time, increasing his comparative advantage in fishing and also his comparative disadvantage in coconut production. In the same fashion, Friday's comparative advantage in coconut production will likely increase over time as the benefits of specialization take hold. His production frontier will become relatively flatter over time. As Crusoe's and Friday's comparative advantages become even more pronounced, the benefits available to them from specialization and trade become even greater.

Check your understanding: Suppose Crusoe could catch 9 fish and gather 9 coconuts per day. How would his absolute and comparative advantages change relative to Friday, and would this make Friday more likely to produce fish?

The theory of comparative advantage outlined above was developed by a British economist, David Ricardo, around 1812.[4] Ricardo noticed that corn (in Britain, a generic word for all grains) was expensive in part because of the British Corn Laws of that time, which forbade the importation of grains from other countries, particularly America. Ricardo used this theory to advocate repeal of these laws; they remained on the books, however, until the 1840s.

In today's economy, the exploitation of comparative advantages through international trade remains a hot political issue. Beginning in the early 1980s, Japanese automobile companies made substantial inroads in the American car market, increasing their share of cars sold from around 15% to approximately 30%. Since that time, American politicians who represent districts in which domestic auto production takes place have advocated restrictions on these imports in order to preserve domestic jobs. Partly as a result of this political pressure, the major Japanese car companies built factories in the United States, so that many cars with a Japanese name, such as Honda and Toyota are in fact manufactured domestically. At this writing in early 2002, American steel manufacturers have convinced Congress to impose steep duties on foreign steel, particularly Russian steel, claiming that these manufacturers are selling steel for less in America than in their own countries (a practice called "dumping"). Japanese dominance in electronics and cameras is legendary. Though not an issue in

4. David Ricardo, *Works I The Works and Correspondence of David Ricardo,* edited by P. Sraffa and M. Dobb. Cambridge University Press, 1951–1955.

the United States, American exports of grains and other foodstuffs are similarly regarded by foreign competitors as a threat to be eliminated by law. The Japanese have long restricted the importing of American rice and beef, because of the political influence of Japanese producers of those goods.

In the United States, we often hear the cry, "Low-priced foreign labor is costing American jobs!" This is usually the basis for the opposition to NAFTA, the North American Free Trade Act, which lowered tariff barriers between the U.S., Canada and Mexico, on this basis. Meanwhile, labor in foreign countries fears "the productive American workers." But we know from the previous analysis that it is *comparative* advantage that produces trade, not differences in absolute wage levels. Here is a numerical example. Suppose American workers earn $10 per hour manufacturing office machines, whereas labor in China is paid $1.00 per hour in the manufacturing sector. How can Americans continue to be employed in this industry? How is it that the United States in fact exports office machines to China? The reason is the same as why Friday, the higher wage (more productive) worker nonetheless finds it in his interest to purchase fish from Crusoe in the preceding example. Even though Friday is more productive than Crusoe in an absolute sense, Friday is the relatively high cost producer of fish, so he finds it to his advantage to trade with Crusoe. The theory of comparative advantage says that it is the marginal cost of producing one good versus some alternative good that produces specialization and trade.

Suppose Chinese workers were to attempt to produce additional office machines. To do this, they would have to shift labor and other productive inputs away from other endeavors, say, the production of clothing. The cost of an additional office machine in China might very well be $1,000 of foregone clothing production. In that case, the marginal cost of domestically produced office machines in China would be $1,000 of clothing. It is probably the case, however, that the Chinese could purchase that same office machine from the United States at less than $1,000, because producing another office machine in the United States would entail a lower valued sacrifice of clothing, say, $500. Absolute wage levels in the United States are much higher than those prevailing in China, but the cost of producing an office machine *in terms of clothing foregone* is less in America than the corresponding alternative cost in China. Chinese labor and the machinery available to them are probably much more suited at the present time for production of clothing than for high-technology items. In that case, even though absolute wages are lower in China than in the United States, the United States still has a comparative advantage in many goods; trade with China is therefore mutually beneficial. Wages in most countries of the world (particularly less developed countries) are lower than wages in the United States, Canada and western Europe, yet these countries import substantial amounts of goods from the United States and other industrialized countries.[5] Low-wage workers do not necessarily take jobs from high-wage workers. If this were not true, there would be no high-wage workers, and one country could not enjoy a higher standard of living than others.

When nations reduce tariff and other barriers to international trade, trade expands. Recall the second theorem of trade in Chap. 4: more trade is not always preferred by all to less trade. With expanded trade with Mexico, for example,

5. The number of jobs alleged to have been "lost" to foreign competition probably exceeds the number of people who ever worked in some of those industries!

the American workers whose comparative advantages closely resemble the comparative advantages of Mexican workers often lose their jobs, as firms choose to use the lower cost labor in another part of the continent. This is why the legislators elected from districts where many of these workers are located typically have opposed NAFTA (the North American Free Trade Act) and other laws reducing international trade barriers. At the same time, however, the demand for workers whose comparative advantages are dissimilar to Mexican workers will increase. Thus expansion of trade leads to a contraction of the domestic industries whose workers most closely resemble the skills (or lack of skills) of foreign workers, while the domestic industries whose workers and capital are different from foreign workers or capital expand. The expansion of trade produces gainers and losers. We know from the above analysis that since total output necessarily expands, the gainers gain by more than the losers lose, so that it is theoretically possible for the gainers to compensate the losers and still have something left over for themselves. Such direct compensation of course never happens. What we do see, however, are laws enacted by Congress to grant extended unemployment benefits and subsidies for retraining to workers injured in this fashion. It is a way society resolves (imperfectly) the conflict of the benefits of expanded trade and the losses some workers incur as a result.

These principles apply to domestic as well as international trade. The reason we do not have similar political quarrels regarding interstate trade is that the commerce clause of the United States Constitution prohibits states from interfering with the movement of either people or goods over state lines (similar prohibitions apply in Canada as well). As improved transportation stimulated trade with farms in California, the wages of some farm workers in other states surely decreased. Consumers as a group have benefited from the expansion of the production possibilities frontier of the economy, but it is not the case that all workers have gained from the expansion of trade. The long-term growth of the standard of living in the Unites States and Canada is testimony, however, to the benefits of increased specialization and trade.

Check your understanding: Many workers in places like Bangladesh earn about 10¢ per hour. Why don't American firms employ these workers for essentially everything that can be exported to the U.S.?

6.3 Increasing Costs at the Extensive Margin

We now generalize the preceding discussion and consider the specialization in a large modern economy. In this case we have many resources—numerous people with differing skills and training, and capital equipment of various kinds, including land and natural resources such as oil, natural gas, forests. We can imagine each resource producing its own production frontier of the types displayed in Figs. 6-1 and 6-2, with many different slopes. These slopes indicate different degrees of comparative advantage (or disadvantage) in each good. With many individuals in command of their own personal resources, or, more generally, who have command over other resources in the economy such as machines (capital) and land, the production possibilities frontier will consist of many more than the two segments *AB* and *BC* in Fig. 6-3. It will instead appear as the approximately smooth bowed out curve depicted in Fig. 6-4. The shape of this frontier, concave to the origin, represents a fundamental observation about costs and production—rising marginal costs.

In Fig. 6-4, society's production frontier *AB* is drawn for publicly and privately provided goods, fancifully labeled guns and butter.[6] Also drawn are vertically parallel lines delineating equal amounts of the good on the horizontal axis, "butter." Point *A* represents an economy devoted 100% to the production of government services; point *B* represents complete specialization in private goods. Suppose now the economy is initially at point *A*, where all resources are engaged in the production of government services, and consider the cost to consumers of providing the first 10 units of private goods, represented by the distance along the horizontal axis to the first vertical line. The cost to consumers of 10 units of butter is the amount of guns that must be given up in order to be able to produce this increment of butter. The production frontier indicates the limits of society's ability to produce these goods. The height of the frontier above 10 units of butter indicates the amount of guns now available. This amount is 90 units of guns, down from 100, when the economy was completely specialized in gun production. The decrease in the amount of guns available, 10, indicates the (marginal) sacrifice of publicly provided goods in order to be able to consume 10 units of butter, i.e., the marginal cost of 10 units of butter.

Consider now the cost of the next 10 units of butter. When 20 units of butter are produced gun production falls to 70. The marginal cost of butter (10 units) has risen to 20 units of guns. Likewise, the marginal cost of the next 10 units of butter is 30 units of guns, production of the latter falling from 70 to 40. It is geometrically apparent that because of the concavity of the production frontier, the

Figure 6-4 *A Production Possibilities Frontier with Many Producers*

This production frontier represents society's production possibilities. The first 10 units of butter require very little sacrifice of guns, because only the most specialized and efficient resources in butter production are used. A decrease of only 10 units of guns occurs, from 100 to 90. The next 10 units of butter require a greater sacrifice of guns, 20 units, and the next 10 units of butter force a reduction of 30 units of guns. Because of specialized resources, marginal costs rise on the *extensive margin.*

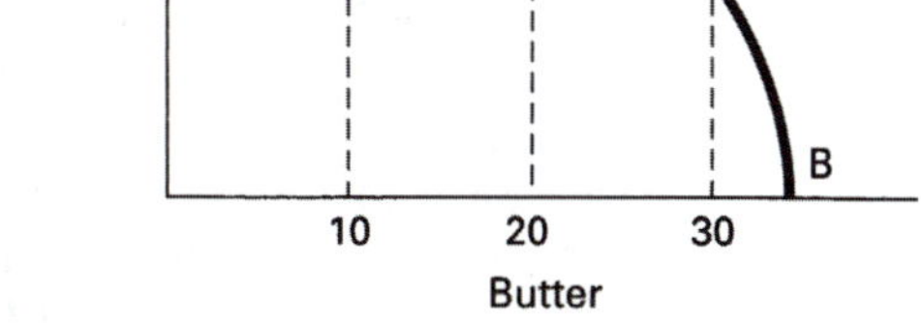

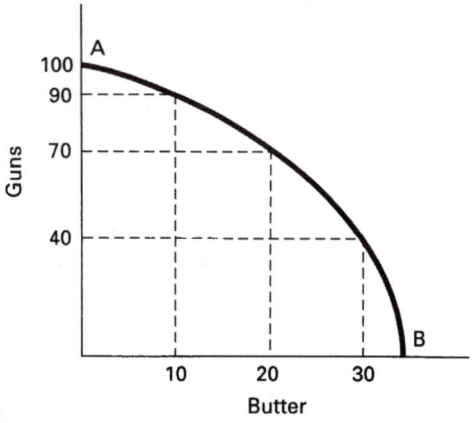

6. Former president Lyndon Johnson used the "guns and butter" metaphor for publicly versus privately provided goods at the beginning of the Vietnam war. He declared we could have more of both—expenditures on the war could be increased without a tax increase, i.e., without a reduction in the amount of private goods available for consumers (not the first time a free lunch was offered by a politician). "Guns vs. butter" is now a common expression. In fact, the term dates to a radio broadcast by Nazi propaganda chief Paul Joseph Goebbels in Berlin, January 17, 1936: "We can do without butter, but, despite our love of peace, not without arms. One cannot shoot with butter but with guns." Later, in the summer of 1936, Hermann Goering said in a radio broadcast, "Guns will make us powerful; butter will only make us fat."

marginal sacrifice of guns increases as more and more butter is produced. The marginal cost of butter rises with increased production levels. In a similar manner, we could derive increasing marginal costs of guns, starting at point *B* and proceeding upward along the production frontier towards point *A*.

Increasing marginal cost does not occur simply because we choose to draw the production frontier in a particular way. We mean to represent, or model the empirical world in a correct fashion. In other words, we believe concavity of the production frontier is the empirically correct shape. But why? This shape is not a foregone conclusion. It is derived from some important observations about technology and the organization of production. Most importantly, productive resources—the talents of individuals, the properties of natural materials, the application of machines and land to productive enterprises—are most often specialized to one or a few tasks, and the ability to replicate, or fully reproduce these resources is generally limited. As greater output is demanded, resources less specialized, and therefore less efficient than those already used must be utilized to produce the additional output. Because less efficient resources are employed, the cost of producing the additional units increases, i.e., the marginal cost of production increases with increased output.

The phenomenon of increasing marginal costs is dependent upon the laws and institutions guiding production. Crusoe and Friday's production frontier was concave because it was to their mutual advantage to have the low cost producer be the first to produce either good, and, we assumed they could and would act in their mutual interest. If laws or institutions induce Crusoe to be the first coconut gatherer and then, only after he can produce no more, does Friday enter this enterprise, then the production frontier would be bowed in, or convex to the origin. Marginal costs would initially be relatively high and then fall with increased production. In modern societies, taxes are sometimes levied on what would be the most efficient resources causing them not to be used first. Alternatively, less efficient resources are sometimes subsidized by the government, so that they are utilized prior to more efficient resources. Or, sometimes firms may possess sufficient monopoly power in a given market, that is, some unique privilege which prevents others from engaging in certain production, that the most efficient resources are not utilized. On an economy-wide basis, these influences would be less pronounced, though we cannot rule them out in specific markets.

Absent the problems just mentioned, individuals in a society with clearly delineated rights over the use of resources will direct those resources to their most advantageous use. Since more is preferred to less, consumers favor producers who can offer a cheaper price. However, the ability to offer a good at a cheaper price can only derive from one's ability to produce a good at a lower cost than some other individual. If resources are directed so that their use is based on where the increase in total output is greatest, those resources with the greatest comparative advantage will be the first used to produce any good. With increasing demand, resources with successively less comparative advantage will be utilized, but those remaining resources with the relatively greatest comparative advantage will be used before those with less comparative advantage. As resources less and less suitable for the production of any particular good are used, the cost of producing the last units necessarily increases. We refer to this phenomenon as **increasing marginal costs**, or **diminishing returns at the extensive margin**.[7]

7. We analyze a separate reason for rising marginal costs within firms, called diminishing returns on the *intensive* margin, in the next chapter.

6.4 Marginal Cost and Supply

We now analyze the important relationship between marginal cost and the supply curve. Consider a firm that owns 10 coal mines. Each mine produces 10 tons of coal per day; however, the mines differ in the ease with which coal is brought to the surface for transport to market. Some mines are very deep and already extensively worked, while others are near the surface and easy to excavate. Suppose the first mine can produce 10 tons of coal at a cost of $5 per ton, mine 2 can produce them at $10 per ton, firm 3 at $15, etc., so that each successively numbered mine's cost per ton of coal increases by $5. The marginal cost of additional output (as we move from one mine to the next) for this firm thus increases, as we have to bring in the less and less efficient mines as output expands.

The situation is depicted in Fig. 6-5. The marginal cost curve consists of a series of "steps" of $5 each, indicating that as production increases beyond the 10 tons for each mine, the firm produces the additional coal at $5 per ton more than with the previous mine. Consider the area under the marginal cost curve. For the first ten tons, this area is 10 × $5 = $50, the total cost of producing those initial ten tons. For the next ten tons, this area is 10 × $10 =$100. The sum of these two areas, $150, equals the total cost of producing the first twenty tons. In like fashion, the area under the marginal cost curve up to any given quantity equals the **total cost** of producing that amount of the good. The total cost of producing forty tons of coal is $50 + $100 + $150 + $200 = $500.[8] This $500 figure represents society's opportunity cost of 40 tons of coal. That is, the labor and other resources that must be used to mine 40 tons of coal could have been used to produce $500 worth of other goods for consumers. The costs for each individual mine are the respective opportunity costs of that labor and other resources, i.e. the value of other goods that could have been produced but for their decision to produce coal.

Figure 6-5 *Increasing Marginal Costs, Reflecting Lesser Access to Inexpensive Coal at Various Mines*

As production increases, coal mines with less accessible coal must be utilized. The cost of extracting coal increases by $5 per ton as each additional 10 tons are extracted.

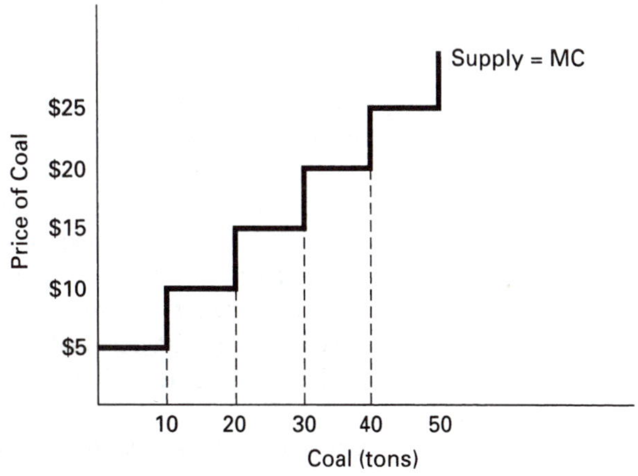

8. Readers who have taken calculus may recognize this argument as evaluating the integral of a function. Letting x = output, marginal cost, by definition is the rate of change of total cost, $C(x)$, with respect to output. That is, $MC(x) = dC(x)/dx = C'(x)$, the first derivative of total cost. The integral of marginal cost, $\int C'(x)dx = C(x)$ is the area beneath the marginal cost curve between 0 and some output level x_0.

Suppose now that the market price of coal is \$20 per ton, and at that price consumers are willing to purchase whatever output this firm chooses to produce. Which mines will produce coal, and what will be the total cost to society of this output? Mine 1 can produce 10 tons of coal at \$5 per ton, and will be able to sell that output at \$20 per ton, earning a \$15 profit on each ton of coal. Thus the firm will happily utilize mine 1 to its limit of 10 tons, without any need for coercion. Likewise, the owners also eagerly use mine 2 to produce 10 tons of coal, since it too will generate a profit, albeit not quite as large a profit as mine 1. Similarly, mine 3 will earn \$5 on each of the 10 tons it produces and will therefore be utilized. In the case of mine 4, the price received equals the cost of production, so it is a matter of indifference as to whether this mine is used or not. We shall assume that in all such situations, the decision is made to produce the good in question.

Notice that the **average cost** of producing 40 tons of coal is only \$500 ÷ 40 = \$12.50. This is less than the market price of \$20. Yet it does *not* pay to increase output any further. It costs the owner \$25 per ton to operate the 5th mine. With a market price of only \$20 per ton, the owner loses money if this mine operates. More importantly, the market price of \$20 indicates that consumers of coal value an additional ton at only \$20. Operating mine 5 costs consumers \$25 worth of goods elsewhere in the economy. Therefore, if the firm uses mine 5, the value of output in the economy would decrease by this excess of costs over consumers' marginal value of coal. For mine 5, this cost differential is \$5; multiplied by its 10 tons of output would yield a loss of mutual benefits of \$50. This cost to the economy would be borne by the owner of this mine, and no coercion would be necessary to induce the owner to leave the mine idle. This coincidence of the private interests of the mine owner and the efficiency of the economy is a critical feature of economies in which individuals who have clearly delineated rights over resources respond to market prices. We discuss this aspect of economies further in the next two chapters. Mines 5 through 10 have marginal costs of production that exceed the market price, and thus they remain idle.

We see that production decisions are based on whether the price received is at least equal to the marginal cost of production. A firm may be earning a little or a lot on previous units produced, but the decision to produce incrementally more or incrementally less is based only on marginal cost, the cost of producing those incremental units. If the market price is \$20, the firm decides to produce until the point where an additional unit would cost more than \$20. *The supply curve of a firm is thus the marginal cost curve of that firm.* Moreover, the analysis is the same whether 1 firm owns the above 10 mines, or whether each mine is separately owned by independent firms. In either case, production takes place until the marginal cost equals the price of the good. If the mines are independently owned, it is still the case that at a market price of \$20 per ton, mines 1 through 4 will engage in production, while the rest will remain idle. If the price were to rise to \$30 per ton, then mines 5 and 6, with marginal costs of \$25 and \$30 per ton would be brought into production regardless of whether they are owned by one firm or by separate firms.

Check your understanding: This firm is making money producing 40 tons of coal. They are more than covering their costs. Why don't they produce more?

At any price, the amount of a good that will be produced by all firms in the industry is the sum of the amounts produced by each firm, each determined by equality of that firm's marginal cost and the market price. In the aggregate, therefore, the supply curve of an industry consisting of many firms of varying sizes and efficiencies, is the **industry marginal cost curve**, formed by the lateral summation of each firm's individual marginal cost curve. This process is the same as that described in Chap. 2 for demand curves.

An important consequence follows when each firm in an industry determines output by choosing that output for which the marginal cost of production equals the market price: *total output is produced at the minimum possible cost.* Suppose there are two firms, each with the 10 coal mines described above, and market price is \$20 per ton. Then each firm will produce where marginal cost equals price (40 tons), and total output will be 80 tons. The total cost to society of producing these 80 tons of coal is therefore 2 × \$500 = \$1,000. Is there some cheaper way for this two-firm economy to produce 80 tons of coal? Suppose a central planner decided to shift 1 ton of production from one firm to the other. If firm 1 produces 1 less ton of coal, this frees up \$20 of resources, since that is what it cost this firm to produce that ton of coal. Firm 2, on the other hand, must increase its production to 41 tons; this requires opening up the 5th mine, for which the marginal cost of coal is \$25. Thus, shifting production around in this manner results in a net loss of \$5. Each ton of coal reallocated to firm 2, up to 10 tons, costs \$5 more to produce than if each firm determined output on the basis of marginal cost equals price. Beyond 10 tons reallocated, the loss is even greater, since now mine 6, with marginal cost of \$30 will have to be utilized.

Minimization of the total cost of any given output level requires that each firm, or each plant within a firm produce output until the marginal costs at each firm or plant are all equal. Otherwise, the output can be rearranged from the relatively high marginal cost firm to the relatively low marginal cost firm, saving resources in the amount of the difference between the two marginal costs. If firm 1 is producing where marginal cost is \$25, and firm 2 is producing where marginal cost is \$15, then by shifting a ton of coal production from firm 1 to firm 2 saves \$10. This procedure for saving cost can continue as long as the marginal costs differ. When the marginal costs are the same, the output is being produced at the minimum possible cost.[9]

We show this important result in Fig. 6-6. Firm 1 and firm 2's marginal cost curves are labeled MC_1 and MC_2. Together, when the price of coal is \$20 per ton, they produce 250 tons, 100 from firm 1 and 150 from firm 2. Suppose a central planner ordered firm 1 to reduce production to 90 tons, and ordered firm 2 to increase production to 160 tons, leaving total production unchanged. Then the decrease in firm 1's total cost is the trapezoidal area below MC_1 between 90 and 100 tons; the increase in firm 2's total cost is the area under MC_2 between 150 and 160 tons. It is obvious that the increase in cost to firm 2 is greater than the savings to firm 1. Thus the total cost of producing the 250 tons is least when each firm produces where its marginal cost equals price.

In summation, the area under the marginal cost curve of any good represents the sum of all the incremental costs of production. It is the cost of the first unit plus that of the second, the third, fourth etc. until all units are counted. Typically, we draw a smooth curve representing marginal cost, abstracting from the discrete increments to output. When we consider large amounts of a good, as is usually

9. We can show this result using elementary calculus. We seek to minimize $C = C_1(q_1) + C_2(q_2)$ where $q_1 + q_2 = q^0$, some arbitrary fixed amount. Equivalently, we minimize $C = C_1(q_1) + C_2(q^0 - q_1)$ by setting the first derivative equal to zero: $dC/dq_1 = C_1'(q_1) + C_2'(q^0 - q_1)(-1) = 0$, or $C_1'(q_1) = C_2'(q_2)$.

Figure 6-6 *Marginal Cost Pricing Results in Minimum Total Cost*

When the market price is $20, firm 1 produces 100 tons of coal and firm 2 produces 150 tons, for a total of 250 tons. Reducing firm 1's production to 90 and increasing firm 2's production to 160 would increase the total cost of producing the 250 tons.

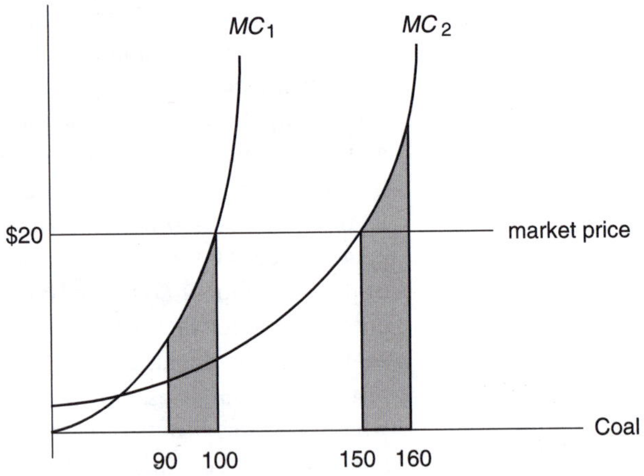

the case in the real economy, individual units are a negligible part of the total. We therefore ignore the discontinuous steps and treat marginal cost as varying in a continuous manner, in the same manner as using smooth curves to represent consumers' marginal values. *The area under the marginal cost curve up to any arbitrary level of output represents the (minimum) total cost of producing that quantity of the good.*

Tradable Pollution Rights

All production involves waste to one degree or another. The Second Law of Thermodynamics assures us that there is no 100% efficient production process. Humans exhale carbon dioxide and carbon monoxide, two well-known poisonous gases. Factories emit smoke and other effluents that we must dispose of in some way. To some extent at present, and to a much greater extent in the past, the atmosphere and rivers adjacent to factories were treated as public dumps. Any person or firm could use the atmosphere to whatever extent was convenient to discharge waste smoke created in the production process. Rivers were treated by many firms as convenient garbage conveyances that lowered the cost of waste removal.

In recent decades, various agencies of state and federal governments have been attempting to reduce pollution through regulation. Many strategies are possible. One scheme is to simply order all industries to reduce pollution by some percentage, say, by one half. The problem with this approach is that some firms will likely be economically unable to exist with these reductions, and will go out of business. Workers in these industries will lose their jobs, and consumers will lose the output these firms once produced. The problem with arbitrary regulations like this is that they do not address the costs and benefits of pollution. Pollution allows consumers to consume greater amounts of goods because of higher production levels. The problem is not that pollution exists (which is inevitable), but that society has not charged producers the full cost their pollution imposes on others.

Recent amendments to the Clean Air Acts enacted in the recent past in the United States allow polluting firms rights to pollute up to a certain amount, and to trade the right to pollute amongst themselves. This is a very interesting and important application of marginal cost analysis. Suppose there are two coal generating firms, *A* and *B,* which between them produce 100 tons of soot per year. Consider the problem of reducing pollution by some absolute amount over all, say, 20 tons of soot. How can this be done at least cost to consumers? One firm, *A,* might easily cut back pollution by 15 tons. That is, the reduction in the marginal product of inputs in production caused by the addition of pollution abatement procedures might be only a small amount. The imposition of antipollution procedures would reduce the firm's rents and cause some reduction in, say, labor inputs, but the firm might easily accommodate these costs. For the other firm, *B,* however, the situation might be quite different. It might be that reduction of pollution for this firm would entail a drastic increase in its marginal cost of producing coal.

Reduction of a "bad" such as pollution is really a form of production. Suppose firm *A* can reduce pollution by 1 ton of soot at a cost of $1,000 worth of output. It can reduce pollution by 20 tons of soot at a cost of $20,000 of output. Firm *B,* on the other hand, finds that the reduction of soot reduces output by $3,000 per ton of soot removed. In this case, having the firms reduce pollution by 10 tons each causes a $40,000 reduction in output: $10,000 from firm *A* and $30,000 from *B*. Suppose, instead, that firm *B* can purchase the right to emit soot from firm *A,* at some mutually agreeable price. Then all of the pollution reduction in this case will be accomplished by firm *A,* and the reduction of output will be only $20,000 instead of $40,000! Since firm *B* is saving $30,000 in the process, we can expect the price of the pollution rights for 10 tons of soot purchased from *A* to be some amount less than this but greater than the $10,000 additional cost to *A*. Whatever the price, however, the reduction of pollution has taken place with the least sacrifice of useful output to consumers.

Let us make the problem a bit more complicated and suppose that when firm *A* reduces pollution by 5,000 tons, it incurs a cost of $1,000 as before, but the next 5,000 tons costs $2,000 in lost output, the next 5,000 tons of soot removed costs $3,000, the next $4,000, and so on. In this case, the first 10,000 tons of coal are most cheaply removed by firm *A,* but the marginal cost of further soot removal for firm *A* has now risen to the level of firm *B* 's cost. It is a matter of indifference as to who would remove the next 5,000 tons, but if we were to try to reduce pollution by 20,000 tons total, it is evident that the cheapest way to do it is for firm *A* to reduce soot pollution by 15,000 tons and firm *B* by 5,000 tons. This minimum cost occurs where the marginal costs pollution reduction of the two firms are equal. If firm *B* were to be allowed to increase soot output by 1,000 tons, it would save $3,000, but now firm *A* would be required to reduce pollution by another 1,000 tons, and this would cost society $4,000 in lost output.

Institution of tradable pollution rights has become a feature of U.S. policy in recent years. The American representatives have proposed these types of regulations at recent international conferences on pollution and global warming. In addition to the costs savings outlined above, this approach gives firms the incentives, in the form of potential sale of pollution rights, to adopt technologies for which the reduction in pollution can be accomplished at low cost.

6.5 The Source of Rents

The marginal cost of production is the minimum amount producers must be compensated in order for them to voluntarily offer additional units of their product for sale. However, producers most often receive payments in excess of this minimum amount. Continuing our numerical example, at a price of \$20, 40 tons of coal are sold. The total revenue received by the sellers of coal, however, is \$20 × 40 = \$800. This is greater by \$300 than the total cost of \$500 of providing these 40 units. This extra \$300 are **rents** to the owners of the more efficient inputs used in the production of this coal. The word rent is used in ordinary parlance usually to mean a payment to a property owner for the right to use that person's land or dwelling. In economics, however, the term means *a payment in excess of what is necessary to call forth production of some good or service.* Rents occur because of the inability to completely replicate resources. Rents are payments to resource owners in excess of what is necessary to call forth production.

We show this situation in Fig.6-7. The owner or owners of each mine each receive \$200 for the 10 tons of coal produced, but their costs differ. Specifically, the owner of mine 1 receives \$150 in rents (\$200 revenue minus \$50 of production costs), firm 2 receives \$100 in rents (\$200 revenue minus \$100 costs), firm 3 receives \$50 in rents (\$200 revenue minus \$150 costs) and firm 4 receives no rents at all, since its production cost equals the price received for each unit. These rents are represented in Fig. 6-7 by the shaded area *above* the marginal cost curve up to the price of \$20. If mine 1 could be infinitely replicated, then the marginal cost of coal would be \$5 per ton at any level of output, no matter how large, and the market price of coal would necessarily fall to \$5 per ton. In that case zero rents would be received, since all mines would be identical. Firm 1 receives the greatest rents because it is the most efficient at producing this good. The differences in the costs of production between a given producer and *the least efficient (highest cost) producer* determines rents. It is these cost differentials that are the source of rents.

Suppose now the demand for this good shifts out so that the price increases by \$10, to \$30, It now pays for mine 5 to produce, and, as before, we assume that mine 6 operates also, even though it receives no rents from so doing. The rents received by the owner(s) of the four mines previously operating are greater by \$10 × 40 units = \$400, and mine 5 now also receives rents of \$5 × 10 units = \$50. Rents therefore increase by \$450, from \$300 to \$750. The 20 additional units of output cost \$550 (\$250 for firm 5 and \$300 for firm 6) bringing the total

Figure 6-7 *Creation of Rents*

Rents to the most efficient producers occur as less and less efficient resources must be used to increase output. When the price of coal is \$20 per ton, the first mine receives a rent of \$15 per ton, the second mine receives \$10 per ton, and the third mine receives \$5 per ton.

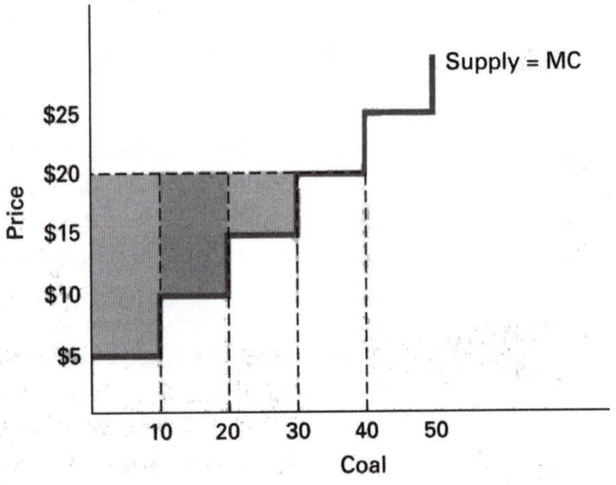

cost for all 60 units to $1,050. That figure, plus the total rents of $750 equals the total expenditure now made by consumers (and received as revenue by the sellers) of $\$30 \times 60 = \$1,800$. In all cases, the rents received by owners of nonreplicable resources are derived from the differences in their productivities and the least efficient resources that are brought into production.

Examples of diminishing returns at the extensive margin and the creation of rents are easy to provide. In the 1930's, oil companies discovered major oil fields in Texas and Oklahoma. As a result, the price of petroleum products fell drastically as these new sources came on line. Since that time, however, the world demand for petroleum has been steadily increasing. As a result, producers have had to resort to less convenient (and therefore more costly) sources of this energy. Oil companies now explore for oil in remote corners of the world. In the past decades oil has been found and produced, for example, in the north slope of Alaska and the North Sea (in the North Atlantic off the coasts of England and Norway). It is much more costly to drill for oil in the ocean, especially in the icy Arctic, or in the frigid north slope of Alaska, than in Oklahoma or Texas. In addition, the cost of shipping this oil to the consumer market is obviously greater than for the less remote sources. As a result, owners of the more convenient or less expensive wells receive rents. These rents equal the value of their cost advantage over the least efficient producer.

Oil produced in the Islamic countries of the Middle East is a low cost source only in a purely technical sense. It costs very little to extract this oil from the ground: in many cases a turn of a spigot suffices. However, the political instability of the region results in uncertainty about the availability of that oil. Thus when these political costs are considered, these may be high-cost sources of oil. This example serves to remind us that costs are not just technological or engineering relationships about production techniques. Costs vary with the institutional framework under which production takes place. A firm operating in Iran will not have the same cost of production as it would in the United States even if the underlying production process were identical in the two locations. The decisions that are allowable are different in the two countries.

Consider also the case of land used to grow wheat. There is some land, particularly the Palouse country of eastern Washington State, and certain areas of the great plains of the United States, Canada, Ukraine and Russia, that is so suitable for this purpose that even if the price of wheat was only a quarter of its present price, it would still pay for farmers to grow wheat on it. Other land is not so fertile, and the price of wheat would have to be higher to induce farmers to voluntarily grow wheat. Lastly, there are farms that just barely manage to provide their owners and employees with enough income, at the current price of wheat, to keep the farm in wheat production. These farms are called the **marginal firms** of this industry. These firms either go out of business or switch to some other activity if the price of their product decreases.

If the demand for wheat was sufficiently small so that it could all be supplied by the most efficient land, the production from this land would constitute the entire market supply, and the market price would equal the marginal cost of producing wheat on this land. If demand increases, this higher consumers' marginal value of wheat induces owners of land formerly used in some other endeavor to switch to wheat production. This new wheat will be produced at the higher marginal cost of the new producers, and will continue until consumers' marginal value of wheat equals the marginal cost of the highest cost producer. But now, the owners of the most fertile wheat land begin to receive rents, because the market price exceeds the minimum they would have to be paid in order to produce. When production increases, farmers utilize land which is successively less specific to wheat production, the marginal cost will rise with increased output. As new farmers produce wheat in response to increasing willingness on the part of consumers to pay for wheat, rents to the most efficient producers increase.

During the colonial period of the United States and on into the early nineteenth century, wheat was grown in New England. That soil is very rocky, and by present day standards, the area is an abysmal place to grow wheat. However, New England in fact had a comparative advantage over the other regions of early America in this regard; the soil and climatic conditions elsewhere were even less conducive for successful wheat farming. With the opening up of the plains states of Ohio and Indiana, the wheat farmers of New England were forced to switch to other crops, or to quit farming altogether. They became extra marginal firms, i.e., firms beyond the margin where the price of the product was sufficiently high to enable profitable production. Later in the nineteenth century, as land farther west was settled, the eastern farms became the marginal farms, and competition from the western plains eventually forced the eastern farmers to switch to crops other than wheat.

Rents occur because of the inability to completely replicate resources, which results in rising marginal costs of production. Since all goods and resources are paid the marginal cost of providing additional amounts of that good, the owners of goods or resources that could be provided at a lower cost receive rents. Although land is the archetypal resource to which the name rent is applied, the most significant resource receiving rents is probably human skills, which economists call human capital. Some of the most dramatic examples are in professional sports. Presently, some dozen or so professional baseball players earn in excess of $10 million dollars per year, not counting the additional income they receive from endorsing products. The minimum salary in the major leagues is around $250,000 per year. The difference represents the difference in productivity (measured in the ability to produce revenues for the owners) of the star players and the marginal players—those just barely qualifying for the major leagues. These superstars (and their counterparts in professional football, basketball and the rest of the entertainment industry) possess skills that are only rarely encountered.

Professional athletes provide sports entertainment to their fans. Some players are better able to do this than others. Moreover, it is not possible to perfectly replicate Ken Griffey Jr., Tiger Woods, and other superstars, past and present. These players provide more entertainment per game than do their teammates. Therefore, each time a new league forms, or the existing leagues expand, the leagues must utilize resources (professional athletes) that are not as efficient in production as those formerly employed. As a result, the cost of providing this form of entertainment rises at the margin, increasing the rents to the players who previously qualified for the established professional league. The marginal cost of providing professional sports games, like all other activities, rises with increasing output. The most efficient resources (the best players) receive rents based on the difference in the marginal value their services in providing entertainment and the marginal value of the least efficient resources (worst players).

Similarly, it is not easy to replicate Tina Turner, Jennifer Lopez, Britney Spears, Whitney Houston and their ilk. Because their talents are so unusual, these stars are highly paid. They receive much more than what they could earn in some other line of work. They receive rents derived from the superiority of their skills over the marginal person or firm in their field of endeavor. If there were a large number of people with comparable talents, these stars would be paid amounts much closer to what they could earn in their next best alternative.

The theory of rent was developed concurrently by two great British economists of the early nineteenth century, the Reverend Thomas R. Malthus, known mainly to the general public for his *Essay On Population,* and David Ricardo, already mentioned above. During the Napoleonic wars, the French embargoed British ports. To offset the loss of imported grain, domestic farmers increased production. Corn (i.e. all grain) and land prices rose to unprecedented levels. Ricardo's analysis of the events is as clear and compelling today as then:

> "If all land had the same properties, if it were unlimited in quantity, and uniform in quality, no charge could be made for its use, unless where it possessed peculiar advantages of situation. It is only, then, because land is not unlimited in quantity and uniform in quality, and because in the progress of population, land of an inferior quality, or less advantageously situated, is called into cultivation, that rent is ever paid for the use of it. When in the progress of society, land of the second degree of fertility is taken into cultivation, rent immediately commences on that of the first quality, and the amount of that rent will depend on the difference in the quality of these two portions of land."[10]

6.6 Rents and Quasi-Rents

Production of output requires resources which have alternative uses. The goods those resources might have instead produced vanish irretrievably. These forgone goods are the cost of the goods produced. In market economies, we observe costs, for example, when firms endeavor to hire workers and capital to carry on trade of some sort. However, cost is not dependent for its existence on such institutions as markets or trade. Even if the resources were available by command of some dictator, it is still the case that they could have been used to produce something else. That something else is the cost.[11]

If there is no production involved in securing the right to consume some good, the payment to the owner of that good is a pure rent, not a cost. Consider a coal mine, and assume the only use for the land in which the mine is located is to mine coal, that is, there is no alternative use of this particular land. If the coal spontaneously appeared on the surface, then payment for its use would constitute a pure rent. These rents arise because people will bid against each other for the right to sell this useful commodity. There is no cost of this coal to society in this case since it is there anyway.

10. David Ricardo, in *Works I (The Works and Correspondence of David Ricardo,* edited by P. Sraffa and M. Dobb. Cambridge University Press, 1951–1955). Quoted in *A History of Economic Theory and Method,* by R. B. Ekelund, Jr. and R. F. Hebert, New York: McGraw Hill, 1975.

11. In the pre civil-war South, some plantation owners utilized slaves. The slaves didn't have to be paid, and they couldn't easily run away. Nonetheless, the slaves were not a *free* resource to their owners. The slaves could be sold, and the money used for improvements in the plantation or in the owner's lifestyle. Most plantations did not in fact use slaves. Nonslave labor was also available for the tasks assigned to slaves. The cost of owning a slave was the forgone output that could have been produced by nonslave labor. For many plantation owners, nonslave labor was the lower cost means of production.

In real coal mines, however, coal does not automatically appear on the surface. Mining firms must employ labor and other resources, all of which have alternative uses, to secure the coal. Therefore, the total expenditure on this coal by consumers consists partially of these costs, and partially of the rents on the coal mine itself, which is the only resource with no alternative use. If, on the other hand, the land on which the coal mine is situated is also fertile and but for the mining activity could be used to grow crops, the payment for the use of the land would not be a rent. In this case, the decision to mine coal on this land prevents consumers from enjoying another useful product, food. Thus even though the mine operator might consider the payment to the landowner for the use of the land a rent in the ordinary parlance, this payment would really be a cost to society in the same way as the payments for other capital and labor.

Quasi-Rents

It is often the case that resources are utilized to build capital goods, for example, machinery or even a whole factory or office building, for some very specific use. Once built, the machine, say, cannot easily be converted to some other use. While steel is in ingot form it has many uses; when it has been transformed into a printing press, it has little utility other than in printing. Once the inputs have been transformed into the final good, it is often very difficult or costly to recreate the inputs in their original form. (The classic example is trying to unscramble an egg!) Thus although the productive inputs may have had alternative uses, the final good may be so specialized as to have only one use.

In their final form, specialized machines or facilities often yield valuable services and thus their owners receive payments for their use. It is also typical, however, that this payment exceeds the minimum amount the owners would demand in order to provide the service, once the equipment is built. The construction costs are all sunk, having occurred in the past, and are irretrievable. The office building still stands and the printing presses can still run at low additional, or marginal expense. Even if it turns out that there is little demand for the presses or office space, it may still be profitable for their owners to employ these facilities, so long as the additional revenues received cover the marginal costs of utilizing them. If the builders of these capital goods have correctly assessed the demand for their services, the payments they receive for their use should be sufficient to cover the cost of fabricating the machines or buildings in the first place, plus the cost of operations, plus a normal return for the risk inherent in investing in such capital. In that case, the actual payment the owners receive will exceed that minimum amount required merely for operating the machines or buildings. Some part of the receipts will therefore have the character of a rent. However, these rents exist only after the fact, that is, after a capital good with a specific use is already in existence. If the owners could not receive these rents, the machinery would never have been built. We call such payments **quasi-rents**. They are rents owners of these resources can receive only in the short run. If taxed or appropriated by others, no such rents will appear in the future. Although these payments are not necessary to call forth the services produced by the good at that moment, the good would not have existed in the first place were it not for the anticipation that such payment would exist.

A current (though not new) public policy debate concerns the pricing of prescription drugs. The federal government, in an effort to mandate some person's idea of a fair price for these often life-saving chemicals, is proposing to set maximum prices (price controls) on some of these pharmaceuticals or to permit the importation of drugs from foreign countries, particularly Canada, where drug prices are set lower by government controls. Many of these drugs sell for prices that vastly exceed their cost of manufacture. Drug manufacturers sometimes make millions or tens of millions of dollars on some of these compounds. What would be the effects of taxing these profits in some way, either through outright levies or through price controls? Drug companies usually invest large sums in the development of new drugs. Much of this research proves fruitless. When a new useful compound is developed, it must be proven safe and effective, through extensive trials on animals and then on humans. The process can take five to ten years. When the drug is finally approved, all these research and development costs are sunk. They cannot be retrieved. The money has been spent.

When the drug companies have a new drug to sell, they decide on a price that will yield them the greatest profits. That price depends mainly on the price of competing drugs on the market. Whether the company spent millions or just stumbled luckily on the discovery of the drug, the price it sets depends only on the current market for compounds such as its own. The cost of manufacturing already developed pills, say, is likely only a small part of the total cost of getting the drug to the market, perhaps only a few cents per pill. In most cases, the price the company receives for these already developed drugs exceeds the marginal cost of manufacture by factors of ten or a hundred or more. Thus for drugs on the market, especially new drugs whose chemical makeup is protected by patents, firms receive rents, sometimes of a substantial nature.

The price that would induce drug firms to produce an already developed drug in most cases is probably only a few cents in most cases, a small fraction of the price the medicines usually sell for. However, we know these profits must be quasi-rents, because no company would expend the resources to develop these drugs if the price they received for the drugs was limited to just what it cost to manufacture the pills. Although firms cannot go back in time and recover sunk costs, they can and do plan ahead when it comes to investment in future drugs. If they do not anticipate profits in excess of development costs, new drugs will not be developed. Thus rents on existing drugs can be largely taxed away without causing the drug to be withdrawn from the market. But such penalties will discourage the development of new medicines.

It appears that most rents in a modern economy are in fact quasi-rents. There are few truly fixed resources—resources whose supply curves are vertical—in a modern economy. Even sites with views are not fixed, as an expenditure of resources often will convert a site without a view to one with a view. People sometimes build houses on stilts in order to raise the floor level over some obstruction. Better architectural planning may convert a site with a poor view to one with a good view. The convenience of a given location may depend greatly on the resources spent to enhance the property, e.g. making the location attractive, providing parking or rapid transit access, etc. If payments for views cannot be received by the owners of these resources, there will be many fewer sites with views or other conveniences. A society that rewards slender, beautiful men and women will have more such persons, through dieting and grooming, than a society with no such rewards. In the long run, resources are not fixed; rather, individuals alter the quantity available by expenditure of resources. We showed in Chap. 5 that an excise tax levied on a fixed resource leads to no misallocation;

the only effect is to transfer rents from the owners of the resource to the general taxpayer. However, supply curves are not permanently vertical, and thus all specific excise taxes will likely involve deadweight losses.

Rent Payments: Sterile Transfers or Allocative Function?

Since rents or quasi-rents constitute payments in excess of the amount needed to call forth the productive use of some resource, such payments are sometimes regarded as useless or sterile transfers of income from the consumers of a resource to its lucky owners. Even in the short run, however, these receipts serve the important economic function of allocating these resources to those individuals who can use them to produce the greatest net gain in value to consumers. We say that rents direct, or allocate resources to their highest value in use.

Suppose some parcel of land is particularly well suited for commercial use because of its proximity to transportation, or to a central business district, etc. Since the land is conveniently located, the person who owns the land will receive rents. Many people will eagerly seek such parcels of land for their own special use. The land has value only because when combined with other productive inputs, some good or service which consumers value is produced. Only consumers create value for resources; value cannot be produced in a vacuum. A shopkeeper is willing to pay rent on a piece of land only if the goods or services produced there are sufficiently valuable to consumers that the resulting sales are sufficient to pay for all costs of production, including the payments for the use of that land. Therefore, the individual willing to pay the highest rent to the landowner is necessarily the person who can use the land so that its aggregate benefit to consumers is as great as possible. If there were further gains from trade to be realized, then others would be willing to pay still higher rents, since some of those additional gains would be available. Thus allocating the land to the highest bidder insures that gains from trade will not be inadvertently lost.

Even if the land had only one use, the conclusion would be the same. Consider the coal mine again. Since the land has no alternative use, payments to its owner constitutes a rent. Different prospective operators, however, have different skills at running the mine. The individuals who are most efficient at mining, i.e., those people with the greatest comparative advantage in operating a coal mine, are precisely the people willing to pay the greatest rent to the land on which the mine sits. Thus, rent payments again serve the important function of directing resources to those who can most efficiently use them, in this case, to produce coal at the least resource cost to the economy. Rent payments are therefore not just sterile transfers of money from one person to another.

In market economies, firms pay the owners of resources for the use of those items, bidding these resources away from their alternative uses. Firm owners thus incur the opportunity cost of these resources, along with any rent payments. Competitive bidding leads to allocation of these resources to the highest bidder. Consumers thus pay the full opportunity cost of the goods, plus rent payments to immobile factors of production. When property rights are well-defined, the highest bidder is necessarily the firm or individual who is combining those resources in the way that adds the greatest aggregate gain in value for consumers, unless the firm is subsidizing that gain out of its own wealth.

Application: Greenbelt Legislation

Many cities in the United States and Canada have experienced a phenomenon known as urban sprawl. As cities have grown, land once used for farming has been converted to urban uses, particularly housing and shopping centers. Farmers have often complained they were driven off the land by high rents, or high land values. These high rents are sometimes attributed to speculation in real estate by property developers. Although the charge has an element of truth in it, the culprits are not the real estate speculators. The culprits are those consumers who value the non-agricultural products that could be produced on this land more highly than the food it would yield.

Land has many uses. It can be used for growing food, for factories, housing, shopping centers, and the like. If competition for its use is by means of price, the highest bidder will get to use the land. In rural areas, the high bidders will likely be farmers (if the land is fertile) or a person with some other agricultural use for the land. It would hardly be profitable to build a shopping center or a factory on fertile land in a remote area where there are few people and a scant labor force. However, as the population of cities increases, the demand for adjacent land for nonagricultural uses increases, producing an outward shift in the demand for land. As a result, the price of land for any use increases. Farmers who are renting their land find that their costs of production increase, in terms of the cost to them of obtaining the rights to use the land, thereby lowering their net return from farming. Farmers who own their own land find increasingly attractive offers to sell or rent their land to non-farmers. In either case, the owners will observe the opportunity cost of the land, by what other people are willing to pay for its use. Eventually, the land will pass from agricultural to urban or suburban use, unless additional, nonprice restrictions are imposed, such as zoning, wetlands restrictions, or type of use restrictions. In that case, one should note, competition will in part shift to these nonprice means, such as qualifying for new rules. The people who ultimately drive the farmers off the land are the other people who would like to use the land. Real estate developers are merely the agents or intermediaries in these transactions. Their sin is to bring these buyers and sellers together. In the process they facilitate the transfer of land away from farming. They cannot produce that result on their own, however. There first must be consumers who would like to use the land for these other purposes before the use of the land can change. Urban sprawlers cause urban sprawl, not the real estate developers.

In a similar manner, it is sometimes argued that high rents are driving small shopkeepers out of business, or words to that effect. The phrase is often meant to convey that if only rents were lower, some businesses, such as art galleries, mom & pop groceries and the like would be more viable, leading to a more pleasant urban environment. The reason rents are high (leaving aside the value judgment inherent in choosing sides in an issue like this) is that other consumers place a higher value on the goods that could also be sold in these same locations than they do on art or personal grocery service. The rents are high because the land is valuable in these other endeavors. It is eagerness of individuals to consume the goods to be sold that creates the rental values on land. Restricting the use of the land discriminates in favor of one group of consumers and against another. By directing resources away from that which produces the highest rent on the land, resources are directed towards relatively lower valued uses, that is, uses that are valued less in the aggregate by consumers than in some other use.

6.7 Economic Efficiency

In Fig. 6-8, we show a hypothetical supply curve of some commodity, say, wheat. Its positive slope expresses the increase in marginal cost due to the inability to completely replicate resources, especially land. Several prices are indicated, starting at \$1.00. At this lowest price, only those farms with the most fertile land produce. As the price is incrementally increased, new production ensues. The total cost of producing that output can be ascertained by multiplying the height of the supply curve by a small increment of production. Starting at the origin, each new incremental increase in output (measured along the horizontal axis), multiplied by the height of the marginal cost curve, and added to the previous total yields the total cost of producing wheat up to that output level. The area *under* the supply curve up to any arbitrary output represents the total cost of producing that output.

Also drawn in Fig. 6-8 is the demand curve for wheat (ignoring for the moment government price supports that effectively raise the price over the price at which the quantity demanded equals the quantity supplied), indicating a market price of *OB* (\$4.00) per bushel and total output of *OE* = *BD*. Since producers sell all units of wheat, *OE,* at price \$4.00 (*OB*), producers' total revenues or receipts are represented by the rectangle *OBDE.* The total cost of producing this wheat, however, is less than this amount, being the area *OADE.* The difference, *ABD,* represents payments to producers in excess of the minimum they would demand to produce *OE.* This area represents the rents to the specialized factors used, in particular, land that is particularly suitable for producing wheat. The price set in the market is the marginal cost of the least efficient, highest cost producer. It is their efforts that must be induced to produce the last units of the good desired by consumers.

The total net benefits from production and trade is the sum of consumers' and producers' rents. It is apparent from Fig. 6-8 that these total gains are as great as possible when the amount of production is *OE,* yielding mutual benefits *ACD.* The gains to both producers and consumers are greatest when the area below the demand curve and above the supply curve is as large as possible. There is always a potential net gain when the amount a consumer is willing to pay for an additional unit of a good exceeds the amount for which someone is willing to sell that

Figure 6-8 *Economic Efficiency*

The supply and demand for some commodity—wheat is shown. The area below the demand curve and above the market price is consumers' surplus; the area above the supply (marginal cost) curve and below the market price represents rents to the sellers; and the area below the supply curve is the total cost of production.

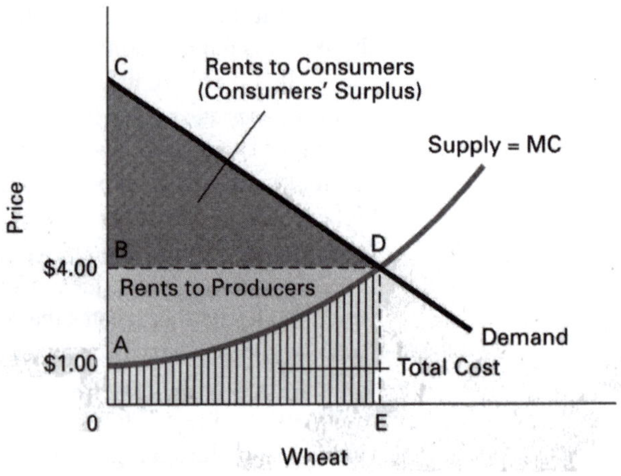

unit. That is, mutual gains exist any time a consumer's marginal value of a good exceeds the marginal opportunity cost of providing that good, a situation that prevails at all production levels less than *OE*. The gains from trade therefore increase as production and trade take place up to *OE*. Beyond that level, however, the marginal opportunity cost of providing the good exceeds the amount that consumers are willing to pay. If person *A* values some item at $10 and *B* values it at $6, and if somehow it's ownership passes from *A* to *B*, there is a net loss of benefits of $4. Beyond *OE*, the sacrifice consumers must make in order to acquire additional units, measured by the area below the supply (marginal cost) curve, is greater than the benefits consumers receive from those additional units (measured by the area below the demand curve). There is therefore a net loss of benefits to consumers whenever production takes place beyond *OE*, where the quantity demanded by consumers equals the quantity supplied by producers.

A very important characteristic of this market equilibrium is that not only is the amount of the good produced efficient, there are no further gains to be had by either rearranging production amongst producers, or by retrading by consumers. Since all producers produce where each firm's *MC* equals the market price, and they all face the same price, the marginal costs for all producers are equal, and so there is no way to produce the quantity *OE* at less resource cost to the economy, as we showed in Fig. 6-6. Likewise, consumers purchase goods until their marginal values (*MV*s) of the good falls to the market price. Since all consumers face the same market price, their *MV*s must therefore all be equal, and thus by the theorems on exchange proved in Chap. 4, there are no further gains to be had by retrading amongst consumers.

As in the case of economies consisting only of exchange, the situation in which all gains from production and trade are exhausted is called *Pareto efficient*, or *Pareto optimal*. Pareto efficient means, as before, that it is not possible to make any individual better off without making someone else worse off. Economics tries to analyze the mechanisms that tend to lead an economy to a Pareto efficient allocation of resources. In other words, under what set of rules, or laws will efficiency most likely occur? Recall from Chap. 5 that excise taxes imposed on markets create a wedge between the prices paid by buyers and the prices received by sellers. This causes a contraction of output to below the efficient level *OE* in Fig. 6-8. A triangular area of deadweight loss is created by the tax. Similarly, price controls and price floors cause output to deviate from the most efficient level. We shall see in Chap. 11. that monopolies likewise raise the price to consumers above *OB*, and thus in a similar way produce these losses of mutual benefits. Likewise, the opposite of a tax, a government subsidy on some good can lead the economy to output greater than *OE* producing similar deadweight losses.

If an economy is not in a Pareto efficient situation, there are mutual gains from trade yet to be realized. The principle that more is preferred to less implies that individuals will not willingly forego these gains; rather, they will endeavor to capture them. It follows therefore that resources are not allocated efficiently only when individuals are unable to get together and transact with each other. If a consumer's marginal value of some good exceeds the marginal cost of providing that good, a seller has an incentive to supply the good. If, on the other hand, there is some law restricting that transaction, or a restriction on a person's freedom to provide the good (e.g., a monopoly right for a particular seller, or perhaps absence of information that a consumer desires the good at an attractive price to sellers), then that mutually beneficial trade might not take place. In the absence of transactions costs, however, mutually advantageous trade must take place; therefore we must look to situations in which transactions costs are substantial to uncover inefficiencies in the economy. We shall explore these important situations beginning in the next chapter.

6.8 The Division of Labor Is Limited by the Extent of the Market

By engaging in specialization, Crusoe and Friday increase their income over that which could be derived from separate production. In modern economies, people specialize to a high degree to take advantage of these gains.

In order for individuals to specialize, however, it must be possible for people to exchange their own production for that of others. Crusoe and Friday want to eat a mixture of fish and coconuts, not just one or the other. What we like to consume is rarely, if ever, what we are best at producing. In modern economies, in which specialization is taken to extreme lengths, the separation of production from consumption decisions is critical. Automobile workers do not want to consume automobile parts, dry cleaners do not want to consume cleaning only. In order for people to increase their income through specialization, it must be possible for individuals to exchange their own production for that of others. However, the ability to do this depends on the extent to which markets for exchange are developed and available.

It is therefore the possibility of exchange that allows people to separate decisions about what they want to consume from decisions about production. Consumers derive the greatest benefits if they produce goods with the highest market value, and then trade these goods for the ones they actually want to consume. If a person instead has to consume what he or she produces, then even with a substantial comparative advantage in one good over others, that person must nonetheless produce some food, some clothing, some shelter, some recreation. This output will not be the most highly valued possible, because concessions to survival, or at least enjoyment of life must be made. If markets exists for the goods they produce, people can produce the goods with the highest market value and then trade those goods for whatever they choose to consume. Thus, the degree of specialization that can occur depends in an important way on the extent to which markets are developed for these goods. Adam Smith put it this way:

> But man has almost constant occasion for the help of his brethren. . . . As it is by treaty, by barter, and by purchase that we obtain the greater part of those mutual good offices which we stand in need of, so it is this same trucking disposition which originally gives occasion to the division of labor . . . so the extent of this division must always be limited by the extent of that power or, in other words, by the extent of the market. When the market is small, no person can have any encouragement to dedicate himself entirely to one employment, for want of the power to exchange all that surplus part of the produce of his own labor, which is over and above his own consumption, for such parts of the produce of other men's labor as he has the occasion for.[12]

12. Adam Smith, *The Wealth of Nations,* 1776, Book I

It is apparent from common experience that the variety of goods and services available in small towns is less than that available in large cities. The variety of courses taught in large universities is greater than that available in small liberal arts colleges.[13] In large cities, specialized medical services are available: there are hand surgeons, neurosurgeons, chest surgeons, and the like. In small towns, none of these specialists could hope to be fully employed, and thus they practice only in larger markets. Moreover, since these specialists do only a narrow, closely related set of operations, and nothing else, their knowledge of those operations and their dexterity can be developed much further than general physicians who might only perform those procedures occasionally.[14]

In remote areas of underdeveloped countries, much production takes place in village economies where almost all the goods and services consumed by the native population is produced right there in their local economy. These villages are only slightly more economically developed than our hypothetical Crusoe-Friday economy. Even if every working person was completely specialized, the number of goods produced could not exceed the number of workers. As a result, the number of goods available for consumption will be smaller in lightly populated areas. In remote areas, specialization will be limited, and therefore incomes will be low, reflecting this lack of specialization. As population grows, and especially as transportation and communication develop so that trade with other villages or cities becomes possible, then a greater degree of specialization can take place. In Seattle Washington, you can buy a *latte* (espresso coffee with steamed milk) with your choice of decaf or regular coffee; single short, single tall, double short, double tall, double-double tall; *grande* (more milk); with either nonfat, 2 percent or whole milk (foamed or plain); optional added vanilla or chocolate; hot or iced, but it's still impossible to purchase a good hot pastrami sandwich on rye.

Suppose you are an attorney, and also a pretty good typist. Will you type your own briefs? You probably will notice that you earn about $100 per hour doing law, but only $20 per hour as a typist, even if you are the best typist in town. So you won't do your own typing, even if you can out-type anybody for miles around. You'll engage in that activity at which you have a comparative advantage. In time you'll become better at lawyering and worse at typing, but you won't make any attempt to change this pattern.

In my house, everything *works,* because I don't do anything myself. With the exception of only the most elementary tasks, such as changing a faucet washer, it doesn't pay for me to engage in household production. When I once attempted to replace a leaky toilet, I learned all the famous mistakes people make when they first apply themselves to such tasks. By the time it was done (badly), I estimated I had earned about $1.25 an hour. I should have stuck to specializing in the good for which I have a comparative advantage—economics—and gain increases in salary through that route, rather than trying to produce income as a plumber.

---

13. Professor Bobby McCormick once told me that there were only twenty-one restaurants in Clemson, South Carolina; nineteen of them served pizza, and the other two were going out of business.

14. Jack Benny once remarked, however, that in the case of playing the violin, you had to practice four hours a day "just to be lousy."

6.9 Specialization, Trade and Economic Growth

The theory of comparative advantage explains why a high degree of specialization characterizes modern production. In addition, concentration on their comparative advantage causes individuals to increase their skills, enhancing the gains societies derive from specialization. Henry George gave an eloquent discussion of these principles over a century ago:

> Here, let us imagine, is an unbounded savannah, stretching off in unbroken sameness. . . . Along comes the wagon of the first immigrant. Where to settle he cannot tell—every acre seems as good as another. . . . Nature is at her very best. He has what, were he in a populous district, would make him rich; but he is very poor. To say nothing of mental craving, which would lead him to welcome the sorriest stranger, he labors under all the material disadvantages of solitude. . . . Though he has cattle, he cannot often have fresh meat, for to get a beefsteak, he must kill a bullock. He must be his own blacksmith, wagonmaker, carpenter and cobbler—in short, a "jack of all trades and master of none." He cannot have his children schooled, for, to do so, he must himself pay and maintain a teacher. Such things as he cannot produce himself, he must buy in quantities and keep on hand, or else go without, for he cannot be constantly leaving his work and making a long journey to the verge of civilization. . . . Under such circumstances, though the nature is prolific, the man is poor. It is an easy matter for him to get enough to eat; but beyond this, his labor will suffice to satisfy only the simplest wants in the rudest way.
>
> Soon there comes another immigrant. Although every quarter of section of the boundless plain is as good as every other . . . there is one place that is clearly better for him than any other, and that is where there is another settler and he may have a neighbor. He settles by the side of the first comer, whose condition is at once greatly improved, and to whom many things are now possible that were once impossible, for two men may help each other to do things that one man could never do.
>
> Another immigrant comes, and guided by the same attraction, settles where there are already two. Another, and another, until around our first comer there are a score of neighbors. Labor has now an effectiveness which, in the solitary state, it could not approach. If heavy work is to be done, the settlers have a log-rolling, and together accomplish in a day what singly would require years. When one kills a bullock, the others take part of it, returning when they kill, and thus have fresh meat all the time. Together they hire a school-master, and the children are taught for a fractional part of what similar teaching would have cost the first settler. It becomes a comparatively easy matter to send to the nearest town, for some one is always going. But there is less need for such journeys. A blacksmith and a wheelwright soon set up shops, and our settler can have his tools repaired for a small part of the labor it formerly cost him. A store is opened and he can get what he wants when he wants it; a post office, soon added, gives him communication with the rest of the world. Then comes a cobbler, a carpenter, a harnessmaker, a doctor; and a little

> church soon arises. Satisfactions become possible that in the solitary state were impossible.
>
> . . . The presence of other settlers—the increase in population—has added to the productiveness, in these things, of labor bestowed on [land], and this added productiveness gives it a superiority over land of equal natural quality where there are as yet no settlers. . . . The value or rent of our settler's land will thus depend on the advantage which it has, from being at the center of population, over that on the verge. . . . The coal and iron fields of Pennsylvania, that today are worth enormous sums, were fifty years ago valueless. . . . The coal and iron beds of Wyoming and Montana, which today are valueless, will, in fifty years from now, be worth millions upon millions, simply because, in the meantime, population will have greatly increased.[15]

Some of the most densely populated areas of the world, such as the urban parts of Hong Kong, are surrounded by very sparsely populated regions. Only a small fraction of all the land in Hong Kong is heavily populated; some parts are practically uninhabited. The cities located in the midsection of North America have dense urban centers, with high-rise apartments and office buildings, even though there are few natural geographical constraints that would prevent expansion into the lower density surroundings. Rather than live in the lower rent outer edges of suburbia, most families choose to live and work in the more densely populated urban areas. In less developed countries, cities are often the scene of the most abject poverty, with large families squeezing into very small spaces. Yet it seems, from the persistence of these patterns, that people find the prospect of moving to the less populated regions even worse. Evidently the gains from specialization afforded by high population density outweigh, for most people, the negative aspects of crowding.

Increased specialization leads to higher incomes, and also to greater interdependence among people. With isolated village economies, a natural disaster in one village, such as a severe hailstorm or earthquake, will have little if any economic effect on other villages. However, with interdependence, events in one sector of the economy have macroeconomic effects on other parts of the economy. If the U.S. automobile industry becomes depressed, with high unemployment occurring in Detroit, then since car manufacturers are major purchasers of steel, steelworkers in Pittsburgh will be laid off and that area may experience recession. With a reduction in steelworkers' incomes, grocery stores from which they purchase food and farmers who supply that food have fewer sales, leading to reduced incomes in those sectors of the economy as well. These multiplier effects are present only in specialized economies. Despite them, all modern economies are specialized because of the vast increase in living standards that specialization permits.

For all its benefits, international trade is one of the most contentious issues nations face. The practice of "outsourcing" jobs to lower cost contractors in foreign countries produces heated arguments in Congress and in presidential debates. When President Bush's economic advisor and Harvard Professor Gregory Mankiw

---

15. Henry George, *Progress and Poverty, (1879)* Originally published by D. Appleton & Co. (only after George agreed to set the plates himself). Available from The Modern Library, Random House, New York. The quoted passages are from *Book IV Chapter II.*

was quoted in the 2004 presidential campaign explaining the benefits of outsourcing as an example of pursuing our comparative advantages, it created quite a political storm. There is a growing industry of outsourcing technical support services electronically to India, where many people speak English. For the first time, perhaps, high-tech and middle-class jobs are being transferred to foreign shores. The people opposing these trends argue something like, "China and India, with their huge populations and low wages can literally produce every commodity the U.S. produces at a lower cost than in the U.S. They will always underbid American firms and drive our standard of living down to theirs. We will never export goods to China or India." The argument usually continues with "What's the use of having lower cost goods if you can't afford to buy them because you've lost your job?" These are serious criticisms and it is important to understand the arguments on both sides.

Although the argument above has been durable, there is not really much new since Adam Smith and David Ricardo first enunciated the principles of specialization and comparative advantage two hundred years ago. Economic growth and trade is unruly. There are gainers and losers at any moment in time. The central question is the extent to which societies will allow their citizens to take advantage of lower priced goods. It is not a new issue. For example, at the beginning of the industrial revolution in England, most weaving was done by workers with individual looms. Cloth was bulky, coarse and expensive. In the first decade of the nineteenth century, manufacturers introduced larger mechanical looms that reduced the amount of labor required to produce sheets of cloth. In addition, the cloth was finer, though apparently less durable. In 1811, some mobs of discontented workers led by someone calling himself Ned Lud broke into some knitting establishments and destroyed their looms. These workers and other who joined their cause became known as Luddites (though who, and if Ned Lud was seems unresolved). They devoted themselves to the destruction of machinery, and the term is used even today to refer to someone opposed to new technology. Their argument was the same as what we hear now in the international trade debates: "What's the use of having lower-priced goods if I have no job?"

In the early years of the American republic, wheat was grown in the New England states. Land in New England is very rocky, and as a result, there are many picturesque stone walls the early settlers built do delineate their property lines. It was backbreaking work clearing those lands, but eventually wheat was grown there. In the first half of the nineteenth century, farmers cultivated land in what was then regarded as the northwest—Ohio, Indiana, Illinois—and states to the south. In the likely case you have never driven across the continental United States (or Canada), let me assure you that the scenery is essentially nonexistent between eastern Ohio and Wyoming. What makes the views boring is exactly what makes the land good for farming—it is flat. Soon, farmers in these states were undercutting prices farmers charged in New England. The wheat industry ceased to exist in the northeast, and moved steadily westward to where it is now concentrated—the western plains states. In the process many farmers suffered losses. If they were politically able, they would have used the same arguments as stated above and would have tried to enact laws preventing the importation of grains from these lower cost producers in the western states. In the United States, the Commerce Clause in the U.S. Constitution prohibits states from restricting the free movement of goods or people across state boundaries, so state-by-state tariffs are not possible. The farmers and other workers who lose their jobs in one state because production is cheaper in another state have no legal recourse. These workers of old simply had to endure the economic change they faced.

The history of the United States and other modern countries is filled with stories of business successes followed by failures. Industries that once flourished sometimes do not even exist in the present. Most of the reason for these changes has to do with technological change. For example, half-century ago, retail businesses purchased mechanical cash registers to make change and to keep track of their daily sales. That's about all these machines did, but they were expensive nonetheless. Maybe you have seen some of the behemoths of the early part of the twentieth century in antique shops. In today's dollars they would cost about $10,000 apiece. The reason they were so expensive is that they consisted of hundreds of gears machined to high tolerances. The workers who produced these and similar machines were highly skilled, and highly paid. In the past generation, all these machines were replaced by electronic terminals that at a fraction of the cost, not only make change, but also keep track of sales by cashier and transmit the sales data to a computer that automatically tracks inventory. The accounting software they use eliminated the jobs of countless bookkeepers. These electronic terminals are manufactured by machines that stamp out component parts by robots. As a result, the cost of retailing and therefore retail prices has fallen, and consumers benefit by these lower prices. Many of the machinists who built the old mechanical devices, on the other hand, have had to accept lower-paying jobs, as the demand for their services is now much less. The electronic revolution, which has brought tremendous gains to consumers, has produced some net losers as well. It's all a part of the process of economic growth.

The fundamental value judgment we face as a modern society is the extent to which we are going to allow consumers to benefit from the availability of lower cost goods, whether these gains derive from technological change or from international trade. When the wheel was invented, people whose comparative advantage was toting things around because they were big and strong suffered a loss in income. Power steering made truck driving available to women, and lowered the incomes of males in that profession. In the 1970s, typesetters at the New York Daily News had a protracted strike because the owners wanted to replace them with electronic word processing. It's easy to be sympathetic with those workers, but we know that a public policy along the lines of what the Luddites were suggesting—preventing these technological improvements from taking place over the years—would mean that we would still be slaving away in the fields for 16 hours a day.

These trade-offs are ultimate resolved through the political system. We provide unemployment compensation to workers who lose their jobs. In the U.S., we have for the most part let domestic industries fail if it was just domestic competition that did them in, but we have always resisted just standing by when it was due to foreign competition. On the other hand congress enacted legislation to provide extended unemployment benefits and job retraining for workers who lost jobs due to NAFTA.

In 1930, with the U.S. economy heading free-fall into the great depression, Congress passed the Hawley-Smoot tariff, which raised tariffs above their already high levels. Because the tariff was stated in actual dollars per unit of a good, as the depression deepened and the price level fell in the early 1930s, the effective tariff rates increased. The effective tariff rate neared 60% in 1933. It had the effect of reducing imports, which is what Congress intended, in order to preserve U.S. jobs. The trouble was, Canada and the European countries retaliated and reduced our exports as well. This had the effect of exporting the U.S. economic depression to Canada and Europe. It is a serious argument that this contributed in a nontrivial way to the rise of fascism in Europe, and ultimately to World War II. After the war, it was a common belief that countries should in the future avoid these "beggar thy neighbor" policies, but many of our leaders today have forgotten that earlier episode.

Hong Kong provides a powerful argument in favor of free trade. After World War II, sovereignty of Hong Kong returned to Britain. Much of the population had left for the mainland during the war, and at war's end, the city had the typically low standard of living common to that part of the world. Britain happened to appoint a governor of Hong Kong who believed in free markets and free trade, in spite of the fact that Britain itself enacted protectionist legislation, imposed widespread wage and price controls, and strongly supported the efforts of unions to prevent plant closures. (Rolls Royce, and the steel industry were classic examples.) Hong Kong pursued none of these policies, and although labor unions were legal, they were an insignificant part of the labor force. Unlike Britain, price controls were very few and far between. Hong Kong refused to retaliate against any country that enacted tariffs on their goods. After 50 years, when the colony was returned to China, the standard of living there actually exceeded that of England, in spite of a steady flow of penniless immigrants into Hong Kong from mainland China. (It's interesting as well that 100 years ago, during the great wave of immigration to America, the per capita income of the U.S. rose every year, even though millions of immigrants with nothing other than the shirts on their backs were entering the U.S.)

Specialization and trade are among the most powerful economic forces. It seems to be part of a basic human instinct to better ourselves through trade with our neighbors. We are unlikely to repeal these tendencies by law, and we will likely have a lower average standard of living to the extent that such restrictions in trading are successful.

CHAPTER SUMMARY

- Modern economies are characterized by a high degree of specialized labor and other resources. In 1776, in *The Wealth of Nations,* Adam Smith gave three reasons for the division of labor. First, specialization increases the dexterity or skill through repetition, second, time is saved by not passing from one task to another, and third, specialization facilitates the invention of machines to take over the routine tasks performed by labor.

- A generation later, David Ricardo enunciated the theory of comparative advantage. Even if one person is absolutely more productive in all tasks than another, it will pay for each individual to specialize in the task in which they are *relatively* most efficient. If trade can take place after production, the highest valued output occurs when each person produces what they do best, and purchases other goods from those whose alternative costs of production are relatively lower.

- Specialization, however, requires trade. It is only through markets that the decisions concerning production can be separated from choices about consumption. It therefore follows that the degree of specialization that can occur, or the division of labor, is limited by the extent of the market.

- The theory of comparative advantage refutes the idea that low wage foreign workers drive American firms out of business and cause loss of jobs. Rather, trade with foreigners enlarges the market and causes further specialization due to comparative advantages. Industries for which Americans have a comparative advantage expand, while others for which firms abroad have comparative advantages contract. Trade benefits some workers and injures others; the value of total output, however, increases.
- The decision to produce one good requires that resources be shifted away from other goods. The marginal cost of output is the decreased output of other goods when additional production of some good occurs. Because resources which have the greatest comparative advantage are utilized first, and these resources cannot be indefinitely replicated, marginal cost increases as output increases. Economists call this phenomenon diminishing returns on the extensive margin.
- Because of rising marginal costs, the relatively efficient resources, such as especially fertile land are paid amounts in excess of the minimum necessary to call forth production. This excess is called rent. These are gains to suppliers in the same way that the difference between a consumer's initial marginal value of some good and the price paid for the good in the market represents a consumer's surplus.
- By maximizing rents, owners direct those resources to those who can use them most efficiently, that is, to generate the greatest net increase in value. This increased value is derived from the usefulness of these resources in satisfying consumers' demand for goods.
- An economy in which the gains from trade are exhausted is called Pareto efficient. In such a situation, it is not possible to make one person better off without making some other person worse off, according to each person's own preferences.
- Economies in which all consumers purchase goods at the same price, and where the price of any good is equal to the marginal cost of production of that good is Pareto efficient. Sales taxes and other laws or regulations that cause consumers' marginal value to differ from the marginal cost of production result in inefficiencies, that is, lost mutual benefits from trade.

REVIEW QUESTIONS

1. Explain clearly the distinction between absolute and comparative advantage.
2. What is the relationship between a person's comparative advantage and his or her marginal cost of producing some good relative to some other person's marginal cost?
3. Why is the area under the marginal cost curve up to some quantity the total cost of producing that quantity of goods?

4. Why is the area above the marginal cost curve up to the market price the rents received by sellers? Why does this represent the increase in the value of resources when employed in this endeavor?

5. Explain why the marginal cost curve is a firm's supply curve.

6. Explain the meaning of economic efficiency (Pareto efficiency) in the context of production and exchange.

PROBLEMS

1. Some say that you can buy virtually anything anyone produces in New York City. It's probably true. What would account for this?

2. Mutt and Jeff find themselves on a deserted island. The only two activities available are fishing and hunting rabbits. In a full day, Mutt can catch 3 fish or 9 rabbits; in the same time, Jeff can catch 4 fish or 2 rabbits. Activities can be divided with no loss of efficiency. When left to their own devices, Mutt consumes 2 fish and Jeff consumes 2 fish also.

   a. How many rabbits can each person consume, acting alone?
   b. What are each individual's marginal costs of fishing and hunting rabbits?
   c. Explain how Mutt and Jeff can improve their standard of living through specialization. If they decide to continue to consume 2 fish each, what is their gain from specialization and trade?

3. Aaron and Charlotte find themselves on a deserted island. The only two activities available are fishing and hunting rabbits. In a full day, Aaron can catch 4 fish or 2 rabbits; in the same time, Charlotte can catch 3 fish or 6 rabbits. Activities can be divided with no loss of efficiency. When left to their own devices, Aaron consumes 2 fish and Charlotte consumes 2 fish also.

   a. How many rabbits can each person consume, acting alone?
   b. What are each individual's marginal costs of fishing and hunting rabbits?
   c. Explain how Aaron and Charlotte can improve their standard of living through specialization. If they decide to continue to consume 2 fish each, what is their gain from specialization and trade?

4. Suppose two countries are composed of populations and resources that are identical, that is, there are no comparative advantages that are apparent. Will these countries ever engage in trade, or will comparative advantages eventually come about? What would lead to the ultimate appearance of comparative advantages possessed by each country?

5. The average wage in places like Bangladesh is only about 10¢ per hour. How is it that American firms don't hire these workers causing American workers to lose their jobs, or experience severe decreases in wages?

6. Explain why a shift in consumer demand leads to a movement *along* the production frontier.

7. Why is it that in primary schools one teacher instructs a class for an entire day in such diverse subjects as spelling, arithmetic, geography, science, etc.,

whereas in secondary schools and in college, these topics are taught by specialists in each field. Why do you suppose primary schools are structured contrary to the gains from division of labor?

8. A recent article in the Wall Street Journal described a small apparel company in Los Angeles that is transferring part of its operations to Mexico, largely in response to the provisions of NAFTA which eliminated quotas on clothing imports from Mexico. The owners commented that wages were much lower in Mexico, $60 a day versus $300 a day in L.A., but absenteeism and labor turnover were much higher in Mexico and the workers' output is less than in L.A. The owners indicated they were transferring the sewing of only their low-end products such as T-shirts to Mexico; the high-end apparel operations were being kept in Los Angeles.

   Analyze the above situation. Why aren't all firms moving all of their operations to Mexico, since wages there are such a small fraction of those in the U.S.? Are there goods we would not buy from low-wage countries such as Mexico? Why is this firm transferring only the low-end sewing to Mexico?

9. Suppose you own a computer firm that has two production facilities; one is more modern than the other and production takes place at lower cost there than at the second facility. Suppose you budget $1 million for production and you want to produce the greatest number of computers for that expenditure. You wind up producing 700 computers at the first facility and 300 at the second. Suppose instead you had decided to produce 1,000 computers at the least total cost. Would your production plans be the same or different? What rule would determine how much to produce in each facility, for each strategy?

10. What is the fundamental reason for the existence of rents?

11. Is the payment of rent on an apartment a rent or a cost? Does it matter if one is referring to an individual to society as a whole?

12. "Since rents are a payment in excess of what is necessary to call forth production, taxation of rents would have no affect on production." Do you agree? How does your answer depend, if at all, on the length of time between the imposition of such a tax and reactions to it, if any?

13. Suppose gold is found on public land, say, in a national forest. The government is considering holding a lottery for the right to mine the gold. An economist suggests instead an auction, with the rights to mine the gold awarded to the highest bidder. What allocative differences might exist between these two mechanisms for assigning rights? Which is apt to involve fewer scarce resources?

14. Many politicians advocate energy independence for the United States, that is, complete reliance on domestic energy supplies.

    a. Does the existence of imports indicate energy dependence?
    b. How is it that a big, powerful, productive country like the U.S. none-the-less imports oil from other countries, most of which are much less developed than the U.S.?
    c. What effect does energy imports have on conservation of domestic energy supplies?

15. Suppose the government builds a dam on some river in order to generate electricity. The dam also creates a lake enhancing recreational use of the land. As a result, rents on that land increase, and campers, hikers, etc., are charged a higher fee for use of this land. Are these increases in use fees measures of costs or benefits created by the dam?

16. California Sea Lions are protected by the Marine Mammal Protection Act. It is illegal to shoot or even to harass sea lions. In the Pacific Northwest, these animals have devastated salmon runs to the extent that certain subspecies of salmon are endangered. What fundamental principals of economics is illustrated by this policy?

17. Evaluate the claim made by a columnist in Newsweek that the government could lower our doctor bills by paying the entire education cost of physicians, thus making it unnecessary for physicians to recover the cost of their education in their fees.

18. The President of Mexico recently "bragged" that Mexico had become self-sufficient in food production due to government subsidies of agriculture. Are the people of Mexico better off economically because of such self-sufficiency?

19. "The steel industry must be protected from cheap foreign imports. If steel does not receive (tariff) protection, foreign imports will drive American producers out of business, thus reducing the number of jobs available to Americans." Evaluate.

20. Does application of comparative advantage mean that the person who can produce the most of some good is the one who will do it?

21. Consider two wood pulp firms with the following marginal cost (MC) schedules. Firm A produces the first ton of pulp at $1 per ton, the 2nd ton at $2 per ton, the 3rd at $3, etc., while firm B produces 2 tons of pulp at $1 per ton, tons 3 and 4 at $2 per ton, and so forth.

    a. If 30 tons of pulp are to be produced, what outputs at each plant would minimize the total cost of the pulp?
    b. Suppose the market price for pulp is $10 per ton. How much will each plant produce?
    c. Suppose now, along with each ton on pulp produced, the firms produce a ton of pollutants, which decrease the value of the surrounding area by $2 per ton. What is the *economically efficient* level of output at each plant? (Be sure to define that term.)
    d. Suppose the government simply ordered the firms to cut back pulp production to 3 tons each. Would that result in efficient use of resources? Explain.

22. At the global warming conference that took place in Kyoto Japan, the United States advocated reductions in emissions of greenhouse gases (principally carbon dioxide). All the proposed measures will of course raise the costs of production. Suppose the countries were to agree that every country will be given a quota of a 10% reduction in greenhouse emissions. The United States further proposed that these emission reductions be tradable.

For example, if Japan did not wish to reduce its emissions by some amount, it could purchase the right to produce more than its quota of emissions from another country, say, the United States. The U.S. would then have to reduce its emissions by its own 10% plus the amount it received from Japan. Thus countries could get cash from other countries by agreeing to reduce emissions by more than 10%, while other countries would pay other countries to take part or all of these emissions reduction mandates off their hands. What do you make of this emissions trading program; in particular, would it improve economic efficiency, and if so, why?

23. (From the fifth grade, but it still gives students fits.) If one boy can mow a lawn in four hours and another can mow it in five, how long will it take them to do it together? Assume no interference or gains from specialization.

QUESTIONS FOR DISCUSSION

1. Where do you stand on NAFTA? Do you think we should extend free trade to the rest of this hemisphere?
2. Suppose the commerce clause in the U.S. constitution had never been included, so that each state had its own tariff commission to protect its domestic industry. How do you think our standard of living would compare to what it is now?
3. The United States and other countries have laws against foreign countries selling goods "below cost." What incentives or disincentives do firms have to sell below cost? Is this a good way to make money?
4. Some prominent American firms have been found to be contracting with firms in the third world that employ children at low wages and for long hours. It is not easy to be unmoved by the conditions under which these people live and work. Should it be our policy that domestic firms should not deal with firms that employ children anywhere in the world? What affect will we have on those children and their families if we pursue this policy?
5. What do you think of the tendency of universities and colleges to promote interdisciplinary courses and programs?
6. "Life would be so much simpler and less stressful if people were more alike." Do you agree? When do differences lead to gains, and when do they lead to losses?

CHAPTER 7

The Law of Diminishing Returns

There is perhaps no more amazing development in human history than the incredible increase in production in the past two centuries. Two hundred years ago, most Americans (and most everyone else as well) earned their living as farmers. Today, only about one percent of Americans earn their living farming. Whereas it used to take most of the population to feed us, now we are fed by a tiny fraction of the workforce. This means the rest can produce goods other than food. The amount of goods any one of us is now able to produce is beyond the wildest speculation of people even just a hundred years ago. Our poorest people now have a standard of living higher than all but the most lavishly wealthy citizens of earlier centuries (and those people didn't have cars and televisions, and if they got appendicitis, they died).

7.1 Inputs and Outputs; Marginal Product

In this chapter, we begin our analysis of the process of production. We also explore how the reasoning we use is important in many aspects of our lives. In Chapter 6, we investigated the phenomenon of diminishing returns at the extensive margin. As output is increased in the economy, we must utilize resources which are less and less efficient in that endeavor. In this chapter we analyze diminishing returns as firms add productive inputs *of the same quality* to given amounts of other resources.

Production takes place when various **inputs**, for example labor, land and machinery (capital) are combined, typically under the direction of some firm owner or manager, to produce some sort of **output**. The inputs are often called **factors of production**; they include anything that in any way contributes to production. Output is the new good that results from the combined actions of the inputs. Outputs are goods or services that are more useful to consumers (i.e., more highly valued) than the total of the input values in their raw state. Outputs can take various forms. Some outputs are the end products that individuals consume directly, such as food and clothing. Others outputs are intermediate goods desired not for their own use, but because they are useful inputs in the production of some other good. For example, tractors are produced not because people want to stand around and admire their beauty or form, but because tractors are useful inputs in the production of food. Even food, i.e., the crops grown by farmers, is not really the end product for consumers because before actual final consumption takes place, someone must transport and retail the raw food, and (usually) cook it, i.e., combine it with labor inputs to produce a meal.

Durable goods, those that last for more than one production period, and which are produced specifically to be inputs in the production of other goods, are called **capital**. More generally, capital comprises any resource that generates income. The human brain is a most important form of capital: the knowledge and skills we possess are a critical part of the process of production. We refer to this kind of capital, not surprisingly, as **human capital**. We refer to the remaining capital in society as nonhuman, or physical capital. A college education, especially in fields with a strong vocational aspect, such as engineering or business, is a direct source of enhanced income for its owner. Land is sometimes accorded its own category (the classical economists referred to land, labor and capital as the three inputs of production) but in reality, land is simply one form of capital. We deal more explicitly and in much greater detail with the process of capital formation in Chapter 10. This very important topic is the foundation of the theory of economic growth.

For now, however, we simplify the process of production and consider just two inputs, labor and capital which are used together to produce useful output. Economists use the term **production function** to denote the relationship between inputs and output. We write

$$y = f(L,K)$$

to express mathematically the statement that the amount of output, y, is a function of (depends in a well defined way) on the level of both labor, L, and capital, K, employed. When we consider only two inputs, we usually think that they enhance each other's effects, that is, they are complementary. For example, the output of laborers will be enhanced if they are provided equipment with which to work, and enhanced further if the equipment is of higher quality. A writer with a word processor can produce more than a writer with only a typewriter, but output using a typewriter will be greater than using a quill pen. Trucks and truck drivers similarly are complementary inputs. More generally, however, the various inputs in production can also be substitutes. For example, typewriters and word processors are substitute inputs, as are men and women in the work force, and professors and teaching assistants.

As in the analysis of consumer behavior, we seek refutable implications based on general empirical laws. Proceeding in an analogous manner, we first distinguish the **marginal product** of a factor input, from its **total product**. Recall that the marginal value of a good is the amount a consumer would pay for an additional unit, whereas its total value is the amount the consumer would pay for all units rather than have none. In the same manner, the marginal product of some productive input, say, labor, is the additional output that is created when an additional unit of labor is applied to a given amount of other inputs. The marginal product of any input is always measured holding the level of other inputs constant.[1] The total product of labor is the difference in output that results when the present amount of labor is used versus when no labor at all is used. If a certain input is critical to production, meaning that no production can take place in its absence, e.g., if no output can occur without at least one worker, then the total product of that input is simply the entire total product.

The marginal product of a factor of production depends on the useful attributes possessed by that factor and by the quantity and quality of other inputs used with that factor. In the case of human labor, useful attributes include a person's training and skills, and other traits such as honesty and the propensity to arrive for work on time. In addition, the marginal product of human labor depends on the quantity and quality of capital that is available for use with labor. The marginal product of a writer or secretary is higher if word processors rather than typewriters are available. The marginal product of an engineer depends on the availability of computers and other equipment. Further, the marginal product of an input depends on the quantities of the various inputs used. It matters whether a person is the first worker hired or the 101st. Lastly, the marginal value of an input to a firm is the value of the marginal product of that input. This incremental value is the additional output produced by that factor, multiplied by the price at which that extra output is sold.

1. Mathematically, the marginal products of labor and capital are, respectively, the first partial derivatives of the production function with respect to labor and capital.

In modern societies, production takes place within firms. It is interesting and important to consider why this is so. An alternative means would be for labor and the owners of capital to contract with each other in the marketplace. Instead, we see workers, managers and owners working within some sort of institutional structure with rights and duties that both groups agree to follow. Workers are expected to show up and leave at certain times, perform certain tasks, and to allow direction and coordination by owners and managers. For the present, we take this organization of production as a given. In the Chapter 9, we investigate why this arrangement is such a pervasive form of production.

The Law of Diminishing Marginal Product

Consider now a farm in a developing country as a representative firm,[2] and assume for simplicity that only two inputs are used, human labor and land. The output, or product of the farm is food, and we show in Table 7-1 the actual quantities forthcoming. The first two columns of this table indicate the number of people working and the resulting total output of the farm. In particular, the numbers in column (2) reveal how much output results when the indicated labor input is combined with a certain amount of capital in the form of land. The outputs resulting from the various levels of labor input are a description of the production function of this farm. Not displayed is the relationship between capital (in this case, land) and output. The numbers in this table assume some given, constant amount of farm land of some specified quality is utilized. It is obvious that the fertility of the land will be an important determinant of output. If the land was more fertile, food output with one or two units of labor might be 5 and 11 units respectively, rather than 3 and 8. In general, the amount and quality of other inputs will be important determinants of the output resulting from the

Table 7-1

(1) Number of laborers	(2) Total Product	(3) Marginal Product	(4) Average Product
1	3	3	3.00
2	8	5	4.00
3	15	7	5.00
4	21	6	5.25
5	26	5	5.20
6	30	4	5.00
7	33	3	4.71
8	35	2	4.38
9	36	1	4.00
10	36	0	3.60
11	35	–1	3.18

2. The word firm is apparently derived from farm, a prominent early example of a firm.

application of any given input, e.g. labor, to the productive process. These other inputs can be either different kinds of labor or various capital inputs, such as the machinery used by the workers. A farm with modern equipment will produce more than one in which the capital inputs are more meager.

The remaining two columns of the table are derived from the first two. Column (3) is called Marginal Product. The marginal product, in this case, of labor is the *incremental* output that occurs when one additional laborer is added.[3] We must emphasize that in this example, labor is added to a fixed parcel of land. Only labor is varying. The marginal product of a factor of production is always defined in terms of changes in that factor applied to fixed amounts of all other factor inputs. In this example, when zero laborers are employed, there is no output. When one laborer is employed, the incremental or marginal output is the entire output of the farm, 3 units of food. When a second laborer is added, total output rises to 8. The marginal product of labor at this point is therefore 8 – 3 = 5. At this level of labor input, the marginal product of labor has increased. When worker number three is added, output rises to 15; the marginal product is therefore 15 – 8 = 7. As additional laborers are added beyond this point, however, the marginal product starts to decrease, and decreases forever after that point. Total output continues to increase as workers are added (up to 10 workers total) but those increases become smaller and smaller. This phenomenon of (eventually) diminishing marginal product is regarded as so universally valid that it has come to be characterized as a law. We state the *law of diminishing marginal product* in this way:

> As one input of production is added to a fixed amount of other inputs, after some point, the marginal product of the variable input continually diminishes.

The law of diminishing returns is a law about the behavior of marginal product, not about total product, or about anything else. In our example, when the eleventh worker is added to the farm, total output actually declines. This might occur if the laborers actually started to interfere with each other at some point, e.g., get in each other's way and hinder the productive process. Too many cooks really can spoil a broth. But decreasing total product is not what the law of diminishing marginal product is about. The law refers only to the behavior of marginal products, as its statement indicates.

Why should we believe that this law is true? This proposition is not a rule of logic or mathematics, nor has anyone claimed divine revelation in its behalf. The law of diminishing marginal product is an empirical generalization about the real world, a statement of a regularity in all observed technological relationships. What evidence speaks for its veracity?

Perhaps the most compelling case for the law of diminishing marginal product is made by considering the consequences of the contrary law. Suppose as workers were added to a firm, marginal products were forever rising. What would we observe? Consider that firms hire workers (or, for that matter, any input) because of mutual gain. That is, workers agree to be employed because it is better than any other alternative (either another job or unemployment), and the

3. The incremental output that occurs when a unit of capital is added to a given amount of labor is likewise called the marginal product of capital, though those numbers are not displayed.

firm agrees to hire the person because it will make more money by so doing than by not hiring the person. If a firm has already decided to hire one person out of its self-interest, then if the second worker adds even more to output than the first, it will be even more advantageous to hire the second worker, assuming wages remain the same. If the marginal product of each successive worker is always greater than that of the previous workers, then if it paid to hire the previous workers, it will surely pay to hire the next worker, and the next worker, and so on, *ad infinitum.* Increasing marginal product with constant wage levels implies infinite firm size. It never pays to stop hiring workers if their marginal products continually increase.[4] The inconsistency of this implication of increasing marginal products with actual observation of real firms is the fundamental evidence for the veracity of the law of diminishing marginal product.[5]

The law does not rule out increasing marginal product over some initial level of factor inputs. We indicate this in Table 7-1, where for up to three workers, marginal product in fact increases. We allow this possibility because it seems consistent with observation. Suppose, for example, the output to be produced is to move 100 pound rocks from one spot to another. One person will likely have zero marginal product in this endeavor, but the addition of a second person will probably allow output to take place. The marginal product will almost certainly increase at that margin. As additional workers are added to the effort, however, their marginal contribution will certainly fall. More fundamentally, initially increasing marginal product derives from the gains from specialization. In the case of carrying a rock, the individual workers are doing an identical task. There is little coordination required. In more substantial processes, however, the presence of additional workers allows specialization to take place to a greater extent. Specialization produces gains by exploiting individual comparative advantages, by the time saved avoiding changes in tasks and through eventual greater dexterity. These effects are reflected in the production function in the total and marginal product schedules. The gains from greater specialization can be expected to at least initially outweigh the disadvantages stemming from the added congestion inherent in applying additional variable inputs (workers) to a fixed amount of the other factors of production.

Column (4) in Table 7-1 displays the average product of the workers for each input level. Average product, as its name implies, is simply the total product divided by the number of workers. It is tempting to think of the marginal product as the output of the last worker. In fact, the output of the last worker is

---

4. Eventually, however, a firm will become so large that its own hiring efforts will bid up wages, producing large but not infinite-sized firms. However, even for large corporations, the effect on wages is not apt to be large. Firms such as Microsoft recruit nationwide, partly to avoid exactly this effect on wages. In the long run, when workers and other firms can migrate, the presence of large firms is unlikely to swamp constantly increasing marginal products.

5. A more fanciful argument suggests that with increasing marginal products, the world's wheat supply could be grown in a flower pot. Suppose one laborer working on an acre of land produces 10 bushels of wheat; two laborers produce 25 so that the marginal product of the second worker is 15 bushels; a third worker adds 20 more bushels, a fourth 25, for a total of 70 bushels. Since four workers can produce 70 bushels on 1 acre, two workers should be able to produce 35 bushels on half an acre, and one worker should produce 17.5 bushels on a quarter acre. Evidently, by squeezing more and more workers onto the same plot of land, and then shrinking the parcel for each worker allows then same output over ever decreasing acreage. This argument, however, also employs an assumption known as constant returns to scale, wherein changes in all factor inputs in the same proportion leads to changes output in exactly that proportion.

the same, if the workers are all identical, as the output of any other worker, and this output level is the average product. Marginal product is the increase in output that occurs when an additional laborer is used; this is a different quantity from the output of any given worker (the first or the last) which is the average product. Note that the average product also increases and then decreases in this example; however, economics asserts no general law about average products.

We refer to diminishing marginal product within a firm as diminishing returns at the intensive margin. It is a different phenomenon than diminishing returns at the extensive margin, which is caused by the inability to replicate efficient resources as output increases. The distinction between the two is due to David Ricardo:

> It often, and indeed commonly happens, that before . . . the inferior lands are cultivated, capital can be employed more productively on those lands which are already in cultivation. It may perhaps be found, that by doubling the original capital employed . . . the produce will not be doubled . . . it may be increased . . . [by something less], and that this quantity exceeds what could be obtained by employing the same capital on [other] land. . . . In such a case, capital will be preferably employed on the old land, and will equally create a rent; for rent is always the difference between the produce obtained by the employment of two equal quantities of capital and labour.[6]

We have discussed in the previous chapter that rents occur at the extensive margin because of the difference in efficiencies in production between some input and the least efficient input of its type that is used. It is also the case that rents are produced at the intensive margin because of diminishing marginal products. In this case, the units of input are of identical efficiency, but their application to a fixed amount of other factors makes the addition to output (marginal product) created by the last unit of variable input employed less than the marginal product of previous units. The effect, therefore, is the same: rents are created representing the difference in the contributions (here, the marginal products) of the successive units. These rents similarly represent the gain in employing these resources in their current use versus their next best alternative.

Check your understanding: Make sure you can distinguish total, marginal and average products. If the marginal product is diminishing forever, does that mean that total product will eventually diminish?

7.2 Profit Maximization and Factor Demand

We now investigate the production decisions of a firm under the assumption that the land which the farm occupies is held as private property. In this case, the land owner decides how many workers to employ, and any profit or rent on the land is kept by the landowner. We say the owner is a "residual claimant" on all rents generated on the land. Under private property, the owner has the undisputed right to receive this income. Since more is preferred to less, the owner chooses

6. David Ricardo, *Works, op. cit.,* quoted in R.B. Ekelund and R.F. Hebert,*op. cit.*

that labor input which maximizes the rent on the land. (Of course actual firms choose the levels of many inputs, what level of skills workers should have, and the level of capital inputs—the types and quantities of machines—in addition to merely the level of one particular type of labor. These more advanced considerations do not change the reasoning that follows in any important way for our present purposes.) It may not be simple or instantaneous to find the input level which results in rent maximization, but the incentive is there to discover it. If the present owner is insufficiently astute to discover it, then if the land is legally transferable (i.e., it can be sold), another owner who is better at farm management is likely to purchase the farm and run it more profitably. A more efficient manager can produce larger rents on the land than someone will less skill. In that case, the more skilled manager can profitably offer the present owner some amount greater than what the less efficient owner can earn for the rights to the land, and the land will eventually pass into the hands of those who can produce the greatest increase in value (rents) from it.

The data in Table 7-1 have been used to construct Table 7-2. In this table, Total Product, Marginal Product and Average Product have been replaced by the values of the total, marginal and average products. Output, or product is a physical unit, e.g., bushels of wheat, or number of head of cattle. The value of total product is the amount that consumers pay for the total output. The value of the marginal product of a factor of production is called its **marginal value product**. It is the number of physical units the firms produces times the per-unit price. We assume here that the market price of this output is not affected by how much this farm decides to produce. Usually, we assume that an increase in output, which increases the amount of the good available to consumers must lower consumers' marginal value of the good and thus its market price. However, if a firm is only a very small part of a large market, its output decisions have only a negligible influence on the total amount of the good available. The effect on market price then can also be assumed to be negligible. For example, the decision by one wheat farmer in the United States either to increase output or go out of business altogether has no measurable effect on the world price of wheat.[7] With this assumption, the values listed in Table 7-2 are all proportional to the corresponding physical quantities displayed in Table 7-1.[8] In the analysis below, we assume the price of the output is $10.00. The values of total, marginal and average product are therefore simply $10 times the physical outputs listed in Table 7-1.

In addition to the columns which are directly multiples of those in Table 7-1, we show columns indicating Total Labor Cost and Rent. Let us assume that this farm can hire all the workers it wants at $40 per day. That is, assume the supply curve of farm workers is a horizontal line at a wage (price) of $40. This assumption means that this farm's decisions with regard to its labor input are a negligible part of the entire labor market, almost surely a safe assumption for virtually all firms of any kind. In this case, column (5), total labor cost, equals the number of laborers times their daily wage of $40. The rent generated by these input (and thus output) decisions is the value of total product minus the

7. Economists refer to such markets as perfectly competitive. We discuss these markets, and imperfectly competitive markets in the next chapters.

8. In the case where one firm is so dominant in a market so that its decision to, say, produce more has the effect of lowering the price of its output, total revenue is not proportional to physical output. We leave the analysis of such monopolistic markets to a later chapter.

Table 7-2

(1) Number of Laborers	(2) Value of Total Product	(3) Value of Marginal Product	(4) Value of Average Product	(5) Total Labor Cost	(6) Rent
1	$ 30.00	$30.00	$30.00	$ 40.00	–$10.00
2	$ 80.00	$50.00	$40.00	$ 80.00	$ 0.00
3	$150.00	$70.00	$50.00	$120.00	$30.00
4	$210.00	$60.00	$52.50	$160.00	$50.00
5	$260.00	$50.00	$52.00	$200.00	$60.00
6	$300.00	$40.00	$50.00	$240.00	$60.00
7	$330.00	$30.00	$47.14	$280.00	$50.00
8	$350.00	$20.00	$43.75	$320.00	$30.00
9	$360.00	$10.00	$40.00	$360.00	$ 0.00
10	$360.00	$ 0.00	$36.00	$400.00	–$40.00
11	$350.00	–$10.00	$31.82	$440.00	–$90.00

total labor cost. (In this example, the only costs are labor costs. In more complex models, the cost of other inputs such as various capital items would also be included.) It is apparent from the table that rents are maximized when the farm utilizes either 5 or 6 workers. For the purposes of this discussion we shall use 6 as the rent maximizing input. In the case where inputs can be continuously varied, so that, say, 5½ units could be used (perhaps 5 full time workers plus one at half time) the firm would hire up to 6 workers. With 6 workers, the total value of output the farm produces is $300.

That rents are maximized when the owner uses six workers is something we can derive without any reference at all to the actual rent column, using more insightful reasoning. Consider the employment decision of the landowner. The owner will hire a worker as long as that person produces more in rents than the $40 it costs to hire that person. Notice that rents are zero when two workers are used. The third worker increases the value of output by $70, yet this person only costs the owner $40. The owner therefore derives $30 additional rents on the land by hiring this worker, and so rents increase to $30. Likewise, the owner makes an additional $20 by hiring the fourth worker since the value of this worker's marginal product is $60, while the additional cost of the worker is only $40. The total rents generated by workers 1 through 6 is the sum of the rents at each input level: –$10 + $10 + $30 + $20 + $10 + $0 = $60. As long as the value of the marginal product of labor is greater than the cost of that labor, a firm owner will employ those workers. It is to their mutual advantage that this be done; no coercion or additional incentive from the state is necessary. The firm will cease hiring additional workers when the value of the marginal product of labor falls to the alternative cost of that labor. *A firm engaging in profit or rent maximization employs factors of production as long as the value of the marginal product of each factor is greater than or equal to the additional cost to the firm of that factor. When the value of the marginal product falls to the wage of that factor, the firm ceases to hire that input.* In symbols, this condition is

$$p \times MP = w \qquad (7\text{-}1)$$

where p is the price of the firm's output and w is the wage of the factor of production.

In the present example, the firm will find it to its advantage to employ six workers but not the seventh. The seventh worker adds only $30 to rents, but costs the owner $40. If, however, wages of workers fell to $30, it would then be in the self-interest of the firm owner to hire that additional worker. If wages in the rest of the economy rise to $50, the firm would cut back to five workers. We see therefore that the firm's demand curve for factors of production must be downward sloping, in analogy to consumer's demand curves for ordinary goods and services. The law of diminishing marginal product implies that the demands for factors of production on the part of rent maximizing firms have the fundamental property of all demand curves: a negative slope. Economists state the **law of factor demand** as:

> If the wage of any factor decreases, the firm will choose to hire additional units (and vice versa), holding other things constant.

Check your understanding: Suppose the firm could vary more than one input at a time. Would relation (7-1) still hold for labor, and what would the corresponding rule be for the other inputs?

7.3 The Behavior of Firms Under Different Rules of Ownership: The Effects of Property Rights on Resource Allocation

We now analyze how the legal and institutional framework in which a firm works affects the process of production. We show that laws and institutions *matter.* In the previous sections, we assumed that land and the other nonlabor resources are private property, and the firm had an owner who could keep the rents produced on the land. While common in the western democracies, this institution has not been universally admired. With private ownership, production is carried to the level where those rents are as large as possible. However, this is not true in many parts of the world, and even in the western democracies, pursuit of pecuniary gain is often restricted by laws, e.g. in regard to pollution, discrimination, wetlands regulations, zoning and the like. Consider therefore two somewhat idealized alternative arrangements under which our hypothetical farm (firm) might operate:

1. Common Ownership of the Land. In many countries and societies, land is regarded as a gift of nature and private ownership is forbidden. In these instances, no person has the right to exclude others from any parcel of land. A very prominent instance of this situation is deep-sea fishing. On the high seas, there are no property rights established in either the fish or other ocean resources, except by occasional international treaties. Beyond each country's territorial and offshore limits, there is in general no law and no legal protection of any natural resource, and in particular, the fish. Anyone who catches fish on the open seas can keep that fish without paying fees to an owner. Even within countries, however, various societies have operated in this fashion. At various times in Mexico, for example, persons could squat on a piece of land and effectively claim ownership and use the land for their own purposes. Much land on Indian reservations in North America is owned communally by a tribal leadership, and individuals have little to say about how land is allocated and used. Individuals in some cases cannot exclude other tribal members from using any land owned by the tribe. In Israel, farms were sometimes organized as a Kibbutz, where anyone who wished could join the Kibbutz, though in more recent years, existing members could restrict the number of newcomers.

2. Socialist Cooperative. This type of enterprise is a workers' democracy in which the laborers in the firm decide how many people to hire (and therefore how much to produce) and how the proceeds will be divided. We assume here that each worker shares equally in the total product, and that the cooperative chooses the amount of labor input for which the gain to each individual is greatest. This is an entirely legal form of ownership in the United States and other western countries. There were also some firms of this type in what was once communist Yugoslavia.

We now show that the allocation of resources varies under the different constraints imposed by the various systems of property rights just described (and private property). That is, the input levels and outputs chosen by firms operating under these different rules are different. We inquire as to why these different outcomes occur, and analyze the economic efficiency of the resulting allocations. We ask if the outputs that result from these legal environments exhaust the gains from trade that are available. We assume as in the case of the competitive firms, that workers can earn $40 per day elsewhere in the economy.

With *common property,* no person owns the land. No individual has the right to exclude any others from the land. Any person wishing to use the land need only stake a claim, but if others also wish to work on the land, the land must be shared. To stylize the situation for convenience, assume the land is managed by a commune and all members of the commune share equally in the output of the land (and their labor). Also, most importantly, anyone who wishes may join the commune. Instead of wages, each worker shares equally in the total output of the farm. (We assume equal productivity of all workers.) Thus each laborer receives the value of the average product of the farm (total product ÷ number of workers). However, since exclusive rights in the land are not present, workers keep joining the commune until their share falls to what they could earn elsewhere. With fewer than 9 workers, the value of average product is greater than the $40 available in the workers' next best alternative. When 9 workers are in the commune, each individual earns $40, and no incentive remains for any additional worker to join. Thus, with no ownership, workers crowd onto the resource that is common property until the average product falls to the wage available elsewhere in the economy. Under common property, 9 workers produce $360 worth of output on the farm.

Under the *socialist cooperative* type of firm, the workers again all have equal ownership shares of the land. The workers decide democratically how many workers there are to be. Each worker receives an equal share of the total output. The distinction between this and common property is that the workers can and do decide to limit the number of people in the coop. The workers do have the right of exclusion, absent in common property. In this case each worker earns the highest income when the average product of the farm is as large as possible. This occurs in our example when 4 workers are employed. The value of total output on the farm is $210 and each worker earns $52.50 per day. This is a greater amount than what they could earn as laborers elsewhere ($40). The workers exclude any further entrants onto the farm, though many individuals eagerly seek the higher income available to members of the cooperative.

Here we have three systems of property rights (though one, common property, is really an absence of rights), and each produces a different level of output. Under private ownership of the land, 6 people work the land producing $300 output; with common property, 9 people work the land producing $360 output, and under the socialist coop arrangement, 4 workers produce $210. Laws matter. The outcomes are different for each set of rules, or laws. All three cannot be economically efficient. What output, and therefore which system, if any, leads to exhaustion of the gains from trade?

To answer this question, we must understand the nature of the $40 wage available to these workers. This market price of this labor means other employers are ready to employ these workers at that wage. If workers decline to work on this farm for $40, it means that they have a more attractive alternative available to them. They either can find other work at $40 or they are searching for better employment, with an expectation of earning more than $40. It means some productive activity is available to the workers, and thus to society, which consumers value at $40 per day. *Therefore, when an individual decides to work on this farm, $40 of output necessarily disappears somewhere else in the economy.* The wage rate of these workers represents the opportunity cost to society of these laborers. Everyone knows that labor is not free, but it is sometimes forgotten that the real basis for this is that workers can *produce* other goods, which consumers also value. Thus in our example, this $40 wage represents what labor could produce, say, in the nonagricultural sector of the economy if they are not employed on this farm. In order to obtain workers to labor on the farms, they must be bid away from their alternative production capabilities in the rest of the economy. In so doing that alternative production irretrievably disappears.

Mutual benefits are exhausted if the total value of output in the combined farm and nonfarm economy is as great as possible. Suppose a worker produces $40 in one line of work but could produce $50 in another. Then consumers could receive more highly valued output if the worker changed jobs. Consumers in principle would be willing to bribe this worker up to $10 to induce him or her to switch to the higher valued output. They would gain up to that amount, and the worker would lose nothing, assuming the worker was indifferent as to which job he or she performed.[9] A system of property rights that somehow induces workers to direct their energies into labor that is valued less by consumers than in other available work is an economically inefficient system.

Consider now the allocation of resources under common property, where land is declared to be free, and no person has the right to exclude others. In particular, consider the net contribution the ninth worker makes to society. By working on the farm, he or she adds $10 to society's output—the value of the marginal product of that ninth worker. In order to produce this $10 of output, this person did not engage in his or her alternative employment, in which $40 of output

9. If the worker is *not indifferent* between the jobs, the gain is not $10. If the $50 job is so odious that the worker would not take it even at, say, $55, then that worker's loss more than offsets the $10 gain to consumers. We assume the wages already reflect these nonpecuniary aspects of the jobs.

would have been produced somewhere else. Therefore, a net loss of $30 has occurred to society because of this worker's decision to engage in farming. The same analysis holds for the seventh and eighth workers as well. When the seventh worker joins the commune, the value of the additional output is $30, whereas the value of goods lost elsewhere in the economy (the worker's alternative cost) is, as before, $40, producing a $10 net loss. The eighth worker similarly produces a net loss of $20 to society. The loss of total output sustained because workers 7, 8 and 9 work on the farm rather than elsewhere is thus $10 + $20 + $30 = $60. This amount is precisely the maximum rent obtainable on the land. *These rents represent the net gains in the value of output over the cost of production. These gains are dissipated by the absence of property rights.* Although $360 worth of farm output is produced, $360 of nonfarm output is foregone. No net gains have occurred. **Dissipation of rents** is a major cause of economic stagnation in societies where property rights over resources are not well defined.

How can it be that what is in a person's own private interest leads to a net loss to society? The only way an individual's private product can differ from the true, total product to society (what economists sometimes call the social product of that person's efforts), is if that person does not capture all of the marginal benefits produced, or pay all of the marginal costs of his or her actions. When firms add workers, they do a subtle form of harm to the other workers (and possibly to some nonhuman inputs). As each worker comes on board, the contributions to output of the other workers are diminished because of the law of diminishing marginal product. As the labor input changes, the average amount that each worker produces eventually declines.

The fifth worker sees a gain of $12 by working on the farm: the $52 average share versus his alternative wage of $40. However, he damages the previous 4 workers by $.50 each—the decrease in their average products from $52.50 – $52.00. Thus the net benefit he creates is $12.00 – $2.00 = $10.00. The sixth worker stands to gain $10 (her average share of $50 less her alternative wage of $40). She, however, lowers the average product of the previous 5 workers by $2 each, from $52 to $50, or $10 total. The sixth worker therefore destroys as much output as she gains by coming to the farm. For the seventh worker and beyond, the damage created by lowering the previous workers' average products is greater than their own gain in coming to the farm. Worker 7, for example, stands to gain $7.14, but he imposes a cost on the previous 6 workers of $2.86 each, for a total cost of $17.16. The net impact of worker 7's decision to work on this farm is thus $7.14 – $17.16 = –$10 (after the rounding error is eliminated). This is exactly the decrease in rents on the land ($60 – $50) that occurs when worker 7 joins the farm.

This important arithmetic can be viewed from a slightly different angle. With five workers, the value of total product is $260 and the value of the average product of each worker is $260 ÷ 5 = $52. When the firm adds the sixth worker, the average amount that the other workers produce is reduced by $2, to $50. The sixth worker thus damages each of the five other workers by $2 each, for a total damage inflicted of $10. This $10 is in fact exactly the difference between the values of the marginal product of the sixth worker ($40) and the average product ($50). In like fashion, the seventh worker damages the previous six by reducing the value of all of their average products by approximately $2.85 cents each, for a total damage of 6 × $2.85 = $17.10. Again, this damage is precisely the difference between the marginal product of seven workers versus their average product. The marginal product differs from the average product because the marginal product takes into account the impact of adding another worker on the previous workers' average productivity. If this impact is ignored, then individuals do not own the full consequences of their actions. this is the source of lost gains from trade.

With common property, where no one can place restrictions on the amount of workers who can toil on a given piece of land, workers have no occasion to act on this damage in order to mitigate its effects. Each individual sees the average product schedule as their own marginal product. They have no incentive or ability to take account of the reduction of other workers' shares (the average products) that their decision to work on the land imposes. No one is held accountable for this damage, nor is there a mechanism by which the workers can take account of the economic harm they inflict on each other. Each worker, in his or her private decision to engage in farming, therefore ignores the diminution in average product of the other workers. No worker ever considers these external effects even though the private cost of an individual's actions are not the same as the true, or social cost.

With common property, the rent on the land is up for grabs, and therefore workers crowd onto the land until the combined return of their own labor plus the return on the land equals their alternative employment possibilities. But at that point (here, 9 workers) the damage to the other workers is so great that the last worker is really adding only $10 to net product while subtracting $40 from society's output elsewhere. *Common property results in overuse of the unowned resource.* With 9 workers, $360 worth of alternative goods are given up in order to produce $360 worth of food. The term overuse means that the total output of society (that is, including the output foregone when workers engage in this activity) would be higher, resulting in further gains from trade, if utilization of the common property was reduced.

Consider now the case of privately owned land, where the landowner chooses the number of workers so as to maximize the rents on the land. The landowner's own private cost of hiring labor and society's alternative cost of employing that labor on the farm are identical: $40. When the owner decides to hire an additional worker, he or she bids the worker away from his or her next best alternative, which is determined by what that person can produce elsewhere in the economy. The owner, without intending it, compares that alternative production with what the worker can produce on the farm. In this case, therefore, maximizing the landowner's rents will be the same as maximizing the total value of output to society. Workers will be directed to activities that produce the largest possible output through the private interest of property owners, without any central direction. We have seen that a private owner of the land employs 6 workers on the farm. These 6 persons could have produced $240 of goods elsewhere in the economy. On the farm, they produce a greater amount, $300, for a net gain in output of $60 over the next best use of these labor inputs. This gain appears as rents (payments in excess of the cost of production) on the land. Moreover, these net gains are greatest precisely when the private ownership solution prevails.

The reason why private ownership leads to the efficient outcome is that unlike workers under common property, who do not have occasion to observe the entire cost of their actions, the landowner captures all the benefits and all the costs of his or her actions. The effect on the average product of other workers when an additional worker is added to the farm is all reflected in the value of the rents on the fixed factor, the land. Because the landowner owns the land, and therefore the rents on the land, the landowner owns all of the net damages and benefits that workers have on each other. Therefore, no misallocation of resources can then occur. Thus in the case of privately owned resources, the invisible hand does indeed work to produce those goods which are valued most highly by consumers, exhausting all possible gains from trade. However, in the absence of well-defined property rights, this outcome is not assured. *Under a system of privately owned resources and competitive markets, the resulting allocation of resources is Pareto efficient.*

Finally, consider the system of socialist cooperatives. In this case, too few workers engage in farming. The self-interest of the co-op members is to exclude the fifth and sixth workers. But the fifth worker would add $50 of farm output, with a loss of only $40 of output elsewhere. This $10 net gain to consumers is lost by excluding worker number 5. The rent on the land is $50 with four workers. Each worker receives one-fourth of this amount, $12.50, in addition to their wage, totaling $52.50 each, the value of average product with four workers. Each worker earns more than their alternative wage, hence other workers will queue up for the right to work on this farm. The members of the co-op will be faced with the rationing problem of deciding which lucky applicants will be admitted to the co-op when a vacancy arises. These new applicants eagerly seek a share of the rents earned by the existing coop members. They compete with each other in order to obtain those rents. If the memberships are decided by, say, lottery, then the rents will be captured by the lucky winner. However, if entrance into the co-op is itself a common property, meaning no clear rules exist for ownership rights for joining the co-op, applicants will expend resources in order to qualify for the rents. For example, applicants might over-qualify themselves by acquiring extra skills or other attributes that the existing members would find attractive. Any actions along these lines will cause the applicant to dissipate the rents that were to be received. They will make expenditures equal to the gain that was to be realized in exactly the same manner that rents on the land are dissipated under common property in land.

Check your understanding: Is it what workers can earn or what they can produce elsewhere that is important to understanding the problem of common property?

Ocean Fishing

As we mentioned earlier, one of the most prominent and important occurrences of common property are with respect to fishing on the high seas. Many species of fish inhabit areas of the ocean that no nation claims. As a result, no individual has the correct incentive to manage these fisheries in a manner that is economically efficient over the long term.

Various species of fish have been fished almost to extinction. The season for a certain type of mackerel is now down to 15 minutes per year. Why is it that we worry about all the halibut disappearing, but we don't worry about ranchers slaughtering all their cattle and having no beef in the future? In order for us to have wheat next year, some wheat that farmers currently produce must be kept aside for feed rather than be consumed. Why do we not worry that without some sort of regulation, we might in some year wind up with no wheat? The difference is that beef and wheat are privately owned, and the owners of the resources used to produce these commodities can and do evaluate what is best not only for the present but also what effect their present actions have on the future.

Everyone might agree that if more than 10 million pounds of some fish are harvested in a given year, the stocks of that fish will begin to seriously erode, and eventually disappear. The problem is how to prevent overfishing of this resource, meaning managing the harvest that takes into account the fishery's long term prospects. If the fish were raised on a private fish farm, for example, as in the case of trout, we would have no such fears. The current and projected future prices of trout would reveal to the owner of the farm the advantages or disadvantages of increased harvesting. If other trout farmers were depleting their stocks, it would become known that in the future, the price of trout would become very high relative to today's price. In that case, many farmers would realize a greater gain by withholding harvesting in favor of waiting for the much higher future prices.

In the case of ocean fish, no individual has the power to decide any aspect of the over-all harvest. It is first come, first served. If you don't harvest the fish, someone else will. There is no private mechanism for restricting the total catch, and some fisheries have neared extinction as a result. Governments have stepped in to manage offshore fisheries via international treaties. A regulatory body determines the sustainable catch and then typically limits the season to a number of days or hours that they estimate it will take fishers to harvest that catch. Up until very recently, the halibut season in the Bering Sea was limited to two 24 hour days, six months apart. These events became known as the halibut derby. In the days or weeks prior to the season, boats would gear up and head out to some desired area. They would bring in as much equipment as they could handle and then fish continuously for 24 hours, with no sleep. It was very arduous work in an extremely cold and dangerous environment.

In the mid 1990s, under the prodding of economists and other fisheries experts, the Canadian government, followed by the U.S. government a year or so later finally replaced this system with a system of exchangeable quotas. Under current law, the regulatory bodies allocate to each fishing boat the right to catch a certain amount of halibut. They can catch these fish any time they want. The advantages of this system over the previous one is that there are now essentially private rights to the halibut. With the derby, too many resources were used to catch the fish, because the fish were common property. Boats could keep only what they caught in the 24 hour period, so they used more labor and capital than they would have had they been able to fish at a more efficient pace. Fresh halibut was available only for a week after the derbies; after that, halibut was available only frozen. With the quotas, not only can the boats use more efficient levels of inputs, there is an incentive for the boats to pass into the hands of those who can catch the fish with the least resources. If some other prospective owner can catch the fish more efficiently than a current owner, the prospective owner can make a larger profit than the existing owners. They can therefore offer to purchase the quota allotment for an amount that will be mutually agreeable. The highest bidders for the rights to catch these fish are precisely the owners who can catch the fish at least cost. Over time, therefore, the cost of catching fish will decline with this system.

An additional response is that private fish farming of ocean fish has begun, and is now an important factor in the supply of fish. Growers are raising Atlantic salmon in large pens on the Pacific coast in Washington state and elsewhere. The price of salmon has plummeted as a result, but the wild salmon that spawn naturally in rivers and streams on the west coast up to Alaska are in decline, due to the common property problem.

Property Rights on the Navajo Reservation

The creation and maintenance of property rights is an important issue in economic development. In particular, the problems of common property in preventing efficient land use can retard economic growth. Economists Gary Libecap and Ron Johnson have analyzed the effects of common property on the economic development of the Navajo Range in New Mexico.[10] They note that the Navajo, who are often cited as in harmony with nature, have had a history of severe overgrazing of their land by sheep. Libecap and Johnson argue that the overgrazing is caused by the policies of the U.S. Interior department and the Navajo Tribal Council, which have made range land a common property.

The Navajo are a loose federation of family clans. They had no history of central authority and have only had a permanent tribal council since 1923, at the behest of the Commissioner of Indian Affairs. The Council was granted authority over most Reservation property, though individual Navajo owned their own sheep. Each family grazed animals within its customary use area, the borders of which were based mainly on verbal agreements. As population grew, competition for range land increased and grazing on neighboring property became commonplace. By 1930, there were an estimated 1,300,000 sheep on the reservation, more than twice the estimated carrying capacity of 513,000. The intense feeding destroyed forage plants and the soil was exposed to damaging wind and water erosion. Because of the diminished feed capacity of the land, Navajo sheep produced only half as much wool as did non-Indian sheep.

As a result of these ecological effects, the newly appointed Commissioner of Indian affairs, John Collier initiated a stock reduction program. In 1933, purchases of excess sheep were begun, especially from owners of the larger herds. In 1935 the market price of sheep rose above the government purchase price and sales became compulsory. By 1948, the stock of Navajo sheep had been reduced to 465,000. These stock reductions were widely resented. The Indian Service issued grazing permits to family heads that allowed each individual permittee to graze at most 350 sheep. However, no boundaries on the grazing areas were defined. As a result, overgrazing continues to this day. Trespass disputes are supposed to be resolved by the Tribal Council, but these hearings are delayed sometimes for many years, and the Council seems loathe to act. As of 1980, the council was still associated with the stock reductions, and the enforcement of boundaries was at a low level.

Although the grazing permits are transferable, the Navajo prefer to transfer them to family members. Also, leasing to non family members is forbidden, further restricting consolidation of the herds. As a result, the herds are much smaller than what is most economically efficient. Herds on non Navajo land are several times larger than Navajo herds. The existence of many small herds are not only inefficient, they also make enforcement of boundaries more difficult. The invention of barbed wire significantly lowered the cost of fencing and was an important factor in the establishment of property rights in the American West. On the Navajo range, however, fencing has been severely restricted by the procedures of

10. Gary D. Libecap and Ron N. Johnson, Legislating Commons: The Navajo Tribal Council and the Navajo Range, *Economic Inquiry,* 18, January 1980, 69–86.

the Tribal Council. The Council requires unanimous approval of all neighbors that might be affected. Even then further approval is required of other committees and officials. As a result, only 3% of the land is fenced.

Libecap and Johnson investigated the data on herd sizes, overgrazing and production. They found that overgrazing was most severe when the herds were smallest. Fencing is used relatively most frequently by owners of large herds. Owners of small herds have more occasion to migrate, because their smaller land holdings are more susceptible to the vagaries of local weather. Overgrazing, as in the past, leads to sheep of less value due to poor nutrition and thus to declines in incomes from sheep raising. As the theory predicts, poorly defined property rights leads to too much use of the resource which is common property. If people do not capture all costs and benefits of their actions, resource allocation will not be efficient. Lack of property rights may be a significant factor in the decline of traditional Navajo culture.

Population Growth

In a provocative article, ecologist Garritt Hardin described the effects of common property as the tragedy of the commons.[11] He used the word tragedy in its literary sense of the remorseless working of things to an unhappy conclusion, despite our knowledge of how it might be prevented. Hardin applied the concept of common property to the problem of global population growth.

Hardin pointed out that if families bore the entire costs of increasing the population, there would be no population problem. When a couple has children, they must provide for them lest the children not survive. In more primitive times, parents who bred too many children might actually leave relatively *fewer* children, because of their inability to provide food and care. However, with the advent of the modern welfare state, the government has undertaken to provide services for children at public expense. Families therefore have a tendency to treat certain services, such as medical services, food and rent supplements, as part of the public domain. At the present time, many fathers in the United States literally abandon their offspring to their mothers, and thus avoid the costs of their actions. Furthermore, many of these mothers wind up on public assistance. In these instances, the costs of raising their children is borne by others in society.

The population problem is therefore a problem of common property. In the same way that land is overused if it is not owned, society's resources are overutilized when no restrictions are placed on their use. Hardin concludes that to couple the concept of freedom to breed with the belief that everyone born has an equal right to the commons is to lock the world into a tragic course of action.

7.4 Applications of Diminishing Marginal Products

We now further apply the law of diminishing marginal product. First, however, we must consider what a firm or some other economic agent does when more than one productive input is variable. Firms in general can vary the levels of

11. Garrett Hardin, The Tragedy of the Commons, *Science,* Vol. 162 (1968), pp. 1243–48.

many inputs, even in the short run. As in the case of only one variable input, however, the firm compares the value of the marginal product of each factor with the wage or rental rate of that factor. The rents to the firm increase any time an input whose marginal value product of exceeds the wage of that factor is utilized to a greater degree. Thus the firm expands its utilization of all inputs until the marginal value product of each factor equals its respective wage.

Suppose there are *two* variable inputs, labor (L) and capital (K) and denote the marginal products of these factors as MP_L and MP_K. Assume the wages of these factors are w_L and w_K, respectively. If the firm sells its output at price p, then each factor will be hired until the value of the marginal products for each factor equal their respective wages:

$$p \times MP_L = w_L$$

and

$$p \times MP_K = w_K$$

By division, these two relations imply

$$\frac{pMP_L}{w_L} = \frac{pMP_K}{w_K} \tag{7-2}$$

Relation (7-2) says that in order to maximize the net benefits produced by the firm, the ratio of the marginal product of each factor (or, equivalently, the value of the marginal product) to its wage must be the same for all factors. Stated differently, to maximize net rents (benefits), the additional product forthcoming from each input per dollar spent on that productive input must be the same for all inputs. The marginal product per dollar spent must be the same for all inputs. Suppose, for example, that by spending \$500 on additional labor, a firm could produce two new computers, but if the firm instead used that \$500 to purchase new equipment, it could produce 3 new computers. In this case, the firm is not allocating labor and capital to its fullest advantage. If the firm spends \$500 *less* on labor and \$500 *more* on capital, there will be a net increase of 1 computer, at the same total expenditure. This kind of beneficial reallocation on productive inputs is possible any time relation (7-2) is violated. When the value of the marginal products per dollar spent on each factor are the same, no rearrangement of the inputs to production can increase output, and thus net rents are as large as possible. We assume here that the prices, or wages of these inputs to production are set in markets and are beyond the control of this firm.

The above logic of maximizing behavior applies more generally than solely in terms of a firm maximizing rents. In a general sense, relation (7-2) says that whenever choices can be made at more than one margin, so that a decision-maker has several decision variables at his or her disposal, the choices that result in the greatest net benefits are those for which the additional net benefits are the same for all variables. Whatever the objective of a person, firm or political entity, the maximization of net benefits requires the equalization of additional net benefits *at every margin.* We now show how this reasoning applies to some important problems and policy issues.

Emergency Medicine The movie and TV series *M*A*S*H* depicted activities in a Mobile Army Surgical Hospital during the Korean war. Doctors in these units do emergency surgery on wounded soldiers, often making life and death decisions. They have to decide both on whom to operate, and to what extent they should operate on any given individual. The objective in these facilities is to save as many lives as possible, that is, to maximize life. Life is the total product these facilities produce.

Although doctors and nurses in actual situations such probably cannot state the preceding principle of maximization, their actions are clearly consistent with that principle. The doctors do not know any of their patients; they weigh each life equally. Often, a soldier is passed over for surgery because he is too far gone. Perhaps 8 hours of surgery might save his life. However, in those same 8 hours, perhaps several other less severely injured personnel could be saved. Saving the 1 severely wounded soldier might cost the lives of several other soldiers. Maximization of the total number of lives saved requires the doctors to equate the marginal product of their services on all patients. Their marginal product is close to zero both for gravely wounded and only mildly wounded soldiers. As a result, both of those categories have lower priority than those whom surgical intervention carries immediate and large benefits.

In field hospitals, the marginal product of surgery beyond that needed to preserve life may be less than the marginal product of initiating surgery on the next patient. If evacuation of wounded is possible, the surgeons may try mainly to stabilize patients enough so that further surgery in a better equipped base hospital can take place at a later time. The operations themselves therefore are not carried out to the extent they would if the injuries had taken place in a civilian accident. In civilian emergencies, the patient is more likely to have a complete operation with no further surgery. The reason is that in the civilian arena (absent some widespread emergency), surgeons are not faced with the same alternative use of their time as in *MASH* units. There are not usually other emergencies awaiting their services.

Health Care Rationing Marginal reasoning has entered current policy debates regarding state-funded medical care. The state of Oregon has recently instituted a plan for rationing medical care using these principles. In order to extend Medicaid benefits to all of the state's poor, they have decided to curtail some very expensive and often not very productive procedures. The state has drawn up a list of 688 medical conditions but will pay for only 568 of them. Some very expensive procedures exist for treating terminally ill patients. These treatments extend the person's life, but often by only a small amount, and the quality of life may be very poor. The plan's proponents argue that the alternative costs—not providing care to other patients—of these procedures are often too high. Some of the procedures that are not covered are aggressive treatment of terminal cancer or AIDS, simultaneous liver and kidney transplants, infertility and the common cold. By directing medical resources towards patients with better prognoses, or where the treatment has relatively greater impact, the total value of the service may be increased. These discussions very clearly depend on important ethical considerations concerning the value of one human being's life versus another's. These decisions, however, are forced upon us by scarcity. We simply cannot pay for all the medical procedures all people would demand at zero cost. The ethical judgments ultimately come down to the same kinds of trade-offs at the margin that economists use to analyze issues such as these.

Medical Research and Orphan Drugs The United States and other governments spend billions of dollars each year to fund medical research. In recent years, Hollywood actors have sometimes testified before Congress that research on certain diseases which afflicted only a relatively small part of the population was underfunded. The drugs that might be developed for such conditions are referred to as orphan drugs, because pharmaceutical companies find them less desirable to develop than drugs for which the potential patient pool is much larger. It is difficult not to be moved by scenes of people suffering for lack of modern drugs. In 1983 the U.S. Congress enacted the Orphan Drug Act to encourage the development of drugs to treat rare diseases, by granting drug manufacturers exclusive selling rights and providing simpler regulatory review. The question is, however, how shall scarce resources be spent on medical research?

There are two separate decisions to be made at the national policy level. The first is to decide how much total funds are to allocated to medical research, and then, the share going to each disease. The total budget is of course decided through the political process. It is always true that if more funds are allocated to medical research, lives will probably be saved. Yet it is also the case that spending money on other programs also saves lives, or improves lives, such as programs to reduce drug addiction, reduce the presence of dangerous substances in our food, provide educational and medical care to the indigent, etc. These programs must compete with all the other possible uses of our tax dollars, such as national defense, the provision of law and justice and all the rest. The use of resources that would produce the largest benefits to consumers would be that for which the marginal product of the tax dollars spent would be equal in each use.

For a given total amount for medical research, the allocation that maximizes benefits to consumers, in terms of potential lives saved through research, is when the marginal product of research into each various disease is the same for every research program. For rare diseases, the marginal product of research dollars may be very small, because only relatively few lives would be saved even with a complete cure. This is the reason for orphan drugs. For widespread ailments such as cancer and heart disease, the potential benefits are huge because many people are afflicted. However, the potential for progress must also be measured. It may be that certain diseases are so difficult to analyze that funds would have higher payoffs if spent on lesser but more tractable conditions. Obviously, the measurement of the marginal products of research is a very difficult process. However, economic reasoning can be a useful guide to allocating funds in this highly emotional area.

Equalize Output per Worker or per Machine? It has long been noted that in World Wars I and II, the most effective naval weapon, by far, was the submarine. Ton for ton, these ships were the most cost-effective way of sinking enemy ships; in fact, submarines accounted for over 90% of all enemy shipping destroyed. This raises an interesting question: why don't navies build only submarines? A more mundane example was provided to the author by a former student whose family managed a Las Vegas casino. It turns out that casinos, not too surprisingly, make most of their slot machine profits on the dollar machines, not on the nickel machines. Indeed, the average profit per slot machine is greatest for the dollar machines, and least for the nickel machines. (There were once penny machines as well, but that was before inflation.) Why, in the face of good accounting data to this effect, do casinos maintain these lower stakes machines? Why not have all dollar machines, since that's where they make the most money?

On a somewhat grander scale, imagine that you are the economics minister of some country. The administration is committed to scientific economic planning in order to further economic growth and improve upon the obvious failings of the previous free market system. Your assistants have gathered data on worker productivity in various industries. In particular, you are informed that the steel industry produced $1 million per day with 10,000 workers, for an output per worker of $100 per day. On the other hand, the farm sector produced, on an average over the year, $3 million per day using 40,000 workers, implying an output per worker of $75 per day. The prime minister demands to know why you are not recommending the immediate transfer of workers from the agricultural sector of the country to the industrial sector, in particular to the steel industry.

The resolution of these puzzles lies with the law of diminishing marginal product. Suppose you own a casino and you want to put in one slot machine. It'll certainly be a dollar machine; probably the second, third and fourth machines will be dollar machines also. However, suppose you have already installed fifty dollar machines. You must now decide whether a fifty-first dollar machine or the first nickel machine will make more money. A casino owner must always compare the *marginal* revenues available from buying an additional machine, not their average profitabilities.

In Fig. 7-1, we show the value of the marginal products of dollar and nickel slot machines. It also indicates the (constant) marginal factor cost of providing these machines, which for convenience we assume to be the same for both machines. The area under these curves is the value of total product; it is the sum of all the values of marginal products up to any given number of machines. The total profit from employing these machines is the value of the total product minus the total cost. This is the shaded area between the value of the *MP* curve and the input supply curve. Note that after a point, the nickel machines become more profitable than still one more dollar machine. Note also, however, that the average profitability of the dollar machines, measured by the average height of the marginal product schedule above the (constant) marginal cost of providing the machines, is greater than the average profitability of the nickel machines. But it clearly does *not* follow that profits would be greatest if the casino

Figure 7-1 *Equalizing Marginal, not Average Products*

The average profitabilities of machines is the average height above the marginal cost. Even though the average is higher for one machine, it does not pay to use only that machine. Maximum value of output occurs when the values of marginal products of each machine are equal to their respective marginal opportunity costs.

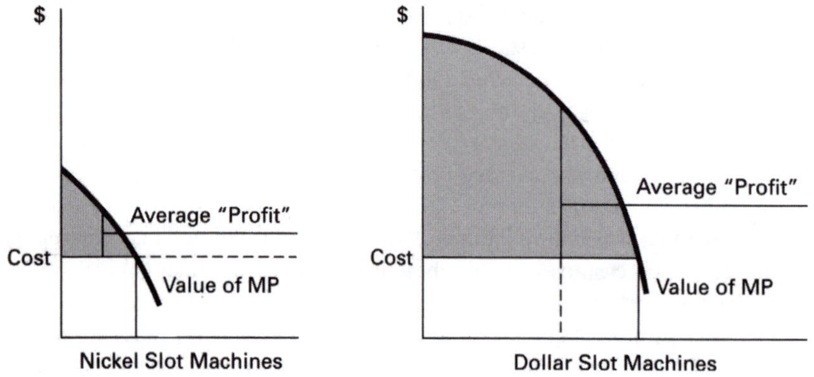

employed only dollar machines. The 100th dollar machine is likely less profitable than to first nickel machine, even if the average of the profits on all dollar machines is greater than the average of the nickel machines. The decision must always be made at the margin, that is, taking into account the number of machines of each type already installed. For the same reason, even if submarines sank 95% of the enemy ships, and the only mission of the navy was to sink enemy ships, a defense planner would still have to weigh the probable effect of adding a few more submarines to a fleet already consisting of, say, 500, against the marginal productivity of the first aircraft carrier. It is likely that a sizable navy (or any other branch of the service) will buy a variety of equipment, even in the face of data such as mentioned above.

In like fashion, output per worker is an average quantity. It is in fact the average product of labor in that industry. The average product of labor is not the same thing as the marginal product of labor. Output per worker does not capture the net impact of adding one worker to the steel industry and removing that worker from the farm. The effects of those actions are given only by the marginal products of labor in those industries. The average products, or outputs per worker, do not include the impact of the addition of workers on the average products of the existing workers. If workers are added to the steel industry in the above example, because of the law of diminishing marginal product, it is not merely the last worker whose product is less, but the average product of all workers decreases. That is why the marginal product is eventually less than the average product. Although the average product of labor might be higher in the steel vs. the wheat industry, the marginal products of labor do not necessarily have to be in that same relationship, and indeed, there is no presumption that it is even likely to be that way. That is why equalizing average products between industries, or trying to achieve the maximum output per worker, even though plausible sounding, are rules which will lead to misallocation of resources. Moreover, economic planners are not likely to be able to secure the kinds of data on marginal products that would be reliable in economic planning. *Query:* How successful do you think you would be explaining the difference between average and marginal quantities to the politicians and the public?

CHAPTER SUMMARY

- The relationship between a firm's inputs, also called factors of production, and the output produced is called a production function. For specified levels of, say, labor (L) and capital (K) a certain output, or total product, occurs.
- The marginal product (MP) of a factor of production is the change in total product that occurs when an additional unit of that input is added to a fixed amount of the other factors.
- As additional units of any factor are added to fixed amounts of the other factors, the marginal product of the variable input eventually declines. This famous generalization is called the law of diminishing marginal product.
- If a firm hires labor at some constant wage rate w, rents to the fixed factors are maximized at the input level where $w = pMP_L$ where p = the price of the firm's output, and MP_L= the marginal product of labor. If the value of the

additional output an input produces (MP_L) is greater than the cost of hiring that extra unit (w), it clearly increases the firm's rents to hire that extra input. Eventually, the value of the marginal product declines due to the law of diminishing marginal product.

- If the land is not owned, so that it is a common property, workers will crowd onto the land until their average product falls to their alternative wage w. This leads to an inefficient level of production, because the value of the worker's marginal product will be less than what the workers could produce elsewhere, measured by their wage. If some workers were to leave the firm and work elsewhere, they would increase the total output of the economy.
- In order to maximize the total value of output with scarce resources, MP/w, the marginal product of each factor divided by its wage must be equal for all variable inputs. This says that the marginal product per dollar spent on each factor must be the same for all factors. If this ratio was larger for, say, labor than for capital, output could be increased by spending a bit less on capital and using the money to purchase more labor.
- Important policy decisions utilize this reasoning. Spending additional dollars on research on some disease necessarily decreases research on other diseases. In order to produce the greatest potential saving of life through disease prevention, the marginal product of research must be the same for all diseases. This may imply, however, that little is spent on some diseases for which the benefits of additional research funds are small, either because the disease is so difficult to cure, or because relatively few persons are afflicted with the disease.

REVIEW QUESTIONS

1. Clearly distinguish total product, marginal product and average product. To which does the law of diminishing "returns" apply?
2. Explain why a privately owned firm sets the value of the marginal product of each input equal to that input's price, or wage.
3. Explain what is meant by common property.
4. What do the rents produced by a competitive firm represent in terms of the alternative value of the resources the firm uses?
5. What do we mean by equating at the margin? Give an example of this type of reasoning.

PROBLEMS

1. The Reverend Thomas Malthus predicted in the early 19th century that due to the law of diminishing marginal product, humanity would always be driven down to subsistence levels of income. Why did his prophesy not come true?

2. Suppose a lake is publicly owned, i.e. a "common property," with "free" fishing for all. The number of fish caught varies with the number of people fishing as follows:

L	TP
1	13
2	25
3	36
4	46
5	55
6	63
7	70
8	76
9	81

Assume the market price of these fish is $10 per fish, and this price is unaffected by the total number of fish caught in this lake. Assume all fishermen can earn $100 per day in their next best alternative. Assume for the moment that there is no depletion of the stock of fish in the lake, for any level of fishing.

a. Explain why common property leads to "too much" fishing.
b. Explain why, if the lake were privately owned the benefits and costs obtained from the owner's decisions about how much fishing to allow would coincide with society's benefits and costs. How much fishing would the owner allow, and would it be an efficient allocation of resources?
c. Suppose now that even at efficient levels of fishing on a current basis, the stock of fish was being depleted. How does this affect your answers to parts a. and b. above?

3. Answer the same questions with the following production function:

L	TP
1	13
2	23
3	30
4	36
5	40
6	42
7+	42

4. You own a supermarket, and your accountants have just informed you that your profits per square foot of store space are greatest for the coffee section, and least for breakfast cereals. Should you therefore expand the coffee and contract the cereal sections?

5. Suppose your next exam consists of 4 questions, equally weighted. Should you therefore spend the same amount of time answering each question?

6. You are running for president on the Republican ticket. In order to win, you need to win a majority of the electoral votes of the 50 states. In each state, the party that receives a plurality of the votes gets *all* the electoral votes, equal to the number of senators (2) plus congressional representatives. Some states, e.g., Utah, Arizona and New Hampshire rarely vote Democratic, and other states, e.g., Massachusetts, Virginia and Minnesota rarely vote Republican.

   a. What strategy should you use for your campaign, e.g., how should you allocate your campaign time in each state? Should you visit each state?
   b. Suppose the electoral college were eliminated, so that presidents would be elected on a straight majority vote. How would that affect campaign strategy?
   c. Suppose you were running on the Democratic ticket. Would your strategy differ, i.e., would you visit different states than if you were a Republican?

7. Many prominent Hollywood actors testified before Congress in behalf of the "Orphan Drug Act.," which gave added patent protection to drugs which were useful only for relatively rare diseases. The actors told compelling stories of people who were condemned to suffer from the ravages of these conditions, and generally blamed the drug companies for "putting profits before people," or words to that effect. How do you react to this testimony? Are more lives saved or benefited by giving special subsidies or rights to research into rare conditions?

8. Each year, major cities in the United States and Canada spend hundreds of millions of dollars on police protection. However, only a small fraction is spent pursuing murderers; much money is spent ticketing speeders and jaywalkers, investigating minor break-ins, etc. If we directed more police resources to catching murderers, we would save lives. Why is it that no police departments devote themselves exclusively to pursuing serious felons such as murderers, rapists, armed robbers and the like?

9. During the 14th century, the Black (Shudder) Death (Bubonic Plague) reduced the population of England by *one third,* in three years. Historians report that afterwards, the prices of goods rose, but wages (incomes) of the survivors rose even more, resulting in higher *real* incomes for the survivors. Also, rents on land fell, and some marginal lands fell into complete disuse. Incidentally, the medium of exchange at the time was mainly metal coin.

   a. What effect did the plague have on *total* (not per capita) output and stock of money?
   b. Explain why the prices of goods would be expected to rise.
   c. Only humans caught the plague. Using the law of diminishing returns, explain why real incomes would increase.
   d. Explain the observation about land rents.

10. "A firm is operating at an efficient level if all workers with one vote each would vote to keep the firm at the present size." Evaluate.

11. During a national plastic emergency, toy manufacturers were allocated 75% of the amount of plastics used in the previous year.
    a. Compare the economic efficiency of this mechanism to allocating plastic by price.
    b. Compare the effect this policy would have on the price of toys versus reducing plastic used through the market.
12. Tobacco production is regulated in the United States. In particular, the right to grow tobacco is limited to certain acreage. Consider that cigarette companies do not own tobacco growing land. Should cigarette companies lobby for removing these restrictions on tobacco acreage?
13. Some Marxists have argued that labor is the ultimate source of the value of all manufactured goods (because some labor had to be used to produce all goods), and therefore payments to capital represent exploitation of labor.
    a. Does capital produce value?
    b. If payments to capital were forbidden, would payments to labor increase?
14. You are the owner of an independent supermarket. Your accountants point out to you that you are making greater profits selling Cheerios than Kellogg's Corn Flakes, but that your profit per box of Cheerios is less than per box of Kellogg's Corn Flakes.
    a. Is this possible? Explain why or why not, with a diagram.
    b. Would these data indicate that you should reduce or eliminate one of these items from your shelves, and if so, which one?
    c. The accountants further point out that both these items have higher profits over-all and per unit than Wolff's brand buckwheat groats (Kasha). Should you be selling Kasha?
15. Suppose you are in charge of allocating research funds for the National Institute of Health. You make a list showing all the diseases afflicting the public and the number of people with each ailment. Assuming you are trying to allocate funds in order to preserve the greatest total amount of life, should you allocate funds in proportion to the number of people in the population with each disease?
16. Salaries for professors in different fields vary considerably across disciplines, even though faculty in these various fields on average work equally hard and are held to the same standards. Professors in the humanities generally earn much less than others, and economists are the highest paid social scientists. What accounts for these pay differences, and can one conclude from these data that, say, that we value the study of economics more than, say, literature?

QUESTIONS FOR DISCUSSION

1. How do you feel about medical rationing plans such as the plan developed by the state of Oregon? Can you propose a more satisfactory way to allocate scarce medical services to the poor?

2. Access to specific classes at universities are never auctioned off to the highest bidder. Classes are simply closed when a certain number of students sign up. As a result, some students are delayed in their progress towards a degree, and sometimes are unable to graduate in a timely fashion. Is there some better way to allocate class space?

CHAPTER 8

Supply in Competitive Markets

The computer industry continues to expand, yet every time we purchase a computer we find that six months later, a better and cheaper model is available. We learn to grit our teeth and smile. What's happening? Is this an increase in demand, and if so, shouldn't that drive the price up, not down? Or is this a supply phenomenon, and we're moving down our demand curves? We next study the workings of competitive markets.

8.1 Competitive Markets

In this chapter we combine the analysis of production and cost and further refine the theory of supply. A supply curve is a schedule which shows what level of production takes place at hypothetical prices. We imagine that the firm is faced by some price determined in the market, and the firm responds to that price by making some output decision. Importantly, we assume the firm's own decisions do not materially affect the market price. Such firms are called **price takers**. They take the price set in the market as given and react to it. Markets in which firms are price takers are called **perfectly competitive**.

How is it that although market prices are determined by the interaction of those who supply and those who demand the various goods in the marketplace, the actions of individual firms can be assumed not to affect the price? Consider first our own influence as consumers of goods. We typically are part of a large buying group. Our own individual actions, while a part of the aggregate demand for the goods we purchase, are only a minuscule part of that demand. If any one of us decided to become a vegetarian, the supermarkets would not notice this decline in their meat sales. They would order the same amount from their wholesalers. Very possibly, at about the same time, someone else decided not to be a vegetarian. Our influence on the market price is so small, we discount it completely. We are price takers in the market for ordinary consumer goods. If we decided to offer supermarkets a price one cent less than the market price for their goods, we would be turned down.

The same reasoning applies to firms that are not a large part of the market they serve. If many other firms sell similar goods in the same market area, the production decisions of individual firms may be so small as to have a negligible affect on market price. The clearest examples of price taking firms are farms producing foodstuffs that are traded internationally, such as wheat, corn and soybeans. Even the largest wheat farmer in the United States supplies only a tiny part of world demand. Wheat is traded around the world, with major producers in many countries, such as the United States, Canada, Argentina, Russia and Ukraine. Farmers are for the most part price takers. They respond to market prices; their own production has no effect on those prices. If they were to attempt to sell their product at even a penny more than the established price, the demand for their output would literally fall to zero, since buyers would easily purchase all they want from other suppliers at the established price.

With other firms, the situation is less clear. It is not true that demand would literally fall to zero if the local supermarket raised its price by a penny on all goods. Most firms have some discretion as to pricing. Moreover, the mix of retail services to offer is often a decision firms make. Some choose to sell at a slightly higher price but provide consumers with faster service at the checkout counters. Some stores sell mostly generic store brands as opposed to nationally advertised brands. These decisions are all evidence that firms are not pure price takers in the literal sense. By contrast, a wheat farmer would never have occasion to make these types of decisions.

The degree to which markets are perfectly competitive is largely an empirical question. There is no completely general answer. In Chapters 11 and 12, we study the behavior of firms that are to some extent **price makers**, that is, they themselves set the price, at least to some extent, in the market. Industries in which only a few firms are present, or where government licensing arrangements have restricted the entry of new firms into the industry are the prime candidates for price making activity. However, we defer discussion of these interesting issues to those later chapters. In this chapter, we treat firms as possessing little or no power to influence market prices on their own. They are one firm in a perfectly competitive industry.

8.2 Diminishing Marginal Product and Rising Marginal Cost

We first investigate the relationship between the law of diminishing marginal product and rising marginal cost. Consider again the production function of the representative firm of the previous chapter. Table 8-1 displays the labor input, total output (total product) and marginal product as before. In addition, however, we show the total, marginal and average costs in the next two columns. Assume as before that the cost of farming on this land consists only of the labor cost. Payment for the use of the land is a pure rent. In Table 8-1, column (4), Total Cost (TC) is the number of workers shown in column (1) times their alternative wage, \$40. Column (5) shows Marginal Cost (MC) and column (6), Average Cost.

The average cost figures in column (6) are simply the total costs in column (4) divided by total output or product, given in column (2):

$$AC = TC \div TP$$

Table 8-1

(1) Number of laborers (*L*)	(2) Total Product (*TP*)	(3) Marginal Product (*MP*)	(4) Total Cost (*TC*)	(5) Marginal Cost *MC*	(6) Average Cost *AC*
1	3	3	\$ 40.00	\$13.33	\$13.33
2	8	5	\$ 80.00	\$ 8.00	\$10.00
3	15	7	\$120.00	\$ 5.71	\$ 8.00
4	21	6	\$60.00	\$ 6.67	\$ 7.62
5	26	5	\$200.00	\$ 8.00	\$ 7.69
6	30	4	\$240.00	\$10.00	\$ 8.00
7	33	3	\$280.00	\$13.33	\$ 8.48
8	35	2	\$320.00	\$20.00	\$ 9.14
9	36	1	\$360.00	\$40.00	\$10.00
10	36	0	\$400.00	—	\$11.11
11	35	–1	\$440.00	—	\$12.57

Average anything is always the total divided by the number of things. Thus, at output level 15, $AC = \$120 \div 15 = \$8.00$, etc. Notice that average cost decreases and then increases, reaching a minimum at around 21 units of output. The reason for this progression is that whereas costs rise in direct proportion to the labor input, i.e. when twice as much labor is used, exactly twice as much cost is incurred, output first increases in greater proportion than the labor input, but then increases in smaller proportion to the labor input, as the law of diminishing marginal product sets in. Thus in the above formula for *AC,* the denominator first increases faster than the numerator, and then slower.

More importantly, turn now to the marginal cost (*MC*) relation. Marginal cost of output is the cost of acquiring an additional unit of output, as distinguished from the average cost, which is a simple ratio defined over all of the units of output. When the first worker is hired, 3 units of output occur at a cost of \$40. The cost of acquiring these three units is therefore $\$40 \div 3 = \$13.33$ per unit. When the second worker is hired, again at an additional cost to the firm of \$40, 5 units of output are added, this being the marginal product of the second worker. In this interval, the marginal cost of output is thus $\$40 \div 5 = \$8.00$. The reason why marginal cost has actually fallen is that when the second worker was added, the addition to output was greater than the previous gain. This production function exhibits initially increasing marginal product. The arithmetic illustrates how the marginal cost of output is determined. When a worker is added to the already existing labor force, the marginal factor (input) cost of that action is the wage rate *w,* in this case \$40. The additional output which results from this action is the marginal product of labor, *MP.* Therefore, the marginal cost of this output is w/MP. In this simple example where only one factor of production can be varied, marginal cost is determined by this simple relation. It says that marginal cost is the cost of the action (in this case adding one worker) per additional output resulting from that action.

Suppose now a firm can choose both the labor and capital input levels in reaching a profit or rent maximum. Denote the wage of labor as w_L and the marginal product of labor as MP_L. Similarly, call the wage (or perhaps a rental rate) of capital as w_K and its marginal product as MP_K. The marginal cost of output when the firm adds a unit of labor is $MC = w_L/MP_L$. If the firm were instead to increase output by increasing its use of capital, the marginal cost would similarly be $MC = w_K/MP_K$. In order to maximize rents, these two ratios must be equal. If the marginal cost of output were cheaper using one input versus the other, the firm would gain by switching to the relatively cheaper input. Thus, when both inputs are variable, marginal cost is determined by the common ratio of wage of each factor divided by its respective marginal product:

$$MC = \frac{w_L}{MP_L} = \frac{w_K}{MP_K} \tag{8-1}$$

Suppose, for example, that by adding labor a firm could add 4 units of output at a cost of \$40; its marginal cost of output in this range is therefore \$10. Suppose also that a unit of capital can be rented for \$50, but that the resulting increase in output is 10 units. Then the marginal cost of output through the use of capital is only \$5. Thus, $w_L/MP_L > w_K/MP_K$. In this case, by cutting back on labor hours by about 1/4 unit, the firm will lose one unit of output at a saving of

1/4 × $40 = $10. It can get that unit of output back by adding about 1/10 unit of capital, at a cost of only $5, thus saving the firm $5 with no decrease in output. The firm thus increases its rents by this rearrangement of its factor inputs. It therefore follows that if a firm is maximizing rents, these ratios of wages to marginal products must be equal, for all variable inputs.

If, as in the above example, the marginal cost of acquiring output is less by using capital than by using labor, the firm can save money and therefore increase its net rents by cutting back on its labor input and increasing its capital input. As it does this, however, the marginal product of labor will rise, due to the law of diminishing marginal product.[1] Therefore, the ratio w_L/MP_L will fall, since the denominator of that fraction is increasing. By the same reasoning, as capital is added, the marginal product of capital will fall, thereby *increasing* the ratio w_K/MP_K. Therefore, as the firm engages in this input rearrangement, the law of diminishing returns acts so as to make the ratios w/MP more nearly equal to each other. Eventually, these ratios must become equal for all variable inputs; at that point, the marginal cost of output is the same whichever input is used, and the net rents of the firm are as large as possible. The equality of w/MP for each variable factor therefore also means that at the rent maximum, if the firm wished to spend an additional dollar on inputs in order to increase output a bit, the firm would be indifferent between using that dollar to hire labor, capital or other variable input, or spreading the dollar around to some or all of the inputs.

In Figure 8-1, we plot marginal cost (*MC*) along with average cost (*AC*). As noted above, the *AC* curve is *U* shaped. The marginal cost curve *MC* first falls and

Figure 8-1 *Average and Marginal Cost Curves*

The average cost curve (*AC*) is *U*-shaped and the marginal cost curve (*MC*) cuts through *AC* at its minimum point. Since marginal cost equals the wage of labor by marginal product, when diminishing marginal product sets in, marginal cost must rise.

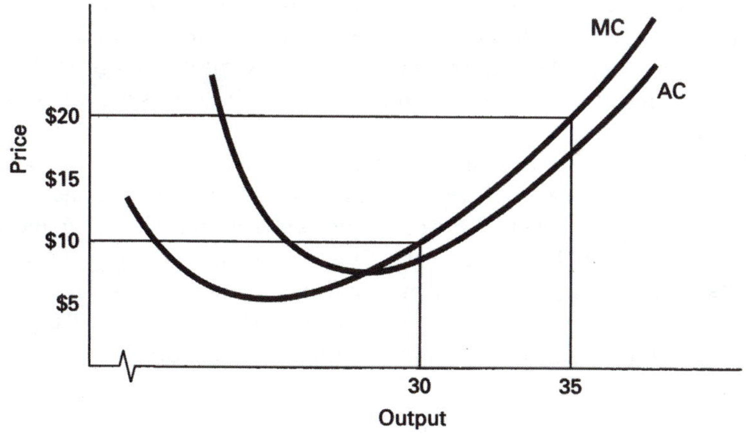

1. This discussion assumes that the firm is operating in the region of diminishing marginal product for each factor, as is necessary for rent maximization.

then rises, passing through AC at the minimum point of the AC curve. It then rises continually. Let us examine the relationship between these curves. First and foremost, *MC eventually rises because of the law of diminishing marginal product.* For every variable input, $MC = w/MP$. The law of diminishing marginal product says that the denominators of all of these ratios decrease as additional units of those inputs are utilized. As the denominator decreases, the expression is made larger. Thus, whichever inputs the firm uses to increase output, marginal cost must eventually rise within each firm, as long as there are some inputs which are not variable. We call this the phenomenon of diminishing returns, or rising marginal cost at the **intensive margin**. Rising marginal cost within the firm is caused by diminishing marginal product of identical units of factor inputs. Rising marginal cost occurs externally to a firm because as output increases, inputs which are less efficient than those previously used are called into production. This source of rising marginal cost, which we studied in Chapter 6, is diminishing returns at the **extensive margin**, and is a separate phenomenon.

If the firm increases all inputs together, the law of diminishing returns does not apply. The law specifically refers to combining increasing amounts of a variable input with a fixed amount of another factor of production. Thus it may be that by expanding all factors, MC actually decreases over some range of output. This is in fact why some industries are dominated by several very large firms. Decreasing average cost is referred to as **increasing returns to scale**, or sometimes, more simply, as *scale economies.* These economies are very apparent in certain industries. It is clearly much cheaper to assemble jet airplanes in large firms with extensive capital inputs than in small neighborhood firms. (However, large firms do subcontract out many components of those jetliners to smaller, and sometimes quite small firms.) At some point, however, it becomes impractical to expand the physical plant beyond its present boundaries, and the law of diminishing marginal product sets in.

The numbers in Table 8-1 produce a graph in which the MC curve intersects the AC curve at the minimum point of the AC curve. This important relation is in fact general for all average and marginal cost curves. It is easy to see why if you think of these quantities as grades on exams. Suppose you have already taken three exams and have obtained an average grade of 80. If your next exam grade, your marginal grade, is higher than that average, it will pull your average up. If it is lower, it will pull the average down. The same is true of average and marginal cost. If marginal cost is lower than average cost, it decreases average cost. If marginal cost is higher than average cost, it increases average cost. Therefore, if AC is falling, MC must be below it, and if AC is rising, MC must be above AC. If AC has a *U* shape, i.e. it has a minimum at some level of output, then it is necessarily falling to the left of that minimum, and therefore $MC<AC$ to the left of that minimum. Similarly, to the right of the minimum, AC is rising and therefore $MC > AC$ in that region. But this means that at the minimum point, $MC = AC$, assuming that there are no discontinuous jumps in either curve.[2] Thus the MC curve passes through the AC curve at the minimum point of AC.

---

2. For those readers with a knowledge of elementary calculus, the following proof of the above relationship between AC and MC may be of some help. Letting y = output, define $TC(y)$, $AC(y)$ and $MC(y)$ to be the total, average and marginal cost functions respectively. By definition, $TC(y) = AC(y)y$. Using the product rule for differentiation, $MC = dTC/dy = AC + y dAC/dy$. Thus $MC > AC$ when AC is increasing ($dAC/dy > 0$) and $MC<AC$ when AC is falling. At the minimum of AC, $dAC/dy = 0$, and thus $AC = MC$.

Check your understanding: Why do we expect the *AC* curve to be *U* shaped? Under what circumstances would it be continually rising?

Fixed vs. Variable Costs

Up to now we have been treating as costs only the amount paid to labor. In general, payments to other factors of production are present as well. The method of payment of these various factors often differs. For example, labor—the services of humans—is really rented. Since the abolition of slavery, it has not been possible literally to own another person's labor. It is possible for firms and individuals to own machines and land, or in general any nonhuman capital. The method by which firms contract with productive inputs for their services therefore varies with the type of input and the legal and institutional setting in which the firm is operating.

One element in these arrangements is whether a firm or individual is committed to paying a factor of production for a specific length of time, or whether the employment contract can be terminated at will by either party. In the case of nonunionized labor, the employer and employee usually agree to the terms of employment informally and verbally. Honesty in dealings between the employer and employee is essentially completely voluntary, depending for its existence on the mutual desire of both parties to continue the relationship. Unionized labor generally operates with written contracts which specify in some detail the wages and working conditions of the employees. Even in this instance, however, workers are rarely given contracts which specify that the employment will continue for some specified period of time, although such agreements are not uncommon in the professions and management. In most cases, an employer who wishes to reduce the number of employees, i.e., reduce the labor input, is free to do so at will, though the terms of dismissal, e.g. by seniority, may vary. Hence, we generally consider labor to be a variable cost. The cost of labor varies as the labor input varies (often in direct proportion—the wage times number of employees).

In contrast, firms employ some factors of production over specified time periods, and a contract is written which says that factor must be paid whether or not the input is used. For example, a firm owner may rent a parcel of land for 3 years at some specified rental rate. (These rental rates, though specified in advance, need not be constant. Often, they are specified to change periodically in proportion to changes in the consumer price index.) In these cases, some part of total costs take on the characteristics of fixed liabilities. Whether the firm produces a great deal or little, makes large profits or operates at a loss, the firm, as long as it is in existence must pay these contractually fixed costs. Such costs affect the *AC* and *MC* curves in ways different from the variable cost of labor.

Suppose that the firm whose production function is displayed in Table 8-1 had entered into an agreement to *rent* the land on which it farmed, for some extended period of time. We previously showed that the maximum rent which could be earned on that land was $60 per day (total product of $300 minus total cost of $240; 6 workers employed). The landowner could therefore charge this rental rate for the use of the land. The rent*er* of this land would have to pay this cost in addition to the labor cost. This payment for the use of the land is not in this case a true cost; rather, it is a transfer of *rents,* since this land is there anyway. It *is* a cost to the firm, since in order to use this land, the firm must bid the land away from other, similar firms. In the case of these rent payments, the amount due, \$60 per day, must be paid regardless of the firm's fortunes at any given moment. These payments are therefore said to be a fixed cost to the firm.

Denote total fixed cost as *TFC;* similarly, let *AFC* represent average fixed cost. By definition, $AFC = TFC \div q$, or, $AFC \times q = TFC$. Since total fixed cost, *TFC,* is just some constant number, this equation has the well known form, $xy =$ constant, which is a rectangular hyperbola. Its graph is shown in Fig. 8-2. When there is very little output, the fixed cost is imposed on a small quantity of product; therefore its effect per unit is quite high. When many units of output are present, the cost is spread over many units and therefore has a small impact.

Since total cost is the sum of total fixed plus total variable cost, the sum of these components per unit, called average total cost, or *ATC,* is the sum of average variable plus average fixed cost:

$$ATC = AVC + AFC$$

These curves are all in Fig. 8-2. The effect of the fixed costs is to shift the *AC* curve upwards, and slightly to the right. The *U* shape is maintained.

However, the existence of fixed costs have no effect at all on the marginal costs of the firm. Marginal cost is the cost of acquiring an additional unit of output. Fixed costs, by definition, occur independently of how much the firm produces, or whether it produces at all. Since they are sunk, and the firm cannot recover them, they cannot affect behavior. The rental payment, the fixed costs in this example, therefore has no effect on the cost of producing an extra unit; it only affects the average cost of production. Consider the exam grade analogy again. Suppose your instructor announces that 10 points will be added to your final average grade, no matter what you score on the exams. Then the impact of

Figure 8-2 *The Various Average Cost Curves and the Marginal Cost Curve*

The marginal cost curve cuts the average variable cost (*AVC*) and the average total cost (*ATC*) curves at their respective minimum points. Average fixed costs, being sunk, are irrelevant except at the time the firm has to decide whether or not to renew them.

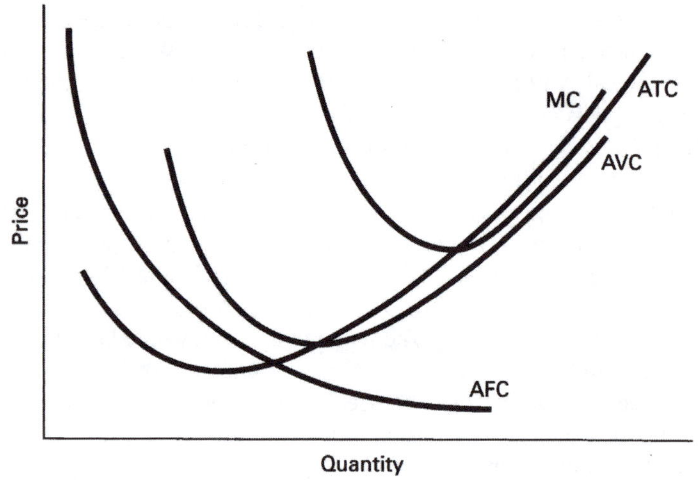

your next exam on your average will be the same; your average, however, will be 10 points higher than it otherwise would be. That is, if your final exam previously would have raised your average grade from 70 to 85 (hope springs eternal), your final exam will still raise your average by 15 points, only now your average will go from 80 to 95. Fixed costs have no effect on marginal costs! The *MC* curve remains unchanged by the existence of fixed costs; *MC* passes through the *AC* and *ATC* curves at their respective minimums.[3]

8.3 Marginal Cost and Supply

We now investigate how a firm determines its output level, and how that output changes when output price changes. Assume again the production structure or function displayed in Table 8-1. We reproduce the table for convenience. Assuming the objective of the firm is to maximize the net rents on the land, how does the firm respond to changes in output price?

Suppose initially the market price of this good is $10. In that case, the total revenue received by the firm is equal to the physical output, q, times the price, $10, or TR = price × quantity = $10 × q = $10q$. We could in principle find the profit maximum by constructing a net rents column for each output, as we did in Table 7-2 in the previous chapter, but a more revealing procedure is to compare the consequences of the firm's incremental decisions to change productions levels. If the firm receives more in revenue from a given action than what that action costs the firm, that action will be undertaken. Suppose the firm is currently producing 15 units and is contemplating increasing production to 21 units (by adding an additional worker). The marginal cost of these separate units, from

Table 8-1

(1) Number of laborers (*L*)	(2) Total Product (*TP*)	(3) Marginal Product (*MP*)	(4) Total Cost (*TC*)	(5) Marginal Cost *MC*	(6) Average Cost *AC*
1	3	3	$ 40.00	$13.33	$13.33
2	8	5	$ 80.00	$ 8.00	$10.00
3	15	7	$120.00	$ 5.71	$ 8.00
4	21	6	$60.00	$ 6.67	$ 7.62
5	26	5	$200.00	$ 8.00	$ 7.69
6	30	4	$240.00	$10.00	$ 8.00
7	33	3	$280.00	$13.33	$ 8.48
8	35	2	$320.00	$20.00	$ 9.14
9	36	1	$360.00	$40.00	$10.00
10	36	0	$400.00	—	$11.11
11	35	–1	$440.00	—	$12.57

3. Again using calculus, this proposition is merely the familiar statement that constants drop out upon differentiation. Letting $C(y) = TVC(y) + TFC$, i.e., total costs = total variable costs plus total fixed costs (a constant, so not dependent on output y), $MC(y) = dTVC/dy + 0$.

the table, is \$6.67. If the firm were to receive an amount greater than \$6.67 for each of these units of output, it would clearly be profitable to produce them. Since the market price is \$10, the firm will be \$3.30 per unit richer by producing units 16 through 21; thus we predict that action. In fact, the price p (\$10) received is greater than or equal to the marginal cost of production up through 30 units (using 6 workers). If the firm chose to be in business at all, it would clearly earn the largest net rents by producing 30 units of output. The maximum rent on the land (the only fixed factor in this example) is $TR - TC = \$300 - \$240 = \$60$.

Suppose now that the price of the product were to rise to \$15. The marginal cost of the thirtieth unit is \$10, but the revenue received from its sale is now \$15. Clearly, it still pays to produce this unit (and all of the previous ones) and, in addition, three more units, which add only \$13.33 each to cost, producing a net rent of \$1.70 on those units. If the market price were to rise to \$20, the firm will similarly expand output to 35 units of output; that is the new point at which the marginal cost of production rises to just the amount of marginal revenue received from the sale of the last unit. Since marginal costs increase with increasing output, when the price of the product rises, the amount produced will also increase. If the price were to rise still further, to \$40, the firm would increase output still further, to 36 units.

The amount the firm decides to produce is determined by the marginal cost curve. In particular, the output chosen is the one for which the marginal cost of output is equal to the price of output. The supply curve of a firm is therefore the marginal cost curve of the firm. Since the marginal cost curves of firms eventually rise, due to the law of diminishing marginal product, the supply response of firms is in the same direction as the price; that is, *supply curves are upward (positively) sloping in output price.* This upward slope is based on diminishing returns at the intensive margin. That is, within individual firms, as identical units of variable factors are added to fixed amounts of other inputs the marginal product of that input falls, raising the marginal cost of output. This source of rising marginal costs is independent of and in addition to the upward slope due to diminishing returns at the extensive margin discussed earlier, where as output increases, less and less efficient resources are utilized.

The Shut-down Decision

In a voluntary exchange economy, firms produce and sell goods when it is in their self-interest to do so. The level of production and sales is similarly determined by self-interest. In deciding how much to produce, the firm's decisions can be formulated as "What does it cost to produce another unit, and what are the benefits?" If, and only if, the benefits of some action, e.g., production, are greater than the costs, then that action will take place. There are, however, several margins of decisions for firms. One is which products to produce, and with what technology. Another is how much to produce, which we discussed in the preceding section. Lastly, there is the question of whether or not to be in business at all, to which we now turn.

In the preceding discussion, we assumed that it was better for the firm to engage in some production rather than none at all. The average cost curves in fact tell us when this is the case. The firm always has the option of temporarily shutting down. In that case total revenue is zero, and total variable cost is zero, but the firm is still liable for its fixed costs. Thus in this case net rents equals the negative of these total fixed costs. In order for the firm to start up production, the results must be better than doing nothing. If the market price p is so low that even when the firm picks the output level that maximizes its rents, it still does worse than doing nothing, the firm will cease production and cease to exist altogether.

Consider Fig. 8-3, which is largely a reproduction of Fig. 8-2, with some added prices and quantities for emphasis. Suppose the price of this good set by the market is \$6.67. The quantity that maximizes the firm's net rents is 21, where price = marginal cost ($p = MC$). However, the firm must be losing money here; the price is below *AVC*. The firm is losing money on every unit it sells. Output will not appear for any price less than the minimum value of average variable cost, \$7.60, indicated by point *A* on the *AVC* curve.

Suppose now the price is greater than \$7.60, say, \$17. This price is above marginal cost for all output levels less than 33, thus the firm makes the greatest profits (rents on the specific factors of production) by producing 33 units of output. This price is also greater than the per-unit variable cost of operating at that level, indicated by the *AVC* curve there. Therefore, producing 33 is a wealth-increasing decision. The rents to the firm are greater at this point than not producing at all. The firm will therefore engage in this production, at least in the short-run. However, the firm is still not making positive net rents. This price is still less than the average total costs of production, given by the *ATC* curve, which is the vertical sum of the *ATC* and *AVC* curves. Therefore, in the range *AC* along the *MC* curve, where average variable costs are covered but not the total costs, the firm will produce, because it is better than not producing, but this can only go on temporarily. In the long run, all costs must be covered, or

Figure 8-3 *The Supply Curve of a Firm*

The marginal cost curve is the supply curve of a firm. However, the section of the curve that is relevant depends on what decisions the firm has available. The firm will open for business if it covers its average variable costs, but it will cease to exist if it does not cover average total costs in the long run. Thus, the section of the marginal cost curve between points *A* and *C*, where only average variable costs are covered, is a supply curve only in the short run.

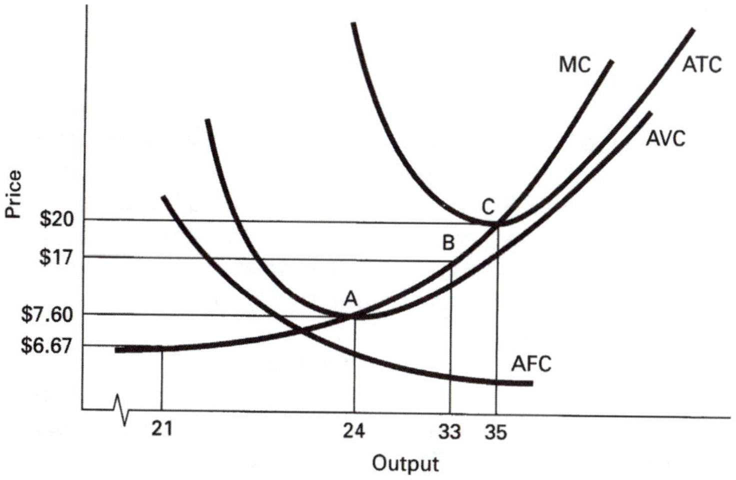

else the firm will go out of business. For all costs to covered, the market price must be greater than or equal to the minimum value of average total cost, \$20, in this example. If the market price is above \$20, then the firm can earn positive profits or net rents.

Let us summarize the above analysis. Firm behavior is dictated by the rule, produce until $p = MC$, since at output less than that amount, the additional revenues from production are greater than the additional costs, and beyond that amount, the additional costs are greater than the additional revenues. The marginal cost curve therefore indicates how much the firm will produce at any given price. However, in order that the firm produce at all, price must be above the minimum level of average variable cost or else the firm will simply shut down temporarily. For prices above this level but below the minimum of average total cost, the *MC* curve indicates the supply of the firm, but only in the short run, since net rents, while greater than that received by not producing at all, are still negative. The *MC* curve is thus the supply curve of the firm for all prices above the minimum of the *AVC* curve (\$7.60 in Fig. 8-3). However in the range *AC, MC* is only a short-run supply curve. In order for the firm to renew its contracts with its fixed inputs, the market price will have to cover all costs. Thus in the long run, the firm will continue to exist only if the market price rises to the minimum of *ATC,* \$20, in this example.

Check your understanding: Suppose you own a restaurant and you have just contracted for one year to pay \$2,000 per month for rent. The waiters, cooks, your own labor and utilities cost you another \$3,000 per month. You find, after a few months, that you are taking in \$4,000 per month in receipts. Do you continue to operate? If yes, for how long?

8.4 Do Firms Really Maximize Profits?

We have, in all of the preceding discussions, maintained the hypothesis that firms maximize profits. We now consider the reasonableness of this assertion. We should note that even though we speak of "the firm" doing this or that, it is really some identifiable humans, not necessarily the owners, who make the firm's decisions. We need ultimately to investigate whether the private interests of these individuals are the same as the owner's interests, though we defer that discussion to Chapter 9. A firm is an organization where production takes place, that is, various inputs are organized and combined so as to increase their value. The owner of the firm is that individual (or group of individuals) who is responsible for the debts of the firm and is the legal **residual claimant** on any amounts received in excess of the legally contracted debts or liabilities. That is, defining profits as the difference between total revenue (*TR*) and total cost (*TC*), the owner is the person who keeps the difference if it happens to be positive, and who must pay the difference to creditors if it is negative. Typically, owners contract with the factor inputs, coordinate their activity and engage in some sort of input activity themselves.

The common term profits must be defined carefully. The first step in a true accounting of profits is to treat the productive activities of the owner as a cost, not as some sort of residual. If the owner is in fact performing the duties of a manager, the value of those services must be included in the costs before any calculation of profits is made. These services can be evaluated by considering the amount some other firm would be willing to pay this individual for the same activity, or the amount this owner would have to pay someone else to replace his or her services. In a similar fashion, any factors that the firm owns outright, so that regular payments to that input do not occur, would similarly have to be evaluated. If the firm owns a computer outright, the fact that the computer is entirely paid for does not alter the fact that by being used by this firm, the computer is not producing output elsewhere, and its use therefore constitutes a cost. The firm could rent or sell the computer to another firm. The owner owns his or her own labor outright, but that labor has alternative uses. The owner could in fact choose to earn a salary working for someone else. Thus the firm would have to include as a cost what it would cost to obtain the services of a similar individual or piece of equipment from others, because these values represent real opportunities foregone.

When all of these true costs have been accounted for, profits, i.e., total revenue minus total cost ($TR - TC$) might still be other than zero because of the uncertainty of outcomes of various decisions. In all real world business enterprises, events are rarely predictable with great accuracy. Fewer, or perhaps more customers than the firm anticipates may show up at any time, and costs may be smaller or larger than anticipated. The vagaries of commercial activities are generally not willingly borne without some compensation. A known, certain income of $40,000 per year will usually be preferred to one which varied unpredictably, even if on average, the income received was the same $40,000. The owner, as residual claimant on all the uncertainties of the firm's activities, positive or negative, will therefore receive a payment in excess of that which a person would receive just for the owner's managerial functions. Thus part of what is typically called profits is really a payment for the acceptance of risk.

After considering all of the above issues, any excess of revenues over the combined alternative costs of the inputs are rents to the immobile or specific factors of production, that is, payments to the factors which cannot be completely replicated. Because people prefer more to less, we expect the owners of these specific factors seek the largest possible payments for their use. We expect that maximization of rents to be a powerful hypothesis in explaining the behavior of real world firms.

Rent maximization, however, is not the only conceivable objective of firms. Attaining prestige for the managers is an alternative objective, and one the firm's owner or managers might substitute for pecuniary profits. There is really little doubt that firms do not maximize rents to the theoretical limits; various other objectives, such as leisure, comfort and perhaps prestige (not easily defined or measured) enter into the decision of what and how much to produce. The pertinent question, however, is whether the hypothesis of rent maximization is a sufficiently close approximation to actual firm behavior to be useful in positive analysis, that is, with which to explain real world events. There are some important reasons to believe it is. If a firm is not pursuing rent maximization, it means another individual can purchase the firm and realize a greater return with the same assets. Firms whose owners are not vigorously pursuing pecuniary gain are therefore prime candidates for either bankruptcy (due to competition from other similar firms) or for takeovers by outsiders. In either case, the surviving firms will operate more closely to the rent maximization limit. The acid test, however, is whether this hypothesis yields implications which are borne out by reality. We therefore hypothesize that firms pursue their pecuniary self-interest and maximize their profits, or net rents, and we try to derive useful implications from that hypothesis. One of the most important implications of rent maximization, as we demonstrated in the previous chapter, is downward sloping factor demand curves. This implication predicts that firms will resist increases in wages, and when such relative prices for, say, labor occur, firms will substitute labor-saving capital for the now more expensive labor.

8.5 The Intensive and Extensive Margins Combined

We now integrate the discussions of diminishing returns on the intensive and extensive margins. Consider the market for wheat, say, and ignore for the moment the institutional features of price supports which are not germane to this discussion. The market is pictured in Fig. 8-4, indicating an initial market equilibrium at point *E,* where the demand curve *D* intersects the supply curve of wheat from farms in North America, *S,* at price \$4 and quantity 40. We take this supply curve to be the **long run supply curve**, meaning that points along it represent outputs that will be produced at given prices when all factors of production can be varied. Suppose crop failures in other countries have shifted the demand for wheat to *D′*. What are the effects on the market for wheat, the wages of labor and the rents on land used to grow wheat?

At the initial equilibrium, firms have adjusted their input (labor and land) levels so that the value of the marginal product of each factor input equals its alternative wage. The supply curve is upward sloping because some factors, here, assumed to be land only, are not completely replicable. In order to produce more wheat, land that is less fertile than previously used land must be utilized. (This might also be true of other factors of production, such as skilled workers or specialized equipment other than land, but we simplify the model and include all these factors under the rubric land.)

The supply curve is the lateral sum of many firms' individual marginal cost curves (not shown). Each firm initially produces where its own marginal cost equals the market price, \$4. However, certain firms have lower per-unit (aver-

Figure 8-4 *Short- and Long-Run Equilibrium*

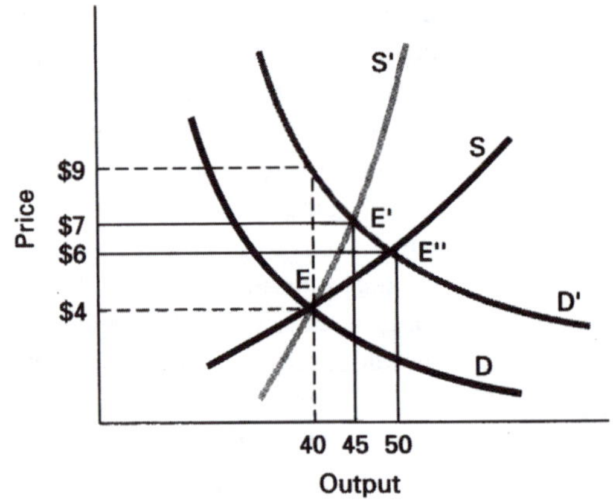

Suppose the demand for some product, for example, wheat, shifts to the right, from *D* to *D'*. In the short run, in which some factors are fixed, existing firms move up their short run *MC* curves, producing a new equilibrium at point *E'*, at output 45 and market price \$7. In the long run, when all factors can be varied, and when new firms can enter the industry, the supply curve becomes more elastic and the equilibrium moves from *E'* to *E''*, with output 50 at price \$6.

age) costs than others, because they possess nonreplicable specialized factor inputs, e.g., especially fertile land. These firms are located along the supply curve to the left of the equilibrium point *E;* they are the firms whose land earn rents. The firms with the most fertile land earn the most rents; these are the firms that enter the market first, when the price of wheat is barely above where the supply curve meets the vertical axis. At the other extreme are the **marginal firms**, whose marginal costs of production above the break-even point are equal to the market price. These firms earn no rents at the current market price. They would abandon wheat farming for some other endeavor, say, sugar beets, if the price were to fall below $4.

Suppose now because of crop failures elsewhere in the world, the demand for North American wheat shifts to D'. In this environment, each firm will start to earn rents, as price will immediately increase. In the very short run, say, within a season, or before shipments can be rerouted from elsewhere, the supply may be almost completely inelastic, raising the price to $9, at the intersection of D' and the vertical supply curve at output 40. Each firm soon seeks to expand production to the new output which maximizes profits, where marginal cost = price. In the short run, however, firms can expand only one input, labor. We assume they can continue to hire all the labor they wish at some wage w_L, but their land input is fixed at its previous level. Recall that profit (rent) maximization implies that firms hire labor until the value of the marginal product equals the wage, or, in symbols, $w_L = p \times MP_L$.

Since the price has increased, and w_L has remained the same, this equality can continue to hold only if MP_L falls. From the law of diminishing marginal product, this can happen only if the firm hires more labor, and applies that labor to its fixed plot of land. Thus, each firm expands output utilizing more labor only. In so doing, they move along their short run marginal cost curve. The lateral sum of these curves is the industry short run supply curve S'. It produces a new market equilibrium at point E', the intersection of S' and D', at the higher price $7 and higher quantity of output 45. At this new price, *all* firms are now receiving rents on their land, even the formerly marginal firms, and the rents received are greater than before.

In the long run, as time elapses, the appearance of rents has a way of attracting a crowd. Points along the original supply curve S beyond (to the right of) point E indicate firms that would be willing to produce, if the price were above $4. In the short run equilibrium, the price *is* above $4, and these other firms will therefore gradually shift their production away from their previous employment to production of wheat. Also, with the passage of time, individual firms adjust their own land inputs to that level yielding the highest rents, in combination with the labor used. In the long run, therefore, output expands to 50, where the original long run supply curve S intersects the new demand curve D', producing a market price eventually of $6. The price becomes lower than its short run price of $7, due to the expansion of output. At the new long run equilibrium, diminishing returns on the extensive margin have taken place to a greater extent. Land that is even less fertile than used by the marginal firms when the price was $4 is now employed in wheat farming. Owners of specific factors (especially fertile land) derive greater rents than before the demand shift. Within each firm, in the long run, both labor and land have been adjusted; it is not possible to state whether diminishing returns on the intensive margin have occurred. It is technically possible that the expansion of each firm has led to larger farms, with fewer workers per acre, though in the case of upward sloping long run supply curves, it is unlikely. We expect that eventually, the ability to expand output is constrained both by diminishing marginal product within the firm (diminishing returns on the *intensive* margin) and incomplete replicability of specific factors of production (diminishing returns on the *extensive* margin).

8.6 Returns to Scale

Although the inability to completely replicate specialized resources is the fundamental reason why supply curves tend to slope upward even when all factors can be varied, other influences sometimes operate to counteract this effect. In particular, the technological aspects of production and gains from specialization sometimes more than offset the limiting effects of specialized resources. For example, a few ditches might be dug at least cost by hiring some unskilled laborers and equipping them each with shovels. At greater levels of production, the digging might be most economically accomplished by hiring one back-hoe and a skilled operator, and the cost per foot of ditch might very well be less than with the small scale shovel operation. The process by which large scale production lowers the unit cost of output is called economies of scale, or, returns to scale. These gains tend to become greater as firms and industries expand. The combined influences of these scale economies may shift the supply curve to the right as firms or industries expand. These returns to large scale production are most apparent when nonrenewable natural resources, such as land of some particular fertility are relatively less important in the production process. In industrial production, especially, economies of scale are significant.

Decreases in the average cost of output due to the application of more efficient technology which occur because of expansion of output *within* a firm are called internal economies of scale. Large scale production allows, for example, the use of assembly-line techniques. In this way, for example, Henry Ford lowered the price of cars so substantially in the early 1920s, that owning a car became feasible for ordinary working people. It is generally possible to purchase all the parts of a modern car in the parts department of a dealership. One could in principle then construct the car as a kit. However, the cost of all the parts comprising a finished automobile is about *three times* the cost of buying the finished car off the lot! It is much cheaper to assemble the car at the factory, using the now famous methods of mass production, and ship the final product to dealers than to ship the parts to consumers for production in small quantities. In agriculture today, crops are grown with fewer labor inputs than our grandparents could have ever imagined. The application of modern machinery is most efficient on large farms, and the application of these modern techniques on mostly large farms have dramatically lowered the cost of food. The small family farm has been rapidly disappearing as a result.

Some instances of cost reductions take place *external* to the firm and are therefore called external economies of scale. Consider for example that in the past generation, electronic equipment has decreased dramatically in price. Desktop computers have decreased in price so substantially that they are now commonplace household items. The invention of the transistor, and the process of etching solid-state circuitry onto smaller and smaller semiconducting chips lowered the cost of numerical computations. As the prices of computers have fallen due to these technological advances, greater numbers of people have purchased computers. In addition, because the market expanded, it has become feasible for firms to specialize in products that could not have been produced when the market was smaller. Moreover, these new firms are often wholly independent of the firms actually producing the final product (the computer). Because the number of chips produced is now so large, the incentives for new firms to discover ways in which these chips can be produced at lower costs are greater. Thus a large market generates conditions which contribute to the further lowering of unit costs.

Word processing was one of the first major applications of desktop computers, because most of the users desired this application. As the number of computer users has expanded, other, more arcane products have appeared. It is now possible, for example, to purchase programs for desktop computers that solve algebraic equations and do calculus, perform sophisticated statistical tests on data, produce detailed architectural drawings, some in simulated three dimensions. Much of this software has been developed by independent computer programmers. They exist only because the market is now so large, enough programs can be sold to reward the costs of development. Thus the large computer market creates conditions for other firms to make computers more useful. These software applications further lower the cost of the output created by the computers.

8.7 Futures Markets

Consider the following scenario, which has in fact happened two or three times in recent decades. Word starts spreading that a frost in Brazil is destroying the coffee trees. Brazil currently produces about one-half the world's supply of coffee; not surprisingly, the price of coffee starts to rise almost immediately. But why in fact should the price of coffee start to rise so soon? There is always a substantial amount of coffee in inventory, and those stocks of coffee are still there, and nothing has occurred on the demand side. Why shouldn't the price of coffee stay right where it is while we use up the current inventory of coffee, and why shouldn't the price rise only when the supply of coffee shifts to the left, reflecting the decrease in coffee production in Brazil? What we actually observe is that the price of coffee immediately spikes upward, by a substantial amount, and then levels off at some new higher price for the duration of the decrease in supply. What would explain this?

What most of us do when we hear that some good is soon going to be in very short supply is to stock up on some extra amounts of that good. We raise our personal inventories of the good. But not only do we do this, professional traders in the market do the same thing. If the good really is going to have a reduced supply in the future, then we all know that the price will be higher in the future than now, and it behooves us to try to get some additional units of the good now, presuming it is storable, while the price is still low. What we are doing is engaging in **speculation** about the future price of the good. In organized markets in many commodities whose prices often change, particularly agricultural goods and mined goods (including petroleum), professional speculators spend their days trying to figure out whether the price of those commodities will increase or decrease in the foreseeable future, and they buy or sell inventories of the goods accordingly. These speculators are among the least popular people in society; together with moneylenders, they share probably the lowest esteem of the general public. One reason for this widespread opinion is that when, say, a frost that kills Brazilian coffee trees or Florida citrus fruit actually happens, newspaper headlines will soon trumpet the idea that speculators are driving up the prices of these goods. The newspapers are correct in so far as they go, but they miss half the story: when the speculators eventually *sell* their inventories of these goods, the price must be consequently be lower than otherwise, because of the increased supply from speculators' inventories.

The motives of speculators is of course to make money, by buying a good when its price is low and selling it when its price is high. But why is someone able to make a living doing this? In a market economy based on mutually advantageous trade, the speculators must be providing a productive service in the economy; else no one would have occasion to use their services. The benefit speculators provide is that they smooth out the flow of consumption for consumers. Recall the discussion in Chapter 2, in Section 2.7, Consumption Over Time. We showed there that the total value consumers place on goods is greater when the good is consumed evenly over time rather than on a "feast and famine" cycle. When a good is in relatively plentiful supply, a consumer's marginal value of the good is low relative to when the good is in shorter supply. By moving consumption from when the good is plentiful to when it is more scarce, the consumer engages in a beneficial trade. If the marginal value of the good is \$1 when the good is plentiful and \$5 when it is not, then the consumer gains the \$4 difference by moving a unit of good from the time of feast to the time of famine. This potential benefit exists as long as the level of consumption is not the same in the two time periods. The greatest benefit derived from consuming the good occurs when the amount consumed in all time periods is the same. It therefore pays for producers to spend some amount of resources to endeavor to even out the flow of goods.

Let us continue with the coffee tree scenario. When rumor starts about destruction of coffee trees, speculators start to purchase coffee at its current low price, in anticipation of selling it later when the price is high. In so doing, they hold current inventories off the market, causing a public relations disaster for themselves as the price rises with this decrease in supply. Of course, sometimes these rumors about weather-related disasters that affect markets turn out not to be true. If that happens, the speculators who started buying coffee at ever-increasing prices discover that the supply of coffee is not going to decrease after all, and are now stuck with excess inventories of coffee. They now have to sell this coffee, and when they do, the supply of coffee will be greater than it otherwise would be, since they temporarily held some off the market. Thus in this case, the price will be less than its long run equilibrium price, and the speculators will therefore lose money in the process. The market penalizes mistakes: if there is no underlying cause that might disturb the market equilibrium, the speculators will lose money trying to manipulate the market.

Suppose now the rumor is correct, and the coffee trees really have started to freeze and die. If the speculators can correctly assess the full extent of the damage and predict the final equilibrium price, they will hold enough coffee off the market to produce this price. Since the gain to consumers is greatest when the flow of consumption is even, finding that amount to withhold now for future sale that makes the price steady produces the largest potential profit for the speculators. But this action produces the largest gains for consumers, by evening out the flow of consumption. Thus if the market is working as efficiently as possible, we should expect the price to rise sharply at the beginning of an anticipated market disturbance of this nature and then to stay at that higher level until the supply is restored.

Have the speculators raised the price of coffee? Definitely not! Nature raised the price of coffee by destroying the coffee trees. If there were no speculators (including households who also withhold coffee from the market, albeit on a smaller scale), the price of coffee would remain low for a while, and then gradually rise as the reduced supply took hold. Consumers would consume at their old levels until the supply decrease raised the price, and then as the price continued to rise, their quantity demanded would continue to fall. The price would rise to a level higher than what occurs with speculation, because the speculators eventually sell their inventories in order to keep the price as steady as possible. Thus the supply of coffee is larger in the future than it would be if the speculators had not held some coffee off the market for sale in the future.

Futures Markets

Many commodities, particularly agricultural commodities, experience seasonal changes in prices. In addition, these commodities are subject to the vagaries of nature and other market uncertainties. Suppose it is the beginning of the planting season, and wheat farmers are trying to decide how much wheat to produce, or possibly even whether to produce wheat or some other commodity. Wheat farmers are experts to some degree in growing wheat; they are less expert in predicting what the price of wheat will be six months hence when the wheat is ready for harvest. If they have to spend their time trying to predict future wheat prices, they will have to divert their time from their comparative advantage, growing wheat, to their comparative disadvantage, predicting wheat markets. Moreover, some individuals are better able to bear risk than others. Anyone who speculates in markets will lose some of the time. No one ever predicts market prices accurately all the time. It is economically efficient to have the risk borne by those individuals best able to do it. These are not likely to be the farmers themselves.

In the United States and other countries with well-developed markets, organized exchanges exist in which traders buy and sell goods for future delivery. It is possible to make contract in the present for wheat that has not yet even been planted. The price of wheat or some other commodity for delivery sometime in the future is called its **futures price**. The price that actually transpires on that date in the future is the *future* price; we cannot know what it is until the date arrives. The current price at the moment is called the **spot price**. In the other sections of this book we have essentially always analyzed spot prices—the prices that exist at any moment in time for current delivery. Every day, at organized exchanges such as the Chicago Board of Trade, the New York Mercantile Exchange and other markets, futures prices of many commodities are determined by traders contracting for sale or delivery of goods in the future. Futures markets enable a wheat farmer to lock in a price of the wheat he or she will deliver, before even the planting season has begun. The farmer can then go about his business of deciding how much wheat to plant, what resources to use, etc., with the secure knowledge of what the price of wheat will be when it comes time to sell it.

Futures prices are printed every day in many newspapers, particularly *The Wall Street Journal*. Here is a typical listing for crude oil; it is from January 1999, when the Asian economies were in recession and crude oil was very cheap. The prices are per barrel (bbl.) of "Sweet Light Crude" listed on the New York Mercantile Exchange.

Date	Price
Feb. 1999	$12.34
Feb. 2000	$14.16
Feb. 2001	$15.51
Dec. 2001	$16.39

The price of petroleum had been approximately $11.00 per barrel in late 1998 and early 1999. The futures prices displayed above indicate that traders expected prices to rise in the not too distant future. Crude oil was being traded at around $12.00 per barrel in early 1999, but no one was willing to promise to sell oil at that low price in the coming months or years. In January 1999, some traders promised to deliver crude oil in February 2001 at $15.51 per barrel; others were promising to purchase oil at that price on that date. Likewise, buyers and sellers were agreeing to exchange oil at $16.39 per barrel in December 2001. In fact, by February 2001, the spot, or current price of oil had risen to approximately $25.50 per barrel. Those traders who had earlier promised to deliver oil at $15.51 per barrel were forced to give this $10 per barrel windfall to the traders who promised to buy the oil at the original contract price of $15.51.

Futures prices cannot deviate very much from the current spot prices, else trading would cease. It couldn't be the case that the spot price of oil is $20 per barrel, but the futures price one month hence is $40 per barrel: no one would sell oil in the present. They would simply store the oil for a month and sell at the much higher price then. The spot price would quickly rise to approximately the near-term futures price. Likewise, if the futures price were much lower than the spot price, the spot price would fall quickly, as producers sold off their inventories as rapidly as feasible.

Here are the futures prices as of April 2004. The current, spot price of this crude oil is approximately $37.00.

Date	Price
Aug. 2004	$35.90
Jan. 2005	$33.64
Dec. 2005	$30.70
Dec. 2006	$29.10

It is clear that oil traders expect the price of oil to be cheaper in the future than in the spring of 2004. Only time will tell if this is correct, and whether the buyers or sellers of these contracts will profit.

Futures markets exist for many commodities (see the listings, for example, in *The Wall Street Journal*) including corn, wheat, soybeans; precious metals such as gold, silver and platinum; energy products, particularly coal, oil and natural gas; and also financial products such as bonds issued by the United States government and other governments around the world. Many people feel that these "speculators" increase the risk in these markets, but we have seen that in a voluntary exchange system, people make money when they produce some good that consumers desire. Nature produces the uncertainty, along with politics, for example, in the oil market. Futures markets provide three benefits to individuals where these markets are not restricted. First, they enable consumers to even out the flow of consumption, raising the total value of these goods. Second, they enable individuals to shift risk to others who are more capable of bearing it. Futures markets provide the ability for individuals to eliminate a large part of the risks they face in production and consumption. Third, futures markets allow individuals to pursue their comparative advantages more completely, by allowing people to specialize in what they do best, for example, production, rather than predicting the future prices of the goods they intend to produce.

CHAPTER SUMMARY

- Perfectly competitive markets are characterized by firms that are *price takers*. These firms are a small enough part of the market in which they operate so that their production decisions do not affect the market price. Competitive firms *respond* to market prices; they cannot individually *make* the price.
- Marginal Cost is the cost of producing an additional unit of output. Average cost is simply the total cost of all units divided by the number of units.
- Some costs are contractually fixed; the firm must pay these regardless of its output. Other costs vary with output. Average total costs are the sum of average fixed plus average variable costs. Average variable and average total costs are "U-shaped" because of scale economies at low levels of output.
- The marginal cost curve always cuts through the average cost curves at the minimum point of those curves.
- With only one variable factor, say, labor (L), marginal cost $MC = w/MP_L$, where w is the wage of labor. In order to produce additional output, the firm hires an additional unit of labor, at a cost of w. The additional output this labor creates is MP_L, so the cost of this additional output is wage divided by marginal product.
- Because of the law of diminishing marginal product, the denominator in the expression for MC declines, and thus MC increases. Since eventually labor adds less and less to output, it costs more at the margin to produce additional output.
- If all factors are variable, w/MP must be equal for all factors, else the firm could save costs by switching to that factor whose marginal cost of output is least.
- Even in the long run when all factors are variable, MC likely increases because eventually factors that are less and less efficient must be utilized.
- The output at which a firm's profits (rents) are maximized is where the marginal cost of output equals price (p). As long as $p > MC$, the firm can earn larger rents by increasing output.
- If demand increases, each firm moves up along its short-run marginal cost curve until output is such that price equals marginal cost. In time, firms can vary more factors of production, and, eventually, new firms can enter the industry. The supply curve becomes flatter, or more elastic and output increases as price comes down.

REVIEW QUESTIONS

1. Make sure you understand the difference between marginal and average costs. Explain why *AC* is falling when *MC* is below it and *AC* is rising when *MC* is above *AC,* and why the two are equal at the minimum point of *AC.*
2. If diminishing marginal product sets in at the very first unit of labor input, what is the shape of the marginal and average cost curves?
3. Why are supply curves flatter, or more elastic in the long run than in the short run?
4. Can supply curves be downward sloping, meaning firms will supply more at a lower price? (Answer: No, but does this mean that marginal cost curves can't be downward sloping?)

PROBLEMS

1. a. Explain why, in the short run, when other productive inputs are fixed, $MC = w/MP$ where MC = marginal cost of output, w = wage of labor, and MP = marginal product of labor.
   b. Explain, therefore, why *MC* rises on the "intensive margin."
   c. Explain the relation between the *MC* curve and a firm's supply curve.
   d. In the long run, when other inputs are variable and new firms can enter the industry, supply curves are flatter (or more elastic) than in the short run. Explain why this is so, and explain why marginal costs rise on this extensive margin.
   e. Turnip farmers are complaining that the price of turnips is too low. They want the government to buy turnips for school lunches. Senator Smith notes that several years ago, they had the same complaint, and when the government imposed a price support above the market price, the farmers were happy for awhile, but now they are upset again, and what's more, there are more of them (farmers and turnips) than ever. Explain what happened.
2. Consider the following Total Product schedule:

L	*TP*
1	13
2	25
3	36
4	46
5	55
6	63
7	70
8	76
9	81

The price of the product is \$10, and the alternative cost of labor is \$100. Calculate the marginal cost of output schedule and explain why it looks the way it does. At what output do the rents of the firm become largest? What is the source of those rents?

3. Answer the same question with the following production function. Here, assume the alternative cost of labor is $50 and the price of the product is $10.

L	*TP*
1	12
2	23
3	30
4	36
5	40
6	42
7+	no additional output

4. Suppose certain land is publicly owned, i.e. a "common property," so that anyone can "squat" on the land and grow crops. The land is most suitable for growing popcorn; the output (in bushels) varies with the number of people farming as follows:

L	TP
1	10
2	20
3	29
4	35
5	40
6	42
7	42
8+	No additional increases in output

Assume the market price of popcorn is $10 per bushel, and this price is unaffected by total output on this land. Assume all farmers can earn $50 per day in their next best alternative. Assume for the moment that there is no depletion of the land, for any level of farming.

a. Explain why common property leads to "too much" popcorn. How many people will farm in this case?
b. Explain why, if the land were owned by a private wealth maximizer, the benefits and costs obtained from the owner's decisions about how much farming to allow would coincide with society's benefits and costs. How much farming would the owner allow, and would it be an efficient allocation of resources?
c. Explain why, in the short run, when other productive inputs are fixed, MC = w/MP where MC = marginal cost of output, w = wage of labor, and MP = marginal product of labor.
d. Explain, therefore, why MC rises on the "intensive margin."
e. Demonstrate that the answer you gave in part b. is where MC = $10, and explain why this occurs.
f. Suppose this same owner has another farm with more fertile land, and for which the marginal cost of growing popcorn is always one half the amount in the first farm, at any given output level. Would the owner use both farms? What rule would determine the amount of output produced on each farm?
g. Suppose it is suddenly found that eating popcorn increases financial success and improves relations with the opposite sex. Analyze the effects of this on quantity of popcorn produced and price. Explain why firms

choose output such that price equals marginal cost. Explain why, therefore, the marginal cost curve is the firm's supply curve.

5. Suppose a firm had two production facilities with differing marginal and average cost schedules. How would one construct the combined marginal cost curve for such a firm, and would this be the firm's supply curve?
6. Explain why the relevant part of the marginal cost curve (*MC*) for determining the quantity supplied changes as the time frame for the firm changes. What is the relevant section of *MC* when all factors can be adjusted, but new firms cannot enter this industry? Is any section relevant in the "very long run" where entry of new firms takes place?
7. Suppose a firm has economies of scale, i.e., average costs of production are lower at higher levels of output. Would the labor and capital used by the firm exhibit the law of diminishing marginal product?
8. Suppose it is suddenly found that Popeye notwithstanding, eating spinach decreases financial success and sours relations with the opposite sex. What effect would this have on the quantity of spinach produced, the price of spinach, employment in the spinach industry, wages of farm workers and rents to landowners, in the short and run and in the long run, when new firms can enter the business?
9. How would the construction of mass transit connecting downtown centers with suburbs affect land rents downtown and in the suburbs?
10. In that same supermarket you own from Chapter 7, it costs more to sell \$10 of meat than to sell \$10 of pet food. Should you contract the meat and expand the pet food department?
11. A great many barges are shipped empty up the Mississippi river. Why would profit maximizing firms do such a thing? Along the same lines, sometimes airlines schedule a flight from one city to another in spite of a persistent very low volume of passengers. Why would they do this?
12. "We regret that an increase in our costs has necessitated that we increase our prices." This is a common statement made by sellers raising their prices. Do cost increases necessitate a price increase? What determines the price of goods?
13. It is sometimes claimed that businesses continue to use their older obsolete equipment because they have so much money tied up in it. Evaluate. Is it inefficient for an airline to use gas-guzzling 727s when more efficient 757s and 767s are available?
14. You own a grocery store and you have just received a shipment of oranges. You hear on the radio that the Florida citrus crop has been severely damaged by frost. Do you change the price of the oranges you already have in stock?
15. Many jewelry stores advertise that they will sell you diamonds at wholesale prices. How reliable is that claim, and why don't other stores, e.g., supermarkets advertise in that manner?
16. Suppose the demand for office space increases. What effect will this have on the cost of providing low cost housing to inner city residents?

17. A small town has three groceries. They are identical except that Joe's has two more checkstands than the others.

    a. Would you expect to save time at Joe's?
    b. Would you expect to save money at Joe's?
    c. In which store would the average amount purchased by consumers be larger?
    d. Which store would you expect to have more customers?
    e. Which store's customers would you expect to be richer?

18. You own two factories for producing computers, a new modern one and an older one. The marginal cost of producing computers in the new factory is always half the marginal cost of producing the same number of computers in the old factories. Do you use both factories? What rule would describe the least cost way of producing a given number of computers?

19. It is common to see advertisements proclaiming that a store is selling "below cost." What could this phrase mean, and does it mean below cost in the economic sense of the word?

QUESTIONS FOR DISCUSSION

1. Some observers note that prices in inner city supermarkets are often higher than prices in more middle class suburban outlets. They claim this is an example of exploitation of the poor and minorities. What do you make of this observation and conclusion? What factors do you suppose affect the relative prices in these stores, and what would make it more likely for supermarkets to exploit the poor versus the rich?

2. It is a common observation that service in the post office is not quite up to the standards at local supermarkets. Do you agree with this, and if so, what might account for these differences? How has the advent of express companies such as Fedex and UPS affected this market?

CHAPTER 9

Property Rights and Transactions Costs

When your grandfather proposed to your grandmother, he had an additional reason than people nowadays have to consider carefully his words. Back then, if he were to break the engagement, his fiancée could sue him for breach of promise. New suitors tended to regard jilted lovers as women of uncertain moral character and therefore damaged goods. It seems that the custom of giving diamonds as engagement presents arose when states struck these laws from the books. The ring became an indemnification against the breach of promise; the young lady got to keep the ring if her intended broke the engagement. It was an interesting private sector response to a change in property rights. In this chapter we study further the effects of property rights on economic activity.

9.1 Introduction

Thus far we have examined a simple, but very powerful model. One of the assumptions of our economic model has been that there is no uncertainty about the terms of any transaction, or about the nature of the goods to be exchanged. In a world without these transactions costs, individuals would never leave mutual benefits unclaimed. It is a denial of "more is preferred to less" to not seek mutual benefits, if the cost of such action is zero. Yet casual observation suggests that many important situations exist where this is not true. For example, when we go to restaurants, movies, and the grocery store, we quite often have to wait in line. Why don't the prices of these services rise to eliminate the queue? Quite often a particular restaurant will habitually have a long line outside, and so we cannot argue that customers showed up unexpectedly. At any moment, some people are unemployed. Why do wage rates not fall to eliminate this surplus? Classrooms, books in the library and other college facilities sit idle during the night. During class time most of the toilets on campus are unemployed, but in between classes there is often a shortage. Why are there no markets, as described in earlier chapters, to eliminate these problems?

Recall that when land is common property, that is, when the right to exclude workers from the land is absent, individuals do not exhaust the gains from trade. Self-interest leads workers to crowd onto the land to an extent whereby their marginal product on that land is less than what they could produce elsewhere. This result is quite general. For example, individuals persistently drive their own cars to work, congesting the streets and highways, even though carpooling or rapid transit would reduce commute times dramatically. The government levies tariffs, which raise the prices of domestic goods to an extent that often produces larger losses to consumers than the total gains to the protected industries. Pollution, rising health costs, the decimation of various ocean fisheries, are all examples of where pure price allocation is not (or has not been) used. It may appear that prices couldn't be used in cases like these. But if individuals are free to use prices, why are they not used? There are many cases where prices are explicitly and conscientiously not used. You probably can't buy a grade in this class. Not only can you not buy a grade, but you cannot sell your student card to a friend. When your future boss tells you to do some task, you are unlikely to respond "what's it worth to you." Your parents probably didn't bid for your labor services around the house. In firms and families, commands are used more than prices to allocate resources. In this chapter we explore what happens when information is not free, transactions costs are not zero, and property rights are imperfectly defined. The answers are quite fascinating. First, we must explore the nature of transactions costs.

9.2 The Coase Theorem

The analysis of transactions costs is intimately tied to the delineation of property rights. In particular, we say goods are held as **private property** if three conditions hold:[1]

- **Exclusivity.** The condition in which an individual has the right to exclude others from use of the good or property
- **Ownership of Income.** The right of individuals to keep the income the property produces.
- **Transferability.** The right of individuals to transfer the property to others at a mutually agreed upon price.

If these conditions are lacking to some degree, gains from trade will be diminished. Instead of pursuing mutually advantageous gains, individuals will spend resources attempting to better secure ownership rights in the goods. Moreover, since each individual has the same incentive to secure these rights, and only one can succeed, wasted resources in the form of duplication of effort is a likely outcome.

Private ownership of resources means, among other things, that the owner can direct the use of that resource. When it is difficult to measure a worker's input, so that shirking is a problem, it means that the owner of the firm does not have complete control over his or her other resources. The circumstance of high transactions costs, where it is difficult for people to contract with each other, e.g., if it is difficult to tell whether the other persons are fully honoring their end of the contract, is equivalent to the case where property rights are not well defined. In either case, resources will be utilized differently than if the rights to use resources were clearly delineated. Thus the analysis of transactions costs is similar, and in many ways equivalent to the analysis of property rights.

The analysis of property rights in economics concerns the effects on resource allocation of changes in these rights. Although the literature on this subject is generations old, a convenient starting point for the modern treatment is Ronald Coase's path breaking 1960 article, "The Problem of Social Cost."[2] Coase began by considering the historically important case of wandering cattle. Specifically, consider the case of a rancher whose property abuts a neighboring farm. The rancher's cattle occasionally wander onto the farmer's land and trample some crops. Coase posed the following question. How does production vary with who has the rights to the land? In particular, if the rancher is liable for all damage his or her cattle (his, for convenience) cause, will production be different than if the farmer must bear the costs? Coase's surprising answer changed the way economists thought about these issues.[3]

---

1. Taken from Steven N.S. Cheung, "A Theory of Price Control," *Journal of Law and Economics,* 17(1): 53–72, April 1974. A similar taxonomy is presented in the first edition of Armen Allen and William Allen's text, *Exchange and Production,* Wadsworth, 1964.

2. Ronald Coase, The Problem of Social Cost, *The Journal of Law and Economics,* October, 1960.

3. Analysis of this issue is sometimes clouded by ethical concerns. It strikes some people as outrageous that a rancher should have the right to destroy a neighbor's crops. However, open range land of this type is historically important in the United States and elsewhere. Lastly, it may be that the rancher occupied a given tract of land first, and at some later date a farmer moved nearby. It could as easily be said, under these circumstances, that the farmer is encroaching on the rancher's land, as the reverse.

To make the analysis more concrete, consider the data in Table 9-1. Column 1 indicates an amount of cattle produced, and column 2 indicates the marginal cost of producing each additional steer.

The figures in column 2 indicate the private cost to the rancher of producing steers. These would include, for example, feed, cowpersons, etc., meaning all the costs to the rancher of raising cattle to maturity and bringing them to market. According to the table, it costs the rancher $100 to raise one steer, an additional $150 to raise a second, $200 to raise a third, and so forth. Not included in these costs, however, are the damages the cattle impose on the neighboring farmer. Each steer tramples $100 worth of crops during its lifetime. These costs, which are external to the rancher, are often referred to as externalities. Thus, the actual cost to society of raising 1 steer is not just the $100 diverted from other uses by the rancher, but also the $100 in crops that never get harvested, yielding a true marginal cost for 1 steer of $200. Similarly, the second steer costs $150 of direct costs to the rancher, plus another $100 of destroyed crops, for a true marginal cost of $250. We refer to the complete, actual cost to society of producing a good as its **social cost**. Likewise, marginal social cost refers to the true, complete cost of producing an additional increment of the good. The private cost is really a misspecification of cost, as it leaves out part of the true effects of producing this good, in particular, the costs imposed on someone else. We consider private costs because it often seems that producers do not in fact always bear all of the costs of their decisions.

Suppose now the market price of mature steers is $300. How many steers will the rancher produce, and how does the answer depend, if at all, on the rancher's liability for crop damage caused by his steers? Assume first that the rancher is liable for all such crop damage. In this case, the figures in column 4, marginal social cost, are also the rancher's own marginal costs of production. For each steer produced, the rancher must compensate the farmer $100 to cover the cost of the ruined crops. The rancher produces 3 steers under these constraints. Production is carried out until marginal cost rises to the market price. The rancher makes $100 on the first steer, $50 on the second, and zero on the third, but, as usual, we assume production is carried out to this limit. He receives total rents of $150 on this production.

Suppose now the rancher is not liable for crop damage. In this case, the rancher does not have to compensate the farmer for the $100 of crops each steer destroys. It appears the private marginal cost figures in column 2 will determine output. In that case, the rancher would produce 5 steers, where the private mar-

Table 9-1

(1) Number of Steers	(2) Marginal Private Cost	(3) Marginal Crop Damage	(4) Social Marginal Cost
1	$100	$100	$200
2	$150	$100	$250
3	$200	$100	$300
4	$250	$100	$350
5	$300	$100	$400
6	$350	$100	$450

ginal cost equals the market price. Coase, showed, however that this conclusion depends on the assumption that *the farmer and rancher are unable to negotiate a mutually beneficial contract with each other.*

When the rancher produces a fourth steer, his rents are potentially \$50: the difference between the market price, \$300, and the private marginal cost of that steer, \$250. However, this steer produces a greater amount of damages—\$100—than the rents received. The farmer would benefit by \$100 if the steer were not produced; the rancher gains only \$50 from producing it. In this situation, where the loser loses more than the gainer gains, the loser can pay the gainer something greater than the potential gain and less than the potential loss, *improving the position of both parties.* For example, if the rancher accepts a payment from the farmer of \$75 to not produce the fourth steer, then the farmer and the rancher each gain \$25. Similarly, since the rancher makes no rents on the sixth steer, any small payment from the farmer will induce him not to produce it, thereby saving the farmer almost \$100 in the process. If damages result from someone's actions, those costs must be weighed against the benefits of the actions. If the costs are larger than the benefits, the parties can contract with each other to avoid these losses.

Assuming, therefore, that the cost of transactions is sufficiently low that the farmer and the rancher can negotiate, *resource allocation is the same, regardless of the assignment of liability.* In this example, the rancher produces 3 steers under either assignment of liability. The wealth of the farmer and rancher are of course affected by who has to pay whom. If the rancher is liable for crop damage, he is worse off, and if the rancher is not liable, the farmer is clearly worse off. The production outcome is the same, however, in either case: 3 steers. This remarkable insight has been dubbed the **Coase Theorem**. It follows because in the absence of transactions costs, the gains from trade must be exhausted. Such inefficient outcomes violate the axioms of behavior, if there are no costs of negotiating.

Consider Fig. 9-1, depicting a private marginal cost curve (MC_P) and a social marginal cost curve (MC_S) for which all costs of producing some good, say, cattle are included. The area under these marginal cost curves are the respective total private and social costs of producing a given quantity. As the marginal social cost curve includes the crop damage, and the private marginal cost curve excludes it, the area between the curves represents the total external cost of cattle, in this case,

Figure 9-1 *The Coase Theorem*

With production between 3 steers and 5, the additional crop damage, *ABCD*, is greater than the additional rents the rancher recieves, *ABD*. Therefore, a mutually beneficial contract exists to eliminate this waste.

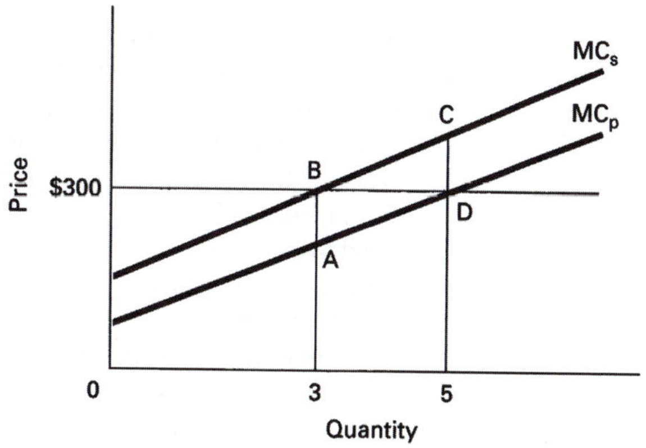

the crop damage. Demand conditions produce a market price of \$300 for cattle. If the rancher is liable for all crop damage, then he treats MC_S as his own private marginal cost function, and maximizes rents by producing 3 steers, the amount for which marginal cost equals price. At this output, total cost is the area under the marginal social cost curve up to this output. It consists partly of direct costs to the rancher, and partly of payments to the farmer for crop damage.

Suppose now the liability of the rancher for crop damage is removed. If he decides to produce beyond 3 steers, the additional rents he receives is the area between MC_P and the market price of \$300. However, beyond 3 steers, this amount is less than the crop damage—the difference between the two marginal cost curves, since MC_S is above the market price in this range. If the output is 5 steers, for example, which occurs if the rancher is oblivious to the crop damage, the total value of the damaged crops is the area *ABCD*. This amount is greater than the addition to rents, *ABD*. This situation, where the marginal damage exceeds the marginal private gains, occurs when, and only when, the marginal social cost function, which by definition includes all these damages, exceeds the market price, measuring consumers' marginal value of this good. This situation is precisely where a mutually beneficial contract exists: the people who are harmed, in this case the farmer, can pay the other parties the entire amount of the damages and still have something left over for themselves.

Notice, however, that there is nothing the farmer can do to induce the rancher not to produce up to 3 steers. The gains to the rancher, e.g., \$200 for the first steer, exceed the crop damage. The farmer could offer the rancher \$100 to not produce the first steer, for example, but the offer will be rejected. More importantly, it is economically efficient that the offer be rejected. The market price of \$300 measures consumers' marginal value of resources in the form of a steer. If the resource cost of producing that steer is only \$200, production of the steer raises the net value of resources by \$100 over their next best alternative, even including the crops that the cattle inadvertently trample. The efficient amount of externalities, i.e., damage to third parties, is not likely to be zero. Sometimes the costs may be less than the benefits they generate.

The rancher and farmer always have an incentive to reduce the dissipation of rents. The actions available to them are not limited to direct negotiations of cash transfers. In some cases, the farmer can simply build a fence around his land. Another option is for one person to buy out the other. If, for example, the rancher is not liable for damages, and contracting output restrictions is somehow very costly, the farm will be more valuable if the farm and ranch are owned by the same person. In that case, the single owner will directly observe the cost of damaged crops, and the value of joint output will be larger than when the farm and ranch are separately owned. This increase in the value of output creates the incentive for a buyout. The purchase price will reflect the increased value of the land. It is immaterial which person buys and which sells. The increase in the value of the farmer's property can be captured by the farmer either by selling to the rancher, or by buying out the rancher and capturing the increased value of the land by restricting the production of cattle to efficient levels. The person who is better able to manage both enterprises will be the buyer.

One of the classic textbook examples of alleged inefficient production due to external effects is the case of beekeepers placing hives in orchards. The beekeepers receive honey from this operation, and the bees pollinate the orchard's fruit trees. Some economists asserted that since the bees provided a free service to the orchard owners, there would be excessive fruit production. The apple growers would be receiving free pollination services and therefore using too much. In fact, upon empirical investigation, economists found that orchard owners and beekeepers regularly contract with each other for their mutual benefit.[4] Moreover, payments go in the direction of the higher net benefits. Cheung's analysis of apple orchards in Washington State revealed that if the increase in apple production was greater than the value of the extra honey production, the orchard owners paid the beekeepers to put hives in the orchards. On other lands, where marketable fruit was not produced, beekeepers paid the landowners for the right to place hives on their property. There seemed to be little dissipation or excessive use of these resources after all; property rights in these resources are well defined, and contracting between the parties prevents dissipation of rents.

Professional Sports

Economists Rodney Fort and James Quirk applied Coase's analysis to professional sports leagues.[5] They analyzed how recent important changes in the players' contracts affected the competitive balance of the leagues. Each team owner has an incentive to field a winning team, because their fans prefer to see their team win rather than lose. However, the league, as a collection of owners, has an incentive to have teams that are fairly evenly matched, because games are most exciting (and attendance highest) when the home team wins a close game over a challenging opponent. If most of the good players wind up on a few teams, fan interest quickly wanes at the weaker franchises, and ultimately at the stronger franchises also, because the games become predictable and boring.

Prior to 1976, a reserve clause bound baseball players to their teams. Once a player signed on with the Yankees, his services were exclusively reserved for the Yankees in the following year. This effectively prevented teams from bidding against each other for players. It was long argued that this prevented the rich teams from buying up the good players and destroying the competitive balance of the league. That argument ignored the possibility that the richer owners could not foresee the consequences of their actions. The Coase theorem suggests that if the owners could negotiate, they would not engage in this type of self-defeating action.

In 1976 an arbitrator provided a means for testing these arguments, by fundamentally weakening the reserve clause. Under the current agreement, when a player has played in the league for 6 years he becomes liberated from the reserve clause, and can be signed by any team. Also, a player is eligible for binding salary arbitration after 5 years in the league. As a result, there has been a tremendous increase in players' salaries, with several well-publicized players making in excess of $8 million per year. Even after adjusting for inflation, these are salaries that were unheard of in the reserve clause days. This *change in property rights* has had the effect of transferring a substantial part of the owners' wealth to players. An interesting economic question is, has this change in rules affected the outcomes of the games?

4. See, e.g., Stephen N.S. Cheung, The Fable of the Bees: An Economic Investigation, *Journal of Law and Economics,* 16:11–33, April, 1973.

5. James Quirk and Rodney D. Fort, Pay Dirt: *The Business of Professional Team Sports,* Princeton: Princeton University Press, 1992.

Quirk and Fort studied whether the competitive balance of the leagues was affected by the restriction on the reserve clause. The anecdotal evidence suggests that a certain amount of unbalance existed prior to the ruling. The New York Yankees were long a dominant American League team, and many other examples of dominant teams exist in earlier decades. The Philadelphia Athletics, St. Louis Browns and the Washington Senators were perennially weak teams in the 1930s and 1940s.[6] Quirk and Fort measured competitive balance by calculating the dispersion of won-loss records around the league average (necessarily .500). If certain teams were dominant, then the measures of dispersion should be high. They found that the measures of competitive balance changed insignificantly after the reserve clause was weakened; if anything, there was more team balance in the leagues after 1976 than before. This example confirms Coase's argument that if the rules (property rights) are well-known and enforceable to all, the changes in those rights will affect the wealth of the participants but not the outcomes.

Marriage and Divorce

Let us now apply this analysis to an important contracting situation faced by most people: marriage and divorce. In 1969 California became the first state to switch to no fault divorce; South Dakota was the last state to switch, in 1985. Prior to these laws, in order for a divorce to take place one party had to commit a "fault." These varied from state to state, but they usually included things like adultery, cruelty and criminal behavior. The important distinction between fault and no fault divorce is that in the former, *both* parties had to agree in order to divorce. One spouse could not leave the marriage without the approval of the other. With no fault divorce, either spouse can terminate the marriage unilaterally, without the agreement of the other. It is enough that there are irreconcilable differences, and only one spouse need establish these differences. This has been an important change in property rights in the past generation.

One of the realities of fault divorce was that it was often hard to prove a fault had been committed, especially if the guilty party didn't wish to be caught. What tended to happen was the couples would agree to a fault and then perjure themselves in court.[7] But why would someone agree to a fault? A person would take this action only because they expected to be compensated. Suppose the husband wanted to leave the marriage.[8] Under the old fault law he would have to pay his wife to agree to some fault. This payment often took the form of a certain percentage of the marital assets and extended alimony payments. For example, the wife may have consented to a divorce for full possession of the house, or custody of the children. The individual most wanting the divorce had to pay the individual who least wanted to divorce. With fault divorce, the property right

6. Around 1910 someone coined the expression, Washington—first in war, first in peace, and last in the American League. See Fort and Quirk, op. cit., page 241.

7. Many have argued this was the major reason legislators changed the law.

8. Historically, it has been the husband who generally breaches the marriage contract and wants the divorce. Can you think of why? (For some clues, see the discussion in Chap.13.) Although the reverse is quite possible and becoming more prevalent, we stick to this older scenario for expository convenience.

over divorce belonged to the one who least wanted the divorce, typically, in the past, the wife. With the new no fault divorce law, grounds aren't required. In our example, if the husband decides to end the marriage, under no fault law, he can just leave. If the wife wants him to stay then *she must pay him!* Hence the property right to divorce has switched from the one who least wants a marriage to the one that most wants it.

This change in liability provides a nice Coase Theorem experiment. We have two worlds, one where the wife holds the property right, while in the other the husband holds the right. Will the divorce rate be the same in those states where the law is fault as in those states where the law is no fault? According to the Coase theorem, when transactions costs are zero, there should be no difference.

Table 9-2 describes a situation where marriage is the efficient outcome. Assume we can measure in dollars the daily net benefits to the husband and wife of marriage and divorce. When married, the benefits to the husband and wife are $50 to each. If they were to divorce, their net daily benefits would be $60 and $30 respectively. Married, their joint benefits are worth $100, $10 more than their joint value divorced, $90. If the gains from exchange are exhausted, this is a couple that will stay together, since more is preferred to less. However, this is also a situation where the husband would prefer a divorce to marriage because his net benefits are greater when divorced. For the wife, the opposite is true, she prefers being married.

Suppose now that this couple lives in is a fault state, i.e., *both* parties must agree to the divorce. This means that the husband must pay his wife to agree to a divorce. The maximum he is willing to pay (i.e., his marginal value for the divorce) is $10. He could, for example, agree to pay these amounts as alimony or as part of some property settlement. However, the wife requires at least $20 to agree to a divorce. Since the husband is unwilling to pay this amount, the wife does not consent to the divorce and the couple remains married. This is the efficient result, since this is when joint benefits are greatest.

Now suppose this couple instead lives in a no fault state. The husband can in this instance unilaterally decide to leave—he does not require his wife's permission. Will the wife be able to convince her husband to stay? Yes, she will. She is willing to pay $20 to have him stay, while he only requires $10 to be convinced. The efficient result happens again: the husband remains and there is no divorce. In this case, however, the wife will actually have to pay him $10+ per day. She can do this, for example, by agreeing to do a disproportionate share of the housework, or, if she is employed in the labor market, she can contribute a disproportionate share of income to the marital community. These differing property rights do affect the husband's and wife's wealth. She is less wealthy and he is more wealthy than what would occur if they lived in a fault state. However, the allocation of resources, in this case, the decision to live as a married couple or to divorce is not affected by the differing rules of liability.

Table 9-2

	Husband	**Wife**
Married	$50	$50
Divorced	$60	$30

Lastly, suppose the numbers in the first row of Table 9-2 for married are interchanged with those in the second row for divorced. Then the joint value married is lower than the joint value divorced. We leave it as an exercise to show that this couple always divorces, no matter what the law is. Again, the rules of divorce will affect the relative wealth of the spouses but not whether they stay together or get divorced. In the absence of transactions costs, the decision to divorce is independent of the distribution of property rights between the couple. Just like in the cattle example where liability does not affect production levels, here the divorce law doesn't affect outcomes either. The outcome is the same, and it is always efficient. The Coase theorem states that in the absence of transactions costs, the allocation of resources is independent of the distribution of property rights. When transactions costs are zero, the gains from trade must be exhausted. Individuals respond to costs and benefits, and the rules of the game change only the initial, and thus the final endowments of individuals, but not the gains from trade.

9.3 Transactions Costs and Property Rights

The Coase theorem holds only when transactions costs are zero. When transactions costs are positive, rules and property rights do matter. If we are to understand how rules, laws, and organizations affect outcomes, we must understand transactions costs.[9] In order to do this, we revisit the definition of property rights.

Property Rights are one's ability to exercise a choice freely.

These choices relate to exclusion of others, deriving income, and selling (transferring) a commodity. The degree of property rights individuals possess hinges on their ability to make these choices. Property rights are not an all-or-nothing affair. Most often our ability to make choices is limited, and in these cases our property rights are therefore limited. We say we own our stereo systems, but we do not have the right to blast them at high volumes when roommates or neighbors are around. We may own a car, but we cannot drive on the wrong side of the street or go through red lights. We usually cannot use our house or apartment to operate a business. You cannot legally sell your student card or driver's license because it legally belongs to the school or state. We are not allowed to dump toxic wastes even on our own private property. Every right is limited to at least some degree.

Property rights are often limited because somebody else is the true holder of the rights. All laws and regulations ultimately distribute property rights to various individuals, and none of us end up with all of them. Other times our rights are limited because it just doesn't pay to enforce them. Trespass is common on private property and roads. If you can use private forest land for weekend hikes without paying for it, you have the economic property right, not the forest company.[10] When rights are too costly for anyone to own, the asset in question is said

---

9. This section draws on Douglas W. Allen "What Are Transactions Costs" *Research In Law and Economics* 1991, and Yoram Barzel, Transactions Costs: Are They Just Costs?, *Zeitschrift fur die gesamte Staatswissenschaft, Journal of Institutional and Theoretical Economics,* March 1985, 4–16.

10. Property rights as we are defining them are not the same as how a lawyer would define them. A legal property right refers to your rights to make decisions *under the law.* I may have the legal property right to sell my car, but if it was stolen last night I no longer have any economic property right to the car.

to be in the *public domain,* or *common property.* There are two important points worth considering with respect to property rights.[11]

1. When there are no property rights, there is no trade and no wealth.

What would a world be like without property rights? Since no one would have any control over any resource, no one could make any decisions. No one would produce anything because as soon as it was made it would be stolen. For the same reason, no one would ever save (i.e., accumulate wealth). Absence of property rights means anarchy. This is one of the reasons why economic rights are so closely linked with legal rights. It is very difficult to trade when one person holds one type of right and someone else holds the other. For example, a friend of mine once had his car stolen. My friend had the legal right to the car, but the thief had the economic rights. (When the police found the car it was locked!) Imagine if the thief had tried to sell the car back to my friend. The conversation might go something like this. Hello, I'm the fellow who stole your car last night, and I'd like to sell it back for $10,000. Just leave the money in small bills in a paper bag under the third bench at the park. Oh, thanks for calling. Unfortunately I have hay fever and the park is really bad for me. Perhaps you could meet me at my house around ten o'clock. This is a transaction that's not going to happen. Neither party is able to enter into an enforceable contract with the other and control the resource in question.[12]

2. When property rights are perfectly defined, the gains from trade are maximized.

This is the Coase theorem again. There is a spectrum of rights ranging from zero to complete, and correspondingly there are wealth levels that range from zero to some maximum. We live in a world that is at neither extreme. Individuals own property but never completely. Given that wealth is always higher when property rights are better defined, however, it is always true that *ceteris paribus* (other things equal), individuals prefer more completely defined rights to less completely defined rights. Therefore, it pays for individuals to make efforts to establish property rights, and once established, to maintain those rights.

These considerations lead to the definition of transactions costs:

> *Transactions costs are the costs of establishing and maintaining property rights.*

These costs include the costs of protection from theft and any concomitant losses that result from such efforts. Property rights are therefore linked in a fundamental way to transactions costs. When property rights are perfect, no effort is required to establish or protect them, and as a result transactions costs are zero. When transactions costs are prohibitive, no one would engage in them and property rights are zero. Finally, when transactions costs are positive, property rights will be incomplete.

Now let's return to the no fault divorce example. It is common knowledge, and research has in fact shown, that the divorce rate increased when states

11. These points were first made by Steven Cheung, The Theory of Rent Control, *Journal of Law and Economics,* 1974.

12. Ransom seems like the obvious thing for a thief to always do. The original owner must be the high marginal valued user of the good, so why not sell it back? Can you think of why children tend to be ransomed rather than automobiles?

enacted no fault divorce laws.[13] Why would divorces have increased? What is wrong with the previous analysis using the simple numbers in Table 9-2? In that discussion we assumed that the property rights of the wife and the husband were perfect because transactions costs were zero. However, property rights are limited in the world we live in. For example, some states have had property laws that stated the owner of a marital asset, for example, the house or car, was the individual who's name was on the title. If the home and other major assets are in the husband's name when the law changes to no fault, the wife may have no wealth to compensate the husband to stay, despite having made some economic contribution to those assets. The law in effect allows the husband to take the wife's wealth. Her property right is incomplete, and this prevents application of the Coase theorem.

Consider also the fairly common situation in which the wife put her husband through medical or law school and was expecting a return on this investment. In only a few jurisdictions do courts recognize a medical or law degree as property (and very recently at that). It therefore has commonly not been divided at divorce, even though extremely valuable to its possessor. When the law switches to no fault, the wife may be unable to compensate her husband because her investment is in his brain and there is no legal remedy to get it back. The no fault law allows husbands in this situation to abscond with their wife's investment, providing an additional incentive to divorce. As a final example, in many traditional marriages, the wife remained in the home for the entire duration of the marriage. During the marriage, the husband spent his time employed, acquiring valuable (and transferable) labor market skills. The wife, however, invested in homemaking skills which have little value in employment outside the home. Historically, this may have been mutually advantageous specialization. With no fault divorce, however, wives in this situation have had few liquid assets with which to compensate their husbands, leading to divorce even when the greatest mutual gains occur when the couple stays married.[14]

Transactions costs are the reason why banks rarely make tuition loans to students. The value of a college education is substantial—over a lifetime, college graduates make several hundred thousand dollars per year more than high school graduates. Therefore, it would be mutually advantageous if banks financed such education, since the increase in the student's wealth would be greater than the costs of the loan. In spite of this, however, such loans rarely occur without the backing of government guarantees. The reason is that the only collateral for the loan is the student's brain. If the student defaults, the only way a bank can collect on the loan would be to sell the student into slavery, an act illegal in the United States since 1865. (College ROTC programs are an exception. The federal government will finance your college education if you agree to serve in the military for four years after graduation. This is a contract you cannot easily break. Because the government has, in this instance, peculiarly strong powers to collect on its loan, these contracts are viable.) In private markets, banks have, on their own, sometimes made loans to medical students. The

---

13. See Douglas W. Allen, Marriage and Divorce: Comment, *American Economic Review* June 1992.

14. A common explanation for why the Coase theorem would not apply is that the husband may simply beat his wife to accepting the poorer circumstance. Can you see how this is also a problem of transactions costs and incomplete property rights?

dropout rate in medical school has always been quite small, and formerly, at least, physicians may have been subject to loss of licensure if found in default.

In cases where many individuals are involved, transactions costs may be so large that rents will always be partially dissipated. Consider the case of airport noise. Jet aircraft are wonderful machines, transporting us great distances in short amounts of time. However, they are also noisy, and this problem is especially acute when the planes fly low and often, for example, around airports. One set of rules is to make the airlines liable for all noise damage they create, by levying fines or charges for each take-off or landing. In that case, the airlines will restrict flights somewhat, until the marginal benefit to them of adding a flight equals the marginal cost, including the charge for noise. People who live near the airport will benefit, but air travelers will lose some convenience in terms of frequency of flights, and perhaps fare increases. The problem this creates is that if full compensation is paid to residents who live near the airport, they lose the incentive to reduce or otherwise mitigate the noise damage on their own. For some areas near the runways, being a repository for noise may be the most highly valued use. If airlines fully compensate residents, the residents lose the incentive to not move too close to the end of the runway, or to install noise insulation. Land that might have been better for industrial purposes (where firms might easily shield the workers from the effects of added airplane noise) might become a site for residential housing. Thus too much noise damage may occur with full compensation if the parties do not further contract.

Consider now the opposite rule, where the airlines are not liable for any noise they create. In this case, they have no incentive to reduce noise at especially inconvenient times, such as three o'clock in the morning. Passengers benefit from the greater frequency of flights (and perhaps lower fares) but residents lose. In this case, land near the airport is treated as common property as far as noise pollution is concerned. As a result, too much such pollution occurs, just as in the case of common ownership of land studied in Chapter 7. Coase pointed out that in instances like these, where transactions cost are not small and thus property rights to silence are not well defined, the rules that result in minimum rent dissipation are not easy to determine. Either assignment of liability produces some dissipation of rents.

Spring floods regularly destroy housing built along many river banks. Ocean waves destroy beach housing with some regularity, and certain regions of the U.S. Gulf Coast are hit by hurricanes every few years. In California and elsewhere, buildings are sometimes built adjacent to or even straddling known major fault lines, subjecting them to severe earthquake damage. In many such cases, when earthquakes strike, the government declares the region a disaster area, qualifying the residents for subsidized loans or outright grants. In a real sense, then, the government assumes partial liability for acts of nature. The situation is the same as when the airlines are liable for all noise damage. While obviously humane, this assignment of liability also has the effect of reducing the incentives to mitigate these damages by appropriate action. Certain areas may be too risky for building, but if society picks up part of the tab for damages, building in these areas is encouraged beyond what is efficient, or with incorrect construction.

This issue became front-page news in the summer of 1993, when large parts of the upper Mississippi River and its tributaries overflowed, producing widescale flooding. Parts of Davenport and Des Moines Iowa were under eight feet of water at various times. The Authorities closed the Mississippi River for navigation for hundreds of miles. In public discussions on the causes and costs of this disaster, it came to light that although the federal government had offered subsidized flood insurance, certain cities along the river had declined to purchase it. They did this because of the cost and because the federal government insisted that coverage would apply only if the cities at risk for flooding took some preventative measures. These steps included building higher levees, which destroyed views of the river and the scenic value of land near the river, and possibly not using some of the land close to the river.

Some part of the flood damage apparently occurred because of specific choices made regarding the trade-offs of better scenery and additional crops during the periods when the river was not flooding, versus the costs of destroyed crops and other losses of income due to business disruption when the river flooded. However, the costs of the flooding were not borne only by those making the choices. The general taxpayer was asked to foot the bill for most of the damage. That is, consumers elsewhere in the economy became liable for the crop damage and income loss. In that case, it can be argued that too much damage occurred. There have been some efforts at legislation to provide payment for flood damages only if certain affirmative measures are taken to reduce the loss when the floods occur. However, these issues are still under debate.

The prices of goods in some cases reflect the external effects; those who purchase such goods receive compensation. The price of housing near airports reflects known airport noise. A person purchasing a house in the flight path receives compensation for this noise by paying a lower price than for equivalent houses not subject to this nuisance.[15] In the same manner, useful attributes, such as living near a convenient bus or transit line are also reflected in the price of housing, thus allocating this land to those who value this convenience most highly. If, on the other hand, a person purchases a house and the airport authority builds a new runway, or rearranges flight paths in a way not anticipated at the time of the sale, then that person suffers a loss in wealth. The resale price of the house will be lower in the future, reflecting these new circumstances.

The classic case of damages to third parties is the factory polluting rivers or the atmosphere. Contracting between the factory owner(s) and residents in the affected area is likely to be difficult or impossible. Many firms have used the atmosphere or adjacent streams as though they were common property. In this case we suspect damages beyond the efficient level. However, these damages are to some extent mitigated by the adjustment of market prices of housing and other goods, and perhaps wages. Since living and working in a polluted area is undesirable, the price of housing will be lower and wages higher than in areas that are less polluted. These price differentials in part, at least, compensate individuals for the damage to their environment. However, if many firms created these conditions, the ability of any one firm to adjust its production to capture the benefits of pollution reduction is slight, and we would expect resource misallocation to be empirically important.

The next sections go through five separate types of transaction cost problems in some detail. In the first three cases we compare the zero transaction cost

15. Home buyers can be expected to self select in the sense that those bothered less by the noise should be the successful bidders for these houses, thereby further reducing the damages. I have often suspected, in particular, that there should be a disproportionate population of hearing impaired persons living near airports, though I know of no study confirming it.

outcome to a situation where there is little or no ability to avoid the transaction cost problem. They are: congestion externalities, public goods, and the prisoner's dilemma. These examples illustrate the generality of transaction cost problems. After these examples, we look at the phenomenon of signaling to show how a simple procedure can both create transactions costs and reduce them. Finally we end up with perhaps the most famous of problems, the one that started it all, the nature of the firm. We don't intend for these examples to be exhaustive, just illustrative. By the end of them you should have some feel for a relatively new branch of economics.

9.4 Highway Congestion[16]

One of the most important instances of dissipation of rents people encounter in their daily lives is the congestion on the nation's highways. These roads, in particular the interstate highway system in the United States and elsewhere are referred to as freeways because no toll is collected for their use. These roads are publicly owned, but more importantly, since no exclusion is exercised over their use, we expect the common property outcome. Indeed this is what happens—as those caught in freeway gridlock can appreciate. The first systematic analysis of highway congestion appeared in an article published in 1924 by Frank H. Knight.[17] Knight's paper is one of the first instances of the modern analysis of the effects of property rights on resource allocation.

Consider a section of freeway that is uncongested during off-peak hours, but congested during rush hours. Suppose for simplicity that all freeway users are traveling to or from work, and when the freeway is not congested, the trip takes a half hour. Beyond a certain density of cars, each additional car on the freeway slows everyone down, and the trip takes longer. Assume further that the trip can be taken on side streets, but that route takes one hour, no matter how many cars are on the streets. Assume in particular the data in Table 9-3. Column 2 shows the travel times on the freeway for the number of cars indicated in column 1. These times are average quantities—they are the times each car takes to get to or from work. The table indicates that up to a density of 5 cars,[18] no effects of congestion occur. At low densities, the interaction between autos is negligible; the presence of one car has no impact on the speeds of others. Beginning with six cars, however, congestion occurs. Each additional car adds 3 minutes to the trip. The effects are not borne just by the additional car entering the freeway: the new car slows *all* cars down by 3 minutes. This imposition of costs on others is the source of the congestion problem.

The figures in column 3 are the total times of travel, for all commuters shown in column 1. For example, when 5 cars use the freeway, their trips each

16. This is one of my favorite problems. I found I gained a much greater understanding of the distinction between marginal and average cost when I got around to working out some numerical examples as appear in the text.

17. Frank H. Knight, Some Fallacies in the Interpretation of Social Cost, *The Quarterly Journal of Economics,* 38, pp. 582–606, 1924. Reprinted in *A.E.A. Readings in Welfare Economics,* K. Arrow and T. Scitovsky, eds., Irwin: Homewood IL, 1969. Knight was a leading theorist at the University of Chicago.

18. This number refers to a number of cars per some length of freeway.

Table 9-3

(1) Number of Cars	(2) Average Travel Time (Minutes)	(3) Total Travel Time (Minutes)	(4) Marginal Travel Time (Minutes)
4	30	120	30
5	30	150	30
6	33	198	48
7	36	252	54
8	39	312	60
9	42	378	66
10	45	450	72
11	48	528	78
12	51	612	84
13	54	702	90
14	57	798	96
15	60	900	102
16	63	1008	108

take 30 minutes, for a total time for all five drivers of 150 minutes. For 6 drivers, the trips take 33 minutes, for a total time cost of $6 \times 33 = 198$. The *marginal* impact of an additional car on the freeway is, by definition, the change in total cost (measured in minutes of travel time) caused by that additional driver. The marginal cost for 6 cars is the difference between 198 minutes total time for 6 drivers and 150 minute total time for 5 drivers. In like fashion, we can calculate the marginal costs of an additional car as the differences between successive total times. However, a much more revealing calculation of marginal cost is important in this analysis.

Up through 5 cars on the freeway, the marginal cost equals the average cost time of 30 minutes, since no car has any impact on another's ability to use the freeway. When the sixth car enters the freeway, however, the situation changes. In addition to her own 33 minute commute, the sixth car slows the other 5 cars down by 3 minutes each, thereby adding 15 minutes to the total travel time. The complete impact of the sixth car on the freeway is therefore $33 + 5 \times 3 = 48$ minutes, as shown in the last column, and derived above by simple calculation of the differences in total times. In like fashion, when the seventh driver enters the freeway, in addition to his own 36 minute commute, he slows the previous 6 cars down by 3 minutes each. The marginal cost of the seventh car is therefore $36 + 6 \times 3 = 52$ minutes. The remaining figures in column 4 are derivable in like fashion.

Algebraically, this calculation of marginal cost is as follows. Let:

$AC(n)$ = average cost (travel time) per commuter, in terms of the number of cars n on the freeway

$TC(n)$ = total cost (travel time) of all commuters, in terms of the number of cars n on the freeway

$MC(n)$ = marginal cost (in terms of travel time) of adding one car, in terms of the number of cars n on the freeway.

Then by definition,

$$TC(n) = n\,AC(n)$$

$$TC(n + 1) = (n + 1)\,AC(n + 1)$$

Since the marginal cost is the change in total cost when an additional car enters the freeway,

$$\begin{aligned} MC(n + 1) &= TC(n + 1) - TC(n) \\ &= (n + 1)\,AC(n + 1) - n\,AC(n) \\ &= AC(n + 1) + n\,AC(n + 1) - n\,AC(n) \end{aligned}$$

yielding

$$MC\,(n + 1) = AC\,(n + 1) + n\,[AC\,(n + 1) - AC\,(n)] \qquad (9\text{-}1)$$

Equation (9-1) says that the marginal cost of any action equals the average cost *plus* the effect that action has on the average cost times the number of individuals involved.[19] It highlights the important distinction between average and marginal costs: marginal cost includes, whereas average cost excludes the impact of one person's actions on others. The marginal cost of a person's presence on a freeway includes the imposition of extra commute time on all the other cars.

Consider now how the freeway will be used. Commuters use the freeway as long as their travel time is less than their commute using the side streets, assumed here to be 1 hour. Since no one restricts access to the freeway, up to 15 cars will enter the freeway, for at that point, the average commute on the freeway is the same as on the side streets, 1 hour. *This is the common property outcome.* It is inefficient because the detrimental effects each driver imposes on other commuters is ignored. The fifteenth car adds 102 minutes of travel time—his own 60 minutes plus 42 more, comprised of the extra 3 minutes he imposes on each of the previous 14 drivers. If he instead took the side streets, he personally would lose no time, and the other 14 drivers would each save 3 minutes. These mutual gains are being lost by his decision to take the freeway. Likewise, when the 9th driver enters the freeway, he saves 18 minutes over taking the side streets (60 minus 42), but he adds 3 minutes time to each of 8 other commuters. His saving of 18 minutes causes 24 minutes of damage to others. In any such situation where the damages an individual causes exceeds the gains, a mutually beneficial trade exists. The losers, if they could trade the time around, would pay the ninth drive something more than the value of 18 minutes (but less than 24), and by so doing, all commuters would be better off. This type of contract exists when the number of drivers is such that the marginal cost of entering the freeway, that is, the additional cost including the extra time imposed on other commuters, exceeds the marginal cost of using the alternative route, the side streets. The economically efficient level of freeway use in this example is 8 cars. When the 8th car enters the freeway that driver saves 21 minutes over the side streets (60 — 39), and imposes

19. In terms of calculus, $TC(x) = xAC(x)$. Using the product rule of differentiation, $TC'(x) = MC(x) = AC + xAC'(x)$.

exactly 21 minutes on the other drivers (the previous 7 times 3 minutes each). The marginal cost of her action is 60 minutes, whether she takes the freeway or the side streets. No rearrangement of routes will be mutually beneficial to all commuters.

With unrestricted access to freeways, as with unrestricted access to land (or any resource) in general, the rents derivable from that resource (in this case, the saving of commute time) are *dissipated.* With no mechanism for restricting access, rents are driven to zero, eliminating the savings in commute time from freeway travel.[20] Although potential gains from trade exist, meaning consumers could in principle get together and arrange a mutually beneficial contract, it is difficult to think commuters entering a freeway could negotiate that contract. But it is the economic role of property rights to internalize these effects on others. If the freeway were owned, meaning some individual had the right to charge for its use and exclude nonpayers, that owner would own all the damages additional drivers impose on others. That is, an owner would receive all the benefits and bear all the costs. By owning all the costs and all the benefits, wealth maximization would lead the owner to restrict the freeway use to its efficient level. The problem of freeway congestion, or perhaps better put, *excessive* freeway congestion is thus a problem of common property. (Even at the efficient level of usage (8 cars), some congestion occurs, slowing down each driver 9 minutes over the uncrowded state. Here, as in most cases, the economically efficient level of external damages is not zero.)

Having identified the source of the congestion problem, the issue is then whether a solution based on individual maximizing behavior is possible. A solution based on unparalleled courtesy, where some drivers voluntarily agree to take the side streets instead of saving time on the freeway is not realistic. Likewise, it is farfetched to imagine freeway drivers entering into an elaborate contract with each other, agreeing on side-payments for not using the freeway. But it is exactly the economic function of private property to provide this solution. Suppose therefore that the freeway is privately owned. The owner can easily restrict access and charge for the service of the freeway by constructing toll booths. What toll would a freeway owner charge, and would it yield the economically efficient level of freeway use?

The amount an owner of freeways can charge a consumer of the freeway is the value of the time saved by taking the freeway versus the side streets. If the freeway is uncongested, commuters save a half hour. How much is that worth? The value of time is the highest valued alternative use of that time to an individual. A person's day is divided amongst working in the marketplace, that is, for wages, working around the house, and leisure. A decrease in commute time means more time for any one of those activities. The value of an increment of time is what it could produce in the highest valued of these alternatives. For example, a person might have the option of staying longer at work, earning extra income. Extra leisure or work around the house might be more valuable still. As more time is saved, the value of this time changes, but let us approximate it at the margin by what a person could earn by staying at work a bit longer. This has

20. In this example, the side streets never become more congested, and thus the entire benefits from having a freeway literally disappear. In reality, freeways relieve traffic congestion on the side streets, lowering travel times there, and thus net benefits persist.

the advantage of objective measurement, though it might overstate the value of a person's time if that individual had no opportunity to increase his or her wealth by extra work.[21]

For computational ease, assume that all commuters earn $6.00 per hour, or $.10 per minute, and that this amount represents the value of time for all concerned. In that case, saving a half hour is worth $3.00, that is, commuters would be willing to pay up to $3.00 to save that much time. If the toll is $3.00, only 5 people will take the freeway, and the owner will collect $15.00 total toll. A sixth driver will not get on the freeway, because then the total cost of the commute on the freeway will exceed the toll-free commute on the side streets, by 30 cents. These six drivers will not pay $3.00 to save 27 minutes; that time is worth only $2.70 each. Table 9-4 shows the potential toll collections.

The maximum toll collection occurs when the toll is set so that the efficient level of freeway use results.[22] If the road is privately owned, the owner, by individual wealth maximization, induces that level of use such that the gains from trade are exhausted. This is not a result the owner intends or even knows about; it is an example of Adam Smith's invisible hand at work. The result occurs because the freeway is now completely private in nature. Ownership of the rents the road produces eliminates the common property problem. When the road is private, the owner owns not only the rents generated, but also all the *damages* inflicted on other drivers as congestion increases. As traffic slows, the freeway produces less aggregate benefits, and so the consumers (commuters) become willing to pay less and less for the right to use the freeway. The aggregate toll is simply the monetary value of these aggregate benefits; the larger these benefits become, the larger the toll the owner can collect. The maximum toll represents the maximum net benefits to commuters.

It seems that even if a private owner would maximize net benefits of the freeway, commuters wouldn't benefit, since the freeway owner would keep all these benefits. However, the government has the power to tax these rents and

Table 9-4

Toll	Number of Cars	Total Toll Collected
$3.00	5	$15.00
$2.70	6	$16.20
$2.40	7	$16.80
$2.10	8	$16.80
$1.80	9	$16.20
$1.50	10	$15.00

21. A person need not have an explicit overtime contract for extra work to be wealth-increasing. All that is necessary is that the extra work ultimately be rewarded with a higher salary, say, for greater skill or productivity.

22. In this example we have eliminated a potential problem of monopoly by assuming that the demand for the freeway (and the sidestreets) is horizontal, i.e., infinitely elastic at the total price of $6.00. This assumption would not be valid if people had differing demands for the freeway, e.g., if they commute different distances to work and differing values of time. Also, the problem of *public goods,* discussed in the next section would be relevant at noncongested times.

redistribute them as it sees fit. *The rents must be collected, in order for the freeway to be efficiently used, but the owner does not have to keep all the rents.*

Mathematical Note[23]

Since one example does not constitute a proof, let the value of time taken up commuting on the side streets (1 hour in our example) be represented by some value p. The toll t a freeway owner can collect for use of the freeway is $t = p - AC(x)$, where $AC(x)$ is the value of the average time each driver takes using the freeway. The total toll collected is

$$T = tx = (p - AC\,(x))x = px—TC(x) \tag{9-2}$$

Note that total cost, $TC(x)$, by definition, is average cost times the number of cars x. Maximum T occurs when the first derivative of this expression equals zero. Recalling that marginal cost is simply the rate of change (first derivative) of total cost,

$$T'\,(x) = p - MC(x) = 0 \tag{9-3}$$

Equation (9-3) is the same condition for profit maximization of any firm; produce where price equals marginal cost. Here, the condition says that the toll is maximized when the number of commuters on the freeway is such that the marginal cost of travel on the freeway equals the alternative cost, p. But this is exactly the condition for economic efficiency. Thus, private ownership, as we expect, results in efficient freeway use.

9.5 Public Goods

An important class of goods exists that have the characteristic of being *jointly consumed* by many individuals at one time. These are goods for which there is *no congestion,* and are what economists call **public goods**. The most famous example of such goods is national defense. The protection we receive from our defense establishment is something all citizens share. If a baby is born, or immigrants move to the country, their presence does not diminish the protection of the residents already present. Similarly, an uncrowded freeway is a public good, in that one person's presence does not detract from another's ability to use the road. Many private services we consume in also have this attribute. Several people can watch a television program, movie or theater production simultaneously without diminishing anyone else's ability to consume the good. The old expression, two can live as cheaply as one, while obviously not entirely true, refers to the fact that many consumption goods, such as housing and furniture are shared by family members. Two people living together can live more cheaply than two individuals living in separate apartments or houses, because some goods, mainly shelter, furniture and fixtures have the property of no congestion and are jointly consumed.

With ordinary goods and services, the efficient production level is where the marginal cost of production equals the market price of the good, reflecting consumers' marginal value of that good. If consumers value a good at $10, then if

23. Readers without rudimentary knowledge of calculus can skip this section.

someone can produce it by diverting less than $10 of resources from other goods, consumers receive this net difference. However, this reasoning applies to goods that only one person can consume. Suppose two people each value a movie at $5 each, and they can both watch the movie at the same time (perhaps they even prefer it that way). Then when the movie is shown, the combined marginal value of the movie to both individuals is $10, the *sum* of the individual marginal values. If one hundred people watch the movie at the same time the marginal benefit produced is likewise the sum of all one hundred of their marginal values. For public goods, therefore, the condition for efficient production is

Sum of consumers' marginal values = marginal cost of production (9-4)

In the case of ordinary goods, such as apples, for which congestion is so extreme that if one person consumes the good, no one else can, market demand curves are formed by laterally summing the individual demand curves, as we showed in Chapter 2. In that case, if one consumer has a marginal value of an apple of $.50 when two apples are consumed, and another's marginal value is $.50 when three apples are consumed, and if five apples are produced at a marginal cost of $.50, we exhaust the gains from trade when the consumers purchase the five apples at that price. The market supply curve intersects the market demand curve at a price of $.50, at the production level of 5 apples.

In the case of public goods, however, the goods are jointly consumed. The way to achieve the Pareto condition (9-4) is to add the individual consumer's demand curves *vertically,* (which we show in Fig. 9-2) so that at a given quantity, we sum their *marginal values,* not their quantities. When the marginal cost curve (the industry supply curve) intersects this aggregate demand curve (at point *E*), the sum of all consumers' marginal values equals the marginal cost of production. This equality defines the quantity of the public good versus the production of competing private goods that exhausts the gains from trade.

While this procedure in principle determines the efficient mix of public versus private goods, the nature of public goods often prevents provision of that quantity using private markets. Many public goods are difficult to sell on a per unit, fee-for-service basis. It's hard to imagine selling units of national defense in a private market. Rather, once provided at a certain level, exclusion of nonpayers is virtually

Figure 9-2 *Efficient Production of Public Goods*

The total demand for goods with no congestion is the (vertical) sum of the marginal values of each consumer, shown as D_T. Efficient production takes place at point *E*, where this demand curve intersects the marginal cost curve of producing the good.

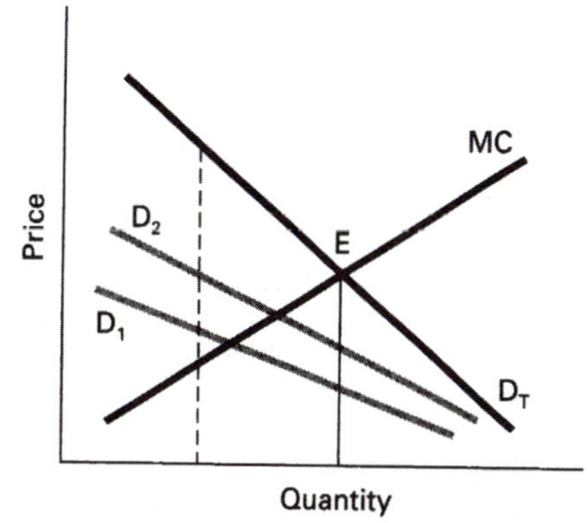

impossible. Public goods were in fact once defined in terms of this inability to exclude free riders.[24] However, exclusion is a separate issue. The attribute that makes public goods distinctive is jointness of consumption. Uncrowded freeways have the attribute of no congestion, yet exclusion is easily enforced by erecting toll booths. Inability to enforce exclusion is a question not of jointness of consumption, but of enforcing property rights. Property rights in information, or ideas, are sometime difficult to enforce. Once an idea is out, anyone can use it. This is one reason for copyright laws—to establish property rights in ideas. However, the public aspect of information is that it is often capable of joint consumption. If a person discovers a way to make a better mousetrap, adding new consumers to this good does not affect the ability of any other consumer to use the information. The marginal cost of allowing other consumers to use the better information is zero.

Consider a bridge (or freeway) that shortens various road trips, and assume the bridge is never congested.[25] Since the bridge is never crowded, the marginal cost to society of an additional car using the bridge is zero. Imagine that consumers have various demands for the services of the bridge. Consumers choose to use the bridge to differing extents depending on the price charged. In the case of goods such as this, however, the efficient price to charge consumers is zero. At any positive price, some consumers choose to forego the services of the bridge. At a positive price, consumers' marginal value of the bridge is greater than zero, even though the marginal cost of providing that service to consumers is zero. Too few bridge services are being provided. Once built, if the bridge is never congested, the efficient allocation is to offer it free to all consumers.

When the bridge is priced at zero, however, no revenues are generated to pay for the bridge. Therefore, no information is elicited as to the values consumers place on the bridge. The efficient number of bridges *to produce* is where the sum of consumers' marginal values of bridges equals the marginal cost of building bridges. However, when the services of the bridges are given away, it becomes impossible to ascertain how much consumers value bridges. It therefore is difficult or impossible to decide how many bridges to build. This problem does not admit of an easy solution. The most efficient solution may very well be to charge a toll to cross the bridge. This may reduce the loss of gains from trade, but some potential gains would still be lost, since some consumers will be dissuaded from using the bridge even though at the margin where the bridge is already built, the marginal cost of providing the service to them is zero.

9.6 The Prisoner's Dilemma

In recent years, the mathematical theory of games has been utilized to analyze contract theory in economics. Game theory is a framework in which two or more individuals compete for certain payoffs which depend explicitly not only on the decisions of the person in question, but on the strategies employed by the other

24. This term probably derives from the practice of sneaking onto empty railroad freight cars and riding to some destination without paying. The practice was often justified by asserting that the train was going there anyway, and the insignificant extra human weight added nothing to the railroad's cost. Unfortunately, if everyone used this reasoning, the railroads could not operate.

25. Harold Hotelling, a famous economist and one of the developers of modern statistical analysis was the first to formulate and analyze this problem in this way.

player(s) as well. A very simple type of game is matching pennies: You and another person each reveal the face of a penny simultaneously. If they are the same (i.e., both heads or both tails), you win the pennies; if they are different, your opponent wins. This, and more complicated games such as poker, where bluffing may be an important strategy, are called zero sum games: what one person wins, another loses. There are no mutual benefits generated, other than the sport of an evening of gambling.

Economics, however, is concerned mainly with situations where mutual benefits exist. The term **nonzero sum game** refers to a model in which two or more individuals compete for payoffs, where mutual benefits are possible. The most famous game of this nature is referred to as the **prisoner's dilemma**, because of the colorful description of the origins of the payoffs. We display the game below in Fig. 9-3, called a payoff matrix. The police have just captured two individuals whom they suspect to have committed a serious crime. The police separate and interrogate the prisoners individually. They cannot communicate or cooperate with each other. Each prisoner has two strategies. One possibility is to stonewall, that is, deny everything; the second option is to confess. We indicate the outcomes in each box. The first number represents the payoff to player 1, the second, to player 2. If both prisoners stonewall, they will be convicted of some lesser crime and will each receive a three-year sentence. This outcome is in the top left-hand corner of the payoff matrix.

One prisoner can make a deal with the police, confess to the crime and turn state's evidence against his or her associate. In this case, the prisoner who confesses will be let off with a very light sentence (1 year), and the partner will receive 15 years. For example, the box in the lower left-hand corner indicates that if player 1 confesses and player 2 stonewalls, player 1 receives 1 year and player 2 receives 15 years. The box in the upper right shows the symmetric result when the prisoners reverse the strategies. Lastly, however, if both players confess, they each receive 10 years.

In this situation, if one considers the total penalties imposed on both prisoners, there is clearly a best strategy. The total penalties (analogous to total costs in an economy) are least if both prisoners stonewall. The police, however, have rigged the payoffs to discourage that outcome. Consider prisoner 1's thoughts on his situation. He has to decide what his partner might do. He might reason as follows. "Suppose my partner, whom I've known since childhood and is my closest buddy, *stonewalls.* If I stonewall also, I'll get three years, but if I confess, I'll only get 1 year (serves him right—what'd he ever do for me anyway). So I'm

Figure 9-3 *The Prisoner's Dilemma*

		Prisoner 2: Stonewall	Prisoner 2: Confess
Prisoner 1	Stonewall	3,3	15,1
	Confess	1,15	10,10

better off if I confess, given that my partner stonewalls. But wait—maybe he's going to cut a deal with the D. A., the dirty rat (I never *could* trust him). Hmmm, if he confesses and I stonewall, I'm going to get 15 years, whereas if I confess also, I'll only get 10 years. So if my partner confesses, I'm better off confessing too, and if my partner stonewalls, I'm also better off confessing. I guess I'll *confess.*" Of course, since the penalties are completely symmetric, prisoner 2 is led to the same conclusion. Each person is better off confessing, for any assumed behavior of his compatriot.

That each player is led to this strategy is the essence of the prisoner's dilemma. This outcome is called a **Nash Equilibrium**, after mathematician and Nobel Laureate in economics, John Nash, who first formulated this idea. Neither player on his own has any incentive to depart from this strategy. Clearly, the best outcome is for both players to stonewall. This is the **cooperative outcome**, for it requires that each player engage in behavior that is wealth-maximizing only if the parties agree not to pursue their opportunistic self-interest. If the prisoners can sign an ironclad contract with each other to not confess, they will opt for this strategy. However, the authorities are usually intent on preventing such collusion. They are interested in keeping transactions cost high, so that prisoners cannot contract to maximize their mutual benefits, (which are rarely society's). Thus, the likely outcome is that one or more of the prisoners will confess, and perhaps both of them, resulting in total jail terms exceeding their combined sentences if they could successfully contract with each other.

In our daily lives, we regularly face prisoner's dilemma situations. When we make a purchase, we worry a bit that perhaps the vendor is cheating us, and not selling us what we anticipate. If we write a check for our purchase, the seller wonders if the check is really good. All transactions contain a certain game element of this nature. We face a choice of cheating or not cheating. In most circumstances, we stand to make a short run gain by cheating the other person, in the same way that each prisoner stands to gain by cheating on his co-conspirator. We call this **opportunistic behavior**. If both consumers and buyers act on this impulse, we will constantly wind up at the noncooperative solution to the prisoner's dilemma game, where gains from trade are lost. The reason most of us in fact don't pursue these selfish strategies is that we repeat most of our transactions. Our behavior signals the other player as to our intentions, a strategy known as *tit-for-tat.* We achieve the cooperative solution by not cheating in the short run, even though in virtually all circumstances, we could get away with some degree of dishonesty. Thus businesses and manufacturers guarantee their merchandise even though they know some consumers cheat them, and buyers pay their bills, even though collection of small bad debts is so costly it rarely pays for businesses to pursue them. When a traveling salesman comes to our door promising us a miracle cleaner, we have less faith that he is honest, because we will likely not transact with him again, nor he with us. With no repeat transactions, achieving the cooperative outcome is more difficult.

Foreign policy decisions are distinctly game-theoretic in nature. For forty-five years after the conclusion of World War II, the United States and the Soviet Union pursued costly armament programs. The choices, to simplify, were to arm or not arm. The cooperative solution, which would have saved each country untold trillions of dollars, would have been to not arm. Unfortunately, each country feared that the other would secretly arm, producing the noncooperative outcome. Many nations around the world who can ill afford costly military equipment are as we speak on an arms buying binge. In recent years, both India and Pakistan have both detonated nuclear weapons. Each is afraid of being the only unarmed state, and none trust their neighbors to abide by the cooperative strategy. Unfortunately, in war, there sometimes may be no repeat transaction, and thus nations perceive the tit-for-tat strategy as too risky. Throughout history, nations have been unable to overcome the suspicion that their neighbors were secretly arming, and have found themselves at the noncooperative outcome.

On a lesser scale, we can analyze the decay of urban neighborhoods with a game theory approach. When you purchase a house, you also buy the neighborhood in which it resides. The value of a house in no small part reflects the quality of the houses that surround it. A brand new home in a run down neighborhood sells for less than in a neighborhood with similar quality homes. If all your neighbors fix up their houses, that is a direct benefit to you; your house will increase in value with no effort on your part. In like fashion, if your neighbors all let their houses deteriorate, the value of your house will fall also, because the neighborhood will deteriorate, even if you keep your house in good repair. We display this game in Fig. 9-4. There are two strategies: fix up, and don't fix up. In each box hypothetical investment rates of return are displayed. The cooperative outcome is where each home owner fixes up their house; in that case, all residents receive a 9% investment yield. If nobody fixes up their houses, the homes slowly deteriorate and owners receive a 4% return. On the other hand, home owners can free ride on the efforts of their neighbors by spending no money fixing up their own houses, but still receiving the benefits of the improving neighborhood from the efforts of their neighbors. In this case, not fixing up one's own house yields a 10% investment yield, while the neighbors, who spend their own money receive only a 2% yield.

Consider now the incentives facing each home owner. They all wonder if it pays to fix up their houses; it can be an expensive mistake if the neighbors do not follow suit, because the neighborhood will go downhill in spite of their singular effort. Even worse, suppose you believe your neighbors will indeed fix up their houses. In that case, if you don't fix up your house, you make a 10% investment yield instead of only a 9% yield if you do fix up. Thus in this case a home owner does better by not fixing up. Moreover, suppose your neighbors do not fix up their houses. Then, again, a home owner receives a higher return, 4% versus 2%, by not fixing up. In either case, a home owner does better by letting the house decay!

While the specific numbers in this example are hypothetical, it is easy to imagine that this mechanism is responsible for the decay of many neighborhoods. No individual home owner finds it in their self interest to prevent the decay, even though all wish that everyone else would take steps to prevent it. If a

Figure 9-4 *Urban Decay*

		Fix Up	Don't Fix Up
You	Fix Up	9%,9%	2%,10%
	Don't Fix Up	10%,2%	4%,4%

contract could be written in which all the home owners in the neighborhood commit to fixing up their houses, the cooperative outcome could be achieved. One mechanism for contracting is the use of zoning laws. Although zoning cannot easily mandate that a person fix up his or her house, zoning laws prevent owners from free riding on the neighborhood in other ways. For example, in a neighborhood composed of single-family housing, any one home owner might benefit by converting their home to a multi-family dwelling. In that case, the neighborhood would still have its single-family character. One multi-family house doesn't change a neighborhood. The owner of the converted home can capture that benefit by renting out part of his or her house. The problem this action creates is that every home owner is aware of this arithmetic. Each would also be inclined to convert their house to multifamily use. But this combined action would change the character of the neighborhood, and in all likelihood lower it. To prevent this, the city often zones a neighborhood as single family only, preventing conversion by law. Zoning therefore is a contract between home owners not to engage in opportunistic behavior—actions that benefit one person by imposing costs on others, and, ultimately, on the opportunist when others copy their behavior. For similar reasons, zoning ordinances often prevent structures from exceeding a certain height (even though it might give one owner an enhanced view), require that buildings be set back from the street in certain amounts, and at given heights, and prevent the establishment of commercial enterprises in residential neighborhoods. These laws are ways in which residents contract with each other not to engage in opportunistic behavior.

Another device for achieving the cooperative outcome is to somehow buy the entire neighborhood. If a neighborhood is currently run down, it might be possible to purchase individual houses at a relatively low price that reflects the current quality of the neighborhood. If a single buyer can purchase enough houses and fix them up, the buyer can change the character of the neighborhood, and capture the benefits in the form of appreciation in the sale price of the fixed up houses in the now improved neighborhood. This strategy is not easy to accomplish in practice, however. If existing home owners catch on to the plan, they will raise their price in a classic hold-up maneuver. In that case, the home owners will capture the benefit of the improved neighborhood instead of the developer, and the plan may be aborted.

As a last example of a game situation, consider the problem of maintaining a monogamous relationship during marriage. An interesting puzzle is, how is it that marriages survive, in the face of diminishing marginal values? At this writing, the author has been married to the same woman for over 36 years. We have already consumed each other for over 13,000 days. Many times, some new woman looks quite attractive to me. The reason is clear: I am comparing the marginal value of the 13,000th unit of my wife with the marginal value of the first unit of some new woman. This is why new acquaintances are sometimes more exciting than our old friends. One reason not to act on adulterous impulses, however, is that the marginal value of the new acquaintance will surely decrease with increased consumption, just as with one's spouse. One reason why we stay married is the tremendous savings in transactions cost obtained by having a relationship with only one person, especially with regards to raising children. Moreover, the daily interactions of two people living together means that this is a repeated game, and so the cooperative solution is relatively more likely to prevail.

Figure 9-5 *The Marriage Dilemma*

		Your Spouse: Be Faithful	Your Spouse: Fool Around
You	Be Faithful	10,10	1,15
	Fool Around	15,1	3,3

There is still an ever-present temptation to engage in opportunistic behavior, in the attempt to have our cake and eat it too. We want to consume both the spouse and the bimbo or gigolo. In marriage, one is faced with two choices: be faithful to your spouse, or fool around. It's difficult to quantify the results of these strategies, but suppose we can measure the excitement and pleasure of these activities. Consider the payoff matrix depicted in Fig. 9-5. If both partners are faithful, the highest joint return is achieved. This is the cooperative solution. However, each spouse has an incentive to cheat on the other—each can have even more excitement by fooling around—but only if your spouse does not fool around also. The highest rate of return occurs when you have an affair and it's just fine with your spouse. However, if both parties have an affair, the lowest combined return occurs. With the numbers in Fig. 9-5, we can see that whether your spouse chooses to be faithful or to fool around, you achieve higher thrills by cheating. The problem is, so does your spouse, and then divorce, the worst outcome for both, is the likely outcome. Couples avoid this outcome by contracting with each other to forsake all others.

9.7 Signals

Have you ever worn a nice suit to an interview? This is an elementary example of signaling. It says you have some modicum of good manners, that you respect the other person enough to dress up for them, etc. Every year around Christmas time economists have their annual meetings, and at these meetings first interviews are done with all of the new Ph.Ds. You can usually tell the interviewees because they're the only ones with new suits. **Signals** provide information. In a world where information is costly, and where people take advantage of other's lack of knowledge, signals can be very useful. In order for something to be a good signal it must be difficult to imitate and it must be relatively more costly for the low quality producer. However, anyone can dress in a suit, and good job candidates have no advantage over the bad ones in that dimension. Hence, dressing in a suit is sometimes not a terribly useful signal.

An interesting example of signaling was provided by the Air Traffic Controllers (ATC) during the 1970's.[26] In 1972 Congress passed a disability act that

26. Michael Staten and John Umbeck, "Information Costs and Incentives to Shirk: Disability Compensation of Air Traffic Controllers," *American Economic Review,* 72, December, 1982, 1023–37.

allowed stress and burn out to count as a disability. This act also increased the disability pay so that for some government employees the tax free disability was higher than their after tax wage. In 1974 Congress modified the rules to allow a worker to choose their own physician. Claims made by ATCs jumped by 150%. This could have been due to the fact that they really were under stress, and the new laws simply lowered the cost of making a claim, but there appears to be more to it. In order to increase the probability of a successful claim, ATCs could signal that they were under stress. Planes suddenly started to come closer together. There are several degrees of closeness, and all of them qualify as evidence of stress. Interestingly, planes were brought closer together, but not to the point where there was a near mid air collision. Most of these errors occurred in the daytime, when the weather was nice, usually with smaller passenger jets, and at non-peak times. This increased the probability that some one else (like a passenger or pilot) would report the error and that the ATC could devote all of his energy to the signal. This is a case where signaling reduced wealth. Congress changed the rules again in 1978, so the skies are friendly once again.

Signals do not always reduce wealth. They are often a way of economizing on costly information. Graduation from college is a signal that a person is intelligent and capable of sustained effort. That information is one of the reasons why college graduates get better jobs than high school graduates. Another reason, of course, is that the knowledge one gets in college is actually useful to employers. There is a lively, ongoing debate in the economics profession as to relative importance of these two components. Graduating *summa cum laude* from a premier school signals that a student is not only intelligent but also extremely motivated and hard working. Many such people still do not succeed exceptionally in private or public employment, and the Unites States and Canada are littered with extremely successful individuals whose school records are unimpressive. But school achievements are correlated to some degree with success in later life, and therefore people use them.

Brand names are another instance of signaling. Probably every college town has some computer stores that assemble components into Windows based computers. They usually provide more bang for the buck than branded computers, such as Dell, IBM and Compaq. They are also generally less reliable, and the stores themselves are less likely to be in business next year than stores that sell the branded items. When a company spends money on advertising, or on a fancy retail facility, that is a signal to consumers that they intend to stay in business for a long time. The costs involved in setting up such an establishment are substantial. The only way the store can recover these costs is to sell many items over a long period of time. They thus signal that they are interested in your *repeat* business. Since customers do not return to stores that engage in opportunistic short run cheating, customers infer that such a store does not intend to misrepresent what they sell, or engage in other nefarious retail tactics.

Being a virgin at the time of marriage was historically a very desirable trait for both women and men, but much more so for women. One reason for its greater importance for women is that it is more verifiable for women than for men. More importantly, what did virginity at marriage signal to one's intended? Couples generally prefer to raise their own children rather than someone else's. A parent is likely to be very upset to find out years later that the child they were raising was fathered or mothered by some other person. However, women always know, absent child stealing, who their child is. They (and perhaps others) were there when it was born. The father is much less easily identified (though DNA testing is now changing that). A woman, if she has been monogamous, can know for certain that the child she is bearing is hers and her husband's, but her husband could never (at least in the past) be certain that the child is his. Being a virgin at marriage is a way that brides signal to their fiancées that they intend not to have someone else's child. The analogous signal for husbands is much less important because everyone can observe the wife's pregnancy and delivery. Virginity at marriage signals fidelity in sexual affairs. With imperfect contraception, what might otherwise be of equal importance to men and women becomes a relatively more important signal for women to engage in. As contraception has improved and with abortion widely available, issues of childbearing can be separated from purely sexual matters. As a result, this particular signal has become less important.

Margaret Brinig used this framework to analyze the practice of giving diamond engagement rings.[27] She noted that diamonds were always available but not commonly given as this type of gift. She noted that her mother had such a ring, but that neither of her grandmothers did, even though her grandfathers were wealthy enough to afford them. Diamond engagement rings became fashionable during the 1930s. Moreover, they accounted for a greater part of a person's wealth than other gifts, and other engagement gifts given prior to that time. Brinig rejects the idea that this was some unaccountable change in tastes, or a result of a successful promotion campaign by the DeBeers diamond exchange (though diamonds had become less expensive because of new discoveries, principally in South Africa). What changed in the 1930s was the elimination of the now almost forgotten legal cause of action, the breach of promise suit.

Prior to 1935, if a man broke off an engagement, he could be sued by his ex-fiancée for breach of promise. The reason for such actions has to do with the value to women of virginity prior to marriage. The famous Kinsey Report of 1948 documented that in the decades between the two world wars women typically remained chaste until engagement, but that almost half lost their virginity after engagement and prior to marriage. A woman who was engaged was presumptively no longer a virgin. This decreased her opportunities in marriage if her engagement was broken off. When this horrible circumstance befell her, the law then allowed her to collect damages. Brinig reports that the trials themselves frequently became public spectacles because of testimony regarding the woman's previous chastity (or lack of same.) Beginning in 1935, however, states began to remove these statutes; a few remain on the books to this day. This shifted the liability of broken engagements from men to women.

In response to this new legal environment, it became common for men to post a bond that they would not break off the engagement. The bond took the form of an expensive diamond engagement ring. If the engagement went forward, the ring became part of the new family's wealth. If the husband broke off the engagement, the jilted fiancée got to keep the diamond as compensation. (The bride-to-be was expected to return the ring if she broke off the engagement.) Brinig found a correlation between the sales of diamonds and states

27. Margaret F. Brinig, Rings and Promises, *Journal of Law, Economics and Organization,* Vol. 6 No. 1, Spring, 1990, 203–15.

where the breach of promise laws were stricken. Diamond engagement rings were thus a private contracting response to a change in the law regarding liability for broken promises. In recent years, sexual activity outside of marriage is no longer unusual. The use of diamonds as a bonding device is now much less important. Not surprisingly, therefore, diamonds are now relatively more frequently purchased for reasons other than engagement, e.g., for anniversary rings, wedding bands and other miscellaneous jewelry.

9.8 The Nature of the Firm

We now come to the issue that started the modern theory of transactions costs. In the preceding discussions about production, we have assumed that production takes place within *firms*. This is indeed the pervasive organization of production in modern societies. It is interesting and important to consider why this is so. An alternative means of production would be for labor and the owners of capital to contract with each other in the marketplace. For example, if a person wanted to build cars, they could contract independently for labor, rent equipment, hire consultants to instruct individuals how to run the machines and coordinate activities, and the like. All activities would take place in a market for productive inputs. But we rarely see this form of production. Instead, we see workers, managers and owners working with either specific or informal rights and duties within some sort of institutional structure. Managers and owners expect workers to show up and leave at certain times, perform certain tasks, and to accept direction and coordination from the owners and managers.

Because production within firms is such a pervasive organizational structure, there must be significant savings over alternative means of production. One of the first discussions of this topic was Ronald Coase's insightful article, The Nature of the Firm.[28] Coase argued compellingly that the fundamental reason for the existence of firms is the *savings in transactions costs* over the alternative of contracting in the market for all services. The cost of production is reduced by organizing factors of production in a central location, and allowing managers to issue directives and orders to workers. Firms can then more fully realize the advantages of specialization and team production.

Firms are largely undemocratic institutions—there are bosses and workers—and the workers agree to take orders from the bosses. Workers rarely vote on what they prefer, and management requests have the quality of commands. Firms operate in this manner for the same reasons that representative government has replaced Athenian democracy (where all citizens vote on all issues): these arrangements provide tremendous savings. Contracting in the marketplace with individual suppliers of inputs in production is more costly than simply gathering these inputs in one or a few central locations, and obtaining their services by directives.

The reason why workers agree to these undemocratic terms, which entail for them a limit on their freedom, is that these lower transactions costs allow workers to receive higher wages, in the same way that a lower sales tax is shared by both buyers and sellers. In addition, gains are realized because laborers' efforts are not

28. Ronald Coase, The Nature of the Firm, *Economica,* November, 1937.

diluted by attention to functions unrelated to their specific tasks. It is perfectly legal in the United States and other countries for firms to be organized, for example, as partnerships, or as workers' cooperatives, where all workers vote on firm policies, with the income of the firm distributed on some per capita basis to workers. These types of cooperatives are in fact observed, but usually for relatively small firms. The reason is obvious: this is such an expensive mechanism for decision making, especially for firms producing several commodities, that large firms with this structure usually fail in the marketplace.[29]

To say that managers or owners issue commands or directives, does not, however, imply that owners are unconstrained in this regard. Although owners can fire, or terminate the contracts of workers, sometimes for any reason at all, workers can also fire the company, by quitting. Virtually all workers currently on a job have some advantage over new entrants because of familiarity with the work place and knowledge of the tasks to be performed. It is almost always costly to fire experienced workers and hire new inexperienced replacements. The new workers are rarely as efficient, and owners must always bear training costs to some extent. In such a setting, the managerial structure that becomes dominant will be one in which mutual benefits are maximized, subject to the constraints imposed by the market for workers and managers, and capital.

A prominent problem for firms is the tendency of all workers (managers included) to shirk, that is, to surreptitiously engage in less effort than what they agreed upon. By shirking, the workers infringe on the rights of the owners.[30] Efforts to prevent this shirking constitute transactions costs. In an organization with many individuals, it is costly, to one degree or another, to monitor the efforts and productivity of workers. Although each worker has this incentive to shirk, it is also apparent that each worker suffers because of the shirking of co-workers. If the combined shirking is substantial enough, the very viability of the firm and the workers' jobs could be at risk. The highest income of the firm, and therefore the highest wages that will be available to workers occurs if there is no shirking. It therefore pays for the workers to agree not to shirk, as long as they can enter into an enforceable contract with other workers to do the same. Workers are thus precisely in the prisoner's dilemma game just discussed. One mechanism to accomplish this is to hire a monitor, that is, a manager, who has the authority to penalize or fire shirking workers. The existence of managers with authority over workers can therefore be explained by the desire to more fully realize the mutually beneficial gains from coordination, given costly measurement of factor inputs.

Every business enterprise incurs some costs associated with monitoring the output of its workers. That is, not only must the wages of the workers be paid, but the firm must divert some of its resources to insure that the laborers are actually working, or working at the agreed upon intensity. As a firm grows in size, these monitoring costs become greater. A firm must choose whether to add additional monitors, or seek some other contractual form which will substitute for additional

---

29. Cooperatives, where the customers own the firm, are common in some types of situations. For example, rural towns often have cooperative general stores. Granaries and apartment blocks are often coops. This appears to be a method of reducing the monopoly power an owner might have over isolated customers.

30. This is sometimes referred to as the principal-agent or agency problem.

human monitoring. We expect diminishing marginal product of monitors; thus at some point other means of accomplishing the same goal might appear.

The structure of firms thus depends on the costs of contracting with productive inputs and the nature of the technology employed. Some firms are small, for example retailers dealing in specialized goods, such as fashion goods, ethnic foods and the like. Some firms are very large, like Boeing and McDonnell-Douglas, because the production of modern, highly complex jetliners is less expensive when carried out in large, integrated facilities than by many small firms trading airplane parts with each other. However, large firms often subcontract with smaller firms to produce parts of the final good. By subcontracting, firms can avoid often costly development of expertise in specialized areas. For example, airplane manufacturers typically subcontract for the engines. They find it cheaper to delegate to firms specializing in certain electronic systems the production of various guidance control components. However, there must be a certain minimum sized market in order for a small specialized firm to exist. If some system is unique to a given airplane, for instance, it will likely be production will take place internally. However, if many airplane manufacturers use a similar product, a separate firm may invest in the expertise to be the low cost producer. Indeed, the number of independent specialized firms seems to increase as the market for their product increases.

One of the hazards of producing a specialized product for only one company is that the firms become beholden to each other. If the sole reason a firm exists is to supply a specialized part to another firm, the quasi rents it derives become subject to expropriation by the buyer. The firm producing the final good may have the ability to squeeze the price below what allows for a return on the now sunk costs of developing the product, even though the firm covers the variable costs of production. In a similar manner, the firm producing the final good, i.e., the firm purchasing the specialized good may be subject to a hold-up. The supplier may be able to charge a higher than competitive price at least in the short run because the lack of that part might cause a bottleneck in production for the buyer.

Firms seek contracts and organizational structures that minimize these transactions costs. For example, whereas newspapers almost always own and operate their own printing presses, magazine publishers sometime own their own presses, but book publishers rarely do. Actual manufacture, i.e., the printing of a newspaper or magazine is a very different operation, requiring different skills and technology, than writing and composing the printed matter. The latter is done in offices by white collar workers, usually professionals, whereas printing is a blue collar trade involving mainly skilled operatives. There is no particular reason to house both these operations under the same roof. However, in the case of newspapers in particular, timeliness is very important. If a book comes out a day, week or even a month late, it is usually not a great concern. Newspapers, on the other hand, must be printed on time if they are to have any value at all. Newspaper owners would thus be subject to holdup tactics of independent printers. They therefore often own their own presses. Book publishers are not subject to holdup and thus they rarely engage in the actual printing. Magazines are of a somewhat intermediate nature, and thus we find some ownership of the printing processes there.[31]

---

31. This example is from Vertical Integration, Appropriable Rents, and the Competitive Contracting Process, by Benjamin Klein, Robert Crawford and Armen Alchian, *The Journal of Law and Economics,* 21, October ,1978, 297–326.

Although most workers are paid on an hourly or weekly basis, many different labor contracts are possible. Among these other arrangements available to employer and employee are, for example, sharecropping and piece rate contracts. Sharecropping is a very common contract in agriculture in the United States and Asia. Under this contract, the landowner leases parcels of land to tenants, or sharecroppers. The sharecroppers farm their parcel and pay some stipulated fraction of the output they produce to the landowner as rent. Why would a landowner choose this form of hiring labor rather than the simple wage contract, or perhaps leasing the land to tenants on a fixed rent basis? An analysis of the transactions costs associated with each type of contract provides some answers.

Suppose you have written a somewhat technical term paper and wish to hire someone else to type it for you. You find that some word processors charge by the hour, others charge per page, and still others charge per word typed. Which contract do you prefer? Each has some undesirable characteristics. If you hire the typist by the hour, you worry that perhaps this person is not typing as fast as he or she might. The typist can shirk, or cheat on the arrangement by typing only moderately fast, and this type of shirking is hard to detect. Suppose, then, you decide on the per page contract. Even here, however, cheating is possible. The typist can make the margins slightly larger to create more pages. Perhaps even more importantly, this contract (and the per word contract) provide little incentive for accuracy and elegance of typing, such as setting up the pages carefully, spelling technical words correctly and doing mathematical notation properly. The per hour contract is better if these aspects are important, because the typist will be rewarded for diligence to those details. No contract is perfect. The one that will be used is the one that maximizes the gains from trade net of all transactions costs.

Consider now the particular case of farms. The landowner can rent out the land on a cash or a share basis. The hired hands can work for wages or for part of the crop. Consider the choice of cash rent or cropshare.[32] The level of output from a farm depends on many things. It certainly depends on the level of effort of the farmer—no effort, no crop. But the quality of soil, the weather, pests, and other random features all play a role in the level of crop. When a farmer owns his own land he manages his soil, even when it means a lower crop in the current year. A farmer does not maximize the size of the current crop; he maximizes the value of his farm. Sometimes, for example, it pays to sacrifice current income by leaving fields fallow in order to replenish the soil. A renter on the other hand, cares less about the long term condition of the soil. When a renter pays cash for a parcel of land, any crop that comes off the land is income to him. A cash renter has an incentive to treat the soil as common property, and although the landowner may try to directly police this overuse, many soil exploitation techniques are very hard to detect. One way to reduce these inefficient incentives for the renter is to provide a share contract. When the renter shares the crop with the landowner there is less incentive to exploit the soil because the share acts like a tax.

If the share contract benefits the landowner (and ultimately the tenant) then why would a landowner ever use a cash rent contract? One problem with share contracts is that it gives the farmer an incentive to underreport output. Every part of a shared crop that is underreported counts as income to the farmer. Just as

32. This section draws on Douglas W. Allen and Dean Lueck, Contracting in Modern Agriculture: Cash Rent vs. Cropshare, *Journal of Law and Economics,* October, 1992, 397–426.

with the case of soil exploitation, the landowner will make some effort to avoid underreporting. However, if the problem is serious enough, a cash rent contract may be chosen instead. Hence when crop theft is important it is expected that a cash rent contract will be chosen, and when soil exploitation is a problem share contracts should be used. This holds for many crops, but consider grass crops versus row crops. Hay, alfalfa, and other grass crops are planted and then harvested several times a year. These crops require little soil manipulation and the output can be sold many ways as well as being used on the local farm for feed. Row crops require extensive soil manipulation, and are generally sold through a local elevator. We therefore expect cash contracts to be relatively more frequent with grass crops, and share contracts relatively more frequent in the production of row crops. Researchers Allen and Lueck confirmed these predictions using data from over three thousand farming contracts in Nebraska and South Dakota.

The actual share in a share contract is determined by the fraction total output that the landowner receives as rent. In the text example presented in Chaps. 7 and 8, rent maximization occurred when six workers were utilized, and the resulting maximum rent was \$60. The value of total output the six workers produced was \$300, total labor costs being 6 × 3\$40 = \$240. Thus the landowner's share of total output = \$60/\$300 = 20%. If there were no differences in the costs of these contracts, the landowner would be indifferent between the standard wage agreement of \$40 per day or a share contract of 20% of the worker's output. On an identical sized farm but with more productive land, the share going to the landowner would be greater, reflecting the higher fraction of rent in total output.

Lastly, a landowner could retain workers on a piece-rate basis. In this case, say if workers are picking apples, the employer pays the workers per bushel of apples picked. There is some equivalent per-bushel price that would yield workers their alternative wage. Counting bushels or baskets of fruit seems like a relatively inexpensive procedure for measuring the output of each worker. However, suppose the fruit has to be picked at the right stage of ripening, and packed carefully to avoid bruising. Paying by the bushel picked provides no incentives to the worker to engage in this kind of time-consuming sorting. Paying workers per hour rewards care in packing, because the workers receive compensation for the extra time it takes to pack carefully. However, for the reasons we mentioned above, this form of remuneration also creates an incentive for shirking on time taken per bushel. In fact, piece-rate contracts are not common in most industries. It is obviously an impossible contract unless the employer can easily measure output. In agriculture, piece-rate payments are possible during harvest, but not during the growing season. In industries where many people work on an assembly line on only a small part of a large production process, or service industries such as engineering or accounting, paying employees on a piece rate basis is clearly impractical or impossible. It is not easy to count, that is, measure in numerical units, the output of a college professor, or the manager of a firm, or a computer designer. Firms therefore generally pay these employees on a salary basis by the week or month.

Two other reasons for the occurrence of sharecropping have to do with the sharing of risk and lowering of the transactions costs associated with financing the rental payments. As these are tangential to the present discussion, we shall only briefly cover these interesting topics. In agriculture, although work must proceed throughout most of the year, the output comes only when the crops are harvested, and this output is often of uncertain amount, depending as it does on the vagaries of the weather. Sharecropping is a means of *sharing* this risk among the landowner and laborers. Most people find risky enterprises less desirable than more certain ones. This arrangement allows the dividing of the risk of uncertain output among more people than just the landowner, or just the tenant, as would be the case if the tenant had agreed to a fixed payment as the rent. Thus sharecropping is a way of lowering the costs of risk; we should expect to find greater incidence of sharecropping with crops more susceptible to varying output due to, say, weather. In pre-communist China, for example, sharecropping was more prevalent in wheat farming than in rice farming, the latter of which largely takes place underground and is therefore less susceptible to weather.[33]

When American slaves were freed in 1865, they were largely devoid of all material wealth of any kind. Their main asset was their ability to do farm work; they possessed essentially no other capital. These people largely became sharecroppers. Since these people had no savings or accumulation of assets, they could hardly make rent payments during the year before the crops were harvested. They were also unlikely to be considered good prospects for loans by the bankers of the day. Sharecropping became the means by which the newly freed slaves were able to contract with landowners to obtain some capital (usually, a mule) and produce cotton and other crops. It was a lower cost form of contracting than a straight wage contract and thus became a prominent form of labor contract in the post-war South.

CHAPTER SUMMARY

- Transactions costs are the costs of establishing and enforcing property rights. They include those extra expenditures we make because of uncertainty about the fulfillment of contracts, when trading with other individuals.
- In a world without transactions costs, all gains from trade are exhausted.
- Property rights serve to lower transactions costs by eliminating competition for the rights to goods. Property is *private* if one can *exclude* others from its use, if the income generated can be *owned* by an individual, and if the property can be *transferred* to others at some mutually agreeable terms.
- The Coase theorem says that in the absence of transactions costs, the assignment of liability to damages created by one individual will not prevent the exhaustion of mutual benefits, though the incomes of the parties involved will be affected.
- If transactions costs are not zero, the assignment of liability that leads to minimum dissipation of gains is not easy to predict; any assignment leads to some incentives to produce excessive damages.
- Rules, liability, laws and regulations can often be explained by individual's maximizing wealth subject to transactions costs.

33. See Stephen N. S. Cheung, *The Theory of Share Tenancy,* Chicago: University of Chicago Press, 1969. However, Allen and Lueck, *op. cit.,* found little evidence in their sample that this is significant.

- Highway congestion is a common property problem. When we get on the freeway, we cause damage to other drivers by slowing them all down a bit. Since no person owns the freeway, no person or institution has the incentive to reduce these damages. Drivers crowd onto the freeway until their *average,* instead of their *marginal* travel costs equal their alternative opportunities.
- *Public* goods are those for which no congestion exists, such as uncrowded freeways, television broadcasts and national defense. An individual consuming such goods does not detract from another's ability to consume the good. In this case, efficient production levels occur where the marginal cost of production equals the sum of all consumers' marginal values of the good. Since the alternative cost of consuming these goods is zero, the efficient price to charge is also zero, making provision of these goods in private markets difficult.
- *Game theory* is a new branch of mathematics that economists are using to analyze problems of contracting. In these situations, strategies of individuals are specifically incorporated into the decisions of others. Reducing or eliminating short-term *opportunistic* behavior can occur if transactions are frequently repeated

REVIEW QUESTIONS

1. State the Coase theorem and explain why it holds only when transactions costs are zero.
2. Explain why pollution problems are problems of property rights.
3. Is all freeway congestion a sign of economic inefficiency? (Answer: No. Explain)
4. What do we mean by a public good? Is this just something the government provides? Is the postal service a public good?
5. What is the prisoner's dilemma, that is, what system of payoffs leads people acting in their own self-interest to wind up at an outcome they and their companion least prefer?

PROBLEMS

1. In 1992, Hurricane Andrew destroyed billions of dollars of homes and other property in southern Florida. Many homes were found not to be built to withstand such storms. The federal government has since provided assistance to those whose insurance was either inadequate or nonexistent. What effect would extensive relief have on the incentives to prepare for the next storm? What steps do private insurers take prior to these occurrences to attempt to minimize their losses?
2. A private firm builds an airport "out in the sticks." As the local region grows, people start building houses closer and closer to the airport, and

begin to encounter airport noise. The courts rule, in a suit brought by home owners, that the airport is liable for all noise damage (pollution) produced during take-offs and landings. To reduce damages, the airport restricts the number of flights per day.

a. What two competing uses does land near the airport have?
b. Explain how the land might be allocated if the court ruled the airport was *not* liable for noise pollution.
c. If transactions costs were zero between the airport and home owners, the land would be used efficiently, even if the airport was not liable for its noise pollution. Explain the mechanism by which this would come about.
d. What incentives do home owners have to reduce the waste caused by noise pollution under the different liability rulings of the court?
e. If the land were seriously misallocated, that is, allocated in a very "inefficient" manner, how might ownership of the land or other contractual relationships change to reduce that inefficiency?

3. Car manufacturers (and others) are liable for design flaws that result in injury or death. that is, if consumers can prove in court that their injuries were caused by such flaws, the manufacturers have to pay damages. In view of this, comment on legislative efforts to force car manufacturers to include extra safety equipment, such as automatic seat belts and air bags, extra padding and reinforcement of the door panels, etc.

4. On a certain section of freeway, 3 cars can travel without impeding each other's speed. They all travel to and from work, and when the freeway is uncongested, the trip takes 30 minutes. Travel on the side streets takes 1 hour. Each succeeding car beyond 3 slows everyone up by an additional 4 minutes. All commuters earn $6.00 per hour, and value their time accordingly.

   a. How many cars will use the freeway if access is unrestricted? Explain why this is an inefficient use of the road.
   b. Recently, some brave politicians have advocated "user-fees," i.e., tolls, on freeways. Explain why such a system could lead to efficient use.
   c. Explain why a private owner would charge a toll that produced efficient use of the freeway. What is that toll in this case?

5. How do your answers in problem 4 change if:

   a. Commuters' time is worth $12 per hour, not $6.
   b. Each car after 3 increases the commute by 5 minutes, instead of 4.
   c. Travel on the side streets took 1.5 hours, not 1 hour.
   d. Side streets become more congested as people avoid the freeway due to the toll.

6. Freeways and other public access facilities are sometimes congested and sometimes not. What structure of tolls would be efficient? Would the same toll be collected at each hour of the day, for example?

7. Suppose the economically efficient toll is collected on a freeway, yet the road is still highly congested. What would account for this?

8. Carpooling is often encouraged to prevent the dissipation of rents due to highway congestion. Do you personally carpool? why or why not? What other costs are imposed by this scheme?

9. Shopping centers often provide "free" parking for customers, even though the land is obviously not free. Why do they do this? Why not charge some efficient toll for parking?

10. Why is it that McDonalds and other fast food outlets pay their employees per hour, rather than per hamburger cooked or served, per table bussed, etc., since that would be more clearly related to their productivity?

11. What items commonly found around the home could be classified as public goods? If two people share a stereo system, how does your answer differ, if at all, on whether their tastes in music are compatible?

12. How do you suppose outcomes of the various prisoner's dilemma games are affected if the game is played repeatedly?

13. How have the no-fault divorce laws affected the incentives to get married in the first place? Are these changes the same for men as for women?

14. Consider a privately owned farm with the following production function:

L	TP
1	10
2	20
3	29
4	35
5	40
6	42
7	42
8+	No additional increases in output

Assume the market price of output is $10 per bushel, and this price is unaffected by total output on this land. Assume all farmers can earn $50 per day in their next best alternative.

a. How many workers will the owner hire on a straight wage contract?
b. Suppose the owner decides to sharecrop the land. How many farmers will the owner employ, and what will be the share taken by the owner?
c. How does your answer depend on the relative costs of these two arrangements?
d. Suppose the government places a cap on the percent share the owner can charge, below what currently prevails. What effect might that have on the type of contract offered?
e. Suppose sharecropping is still the dominant contract, even with the restriction. It is noticed that labor inputs and agricultural output increases. Is this a sign of greater economic efficiency? (Hint: Where are these extra laborers coming from?)

15. When teams draft players in the National Football League, they tend to bid for the services of players in particular positions. For example, a team may decide its greatest deficiency is at quarterback, and it will select a player for that position. Another strategy, however, since the teams gain the exclusive right to player's services, is to select the player with the greatest market value and then *trade* that player for whatever players fit the team's demands at the time. If transactions costs were zero, which strategy would the owners

follow? Would the team a player winds up on depend on which team first selected him in the draft? If these outcomes do not occur, what does this say about the existence of important transactions costs in these negotiations?

QUESTIONS FOR DISCUSSION

1. When the Soviet Union dissolved a decade ago, there was general agreement that the old style central planning had to be eliminated, and private property and capitalism encouraged. At the century's end, Russia and many former Soviet states are in a chaotic state, with very limited markets and with considerable corruption and mob influence. Discuss these problems from the standpoint of establishing well-defined property rights in these former Soviet states.
2. Earlier in the book we discussed price and rent controls. These restrictions represent an attenuation of property rights. What can we expect in the way of rent dissipation and efficient outcomes as a result? Why do governments impose these controls, and do you favor them?

CHAPTER 10

Interest Rates and Capital Values

If either we or our parents had bought stock in Microsoft when it first went public in 1984, we probably wouldn't have to be sitting here struggling over some economics text. We might already be retired. But does this mean we should rush out and buy thousands of dollars of Microsoft stock now? Should you trust your money instead to some stockbroker who calls you out of the blue and tells you how wonderfully his company's investments have done? He spends his days cold calling strangers trying to get them to invest. What's wrong with this picture? If his advice is so good, why does he have to work long hours as a salesman each day? In this chapter we study the markets for choices people make over multiple time periods.

10.1 Consumption Over Time

The analyses of previous chapters have all concerned choices among contemporaneous commodities. That is, the trade-offs in production and consumption all take place in the same time period. Consumers choose which goods (and how much) to consume and producers choose which goods and how much to produce in that time period. An important choice individuals make, however, relates to consumption *over time.* For example, how does one allocate the income we earn in different time periods to consumption during one particular year? The decision to go to college means lower consumption in the present in return for probable higher income, and thus higher consumption in the future. Putting money in the bank or investing in stocks is similarly a decision to trade present consumption for future consumption. Borrowing to finance a car or a new stereo system allows one to consume these goods sooner than if one waited until the entire amount had been accumulated, but consumption is necessarily lowered in the future as we repay the loans. In Chapter 2 we showed that the law of demand implies that individuals attempt to smooth out their consumption over time. That is, if income is received in an erratic fashion, individuals borrow and lend so as to lower consumption when income is relatively high and raise consumption when income is relatively low. Saving for a rainy day is a behavior implied by diminishing marginal values. When income is high relative to some other time period, the marginal value of consumption is relatively low; when income is relatively low, the marginal value of consumption is high. Gains from trade across time periods occur because the marginal values are initially different. If income is transferred from when income is high to when income is low, consumption which is initially low valued becomes relatively higher valued consumption. The difference between the initial values measures the net gain to the consumer from the transfer.

10.2 The Price of Present Consumption

In order for consumers to transfer income over time, a market must exist in which borrowing and lending take place. The price at which these loans take place takes the form of charging **interest** on the amount borrowed. Probably no other price has engendered as much hostility from organized groups, in particular, religious organizations and governments, as this particular fee. Interest payments are the amounts in excess of the amounts we originally borrowed when we repay the loans. Antipathy toward the charging of interest on loans is long-standing. Thomas Aquinas argued that since money was simply being exchanged for money, money was therefore barren and charging for its use was immoral. On this basis, the medieval Christian Church forbade charging interest. Even when legal, the practice is almost uniformly regarded with suspicion and disfavor. The amount that can be charged for loans is almost everywhere proscribed to one degree or another. In the United States today, every state has some sort of usury law, which establishes maximum rates on various types of loans. The outstanding question this raises is why interest rates have persisted in the face of such long-standing hostility. Interest must serve some important function, else the practice would have long since disappeared.

Suppose I tell you that I would like to borrow $100 from you. I'll pay you back the $100 in a year (honestly, I really will, I guarantee it). Will any of you do it? If your answer is yes, I can be contacted at the Department of Economics at the University of Washington, Seattle, WA 98195. Maybe we'll make it $1,000 for two years. I eagerly await your loan. In fact, few people will enter into such a contract, even if repayment is certain. Even the United States government, which has never defaulted on a loan, has to pay interest on its loans. Why?

The fundamental reason why none of us engage in these types of interest-free loans is that they violate the axiom that more is preferred to less. If we have $100 now, we have the choice of either spending it in the present or saving it for later consumption. If we have access to the money only after a year has elapsed, we have fewer opportunities than if we have it now. If we have the money now we can always choose not to spend it for a year, but the reverse choice is not available. If we have access to the money only after a year, we cannot choose to consume it now. *Having income now is preferable to having it in the future.* Income in the present is "more" than income in the future.[1]

Since income now is preferred to income in the future, all individuals would prefer to transfer at least some future income to the present, by borrowing from others, if all that is required in return is repayment of the same amount in the future. However, while a few individuals might be able to transfer future income to the present in this manner, it is impossible for everyone to accomplish this. Someone has to be willing to lend money to all these people. The potential lenders, however, themselves wish to transfer income from the future to the present. Competition for additional funds in the present therefore produces a willingness on the part of some individuals to pay a premium to lenders for the right to secure these funds. This is the origin of interest payments. Irving Fisher, a great economist of the early 20th century, stated that interest is the **premium for earlier availability of funds.**[2]

Shown in Fig. 10-1 is a supply and demand curve for present consumption. The **price of present consumption** is the number of units of future consumption a person must give up in order to consume 1 unit (for example, $1) of present consumption. Unless some amount of future consumption is promised in return,

---

1. This argument requires the ability to costlessly store our wealth. If we have to pay some one to hold our wealth over from one time period to the next, then it may be preferable to receive income as a stream of payments rather than all at once.

2. Irving Fisher, *The Theory of Interest,* August M. Kelley, New York, 1970. (First edition, The Macmillan Co., New York, 1930.) This book is so clear, it deludes you into thinking you knew it all along.

Figure 10-1 *The Market Price of Present Consumption*

At any moment in time, some people wish to transfer income from the future to the present. Others, for a price, will supply present income. A market price p is established for income in the present, in terms of income one year in the future. This price always exceeds unity, thus, we write $p = 1 + i$, where i = interest rate.

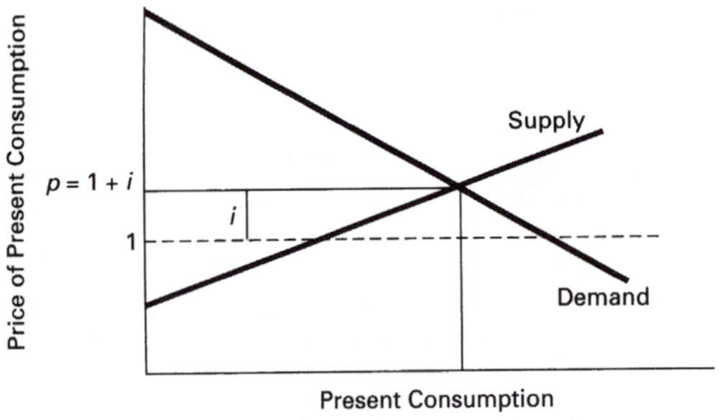

no person would be willing to give up present consumption. The price "1" means that $1 of future consumption is given up for $1 of present consumption. At some price (perhaps below unity—though this theoretical possibility is not considered likely) some individuals in society become willing to enter into a contract to supply present consumption, that is, trade present consumption in return for future consumption. In a society with many buyers and sellers, that is, many borrowers and lenders, a market price p will be established for a unit of present consumption. Markets in which borrowing and lending take place are called **capital markets**. In all empirically observed cases, the price of present consumption (the number of units of future consumption foregone) has exceeded unity. As a result, we write the price of present consumption as $p = 1 + i$, where i is the rate of interest. The fundamental reason for the existence of a positive interest rate is the propensity for individuals to prefer income now rather than in the future (though later we discuss a reason due to our ability to produce income in the future by withholding present consumption). The interest rate is simply the price set in the market for transferring future income to the present.

10.3 Present and Future Values

Suppose a person borrows some amount, say, $100. He or she agrees to repay it a year later. We refer to the amount of the loan as the principal of the loan. If the interest rate is some amount, say, 6%, the amount due at the end of the year is $\$100 + .06 \times \$100 = \$106$. This larger amount is the **future value** of the $100 principal amount. When we put money into an interest-bearing account, such as a savings account or money market fund, we lend money to that institution at some interest rate. If we place $100 in such an account for 1 year at 6% interest, at the end of the year the fund will have grown to $106, meaning the borrowers will owe us that much. If we leave the money in the account for an additional year, we will receive an additional 6% on the new principal of $106 assuming no change in the interest rate. The term **compound interest** refers to getting (or paying) interest on the accumulated principal, not just on the original amount ($100). After 2 years, therefore, the fund will have grown to $106 + .06 × $106 = $112.36. Payment of interest, year after year, on only the original principal is called simple interest and is uncommon today due to the advent of high-speed computers. In this text, interest always means compound interest.

More generally, if some principal P is invested in an account paying i percent interest, after 1 year the account will be worth $P + iP = P(1 + i)$, its future value (FV). The original principal is the **present value** (PV) of this future amount. At 6% interest, the future value of $100 one year from now is $106; the present value of $106 due in 1 year is $100. If the accumulated principal is left in the account to collect interest for another year, the fund will grow to

$$FV = P(1 + i) + iP(1 + i) = P(1 + i)^2$$

In like fashion one can easily show that if a sum is left to accumulate interest for n years,

$$FV = P(1 + i)^n \tag{10-1}$$

Alternatively,

$$PV = \frac{FV}{(1+i)^n} \tag{10-2}$$

Equation (10-1) indicates how a present principal P (or PV) grows, through the accumulation of interest (and interest on the accumulated interest) into a future amount FV. Equation (10-2) is obviously the same equation, but rearranged to show how a present value is derived from a future value. Equation (10-1) is forward looking; (10-2) is backward looking. Equation (10-2) answers the question, "How many dollars do I need right now in order to have some amount, FV, n years in the future, assuming a constant interest rate i throughout?" This amount is the *present value* of that future sum.

Tables 10-1 and 10-2 display the future and present values of one dollar for various interest rates and numbers of years. The values are all derived using equations (10-1) and (10-2) respectively. The numbers in these tables show amounts paid or received at the end of the year. For example, in Table 10-1, if $1 were left in an account paying 5% interest for 10 years, it would grow to $1.63. If $100 were left in such an account, it would grow to $162.90 in 10 years, by simple multiplication. In like fashion, if one wanted to have $100 in 10 years, and a 5% investment were available, Table 10-2 shows that the amount of money you need to set aside now is $100 × .614 = $61.40. At 7% interest, the amount you need now in order to have $100 in 10 years is only $100 × .508 = $50.80. With a higher interest rate, the present value of a future sum is lower, because fewer dollars are required to grow into some specified future sum when the accumulation each year is higher.

On a more conceptual level, the present value of some future sum represents the price of that future amount. The price of consuming $1 one year from now is the amount you have to give up right now in order to do that; at 5% interest, this

Table 10-1 *Future Value of $1 paid or received in n years at interest rate i*

Number of Years (n)	3%	5%	6%	7%	8%	9%	10%	12%	15%	20%
1	1.030	1.050	1.060	1.070	1.080	1.090	1.100	1.120	1.150	1.200
2	1.061	1.103	1.124	1.145	1.166	1.188	1.210	1.254	1.323	1.440
3	1.093	1.158	1.191	1.225	1.260	1.295	1.331	1.405	1.521	1.728
4	1.126	1.216	1.262	1.311	1.360	1.412	1.464	1.574	1.749	2.074
5	1.159	1.276	1.338	1.403	1.469	1.539	1.611	1.762	2.011	2.488
6	1.194	1.340	1.419	1.501	1.587	1.677	1.772	1.974	2.313	2.986
7	1.230	1.407	1.504	1.606	1.714	1.828	1.949	2.211	2.660	3.583
8	1.267	1.477	1.594	1.718	1.851	1.993	2.144	2.476	3.059	4.300
9	1.305	1.551	1.689	1.838	1.999	2.172	2.358	2.773	3.518	5.160
10	1.344	1.629	1.791	1.967	2.159	2.367	2.594	3.106	4.046	6.192
11	1.384	1.710	1.898	2.105	2.332	2.58	2.853	3.479	4.652	7.430
12	1.426	1.796	2.012	2.252	2.518	2.813	3.138	3.896	5.350	8.916
13	1.469	1.886	2.133	2.410	2.720	3.066	3.452	4.363	6.153	10.700
14	1.513	1.980	2.261	2.579	2.937	3.342	3.797	4.887	7.076	12.840
15	1.558	2.079	2.397	2.759	3.172	3.642	4.177	5.474	8.137	15.410
16	1.605	2.183	2.540	2.952	3.426	3.970	4.595	6.130	9.358	18.490
17	1.653	2.292	2.693	3.159	3.700	4.328	5.054	6.866	10.760	22.190
18	1.702	2.407	2.854	3.380	3.996	4.717	5.560	7.690	12.380	26.620
19	1.754	2.527	3.026	3.617	4.316	5.142	6.116	8.613	14.230	31.950
20	1.806	2.653	3.027	3.870	4.661	5.604	6.727	9.646	16.370	38.340
21	1.860	2.786	3.400	4.141	5.034	6.109	7.400	10.800	18.820	46.010
22	1.916	2.925	3.604	4.430	5.437	6.659	8.140	12.100	21.640	55.210
23	1.974	3.072	3.820	4.741	5.871	7.258	8.954	13.550	24.890	66.250
24	2.033	3.225	4.049	5.072	6.341	7.911	9.850	15.180	28.630	79.500
25	2.094	3.386	4.292	5.427	6.848	8.623	10.830	17.000	32.920	95.400
26	2.157	3.556	4.549	5.807	7.396	9.400	11.920	19.040	37.860	114.500
27	2.221	3.733	4.822	6.214	7.988	10.250	13.110	21.320	43.540	137.400
28	2.288	3.920	5.112	6.649	8.627	11.170	14.420	23.880	50.070	164.800
29	2.357	4.116	5.418	7.114	9.317	12.170	15.860	26.750	57.580	197.800
30	2.427	4.322	5.743	7.612	10.060	13.270	17.450	29.960	66.210	237.400
35	2.814	5.516	7.686	10.680	14.790	20.410	28.100	52.800	133.200	590.700
40	3.262	7.040	10.290	14.970	21.720	31.410	45.260	93.050	267.900	1470.000
45	3.782	8.985	13.760	21.000	31.920	48.330	72.890	164.000	538.800	3657.000
50	4.384	11.470	18.420	29.460	46.900	74.360	117.400	289.000	1084.000	9100.000

amount is $.952. The price of a future dollar is something less than a dollar, because when interest is available, you need less than one dollar now in order to have one dollar some time in the future. Dollars today are not the same good as dollars in the future. They have different prices because consumers value them differently. Their prices are measured by their respective present values. The price of $1 to be paid or received a year from now is given by equation (10-2) above.

Table 10-2 *Present Value of $1 paid or received in n years at interest rate i*

Number of Years (n)	3%	5%	6%	7%	8%	9%	10%	12%	15%	20%
1	0.971	0.952	0.943	0.935	0.926	0.917	0.909	0.893	0.870	0.833
2	0.943	0.907	0.890	0.873	0.857	0.842	0.826	0.797	0.756	0.694
3	0.915	0.864	0.840	0.816	0.794	0.772	0.751	0.712	0.658	0.579
4	0.888	0.823	0.792	0.763	0.735	0.708	0.683	0.636	0.572	0.482
5	0.863	0.784	0.747	0.713	0.681	0.650	0.621	0.567	0.497	0.402
6	0.837	0.746	0.705	0.666	0.630	0.596	0.564	0.507	0.432	0.335
7	0.813	0.711	0.665	0.623	0.583	0.547	0.513	0.452	0.376	0.279
8	0.789	0.677	0.627	0.582	0.540	0.502	0.467	0.404	0.327	0.233
9	0.766	0.645	0.592	0.544	0.500	0.460	0.424	0.361	0.284	0.194
10	0.744	0.614	0.558	0.508	0.463	0.422	0.386	0.322	0.247	0.162
11	0.722	0.585	0.527	0.475	0.429	0.388	0.350	0.287	0.215	0.135
12	0.701	0.557	0.497	0.444	0.397	0.356	0.319	0.257	0.187	0.112
13	0.681	0.530	0.469	0.415	0.368	0.326	0.290	0.229	0.163	0.093
14	0.661	0.505	0.442	0.388	0.340	0.299	0.263	0.205	0.141	0.078
15	0.642	0.481	0.417	0.362	0.315	0.275	0.239	0.183	0.123	0.065
16	0.623	0.458	0.394	0.339	0.292	0.252	0.218	0.163	0.107	0.054
17	0.605	0.436	0.371	0.317	0.270	0.231	0.198	0.146	0.093	0.045
18	0.587	0.416	0.350	0.296	0.250	0.212	0.180	0.130	0.081	0.038
19	0.570	0.396	0.331	0.277	0.232	0.194	0.164	0.116	0.070	0.031
20	0.554	0.377	0.312	0.258	0.215	0.178	0.149	0.104	0.061	0.026
21	0.538	0.359	0.294	0.242	0.199	0.164	0.135	0.093	0.053	0.022
22	0.522	0.342	0.278	0.226	0.184	0.150	0.123	0.083	0.046	0.018
23	0.507	0.326	0.262	0.211	0.170	0.138	0.112	0.074	0.040	0.015
24	0.492	0.310	0.247	0.197	0.158	0.126	0.102	0.066	0.035	0.013
25	0.478	0.295	0.233	0.184	0.146	0.116	0.092	0.059	0.030	0.010
26	0.464	0.281	0.220	0.172	0.135	0.106	0.084	0.053	0.026	0.009
27	0.450	0.268	0.207	0.161	0.125	0.098	0.076	0.047	0.023	0.007
28	0.437	0.255	0.196	0.150	0.116	0.090	0.069	0.042	0.020	0.006
29	0.424	0.243	0.185	0.141	0.107	0.082	0.063	0.037	0.017	0.005
30	0.412	0.231	0.174	0.131	0.099	0.075	0.057	0.033	0.015	0.004
35	0.355	0.181	0.130	0.094	0.068	0.049	0.036	0.019	0.008	0.002
40	0.307	0.142	0.097	0.067	0.046	0.032	0.022	0.011	0.004	0.001
45	0.264	0.111	0.073	0.048	0.031	0.021	0.014	0.006	0.002	0.000
50	0.228	0.087	0.054	0.034	0.021	0.013	0.009	0.003	0.001	0.000

Annuities

Many states now run lotteries in which some sum, say, a million dollars is represented as the prize. In fact, what many states typically pay instead is $40,000 per year for 25 years. How much is that sort of prize really worth? That is, how does one add up payments occurring in different years in a meaningful way? A dollar received today is not the same commodity as a dollar received twenty years from today. To simply add the two together is akin to adding apples and oranges. In order to accomplish this summation, a common unit of measure must be established. For example, economists in almost all countries have occasion to measure the total output of the economy. Apple output is added to orange output by multiplying the physical output of each commodity by its price, yielding the total values of each good (that is, total expenditures on each good). The value of apples produced plus the value of oranges produced (plus the values of all other goods) all have the common unit of dollars (or whatever the currency of the country is). These values can then be meaningfully summed.

In a similar way, dollars today can be added to dollars received in the future if the amounts are all converted to a common unit, say, prices of goods in the present. If the \$40,000 lottery payment received one year from now is multiplied by the price of a future dollar, $1/(1 + i)$, the resulting amount is the value of that payment today. Likewise, the payment received in two years can be converted to today's dollars by multiplying that payment by its price, $1/(1 + i)^2$. By multiplying each payment by its price in terms of dollars today, the payments can be meaningfully summed. All payments will have been converted to a common unit, today's dollars.

In the case of a lottery as described above, with the payments coming at the end of each year, if some interest rate i is available throughout the entire time period, the present value of all payments is

$$PV = \frac{\$40{,}000}{(1+i)} + \frac{\$40{,}000}{(1+i)^2} + \ldots + \frac{\$40{,}000}{(1+i)^n}$$

If the interest rate is 8%, this lottery is worth only \$427,000, less than half its advertised value. Another way of looking at this sum is that it represents the amount of money that has to be set aside right now so that out of interest and principal, 25 annual payments of \$40,000 each can be made, and, when the last payment is made, the fund runs out of money. In the twenty-fifth year, for example, the fund has to be accumulating interest on the remaining principle so that at the end of that year, exactly \$40,000 is available to make the last payment.

This type of payment is called an **annuity**. An annuity is a series of payments occurring at regular intervals. Annuities are traded in the market; their price is the present value of the specified stream of payments at interest rates reflecting the current market for funds. In general, if some constant amount A is to be received at the end of each of n years, the present value of that annuity with interest rate i, is

$$PV = \frac{A}{(1+i)} + \frac{A}{(1+i)^2} + \ldots + \frac{A}{(1+i)^n} \tag{10-3}$$

In practice, no one adds these individual sums anymore; these formulas are all programmed into business or financial calculators. Equation (10-3) is a geometric series: each term equals the previous one multiplied by $1/(1 + i)$. An alternative expression, based on the formula for the sum of a geometric series,[3] is

3. Let $S = a + ar^1 + \ldots + ar^{n-1}$. Multiply through by r, and subtract the resulting expression from the above. This yields $S(1 - r) = a - ar^n$. Factoring, and dividing by $(1 - r)$ yields $S = (a/(1 - r))[1 - r^n]$. In equation (11-3), $r = 1/(1 + i)$ and therefore $1 - r = i/(1 + i)$. The first term in the annuity expression is $a = A/(1 + i)$ and thus $a/(1 - r) = 1/i$, producing equation (10-4).

$$PV = \frac{A}{i}\left[1 - \frac{1}{(1+i)^n}\right] \tag{10-4}$$

Table 10-3 presents the values of annuities of $1, paid at the end of the year, for various durations and interest rates. For example, the present value of an annuity of $1 per year for 5 years, at 7% interest, is $4.10. An annuity that pays

Table 10-3 *Present Value of $1 annuity paid or received at the end of the year, for n years at interest rate i*

Number of Years (n)	3%	5%	6%	7%	8%	9%	10%	12%	15%	20%
1	0.971	0.952	0.943	0.935	0.926	0.917	0.909	0.893	0.870	0.833
2	1.913	1.859	1.833	1.808	1.783	1.759	1.736	1.690	1.626	1.528
3	2.829	2.723	2.673	2.624	2.577	2.531	2.487	2.402	2.283	2.106
4	3.717	3.546	3.465	3.387	3.312	3.240	3.170	3.037	2.855	2.589
5	4.580	4.329	4.212	4.100	3.993	3.890	3.791	3.605	3.352	2.991
6	5.417	5.076	4.917	4.767	4.623	4.486	4.355	4.111	3.784	3.326
7	6.230	5.786	5.582	5.389	5.206	5.033	4.868	4.564	4.160	3.605
8	7.020	6.463	6.210	5.971	5.747	5.535	5.335	4.968	4.487	3.837
9	7.786	7.108	6.802	6.515	6.247	5.995	5.759	5.328	4.772	4.031
10	8.530	7.722	7.360	7.024	6.710	6.418	6.145	5.650	5.019	4.192
11	9.253	8.306	7.887	7.499	7.139	6.805	6.495	5.938	5.234	4.327
12	9.954	8.863	8.384	7.943	7.536	7.161	6.814	6.194	5.421	4.439
13	10.635	9.394	8.853	8.358	7.904	7.487	7.103	6.424	5.583	4.533
14	11.296	9.899	9.295	8.745	8.244	7.786	7.367	6.628	5.724	4.611
15	11.938	10.380	9.712	9.108	8.559	8.061	7.606	6.811	5.847	4.675
16	12.561	10.838	10.106	9.447	8.851	8.313	7.824	6.974	5.954	4.730
17	13.166	11.274	10.477	9.763	9.122	8.544	8.022	7.120	6.047	4.775
18	13.754	11.690	10.828	10.059	9.372	8.756	8.201	7.250	6.128	4.812
19	14.324	12.085	11.158	10.336	9.604	8.950	8.365	7.366	6.198	4.843
20	14.877	12.462	11.470	10.594	9.818	9.129	8.514	7.469	6.259	4.870
21	15.415	12.821	11.764	10.836	10.017	9.292	8.649	7.562	6.312	4.891
22	15.937	13.163	12.042	11.061	10.201	9.442	8.772	7.645	6.359	4.909
23	16.444	13.489	12.303	11.272	10.371	9.580	8.883	7.718	6.399	4.925
24	16.936	13.799	12.550	11.469	10.529	9.707	8.985	7.784	6.434	4.937
25	17.413	14.094	12.783	11.654	10.675	9.823	9.077	7.843	6.464	4.948
26	17.877	14.375	13.003	11.826	10.810	9.929	9.161	7.896	6.491	4.956
27	18.327	14.643	13.211	11.987	10.935	10.027	9.237	7.943	6.514	4.964
28	18.764	14.898	13.406	12.137	11.051	10.116	9.307	7.984	6.534	4.970
29	19.188	15.141	13.591	12.278	11.158	10.198	9.370	8.022	6.551	4.975
30	19.600	15.372	13.765	12.409	11.258	10.274	9.427	8.055	6.566	4.979
35	21.487	16.374	14.498	12.948	11.655	10.567	9.644	8.176	6.617	4.992
40	23.115	17.159	15.046	13.332	11.925	10.757	9.779	8.244	6.642	4.997
45	24.519	17.774	15.456	13.606	12.108	10.881	9.863	8.283	6.654	4.999
50	25.730	18.256	15.762	13.801	12.233	10.962	9.915	8.304	6.661	4.999

$100 per year for 5 years at 7% interest is worth $410.00. Annuities of any constant amount *A* are found by multiplying the values in Table 10-3 by *A*. By contrast, the numbers in Table 10-4 are the amounts that must be paid or received at the end of each of *n* years, at interest rate *i*, such that their present values sum to $1. These numbers are the reciprocals of the values in Table 10-3. They indicate, for example, that an annuity of $0.244 paid or received at the end of every year for 5 years in an account paying 7% interest rate has a present value of $1. An annuity of $24.40 per year for 5 years at 7 percent interest has a present value of $100.

Table 10-4 *Required Payments paid or received each year at the end of year for n years at interest rate i, per $1 present value*

Number of Years (n)	3%	5%	6%	7%	8%	9%	10%	12%	15%	20%
1	1.030	1.050	1.060	1.070	1.080	1.090	1.100	1.120	1.150	1.200
2	0.523	0.538	0.545	0.553	0.561	0.568	0.576	0.592	0.615	0.655
3	0.354	0.367	0.374	0.381	0.388	0.395	0.402	0.416	0.438	0.475
4	0.269	0.282	0.289	0.295	0.302	0.309	0.315	0.329	0.350	0.386
5	0.218	0.231	0.237	0.244	0.250	0.257	0.264	0.277	0.298	0.334
6	0.185	0.197	0.203	0.210	0.216	0.223	0.230	0.243	0.264	0.301
7	0.161	0.173	0.179	0.186	0.192	0.199	0.205	0.219	0.240	0.277
8	0.142	0.155	0.161	0.167	0.174	0.181	0.187	0.201	0.223	0.261
9	0.128	0.141	0.147	0.153	0.160	0.167	0.174	0.188	0.210	0.248
10	0.117	0.130	0.136	0.142	0.149	0.156	0.163	0.177	0.199	0.239
11	0.108	0.120	0.127	0.133	0.140	0.147	0.154	0.168	0.191	0.231
12	0.100	0.113	0.119	0.126	0.133	0.140	0.147	0.161	0.184	0.225
13	0.094	0.106	0.113	0.120	0.127	0.134	0.141	0.156	0.179	0.221
14	0.089	0.101	0.108	0.114	0.121	0.128	0.136	0.151	0.175	0.217
15	0.084	0.096	0.103	0.110	0.117	0.124	0.131	0.147	0.171	0.214
16	0.080	0.092	0.099	0.106	0.113	0.120	0.128	0.143	0.168	0.211
17	0.076	0.089	0.095	0.102	0.110	0.117	0.125	0.140	0.165	0.209
18	0.073	0.086	0.092	0.099	0.107	0.114	0.122	0.138	0.163	0.208
19	0.070	0.083	0.090	0.097	0.104	0.112	0.120	0.136	0.161	0.206
20	0.067	0.080	0.087	0.094	0.102	0.110	0.117	0.134	0.160	0.205
21	0.065	0.078	0.085	0.092	0.100	0.108	0.116	0.132	0.158	0.204
22	0.063	0.076	0.083	0.090	0.098	0.106	0.114	0.131	0.157	0.204
23	0.061	0.074	0.081	0.089	0.096	0.104	0.113	0.130	0.156	0.203
24	0.059	0.072	0.080	0.087	0.095	0.103	0.111	0.128	0.155	0.203
25	0.057	0.071	0.078	0.086	0.094	0.102	0.110	0.127	0.155	0.202
26	0.056	0.070	0.077	0.085	0.093	0.101	0.109	0.127	0.154	0.202
27	0.055	0.068	0.076	0.083	0.091	0.100	0.108	0.126	0.154	0.201
28	0.053	0.067	0.075	0.082	0.090	0.099	0.107	0.125	0.153	0.201
29	0.052	0.066	0.074	0.081	0.090	0.098	0.107	0.125	0.153	0.201
30	0.051	0.065	0.073	0.081	0.089	0.097	0.106	0.124	0.152	0.201
35	0.047	0.061	0.069	0.077	0.086	0.095	0.104	0.122	0.151	0.200
40	0.043	0.058	0.066	0.075	0.084	0.093	0.102	0.121	0.151	0.200
45	0.041	0.056	0.065	0.073	0.083	0.092	0.101	0.121	0.150	0.200
50	0.039	0.055	0.063	0.072	0.082	0.091	0.101	0.120	0.150	0.200

Example 1: Consider the million dollar lottery, and suppose the first payment comes at the end of the first year. Using Table 10-3, reading across the row for 25 years gives the present value of twenty payments of \$1 received at the end of the next twenty years at the various interest rates indicated by the column headings. If an 8% interest yield is available throughout, the present value of these twenty payments is \$10.675. The present value of twenty-five such payments of \$40,000 is therefore 40,000 × \$10.675 = \$427,000. The state of Washington in fact presently offers a cash buyout of \$500,000 (before taxes) for winners of the above lottery. If the state can earn only 7%, the present value of the lottery is greater: 40,000 × 11.654 = \$466,160. The arithmetic reason why the lottery is worth more if interest rates are lower is that with lower interest yields, more money has to be set aside now in order to accumulate to any fixed sum in the future. On a more conceptual level, if the rate of interest is relatively low, so that the present dollar is worth relatively less than when the interest rate is high, then future amounts are worth relatively more. With very high premiums for earlier availability, the future is worth relatively less, and the value of an annuity, which pays amounts in the future falls.

Check your understanding: If the first payment of \$40,000 is made immediately and then 24 more payments are made at the end of each following year, show that the present values of this prize at 7% and 8% interest are \$498,760 and \$461,160, respectively.

Example 2: Suppose you wish to purchase a car for \$10,000 (tax and license included). You could save for a number of years until you have the cash in hand, but that means you won't get to consume the car for some time. Since the car is going to last several years (probably more than a decade), you can pay for the car as you consume it by taking out a loan and repaying the loan in the next several years. In this way, you can even out the flow of consumption of other goods, rather than having to forego \$10,000 of those other goods the year you purchase the car. Suppose, therefore, you decide to borrow the \$10,000 and repay it over 4 years. Although these loans are always structured with monthly payments, for simplicity, assume you will have to repay the loan in 4 annual payments beginning a year from now. Assume further that the prevailing interest rate on these loans is 10 percent.[4] Using Table 10-4, 4 payments of \$.315 at the end of the next 4 years have a combined present value of \$1.00. The annual payment necessary for a \$10,000 loan is therefore 10,000 × \$.315 = \$3,150. The car dealer will be indifferent between receiving \$10,000 cash now or a note to pay \$3,150 per year for 4 years. Their indifference is due to their being able to sell your note on the financial market for \$10,000 cash. Your note is worth \$10,000 assuming 10 percent interest correctly reflects the prevailing interest on these types of loans.

Notice that your total payments exceed the \$10,000 principal of the loan: 4 × \$3,150 = \$12,600. The federal government requires the lender to disclose this amount and its excess over the original principal, \$2,600. Consumer groups caution that you pay more for the good if you borrow, and you pay more, the longer you borrow for, or words to that effect. They make the mistake of adding apples and oranges. It is equal nonsense to add today's dollars to dollars paid or

---

4. Monthly payments are calculated by using the interest rate divided by 12 (for example, 10%/12 = .833%) and using 12 times the number of years (for example, 48 months).

received in two or three or four years. The interest on the loan represents the premium you pay in order to be able to consume the car *now* rather than in the future. The alternative (usually) is to forego consumption of the car while you decrease consumption of other goods in order to save the $10,000 required to make the purchase.

Here now is a harder question. At the end of one year, how much do you owe on the loan? That is, suppose you have just made your first annual payment of $3,150, and your rich doting aunt (bless her soul) gives you a gift which is more than adequate to repay the loan in full. How much do you owe the loan company? You find to your possible dismay that the amount owing is more than $10,000 – $3,150 = $6,850. In the just concluded first year of the loan, you had the use of the loan company's $10,000 for one year. The charge for that use at 10 percent interest is .10 × $10,000 = $1,000. Thus the $3,150 payment covered the $1,000 interest charge, leaving only $2,150 for reduction of the principal. The amount owing is thus $10,000 – $2,150 = $7,850. Alternatively, at the end of the first year, you owe the loan company a three-year annuity of $3,150 per year, at 10 percent interest. Using Table 10-3, the present value of such an annuity is 3,150 × $2.487 = $7,834 the same result but for rounding error present in these tables. (In real life, these calculations are made to sufficient decimal places to eliminate this arithmetic problem.)

Example 3: Suppose now the car dealership offers you a choice of tires: you can purchase premium tires for $100 each, or economy tires for $50 each. The premium tires last 50,000 miles, while the economy tires only last 20,000 miles. Some years ago, a leading consumer magazine advised buyers to purchase the premium tires because they were cheaper per 100 miles driven. That is, by arithmetic, the premium tire costs $100 ÷ 50,000 miles = 20¢ per 100 miles. The economy tire costs $50 ÷ 20,000 miles = 25¢ per 100 miles. But this advice ignores the important fact that the cost of the tires comes right now—at the time of purchase—whereas the benefits occur in the future, perhaps many years from the present. The preceding arithmetic would be adequate for, say, owners of taxicabs, traveling salespeople, police departments and others who would use up these tires within a year anyway. However, for individuals who use their cars only occasionally, or who commute via rapid transit, the costs of the tire come perhaps many years before the benefits. A correct calculation must compare costs and benefits during the same time periods.

Assume then that a typical consumer drives 10,000 miles per year. The premium tire will last 5 years, the economy tire 2 years. Assume also that the relevant interest rate is 10 percent, meaning that the price of a dollar received one year from now is $1 ÷ 1.10 = $.909, the price of a dollar received in 2 years is $1 ÷ $(1.10)^2$ = $.826, etc. How much does owning these tires cost *per year*? This question is equivalent to asking, suppose the dealer was willing to rent the tires to you. How much would they charge per year? The equivalent rental charge for the premium tire is the annual amount which, if paid for five years has a present value of $100. Using Table 10-4, using the 10% interest column and the row for 5 years, 5 annual payments of $.264 have a present value of $1. Therefore, the annuity having a present value of $100 is 100 × $.264 = $26.40. (This is equivalent to 26.40¢ per 100 miles.) Similarly, the rental charge for the economy tire is the amount which, if paid at the end of the year for two years has a present value of $50. Again using the 10% column but the row for 2 years, this annuity amount is 50 × $.576 = $28.80, or 28.80¢ per 100 miles. Thus with these assumptions, the premium tire is indeed cheaper per year than the economy tire, but not by as much 5¢ per 100 miles as the simple arithmetic in the preceding paragraph would indicate.

Suppose now the consumer is going to drive only 5,000 miles per year, so that the premium tires will last 10 years and the economy tire 4 years. Now, the benefits of the premium tire come even further in the future. We expect the premium tire to become relatively more expensive. Again using the 10% interest column in Table 10-4, but 10 years for the premium tire and 4 years for the economy tire, the annual rental charges for the premium and economy tires are, respectively, $100 \times \$.163 = \$16.30$ and $50 \times \$.315 = \$15.75$. Thus the economy tire is now the less expensive tire. Finally, suppose the driver again drives 10,000 miles per year, but the interest rate is 20%. This high interest rate indicates a very high premium for earlier availability of income. We thus expect that the premium tire, whose benefits come relatively further in the future, should become relatively more expensive. Using the 20% interest column in Table 10-4 and the rows for 5 and 2 years, the annual costs for the premium and economy tires are, respectively, $100 \times \$.334 = \$33.40$ and $50 \times \$.655 = \$32.75$. The economy tire has indeed become relatively (and absolutely) cheaper than the premium tire.

Finally, here is one last question. Suppose, you are the manufacturer of the premium tires and, to make life relatively easy, suppose all consumers drive 10,000 miles per year and the appropriate interest rate is 10% for all consumers. Your chemists inform you that they have found a way to make a super premium tire that lasts 60,000 miles instead of only 50,000 miles, but the tires will be more expensive. How much more can you charge for these new tires? With these assumptions, the best deal for consumers is to pay the equivalent of \$26.40 per year per tire. If the tire lasts a sixth year, consumers will be willing to pay the present value of \$26.40, paid at the end of 6 years at 10% interest. Using Table 10-2, this amount is $26.40 \times \$.564 = \$14.89$. Therefore, if you can manufacture the new tire for less than \$114.89, you can profit by introducing it and selling it for up to this amount.

Example 4: A private bank operating in its own interest is willing to lend you \$10,000 per year at 10% interest, for 4 years, beginning in 1 year, towards college tuition costs. (You are lucky enough to go to a school that wants its tuition at the *end* of the academic year.) You have to repay the loan in 5 equal payments beginning 6 years from now. How much will you have to pay per year?

This is a very common problem in financial analysis. It is usefully pictured using a time line shown in Fig. 10-2.

In Fig. 10-2, we indicate the present as time 0 and delineate years 1 through 10 along the horizontal axis. The vertical lines above the axis indicate amounts received; those below indicate amounts paid out. The time line shows \$10,000 (\$10K) received at the end of years 1 through 4. Beginning at the end of year six, 5 payments of some amount \$A, yet to be determined, must be paid to the bank, ending at the end of the tenth year.

To answer this question, consider first what it means to repay the loan. The bank is extending you 4 payments of \$10,000 each, but these payments are coming in the future. The amount the bank has to set aside right now in order to make these payments to you is the present value of this four-year annuity. Using Table 10-3, with 10% interest for 4 years, this present value is $\$10{,}000 \times 3.17 = \$31{,}700$. Repaying the loan means that the present value of your payments equals this

Figure 10-2 *Time Line*

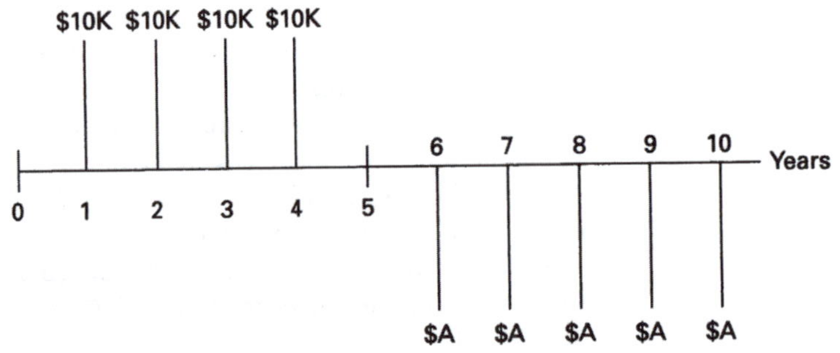

amount. Alternatively, treating amounts received as positive numbers and those paid out as negative numbers, the present value of all payments indicated on the time line must sum to zero.

Your payments to the bank consist of a five-year annuity, but the annuity starts in the future. We therefore split the calculation into two parts. It is easiest to move the present to one year after graduation, that is, at the end of year 5, shown as the small vertical line on the time line. At that moment, you owe the bank the future value of $31,700, at 10% interest for 5 years. This future amount, using Table 10-1, is $\$31{,}700 \times (1.10)^5 = \$31{,}700 \times 1.611 = \$51{,}069$. The present value (as of the end of year 5) of your repayment annuity must equal this amount. (Note that at the end of year 5, your first payment starts at the end of the next year, as required in order to use these tables.) Using Table 10-4, with 10% interest and 5 years, the annual payments required (depicted as $*A* on the time line) are $51{,}069 \times \$.264 = \$13{,}482$.

Suppose now, as often happens with student loans, the government offers you the same type of loan, but with repayment calculated at some below-market interest rate, say, 3%. How much will you now have to pay beginning in year 6, and what is the benefit to you of this lower interest rate? The loan is now a four year annuity at 3% interest; using Table 10-3, its present value is $10{,}000 \times \$3.717 = \$37{,}170$. Using Table 10-1, its accumulated value at the end of year five is $\$37{,}170 \times (1.03)^5 = \$37{,}170 \times 1.159 = \$43{,}080$. This amount must equal the present value of your five payments, calculated at 3% interest. Using Table 10-4, this annual amount is $43{,}080 \times \$.218 = \$9{,}391$.

Thus if you get a student loan at 3% interest instead of the market rate of 10%, you have to pay only $9,391 at the end of years 6 through 10 instead of $13,482. This is a saving of $4,091 per year. The present value of these payments is the benefit to you today of this government program. This present value must be calculated at the market rate, 10%. Using Table 10-3, the present value of this 5 year annuity (where the present means 1 year prior to receipt of the first payment) is $\$4{,}091 \times \$3.791 = \$15{,}509$. This is the present value at the beginning of year 6 (that is, 5 years from the present). This must be further reduced to its present value today. Using Table 10-2, the present value today is $\$15{,}509 \times .621 = \$9{,}631$. This amount is the value to you of this program. Alternatively, it is the amount taxpayers have to set aside right now, in some 10% interest-bearing account, to finance your subsidized student loan. The present value of your repayments in years 6 through10, plus $9,631 right now equals the present value of the four payments to you of \$10,000 at the end of years 1 through 4.

Example 5: Soon after the so-called energy crisis of the early 1970s, the federal government in the United States enacted laws to promote energy efficiency. In the case of cars, the auto companies have been required to meet Corporate Average Fleet Equivalency (CAFE) standards. These regulations force the car companies to produce cars so that the average miles per gallon (mpg) for the fleet of cars produced by each company meets some ever-increasing standard. To the surprise of many regulators, the auto companies voluntarily exceeded the mandated standards for most years. In 1973, the fleet average for American cars was about 13 mpg; by the late 1980s, the average exceeded 26 mpg, more than double the figure of only a little over a decade earlier. (This average has persisted to the present, but the government (specifically the EPA) has excluded the new sports utility vehicles (SUVs) from the calculation. If SUVs were included, the average would be lower.) What incentives do the auto companies have for developing cars that get higher mileage? We consumers prefer cars that get better mileage, because we know it saves us money when we drive. We are therefore willing to pay more for a car that gets better mileage, other things equal. How much more are we willing to pay?

Suppose a typical consumer (you or me) drives 10,000 miles per year. How much gasoline do we save if our new car gets 14 mpg instead of only 13? At 13 mpg, we use $10{,}000 \div 13 = 769$ gallons per year; at 14 mpg, we use $10{,}000 \div 14 = 714$ gallons per year. Thus we save 55 gallons per year by driving the better mileage car. The value of this savings depends on the price of gasoline. The more expensive gasoline is, the more we stand to save. An important first lesson therefore is that the importance of the CAFE standards in any policy discussion depends upon the price of gasoline. In 1972, the real price of gasoline was about where it has been in the early part of the 1990s, about \$1.43 per gallon in 2004 prices. Thus a consumer would stand to save $55 \times \$1.43 = \$78.65$ per year. The value of this savings over the life of the car is the present value of an annuity of \$78.65 for the average amount of years cars are driven, say, 10 years. Using Table 10-3, and assuming 10% interest is appropriate for evaluating investments of this nature, the present value of the gasoline saved over the life of the car is $78.65 \times \$6.145 = \$483$. That is, a consumer would be willing to pay up this amount for a car that was identical in handling aspects to another car, but which got 14 mpg instead of only 13 mpg.

Consider now the incentives this creates for the automobile companies. If the company can expect to sell 1 million vehicles with this improved technology, it could conceivably earn \$483,000,000! Moreover, the company could receive this every year, until the technology became obsolete. It therefore would pay for the company to invest up to that amount in the present to develop such technology. It wouldn't need federal mandates or any other coercive scheme to induce it to explore such an improvement. Indeed, this is what has happened in the twenty-five plus years of these CAFE standards. In the early years especially, when gasoline was relatively high priced, the automobile companies quickly found it to their advantage to sell cars that got better mileage. These were by and large the cars consumers wanted in those years. When the price of gasoline fell dramatically in the late 1980s and again in the 1990s, luxury and performance cars became more popular, and then the government standards started to impinge on the fleet composition.

Lastly, the arithmetic changes as mileage improves. The gains from getting 27 mpg instead of only 26 are $10{,}000 \times 26 = 384.61$ gallons versus $10{,}000 \div 27 = 370.37$ gallons, a net savings of only 14.24 gallons per year! At $1.43 per gallon, this is an annual saving of $20.36. Over the 10-year life of the car, this has a present value of $\$20.36 \times \$6.145 = \$125.11$. Moreover, it seems reasonable that the marginal cost of achieving further increases in miles per gallon should generally rise. If the government forces automobile manufacturers to produce cars that get better mileage than the companies would choose to produce on their own, it may be the case that consumers are receiving benefits of lower value than their opportunity costs.

Recently, Toyota and Honda have developed new hybrid cars that use both electric and gas engines. When a two-ton car is traveling even at city speeds, it develops considerable kinetic energy; that energy is dissipated as waste heat when we apply the brakes. The hybrid cars use that energy to charge the car's batteries. The batteries supply electricity to the electric motor for initial acceleration in stop-and-go city traffic; the gasoline engine kicks in at cruising speed or on the highway. In 2004, Toyota rolled out the new mid-sized Prius, which the EPA rates as 52 mpg on the highway and 60 in the city. The car appears to be about the same size as the Toyota Corolla. The Corolla, which is rated at 38 mpg on the highway and about 25 in the city, costs probably $5,000 to $6,000 less than the Prius, but with gasoline prices near $2.00 per gallon at this writing, the Prius is proving to be very popular. At this gas price, if one drives 10,000 miles per year, the gas saving (say, 55mpg versus 30mpg on average) is about $300 per year (do the math!). The present value of these savings still seems to be less than the price differential for a comparable car, but the difference is narrowing. It will be very interesting to see how consumers react to this car. It will clearly depend to some extent on whether gasoline prices remain at their present high levels. Also, as production of these new energy systems increases, scale economies will cause their price to drop.

Perpetuities

A **perpetuity** is an annuity that lasts *forever.* A promise to receive a sum of money each year for the indefinite future is not, in fact, worth an infinite amount. In equation (10-3), as n gets indefinitely larger, the term $1/(1 + i)^n$ approaches zero, since this represents a number less than unity raised to larger and larger powers. If some amount A is to be received at the end of every year, forever, the present value of that sum is simply

$$PV = \frac{A}{i} \tag{10-5}$$

This equation has an easy intuitive explanation. Suppose you are in possession of $1,000 and interest of 10% per year is available indefinitely. Then by putting your money in such an account, at the end of a year you will have earned $.10 \times \$1{,}000 = \$100$. You take the money out and have a party. This leaves the original $1,000 in the bank. In one more year, another $100 will have been earned; you take it out and have another party. This process can be repeated indefinitely. Having $1,000 in hand enables one to consume $100 forever, if interest is 10%. Alternatively, the right to receive \$100 forever is worth \$1,000, at 10% interest. With some principal PV and prevailing interest rate i, an annual interest payment of $A = PV \times i$ is available every year. Dividing both sides of this equation by i yields equation (10-5).

Equation (10-5) is a very useful formula because of its simplicity. Although forever is infinitely longer than, say, 40 or 50 years, the years after 40 or 50 years count for little in terms of present value, at interest rates commonly encountered. Look at the last several lines in Table 10-3. The present value of a \$1 annuity for 50 years at 10% interest is \$9.91. The value of a perpetuity of \$1, at 10% interest, is \$1/.10 = \$10.00. The difference between 50 years and infinity is \$.09 out of \$10.00—less than 1%! The first fifty years of a perpetual stream of payments at 10% interest accounts for over 99% of the value. Similar results occur for other interest rates. The evaluation of projects of long duration can therefore often be approximated using the simple formula $PV = A/i$.[5]

The Meaning of Wealth

The present value of a stream of future payments is often referred to as the *capitalized value* of those payments. The term **capital**, or equivalently, **asset** refers to a resource that generates income. We typically think of capital as machines that increase the productivity of labor. A computer is capital, because with it, a person can often produce greater income than without it. This greater income derives from the ability of the computer to produce greater output than without it. The value of capital is the present value of the income it produces, now and in the future, for however long the capital lasts. A word processor enables a writer to complete a manuscript in less time, and with less secretarial help, than does a typewriter. The value of the word processor, at the very least, is the present value of these savings in costs over the life of the computer.

The term **wealth** refers to the net value of a person's entire stock of capital. If a person also owes a stream of payments, the present value of those payments, called *liabilities,* must obviously be netted out. We commonly consider a person's wealth as the value of the tangible property they own, such as holdings of cash, savings accounts, stocks and bonds, land, real estate. However, for many (perhaps most) individuals, the most important capital, or assets we own are our skills and education. The human brain is the single most important piece of capital in creation. Data compiled by the United States Census Bureau indicate that college graduates on average earn, over their working lives, approximately two-thirds more than high school graduates. Some of this income derives from the naturally higher talents of the pool of people with college potential, the rest from the skills acquired in college. This relatively high human capital increases one's ability to produce useful goods for consumers, and therefore to produce higher income. The picture is very clear for those studying engineering, business, computer science similar disciplines. Even general liberal arts skills, such as the ability to read and understand some written material, to write a clear paragraph, are

5. The famous French mathematician Blaise Pascal once argued that, considering the infinity of afterlife, prudence dictated participation in religion. He neglected to take discounting to present value into consideration, which is why the young frequently ignore his advice and the old take it. Discounting also explains the expression from World War II, "There are no atheists in foxholes." However, it was commonly observed that the religious fervor faded as the enemy withdrew.

scarce resources paying dividends (quasi-rents) to their owners. It is not for our brawn that most of us find employment; in the main it is for our abilities to solve problems, that is, understand a task and to carry it out.

After World War II, the countries of Europe and Asia were devastated. It is horrific to see pictures of German and Japanese cities in 1945. It is exceptional to find in those pictures a building with a roof still intact. In addition to the loss of life sustained, the physical capital of Germany and Japan was substantially destroyed. Yet today, these countries are two of the most prosperous on earth. What accounts for this? For many Americans, the reason lies in the assistance given these countries by the United States after the war. The United States instituted a large aid program, the Marshall Plan (named after General George C. Marshall, who directed the program) at war's end which provided food and other goods to these nations. However, the amounts given were only a few percentage points of their gross national product, and like amounts have been given to other countries with no such dramatic results. The key lies in the fact that although the war destroyed *physical* capital, the knowledge and basic institutions of law and property were left largely intact. The *human* capital of the Germans and Japanese, those qualities that enabled them to become superpowers in the first place, was not destroyed in the war. The airplane factories may have been destroyed, but the knowledge of how to build airplanes, cars and eventually computers was not destroyed, nor was the ability to enter into binding contracts for mutual benefit. The human capital of these countries enabled them to rebuild; it is the lack of such capital in the third world that hinders those countries from doing likewise. The postwar experiences of Germany and Japan attest to the importance of human capital in the overall wealth of nations.

10.4 Determination of the Interest Rate

Irving Fisher wrote that people are "impatient" (he in fact included it in the subtitle of his book), meaning we prefer present consumption to the same amount of future consumption. If we can costlessly store wealth, it is always preferable to have wealth now, say in the form of money, rather than in the future, simply as a consequence of more being preferred to less. If one has money now, one can always choose not to consume it for a while. The set of opportunities for consumption is necessarily larger if the money is in hand, as opposed to becoming available in the future, assuming there is no cost of insuring against theft. *Impatience,* however, means something else. It refers to preferences, not opportunities. Impatience means that a given level of income generates less satisfaction, or utility, if it is consumed in the future rather than in the present. Impatience is an expression of time preference.

Though economists typically allow for it, the existence of time preference is controversial, and empirically unconfirmed. It implies a myopia concerning the future. Since we know the future will arrive someday, why should the future count for less than the present in our preferences for consumption? If we shift consumption to an earlier time period by borrowing, will we not regret that trade when the future arrives, and can we not anticipate this regret?

We have repeatedly emphasized the importance of explanations based on changes in constraints, rather than those that depend on *ad hoc* changes in tastes. Suppose, therefore, we wish to specify that individual tastes do not change over time. Then the trade-offs a consumer would be willing to make with regard to present versus future consumption should not depend on the *date,* that is, the time identifier. That is, an individual's marginal value of present consumption, that is, their willingness to sacrifice a unit of present consumption in return for some (usually higher) amount of future consumption, should depend only on the levels of consumption in each time period, not whether this evaluation is taking place in 2000, 2005 or 2010.

Economist Robert Strotz of Northwestern University has argued compellingly that if, in some succeeding year, an individual could be predicted to change their weighting scheme for consumption in future years, then the original n -period preferences would essentially be inconsistent with itself and irrelevant.[6] Suppose, for example, an individual were to decide right now, in the present, that he or she would consume wealth evenly for two years, and then in year three, consume one half the remaining wealth, with constant consumption thereafter. Suppose two years pass, and year three is now the present. Will the individual go forward with the original plan? Such a consumption plan implies an inexplicable change in tastes. Suddenly, in a given year, the consumer is willing to sacrifice a much greater amount of future consumption than previously (or henceforth), in order to obtain a given amount of present consumption. It would be inconsistent with the paradigm of economics to allow such arbitrary taste changes. Therefore, economists impose this important property—dynamic consistency—on intertemporal choices. Specifically, we say that *the marginal value of consumption in any period, in terms of foregone future consumption, is independent of the date,* that is, dependent only on the consumption levels in the two time periods.[7] In this way we rule out sudden, inexplicable changes in individual borrowing, saving and consumption.

We now inquire specifically why the real interest rate is positive, and whether it could reasonably be negative. In so doing, we follow two famous economists of the early twentieth century, Irving Fisher and E. Bohm-Bawerk.[8] We consider in turn, the effects of time preference, economic growth and the conditions of production, that is, the ability of society to increase future consumption by producing goods in the present which enhance future productivity.

Consider first whether a negative real interest rate can prevail. Consider a pure trading economy, such as a World War II prisoner of war camp, in which no production takes place. Rather, income arrives periodically in the form of Red Cross packages. Suppose, in addition, it is impossible to store wealth for anything but a brief time period. The individuals in the camp all attempt to even out their flow of consumption. Suppose it becomes known that incomes will be declining in the future. In that case, each person would try to trade some present consumption for future consumption. Individuals could make such trades by sacrificing presently available goods in return for sharing another person's Red Cross parcels in the future. In the

6. Robert Strotz, Myopia and Inconsistency in Dynamic Utility Maximization, *Review of Economic Studies,* 23, No. 3, (1956) 165–80.

7. Strotz went on to say that if such changes in marginal rates of substitution between two time periods were anticipated, a consumer might rationally plan ahead to prevent these changes in plans, by, for example tying up his or her wealth in trusts containing penalties for changing the original consumption plan. We shall not explore this aspect of the problem here.

8. Bohm-Bawerk, E., *Capital and Interest,* translated by William Smart, as *The Positive Theory of Capital,* Books for Libraries Press, Freeport, N.Y., 1971.

absence of preferences for earlier consumption, the simultaneous efforts of all individuals to transfer consumption to the future would lead to a negative interest rate. However, crucial to this outcome is the assumption that wealth cannot be stored. If wealth can be costlessly stored, the real interest rate could never be negative. One would never in that case lend, say, $100 today in return for $95 next year; it would suffice simply to store the $100 for a year. However, if the $100 cash could be easily stolen, or if no asset could be saved for the future, this procedure might not be possible. Thus a negative real interest rate could only exist if sufficient individuals wished to shift income to the future, for example in anticipation of falling incomes, and if it is costly to store wealth over that time period.

Suppose now that economic growth is taking place, so that individuals anticipate future incomes will be higher than present income. In this case, the desire to even out consumption would lead individuals to try to contract with each other to shift future consumption to the present. Any one person can do this by promising to trade some amount of future income to another person, in return for receiving income in the present from that person. However, whereas it is possible for some of the individuals in the economy to accomplish this, it is impossible for all to do so. It is impossible for everyone to consume more in the present than is available. Individuals are not really consuming next year's income; they are simply trading with other persons in the same economy. Next year's income cannot be consumed until it is produced. The simultaneous effort to transfer future income to the present will create a premium for sacrificing present consumption. As this premium increases, more individuals will be willing to make the sacrifice. Exhaustion of the gains from trade will lead to that premium, that is, a price of present consumption in terms of future consumption foregone, for which all individuals' marginal values of present consumption are the same.

Similar reasoning applies if individuals have positive rates of time preference. This is simply another reason why consumers would wish to transfer future income to the present. The same analysis as in the above paragraph applies; the simultaneous efforts to accomplish this will create a positive price for earlier availability of goods.

The preceding analysis takes future income as exogenous, that is, determined by influences beyond our theory. We have assumed up to this point that individuals can do nothing to affect the levels of future income which would become available. Let us now incorporate this important aspect into the analysis. It is possible to increase future income by diverting present income to the production of capital goods. These goods may yield no consumption in and of themselves, but they increase the marginal product of other inputs in production, so that larger incomes can be produced in the future. The diversion of resources into the production of farm equipment, computers, education and the like reduces society's present consumption, but leads to higher future incomes. The ability to accomplish this roundabout production affects the rate of interest.

The simplest theoretical device along these lines is perhaps that devised by Frank Knight. Knight contemplated Robinson Crusoe, stranded on an island, with a food supply consisting of an edible *Crusonia* bush which grows at some constant rate r, say 10% per year. It grows at this constant rate no matter how small or large it is, that is, no matter how much of the bush Crusoe should partake at any given time. Crusoe is unable to affect the growth of this plant in any way. We depict this situation in Fig. 10-3. Current consumption is plotted along the horizontal axis;

Figure 10-3 *Production Frontier Exhibiting Constant Marginal Cost of Converting Present Consumption into Future Consumption*

In this case, the interest rate will always have the constant value *r*.

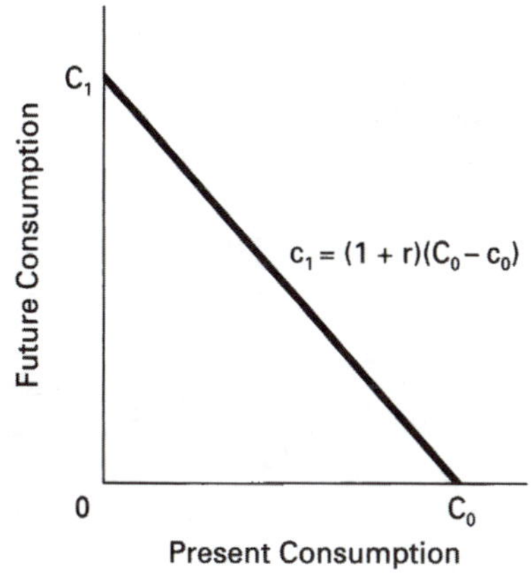

future consumption is plotted vertically. The entire bush consists of a level of consumption C_0, which if consumed, would lead to starvation. If none is eaten, $C_1 = (1 + r)C_0$ is available in the next time period. Crusoe's production frontier is the straight line defined by the edible bush, with slope $-(1 + r)$. His marginal cost of present consumption is constant at $1 + r$ units of future consumption. His supply curve of present consumption is constant at this level. Therefore, no matter what preferences Crusoe might have for consumption now versus consumption in the future, his marginal value of present consumption must be $-(1 + r)$.[9] In this case, production conditions completely determine the real rate of interest. With pervasive technology of this sort, so that any number of individuals could trade present for future consumption along this linear frontier, the rate of interest in a many-person economy would be the constant growth rate, *r*.

Assume now that production is such that current and future consumption can be produced along some concave frontier, as shown in Fig. 10-4. In this case, the rate of time preference, if present, and the (changing) marginal cost of transforming present consumption into future consumption determine the interest rate. In a many-person economy, the production frontier defines the marginal cost (supply) curve of present consumption in terms of future consumption foregone; the preferences of individuals would determine the demand for present consumption. Exhaustion of gains from exchange would lead to the establishment of a single market price of present consumption, where the supply of present consumption equaled the quantity demanded. For all participants in the market, the marginal subjective value of present consumption in terms of foregone future consumption would then equal the marginal opportunity cost, in terms of future consumption foregone, of providing that level of present consumption.

9. If the bush in fact *shrank* at some rate *s*, and any part spoiled once removed from the bush, so that storage was impossible, then Crusoe would face a negative real rate of interest *s*.

Figure 10-4 *Rising Marginal Cost of Converting Present Consumption Into Future Consumption*

In this case, the interaction of consumers' willingness to trade off present consumption for future consumption and society's ability to do so determines the interest rate, as the above frontier indicates.

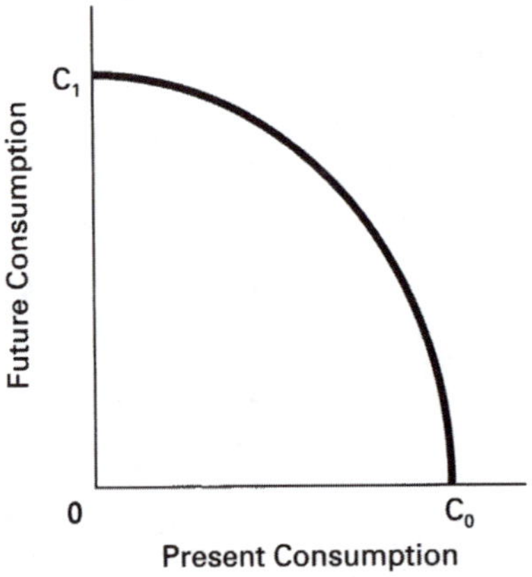

10.5 Real versus Nominal Interest Rates

In the previous discussion we dealt with capital values and the interest rate in terms of trading off some real amount of consumption in one time period for some real amount of consumption in another time period. Most commonly, however, borrowers and lenders state contracts in *nominal* terms, that is, in terms of the monetary unit of account, such as dollars. Such contracts are always forward-looking, meaning repayment of a loan will take place in the future, not in the past. If loan contracts are stated in dollars, the borrowers and lenders attempt to incorporate into the contract any anticipated change in the purchasing power of dollars over the life of the contract, that is, any change in the value of dollars relative to goods. Whatever unit specified in the contract, for example, gold, the parties will attempt to incorporate anticipated changes in the price of that commodity, in this case, gold. We say anticipated changes because when the contract is formed, the actual change in the value of the monetary unit cannot be known. The rate of interest, fully adjusted for any changes in the purchasing power of the loan contract's unit of account, is called the **real rate of interest;** it is what we have been dealing with thus far.

Suppose you contemplate loaning a friend \$100 at 3% interest. You expect repayment of \$103 in one year; you do not fear for repayment. Suppose, however, inflation has been occurring at a 5% annual rate. You, your friend and everyone else expect it to continue at that rate. In 1 year, \$100 will be able to purchase only what \$95 can buy now. When your friend repays your loan with \$103 a year from now, the purchasing power of that \$103 will have decreased by 5%, to about \$98. You will have in fact made a loan at a negative real interest rate of about –2%!

In general, suppose the true, Fisherian premium for earlier availability of goods is some number r. A secure loan of some amount P for 1 year would bear an interest premium of rP so that the borrower repays $P(1 + r)$ at the end of the year. Suppose, however, inflation is anticipated to occur at g% per year, meaning, at year's end, it will take $1 + g$ dollars to purchase what now costs 1 dollar.

Then in order to repay the loan so that the borrower truly receives $P(1 + r)$ more in goods, the borrower must repay that amount increased by $g\%$, or $P(1 + r)(1 + g) = P(1 + r + g + rg)$. For the small values of r and g commonly encountered, for example, $r = .02$, $g = .06$ (2% real rate of interest, 6% inflation), the term rg is insignificant and can be ignored (with these numbers, $rg = .0012$, about a tenth of 1 percent). In that case, therefore, with inflation anticipated to be $g\%$ per year, a secure loan will trade at a market interest rate of $r + g$, the sum of the real rate of interest and the anticipated annual rate of inflation.[10]

The combined effect of real interest rate r and anticipated inflation rate g yields a *nominal* or *money* interest rate of i given by

$$i = r + \text{anticipated rate of inflation} \tag{10-6}$$

Equation (10-6) is generally known as the Fisher equation, after Irving Fisher who first propounded it in 1906.[11] Estimation of the real rate of interest has been the subject of substantial research. The real rate has been variously estimated in the 0% to 2% range (perhaps higher in the 1980s and parts of the 1990s), though its value and the extent of its variation over time are the subject of ongoing research.

Market rates of interest also incorporate a premium for the riskiness of the loan. Risk increases the variability of income. We have shown that risk, which produces varying income, is less desirable than income which is steady at the average of the varying income. For this reason, there is a risk premium for risky loans in the market. The premium for risk is evident in the market for capital. The United States government is able to borrow from the public at a rate lower than any other borrower. This is because the United States has never defaulted on its debts, and it has the power to tax to pay its debts. Established corporations have to pay a higher interest rate, and those wishing to borrow money to start a new business, or to finance the purchase of household goods have to pay a still higher rate. Thus a more complete version of the Fisher equation is:

$$i = r + \text{anticipated inflation} + \text{risk premium} \tag{10-7}$$

The measurement of these quantities is the subject of much current research.

Stocks and Bonds

Corporations wishing to raise funds can do so by selling stocks and bonds to the general public. **Bonds** are promises to pay certain specified amounts in the future; usually quarterly interest payments for up to 30 years. The obligations of bonds are stated in nominal or money terms, that is, in terms of a fixed number of dollars (or other currency, in other countries) for a fixed period of time. For example, a

10. With continuous compounding of interest, a loan of initial principal P, earning $r\%$ per year will have a future value after t years of Pe^{rt}. Any nominal amount P today would depreciate at that rate; in t years, its value would be Pe^{-gt}. The combined effect of real interest and inflation would produce a future value of $Pe^{rt}e^{-gt} = Pe^{(r-g)t}$. To offset the effect of anticipated inflation, interest would be set at r + g; in that case, the future value would be restored to Pe^{rt}, if the rate of inflation actually was g.

11. Irving Fisher, *The Rate of Interest*, 1906. Letting p be the general price level, the anticipated rate of inflation is generally written $E[(1/p)(dp/dt)]$, where E denotes the (mathematical) expected value.

corporation can sell a bond which promises the bearer annual payments of $1,000 for 30 years, after which the original principal is returned. The persons purchasing these bonds are lending money to the corporation; they are creditors of the corporation. The bonds are traded in organized markets such as the New York Stock Exchange.[12] If a bond paying $1,000 per year for 30 years sells for $10,000, the interest yield is 10% for the term of the bond, in this case, 30 years. These interest payments are a legal obligation, or liability of the corporation. The corporation guarantees that the interest payments will be paid before the owners of the corporations keep any profits for themselves. If the corporation cannot meet these obligations, it is **bankrupt**, and the creditors can sell its assets (capital) and use the proceeds to pay its debts.[13] The interest payments on bonds do not vary with either the fortunes of the corporation, except for bankruptcy, and are the same regardless of changes in the purchasing power of the dollar due to inflation.

Not all bonds are safe, however, and some are more risky than others. The interest rate it pays reflects the riskiness of that particular bond relative to other investments. For example, the bonds that corporations issue pay higher interest than bonds the U.S. government issues for the same time period. This reflects the public's anticipation that the U.S. government is less likely to default on its debts than any private corporation. Also, various rating services such as Moodys and Standard and Poors rate corporate bonds. The interest corporations must pay on their bonds generally increases as their ratings worsen.

Stocks, on the other hand, are shares of ownership, or **equity**, in the corporation. If a million shares are issued and you purchase 100 of them, you own one ten-thousandth of the lifetime profits and losses of the corporation. The corporate executives are in general under no legal obligation to pay out profits to shareholders. These payments are called **dividends** and are discretionary. The corporate managers may decide that the money could be more usefully utilized by reinvestment in new plant and equipment, by which they hope to generate even larger dividends in the future. Moreover, all interest payments currently due on bonds must be paid before any dividends can be declared. It is obvious, therefore, that ownership of stocks is a more risky investment than ownership of the same corporation's bonds. The average long-term yield on equity capital, that is, stocks, for which dividends are contingent upon the existence of corporate profits, has been greater than the average long-term yields on bonds, reflecting the greater risk of stocks vs. bonds.

Unlike the interest payments on bonds, which specify fixed dollar amounts, dividends vary with the profitability of the corporation, and therefore, implicitly, with changes in the purchasing power of the dollar. If inflation raises the average price level in the future, the profits of the corporation, which are based on the prices of its inputs and outputs[14] will tend to move proportionately. Uncertain

12. Nowadays, individual brokers have computers connected to central clearing houses, and financial instruments such as these are traded electronically.

13. In some cases, with the approval of a court, a corporation can declare Chapter 11 bankruptcy, referring to a section of U.S. bankruptcy law. This allows a firm to continue operating without paying its debts. At this writing, a number of airlines are in Chapter 11 bankruptcy, yet they continue to fly in spite of not paying their creditors. This tactic is allowed when the company convinces a bankruptcy court that the firm's financial difficulties are temporary, and given some time to reorganize, the company will become solvent again and be able to meet its obligations.

14. Profits also depend on the firm's debt structure, but more on that in a bit.

inflation, therefore, can affect the prices of a corporation's stocks and bonds relative to each other.

The values of both stocks and bonds are the present values of the anticipated payments they promise. The price set in the market for these instruments varies with investors' confidence that the promises will be kept, that is, that the payments will actually be made. Also, present values depend upon market interest rates, for changes in the real and nominal rates change may affect the present value of future obligations.

Consider first the case of bonds, which are promises to pay stipulated amounts of dollars in the future. Suppose you have just purchased a 1 year bond issued by the United States government. These issues are called Treasury Bonds; bonds whose term is less than a year are called Treasury Bills. At this writing, these bonds are paying a bit under 5% interest. If one were to lend the U.S. government \$10,000 by purchasing one of these bonds, they will pay you \$10,500 in one year. Lending money to the U.S. government is in general the safest investment one can make, at least in terms of the likelihood of being paid. The U.S. government has never defaulted on any loan. Why do these bonds pay 5%, and why, during the mid 1980s did they pay 8%, given the security of the loan? In the case of these bonds, the risk premium is close to zero so that the original Fisher equation, equation (10-6) applies. The market rate reflects the real rate of interest plus the anticipated rate of inflation for the coming year. A rate of 5% on a 1 year U.S. government bond indicates the market anticipates inflation of 3% to 4% in the coming year. If you buy this bond, and inflation turns out to be greater than this amount, say, 6%, then you will have loaned the government money at a *minus* 1% real rate of interest, since the dollars repaid have 6% less purchasing power than those you lent out a year ago. On the other hand, if inflation completely abates, you will have received a real return of 5%, quite nice for an extremely secure loan.

This simple transaction highlights the risk inherent in all loans specified in nominal dollars. Even if repayment is not a major concern, the loan is risky if the rate of inflation is uncertain. With short-term bonds with, say, terms of less than a year, this risk is not great, because the rate of inflation usually does not change rapidly. For long-term bonds, however, this risk can be substantial. The longest term bonds sold by the U.S. government are for thirty years. When you purchase these bonds, you are making a thirty-year bet about the rate of inflation. Currently (mid 1999), these bonds pay about 6% interest. This means that if you purchase one of these \$10,000 bonds, the government will pay you \$600 per year for 30 years, and then give you back your \$10,000. Is this a deal or isn't it? You are locking in 6% interest. If inflation goes away and stays away for 30 years, this will be one of the best investments you ever make: 6% *real* interest. On the other hand, inflation hit 12% per year around 1980; no one believes it couldn't happen again. If inflation reaches these rates again and stays in that range, the dollars the government will be paying you will depreciate by 12% per year in purchasing power. In 6 years dollar bills will be worth about \$.50, in another 6 years, a quarter, and by the end of the 30 year period, your \$10,000 will have the same purchasing power as $\$10{,}000/(1.12)^{30} = \$337.78$! It will have been a disastrous loan—a commitment to receive approximately minus 5% per year for 30 years.

The rate of interest on any bond currently transacted reflects the anticipated inflation rate over the term of the bond, and, of course, the perceived riskiness of the bond. If the anticipated inflation rate changes during the life of the bond (as it surely will), then market interest rates also will change, which will in turn change the value of the bond. To take the simplest example, suppose you have just purchased a $10,000 (its printed, or face value) one-year U.S. Treasury bond which is currently paying 5% interest. The next day, inflation is reported to be running at a 9% annual rate. The interest rates on one-year Treasury bonds rise to 10%, to reflect this new information. You are now holding a promise from the government to pay you $10,500 at the end of a year. But now, with 10% interest, the present value of this amount is $10,500/(1.10) = $9,545.45. The value of the bond *falls* because of the increase in interest rates; it now takes only $9,545.45 to reach $10,500 in year. We can understand the reason for the decrease in price simply in terms of dividing a given amount, the future value of the bond, by a larger number, reflecting a higher interest rate. More importantly, though, the price of the bond decreases because the real value of the obligation has diminished. The $10,500 is going to be able to purchase approximately 5% less actual goods than we originally believed. The issuer of the bond, the U.S. government in this case, has to give up fewer actual resources than either it or we originally anticipated in order to pay off the bond.

With long term bonds, the effect is even more dramatic. Suppose you purchase a $10,000, 30 year bond paying 6% interest; the government will pay you $600 per year for 30 years and then return your $10,000. Suppose interest rates rise to 12%. Now, an investment of only $5,000 will generate $600 per year. At this interest rate, a 30 year bond is almost a perpetuity, and the bond will fall in price to just slightly greater than half its original value. Over time, since the government will ultimately redeem your bond at its original price of $10,000, its price will rise towards that value.

Government and corporate bonds are bought and sold every day. If you purchase a bond and interest rates rise, you suffer a once and for all loss of wealth. It cannot be retrieved. You can either accept the lower interest payments you contracted for, or you can sell the bond at its now lower price. The decrease in the price of the bond is the present value of the difference in interest payments available now versus what is stated on the bond, plus the difference in present value of the face value of the bond upon redemption. If interest rates fall after you purchase a bond, you receive a once and for all increase in wealth.

Consider now the case of corporate stocks. A stock represents the right to receive a share of the future profits of some corporation. All public information about that corporation is capitalized into its current price. If some news is published indicating either poorer or better prospects for the company, this information spreads with electronic speed to brokers around the country and the price of the stock starts to change almost immediately. You can't make some unusual amount of money by purchasing the stock of some company about which *Fortune Magazine, The Wall Street Journal* and *Business Week* magazine have just published glowing articles concerning the new patent it has acquired for changing lead into gold. The price has already risen to reflect these anticipated higher profits. If the company makes even larger profits than anticipated at the time of purchase, the price of the stock will rise further. The only way to make money in the stock market is to have information that other investors do not have. If, for example, you are the treasurer or some other officer of a corporation, you have *inside information* about the company. You could profit by buying or selling the stock before any of this news reaches the market. This type of insider trading is in fact illegal, and the government applies strict penalties to those caught doing it. Other than inside information, the only way to do better than the average of the stock market is to truly have a better theory than do others about what affects the value of some company. Very few people seem to be possessed of such insights.

Consider the following proposition: "Invest in land. Population grows steadily, increasing the congestion of people on the land. Therefore, rental rates and the price of land will rise in the future, yielding a profitable investment." This advice has been widely offered; many people in the in various parts of the United States have found out it is unfortunately not universally true. The fallacy in the argument is that even if everything we hypothesized about rents is true, the price of the land when it is first sold reflects this information. Competition between buyers for these future rents bids up the current price of the land. Buying land will be no more profitable than buying other investments of the same riskiness. Only if some unforeseen events occur, such as unusual in-migration to a certain area, will the land yield a higher than normal rate of return.

10.6 The Price of Assets

The ratio of the price of publicly traded corporate stocks to current earnings is reported daily on the stock market tables as the price-earnings (P/E) ratio. Historically, the typical numbers have been 8 to 15; 5 is considered low, and 20 has been high, though in recent years the stock market as a whole has had an average P/E ratio of close to 30. Consider this ratio in terms of equation (10-5) for the value of a perpetuity. Assume for the moment the current earnings are not unusually high or low due to some once-and-for-all event, so that they represent some permanent level of earnings. Then these earnings, E, divided by an interest rate i reflecting the real rate of interest plus the premium for risk, yields the present value of the corporation, treating the earnings as a perpetual stream. When divided by the number of shares of stock outstanding, this ratio yields the value of a share of stock. Algebraically,

$$PV = \frac{E}{i}$$

or, rearranging,

$$i = \frac{\textit{Earnings per share}}{\textit{price of a share}} = \frac{1}{\textit{P/E Ratio}} \qquad (10\text{-}8)$$

The reciprocal of the price-earnings ratio thus represent rates of return on equity capital, that is, the interest rate reflecting the opportunity cost of investing those corporations, taking into account their riskiness, and assuming that the current earnings are in fact typical. A price-earnings ratio of 5, for example, implies an interest rate of 20%, reflecting substantial uncertainty regarding the future prospects of that company (again, assuming the current earnings are not unusual.) Small retail businesses, most of which disappear within a few years, are examples of firms whose price-earnings ratio would be less than 5. When such firms are sold, the buyer usually pays 2 to 5 times the current profits (excluding the owner's salary, as that is not a rent) for ownership of all future rents. Of course the number can vary depending on individual circumstance. On the other hand, new stock issues for corporations which are perceived to have substantial prospects for growth sell for many times the anticipated initial earnings.

Example: The Value of a Business Suppose after kicking around for a few years in entry-level jobs unrelated to your B.A. in metaphysics, you and a friend decide to pursue your long held dreams of opening a restaurant which will serve incredibly delicious food at modest prices. You could try to start from scratch, renting a location, fixing up the premises, putting in a kitchen, etc. This, however, turns out to be a very costly endeavor. Moreover, even if you do serve the city's finest foods at McDonald's prices, it will take awhile before the public finds out about it. In the meantime, your creditors (most likely relatives, whom God had informed that they had too much cash) will be anxiously awaiting the first payment on their loans. Another strategy is to purchase some already existing restaurant. The advantage of this is people already know of the restaurant's existence and location; changing it to suit your own concept is a less risky venture than starting *de novo.* Fortunately, the existing owner of a restaurant in your image is nearing retirement and is interested in finding a buyer. How much should you pay for the restaurant? That is, how much do ongoing businesses sell for in the market, and why?

As a first step you get the owner's financial records. They show that in the past several years, he has had gross receipts (revenues) of $300,00 per year, and a profit averaging $50,000 per year after all expenses. That is, after paying his employees, rent, utilities, etc., the owner gets to keep $50,000 per year in taxable income. The restaurant also has equipment that could be sold for about $25,000. The owner tells you that a common rule of thumb is that the sale price of a business is 1 year's gross, and thus offers to sell for $300,000. How do you react?

What you are purchasing is the right to receive the quasi-rents specific to this restaurant. These rents exist because the public is already informed about the restaurant, they have an established pattern of going to this restaurant because it has a certain reputation regarding the quality food they serve and the prices they charge. The asset you are intending to purchase is called the *goodwill* of the business, and, perhaps, some tangible assets such as equipment. A buyer would always be willing to pay at least as much as the scrap value of all the tangible assets; however, most businesses that actually trade in the marketplace sell for more than that amount. The price of any asset is the present value of the net income it is expected to generate in the future; in this case, the price of the restaurant is the present value of its anticipated future net rents.

The net rents obviously have no direct relationship to the gross receipts of the business. You don't get to eat the gross receipts; you can only consume what is left over after paying all the bills.[15] What about the $50,000 profit, then? Does this number represent the net rents from the business? The owner has neglected to pay himself a salary. If he is a sole proprietor (as opposed to being a corporation) this is perfectly legal. However, it is also misleading. The owner has to *work,* probably long hours at that, in order to produce this $50,000. Some part of these profits is

15. Unless, as reputed mobster Joe Bonnano (Joe Bananas) once said, If you don't pay your expenses, then your gross is your net.

really the owner's salary for his efforts. If he wanted to work that hard managing some other person's restaurant, he could earn a competitive wage in the labor market. In fact, managers of small enterprises in the United States earn about $30,000 per year. The right to receive $30,000 per year in this restaurant from working 12 hours per day six days a week is not worth a dime. A capable manager can earn that much elsewhere, for that level of effort. The only thing a prospective buyer will pay for is the right to earn something in excess of what they could earn by similar efforts elsewhere. In this case, these net rents are $20,000 per year, the excess of the income produced over the opportunity cost of the owner/manager.

What then is it worth to be able to receive $20,000 per year more than one's next best alternative? We treat this asset as a perpetuity. Its price is $P = \$20{,}000/i$, where i is some interest yield appropriate for small businesses of this type. Alternatively, $P = \$20{,}000 \times$ some appropriate P/E ratio. As the plethora of used restaurant equipment for sale attests, this is a very risky business. A risk adjusted interest rate of .20 (equivalent to a price-earnings multiple of 5) is probably generous. More likely, a P/E ratio of 3 ($i = .333$) is more appropriate. Thus the likely selling price of this restaurant is in the range of $60,000 to $100,000. What about the equipment that could easily be sold for $25,000? This is part of what makes the restaurant worth $60,000 to $100,000. You can't get the net rents of the restaurant *plus* $25,000 for the equipment; you can get only one or the other. The value of the restaurant (or any business) is the larger of these two values. If the scrap value of the assets is greater than the present value of the net rents, the economically efficient (and wealth-increasing) thing to do is to sell the assets and go out of business.

10.7 The Fisher Separation Theorem

Suppose consumers can choose amongst alternative income plans, so that the income earned in a given year is part of a long-term decision. For example, individuals make career choices in which patterns of income often differ substantially. A person could enter the labor force right after high school and immediately start earning income in some trade. Alternatively, the individual can attend college and perhaps a graduate or professional school, e.g. law or medicine. In that case, income will be very low in the present, but eventually higher than that produced with no post-high school training. Or, several business investments might be possible, with varying cash flows, some occurring relatively early, while with others, negative cash flows in the near term but large profits later on. What investment strategy is implied by the postulates of behavior?

Recall the discussion of Robinson Crusoe and Friday and the gains from pursuing their comparative advantages. As long as Crusoe and Friday could trade with each other, so they did not have to consume what they individually produced, they could benefit from producing the good that generated the highest income. This good is the one for which they have a comparative advantage. With extensive markets, individuals' production decisions can be separated from their consumption decisions. They can first produce the goods that maximize their income, and then decide how to consume that income. As long as we get paid in money, and can use that money to purchase any good within our budget, more income is preferred to less, other things being equal. Only if production of some good gives us some special entitlement to consume that good, would this logic fail. With well-developed (extensive) markets, these special entitlements do not appear. Producers generally derive the largest rents by selling to the highest bidder, not to their own employees. Thus in modern economies, people specialize in what they do best, and trade for the commodities they wish to consume.

For the same reasons, with well developed capital markets, in which borrowing and lending easily take place, consumers derive their most preferred consumption plan by first choosing that income stream that maximizes wealth, and then rearranging consumption through borrowing or lending so as to achieve the particular stream of consumption they desire. This famous result is known as the Fisher Separation Theorem, after Irving Fisher, who first propounded it.[16] With extensive markets, increases in income or wealth are always desirable.

Suppose, for example, a person is indifferent between being a physician or a model. The modeling career pays a great deal while a person is young and good-looking, but less as one ages. The income a physician derives is very low (negative, perhaps) for up to 10 years, while the individual pursues studies in college, medical school and residency. At the end of that time, income rises, exceeding that available to a model. The income available to such an individual at a given age will differ greatly between the two careers. A person who craved immediate gratification might choose the modeling career; one with great impulse control might choose the medical career. Suppose, however, this person can borrow or lend as much as desired at the market rate of interest. In that case, he or she could rearrange consumption in any way desired. The career that allows the highest level of consumption is the one for which the present value of all the future lifetime income is highest. In other words, the career for which the person's wealth is largest is also the one that allows the greatest benefits from consumption. With extensive capital markets, production and consumption decisions are again separable. In that case, maximizing wealth also maximizes consumption possibilities, and individuals will chose the career that maximizes wealth.[17] We must assume in this analysis that an individual does not have specific preferences with regard to the various investment or income streams available. In the case of career choice particularly, we must apply the theorem with caution, since individuals commonly are not indifferent to the nonpecuniary aspects of the various careers. However, the theorem still applies at the margin: as the pecuniary wealth of some career increases relative to others, more individuals will be attracted to it. If the lifetime incomes of doctors fall relative to modeling, some individuals who are capable of either career and who might have opted for medicine will instead choose to become models.

10.8 Stocks and Flows

For the most part, goods that provide income in the future are durable. Capital can consist of intermediate goods that individuals use only once in some productive process, but interest rates and time preference are not directly relevant for such goods. Most interest (no pun intended) in capital goods focuses on those goods which last over several or many time periods. In that case we have to dis-

16. See Fisher, *The Theory of Interest,* op. cit.

17. The above argument assumes that the individual can borrow and lend at the same rate. Typically, individuals borrow at a higher rate of interest than they lend at, in which case, maximization of wealth may not be implied.

tinguish the physical item, called the **stock**, from the **flow** of service (per unit time) derived from the stock.

A convenient illustration of these concepts is the distinction between a house, and the flow of housing services we derive from owning or renting a house. When we rent housing, we purchase the service flow for some period of time. If we purchase the house itself, we are purchasing the stock. Owning the stock (the house) entitles you to consume the entire future service flow for the duration of the existence of the stock, and also obligates you to pay any costs associated with ownership such as property taxes and maintenance. The price of the stock is therefore the present value of the anticipated net rents (value of service flow, per unit time, net of costs) for the indefinite future.

Let us investigate how changes in interest rates affect the prices and quantities of stocks and flows, and the rate of investment.[18] In Fig. 10-5, panel (a), we depict the supply and demand for *housing,* the service flow of shelter. The supply curve is drawn vertically, to represent that the supply of housing units is very large and cannot change a great deal in the short run. Of course, at any moment of time, some houses are being demolished and others are being built. For simplicity, assume that this supply curve represents a steady state of net housing supply. The demand for the service flow of housing is derived from the desire to be warm and dry. It is one of many goods consumers desire at a moment in time. The fact that houses are sometimes rented and sometimes purchased has to do with minimizing the transactions costs associated with obtaining shelter in these various ways. The market for shelter produces a market rental price R.

Suppose now the interest rate (the real rate plus the risk premium) falls, from i_0 to i_1, due to some exogenous factor, say, lowered anticipated future economic growth or greater security regarding the existence of future income. Changes in the real interest rate would have no predictable effect on the demand for housing relative to other contemporaneous goods. A fall in the interest rate is a decrease in the price of present relative to future consumption. There is no reason why the mix of current goods, that is, the amount of shelter versus food and clothing a person consumes should be affected in any particular way. Thus we would expect no change in the rental price R. In panel (b), however, we show the demand and supply of *houses.* The market price P is the present value of net rents. Assume that houses last a long time so that its services can be approximated as a perpetuity, and assume some annual costs or other obligations such as taxes and maintenance occur in the amount C. Then the price of the house is the present value of the net rentals on the house, or

$$P = \frac{R - C}{i} \tag{10-9}$$

Costs C are represented by the shaded part of total annual rents in panel (a). A fall in i means the premium for present consumption has fallen; future consumption is now relatively more highly valued. Therefore, any asset that generates future income is now more highly valued. The demand for owning such an asset therefore shifts out, as shown in shown in panel (b). The price P of the

18. This discussion is adapted from James Witte's, The Microfoundations of the Social Investment Function, *Journal of Political Economy,* 71: 441–56, October, 1956.

Figure 10-5 *Stocks and Flows*

Panel (a) shows the supply and demand curves for the flow of housing services. These curves are not affected by changes in interest rates because they describe flows in the present. Using equation (10-5), the demand for the stock of houses shifts up in panel (b) when the interest rate falls. The quantity of new houses supplied therefore increases due to the increase in the price of houses, as shown in panel (c).

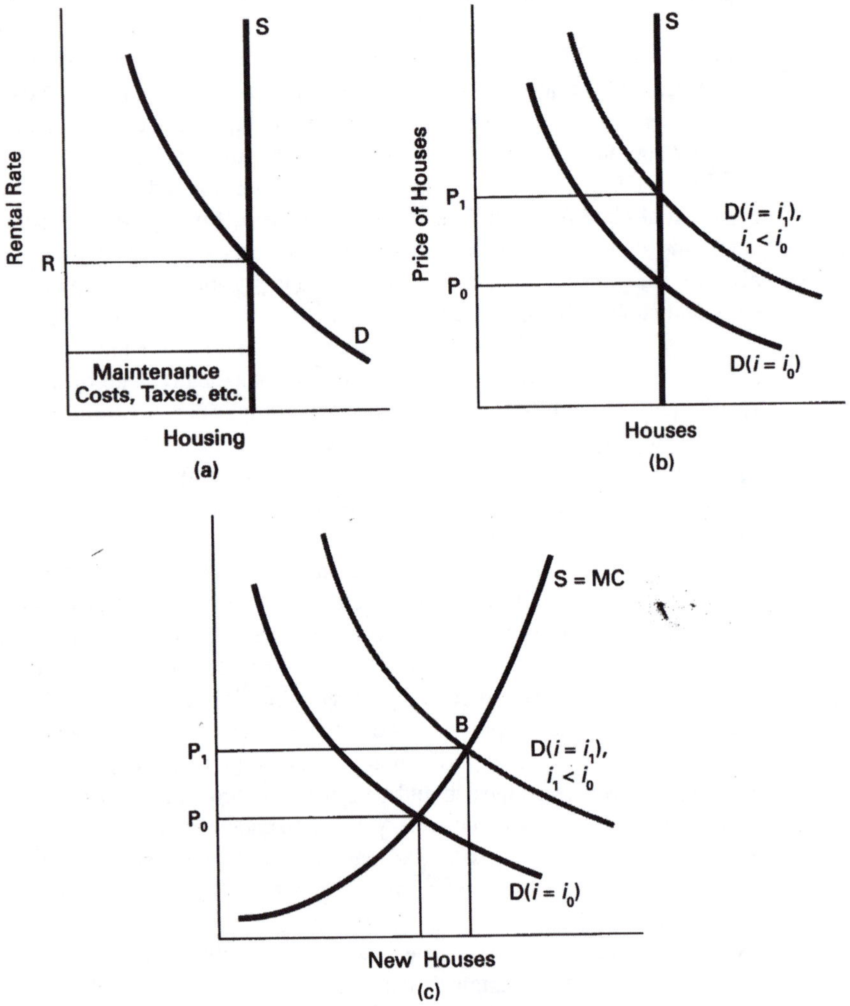

house, (the stock) representing the present value of all anticipated future housing services, therefore rises.

The proper interest rate to use in these formulas is the rate that reflects the opportunity cost of the funds in terms of their use either in alternative investment projects or in the production of present consumption. Consider a building with a prospective long life and total current net rentals of $R - C$. If we expect the rentals and costs to keep pace with inflation, meaning we expect $R - C$ to increase at the same rate as the inflation rate, use of a nominal rate which included anticipated inflation would understate the price P of the building. In the formula $P = (R - C)/i$, $R - C$ is assumed to be constant forever. In this formula, inflation is removed from both the numerator and the denominator. We use the real rental rate in the numerator and the real rate of interest in the denominator. However, the *risk* associated with the level of future rents, based on actual uncertainty about the future, is part of the opportunity cost of using present funds to build capital which we hope will produce income in the future. Risk means that there is some chance that part or all of the current consumption sacrificed to build an asset may be for naught; the anticipated future income may never fully materialize. Thus the appropriate interest rate in these calculations is the real rate plus the risk premium. It is commonly observed, for example, in real estate evaluations, that relatively new buildings sell for approximately 10 to 11 times current rentals. This implies a capitalization (interest) rate of approximately 9% to 10%. Assuming a real interest rate of approximately .01 – .02, this implies a risk premium for such assets of approximately 0.08.

An increase in the current price of houses has an obvious effect on the market for new houses. In panel (c), we show the demand and supply of new houses. When the price of houses increases, production will increase until the marginal cost of producing new houses equals consumers' marginal values of new houses, at point *B*. The housing stock will start to rise above its previous level. In the short run, there will be a negligible effect on rentals, as the housing stock is already very large. Over time, however, the housing stock will increase above its former level, increasing the supply of housing services and thereby lowering housing rental prices. If the new rate of interest is permanently lower, some new, larger, steady state stock of houses and housing supply will exist.

We can address other questions using this same framework. In 1978, voters in California passed the famous Proposition 13 which drastically lowered property taxes. It was sold to the voting public partly as a means to reduce rental prices. Of course, considering panel (a) above, it could do no such thing in the short run, since neither the supply nor the demand for housing services was affected by the new law. However, by lowering the costs *C* of housing ownership, net rents to property owners were increased. We would therefore expect the price of houses to rise, as implied by equation (10-9), producing increased new construction of houses. In the long run, rental prices would decrease, but only due to the larger supply of housing services resulting from the larger housing stock. In the case of the actual Proposition 13, however, the law applied only to existing owners; property taxes are adjusted when the house is sold, thus nullifying this effect (in addition to providing a powerful disincentive to sell one's house).[19]

Consider also that at present, in the United States, mortgage interest on one's own home is a deductible item for income tax purposes. That is, if a married couple earns $50,000 per year and pays $10,000 in interest payments in one year, then in addition to the other deductions (such as charitable contributions, exemptions for children, etc.) home owners can deduct the $10,000 interest payment in determining their *taxable* income. (In Canada, mortgage interest is not deductible.) The effect of this deduction is to lower one's tax liability by whatever the taxes would have been on the extra $10,000. If a couple pays 28% of

19. On the other hand, many local property taxes are directly tied to local community services, such as schools. People move to certain cities and neighborhoods specifically to pay those taxes, that is, to be able to consume the local services they provide. In that case, defeat of, say, a school levy might actually depress house prices, if the main purpose of moving to that locale was to consume the local school district.

their income over about $30,000 (the current marginal rate), then this deduction saves the couple $2,800 per year. Suppose this deductibility were removed. Existing home owners would suffer a once-and-for-all loss of wealth equal to the present value of the future increased tax liability.[20] The demand for houses (the stock) would therefore shift down by some amount representing the effect on the marginal home owner. The change in the tax law would have no effect on prospective first-time home owners; the increase in their tax obligations will be capitalized into a lower purchase price of the house. The change would affect people in the business of new home construction; by lowering the price of new houses, new construction would be reduced. In the long run, therefore, the housing stock would be smaller, resulting in an increase in rental prices (or, in the case of owner-occupied housing, imputed rental prices.)

Inflation and Asset Prices

Lastly, consider how inflation affects the relative price of assets, and in particular houses. It is commonly said that houses offer protection against inflation. The germ of truth in that proposition is that assets denominated in real terms, sometimes houses and other property, are unaffected by inflation. As the general price level rises, the price of these assets will rise as well. Ownership of these assets, however, often involves contracts that are stated in nominal terms. If a home (or any piece of capital) was financed by a loan, the interest charged reflected the anticipated inflation rate at the time the loan was negotiated. The mortgage payments are stated in terms of a fixed amount of dollars to be paid per month. If the rate of inflation increases unexpectedly, the real value of the debt decreases, because the dollars used to repay the loan are now worth a smaller amount than originally believed, producing a windfall gain to the debtors, and a corresponding loss to the creditors. If inflation decreases unexpectedly, the wealth transfer goes from debtor to creditor. The crux of the matter is that only *anticipated* inflation can be hedged in any contract stated in money, or nominal terms. The anticipated rate of decline in the purchasing power of future receipts is capitalized into the loan agreement through the nominal interest rate. The value of business firms may therefore depend on the manner in which their debt is financed. Those firms with high debt to equity ratios will be relatively sensitive to changes in the inflation rate. On the other hand, the present value of government pension plans (social security, railroad retirement, civil service and military pensions), which are all specifically indexed to the rate of inflation, are largely unaffected by unanticipated inflation.

Inflation does have real effects, because in a modern economy laws and contracts are inevitably stated at least partly in nominal terms. It is unlikely that everything can be indexed, although the incentives to do so increase as the inflation rate increases. An outstanding example of how inflation can affect the value of capital is the way the United States' tax laws treat depreciation. Depreciation of assets must be based on its historical cost, not its replacement value. Suppose a firm purchases some equipment for $100,000 with an expected life of 5 years. The government allows the firm to deduct $20,000 per year from gross receipts

20. Assuming, of course, that this change is not simply in lieu of some other tax increase. The actual amount would vary with the tax bracket of the marginal home purchasers.

for 5 years, reflecting the fact that the machine is wearing out at that rate. Suppose, however, inflation is raging, doubling the price level each year. Then the depreciation that would correctly reflect the cost of this equipment wearing out (and its eventual replacement) is $40,000 in year 2, $80,000 in year 3, and so forth. The tax laws, however, still insist that only $20,000 be deducted each year, an amount less in real terms than in the case where there is no inflation. Because of the insistence that only the historical cost be used as a basis for depreciation, depreciation is understated. Measured corporate profits are therefore too high in subsequent years. Consequently, an increase in the inflation rate increases the tax liability of the corporation, even with no change in the tax laws, thus reducing present value of future real rents. Inflation, on this account, is apt to lower corporate stock prices.[21] Additionally, inflation produces spurious taxable capital gains. A house purchased at $100,000 in the 1980s and sold for $200,000 in the 1990s when the price level had doubled, would create a tax liability on the $100,000 gain, even though no real gain (in terms of relative prices) actually exists.[22]

Two important assets, owner-occupied houses and gold, cannot be depreciated for tax purposes. At any moment in time, some existing relative price structure exists for these assets and depreciable assets. If the rate of inflation unexpectedly increases, gold and owner-occupied houses, which are not depreciable, are not subject to the increased tax caused by the depreciation rules. Therefore, we would expect to see the prices of these assets rise relative to depreciable assets. Purchasers of homes, however, can be liquidity constrained, at higher rates of inflation. Mortgage contracts are typically structured with fixed nominal monthly payments. Inflation causes the real value of these payments to decrease over time. Alternatively, inflation shifts the burden of the loan repayment from the future to the present. As the nominal rate of interest increases in response to increased anticipated inflation, this shift in the burden increases, and, at double-digit rates, could easily exceed a family's current income. This would depress the demand for owner-occupied housing, though mortgage contracts would soon be indexed to inflation if this problem became severe or protracted. Since gold is divisible, it would not be subject to this constraint, and thus its price might rise relative to house prices as inflation increased.

CHAPTER SUMMARY

- In addition to choosing amongst contemporaneous goods, individuals make decisions regarding the timing of consumption *over time.*
- Income available in the present is preferable to income received in the future, since greater opportunities for consumption are present if the income is available now. This creates a *premium for earlier availability of income,* called the *real interest rate.*

---

21. Some have argued that this accounts for the decrease in the real value of stocks traded on the U.S. stock exchanges.

22. In the case of owner-occupied housing, the capital gains tax in the United States can be avoided or delayed by purchasing another house of greater or equal value.

- The marginal value of present consumption is the amount of future consumption that a person is willing to forego in order to have an extra unit of present consumption. As is the case with all goods, this marginal value decreases producing a downward sloping demand curve for present consumption.

- Capital markets exist in which present consumption is traded, through borrowing and lending. In virtually all situations, a positive price of present consumption emerges. The price of present consumption in terms of future consumption foregone is some number greater than 1; the difference between this price and unity is the interest rate.

- The present value of some future amount is the amount that must be set aside now, called the *principal,* so that with continuous reinvestment of interest earnings, the principal will grow into the required amount. The further into the future, and the higher the interest rate, the less will be the present value of that amount.

- An annuity is a stream of constant, or predictable amounts occurring at regular intervals in the future. The price of an annuity is the sum of the present values of each payment.

- A perpetuity is an annuity that lasts forever. At some constant interest rate i, the price, or present value of a perpetuity of \$$A$ per year is A/i. At commonly encountered interest rates, the values of annuities lasting over a generation of time can be closely approximated by the perpetuity formula.

- *Capital* is any good that produces income in the future; the price of such an asset is the present value of the anticipated income. The *wealth* of an individual, or institution, or country is the present or capitalized value of the assets of that entity.

- Market, or nominal interest rates reflect the real rate of interest (the premium for earlier availability), the anticipated inflation rate, and a risk premium.

- Bonds are legal obligations of corporations and governments. They must be paid before owners receive payment for their services. Stocks are shares in the ownership or equity of some corporation; dividends are not promised, and are paid only after all contractual debts of the corporation are paid. Stocks are therefore riskier than bonds, but because of that, their average yield is higher.

- With established capital markets, individuals can achieve the highest standard of living by choosing income streams that have the highest *wealth,* and then borrowing or lending to rearrange consumption in the most desired way. This famous result is known as the Fisher Separation Theorem.

- Income or some good or service received *per unit time* is called a *flow.* The asset that produces such a flow is called a *stock.* The price of the stock is the present value of the income or service flow. For example, the price of a house is the present value of the net rentals that can be received from the house.

REVIEW QUESTIONS

1. Why is there an interest rate?
2. What is the difference between real and the nominal interest rates?
3. What is the Fisher equation, relating nominal to real interest rates, and what does it mean?
4. What is present value?
5. What are annuities and perpetuities?
6. If we are contemplating whether to invest in some enterprise with some expected flow of incomes in the future, why can we not simply add up all those future incomes to evaluate the project?
7. When we take out a loan, we have to repay more than the original price. What accounts for this, and does this mean we shouldn't take out loans? Why do people borrow?
8. Why is only the real rate plus the risk premium (and not the factor for anticipated inflation) used in the denominator of the perpetuity formula?
9. What are corporate stocks and bonds, and how are they different?
10. Under what circumstances does the P/E ratio of a publicly traded corporation's stock indicate the riskiness of investing in that stock?
11. Distinguish stocks from flows. What happens in flow markets when the interest changes?

PROBLEMS

1. (For math jocks only) If some amount grows at g % per year, compounded, the original principal will double in approximately $72/g$ years. Prove this famous Rule of 72.
2. Consider the value of a state lottery, as described preceding equation (10–3). Suppose the first payment is received immediately, instead of after one year. How must the formula for the present value of the lottery be revised? At 8% interest, what effect does this have on the present value of a lottery paying 25 payments of $40,000 per year?
3. Publisher's Clearinghouse offers at the time of this writing a $10 million prize for winners of their sweepstakes. In the Official Rules enclosed with my CONFIDENTIAL Prize Acceptance Affidavit, it states that the prizewinner will receive $500,000 the first year, $250,000 a year thereafter, plus a final payment of $2.5 million in the 30th year.
   a. Assume (generously) the payments come at the *beginning* of each year. What is the present value of this lottery, assuming one lives to collect it, at 7% and 10% interest?

b. The American Family Sweepstakes featuring Ed McMahon also offers a $10 million lottery, but their payout is $333,333.33 per year for 30 years. Again assuming that the checks arrive at the beginning of each year, what is the present value of this lottery at 7% and 10% interest?
c. Is there any reasonable interest rate that would make the present values of the two lotteries equal? Why or why not?

4. A private bank operating in its own interest is willing to lend you $10,000 per year at 8% interest, for 4 years, beginning in 1 year, towards college tuition costs. You have to repay the loan in 5 equal payments beginning 6 years from now.

   a. What is the present value of this loan?
   b. How much will you have to pay per year?
   c. The government now offers you the same terms, except at 5% interest. How much will you now have to pay beginning in year 6, and what is the present value of these payments?
   d. What is the value of the government program to you?

5. Home mortgages are based on fixed monthly payments. If inflation increases nominal interest rates, explain why this shifts the burden of loan repayment to the present.

6. Suppose sheep could reproduce so as to increase the stock of sheep 10% per year, forever. Would the real rate of interest rise to 10%?

7. Utility companies in recent years have extended interest-free loans to customers to promote installation of energy-saving furnaces and hot water heaters. Suppose the utility company loans you $2,000 for such purposes, and allows you to repay the loan in 4 equal annual payments of $500, beginning 1 year from now. What is the amount of the subsidy you receive?

8. *The Price of Assets* After some years of managing a restaurant specializing in Armenian food, earning $25,000.00 per year for your efforts, you decide to go into business for yourself. You have the option of renting some space and creating a restaurant in it, or purchasing a going concern. If you open your own restaurant, you have the costs of setting up the place, and also the problem of informing consumers that it exists, and that it is a nice place to dine. A comparable, privately-owned, well-known Armenian restaurant is for sale. The owner shows you her financial records and they show annual revenues in excess of all expenditures by the owner on help, supplies and rent of $45,000. Assume the restaurant has $70,000 worth of fixtures and furnishings, and it is possible to set up a comparable restaurant for $100,000.

   a. What would be the likely market value of the restaurant? You *must* supply a numerical figure and explain how you arrived at that answer.
   b. How would your answer be affected by an increase in the *real* rate of interest (the premium for earlier availability of goods)?
   c. How would your answer be affected by an increase in the nominal or market rate of interest due to widespread anticipation of future inflation?
   d. Suppose immigration of Armenians to this area is to be substantially increased, beginning in three years. What affect would this have on the

annual profits of the restaurant now and in the future, and on the price the restaurant will sell for?

9. *Present Values and Energy conservation* Since the mid 1970s, the federal government has mandated mileage standards for automobiles: the average of the miles per gallon achieved by the cars sold by each manufacturer has to exceed a certain level. These mileage standards have been steadily raised.

   a. Suppose GM produced a car that was identical to its competitors' in comfort, handling etc., but which got more miles per gallon. How would this affect the price of GM's and its competitors' cars?
   b. How much would it be worth to GM or one of its competitors to produce a car that got one mile per gallon more than the previous model, other things equal? Make several assumptions you feel are reasonable, and derive a numerical answer for each assumption so that you can observe the sensitivity of your answer to the specific assumptions made.
   c. Evaluate these mileage standards with respect to their role in efficient allocation of resources to energy conservation.

10. A young woman of extraordinary intelligence and beauty is trying to choose one of three following professions. First, she could be an entertainer, with an income stream higher in the early years but falling as she gets older; second, she could become a teacher with a constant income stream, and lastly, she could go to medical school and become a doctor, in which case her income would be low for many years but would then rise after completion of residency. Assume she wants to maximize her pecuniary wealth (that is, the nonpecuniary aspects of these professions do not matter to her) and that she can borrow and lend to adjust the shape of each income stream. Suppose further, the income streams can be ranked in the following order: the total sum of dollars to be received is greatest as a doctor, next as an entertainer and lowest as a teacher. State whether the following statements are true or false, and why. (The answers to these questions are gender neutral.)

    a. If the rate of interest is zero, she chooses to be a medical student.
    b. A high rate of interest may give her a greater wealth as an entertainer.
    c. At any rate of interest, she will not become a teacher.
    d. There is some positive interest rate which makes the present wealth of being a doctor equal to that of an entertainer.
    e. There is a positive rate of interest which makes the present wealth of being an entertainer equal to that of being a teacher.

11. Suppose you own both stocks and bonds issued by Natural Fruits, Inc., a large apple-growing corporation. Explain the effects on:

    i. the price of apples
    ii. the value of your shares of stock
    iii. the value of your bonds

    of the following events:

    a. an increase in the real rate of interest
    b. an increase in the nominal rate of interest, due to anticipated higher inflation

c. the announcement of a new hybrid that will greatly increase the number of apples per tree, when these new trees reach maturity in 10 years.

12. In a small country, trees are grown with the characteristics shown in the table below. For the first 19 years, the trees have either negative or zero harvest value over planting and maintenance costs. After 26 years, growth ceases. The numbers displayed in Column (2) are recoverable board-feet, which have a permanent market value of 1$ per board-foot. Column (3) gives the % growth in volume (and thus value) of the trees, from the previous year. Tree plantings are staggered at one year intervals, so that the same number of trees mature each year. Column (4), board-feet divided by years of growth, gives the average sustained yield of the land when the trees are harvested in that year.

    Derive and explain the age at which the trees will be harvested, and analyze the allocative efficiency of the following three harvesting plans. Each plan implies harvest at different ages of the trees. *Assume the economy has available to it investments of like risk to forestry, and which have expected interest yields of 15%.*

    i. Maximize the total value of trees harvested each year.
    ii. Maximize average sustained yield.
    iii. Maximize net present value of the trees.

(1) Years	(2) Value of Lumber	(3) % Growth from Previous Year	(4) Average Sustained Yield, Per Year
19	$0	0.0	$ 0
20	5,000	—	250
21	10,000	100.0%	476
22	13,000	30.0	591
23	15,000	15.4	652
24	16,500	10.0	688
25	17,500	6.0	700
26	18,000	3.0	692
27	18,000	0.0	667

13. Suppose a frost destroys a significant part of the Brazilian coffee trees.

    a. Using supply and demand diagrams, explain the effect on prices and quantities sold of coffee and tea.
    b. Upon hearing the news, speculators (and homemakers) start withholding large amounts of coffee for future sale, reducing the supply below what it would be but for their actions. Why do they do this, considering that the current supply of coffee is coming mainly from inventories not affected by the frost?
    c. What benefits to consumers, if any, are produced by this speculation?
    d. Suppose the news turns out to be wrong, and the coffee trees are fine. What affect will this have on speculators' wealth?

14. *Trucking Regulation* The trucking industry is currently regulated within many states, and entry in that business is restricted. Licenses to operate on certain routes are restricted. These licenses are transferable and sell for some price, say $50,000, in the market.

a. What does the value of the license represent?
b. Suppose you inherited your license from your father. Explain why the license still costs you $50,000.
c. Suppose the real interest rate rises. How would this affect current trucking rates and license prices?
d. Suppose nominal, or money interest rates rise, due to a fear of increased inflation. How would this affect current trucking rates and license prices?
e. Suppose that beginning in five years, the number of licenses is to be substantially increased. What effect, if any, would there be on current trucking rates and on license prices?

15. *The Economics of Housing*

a. Carefully distinguish in terms of stocks versus flows, the terms house and housing. How is the purchase price of a house related to the price of housing?
b. Explain the difference between *real* interest rates and those observed in the market, that is, *nominal* interest rates.
c. Explain why changes in the real rate of interest might be expected to *not* affect the price of housing but *would* affect the price of houses.
d. How would a rise in the real interest rate affect existing homeowners, prospective buyers of houses, and people in the construction business?
e. Suppose the interest on home mortgages is no longer a deductible item when income taxes are calculated. How would this affect present homeowners and first-time future home purchasers?
f. How would greenbelt legislation, which restricts *future* building of housing developments in suburban areas affect rental rates and the price of houses?
g. How would an increase in state property taxes affect the rental rate on housing and the price of houses?
h. How would passage of local taxes to finance local schools and other municipal services affect the price of houses in that area?
i. A newsperson once said that houses were getting so expensive, soon no one would be able to afford them. Evaluate. (Also, compare with the statement attributed to Yogi Berra, explaining why he didn't want to go to a certain restaurant, Oh, no one goes there any more. It's too crowded.)

16. *Present values and the Stock Market* You have recently purchased some shares of General Motors (GM) common stock, and also some GM bonds with a maturity of date of 30 years from now. (The stocks pay dividends according to how much profits GM makes, while the bonds are promises to pay a certain fixed dollar amount each year.) Explain how each of the following events would affect the price of these assets and your wealth:

a. A new, widespread belief that double-digit inflation will reoccur.
b. Passage of a new law reducing the level of anti-pollution devices required on cars produced after 1997.
c. A sudden, widespread, increased desire for earlier availability of goods.

17. *Hey Taxi!* A few years ago, the city of Seattle deregulated the taxi industry, but has recently reregulated fares. One of the lingering issues is the number of taxi licenses to issue. The city is mindful of the New York City

experience, where issuance of new licenses (called medallions there) ceased in 1940. These medallions are transferable, and currently sell for about $100,000.

a. What does the value of the medallion represent?
b. Suppose you inherited your medallion from your father. Explain why the medallion still costs you $100,000.
c. Is the value of the medallion a fixed or a variable cost, and how, therefore, would it affect the manner or intensity of operation of the taxi by the owner?
d. Suppose the real interest rate rises. How would this affect current taxi fares and medallion prices?
e. Suppose nominal, or money interest rates rise, due to a fear of increased inflation. How would this affect current taxi fares and medallion prices?
f. Suppose that beginning in five years, the number of medallions is to be substantially increased. Would there be any immediate effect on fares and the price of medallions?
g. Suppose each current medallion holder is given another medallion. How will this affect the wealth of these medallion owners?

18. Suppose you own an apartment complex that generates *R* per year in net rentals.[23] It can be sold outright for some price *P;* alternatively, shares of ownership can be sold.

    a. Plotting present consumption on the horizontal axis and future consumption (assumed infinite) on the vertical axis, indicate the feasible consumption points generated by selling ownership shares.
    b. Suppose you hear that the value of the complex has fallen in half. This could be due to either a doubling of the interest rate or that half the complex has burned down. Under what conditions, if any, would you be indifferent to the cause of this wealth loss?

19. Suppose in some country, borrowing and lending in the money market were prohibited by law. Would an interest rate still exist? What observations would tend to confirm your answer?

20. Some people have argued that the reason for the rapid post World War II recovery for Germany and Japan was that the allies destroyed their old, obsolete capital, so they could then build newer, more modern capital, which was of course more productive than the older capital. What do you think of this argument?

21. You and a friend, recent high school graduates, are discussing career choice. Your friend says, I can work as a carpenter starting this summer and earn $35,000 per year on average. That will put me $100,000 ahead of where I'd be if I went to college for 4 years, to say nothing of the $10,000 per year tuition and expenses in a state university. That's true, you say, but as a college graduate you'll earn an average of $45,000 per year. Over your remaining 40 working years, you'll be ahead $10,000 per year. You'll be ahead $400,000 less the college expenses.

23. Adapted from Alchian & Allen, *Exchange and Production,* (Belmont, CA: Wadsworth)

a. What is, in fact, the major cost of going to college?
b. Explain the errors in the above reasoning, and explain how one would decide matters such as this.

22. TV shows often have a season of only 13 weeks. When television was new, the runs of new episodes were much longer, usually, 26 weeks. Every now and then, someone in Congress proposes to limit the number of times TV shows can be rerun, in an effort to stimulate new production. Discuss the effects of such a law on:

    a. the prices paid for TV shows
    b. the incomes of TV stars
    c. the incomes of actors who obtain jobs through central casting
    d. avid soap opera viewers
    e. avid viewers of expensive prime time shows.

23. In his book, *The New Industrial State,* John Kenneth Galbraith stated that large corporations have so much of their own funds they don't have to borrow in the capital funds market to make new investments. They are therefore immune to changes in interest rates and their investments are therefore not affected by changes in market interest rates. Evaluate this claim.

24. People often accuse speculators of driving up land prices. Can they do so? Are housing prices permanently higher because of the actions of land speculators?

25. "There's no better time than now to buy diamonds. Political changes in South Africa, where most diamonds are mined, will raise wages of miners and therefore prices of diamonds in the future. Come into Silberberg's Diamond Store now and save!" Evaluate.

26. What effect would an increase in the real rate of interest have on

    a. the durability of goods produced
    b. college enrollments?

27. "Banks can charge higher interest rates for riskier loans. Therefore banks can make a higher rate of return by lending to riskier clients." Evaluate.

28. States and municipalities are able to issue bonds whose interest is tax free when the bonds are used to finance public works projects. Should you buy these bonds? For whom are they a relatively better deal, young people just starting a career or successful professionals and business persons?

29. *Union dues* [Note: In this problem, the fundamental diagram is a supply and demand curve for labor, where the amount of labor is plotted on the horizontal axis, and the price of labor, i.e., the wage, is plotted vertically.] A certain industry can hire all the non-union workers it wants at a wage of $10 per hour. The workers then form a union, and successfully raise wages to $11 per hour. Workers are now hired through a union hiring hall; no one can be employed without joining the union.

    a. What will happen to the number of workers who wish to work in this industry now?
    b. What "rationing," or "discrimination" problem will the union have?

c. Approximately how much would a young worker be willing to pay, as a *once and for all, lifetime* initiation fee, for the right to join this union? You *must* supply a numerical answer, or at least a formula, and explain why you chose it.

d. What effects would the following events have on the *current* union wages paid and the size of the initiation fee:

   i. an increase in the real rate of interest

   ii. an increase in the inflation rate

   iii. the prospect of technological change which would *in five years* allow unskilled workers to do the jobs now performed by workers in this union

QUESTIONS FOR DISCUSSION

1. Many states have laws setting maximum interest rates. Do you favor such laws? What effect, if any, do such laws have on the prevalence of "loan sharking?"

2. U.S. law presently requires federally chartered banks to allocate funds specifically to local neighborhoods the bank serves. Do you think this is a good idea?

3. The U.S. government often subsidizes and financially backs in one way or the other, through the World Bank or the International Monetary Fund (IMF), various loans to governments and others in developing countries. So people allege this contributed to the collapse in the late 1990s of many Far Eastern economies, by encouraging loans to unworthy borrowers. Do you favor this policy? What are its benefits and costs?

CHAPTER 11

Monopoly

Maybe you've noticed that many airlines will sell you a cheaper ticket if you agree to stay over Saturday night. What's going on here—do they just like people who spend weekends away from home? Suppose you hold a patent for a type of fuel cell that supplies power for environmentally friendly cars. The government and industry are beginning to purchase large numbers of these items from you. Your engineers suddenly tell you they can, at the same cost, make these fuel cells last twice as long. Would you produce this new product, or is it in your interest to suppress it? In this chapter we discuss the perhaps surprising answers to these questions and other aspects of monopoly behavior.

11.1 Monopoly versus Competition

In Chapter 8 we analyzed the behavior of firms operating in a perfectly competitive industry. Such firms are price takers. The owners of these firms have no power individually to set the price of their output. This price is determined by the impersonal interaction of many suppliers and many consumers. The classic example of such a firm would be a wheat farmer (and most other farmers selling in a national or world market). A huge amount of wheat is produced each growing season. It is literally traded on a world-wide basis. Moreover, wheat is easily stored, so that newly produced wheat competes with wheat in storage. No single farmer, or even a group of farmers can affect the world price by withholding part or even all of his or her production from the market. These firms can only respond to the price in today's market, and to anticipated future market prices. We refer to industries composed of such firms as perfectly competitive. The term competitive firm is taken to mean one firm operating in a perfectly competitive environment.

Since competitive firms respond to prices, it is meaningful to consider the amount of output the firm would choose to produce at various hypothetical prices. This schedule of output as a function of price, $q = s(p)$ is the firm's supply curve. This curve is the upward portion of a firm's marginal cost function, subject to the proviso that in the short run, average variable costs are covered. The reason for these rules is that the profit maximum for a competitive firm occurs where marginal cost becomes equal to output price. If price exceeds the cost of producing additional output, the firm can increase its profits (rents) by producing that additional output. Likewise, if output price is less than marginal cost, the firm would increase its rents by decreasing the amount produced. In the long run, so-called fixed costs are renegotiable, and become part of marginal cost and must then be considered.

The polar opposite of perfect competition is an industry composed of just a single firm. Such a firm is called a **monopolist**, the term **monopoly** being derived from Greek and meaning, literally, one seller. In contrast to competitive firms, monopolistic firms do not respond to a price set in the market; rather, they themselves decide, on the basis of how much output they choose to produce, what the price of the product will be. A monopolistic firm faces the industry demand for its product. That demand curve is the usual aggregate demand schedule derived from individual demands; it is downward sloping. Figure 11-1 shows a hypothetical demand curve for a monopolistic firm. Since the monopolist can choose to produce a little or a lot, the price that the output sells for can be low if the monopolist chooses to produce a great deal, or high if the monopolist

Figure 11-1 *Pricing Possibilities for a Monopolist*

A monopolist, being the only seller in a market, chooses the price in deciding how much to produce. The monopolist is a price maker; competitive firms are price takers.

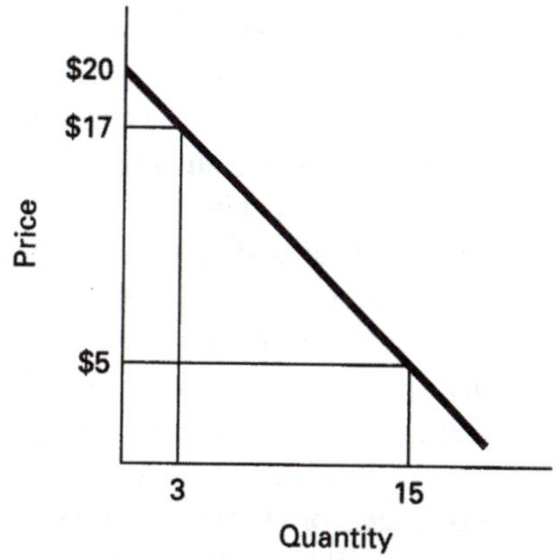

chooses to produce very little. If, for example, the monopolist chooses to produce a few units of output, say 3 units, the price will be relatively high, shown as $17. This is close to the reservation price of consumers of $20. If the monopolist chooses to saturate the market and produce 15 units, where consumers' marginal values of the good is close to zero, the price will be the relatively low value $5.[1]

In this case, where the firm itself determines what price to set, it makes no sense to speak of a supply curve. The firm doesn't respond to hypothetical market prices, it sets the price itself. The decision about output level and output price are really the same, since either one determines the other through the demand curve. How then does a monopolistic firm decide how much to produce? We can be sure that the firm won't price itself out of the market entirely, by choosing a price close to consumers' reservation price, nor will the firm give the product away free (even though it would sell many units). What pricing strategy maximizes the firm's rents?

The reason why we make this inquiry is not so that we can all be good monopolists should we be so fortunate to someday be the sole supplier of some highly valued consumer product. Rather, because monopolies generally charge higher prices for goods than do competitive firms with the same costs, we suspect that in addition to transferring rents from consumers to themselves, monopolies can have adverse effects on economic efficiency. However, recognizing monopolistic behavior is rarely straightforward. We make this investigation partly because we want to be able to recognize monopolistic behavior when it occurs. In the United States and most other countries, monopolistic pricing is for the most part illegal. In order to determine that a given firm is acting monopolistically, we have to be able to identify what pricing strategies are uniquely monopolistic. We shall see that several types of actions are possible for monopolists, and the policies they adopt are likely to vary on the basis of certain aspects of costs.

---

1. A firm that is sufficiently large so that its decisions as to how much to *buy* affect the price of items purchased is called a *monopsonist*. For example, a large firm might bid up the price of labor in some market as it expanded employment. We leave these monopsony problems to a more advanced text.

Monopolies are easier to describe on paper than to identify in the real world. The problem is that with the exception of some agricultural firms, for example wheat farmers who sell wheat identical to other farmer's wheat in an international market, virtually all firms face a demand curve that is downward sloping to at least some degree. The corner dry cleaner could probably raise their prices a bit without losing all business to a competitor. Retailers always have some advantage over others not located in the same neighborhood. If the market is construed narrowly enough, then all firms become monopolists. There are rarely two retailers of the same type, e.g., two cleaners, two hardware stores, two groceries on the same city block. If the market in which they operate is defined as that city block, then they are all monopolists. Yet no economist would regard these firms as monopolists. Sometimes, however, the answer is not clear. Since monopolies are generally illegal and substantial penalties can sometimes be extracted from firms whom the courts have deemed monopolistic, the identification of markets and monopoly power sometimes becomes the focus of large lawsuits. For example, until the age of personal computers, the IBM corporation was completely dominant in the market for computers. In early 1969, on the last day of President Lyndon Johnson's administration, the Justice department filed an anti-trust suit against IBM. The case was fought in the courts until 1982, when the Reagan administration dropped the suit on the basis that it was without merit. Was IBM a monopoly? IBM had achieved its position by selling computers and computing services for *less* than what other firms had been able charge. At this writing, the government is in trial against the Microsoft Corporation over essentially the same issues. Microsoft's Windows software is currently installed on approximately 95% of home personal computers. Microsoft argues this came about because this software was better and cheaper than the competition. It is a problem about which reasonable people can disagree.

The possibility that new firms can enter a market is always present to some degree, and this affects a firm's pricing decisions. If a firm is the only producer of some good, but new firms could easily form to supply the good at about the same price, is the existing firm a monopolist? There are always firms competing on the fringe. When markets are **contestable**, economists tend to downplay the existence of monopolies. In recent years, IBM's dominant position has in fact changed dramatically due to the development of inexpensive personal computers (PC's) and competition from relatively new firms such as Apple, Dell, Compaq, HP and the like.

The existence of monopoly depends on the presence of not just identical goods supplied by other firms, but also on the presence of similar goods in the market. The Kimberly Clark Corporation has a monopoly on "Kleenex" brand tissues. No other company can use this copyrighted trademark. Yet we do not consider Kleenex to be a monopoly because of the presence of many similar brands, and also cloth tissues. In the 1980s, the Fotomat corporation installed small kiosks on street corners where customers dropped off film for processing. Fotomat was sued under the antitrust statutes because they were alleged to have a monopoly in street corner developing. The firm argued it had no monopoly power at all since it competed with all of the neighborhood processing stores, e.g., most pharmacies, discount houses, etc. The service provided by the regular retail stores was not the exact same service, but was similar. Fotomat nevertheless lost the case, and, though small consolation indeed, vindicated its contention of lack of monopoly profits by soon going bankrupt. We shall defer these interesting problems of determining monopoly power and proceed with the analysis of firms that face downward sloping demand curves.

Reasons for Monopoly

It's not easy to somehow become the sole supplier of some good. Usually, markets are characterized by many firms competing with each other for consumers' dollars. What would account for the emergence of a single firm in some industry? For this to occur, there must be **barriers to entry** into that industry. Otherwise, either new firms or existing firms producing a similar product would enter this line of business and destroy the monopoly position of the original firm. These barriers, or restrictions on the abilities of other firms to compete can occur because of the actions of governments or government agencies, or because the underlying technology results in a single firm being the least cost method of producing the good. We discuss two prominent legal restrictions on entry and one major reason stemming from cost considerations.

1. *Government Licensure* The simplest reason why monopolies sometimes exist is that governments occasionally grant a firm the exclusive right to serve a given market. Prior to 1978, the Civil Aeronautics Board (CAB) regulated domestic airlines in the United States. The CAB allocated routes and set air fares between all domestic cities in the U.S. Frequently, only one airline was allowed to fly between two cities, even though other airlines routinely petitioned for that right. These are instances of government-created monopolies. The interstate trucking industry was regulated in a similar manner by the Interstate Commerce Commission (ICC) until the mid 1980s, with similar results.[2] Many states presently grant exclusive trucking rights to firms serving two destinations within that state. Perhaps the most famous licensed monopoly in history is the Hudson's Bay Company, which was formed in 1670 by Royal Charter of King Charles II of England. The British Crown gave the company the exclusive right to trade in all territories draining into Hudson's Bay in Canada, an immense territory. The company is still in existence, and in the same general line of business, though minus the exclusive trading rights.[3] The United States government gave itself a monopoly in postal service in 1872 when it passed the Private Express Statute. This law forbids anyone other than the federal government from operating a postal service. (Its first victim was the famed Pony Express, a private operation.) Today, it is legal to use express services such as Federal Express, Airborne, etc., as long as the shipment is considered urgent. If the shipment does not require an immediate response, it is against the law and shippers have been fined amounts equaling the postage that would have been collected on all such shipments if they had been sent by first class mail.

Government licensure most often reduces the number of firms in an industry, but not necessarily down to a single firm. Many people argue that government

2. The ICC was in some ways particularly perverse. Trucking companies were often granted the exclusive right to ship a particular good from city A to city B (usually via something other than the shortest route), but were not allowed to ship any goods from B to A! They had to return the trucks empty. The CAB, at least, never said that airlines could fly passengers only East to West, or only North to South, but not the other way.

3. For a fascinating discussion of the history of this company and the way it responded to changing economic conditions, see *Economics, Organization and Management* by Paul Milgrom and John Roberts (Prentice-Hall, 1992).

licensure of teachers, lawyers and doctors unduly reduces the number of such practitioners and raises the cost of their services to consumers. With entry into the market restricted, the regulations may create a market which is not perfectly competitive, but not monopolistic either. Industries in which only a few firms are dominant are sometimes referred to as **oligopolies** (literally, few sellers). We analyze such markets in Chapter 12.

2. *Patents and Copyrights* The framers of the U.S. constitution recognized that ideas were easily stolen, and that this might deter individuals from spending their resources in the quest of improving technology, developing new products, creating new written works and the like. People are unlikely to invest their life savings in order to develop a new word processing program, if everyone can without cost or legal penalty copy the program onto their own computers. In order to encourage the development of these new tools and ideas, inventors are allowed to **patent** the devices they develop which achieve a certain end. Similarly, authors can **copyright** their written works, so that others must pay some fee for the use of that work. (The distinction between patents and copyrights is not always clear, though consider the following. If a company develops a new way of etching a computer circuit onto a silicon chip, it can patent that process. It cannot patent the very idea of using silicon for computer chips; it can only patent a particular process for achieving the result. On the other hand, the software (computer programs) that operates the circuits can be copyrighted.) In both cases, these laws assign ownership, or property rights to certain ideas. The owner can thus charge for the use of these tools and benefit from their development. A patent usually lasts for 17 years, after which the invention reverts to public domain (becomes common property); copyrights last for 50 years beyond the author's lifetime.[4]

The framers of the constitution were aware that these laws created the possibility of monopoly in the markets for goods using these patents or copyrights. For example, the Polaroid corporation holds a patent on the only commercially viable process for developing pictures in about a minute. They therefore have a monopoly on such cameras and film. Microsoft has a copyright on the MS-DOS and Windows operating system for personal computers. The company's founder and co-developer of these operating systems, Bill Gates, has become a billionaire many times over from the profits these programs generate, which are used on tens of millions of personal computers (PCs) worldwide. Pearson Custom Publishing has a monopoly in Principles of Microeconomics texts written by Eugene Silberberg, though Silberberg's profits are reputed to be less than Bill Gates.'

The extent to which these patents create important instances of monopoly power is an empirical question, and open to debate. Some have argued, for example, that the dominance of Microsoft's operating systems in the PC market has created an illegal monopoly. However, Microsoft has to compete with Apple, UNIX, Linux and other operating systems. Also there is the possibility that someone might develop a still better system that would replace theirs. Likewise, Polaroid must still compete with cameras using ordinary film, for which processing time has sharply decreased in recent years. Silberberg's text must compete with other texts of a similar nature. Thus although economists agree

4. It may surprise you to find out that the song Happy Birthday is still under copyright and you may owe its composers royalties for all those birthday parties you once attended and used their product.

Figure 11-2 *Decreasing Average Cost*

When average cost continually decreases as output increases, one firm will eventually drive all others out of business by producing the entire output of the industry.

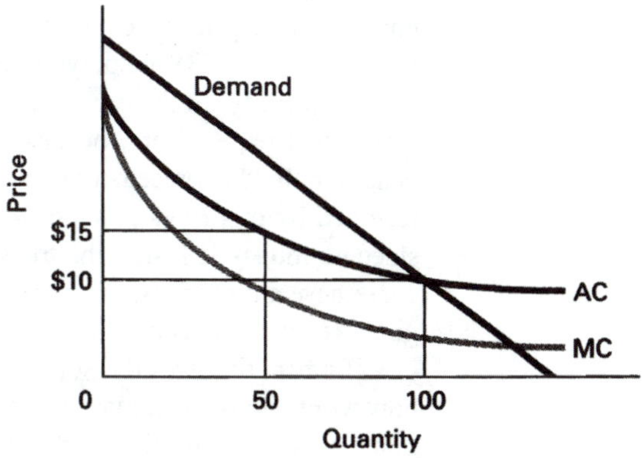

that the potential for monopoly domination exists with patents and copyrights, the empirical significance of the problem is less easy to evaluate.

3. *Decreasing Cost Industries* The most prominent reason for the emergence of a single, dominant firm in an industry for other than legal reasons, is the presence of decreasing average costs of production. Consider Fig. 11-2, which shows a market demand curve for some good, and the average and marginal cost curves for an individual firm producing that good. In this case, a single firm can always produce the good at less cost than if two or more firms entered the market.

If one firm produced 100 units, the average cost of the units would be $10. If two firms each produced 50 units, the average cost would be $15. But then, one firm could profit by increasing output and undercutting the other's price because of the lower unit cost. Eventually, one firm would drive all the others out of business and produce the entire output itself.

The various utilities (gas, water, electricity, telephone services) are the most prominent examples of industries in which decreasing average costs seem to be the case. The provision of these services, say, electricity, involves substantial set-up costs such as electrical generators and power lines, which are then largely fixed, that is, independent of the amount of electricity produced. The marginal cost of generating additional units of electricity are small, producing decreasing average total cost as output increases. If two firms were to provide the same neighborhood with electricity, the cost would likely be higher than if one firm provided it all. It is therefore likely that the market for electricity and the other utilities would consist of a single dominant firm in each of these products. Because people have been concerned that the resulting private monopolies might charge consumers unduly high prices, these services are generally provided either as government-run monopolies or as private firms regulated by government agencies.

11.2 Monopolistic Pricing

To better illustrate the issues, consider the demand schedule first used in Chapter 2, displayed in Table 11-1. Column (1) indicates a schedule of prices running from $10 down to $0, and the quantities consumers purchase at those prices are in column (2). At prices equal to or above \$11, consumers make no purchases; \$11 is the reservation price. When price is lowered to \$10, consumers purchase 1 unit; when the price is lowered further to \$9, consumers purchase 2 units, and so forth. Column (3) displays the amount consumers spend for all units, price × quantity. In the earlier chapters on consumer theory, we called this construct total expenditure, because we were at that time focusing on consumer behavior. In the present context, this total expenditure is the **total revenue** received by this monopolistic firm. Total revenue is exactly total expenditure, since no money is lost in the transaction. From the standpoint of the firm, however, these are receipts, not expenditures. We will discuss the last column, Marginal Revenue (*MR*) in a moment.

If a firm that was the sole supplier of some good faced this demand curve, how would it go about maximizing the rents derivable from that monopoly position? What it would like to do, if it could, would be to charge \$10 for the first unit sold, \$9 for the second, \$8 for the third, and so on, as long as these amounts received were greater than the cost of providing each additional unit. This pricing strategy is known as **perfect** or **first degree price discrimination**; it clearly yields the maximum possible rents. For each unit sold, consumers pay their marginal value of that unit, the maximum amount of other goods (measured in money) they are willing to forego in order to obtain another unit of this good. Although this is clearly the rent maximizing pricing structure, we rarely, if ever observe it in the real world. The fundamental reason why this behavior is so rare is that in order for it to occur, the monopolist must actually know how much consumers are willing to pay for each succeeding unit. Detailed knowledge of this sort about consumers' demand curves is very difficult to secure. Consumers are always reluctant to reveal to sellers the maximum they would pay for given units. These marginal values would have to be estimated by varying the price and observing the quantities purchased. In addition to this estimation problem, the price discrimination between consumers would break down if the consumers who pay only, say, \$3 for one unit, could resell the good to those who would pay a higher amount.

Table 11-1

(1) Price	(2) Quantity	(3) Total Revenue	(4) Marginal Revenue
10	1	10	10
9	2	18	8
8	3	24	6
7	4	28	4
6	5	30	2
5	6	30	0
4	7	28	–2
3	8	24	–4
2	9	18	–6
1	10	10	–8
0	11	0	–10

For the present, therefore, let us exclude the possibility of price discrimination, that is, charging different amounts to either the same consumer, or between consumers, for identical units of the same good. We inquire as to what single price would maximize the monopolist's rents. Recall from Chapter 3 that total expenditure (total revenue) is at a maximum when the elasticity of demand is unity. Therefore, if there were no costs of production, the largest rents would occur by setting the price at the level where the demand curve was unitary elastic. (For straight line demand curves, this occurs at the midpoint of the demand curve.) At that price and quantity, consumers' total expenditure (total revenue to a monopolistic firm) and thus profits, since there are no costs, are maximized. However, in the presence of costs of production, the rent maximizing price cannot be determined from the demand curve alone. The cost of production must also be considered. We know as a general rule that net benefits (in this case rents to the firm) are largest whenever the incremental benefits accruing to the resource owner from any given action fall to the level of the incremental costs of that action. In particular, if a firm can, by producing an additional unit of a good receive an increase in revenue greater than the cost of producing that unit, its rents will increase if it produces the unit. This logic implies that rents to the firm increase until the additional revenue that the firm receives from the sale of the good, which we call **marginal revenue**, falls to the level of marginal cost.

For the demand curve displayed in Table 11-1, the additional, or marginal revenue the firm receives when it endeavors to sell an additional unit of output is shown in column (4). When the price is \$10, 1 unit is sold; producing revenue of \$10. If the firm lowers the price to \$9, the firm sells 2 units and receives \$18 in total revenue. The incremental revenue the firm receives by selling the second unit is \$8, the difference between the revenue that occurs when 2 units are sold versus when 1 less is sold. If the firm further lowers its price to \$8, consumers are induced to purchase a third unit, producing total revenue of \$24. Since revenue increases from \$18 to \$24 when the third unit is sold, the marginal revenue of 3 units of the good is \$6 = \$24 – \$18. All of the numbers in column (4) are the differences between the total revenue at that level of output and the total revenue accruing to the firm when 1 less unit is sold.

In every instance (except for the first unit), the marginal revenue associated with a given output level is less than consumers' marginal value of the good at that quantity, indicated by the price charged. Consider the change in revenue when price is lowered from \$10 to \$9. Previously, the first (and only) unit sold generated \$10 in revenue. Although a second unit is now sold for \$9, the firm now *loses* \$1 on the first unit, because its price falls by \$1, from \$10 to \$9. Thus marginal revenue $MR = \$9 - 1 \times \$1 = \$8$. If the price is lowered to \$8, the firm receives \$8 in additional revenue from that third unit it sells. However, the previous 2 units now sell for \$8 instead of \$9, so the firm loses \$1 on each of them. Thus $MR = \$8 - 2 \times \$1 = \$6$, as shown in the table. If the price is lowered to \$7, $MR = \$7 - 3 \times \$1 = \$4$, and so forth. The reason why marginal revenue is less than price is that in the absence of the ability to perfectly price discriminate, in order to induce consumers to purchase an additional unit, a monopolist must lower the price on all units sold. The monopolist cannot simply lower the price of the last unit offered. When a lower price is set, all units are sold at that lower price. The revenue from the sale of the previous units sold therefore decreases by the amount of those units times the decrease in price. If there were no costs of production, the monopolist would evidently set a price of either \$5 or \$6, and receive maximum revenue of \$30.

We have utilized this same reasoning with regard to marginal and average quantities on two previous occasions. In the analysis of common property in Chapter 7, we discussed why the marginal product (*MP*) is less than average product (*AP*), when *MP* is falling. When the firm hires an additional laborer, that person lowers the marginal product of all the previous workers, because of the law of diminishing returns. Under common property, when the average product equals the alternative wage, the marginal product is less than that alternative wage. Likewise, in the analysis of freeway congestion in Chapter 9, when an additional car enters a crowded highway, it slows all the cars already on the road. The marginal cost of a car entering the freeway is the average travel time plus the product of the number of cars formerly on the road and amount each is slowed down. For this reason, the marginal cost is greater than the average cost. In the present instance, the price paid by consumers is the average revenue received by the firm, since it is the per unit amount received by the firm. Marginal revenue is this amount adjusted by the decrease in price received on all the other units sold, and so marginal revenue is less than the price.

As we showed in Chapter 3, marginal revenue is closely related to the elasticity of demand at that quantity level. We can show the result easily using calculus (but it is virtually impossible to show without it).[5] Define the demand curve in terms of quantity for mathematical convenience, as $p = p(q)$; total revenue (expenditure) $TR = p(q)q$. Using the product rule for differentiation, the change in revenue as quantity changes, *MR*, is the derivative of *TR* with respect to q:

$$MR = TR' = p + q\left(\frac{dp}{dq}\right) = p\left[1 + \left(\frac{q}{p}\right)\left(\frac{dp}{dq}\right)\right] = p\left[1 + \frac{1}{\epsilon}\right] \tag{11-1}$$

Note that when $\epsilon = -1$, $MR = 0$. At this point, *TR* (total revenue) is at a maximum. When $\epsilon = -2$, say, $MR' = p/2 > 0$, so *TR* increases as q increases (equivalently, as p decreases). We leave it as an exercise to show that with a linear demand curve $q = a - bp$, $\epsilon = -p/[(a/b) - p]$; $\epsilon = -1$ when $p = a/2b$, the midpoint of the demand curve.

Suppose now for simplicity the marginal cost of production is constant at \$3. That is, additional units of output can be produced a \$3, at any level of output. What is the profit-maximizing price and output level, assuming only a single price can be charged? The monopolist clearly makes money producing the first unit of the good. He (or she) can charge \$10 for this unit thus making a \$7 profit. If the monopolist decides to sell 2 units, he will set a price of \$9, *but \$9 is not the additional revenue he receives from selling a second unit.* Revenue increases by only \$8 over selling 1 unit, because the price of the first unit is reduced from \$10 to \$9. Notice in Table 11-1 that at 2 units of output, $MR = \$8$. However, since marginal revenue still exceeds the marginal cost of producing 2 units (\$3), monopoly rents are still increasing. In like fashion, the marginal revenue derived from the sale of the good is greater than the marginal cost of production for units 1 through 4, so total rents no longer increase. Profit or rent

5. Those without knowledge of elementary calculus can skip this derivation. Equation (11-1) is, however, an important result to keep in mind.

maximization occurs when $MR = MC$. Allowing for fractional units as in past calculations of this sort implies profit maximization at 4 units of output.

Figure 11-3 shows the pricing strategy for monopolists.[6] Again, we assume for simplicity the marginal cost curve is constant at \$3. The consumers' demand curve corresponds to the numbers used in Table 11-1. The marginal revenue curve *MR* corresponds to the numbers in column (4) in Table 11-1. The height of this curve shows the additional revenue received by firm from selling an incremental unit of output. For example, at 4 units of output, *MR* is \$3, but the price the monopolist charges consumers is \$7. If the monopolist were to try to sell a 5th unit, he or she would have to lower the price to \$6. However, the price of the preceding 4 units sold must also be lowered by \$1 each, and so *MR* is lower than the price, by the \$1 for each of those 4 previous units. Thus at 5 units of output, $MR = \$2$.

In Fig. 11-3, the profit-maximizing output for the monopolist is 4 units. This is the point where $MC = MR$. At output levels less than 4, the additional revenue gained by producing an increment of output, measured by the height of *MR*, is greater than the incremental cost of that output, measured by the height of *MC*. Thus greater net rents will accrue to the monopolist if that additional output is produced. Likewise, at output levels greater than 4 units, where $MC > MR$, the monopolist would gain by lowering output.

The *price* at which the monopolist sells this output is \$7. At this price, consumers voluntarily purchase all that the monopolist wishes to sell, 4 units. Price is greater than the marginal revenue by \$3. The total expenditure by consumers on this good, which is equal to the firm's total revenue (*TR*), is \$28. The total cost (*TC*) of producing 4 units (excluding fixed, or sunk costs) is the area under the *MC* curve between 0 and 4 units. Similarly, just as total cost is the area under the marginal cost curve, total revenue is the area under the marginal revenue curve. Monopoly rents are therefore the area *ABC*, the sum of the differences

Figure 11-3 *Monopoly Pricing*

A monopolist chooses the output where $MR = MC$. Using the numbers in Table 11-1, this is at 4 units of output. The price charged is the height of the demand curve at 4 units, \$7.

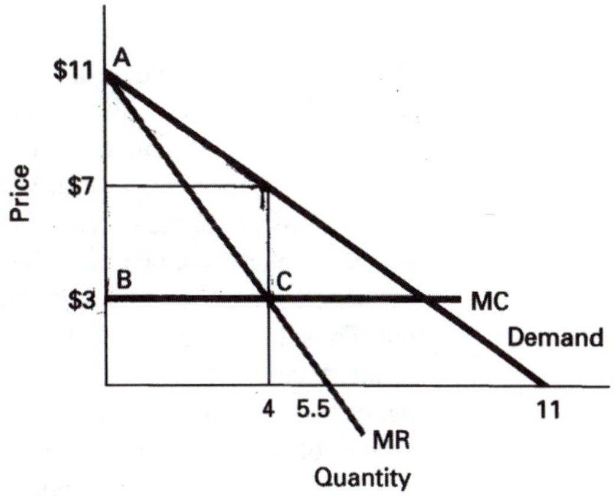

6. Because we use discrete numbers in this example, the actual marginal revenues are a little off. The demand curve in this example is $p = 11 - q$, $TR = pq = 11q - q^2$, $MR = d(TR)/dq = 11 - 2q$. Thus allowing for fractional units, when $q = 4$, $MR = 3$.

between *TR* and *TC*. That is, *ABC* is the sum of the excess of *MR* over *MC* for incremental outputs. When production just begins, this excess, representing the rents derivable on the first unit, is *AB*. As production continues, these rents diminish, until they become zero at point *C*, where $MC = MR$. It is clear that the monopoly rents, measured by the area between *MC* and *MR* are greatest when output is 4 units.

A monopolist will never choose to produce a quantity in the inelastic portion of the demand curve, because the firm could always increase profits by decreasing output. With inelastic demand, lower output implies both lower total cost and higher total revenue, hence higher total profits. Since the marginal cost of production must be positive, and the quantity chosen by the monopolist is where $MR = MC$, marginal revenue must be positive as well. Using equation (11-1), it follows that the elasticity of demand must be greater than 1 in absolute value terms: $MR = p[1 + 1/\epsilon] > 0$ and since $p > 0$, $\epsilon < -1$. A monopolist always prices the product so that consumers are in the elastic portion of the demand curve. For the case of straight line demand curves, such as in Fig. 11-3, *MR* intersects the horizontal axis at half the distance to *OC′*. (Thus for straight line demands, the slope of *MR* is twice the slope of the demand curve.) At the midpoint of the demand curve (not shown), the demand is unitary elastic; this is the point of maximum total revenue or expenditure, but not maximum total profits. At quantities less than this amount, 5.5 units, demand is elastic; total revenue increases as quantity increases and thus *MR* is positive. At quantities greater than halfway along the demand curve, demand is inelastic, so increases in quantity decrease total revenue, and thus *MR* is negative.

11.3 Monopoly and Efficiency

In our previous analysis of competitive markets, the creation of rents has meant the production of goods in excess of the alternative value of the resources used up. It means that net benefits are being generated. It might be tempting, therefore, to conclude that since monopoly rents are greatest at 4 units of output, that this level of output is economically efficient. However, as we have shown previously, the economically efficient level of output is where consumers' marginal value of each good equals the marginal alternative cost of that good. This output level is 7 units, where the consumer demand curve intersects the marginal cost curve. At 4 units of output, where the monopolist chooses to operate, consumers' marginal values of the good still exceed the marginal value of the resources used. Net benefits of \$3, the excess of marginal value over marginal cost are available on incremental production at that point. As production increases further, these net benefits, measured by $MR - MC$, decrease, becoming zero at 7 units of output. Thus the sale of this good by a monopolist results in the loss of net benefits of the triangular area *DCE* in Fig. 11-4. This welfare or deadweight loss is analogous to that caused by the imposition of a sales tax. A monopoly is one of a variety of legal or economic institutions that can cause the economy to move away from a Pareto efficient point, where all gains from exchange are exhausted.

The analysis of Coase suggests that lost gains from trade can only persist when transactions costs are high. As in the case of the wandering cattle discussed in Chapter 9, the potential for gains from trade should lead the parties involved to seek some sort of contract to capture at least some of these mutual

Figure 11-4 *Inefficiency Due to Monopoly Pricing*

The economically efficient output, where consumers' marginal values equal the marginal cost of production, is 8 units. A monopolist, however, produces 4 units. This monopolistic contraction of output results in a deadweight loss of mutual benefits represented by the area *DCE*.

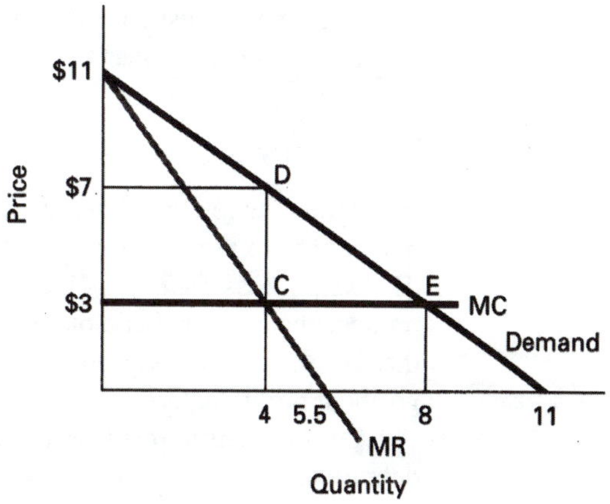

benefits. Indeed, this deadweight loss would not exist if the monopolist could perfectly price discriminate among his or her customers. Price discrimination, however, is never easy to do. Contracting with consumers in this fashion requires considerable knowledge, and perhaps stealth. It is such a more expensive contract than simply setting a single price, it rarely, if ever appears. Thus high transactions costs prevent complete exhaustion of mutual benefits.

The problem of monopoly, from the standpoint of scientific economics, is the potential loss of efficiency it creates, measured by the area *DCE* in Fig. 11-4. In the public's mind, the problem most likely is the perceived injustice of some person or corporation receiving these rents. This, of course, is a value judgment which we leave to the reader. We should be kept in mind, however, that although monopolists may receive these rents, they do not necessarily have to keep them. The government usually has ample means to rearrange the distribution of income through taxation. Thus the problem of allocative inefficiency can in principle be separated from questions about equitable distributions of income.

A few attempts have been made by economists to estimate the size of the deadweight welfare loss in the U.S. economy. In a famous study, Arnold Harberger of the University of Chicago attempted to add up the triangular areas of deadweight loss for 73 industries.[7] Harberger estimated the average cost (*AC*) in each industry and calculated the amount by which price exceeded that value. By using an estimate of the elasticity of demand, he then estimated the amount by which output would increase if price were lowered to *AC*. He thus had a measure of the change in output and price caused by possible monopoly power in each industry. Using the formula for the area of a triangle (½ base × height) he calculated the areas of deadweight loss for each industry. His calculations showed a welfare loss of only 0.1 percent of the gross national product. That is, the potential costs of monopoly were only a tiny portion of the output of the entire economy. Other

7. Arnold C. Harberger, Monopoly and Resource Allocation, *American Economic Review, 44,* May, 1954, 77–87. Harberger expanded his analysis to the distortionary effects of taxes in a later article, Taxation, Resource Allocation and Welfare, in *The Role of Direct and Indirect Taxes in the Federal Revenue System,* Princeton, 1964.

economists have criticized Harberger's calculations on the grounds that it ignored the expenditure of resources to obtain monopolies and because the behavior of the owners of monopolistic firms might be less efficient than the owners of competitive firms. It is still an open question.

Monopoly and Factor Markets

Apart from the loss of potential gains from trade due to monopolistic contraction of output from the level where price equals marginal cost, depicted as the area of deadweight loss *DCE*, it is important to inquire as to whether such a firm will produce that monopolistic output level efficiently, that is, at least cost. That is, is there some further loss to be expected from the way a monopolistic firm would go about hiring factors of production and arranging for production?

Consider a firm that tries to maximize its net rents, or profits, which are, by definition, total revenue minus total costs. In symbols,

$$profits = \pi(q) = TR(q) - TC(q)$$

where total revenue *TR,* and total cost *TC* are shown explicitly to depend on the level of output q produced. Once the firm decides what output to produce, the total revenue, $TR(q)$ gained from the sale of that output is determined. The quantity produced will be the profit-maximizing output for a monopolist. At that output, price is determined by the demand curve. By multiplication of price times quantity, total revenue is implied. Since $TR(q)$ is now a fixed number, maximization of profits requires that at that output level, total costs, $TC(q)$ be as small as possible. That is, *profit maximization requires that whatever the profit-maximizing level of output turns out to be, it must produced at the minimum cost.* Profits can always increase if the same output (and therefore the same revenue) is available at less cost. This reasoning does not mean that monopolists seek to reduce costs by cheapening the product, or otherwise adulterating it in ways a competitive firm would not. Profit maximization simply requires minimizing at the cost of whatever output the firm chooses to produce.

The preceding analysis implies that monopolistic firms are inefficient in terms of the output they choose to produce (they produce too little), but not in the means by which that output is produced. We expect them to use the same inputs in production, and in the same proportion, as would a competitive firm that chose that particular output level. Consider again the reasoning we discussed in Chapter 7 by which firms decide what input levels they use. If a firm produces output q with two inputs, labor (L) and capital (K), the firm will hire these inputs until the value to the firm of the additional output produced by each factor equals the respective cost, or wage of that factor. In the case of competitive firms, where all output is sold at the market price p, the value of the additional output produced by, say, labor, is the marginal product of labor times the price of the good. Thus, for competitive firms,

$$p \times MP_L = w_L \text{ and } p \times MP_K = w_K \tag{11-2}$$

where again, MP_L and MP_K are the marginal products of labor and capital, and w_L and w_K are the unit wages paid to labor and capital. By division, we find the marginal cost of producing output is the same for either input:

$$MC = \frac{w_L}{MP_L} = \frac{w_K}{MP_K} \quad (11\text{-}3)$$

In the case of monopolistic firms, however, as the firm tries to sell additional output, the price of the product falls. The additional revenue the firm receives from expanding output is not the output price *p*, but rather marginal revenue *MR*. Therefore, for a monopolistic firm, the value of the additional product is *MR* times marginal product, rather than price times marginal product. Modifying equation (11-2) in this way, the firm hires additional units of each factor until

$$MR \times MP_L = w_L \text{ and } MR \times MP_K = w_K \quad (11\text{-}4)$$

Performing the same kind of division as before, the marginal cost of output is again the same for either input. Thus at the profit maximum,

$$MR = MC = \frac{w_L}{MP_L} = \frac{w_K}{MP_K} \quad (11\text{-}5)$$

Equation (11-3) thus applies to monopolistic as well as competitive firms. Therefore, the presence of monopoly in the output market does not imply any loss of mutual benefits in the input or factor markets. If the input markets are competitive, meaning the input prices are not affected by the decisions of any one firm, then resources are allocated efficiently there, given the output level chosen by the monopolistic firm.

Monopoly and the Characteristics of Goods

An important question in the theory of monopoly is whether industries characterized by such firms instead of perfect competitors produce either a different mix of goods or alter the characteristics of the goods, such as their quality or durability. In particular, economic commentators have sometimes claimed that monopolists would tend not to introduce new products, say more durable ones, that would cause fewer units to be sold. Consider the following problem, first posed in this manner by Professor Jack Hirshleifer of UCLA. Suppose you are the only producer of incandescent light bulbs because of a patent owned by your company. (This characterizes General Electric's position in the light bulb industry in the first part of the 20th century.) Suppose your engineers suddenly inform you that they have discovered a way to make the bulbs last twice as long, at no additional expense. Would you produce the new bulbs, or would you try to suppress the invention?

One's first reaction to this question often is that the firm would suppress the invention, because with more durable bulbs, fewer will be sold, leading to lower profits. This reasoning, however, ignores the possibility that the firm can charge more for the new bulbs, and also, as we shall see, ignores the law of demand. Consider first that what consumers desire is not the bulb *per se,* but rather the light the bulb produces. Consumers have a demand for well-lit rooms, that is, a demand for light. The demand for light *bulbs* is derived from the pleasure accompanying the availability of light. Figure 11-5 depicts a downward sloping

Figure 11-5 *The Demand for Light*

The demand for light bulbs comes from the demand for light. If the service consumers desire can be produced at lower cost, a monopolist stands to gain, since she or he can produce the same output at lower cost. With the lower *MC* curve, monopoly rents expand from *ABC* to *ADE*. Thus monopolists are not likely to suppress cost-saving inventions.

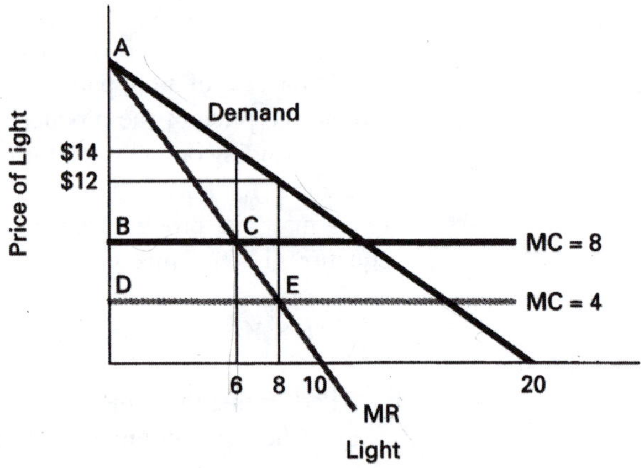

demand curve faced by a monopolistic producer of light bulbs. Notice that the quantity on the horizontal axis is light, not light bulbs. Consumers have a downward sloping demand curve for light, as they do for all goods. Also drawn are two marginal cost curves, drawn horizontally for convenience. The marginal cost of producing light (via bulbs) is assumed constant for simplicity. Prior to the discovery of the new bulbs, the marginal cost of additional units of light is $8 per unit of light. The monopolist produces 6 units of light, the quantity where the marginal cost of producing light equals the marginal revenue received (point *C*), and sets charges $14 per unit of light. Some price of light bulbs is implied by this price of light, but we defer discussion of this.

The monopolist's profits (more correctly, the rents he or she receives due the patent on light bulbs) consist of total revenue less total cost at 6 units of output. Total revenue is the area under the marginal revenue curve (*MR*); total cost is the area under the marginal cost curve $MC = 8$. Net rents on the patent are therefore the triangular area *ABC*.

Consider now the situation when the engineers produce a more durable light bulb, say, one that lasts twice as long. The marginal cost of producing light is now one-half of the previous cost. It is depicted by the lower marginal cost curve, $MC = 4$. The new profit maximum occurs at point *E*, where *MR* intersects this marginal cost curve. Output of light expands to 8 units, and the price of light falls to $12. The net rents to the firm are now necessarily larger. With the lower marginal cost of producing light, net rents become the larger area *ADE*.

How do these additional profits come about? Recall that a firm can always benefit by lowering the cost of the profit-maximizing level of output. In this case, the engineers have discovered a way of producing the same amount of light at half the price. Since this on its own would save half the cost of that output, profits must increase by this cost saving. Since the new bulbs last twice as long as the old ones, consumers would be willing to pay up to twice as much for the new bulbs. But in addition, since the marginal cost of producing light has decreased, the price at which light is sold at decreases as well, from $14 to $12. Because of the law of demand, the amount of light consumers demand necessarily increases. With the lower price of light, the new bulbs will sell for less than twice the old price.

It is ambiguous as to whether the amount of new bulbs sold is greater or less than the amount the monopolist sold previously. If, due to the lower price of light, the amount of light consumed expands in greater proportion than the increase in durability of the bulb, then not only will more light be consumed, but more light bulbs as well. In any case, if the invention is utilized, more light will be consumed, consumers will receive a greater amount of consumers' surplus, and the monopolist will receive greater net rents on his or her patents. Therefore, it is likely that a monopolist will not suppress a cost-saving invention such as this.

In the early twentieth century, the Safety Razor was invented by a traveling salesman, King C. Gillette. It consisted of a flexible thin two-edged blade and a small holder. Previously, the straight blade was the primary tool for shaving as is still sometimes done in barber shops. The safety razor was a vast improvement in comfort and safety, and probably contributed to the large scale disappearance of beards. The device remained essentially the same for a half century, though the blades improved. The best blades on the market yielded about three shaves each; then a new blade had to be used. Those of us old enough to remember regarded the fourth shave as a close approximation to Russian Roulette. By the early 1960s, the Gillette company was the dominant producer of safety razors, supplying about ninety percent of the market. At that time, Gillette patented a stainless steel blade that gave 10 or more shaves per blade. In fact, the important patent concerned coating the sides of the blade with the newly invented nonstick plastic Teflon which lowered the friction associated with cutting through the hair, and dramatically improved the comfort and safety of the device. (The first blades were produced by the Wilkinson Sword Company of Great Britain with a royalty to Gillette.) Why, however, would a company produce a product which would almost certainly lead to less blades sold when it had the ability (at least for a while) to suppress that invention?

The preceding analysis shows why Gillette could make more money with the new blade than with the older technology. Consumers demand shaves. The demand for razors is derived from this goal. The new blades lowered the cost of shaves. The quantity of shaves consumed and the available consumers' surplus therefore increased. With a lower price of shaves, some consumers shifted from electric devices to the new blade technology. Consumers snapped up these new blades at 15¢ apiece, even though the older Blue Blades sold for 5¢. Gillette was thus able to increase its own rents due to the patent.[8]

In the preceding examples, not only does the producer gain by introducing the cost-saving invention, but consumers gain as well. If a horizontal marginal cost curve is shifted down, then, unambiguously, both monopoly rents and consumers' surplus increase. However, for more general cost relations, greater net benefits for consumers is not implied. It is always the case that a producer gains if the same output can be produced at a lower total cost. Total revenue is unaffected and total cost decreases, increasing net profit. Since total cost by definition is average cost times total output, lowering the total cost of a given output level is equivalent to lowering the average cost curve. In the simple examples

8. As an interesting sidelight, stainless steel blades (without the Teflon) were introduced and withdrawn a generation earlier. They were much more expensive than ordinary steel blades and consumers found them not worthwhile. When the Teflon coating idea came along, it was a *cost saving* innovation to coat stainless blades, because the cost of the coating *per shave* is lower with the more durable blade.

above, the average and marginal cost curves were identical, being constant at some level. Lowering the average cost curve necessarily lowered the marginal cost curve producing greater benefits for consumers as well as for the producer. For the more general case of U-shaped average cost curves, however, a new technology might lower the cost of the initial units a great deal, but, near the old output level, actually raise marginal cost above its old level, still yielding lower total costs for that output. In this case, the producer gains by utilizing the new technology, but since the marginal cost curve in the relevant range of output is now higher than previously, consumers can be made worse off. Whether or not this is a significant empirical issue is an empirical question.

Monopolies and the Incentive to Invent

The preceding analysis started at the point at which an invention had already been created, with all costs of development already sunk, and then asked whether a monopolistic firm would avail itself of that invention. However, technological change does not occur out of thin air; research and development (R&D) costs inevitably accompany the invention of new goods or new techniques for production. Therefore, it is important to inquire as to whether the incentives to invent (produce technological change) are affected by industry structure. In particular, if a firm has a monopoly in some industry, would the firm's monopoly position lead it to spend less resources on R&D than it would if the firm faced many competitors?

Though there is an extensive literature on this subject, the question does not admit an easy answer. One important issue affecting the outcome is the degree to which firms can capture the benefits of their expenditures on innovation. Suppose a firm currently sells 100,000 units of some good. If it figured out a way to produce the good at $1 less per unit, it would stand to make $100,000 additional profits in the current year alone. If the firm could patent the invention, the value of the patent would be the present value of the increased profits derived from its use over the life of the patent. Treating these future receipts as a perpetuity for convenience, with an equity rate of return (real interest rate plus a risk premium) of 10%, the present value of the patent might be, say, $\$100{,}000 \div .10 = \$1{,}000{,}000$. Thus under these conditions, the firm would be willing to spend up to a million dollars in order to develop such an innovation.

Ideas, however, are easily stolen, even if one has a valid patent. A firm or person can patent a particular process for achieving some result, but there may be similar processes not covered by the patent. Once a firm has demonstrated a more efficient technique, competitors may be able to largely duplicate the process without violating the patent. That is, information often falls into the public domain and becomes common property despite the efforts to enforce ownership. In that case, the return from developing the invention may be greatly diminished, thereby reducing the incentive to engage in R&D. However, the enforcement of rights to the innovation may be less costly if the firm has a monopoly in the good which uses the patented process. In that case, a monopoly would have a greater incentive to engage in R&D than would a firm in a competitive industry. This problem is similar to the common property problem in ocean fishing, where it does not pay for any one fisherman to invest in saving fish for the future, because enforcing rights in the additional future fish created is next to impossible.

A further issue is the dissipation of rents that may accompany the race to develop new patentable processes. Suppose no one yet knows how to reduce the cost of the preceding product by $1. In an industry of many firms each producing the 100,000 units of the good, each firm has an incentive of up to $1,000,000 to develop the cost-saving innovation. The danger is that the research could take the form of a "race to the pole," where only the winner—the single firm that develops the invention first—is able to patent the process, and the resources spent by the competing firms in the development race are therefore lost. In this situation, the uncertainty of who will be first to develop a new process creates a common property problem. Too many resources are used to produce the ultimate innovation: the research expenditures of the successful firm plus the research expenditures of all the unsuccessful firms as well. The combined expenditures of the unsuccessful firms could total even more than the net benefits to consumers from the invention. This dissipation of rents may be avoided if the firm is a monopolist. However, new firms always have an incentive to try to move into an industry by creating a new process or good using some cost-reducing patent. In fact, R&D is probably one of the more important anti-monopoly devices available in the private market. The extent to which these issues are empirically important is the subject of ongoing research in economics.

Patents and Market Structure

Suppose you own one of the preceding firms producing 100,000 units of a good, and suppose there are 9 other firms producing like amounts of the same good, in perfect competition with your firm, so that 1,000,000 units of the good are sold each year. Suppose you patent a process for lowering the cost of the good by $1. Does this create an incentive to monopolize the industry? As with much of this analysis, the answer is indeterminate.

There are two prominent methods by which you can exploit the new production process, ignoring any antitrust actions of the government for the moment. One strategy is to attempt to monopolize the industry by selling thc good for slightly less than that all other firms. The other is to *license* the process to your competitors. If firms have constant costs, that is, horizontal marginal cost schedules, then lowering the price of the good by just a little will drive all the other firms out of the industry. If your firm can expand output at the same marginal cost, without any increase, your firm then stands to make almost a $1 profit on the total industry output, or $1,000,000 total. However, at your new marginal cost level, the old price might actually be above the monopoly price. In that case, additional profits are available by lowering the price and expanding the amount sold due to the law of demand. (The firm could not charge a monopoly price above the original price because the old firms would reenter the industry.) If all this holds true, and there is no violation of the antitrust statutes, then a monopolistic industry is the likely outcome.

Suppose, however, all firms (yours included) have upward sloping marginal cost curves, so that the marginal cost of production rises with increased output. In this case, although you could sell the product for a dollar less than everyone else initially, as you tried to expand output to take advantage of the disappearance of firms from the market, your marginal cost rises to the old level. If these costs rise fairly quickly, then the same firms will likely be able to compete with you as before. Your invention shifts your marginal cost curve down (or to the right), shifting the industry supply curve to the right, and thereby lowering the market price and increasing the amount sold. Each firm sells the good where price equals marginal cost. However, with your lower costs, you now derive greater rents on the specific factors of production in your firm, in particular, the patented process, while the other firms derive smaller rents on their specific factors or the entrepreneurial abilities of the owners. With these assumptions, the industry remains perfectly competitive.

Finally, consider the possibility of licensing rights to your patent to your competitors. Each firm would be willing to pay an annual fee equal to the amount saved by using the patent. This amount depends on the shape of the marginal cost curves with and without the patent. With horizontal (constant) marginal cost, each firm derives no rents from producing and selling this good. It might be costly to exit the industry and thus the other firms might pay something for the patent in order to avoid that fate. With rising marginal costs for each firm, use of the patent allows greater profits; the firm would therefore be willing to pay up to the amount of those greater profits. Or, a firm could pay a once-and-for-all license fee in the amount of the present value of all future increased rents. However, the decision by the firm with the patent to offer licenses depends on whether their increase in rents is greater by that route versus possibly monopolizing the industry.

11.4 Price Discrimination

Firms that face downward sloping demand curves have more than one strategy for exploiting their market power, that is, their power to set prices and alter the terms of trade in their own favor. One strategy is to adopt the simple monopoly pricing strategy described in Fig. 11-4. This strategy produces larger net rents to the firm than competitive pricing, because the firm is able to capture some consumers' surplus in the process. That is, some benefits that would go to consumers as consumers' surplus, if the market consists of many firms, now goes to the seller in the form of monopoly rents. However, simple monopoly pricing leaves potential gains from trade unexploited. In Fig. 11-4, these gains comprise the area *DCE,* and represent losses of efficiency in the economy. But this raises another, perhaps more fundamental question. Why would a firm that was either lucky enough or clever enough to have a monopoly position in some market leave these further gains from trade on the table? Why not attempt, by some more complex pricing schemes, to extract additional consumers' surplus and producer rents from the triangle of lost benefits *DCE*?

One method by which firms with the power to set prices attempt to increase their net rents is to engage in **price discrimination**. This term refers to any pricing scheme by which some consumers pay a different amount for the identical goods or services than other consumers. Firms sometimes are able to identify certain groups of buyers whose demand for their product is relatively more inelastic than other buyers. For example, many people who drive their cars to and from work could easily commute on public transit and, faced with small increases in the cost of commuting by auto, would switch transport modes. Others, such as outside sales representatives may use their car a great deal to see widely dispersed customers; these consumers would continue to use their cars even faced with substantial increases in the price of gasoline. Yet all these consumers pay the same price for gasoline, and for their cars. No individual firm is able to exploit the relative inelasticity of the latter group's demand. The reason for this uniform price is easy to understand. Suppose the consumers with the relatively inelastic demand (the salespersons) were in fact all known to all sellers (quite a heroic assumption, in fact). If one firm decided to charge them a higher price than other consumers, it would immediately be in the self-interest of another seller to charge just a bit less. This slightly lower price would still exceed this firm's marginal cost, and thus that firm's profits would increase. But another firm would soon undercut the second firm, and so on and so on, until the price is reduced to each firm's marginal cost of production.

A firm that is the sole supplier of a good, however, has selling options not available to perfect competitors. If, at relatively modest expense, the firm can identify customers according to the intensity of their demands, the firm may be able to increase its profits by separating the two (or more) segments of the market, and charging relatively higher prices to those consumers whose demands are relatively least elastic. However, the firm can't simply ask its customers if they are especially anxious to consume the good, and charge a higher price to those who respond affirmatively. Consumers will not cooperate in this endeavor. In order to be able to separate the market, some mechanism must exist so that consumers can identify the consumers with the more intense demand in spite of themselves.

Suppose for the moment that the consumers of some good indeed fall into two easily identifiable distinct groups. Some consumers, say, can relatively easily avoid the consumption of this good by using some substitute. Another group of consumers finds the alternative goods to be poor substitutes. These two groups of consumers can be characterized as having differing elasticities of demand at the same consumption levels. The first group's demand is relatively less elastic than the second's. How can such a firm exploit this information about consumers' preferences? A monopolistic firm in this situation essentially faces *two* demand curves:

$$q_1 = q_1(p_1)$$

$$q_2 = q_2(p_2)$$

This firm is able, if it wishes, to charge these customers different prices, depending on which group they are in. The firm charges price p_1 in market 1 and sells quantity q_1 there, and charges price p_2 to the consumers in the second market, and sells quantity q_2 there. The total output produced by the firm is the total sold in both markets, $q = q_1 + q_2$.

Since the firm faces two demand curves, it is confronted with two marginal revenue curves as well. Call these curves MR_1 and MR_2 respectively. Suppose the firm could, by selling 1 more unit in market 1 derive additional revenue of \$100, and suppose further that selling that last unit in market 2 would instead produce additional revenue of \$200. Then it is obvious that the firm will make derive larger profits if it sells that unit in the second market rather than the first. Moreover, suppose that at its current output level, the marginal revenue in the second market exceeds marginal revenue in the first market. Then it would pay for the firm to reallocate its output away from market 1 and into market 2. The loss of revenue in the first market will be more than offset by the gain in additional revenue in the second market. Anytime the marginal revenue is greater in one market than in another, the firm, without changing its total output, can increase its total revenue by transferring output from the market where MR is relatively low to the market where MR is relatively high. As the firm sells less in, say, market 1, MR_1 starts to rise. Likewise, as more is sold in market 2, MR_2 begins to fall. Eventually, there will be no differences in these values left to exploit. When $MR_1 = MR_2$, then for that particular output level, the total revenue of the firm is a large as possible.

What remains to be solved is exactly what output is best, from the firm's standpoint, to produce. We have already shown that profits are greatest when $MR = MC$. Since the firm is allocating output between the two markets so that marginal revenue is the same in both markets, the output that maximizes the firm's profits is where that common value of marginal revenue equals the firm's marginal cost of production. Thus, for a discriminating monopolist, profit maximization takes place where

$$MR_1 = MR_2 = MC \tag{11-6}$$

In other words, the monopolist always allocates output so that the marginal revenues in the two markets are equal, and produces the output level for which that common value of marginal revenue equals marginal cost.

Consider now what the equality of marginal revenues implies for the prices charged consumers in these two markets. Using equation (11-1), the first equality in equation (11-6) becomes

$$p_1[1 + 1/\epsilon_1] = p_2[1 + 1/\epsilon_2] \tag{11-7}$$

where p_1 and ϵ_1 are, respectively, the price charged and the elasticity of demand for the group of consumers in market 1; likewise p_2 and ϵ_2 are the price charged and the elasticity of demand in market 2. Equation (11-7) implies that consumers in the market with the more elastic demand will be charged a relatively lower price. Recall that a monopolist will never sell at a price where the demand is inelastic. Thus, the values of ϵ_1 and ϵ_2 must both be less than –1 (between –1 and $-\infty$). Suppose for example, $\epsilon_1 = -4$, whereas $\epsilon_2 = -2$. The demand in market 1 is relatively more elastic. Putting these values in equation (11-7) yields

$$p_1[1 + (1/-4)] = p_2[1 + (1/-2)]$$

and, after some arithmetic,

$$p_1 = \frac{\frac{1}{2}}{\frac{3}{4}} p_2 = \frac{2}{3} p_2$$

Thus with these values, the price the firm charges consumers in the market where demand is relatively more elastic, market 1, is only ⅔ the price charged in market 2, whose consumers are more committed to purchasing this good, as measured by their relatively less elastic demand. This result agrees with our intuition. The consumers who can more easily avoid this good, the ones with the more elastic demand, are charged a lower price than those who find the alternative goods relatively poor substitutes.

The market for air travel provides an interesting illustration of these ideas in actual practice (although the example is somewhat problematic for reasons we discuss shortly). Beginning in 1938 and ending in 1978, domestic airlines in the United States were regulated by the Civil Aeronautics Board (CAB). Under those regulations, a certain airline would often be granted the exclusive right to fly between two cities. Entry of new airlines essentially ceased; no new major (trunk) carriers were created during the entire period of regulation. Fares had to be approved by the CAB, and requests for price *decreases* on the part of competitors were routinely turned down. Under these regulatory conditions, various airlines had monopolies on air travel over given routes. A pattern of pricing emerged offering consumers who booked tickets well in advance of travel and who stayed over Saturday night a deep discount off of the regular coach fare. Why did the airlines adopt such a pricing strategy, as opposed to establishing some uniform monopoly price over a given route?

One group of fliers, families on vacation, is able to book reservations well in advance, and can plan alternate trips or destinations relatively easily. A second group of air travelers, business people, who are likely to be going to meetings or seeing distant clients, have much less flexibility in arranging trips. They typically call their travel agent and say things like "I need to go to Chicago tomorrow, then on to New Orleans, and return the following day." Moreover, business people rarely stay over weekends, while families on vacation frequently return during a following week. The vacationers clearly have a more elastic demand for air travel than the business people. What is required for price discrimination is, in the first place, a low-cost mechanism for identifying which consumers belong to which group. It is not possible to accomplish this identification simply by asking what type of traveler a person is; they will always claim to be a family on vacation.

In this particular market, however, the nature of the ticket customers request identifies the type of consumer they are. Customers who purchase tickets well in advance of travel are almost surely not business people on their way to important meetings. Likewise, customers who want to get somewhere tomorrow and return shortly thereafter are almost surely not vacationers. Airline travelers *self-select* (approximately, of course) into the two groups by the type of ticket requested. Therefore, if some restriction on purchasing the low-priced tickets can be devised that is easily satisfied by the vacationers and not easily satisfied by the business people, the airlines could accomplish the tricky task of separating the market. The mechanism that emerged was the requirement of advance sale with Saturday stopover in order to get the discount fares. By using this device, the market for air travelers has apparently been effectively separated. Business travelers, with the relatively less elastic demand, pay higher prices for air travel than do vacationers on the identical flights.

Although this explanation of airline pricing follows easily from the assumption of monopoly power during regulation, the pricing strategy continues to this day, when the airlines have been largely deregulated. Routes are no longer protected, and new airlines now enter and leave specific routes fairly routinely. The discounts for early ticket purchase and nonrefundability can be explained at least in principle by competitive cost cutting. It is common to see firms offer price discounts for advance purchase and nonrefundability; this reduces their uncertainty about the demand for their product or service and therefore allows more accurate (and thus cheaper) production planning. Theater goers, for example, often purchase nonrefundable tickets in advance, and ticket prices are higher at the door. The troubling aspect of airline pricing is the persistence of the Saturday stayover in the face of deregulation. However, gates at airports for planes are in some cases very restricted in supply, so the threat of potential competition may not be very great over some routes. It may be, therefore, that given the costs of setting up a schedule and instituting flights over a given route, the airlines still have sufficient monopoly power (effectively face a downward sloping demand curve) so that continued price discrimination is possible.

Other Forms of Price Discrimination

Although it is easiest to think of price discrimination in terms of observable differences in prices charged consumers, most price discrimination is more subtle. In addition to the "two-part" pricing scheme we just described, firms have devised more complicated strategies for separating buyers from their consumers' surplus. Consider for example how the Disney Corporation, which among other things runs Disneyland and Disney World, two theme parks with somewhat unique characteristics because of the trademark protection of the Disney cartoon characters, charges customers for entrance and use of these parks. Historically, Disney has at some times charged a high price for admission, and low or zero prices for the rides in Disneyland, and at other times has charged a relatively low admission price and high prices for the rides. What pricing scheme would lead to the greatest profits? Suppose you were the Polaroid Land Camera company, with patent protection on cameras that develop pictures in a minute. Would you sell the cameras cheap and charge consumers high prices for the film, or would you make the cameras expensive and the film cheap?

We analyze this problem using a famous antitrust case.[9] Computers were developed in the United States by the IBM corporation and by Sperry Rand (later Remington Rand) in the early part of the twentieth century. By the 1950s, IBM held a commanding market share in the industry. Most people in the 1950s through the 1970s in fact used the term "IBM machine" to *mean* computer. Computers in those days used IBM cards for data input. Data was entered on these cards by punching small rectangular holes in identifiable locations, and then this pattern was read by mechanical devices and converted to electronic form. The computers were useless without the cards and the mechanical data processors. IBM insisted that its customers purchase these cards from IBM and not from outside purveyors, claiming that its reputation would be damaged by faulty cards. Its profits on these cards was apparently substantial, as stipulated in documents filed in various court cases which alleged that IBM was trying to extend its monopoly position. IBM was apparently selling these cards at prices exceeding the marginal cost of the cards. Why did they attempt to extract monopoly rents by this means, as opposed to simply charging a higher price for sale or rental of the machines themselves?

Consider Fig. 11-6, which depicts a firm's marginal cost curve intersecting the industry demand curve at some point D. If the firm acted as a competitive firm, it would sell 20 units at $10 per unit, where marginal cost = price. In this case, consumers would derive consumers' surplus of *CBD* and the firm would receive rents of *ABD* on its specific factors of production. Gains from exchange

9. See John S. McGee, *Industrial Organization,* Prentice-Hall, 1988, for some fascinating reading on this and other anti-trust cases.

Figure 11-6 *All or Nothing Pricing via License Fees*

A monopolistic firm can try to extract consumer's surplus from its customers by selling the right to consume the good. Consumers would be willing to pay the consumer's surplus they receive, *CBD,* for the right to purchase as many units as they want (20) at price $10. With this pricing mechanism, there are no deadweight losses. This strategy is most practical if consumers have similar demand curves for the product, though it is not common.

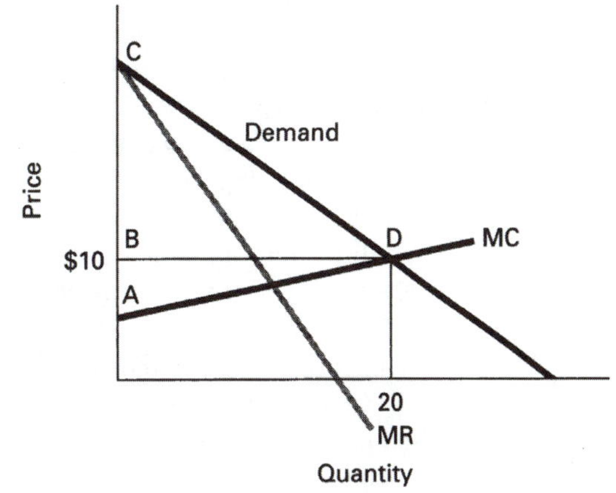

would be exhausted, but the firm would not receive any gains from its monopoly position in the market. Suppose now the firm knew the position of the demand curve. One scheme for capturing all of the consumers' surplus is to engage in perfect price discrimination, as we discussed at the beginning of this chapter. Consumers would be charged prices close to their reservation prices for the initial units, and gradually lower prices for increased quantities, moving down the demand curve until point *D* is reached. However, this grandiose scheme has rarely, if ever, been used. It would require extensive knowledge of all consumer's marginal values of the good at all quantities—quite a tall order.

However, suppose it is the case that all consumers' demands for this good are identical. For the moment, let the demand curve depicted represent the demand curve for any one consumer of this good. Then the firm could extract the entire consumers' surplus by the device of first charging a *license fee* for the right to purchase any units of the good at all, and then charging a price per unit actually purchased. The consumer derives consumer's surplus in the amount *CBD* dollars when $10 is charged. Therefore, the consumer would be willing to pay up to *CBD for the right to consume 20 units at price $10 per unit.* Therefore, by charging its customers first a license fee in the amount of *CBD* for *the right* to purchase the good at $10, and then offering as many units as the consumer desires at that price, the firm receives the entire area under the demand curve as revenue from the sale of this good. It could repeat this with all its customers, and therefore capture all of the potential gains from trade for itself.[10]

Notice that in order to effect this strategy, the firm need not know beforehand the actual shape or height of the demand curve. It has to believe the demand for the good is similar across consumers. In that case, with some experimentation regarding the setting of the license fee, the firm might reasonably approximate the theoretical limit of rent expropriation. Notice also that the largest rents are derivable when the firm sets price = *MC.* If the price charged is above marginal cost, then some area of mutual benefits is lost, because consumers will purchase less than 20 units. In order to capture the entire area *CBD,* consumers must

10. Strictly speaking, the license fee would be the *present value* of *CBD.*

be induced to purchase 20 units, no more and no less. This is accomplished by setting price equal to $10.

License fees are common in the software industry. Consumers pay a once and for all fee for the right to install and use a computer program on the customer's computer. Thereafter, the price of using the software is effectively zero, reflecting the inability of the software developer to meter the use of the program, but also the approximately zero marginal cost of actually using an already installed program. Golf clubs around the country usually charge a large once and for all fee for joining plus relatively high annual dues, but a low price for actually playing a game of golf on a given day. This is consistent with the general lack of available golf courses in metropolitan areas, giving private clubs some monopoly power, and the license fee pricing strategy just discussed.

Consider now the case of IBM machines which ran only with IBM cards, and perhaps the case of film which can be developed in a minute, but only in a patented camera. In these cases, the purchase of the computer or camera is equivalent the license fee. Buying the computer gives one access to computing, the camera gives one access to pictures in a minute. If all consumers were identical, the producers of these computers, say, would maximize their rents by charging the area of consumer's surplus, *BCD,* for the machine itself. The cards would then be sold at the marginal cost of producing the cards. If this marginal cost were constant, the computer company would not even care if the customer purchased the IBM cards from them or from some outside vendor, since no rents could be earned on sale of the cards. Likewise, the Polaroid camera company would derive the largest return on its patented process for charging a high price for the camera, and a low price (the marginal production cost) for the film.

Suppose, now, that consumers are not alike. Some wish to do extensive computing, say, and others have only a light to moderate demand. If the computer company could identify which consumers were which, it might get away with charging a higher computer price to those customers whose demand is greatest. This information, however, might get around to consumers, and the anti-trust authorities tend to look on such pricing schemes with great disdain. What IBM apparently did, was to charge a price *in excess of MC* for the cards. By so doing, they gave up part of the area of mutual gains. But this price structure allowed them to discriminate between the intensive users versus those with lower demand. *The cards were a metering device for measuring the intensity of demand.*[11] The relatively heavy computer users used more cards in the process. By charging in excess of *MC* for the cards, IBM was able to differentially capture some of consumer's surplus from their customers. If the same fee were charged to all, the light users would have abandoned the use of computers altogether. With this pricing system, the heavy users paid more for the computers than did the light users, though it came about through the price of the cards. It is probably for this reason that IBM strenuously resisted efforts on the part of its customers to purchase their cards from less expensive, peripheral vendors.[12]

11. This argument is due to Professor Aaron Director, who taught for many years at the University of Chicago Law School, and who was an editor of the *Journal of Law and Economics* published there.

12. IBM's position on this matter was that peripheral vendors sold a less reliable product, which would in turn damage IBM's reputation for quality. See John S. McGee, *Industrial Organization,* op. cit.

This technique has been tried by others. The Chicken Delight corporation, for example, once had extensive franchised outlets on the West Coast. The company sold ready-to-eat chicken. The corporate office insisted that the individual franchisees purchase their paper goods (napkins, etc.) from Chicken Delight, and no one else. The franchisees resisted because they found they could purchase the same goods cheaper at the local discount chain. In this case, the parent corporation was price discriminating in setting fees for being a member of this franchise, using the paper goods the same way IBM used the computer cards. Since the busier franchisees had more customers, they also used more napkins, and so the parent corporation was able to meter the success of the individual outlet by the amount of paper goods used, and to charge a variable royalty fee on that basis. This technique for price discriminating has been tried by many franchisers at various times.

Price Discrimination and Efficiency

Price discrimination is almost universally regarded with disdain, mainly on ethical grounds. The practice treats people differently—charging people different amounts for the same good. It rubs against many people's egalitarian sensitivities. From the standpoint of economics, these are value judgments and are left to individuals to decide for themselves. Economics does inquire, however, whether price discrimination promotes or impedes economic efficiency. That is, if price discrimination is forbidden (which it is, under United State antitrust law), does this enhance the realization of mutual gains from exchange? The answer, unfortunately, is generally unclear, except that it is possible to state unambiguously that price discrimination certainly does not imply less efficiency. Moreover, some compelling arguments have been made in its favor.

Consider again the case of perfect, or first degree price discrimination, where the monopolist captures the entire area under the demand curve by charging consumers successively lower prices for each additional unit purchased. This pricing strategy is in fact economically efficient. Output is produced where price equals marginal cost (point *D* in Fig. 11-6). With no further actions, the monopolist reaps all the mutual benefits, but it is still the case that the efficient level of production has taken place. What many people might object to is the resulting distribution of income—all the rents go to the monopolist. However, the government has the power to redistribute those monopoly rents through the use of taxes. The problem of *allocation* is often separable from that of *distribution.* In comparison with the single price monopoly solution, in which too little output is produced, first degree price discrimination plus some redistribution of rents to consumers leads to greater net benefits to the firm and all consumers concerned, because the area of deadweight loss is eliminated. Of course, the ability of the firm to engage in this degree of price discrimination, and the likelihood of the government coming up with the appropriate tax scheme with which to compensate consumers is easily questioned. However, the example shows that price discrimination is not *per se* inefficient.

Consider now the more difficult case of two-part price discrimination. In this case, some consumers pay more than the simple monopoly price while others pay less. In comparison with simple monopoly, therefore, some consumers gain while others lose. The net effect of this type of price discrimination is therefore ambiguous. There are, however, some famous special cases. An important question is how this type of price discrimination affects the level of output produced by the monopolist. If output decreases on account of price discrimination, then the area of deadweight loss is certainly increased, leading to further diminution of mutual benefits.

Suppose instead that price discrimination leads to no change in total output. That is, the same output appears when the firm price discriminates as with simple monopoly pricing. It is well known that this is the outcome when the demand curves in the two separated markets are both linear.[13] In this case, price discrimination again leads to efficiency losses. With simple monopoly pricing, too little output is of course produced, leading to inefficiency on those grounds. However, there is no further loss of mutual benefits. Recall that mutual benefits exist when and only when consumers' marginal values of some good differ. With a single (monopoly) price, all consumers purchase the good until their marginal values fall to this same price, and thus no further benefits exist in terms of consumers retrading the good amongst themselves. Thus although too little is produced for overall efficiency, there are no further losses. Contrast this with the case of price discrimination when the same total output is produced. With the same monopoly output, the identical deadweight loss of efficiency occurs due to too little production. However, since consumers now face different prices, it would be possible for consumers to generate mutual benefits for themselves by retrading the good amongst themselves. Some consumers who purchased the good at the low price could resell the good to those who purchased it at the high price, at some mutually agreeable intermediate price. Since the same deadweight loss occurs in any case, and price discrimination produces a situation where still further mutual benefits are possible, it must be the case that when output is unchanged by price discrimination, a greater amount of mutual losses occur with price discrimination than with single monopoly pricing.

Suppose, however, price discrimination actually leads to greater output (as it does in its limiting case of perfect, or first degree price discrimination). Then it is possible that price discrimination reduces the losses created by monopoly (we say, it is *welfare* or *efficiency increasing*). The increased output reduces the area of deadweight losses due to monopolistic contraction of output. However, since efficiency is necessarily lower in the special case where output is unchanged by price discrimination, small increases in output accompanying price discrimination could still be less efficient than simple monopoly. If output expands sufficiently, the resulting reduction in deadweight loss might more than offset the losses created by unequal consumers' marginal values.

Some economists have defended various instances of apparent price discrimination on the grounds that it is or was welfare increasing. Before the widespread appearance of medical insurance, many physicians charged their more well-to-do patients higher prices for medical services than their poorer patients. Doctors claimed that only by this means were they able to serve patients who could only pay little or nothing for their services. The late Professor Reuben Kessel, then of the University of Chicago, argued in a famous paper that licensing of doctors, that is, forbidding the practice of medicine by anyone other than a licensed physician, allowed artificial restrictions on entry into the medical profession, creating monopoly rents for physicians. Even so, price discrimination

13. The first person to demonstrate this result was Joan Robinson, in *The Economics of Imperfect Competition,* published in 1933.

could not occur unless physicians had a mechanism for preventing price cutting by other doctors. Kessel argued that the ability of the American Medical Association (the AMA) to control access to hospital privileges provided that enforcement mechanism. Doctors who did not go along with the arrangement could in principle be denied access to hospitals, diminishing their abilities to earn income, especially in the surgical fields.[14]

Consider also the pattern of airline prices discussed previously. In the days of regulation, the airlines sometimes had youth fares. Persons under 21 were given discounts, though in some instances this was for standby travel only. Even today, senior citizens are given discounts not available to others. It could be that the airlines do these things because they like youths and seniors. However, it seems more likely that such discriminatory practices occur because separation of the market into these segments has proved profitable. Youths and especially retired persons are groups of potential customers with more flexible schedules and therefore more elastic demands for air travel. It is not surprising to see these consumers paying a lower price than middle-aged travelers, whether on business or not. By making airline travel more available to these groups, such price discrimination might be welfare increasing.

CHAPTER SUMMARY

- Monopoly is the polar opposite case of perfect competition. The industry consists of a single firm that decides what price to set, based on the demand curve it faces and its marginal cost curve.
- Monopolies are easier to define on paper than in actual practice. If the industry is defined narrowly enough, say, all firms on a given block, then all firms would be defined as monopolists. Similarly, owners of trademarks and brand names might be misclassified as monopolists.
- A critical question is the availability of close substitutes. With many similar goods available, a firm would probably not be a monopolist, even if no other firm produced exactly the same good. Also, the existence of *potential* competitors is an important determinant of a firm's monopoly power.
- Government licensure is one reason for monopolies. Sometimes the government prevents competition by restricting the number of firms that can enter a certain business.
- Patents and copyrights can also give some firms monopoly power. The framers of the U. S. constitution realized this but felt (with some justification) that invention and innovation would be difficult without this protection of intellectual property.
- Decreasing average costs with increasing output is another reason for monopoly. A large firm can sell at a lower price than a small firm, so the industry tends to be dominated by one large firm.

14. See Reuben Kessel, Price Discrimination in Medicine, *Journal of Law and Economics,* October, 1958, 20–53.

- A monopolist sells at the output where marginal revenue (*MR*) equals marginal cost (*MC*). If the additional revenue received from selling an additional unit of output exceeds what it costs to produce that unit, the firm benefits by producing it. Profits are at a maximum when the additional revenue received from selling a unit of output equals what it costs to produce that last unit.
- Marginal revenue is everywhere less than price, because in order to sell more units, the monopolist must not only lower the price of that last unit, it must lower the price on all the previous units sold as well. As a result, the output level is less than where marginal cost equals consumers' marginal value of the good, the height of the demand curve at that output. As a result, monopolists sell less output than the efficient output level where price equals marginal cost.
- Although monopolists produce an inefficiently low level of output, they make the largest profits by producing that output at least cost. Thus wealth maximization implies there are no additional costs of monopoly beyond contraction of output.
- Because monopolists have an incentive to produce any good or service at least cost, cost saving innovations will generally be adopted by such firms. Since ideas are often expropriable by competitors, monopolists may have an advantage over firms in competitive industries in capturing the benefits of their own research and development costs.
- Monopolists can sometimes increase their profits by price discrimination. If the firm can identify and separate consumers whose demand is relatively inelastic from those whose demand is more elastic, then selling goods at a higher price to the first group produces greater monopoly profits. It may or may not lead to less economic efficiency, and might possibly increase economic efficiency.
- Price discrimination can be subtle. One famous explanation for why a franchiser, for example, would insist that a franchisee's paper goods be purchased from the parent company at prices above marginal cost (and above the retail discount house price) is that it allows the parent company to charge a higher franchise fee to the busier (and thus more profitable) outlets.

REVIEW QUESTIONS

1. What is a monopoly? Is it ever the case that a firm produces a good for which literally no comparable good exists?
2. Explain why a monopolist sets $MR = MC$
3. Why will a monopolist never set a price in the inelastic part of the demand curve?
4. Explain why economists say that monopolists produce too little, and be sure you are clear about what that means.
5. Explain what perfect or third degree price discrimination is and why it leads to an efficient allocation.

6. Explain why a discriminating monopolist sets the marginal revenues in the two separate markets equal to each other and to marginal cost.
7. Explain why if price discrimination results in the same production level, price discrimination is welfare decreasing relative to simple monopoly.
8. What is the fundamental reason why monopolists probably will not suppress cost-saving inventions?

PROBLEMS

1. Show that with a linear demand curve $q = a - bp$, $\epsilon = -p/[(a/b) - p]$; $\epsilon = -1$ when $p = a/2b$, the midpoint of the demand curve.
2. Explain why no supply curve exists for a monopolist.
3. Why doesn't a monopolistic firm produce the level of output such that the demand elasticity is unity, since that is where the largest revenue is generated?
4. Explain why monopolistic industries are apt to lead to "deadweight losses," i.e., economic inefficiency.
5. Since patents and copyrights are legal grants of potentially monopoly power, why do economists defend them on efficiency grounds? Have you ever illegally copied a copyrighted computer program onto your computer? What effects does such activity have on the development of intellectual property?
6. Explain why a monopolistic firm's marginal revenue curve lies below the demand curve. Would this be true if the firm could price discriminate perfectly among consumers?
7. Suppose two firms located in completely separated markets produce the same product. They use the same inputs and face the same input prices. However, one firm is a monopolist in its market, while the other firm is in a perfectly competitive market. If both firms produce the same amount of output, will they use the identical levels of inputs? Explain.
8. Suppose a monopolistic firm operates two plants, with marginal cost curves MC_1 and MC_2 respectively, and faces a marginal revenue curve MR. Explain why the firm would operate the plants at outputs where $MC_1 = MC_2 = MR$. That is, the firm will utilize each plant so that the marginal costs are equal, and that common value of marginal cost will be equal to marginal revenue.
9. Is it true that monopolists tend to produce goods that are less durable than what perfectly competitive firms would produce?
10. Would a monopolistic firm ever sell a good at a low price in one market when it can get a higher price in another market?
11. Suppose one firm was the only retail supermarket in the area, while another had a monopoly in funeral services in that town. Which firm do you suppose would be more likely to engage in price discrimination, and why?

12. Suppose a monopolistic firm is found to be polluting the atmosphere. The government decides to tax the monopolist in order to encourage the monopolist to reduce the level of pollution produced.

    a. The government could of course tax the monopolist out of business altogether, thus reducing pollution produced to zero. Is this likely to be an efficient solution?

    b. Suppose the government levies some percent tax on the monopolistst's profits, e.g., 20% of profits. How will that affect output and the amount of pollution produced?

    c. What taxation measures should the government take to reduce pollution? Is your solution consistent with increasing overall economic efficiency?

13. Price discrimination is regarded unfavorably by the public, and is for the most part illegal under U.S. antitrust laws. When a monopoly will exist no matter what, does price discrimination necessarily compound the problem of inefficiency?

14. Suppose that by sufficient lobbying, a firm may get the government to grant it a monopoly in some market. Why is the amount of loss due to monopoly greater than the standard "deadweight loss" triangle where consumers' marginal values exceed marginal cost?

15. Many movie theaters charge less for children under certain ages, and for adults over certain ages (senior citizens). Is this a sign that movie theater owners like small children and older adults more than young and middle-aged people? If not, why do they adopt this pricing strategy?

CHAPTER 12

Imperfect Competition

There's this great scene in the movie Moscow on the Hudson, where Robin Williams, playing a Russian circus musician who has just defected to the United States is sent out to buy some coffee for the family who has taken him in. He sees one brand of coffee after another on the shelves—something he never saw in the Soviet Union—and he becomes more and more frantic because he previously never had more than one brand to choose from. He finally hyperventilates and passes out. Multiple brands of goods are a hallmark of free market economies. Does this represent waste, with Coca Cola and Pepsi each spending millions to get us to drink their brand? What function, if any, do these and other brand names serve for consumers?

12.1 Monopolistic Competition

In the preceding chapter we analyzed a polar case of market structure, monopoly, where an industry consists of only one firm which decides for itself what the profit-maximizing price and output shall be. We contrasted this with perfect competition, where many firms sell essentially the same product and no single firm, through its own actions, can affect the price of the product. Between these two extremes is a continuum of cases where more than one, but less than many firms all sell the same or a similar product. If the firms are few enough in number, it may be advantageous for the firms to act in unison on prices and other output decisions. That is, the firms may be able to increase their profits by emulating the behavior of a monopolist. In order to do this, they have to *collude,* that is, to coordinate, in secret (because these actions are almost always illegal) their collective output and pricing decisions. If the firms can successfully contract with each other to emulate in some way the decisions of a monopolist and prevent the entry of new firms, they can share the resulting monopoly profits and increase their wealth as compared with competitive behavior. We shall deal with these types of industries—**oligopolies**—(literally, from the Greek, *few sellers*), later in the chapter.

Absent such collusion, each firm competes with the other firms in the industry, as in the case of perfect competition. However, the product that each firm sells may not be identical to that of its competitors. The computer hardware industry, for example, seems highly competitive at present. In addition to the Apple computers, there are dozens of firms making Microsoft Windows based personal computers (PCs). The prices seems to drop almost every other week. Though Windows is the dominant software for home PCs, several other operating systems such as UNIX, Apple, and the newer Linux are available. There are also many other firms such as Hewlett-Packard, IBM, Digital Equipment, Cray, Prime etc. that manufacture more advanced computers for industry and research. These machines (in a given class of specifications) are similar but not identical. In addition, the ancillary services offered by the manufacturers are not identical. Some companies (for example, IBM) have a large network of support staff to help customers, and will probably be around in at least the near future, should something in the computer need repair. Other companies are "fly-by-night" operations that assemble the computers in someone's garage, using components of uncertain quality. You usually get the most bang for the buck with these unknown brands as long as nothing goes wrong, in which case large service costs may be encountered. Some brands or stores sell walk-in service with replacement machines available, whereas others require service by mail.

Each manufacturer has a monopoly in its own brand. No one can sell Apple computers except Apple. These brand differences are a component of what is referred to as **product differentiation**. It means, among other things, that each firm faces a demand curve that is downward sloping at least to some degree, as opposed to horizontal for firms in perfect competition. For this reason, economists frequently attach the modifier monopolistic to the term competition to industries composed of firms selling differentiated products that are not seen as perfect substitutes by consumers.[1] The entire phrase "monopolistic competition" is used because we recognize that the situation faced by computer firms, say, is different from both the cases of the wheat farmer selling a product literally identical to others in a world market, and, for example, the monopoly position of the phone company. Each of the computer firms must compete with other manufacturers selling goods of a very similar nature. The demand curve each firm faces, while downward sloping to some degree, is likely to be highly elastic due to the ready availability of close substitutes. By contrast, while there are means of communicating other than by phone, there is no alternative service as directly comparable to telephones as are different brands of computers to each other. Moreover, even if another firm could legally enter the local telephone business, important cost considerations (for example, very high set-up costs for such an operation) make this a difficult prospect.

Economists generally agree that in industries consisting of many firms selling similar though not identical products, monopolistic profits are soon destroyed by the entry of firms selling closely related goods. It would be difficult to argue, for example, that the Dell computer corporation derives monopoly profits from its brand name. This would show up as an enduring high rate of return for its investors, and other companies would immediately copy their strategies with their own brands. Compaq, Dell or other brands in this industry can only derive rents from their specific factors of production, if any, which enable them to produce computers more efficiently than other firms.

Though profits of these monopolistically competitive firms are zero in the long run, economists have debated whether product differentiation creates monopolistic inefficiency. If one applies the traditional monopoly diagram (Fig. 11-3) to firms in these differentiated industries, then even with zero profits, the price charged to consumers exceeds the marginal cost of production at the output produced. If that is the case, the output produced is too small, and apparent mutual benefits are going unclaimed. Inefficiency, however, implies that some alternate economic organization, or further contracting among consumers and producers would yield mutual benefits. This would be plausible if product differentiation were imposed on an industry from the outside, or if it created some lingering problem of common property. Neither of these explanations seems promising. In unregulated industries, this pattern of production is more likely a consequence of attempts to secure, rather than to reduce mutual benefits from exchange. The question of efficiency cannot be addressed without inquiring into the causes of product differentiation.

1. The term monopolistic competition is a bit *oxymoronic,* like jumbo shrimp, political ethics and the like.

Reasons for Product Differentiation[2]

In a small market only a few or perhaps a single type of some good may be offered. The general stores of the American frontier west sold only a limited variety of the goods carried, perhaps only a single type of soap, one brand or style of jeans, some elementary foodstuffs, etc. In modern markets, especially in metropolitan areas, product differentiation is carried to a seemingly vast extent. There are close to one hundred different types of breakfast cereals sold daily in the supermarket where I shop. There are dozens of types of beer and wine sold; about a dozen makers of ice cream each sell a dozen or more flavors in each of several types of frozen desserts-premium (high butter fat) ice cream, lower fat ice cream, low fat and no fat frozen yogurt and the like. Soaps come in dozens of colors, shapes and scents, and toothpaste is now offered in tubes and pumps, and varying degrees of abrasiveness, flavor and decay and plaque preventing additives.

The tremendous variety of goods offered for sale is such a pervasive phenomenon we hardly stop to consider why it has come about. It's actually news (sort of a "man bites dog" story) when some company decides to sell unbranded, or generic goods. In recent years, generic beer and cigarettes appeared in the market, but without much success. Corporations often spend millions of dollars promoting their own brand of some commodity, such as soft drinks, beer, or breakfast cereals. These advertising expenditures are viewed with suspicion by those who regard them either as wasteful or as nefarious attempts to monopolize some market. Why has all this product differentiation come about?

There are at least three important reasons why product differentiation exists.

1) *Preferences for goods vary across consumers.* Consumers have different tastes for most goods. Although differences in consumer products seem trivial to some, such as the color of one's detergent, these differences are not trivial to all consumers. In a famous instant coffee advertisement, the Folgers company supposedly substituted their instant product for fresh brewed coffee at a well-known restaurant. At least some customers allegedly did not notice the difference. In fact, many people cannot distinguish instant from brewed coffee, butter from margarine, diamonds from cubic zirconia, or Ralph Lauren from J.C. Penney's own house brands. People over the age of thirty generally cannot distinguish one new rock band from another. However, many other people can and do make these distinctions. Because these goods are perceived as different to many consumers, producers have an interest in accommodating those preferences. In large markets, where specialization is possible, it is common that enough separate consumers exist so as to make it worthwhile for producers to engage in the kind of specialized production valued by those consumers. If it were the case that literally no consumers could distinguish instant from fresh brewed coffee, then only one of those products would be produced—whichever was cheapest.

Sometimes people argue that consumers' demands for these goods would not exist but for the tremendous advertising producers engage in to promote their wares. It is true, of course, that if consumers were unaware of certain products, they wouldn't buy them, and product differentiation would be less. Advertising provides information about the existence of goods and also about their attributes. If information were free, informational advertising would indeed be a waste, but

2. Much of this derives from Yoram Barzel, "Meassurement cost and the Organization of Markets," *The Journal of Law and Economics* 25, April 1982, 27–48.

then again, if consumers already had all this information, the information would not likely be produced, since it lowers a firm's profits to create any unwanted good. Some advertising, however, seems intended only to convince us to buy one brand rather than another, for example, to buy Pepsi rather than Coca Cola. Moreover, some advertising seems blatantly false, or at best misleading.

It is not easy to distinguish this persuasive advertising from strictly informational advertising. People rarely want to consume information in some plain, technological fashion. We tend to prefer ads with memorable jingles featuring attractive people. Even for the most useful and beneficial products we can imagine, consumers sometimes have to be prodded over and over before they choose to make a purchase. All advertising is meant to persuade us to purchase a seller's products. If information was free, no advertising would take place. Misleading advertising is another consequence of costly information. Lastly, it is a very costly and risky strategy to try to persuade consumers to purchase goods they truly do not want. Ford Motor Company's famous Edsel fiasco, IBM's all but forgotten PC Jr., the tens of millions of dollars promoting movies such as Ishtar, Heaven's Gate and other notable box office bombs are testimony to consumer resistance to unwanted goods. It is hard enough to persuade consumers to purchase goods that are actually useful to them; convincing consumers to purchase goods they don't want is much more costly still, and a very risky business strategy.

2) *Even if preferences were the same for all consumers, differences in income produce different demands for goods.* On a recent trip to a store selling audio equipment, I noticed that each manufacturer had CD players and receivers priced from about $100 up to several hundreds of dollars or more. The same was true of virtually everything they sold. It seems clear that this instance of product differentiation is driven mainly by the variability in incomes of the consumers. The particular models of the same category of a good all do the same basic thing. CD players read encoded binary information for amplification in the receiver, which translates a signal to the speaker to convert varying electrical signals to audible sound. The more expensive equipment is able to recognize more subtle distinctions in frequencies and volume than the cheap stuff. Many people can hardly hear the difference. It seems likely that if everyone's incomes were the same, the degree of quality differences, in terms of the technical specifications of the equipment produced would be much smaller. It is of course true that some consumers would value subtle differences in the quality of reproduced music more highly than others with the same income. However, given that even the base models do a remarkably good job (author's assessment of this equipment), it seems that the budget of the consumer plays a relatively large role in the decision.

It is easy to find other examples where income differences likely account for a relatively large part of product differentiation. Although one can get from point *A* to point *B* in either a Ford Escort or a Mercedes, people with high incomes tend to choose cars like the latter rather than the former. It's not likely a case of different consumers' preferences for Mercedes. Even within the same brand, cars come with a variety of options, such as air conditioning, power windows, a more powerful engine. These options can amount to 50% of the price of a new car. People with very limited incomes seem to purchase cars with very few options, if any. Thus some part of the diversity of automobiles is driven by differences in consumer's incomes. As a last example, consider the variety of clothing available. Two similar looking suits or dresses can have very disparate prices depending upon the fabric used. A suit with very fine wool costs hundreds of dollars more than one with coarser fabric. A dress made of silk can be several times as expensive as the same dress made out of polyester, though the appearance is similar to many. The choices people make for these items seem likely to be based to an important degree on incomes.

3) *Information about product quality is difficult (costly) to obtain, and that information is most easily provided to consumers by the creation of easily identifiable brand names.* When we purchase goods in the market, we are always concerned that we may not be getting exactly what the seller is representing. Often, the seller has better information about the quality of the product than does the buyer. This **asymmetry of information** creates a potential for lost gains from trade, because consumers, not knowing the actual quality of the goods offered, will only pay an amount for the worst assumed quality. As a result, sellers will be reluctant to offer premium goods. The problem is illustrated by the used car market. In a famous article, Professor George Ackerloff of the University of California at Berkeley argued that people traded in lemons more frequently than cars that were running well. Because consumers have difficulty determining which used cars were lemons, the price of good used cars is less than their true worth. However, this discourages some sellers of good used cars from engaging in mutually beneficial trade with buyers who would prefer those cars to the more expensive new ones.

Suppose many independently owned producers all sold personal computers (PCs) which had no identifying marks, other than some alleged technical specifications. That is, consumers could not tell which producer actually made a given machine offered for sale. Some things about the computer are easy to observe. It's easy to check if the monitor size, whether or not a DVD-ROM drive has been installed, and which software has been installed. It is less easy to check that there really is a 12 GB hard drive, and not a 4 GB drive, whether there really is 128 MB 100MHz SDRAM, and that it runs at 1,000 MHz, not 500 MHz. Much more difficult still is the problem of assessing the long run durability of the monitor, hard drive and the electronic components, failure of which would lead to substantial repair costs. The problem is, how can sellers assure buyers that the goods are of the stated quality? If the producer of the machines is unknown even to the retailer, it will be impossible to offer any guarantees to the consumer other than as to the minimum imaginable quality. In this situation, no manufacturer can capture the benefits of producing a relatively high-quality computer. Consumers who might wind up with the better machine would regard their good fortune only as the luck of the draw. More importantly, consumers have limited mechanisms for rewarding this manufacturer for the expense in producing a high quality machine through repeat purchase, or by recommending the product to others, nor can consumers punish the manufacturer for producing a shoddy product. Producers therefore will not spend the extra resources necessary to produce a superior product.[3]

---

3. A similar phenomenon occurs when "low quality" money (for example, paper Confederate dollars) is issued at a legally fixed price relative to high quality money (historically, gold). In addition to its use as currency, gold can be used for jewelry and other goods. It thus has some market price in terms of other goods. As the supply of paper money increases relative to gold, the value of paper money falls and the amount of goods that can be purchased with a dollar of gold also falls. If the supply of paper money is increased enough, the monetary value of gold will fall below its market price in terms of other goods. Usually, the authorities insist that a dollar is a dollar is a dollar. In that case, consumers soon stop using gold as currency, since it is more valuable in jewelry, etc. This proposition is known as *Gresham's Law,* or more popularly, that bad money drives out good money. Note, however, the importance of the price control on gold (fixing its price in terms of paper money) in arriving at this outcome.

When mutual gains from trade are potentially available, people try to devise institutions that allow those gains to take place. Consumers and producers have a mutual interest in devising ways to produce highly valued information about the quality of a product, so that higher quality goods can be produced. One mechanism for capturing the benefits of producing a more reliable product is for the manufacturer to identify its product with a brand name. Compaq was a small company at the beginning of the PC revolution. It sold machines compatible with IBM computers using the operating system developed by Microsoft. IBM, of course, had a long-established reputation of producing high-quality products with an extensive service network. A new company cannot easily convince consumers that its products are as good as the established market leader. It can offer a very strong warranty and try to market its products in stores which already have a reputation for selling quality goods, but people can't really tell if a product is high quality until it has been around for awhile. Compaq therefore initially offered its computers at prices much below those for similar machines from IBM. As consumers gained experience with upstart companies such as Compaq, they were able to sort out which produced more reliable products. In time, those companies were able to capture the benefits of their higher quality products by charging a price closer to IBM's for the same technical specifications. More recently, the Dell Computer Corporation and Gateway computers have pursued the same strategy, offering attractive prices via mail order sales. The lower prices they charged were compensation to the consumers who took a chance on dealing with these new companies through the mails, or later, on-line.

Brand names create property rights in information consumers desire. This information is valuable to consumers when their marginal values of high quality goods are substantially greater than their marginal values of the low quality goods of the same general type, and when consumers cannot readily procure this information on their own. Consumers can readily determine the size of a computer screen, thus the value of additional information about this feature from the producer (that is, marginal value of this information) is low. Information that the computer will run smoothly for 5 years is not readily available, and it is therefore the type of information conveyed to consumers by the trademark brand. Consumers trust a brand name because the producers know that consumers have the ability to punish the producer for a disappointing product by withholding future purchases and urging their acquaintances to do so as well.

Moreover, brand names may create an exclusive right in improvements to the product. If a particular company devises a way to make the computer run faster, it can advertise this feature under its brand name. Of course, if the improvement is patentable, the company may be able to secure even stronger long run rights to the improvement. However, in many cases, even a patentable improvement is easily copied. Brand names give a producer at least some degree of **capturability** for their expenditures to improve technology. These trademarks are therefore often very valuable to companies. Firms jealously guard them, and major lawsuits are sometimes pursued if some person or other company causes a decrease in the value of a firm's brand name.

Lastly, consider the task of determining the price for the particular products sold by some manufacturer. In textbooks, the task is easy: determine the output where marginal cost equals marginal revenue, and set the price at the height of the demand curve at that output. In the real world, this is not so easy. The demand curve is not known with any degree of certainty, and thus neither is the marginal revenue curve. On the production side, even if firms have good accounting data, estimates of marginal cost, as opposed to the totals and averages usually available from accounting data, are never easily obtained. As a result, firms experiment with various price and output combinations, looking for the decisions that maximize rents. What firms do not want to do is allow competing firms to "free-ride" on this valuable information. Indeed, if firms could easily copy their competitor's decisions about price and output, no firm would invest its own resources to produce that information. That is, this information would fall into the public domain. As a result of this absence of property rights, too little information (less than the amount at which the marginal cost of producing it equals consumers' marginal value of this information) would be produced. This means that output will often be produced at inefficient levels, that is, not where consumers' marginal values of the good equals marginal cost. Product differentiation and brand names allow firms to capture at least part of their expenditures on pricing. Because each firm's product is different from others', and not easily measured, the price of one company's CD player, say, does not translate as easily into the price of a competitor's unit. Thus price is less easily appropriated without compensation, alleviating to some degree the common property problem associated with price determination.

Monopolisticly competitive markets are characterized by *contestability.* No firm can use another's trademark or produce an identical product without permission, but other firms can enter the industry and produce similar products. Entry of these new firms eliminates monopoly profits, so the adjective monopolistic is really something of a misnomer. This environment in fact is the dominant industry structure for production in the United States, Canada and most Western countries. The lingering issue of economic efficiency, while in some dispute, seems to revolve around correctly specifying the marginal cost function (*MC*). If we employ the standard monopoly diagram (Fig. 11-3) for this discussion, the inevitable conclusion is that these industries are inefficient since each firm produces less than the output where price equals marginal cost. However, it must be asked whether the marginal cost curve has been correctly defined. In the standard diagram, *MC* refers to costs of additional output only. These production costs omit the important costs of establishing rights to the particular attributes of a firm's goods, which is an essential component of production. Absent these rights, production of all but the most elementary goods (those with transparently observable attributes) will cease. The true, that is, correctly specified marginal cost of output *must* include these other costs, since output decisions depend on them in essential ways. Although the products themselves are differentiated, the attributes desired by consumers (durability, accurate reproduction of sound in stereo systems, etc.) are competitively produced. Firms produce these attributes until their marginal cost equals the price of the attributes. Thus we can perhaps regard these monopolisticly competitive industries as perfect competitors of attributes of consumer goods, which come packaged in various forms under different firm's trademarks. It is difficult to conceive of production taking place absent these institutions, and thus pronouncements of inefficiency should be made only with the greatest caution.

12.2 Cartels and Collusion

We now move towards the monopoly end of the continuum between many sellers and one seller in a given market. When only a few sellers are present, it may be possible for them to coordinate their pricing and output policies for mutual gain. In particular, it may be possible for the firms to form a **cartel**, and increase profits to the firms by restricting output, thereby raising the price above competitive levels. This action—**collusion**—is generally illegal. However, illegality has rarely been an absolute deterrent when large profits are involved, so we explore the problems and returns for this type of behavior. We discuss U.S. law on this and related subjects in the next section.

To make things as simple as possible, consider the case where there are exactly two firms which presently produce an identical product. Assume each firm's marginal cost of production is constant at \$100, that is, $MC = 100$. The market demand curve is $p = 300 - x$, where p is price and x is the total of the two firm's outputs. Figure 12-1 shows this situation.

If the firms act as perfect competitors, they produce where price equals marginal cost. Since MC is constant at 100, the price cannot exceed this amount. If either firm attempted to charge more than this amount, the other firm would immediately undercut it and get all the customers. As a result, neither firm is able in this situation to derive any rents from its production. In the more general case where specific factors of production are present so that the marginal cost curves are upward sloping, the firms do earn rents on those nonreplicable inputs, but they derive no monopolistic rents. At price = 100, 200 units of output are produced, presumably 100 by each firm.[4]

It will soon occur to the owners of these firms that as long as they continue to produce 200 units of output, then by the law of demand, the price can never rise above \$100, and thus rents will always be zero. The only way to increase their profits is to restrict the total quantity produced to below 200. In order to accomplish this, the firms have to collude. They have to both agree to restrict output to below what either would do acting independently. The largest rent available is that which a single monopolist would derive. If only one firm operated in this market, it would set output where marginal cost equals marginal revenue ($MC = MR$). The marginal revenue curve is shown in Fig. 12-1. It starts at

Figure 12-1 *Competition and Collusion with Two Firms*

Two firms, each with constant marginal cost of \$100, could conceivably collude and sell 100 units at \$200 per unit, the monopoly outcome. However, they would have to police each other closely, because each could gain by cheating on the arrangement.

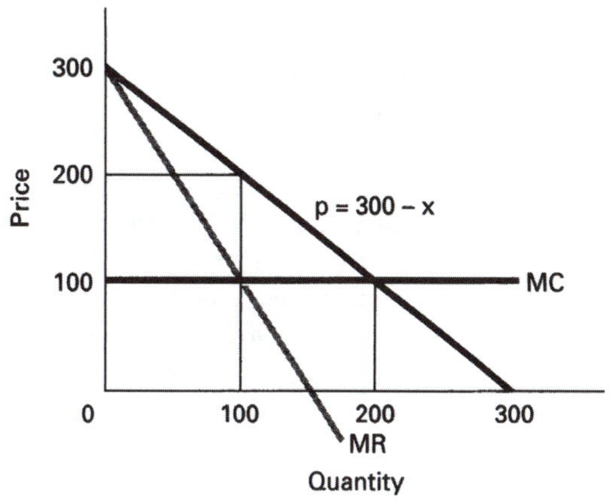

4. With literally constant marginal costs, there really is no way to determine the individual outputs of each firm, since $p = MC$ at every output level.

the vertical intercept of $300 and, as we showed in the previous chapter, it declines at twice the slope of the demand curve. It thus intercepts the quantity axis where output $x = 150$. The equation of the marginal revenue curve is $MR = 300 - 2x$. For outputs less than 150, and thus prices above $150, the demand curve is *elastic;* at prices below $150 and thus outputs greater than 150 units, the demand is *inelastic.*

The output for which $MR = MC$ is where $300 - 2x = 100$. The output that satisfies this equation is $x = 100$, shown as point E in Fig. 12-1, where the MR curve intersects MC. If the two firms can agree to produce 50 units each, they can sell the combined output of 100 units at $200 per unit, determined by the height of the demand curve at that quantity. Each firm therefore receives $200 on 50 units sold, for a total revenue of $10,000; each firms' total cost is $\$100 \times 50 =$ $5,000. Thus each firm stands to make $5,000 monopoly rents, a total for both firms of $10,000 from this collusion.

However, it is easier to cook up this scheme than to actually put it into effect. Each firm has to restrain itself and not produce more than 50 units. At 100 total units produced, the price exceeds the marginal cost of production by $100. This excess of price over marginal cost creates a strong temptation for each firm to cheat on the arrangement, and sell a few (or perhaps many) additional units to customers at a price slightly below $200. They can get away with it as long as the other firm doesn't find out, or worse, as long as the other firm also doesn't cheat. If each firm starts to offer secret deals to their customers, the cartel will soon fall apart and price will fall towards the competitive price of $100. Indeed, cheating on the cartel agreements is the pre-eminent reason why such cartels fall apart. [Query: Suppose, because you were so incredibly clever at this game, you knew for certain that the other firm would always sell 50 units at $200 each, and that you could cheat on the arrangement with impunity. How many units would you sell, and at what price? What monopoly rent would you receive?]

Perhaps the most famous cartel of recent times is OPEC, the Organization of Petroleum Exporting Countries, composed mainly of the Middle Eastern states and Venezuela. In late 1973, following the war with Israel, the Arab states in the Middle East embargoed oil to the United States, and endeavored to raise the price of petroleum by restricting the total output produced by the cartel. It seemed to work for a while. However, it was soon discovered, even during the early embargo days, that one of the most fanatically anti-American countries, Libya, was secretly exporting oil to the U.S.

In the past decades, these countries have held meeting after meeting trying to figure out an effective way to restrict total output. Every time they have agreed on production quotas for each country, they have found that the members routinely ignored their promises and produced more than their share, destroying the monopoly price. As we pointed out in Chapter 3, the price of petroleum at the present time is no higher, and perhaps lower than it was when this cartel first endeavored to raise price through collusion.

In a famous case, usually referred to as GE-Westinghouse, about 30 U.S. manufacturers of heavy electrical equipment conspired to fix prices beginning in the 1950s.[5] Annual sales of this equipment totaled about $2 billion. This was one of those rare instances in which it was absolutely clear that the firms did collude.

5. This discussion is adapted from the highly entertaining account provided by John McGee in *Industrial Organization,* Prentice-Hall, 1988.

The government obtained copies of minutes of meetings in which various pricing schemes were discussed and agreed upon. The issue, still under debate, is the extent to which the agreements were carried out and the degree of harm done to the buyers of these products. Almost from the start, salespeople were offering their customers "sweetheart" deals under the table, throwing in extra merchandise "free," effectively lowering the cartel price. An independent analysis concluded that the collusion had little effect.[6] The Federal Trade Commission, one of the investigating agencies of the federal government concluded that overall, the conspiracy raised profitability by 4 percentage points. Except for insulators and circuit breakers, the government concluded the conspiratorial meetings did not raise profits significantly.

Although the GE-Westinghouse case is much too involved to discuss here, it illustrates the classic problem of organizing an effective cartel: policing the arrangement amongst the conspirators. This is not to say that cartels are never effective. They are most effective in the short run, but over time, the temptations to cheat seem to grow. The case also highlighted another feature of these arrangements. Apparently, the firms that gained the most from the collusion were the firms that did *not* participate. Raising the price of certain items above their competitive levels, that is, above marginal cost, allowed firms not in the arrangement to also charge higher prices and thus to earn above normal profits. In the same fashion, if OPEC truly manages to raise oil prices by contracting their output, this creates a windfall gain for American, Canadian and other oil firms not in OPEC. Moreover, the ability of a cartel to raise its price is constrained by the degree to which firms outside the cartel can expand their own output. If the supply curves of firms outside the cartel are very elastic, then the ability to form an effective cartel is very limited.

The problems inherent in policing cartel behavior are exacerbated when the participating firms are of different sizes, or have different cost structures. Suppose firm 1 is a large firm with low average costs that produces most of the output when the market is competitive, whereas firm 2 is a small relatively high cost firm whose marginal cost function is rising rapidly. If the firms collude, firm 1 with have to contract output much more than firm 2. The gains from establishing the cartel may be larger for the small firm than for the large one. It may be the case, though generalities are difficult to establish, that the gains from cheating on the arrangement will be much greater for the large firm, the one with the relatively elastic marginal cost curve. In these kinds of cases, collusion can be a very contentious affair. The OPEC countries exhibit some of these characteristics. Saudi Arabia has huge oil reserves—enough for the next two centuries at present consumption levels—and large pumping capacity. Its interests are not the same as a smaller member. Saudi Arabia can, on its own, affect the world price of oil by adjusting its output. However, if it voluntarily does this, it creates a windfall for the smaller producers who then increase production to take advantage of the higher price. Political considerations can be important as well. If a ruler of one of these countries is not too secure about his political future, he has an incentive to produce at high levels to make the money now rather than leave the oil in the ground for future rulers.

Perhaps the most successful strategy for forming and maintaining a cartel is to legitimize it under the umbrella of government regulation. A certain amount

6. Ralph G. M. Sultan, *Pricing in the Electrical Oligopoly,* Harvard University Press, 1974, 1975.

of business regulation has occurred because the affected businesses themselves lobbied Congress (or state or provincial legislatures) for price and quantity regulation. Many economists feel the government's regulation of the transportation industry has been of this nature. In the nineteenth century, when railroads arguably had monopoly power over various routes (the exceptions were routes that paralleled inland waterways, such as along the Mississippi and Ohio rivers) they were largely unregulated. In the early twentieth century, with the advent of motor vehicles and trucking, the railroads lobbied for rate and route regulation for themselves and for trucking companies. The Interstate Commerce Commission (ICC), established in 1887 in large part due to public concern over monopolistic practices of the railroads, was given important rate-making powers in 1906 and 1913 when trucks started to become important competitors. The ICC created property rights in routes for railroads and truckers and established the fares over those routes. That is, specified truckers and railroads were given the exclusive right to serve given routes, and entry of new firms was severely restricted. If a new firm wished to serve some route, the ICC would hold hearings as to whether the new firm was needed. All the existing firms would show up and testify as to why service was already more than adequate. Usually, the requests were turned down. As a result, firms in these industries were able to charge monopolistic prices and derived large rents from ownership of lucrative routes.

Government regulation of the transportation industry achieved for the participating firms what they could not have achieved on their own. It is very difficult to maintain a cartel in trucking; entry into the industry is easily accomplished by leasing a truck and offering one's services. There is hardly a case to be made that some danger of monopolization was ever present. Moreover, it would have been a violation of antitrust law for companies to get together and divide up markets between themselves, restrict the entry of new firms and form agreements on prices. In the absence of regulations, owners of firms in the U.S. can be sent to jail for those practices. Yet this is exactly what transport firms managed to accomplish under the legal protection of regulation. In recent decades (beginning in 1978 for the airlines, and the early 1980s for truckers) transportation has been largely deregulated at the federal level. As a result, the number of firms in these industries has increased dramatically, confirming the existence of previous artificial rents in those industries. These industries now seem more competitive than previously.

The ingenuity of schemes to fix prices is impressive testimony to the creative genius of the human mind. In the GE-Westinghouse case, after the case was initially closed, GE issued a revised price book and published all existing price quotations. It also allowed customers to check the pricing book to see if anyone was receiving discounts they were not. The following year, Westinghouse published a similar book and announced its prices. The government then accused GE of *signaling* Westinghouse that it was abandoning secret price-cutting, and accused Westinghouse of agreeing to reciprocate. These public price quotes were eventually eliminated.

In 1990 various Ivy League colleges were indicted by the U.S. Department of Justice for colluding to fix prices of tuition and engaging in illegal price discrimination. The government charged that the colleges were forming secret, explicit agreements setting tuition rates. The colleges then engaged in price discrimination by offering tuition discounts (scholarships) to students depending in part on family income. In a process called overlap, the Ivies and other schools in the Northeast met every April, compared notes on various applicants, and adjusted aid so that the tuition would be the same for every school. Offering scholarships to students of especial promise, or to diversify the student body would not in itself be illegal price discrimination. The charges against the school were that they conspired to set a monopolisticly high tuition base price, and then discriminated through the use of partial scholarships on the basis of willingness to pay. The alleged result was that students from relatively high income families paid higher tuition than they would have without the agreements. The schools argued that the practice enabled disadvantaged and minority students to attend these premier schools. Many African-American groups supported the practice. The defense argued, and Congress and an appeals court agreed in 1992-'93, that the social benefits of the practice should be weighed against the otherwise illegal collusion. The case settled in 1995. The schools are allowed to set average aid levels, but not on an individual student basis.

Other mechanisms to fix prices include rigging bids for certain projects so as to establish higher prices for similar work. A practice known as **basing point pricin**g establishes prices of delivered goods including an amount for transportation from a given production locale, whether or not the producer is located there. The most famous instance of this was the pricing of steel in the early twentieth century—a system known as Pittsburgh Plus. The delivered price of steel included a transportation charge based on the distance from Pittsburgh, the center of steel production, regardless of where the actual steel manufacturer was located. The degree to which these practices are exclusively the result of attempts to form cartels, as opposed to cost-cutting strategies in competitive industries with imperfect information, and the degree of actual harm to consumers is a subject of ongoing research.

12.3 Antitrust Policy[7]

A strategy we have not yet discussed by which firms seek to derive monopoly profits is for the firms in a given industry to *merge* into a single unit. For example, rather than each of two firms agreeing to produce only 50 units of output, and then spending resources policing the behavior of the other firm, the firms can agree to form a single firm. The firm can issue corporate shares and divide them equally between the owners. In this way, the problem of cartel members cheating on the arrangements is overcome; the firm simply operates as an actual monopoly.

This strategy is so appealing, it in fact became a dominant feature in various industries in the United States in the nineteenth century. In corporate forms of business, in which shares of stock are issued, most of the shares typically are owned in small amounts by many disinterested and unorganized individuals. It is therefore often possible to effectively control the corporation by owning perhaps only 10 or 20 percent of the shares. Moreover, it is possible for the owners of one

7. Four excellent sources, from which most of this discussion derives, are Robert Bork, *The Antitrust Paradox,* (New York: The Free Press, 1978, 1993), Ernest Gelhorn, *Antitrust Law and Economics, 3r ed.,* (St. Paul, MN: West Publishing Co., 1986), John S. McGee, *Industrial Organization,* (Engelwood Cliffs, NJ: Prentice Hall, 1988), and Stephen F. Ross, *Principles of Antitrust Law,* (Westbury, NY: The Foundation Press, Inc., 1993).

firm to acquire a dominant interest in another firm, which in turn might acquire a dominant interest in still another, and so forth, so that an individual or small group of individuals ultimately can control the majority of output in a given industry. These business combinations, called **trusts** in the nineteenth century (from which we derive the term "antitrust"), became prominent in several industries. John D. Rockefeller's Standard Oil Company eventually controlled 90% of the petroleum sold in the United States; U.S. Steel, formed by Andrew Carnegie and J.P. Morgan eventually produced about two thirds of all steel in the early part of the twentieth century.

When firms selling a similar product combine into a single firm, we call this a **horizontal merger**. Antitrust law and economic theory distinguish such mergers from those in which firms engaging in successive stages of production of some final good combine. Such mergers are called *vertical,* and the resulting firm is referred to as **vertically integrated**. For example, some (but not all) oil companies own their own oil fields, pump the crude oil out of the ground, refine it in their own refineries, ship it to retailers in their own trucks and market the gasoline in retail stations owned by the company. These are archetypal vertically integrated firms. Some oil companies, however, do little other than retail other company's products under their own brand name; some produce their own oil but leave refining and retailing to others. Why such firm structures appear, and to what extent, if any, they are motivated by monopolistic considerations are important issues in the economics of industrial organization and market structure and the laws which constrain them.

Throughout the first one hundred years history of the United States, there were few if any federal laws restricting the formation of these business combinations. In the late nineteenth century, with the appearance of trusts in some major industries, a popular sentiment emerged to restrict by law the formation of monopolies and cartels. A brief history of these important antitrust laws and some important court cases which defined their scope (and their ambiguities) follows.[8] There are five major legislative actions which constitute the bulk of the antitrust statutes in the United States: the Sherman Act, passed in 1890, The Clayton and Federal Trade Commission Acts of 1914, the Robinson-Patman Act of 1936, and the Celler-Kefauver Merger Act of 1950. The legislative intent of these laws is not always clear; scholars and lawyers have debated them since they appeared. Moreover, the courts have principally defined the extent and scope of these laws as cases have been brought by either the government or private parties. In this section we briefly outline this history and discuss some business practices which scholars and the various courts have found difficult to evaluate in terms of the degree to which they represent monopolistic or collusive behavior.

Prior to the enactment of the Sherman Act in 1890, commercial law in the United States was based on American and English court rulings and precedents known as the *Common Law.* There was little *statutory* law, that is, actual statutes enacted by legislatures or Congress which regulated business transactions. One of the earliest court rulings relating to **restraint of trade** dates to the year 1414. An English court ruled that a contract that sought to prevent John Dyer (Dier) from practicing . . . his art of a dyer's craft within the town . . . for half a year

8. At the end of the chapter we list citations to all the antitrust cases in this chapter.

(possibly imposed by his guild) was void under the common law. However, over time, the courts also recognized that certain restraints of trade were useful not only to the parties directly involved, but also to the public at large. For example, suppose person *A* intends to purchase a business from person *B*. It is a common condition that the seller not immediately turn around and open a competing establishment. That would destroy the value of what the seller was proffering. This type of restraint was upheld by an English court in 1711 in a case known as Mitchel v. Reynolds [1 P.Wms 181, 24 Eng.Rep. 347 (1711).] What made this particular ruling important is that the court enunciated a **rule of reason** regarding restraints of trade. In deciding, the court asked, "Were the restraints *reasonable*?" It distinguished between general (invalid) restraints, for example, when sellers act to prevent others from engaging in trade for no purpose other than to restrict competition, and particular or ancillary (valid) restraints which served some lawful purpose, such as facilitating the sale of a business.

These early rulings were carried over to American and Canadian common law as well. However, common law evolved along different lines in England than in America. In England, the courts seem to have gradually decided that the participants themselves best knew what was desirable (otherwise, why would they be doing it). The English courts allowed so many exceptions to the rule of reason that virtually all restraints of trade became valid. Price fixing was generally allowed, and the House of Lords even upheld a covenant not to compete on a world-wide basis. American common law was less receptive to these practices. Wholesale covenants not to compete, price fixing, refusals to deal and territorial restrictions were generally struck down. These actions were regarded by the courts as illegal *per se,* that is, not subject to a test of their reasonableness.

The *Sherman Act* of 1890 was intended by its framers to incorporate this view of common law into statutory law. It is the first major antitrust statute passed by the U.S. Congress. Its important sections are as follows.

> Sec. 1. Every contract, combination in the form of trust or otherwise, or conspiracy, in restraint of trade or commerce . . . is declared to be illegal.
>
> Every person who shall make any contract or engage in any combination or conspiracy declared to be illegal shall be deemed guilty of a felony, . . . and face fines and/or imprisonment.
>
> Sec. 2. Every person who shall monopolize, or attempt to monopolize or combine or conspire with any other person or persons to monopolize . . . trade . . . are guilty of felonies. Private parties can bring civil suit under this (and other) statutes, and damages can be awarded to the injured parties.

One of the first cases brought under the Sherman Act was the Addyston Pipe Case, in 1898. This was a bid-rigging cartel which sold cast iron pipe to utility companies. The defendants were caught red-handed because a stenographer turned over documents to the government. The opinion was written by then appeals court judge William Howard Taft, later to become Chief Justice of the United States (that is, of the U.S. Supreme Court), and still later, President of the United States. One of the first issues to be decided was whether manufacturing was in fact interstate commerce. The U.S. constitution gives Congress the right to regulate *interstate* commerce only; commerce taking place wholly within the confines of one state is outside the purview of any federal law. Indeed, a few years earlier, the Court had ruled in the *Knight* case (1895) that sugar manufacturing was not interstate or foreign commerce.[9] Taft ruled, however, that the behavior was actionable under the Sherman law because it was a restraint of trade in the flow of commerce and tended towards monopoly.

An important irony of the Addyston case is that at the time of the cartel's actions, the firms involved controlled only 30% of the market. After the trial, four of the six defendants merged to form the American Pipe and Foundry Company, which was then acquired by another company, United Pipe and Foundry, which also acquired the remaining two defendants. Ultimately, this single firm controlled almost 75% of national capacity, though the share fell to about 40% in the 1920s. Fifty years later, in 1948, the government brought an action against the emergent firm for restraint of trade and monopoly. Thus it is not clear that the government's action against the original cartel was a benefit to consumers.

In later court rulings, the Court grappled further with the meaning of "restraint of trade." It noted that virtually all business contracts could be interpreted as restraint of trade. Contracts of the most innocuous type between buyer and seller routinely specified that a given firm, say, had to be supplied with some input before others could be served, or that a given firm would purchase some given amount or percent of the output of some firm. All such clauses in some way restrain the actions of firms. The court grappled with this issue, among others, in the famous Standard Oil of New Jersey (SONJ) case of 1911. John D. Rockefeller had formed this firm out of several others. By the first decade of the twentieth century, the firm's pipelines made it the sole purchaser of crude oil in many oil fields. Also, the firm's refineries produced over 85% of the refined illuminating oil (kerosene), the leading product at that time. In 1906 the government brought suit against the firm. The decision in 1911 ordered the dissolution of SONJ into about 30 companies. Importantly, the Court ruled that only those restraints that unreasonably restrained trade or which were anticompetitive in nature were illegal. The Court thus adopted a *rule of reason* for deciding antitrust cases. However, the difficulty in determining which trade practices were unreasonable and which were not caused critics of the Court to wonder if the Sherman Act would soon be gutted. Moreover, ambiguous law inevitably creates lawsuits, and many wondered if resources would be uselessly spent on antitrust suits of dubious merit.

These became issues in the presidential campaign of 1912. Although scholars tend to applaud laws which are based on human intelligence and reason, what is reasonable is almost always subject to debate. Many people (presidential candidate Woodrow Wilson included) felt, therefore, that it might be better to specify identifiable practices that would be illegal *per se*. However, Wilson apparently became persuaded (in part by his then advisor and future Supreme Court Justice Louis Brandeis) that an enumeration of all prohibited practices was impractical. Many in Congress feared that such an enumeration would end up legitimizing certain actions not enumerated, and would ultimately be contrary to the intent of the law.[10]

---

9. The definition of *interstate* commerce was drawn very narrowly in the early years of antitrust law. However, it was expanded over the years, so that now, if, for example, a local laundry bought its hangers from a manufacturer in another state, the courts would likely deem it to be engaging in interstate commerce, and federal law on interstate commerce would apply.

10. A conference committee stated its concerns as follows. "It is impossible to frame definitions which embrace all unfair practices. There is no limit to human inventiveness in this field. . . . If congress were to adopt the method of definition, it would undertake an endless task." (63rd Congress, 2nd sess. H.R. Rep No. 1142, 18-29 (1914).

In 1914 Congress passed the Clayton Act. The Clayton Act declared four restrictive acts illegal but not criminal. Importantly, however, the law specified that these monopolistic acts were illegal only "... where the effect ... may be to substantially lessen competition" or "tend to create a monopoly in any line of commerce."

Section 2 outlaws price discrimination, that is, selling a good at different prices to different (but similarly situated) customers. Section 3 outlaws tying and full-line forcing contracts, in which buyers must purchase some packaged group of the seller's commodities, rather than being able to pick and choose among the various goods offered for sale. Sections 7 and 8 restrict corporate mergers and interlocking directorates, for example, where the same individuals sit on the corporate boards of related companies. The Act allows injured firms to collect damages equal to three times the harm proven in court (treble damages). The Clayton Act, and the Robinson-Patman Act which amended it, were intended to prevent monopoly problems before they started.

In a companion law, Congress established the Federal Trade Commission (FTC) whose duty it was to enforce the provisions of the Sherman and Clayton acts. The FTC Act declared that "... unfair methods of competition in or affecting commerce, and unfair or deceptive acts or practices in or affecting commerce are hereby declared illegal." The FTC was thus charged, in particular, with investigating alleged unfair business practices.[11] The responsibilities of the FTC in some cases duplicate those of the Justice Department, and businesses can and have been pursued by both agencies at the same time. Around 1991, the Microsoft Corporation, developer of MS-DOS and Windows software, was investigated by the FTC. The FTC found there was too little evidence of wrongdoing to proceed. Nonetheless, shortly thereafter, the Justice Department, headed by new appointees in the Clinton administration, decided to open its own investigation.

One prominent application of the Sherman Act in the early years was to prosecute labor unions for restraint of trade. Unions are groups of sellers (of labor) who bargain collectively, that is, in concert with each other, in order to raise the price of the service they sell (labor). They also strive mightily to prevent employers from hiring nonunion replacement workers. Stated thusly, labor unions fit the definition of a conspiracy among sellers of the same product or service to restrain trade and monopolize a market. The Clayton Act asserted that "the labor of a human being is not a commodity or article of commerce," a proposition of dubious economic validity, but which was intended simply to exempt labor from the reach of the antitrust laws. Further clarifying exemptions were enacted during the 1930s, in particular, the Norris-LaGuardia Act of 1932.

The provisions of the Clayton Act were easier to state on paper than to interpret in practice. For one thing, the concept of what is "injurious to competition" is not easily elucidated. What supermarket owner, for example, wouldn't be pleased if the supermarket a few blocks away closed? Entry of new firms occurs precisely because they perceive rents to be garnered. These actions thus necessarily lower the rents, that is, measured profits of the other firms in the same market. As a result, when asked, firms eagerly testify that the actions of their competitors harm them to some degree.

---

11. The FTC is also empowered to investigate false and misleading advertising and was thus one of the first consumer protection laws enacted by Congress.

Particularly troubling was Section 2 of the Clayton Act which restricted price discrimination. This section was intended to prevent a firm from gaining a monopoly by price-cutting in a particular market. In the 1920s and 1930s, Kroger and A&P, in particular, developed the first supermarkets. In addition to lowering costs by allowing customers to select merchandise by themselves, these food chains were able to reduce wholesale costs by volume purchases. They were vigorously opposed by the owners of "mom and pop" stores, who (accurately) saw the supermarkets as a threat to their existence. The Clayton Act, however, could not be used to prevent the chains from buying and selling at prices below the what the mom and pop stores charged, since no actual price discrimination was involved.

In 1936, this section was amended by the Robinson-Patman Act.[12] Although the Robinson-Patman Act is usually categorized as an antitrust law, its legislative history reveals that it was mainly an act to prevent large food chains from driving the mom and pop grocery stores out of business. The 1930s was a time of widespread economic hardship, the great depression. Many businesses failed and workers lost their jobs in unparalleled numbers. The prospect of small firms being driven out of business by large corporations, never a pretty picture, probably weighed heavily on people's minds. The Robinson-Patman Act was drafted by a representative of the National American Wholesale Grocers Association. This group represented the small grocers, which opposed the emerging chain stores such as Kroger and A&P. Congressman Patman, in a speech arguing for the bill declared that "there is no place for chain stores in the United States." The intent of the legislation was that firms that sold at *lower* prices than their competitors could be prosecuted for attempting to monopolize the market, unless they could show that the price differences were based on identifiable cost differences.

The Robinson-Patman act did not merely outlaw price *discrimination.* Although the language of the law is couched in terms of price discrimination, its effect seems to have been to reduce or eliminate price *differences.* Formerly, firms could only be penalized for selling goods at too high a price. Under Robinson-Patman, they could now also be liable for treble damages for selling at prices that were too *low,* unless they could prove a cost basis in court. This is usually a very arduous and costly process, and therefore such price differences are sometimes avoided by firms. Consider, for example, the problem of determining the average variable cost of this textbook. The marginal cost of just printing the final text is only a couple of dollars. How does one calculate the cost of author's time writing the text, learning the material in the first place, and the cost of the editors? The problem is even more severe for more complex items such as pharmaceuticals. How does one build in the research cost of drugs that didn't pan out, costs of advertising and the like? Robinson-Patman's sponsors wanted the retail chains to purchase from their wholesalers, and to retail the goods at the same prices the mom and pops charged, so as to not drive them out of business. The prevalence of "store brands" in the retail chains is in part a response to this law. By establishing these wholly owned trademarks, the chains were able to avoid some of the reach of the law and purchase and price those items below the prices of the goods sold under different brands by the smaller retailers.

---

12. Curiously, the Act applies only to sales of "tangible commodities" and not to services such as visits to a doctor, or intangibles such as electricity or newspaper advertising.

The Robinson-Patman Act allows a firm to lower its price in order "to meet the competition." However, lowering prices to meet the competition inevitably harmed the competitors whose price was being met, and who would always testify to such harm if the courts asked. Moreover, price differences attributable *solely* to brand names have not been sufficient protection from this statute. Section 2(c) states that receiving commissions, brokerage fees and the like are prohibited "except for services rendered . . . either to the other party to such transactions or to an intermediary . . . acting . . . in behalf . . . or subject to . . . direct or indirect control, of any party to such transaction other than the person by whom such compensation is so granted or paid." If the meaning of these phrases is not immediately clear to you, you can be comforted by the extensive litigation that arose because its meaning was not clear to others as well. However, the intent of these words was to prevent firms such as the retail food chain stores from doing their own wholesaling and purchasing functions.

The Robinson-Patman Act was an attempt, which ultimately failed, to prevent consumers from enjoying lower retail prices for food at supermarkets. However, many actions have been and continue to be brought under this law. Economists tend to regard them unfavorably. The Sherman and Clayton Acts, despite interpretations and court rulings that appear injurious to consumers, seem originally intended to prevent firms from selling at monopolistic prices considered too high. The Robinson-Patman amendments seem to have added, as a public policy objective, the protection of small businesses against large ones, even if harm occurred to consumers.

Mergers, Acquisitions and Industry Concentration

Beginning with the Standard Oil of New Jersey case in 1911 (SONJ), the Supreme Court has regarded very large corporations, or bigness with suspicion, both with respect to absolute size and to market share in its product line. The court agreed that SONJ was an efficient firm, that a significant part of the reason for its size were the economies of large scale production in that industry, that its refineries were efficient, etc. The court worried, however, (especially in view of alleged nefarious means by which this size was acquired) that SONJ's sheer size ". . . gives rise, in and of itself . . . to the *prima facie* presumption of intent and purpose to maintain the dominance over the oil industry not as a result of normal methods of industrial development, but by new means of combination . . . with the purpose of excluding others from the trade and thus centralizing . . . a perpetual control over the movements of petroleum in the channels of interstate commerce." The Court feared, in essence, that SONJ's size would allow it to be a permanent monopoly. The Court reaffirmed this reasoning in the American Tobacco Company case of the same year.

In 1920, a later Court in a four to three decision ruled oppositely, in the case of U.S. Steel. Formed by mergers and acquisitions in 1901, this company had 60 to 70 percent of the steel ingot market, but its share had fallen to about 50 percent at the time of the suit. The Court found that U.S. Steel had not engaged in any abusive or predatory practices. Although a majority felt the company actually had *intended* to monopolize the market, it hadn't succeeded. The Court went on to declare that "The law does not make mere size an offense, or the existence of unexerted power an offense. It . . . requires overt acts and trusts . . . [The law] does not compel competition or require all that is possible."

Section 2 of the Sherman Act became something of a dead letter for the next twenty-five years.

A generation later, in the ALCOA case of 1945, a Circuit (Appeals) Court, acting under special legislation as the Supreme Court again swung back towards a "big is bad" position, in a ruling written by Judge Learned Hand. The circuit court in ALCOA was acting as the Supreme Court because many Supreme Court Justices had disqualified themselves from hearing the case. The Aluminum Corporation of America, originally formed in 1895, becoming ALCOA in 1907, had held patents in the production of aluminum ingots which expired in 1909. It had entered into agreements with foreign corporations setting market quotas. Also, since aluminum production requires very large amounts of electricity, the companies had entered into several exclusive dealings contracts with power companies early in the twentieth century. The government had filed suit in 1912 under the Sherman Act and most of these agreements had been struck down. In 1945, the Court was considering the behavior of ALCOA since the 1912 ruling.

An important issue in *ALCOA* was the determination of market share. The company's share of new (virgin) ingot was never below 80 percent of the market, and had been over 90 percent during the 1930s. However, virgin ingot competed with scrap (secondary) aluminum and with imported aluminum. The lower court, which had ruled in ALCOA's favor, included these other sources of ingot and computed ALCOA's market share at only 33 percent. Judge Hand excluded these competing sources of aluminum and concluded that 90 percent of the market was enough to infer the existence of monopoly. He also ignored non-aluminum substitutes such as steel and other materials. Hand agreed that the threat of foreign competition had prevented ALCOA from raising prices, that the company had not been especially profitable, earning only about a 10% return on its capital, and that it had acquired its commanding position in the market because of its efficiency. Even if monopoly had been "thrust upon it," and that "we need charge it with no moral derelictions since 1912," Hand ruled that nonetheless "ALCOA's size was 'magnified' to make it a monopoly. . . ." Hand also acknowledged that the court didn't intend to penalize efficiency, or turn on a winner, creating some ambiguity in the ruling.

Judge Hand's remedy for ALCOA's alleged monopoly is interesting as well. Hand acknowledged that dissolution of the company would probably harm consumers, since ALCOA's size was due to economies of scale. Also, with the emergence of new aluminum companies (Kaiser and Reynolds) arising from the World War II induced increase in aluminum production capacity, the Court felt that ALCOA was probably no longer a monopolist. The Court ordered the company to compete less aggressively with its new competitors. The implication remained, however, that a firm that became dominant because it served consumers well, and whose lower prices due to greater efficiency drove other firms out of business, could be sued for those actions under the Sherman Act, even though the government couldn't prove any monopolistic actions.

In 1965, the Justice Department filed suit against IBM using Judge Hand's reasoning. IBM had become the dominant computer firm largely because it sold computers for less than others; its machines were widely regarded as the best (and least expensive) on the market. Worthy competitors such as GE, RCA and Xerox entered the field and left. The government again ignored the existence of substitute products (in this case Plug-in modules) and foreign competition in computing market share. The government went so far as to include *competitors' peripherals* as part of IBM's market share, on the grounds that IBM might someday incorporate such products into its own line. Ultimately, in 1982, with a new head at the Department of Justice, the government abandoned the case for lack of merit. The philosophy that big was necessarily bad has gradually lost favor in the law and among economists.

In the early 1990s, the FTC and the Justice Department have investigated the Microsoft Corporation on similar grounds. Microsoft's MS-DOS and Windows software has a commanding market share in personal computers. A competitor, Novell, which manufactures a clone of MS-DOS called DR-DOS charged that Microsoft's policy of offering price discounts to companies that agree to load MS-DOS onto its entire line of machines is anticompetitive. Moreover, Novell also accused Microsoft of unfair trade practices by designing its Windows 3.1 software so that it could not be used with Novell's system. Micrososft claimed that it is not obligated to design a system that would run on its competitors' software. The FTC, on a 2-2 vote declined to accept a staff recommendation to proceed on this complaint. Shortly thereafter, however, the Justice Department decided to launch its own investigation with regard to Microsoft's Windows 97 operating system. The government charges, among other things, that Microsoft is illegally *bundling* its internet explorer with Windows. Microsoft claims this is an integral part of its Windows package. The case is still in court as of this writing. Should Microsoft have proceeded more cautiously, not lowering the prices of its operating systems, not integrating new features thus allowing more entry and perhaps more costly computers and applications software?

One of the most troubling cases for economists is *Brown Shoe,* which the Supreme Court decided in 1962. Chief Justice Earl Warren wrote the majority decision. In 1955, the Brown Shoe Company undertook to acquire Kinney Shoes. In 1958, there were 872 firms manufacturing shoes in the United States, down from 1,077 in 1947. The Court concluded that although combining Brown and Kinney's manufacturing capacities—4.0 percent and 0.5 percent, respectively—would not harm competition in manufacturing, the vertical integration would be anticompetitive. Moreover, merger of retailing—1.6 percent by number of pairs and 1.2 percent by dollar volume—*would* tend to lessen competition. Justice Warren worried about the downward trend, and that ". . . a small number of large companies occupied a commanding position." The four largest firms produced 23 percent of U.S. output; the largest 24 produced only 35 percent. This did not count imports, which were substantial. The Court assumed that manufacturers of women's shoes could not produce men's shoes, or children's shoes. It treated these manufacturing activities as separate markets, but the as same market for retailing. The Court also counted only shoe stores in its measures of market share, excluding department stores, even though the latter accounted for most shoe sales. Warren feared that many mergers were under way and that it would have a harmful effect on family style small businesses, an economic way of life and local control. With regard to consumers, the Court noted that consumers might benefit from the store brands offered by an integrated company such as Brown-Kinney. "But we cannot fail to recognize Congress' desire to promote competition through the protection of viable, small locally owned businesses. . . . Congress appreciated that occasional higher costs and prices might result from the maintenance of fragmented industries and markets. . . ." When faced with a choice between consumers' welfare and encouraging small enterprises, the Warren Court chose small business.

The issue of market share was given a more economically sensible treatment in the *Cellophane* case of 1965. In 1923, the Du Pont company bought patent rights to cellophane (at the time the only clear wrap for foods) from a French Company, La Cellophane, then the only producer. In 1925, two employees of La Cellophane started their own company and established a subsidiary, the Sylvania Industrial Corporation of America. In 1927, Du Pont discovered a way of moisture-proofing cellophane, and Sylvania soon came up with a copy. Until 1951, Du Pont and Sylvania were the only two producers of this product, with Du Pont having about three quarters of the market. The Supreme Court (which might have dismissed the case because of patent protection) ruled, however, that the relevant market was not just cellophane, but "flexible wrapping." These other products included aluminum foil, Saran wrap and other plastic wraps and waxed paper. The Supreme Court agreed with the lower court's determination that Du Pont's cellophane was less than 20 percent of the flexible wrapping market and thus not a monopoly.[13]

Current antitrust law regarding market shares is summarized by the FTC *Merger Guidelines,* adopted during the Reagan Administration and revised somewhat in 1992. These rules call for the calculation of a *Herfindahl-Hirschman* index (HH). This index calls for calculating the percentage share of the market for each firm, squaring those percentages, and summing them. For an industry with just 1 firm, $HH = 100^2 = 10{,}000$. An industry composed of two firms with equal market shares would yield $HH = 50^2 + 50^2 = 5{,}000$. An industry of 5 firms with 20% shares yields $HH = 5 \times 20^2 = 2{,}000$. Thus HH has a maximum value of 10,000, for a monopolistic industry, and approaches zero as the number of firms increases. The FTC's current policy is that industries with HH below 1,000 are considered "unconcentrated," and mergers are generally allowed without government challenge. For HH above 1,000 but below 1,800, the industry is considered moderately concentrated, and mergers will be challenged if the merger raises HH by more than 100. Industries with $HH > 1{,}800$ are considered "concentrated," and mergers are challenged if the merger would raise HH by more than 50. These rules provide some predictability to the government's actions, which saves resources. However, HH is not a completely reliable guide to actual monopolistic or collusive behavior. The index fails to account for *potential* competition, which may be very real and may thus severely constrain the behavior of firms presently in the industry. Also, the definition of the industry may be subjective for many firms engaging in production of many unrelated goods. Lastly, while the HH guidelines characterize the FTC's policy at the moment, private litigants are free to proceed with whatever civil antitrust suits they deem worthwhile.

Predatory Pricing

A strategy for gaining a monopoly position that figures prominently in antitrust history is known as **predatory pricing**. In theory, a firm attempts to drive its competitors out of business by selling below cost. Once the other firms have

13. The Court also used some reasoning regarded as highly suspect by economists. It noted that the cross elasticities of demand between cellophane and its competing products was very high. That is, a small decrease in the price of Saran wrap would induce a large decrease in the quantity of cellophane consumed. However, the Court ignored the fact that this would equally likely be true at a monopoly price of cellophane as at a competitive price. The high cross elasticities do not really imply an absence of monopoly power.

gone bankrupt, the predator firm purchases the victims' assets at "fire-sale" prices and enjoys monopoly profits. Although consumers may benefit from the low prices while the predatory pricing takes place, consumers ultimately lose because of the inefficiency due to high monopolistic prices in the future. The most famous alleged instance of this tactic is the formation of the Standard Oil of New Jersey (SONJ) company by John D. Rockefeller in the late nineteenth and early twentieth centuries. Indeed, the Supreme Court, in its 1911 rulings upholding the lower court's order to dissolve SONJ into about 30 smaller firms cited the alleged predatory practices in its opinion. The Court feared that SONJ would do almost anything to maintain a permanent monopoly. The story, however, is easier to tell than to justify either in theory or in actual practice.

The strategy of losing money by selling below cost in order to acquire a monopoly is regarded with suspicion by most economists because it is not easy to empirically determine if it is actually occurring, and because if it is actually happening, it is not easy to reconcile with a firm's desire to maximize wealth. Consider some large firm that intends to monopolize its market. Assume there are several smaller firms that produce the same good. By whatever means the large firm manages to acquire its monopoly, its increase in wealth once it acquires it is the present value of its monopoly rents the day it becomes a monopolist. These will be the same no matter how the firm achieved its monopoly position. It follows that beginning when the firm still has competitors, the firm's wealth will be largest if it achieves its monopoly power in the least cost manner. The question is, does predatory pricing meet this test?

In a classic paper, John McGee argued that predatory pricing is an expensive way to acquire a monopoly and therefore unlikely to be observed.[14] The tactic has to be weighed against alternative means of monopolization, for example, by merging, perhaps through simply purchasing the competing firms. Assume initially that the two firms have the same cost structures. The preying firm is likely larger than the victim. If goods are to be sold below cost, not only do both firms lose money, the larger firm, the predator, loses more money than the victim. Moreover, as the price falls, the quantity demanded rises because of the law of demand, increasing the cost of this subsidization even further. If the predator firm's average costs are below the victim's, then selling below the average cost of the victim is not predatory pricing—it is simply competition. If the predator's average costs are above those of the victim's, the losses to the predator are even larger than in the case when the two firms have the same costs. This raises a question about whether selling below cost is really a credible threat. Would a firm ever choose this strategy over the seeming less expensive route of simply purchasing the competitor?

What is the wealth-maximizing response of the supposed victim faced with such a campaign? The victim knows that this is only a campaign, after which prices will rise. It therefore pays to "stick it out," and not to fold. If the preying firm actually sells below average variable cost, the victim can shut down temporarily. The predator then suffers an even greater loss because it now has to sell even the victim's output at prices below average variable cost. Even if the victim is so squeezed financially that it must declare bankruptcy, the predator is faced

14. "Predatory Pricing: The Standard Oil (N.J.) Case," *Journal of Law and Economics,* 1, October 1958, 137–69. See also Predatory Pricing Revisited, *Journal of Law and Economics,* 23, October 1980, 289–330.

with potential entrants in the purchase of the victim's plant and equipment. Another firm could enter the business and start the whole process over again.

Empirical implementation of either legal tests for predatory pricing, or economic analyses of historical events is a daunting task. Consider, for example, what "selling below cost" might actually mean. Many firms, during their start-up periods lose money. They make investments in plant and equipment, spend money on advertising in order to attract customers, and outlay various sums for training workers. At the end of the year, when the accountants divide total cost by units of product or service sold, they find this amount to exceed the price at which the goods were sold. They sold below their average total costs. Of course no firm intends to lose money forever. The owners probably started the firm because they thought some other firm's profits were so large that the market could absorb another firm. The firm makes these investments because it expects to earn positive profits in the future. This firm, by entering the industry, intends to gain some rents now going to existing firms. It therefore necessarily *intends* to harm the existing firms. Is this predatory pricing? Actions are "predatory" only if the firm would not have undertaken them but for its intent to receive monopoly profits later. But in the absence of ability to read minds, our ability to tell what the firm is doing is limited by the actual outcomes. Distinguishing the outcomes of predatory pricing and normal rivalrous competition is easier said than done.

The empirical evidence that exists has tended to support the McGee hypothesis that predatory pricing is such a costly strategy it will be rarely observed, though no definitive conclusion is available. McGee investigated the trial record in the original SONJ case in 1911. The actual testimony was that Standard Oil, despite the folklore that has surrounded this case, did *not* use predatory pricing; it used the cheaper alternative of acquisitions and mergers. John D. Rockefeller simply bought out his competitors at prices they regarded as favorable. Moreover, this all occurred at a time when such mergers were thought to be legal, so that one cannot argue that predatory pricing was an attempt to evade the reach of antitrust laws.

Recently, Malcom R. Burns has argued that predatory pricing may be plausible when the predator can convince a succession of competitors that it is futile to resist a predatory campaign.[15] With peaceful mergers, as the dominant firm enlarges, the industry gradually becomes more monopolized. The remaining firms can then resort to a holdout strategy, increasing their acquisition price. It may be the case, therefore, with a dominant firm trying to acquire many competitors, that a successful predation with the first firm, or perhaps a few firms may entice the remaining firms into agreeing to be bought out, reducing the total cost of acquiring the monopoly. Alternatively, a firm might use a bogus company to secretly sell goods below average cost, in order to convince competitors that the price charged really represented their average costs. (This strategy would be especially appealing when faced with laws hostile to mergers and monopolies.) This might convince firms to sell out at a lower price than with a peaceful acquisition.

Burns studied James Buchanan Duke's mergers that created the American Tobacco Company in 1890. Using sophisticated econometric analysis, he found evidence that predatory pricing had been used, including the use of bogus companies, to disguise the true level of average costs. American Tobacco acquired a

15. Malcom R. Burns, "Predatory Pricing and the Acquisition Cost of Competitors," *Journal of Political Economy,* 94, No. 2, April 1986, 266–96.

notorious reputation in the contemporary press for such dealings, which were exactly what it intended. Such a reputation is precisely the aim of a predatory campaign. Burns concedes that the conclusions also confirm merely that increased rivalry between firms lowers all of their values, an outcome consistent with a competitive industry. Also, there is no data which would show what the costs to American Tobacco would have been if it attempted its mergers by peaceful acquisition. However, the results do confirm the impression at the time that predatory pricing was used.

Tie-In Sales and Block Booking

Lastly, consider the practice of "block booking," an example of a tie-in sale that the courts have frowned upon. There is no simple answer regarding the extent to which such booking is a result of monopoly. This involves "bundling" several goods together and offering the package to consumers as an all or nothing choice. Tie-ins, or full-line forcing are generally considered illegal under the Clayton Act. Some restaurants, for example, offer a "prix-fixe," (fixed price) four or five course dinner. Substitutions are generally not allowed. No one accuses restaurants of having monopoly power. Certain items sold on cars are simply not optional. You can hardly buy any car without movable and reclining front seats, a tachometer (it measures the speed of the engine), spare tires and a jack. These are not evidence of monopoly power. Consumers desire these items, and it therefore saves resources and lowers prices to consumers to package goods in this way, even though there may be some consumers who would prefer a more stripped down version of some good.

The most famous cases involving this practice were directed against the movie industry. Since at least 1916, movie companies offered pictures to theaters on this basis. With the advent of television after World War II, movie companies also offered blocks of movies to TV stations. The blocks were often sold even before the movies were produced. The theaters or TV stations could not pick and choose which movies to rent; they had to take all of them or none. In the *Paramount* (1948) and Loew's (1962) cases the Supreme Court struck down this practice. The Court ruled that such bundling "extends monopoly power." The Court felt that block booking "adds to the monopoly of a single copyrighted picture that of another copyrighted picture" (*Paramount*). Additionally, the Court stated that "the antitrust laws do not permit a compounding of statutorily conferred monopoly" (*Loew's*).

In the Loew's case. Justice Arthur Goldberg, writing for the Court, stated "To use the trial court's apt example, forcing a television station which wants 'Gone with the Wind' to take 'Getting Gertie's Garter' as well is taking undue advantage of the fact that to television as well as motion picture viewers there is but one 'Gone with the Wind'".[16] However, at the time, feature films were a very small part of a typical station's programming, and the blocks were only 8 percent of that total.

---

16. Justice Goldberg's attempt at levity was quoted by Nobel Laureate George Stigler in his famous debunking of the extension of monoploy argument, United States vs. Loew's Inc.: "A Note on Block Booking," *Supreme Court Review,* 1963. Since that time, it has been assumed that Loew's actually block booked these two films. However, *Gone with the Wind* was produced in 1939 by MGM (which was owned by Loew's) and David Selznick, and *Getting Gertie's Garter,* a bit of 1940s fluff, was produced in 1945 by United Artists. The trial court's remark was probably a bit of artful hyperbole.

Economists regard with great skepticism the hypothesis that a monopolist can extend power to some other product that is competitively produced. A movie company, by virtue of its copyright, possesses a legal monopoly on any film it produces. If it finds itself with a hit, such as MGM/Selznick had with *Gone with the Wind* (*GWTW*), it could presumably charge an appropriately high price for that film and derive rents from its unusually superior (to consumers) qualities. How could a monopoly on *GWTW* increase profits on other, undistinguished films, or in the theater business? If Loew's bundled *GWTW* with another film and charged a single price for both films, then some profit-maximizing price exists for both films. If theaters rent *GWTW* at less than its monopoly price, they will pay too much for the other. Economists have propounded two hypotheses to explain block booking, one based on price discrimination, and more recently one based on cost savings.

Price Discrimination In the 1950s, Aaron Director of the University of Chicago argued that if these movies appealed differently to different audiences, block booking could increase profits for the movie company. In the 1930s and 1940s, before the major advent of television, average weekly movie attendance was 90 million people, over half the population of the U.S. at that time. Movies theaters exhibited certain films for contractually specified times in specified areas. "First-run" theaters were the large relatively expensive movie theaters with the best systems, and accounted for up to half of the film's rental receipts. Films were then shown in neighborhood "second-run" theaters. The neighborhood theaters provided a service similar to that provided by television today. They showed double bills and short features, and changed programs often, usually once or twice a week.

Suppose there are two distinct audiences, the "high brows" that like to go to fancy theaters for first-run movies such as *GWTW*, and the "low brows," who prefer movies like the fabled *GERTIE*. Suppose the maximums these consumers are willing to pay for the two movies are as shown in Table 12-1. For convenience, suppose there are 1,000 potential consumers of each movie. The numbers in the table indicate the maximum amounts these audiences would pay to see these movies (1,000 times each individual's total value of these films).

As in all cases of monopolistic price discrimination, if the seller has complete information about consumers' preferences, he can collect each consumer's entire consumer's surplus by setting the price equal to the consumer's total value. In this example, Loew's would show *GWTW* in fancy theaters first, at a $7 admission price and then in the second run neighborhood theaters (where only the low brows attend) at a $4 ticket price. Likewise, *GERTIE* would be shown in two types of theaters, at $2 for the high brows and $3 for the low brows. Loew's would collect $16,000 gross rentals by this procedure. This is the maximum profit the movie company can make—it has extracted all the consumers' surplus there is.

However, movie companies never have this much information. Suppose they decide to sell these movies separately, but at a single price for each movie. Then they can receive maximum rental on *GWTW* by charging $4 admission.

Table 12-1

	GWTW	GERTIE
High Brows	$7,000	$2,000
Low Brows	$4,000	$3,000

The low brows and the high brows attend, yielding $8,000 in rentals. Likewise, by charging $2 for *GERTIE,* both audiences attend and the movie company receives $4,000, for a total rental for both movies of $12,000.

Suppose, however, the movie company correctly perceives that the two audiences favor these movies differently. Notice that the high brows value *GWTW* oppositely to *GERTIE,* 7/4 versus 2/3. The film maker can *block book* these movies at $7,000 for the two movies—take them both or leave them. The low brows and the high brows are both willing to spend $7 each to see both movies rather than none. In this case, the low brows receive no consumer's surplus while the high brows still receive $2 apiece on the block. The total take for the movie producer is thus $14,000, less than the unachievable perfect discrimination strategy but more than with individual pricing. Even with a somewhat smaller block price, the movie company does better with this procedure than by single price sales of each movie. Thus price discrimination in this form is a possible explanation for this price structure.

Cost Savings Recently, economists Ben Klein and Roy Kenney have criticized the price discrimination explanation of block booking.[17] They argue that the facts do not support the hypothesis and that a more plausible explanation is available. The price discrimination hypothesis is most plausible when producers face only one exhibitor in each market, and where the film producers have better information about the market than the exhibitors. In fact, the opposite was most always true. The local exhibitors had better information about what types of movies were favored in their own markets, and many exhibitors were available. Under these conditions, the producers should put these movies up for competitive bidding by exhibitors. This is what in fact happened, and these competitive bids dictated the prices of the films. Of course, since the films were block booked, the films were "average priced," that is, total bid divided by the number of films represented an average price for one film. These bids varied widely by the market served.

Klein and Kenney argue that block booking was a way of saving transactions costs, in particular, a way of avoiding costly duplication of effort evaluating the prospects of films. Producers and exhibitors have always found it very difficult to predict a film's market success. The stories are legion. When George Lucas was trying to get the original *Star Wars* movie produced, he was turned down by every studio except Twentieth-Century Fox, which nervously accepted it. Nobody predicted the ultimate success of *Rocky Horror Picture Show.* The sure-fire box office draw Arnold Schwartzenegger bombed expensively in *The Last Action Hero.* When a product's qualities are not apparent, the buyer and the seller each have an incentive to measure and evaluate the good. If they both measure the good and come up with the same evaluation, then the effort was needlessly duplicated. A reduction in these costs would allow the buyer and the seller to share in additional gains from trade, in a manner analogous to the gains from reducing any transaction cost or sales tax. The question is, what mechanism is there to avoid this duplication?

If the films are offered separately, the film company will necessarily evaluate the film in order to know what to ask as a rental price. Likewise, exhibitors will do their own evaluations so they can better judge what to bid for the films. Block booking is a form of blind selling that, in the case of movies, relies on the

---

17. Roy Kenney and Benjamin Klein, The Economics of Block Booking, *Journal of Law and Economics,* 26, October 1983, 497–540.

brand name capital of the producer to establish an average price. Some films turn out to be bargains, some are overpriced. However, by denying inspection of the goods, duplication of effort is eliminated. This same type of savings occurs in supermarkets daily. Potatoes and apples are commonly bundled in opaque bags. When we purchase them this way, the per pound price of these goods is generally much cheaper than when the produce is available for individual inspection. At the end of fashion seasons, clothing manufacturers sell their left over goods to jobbers, who purchase the entire lot with only scant inspection. It saves having the manufacturer and the jobber both measuring each piece. Trade-in values for used cars are most commonly determined by using a blue book, which is a listing of average values by model, year, etc. It is less costly in the long run to do this than for the seller and the buyer to each hire their own mechanics and inspect every car. Confirmation of these cost savings in the case of the movie industry is provided by an interval of time prior to the decision in *Paramount.* Eight years earlier, in 1940, the FTC ordered the producers to have screenings available to exhibitors. These were provided, but rarely attended.

Klein and Kenney argue that this type of cost saving similarly explains the organization of the diamond market by the Central Selling Organization of the De Beers company in South Africa. Almost 90 percent of the world's diamonds are marketed by De Beers, even though they produce less than half of those diamonds. Independent mines are free to sell their stones to the highest bidder in world markets, and some do. De Beers has an interesting arrangement with its customers, who they carefully screen for financial stability. These wholesalers specify a range of qualities and quantities they wish to buy. However, they are allowed to view only a sight of diamonds, consisting of a very small sampling of the diamonds they intend to buy. They can reject the purchase on the basis of the sight, but then they are forever foreclosed from purchasing diamonds from De Beers. This arrangement has persisted over many decades. With this block booking of diamonds, only De Beers measures the diamonds and uses its brand name to assure its buyers that it is not engaging in opportunistic cheating. Costly measurement and duplication of effort is avoided, and the producers and dealers (and ultimately consumers) can share in the reduced transactions costs.

Transactions that are complicated and which involve specifications of exclusive areas, minimum or maximum prices to be set, and other clauses which do not appear in some simple model of perfect competition are often regarded with suspicion by the courts. However, economists are now less likely to assume these practices are the result of monopolies or attempts to monopolize. These practices may be attempts to reduce transactions costs in the face of uncertainty about the product and the reliability of parties to a transaction. It is an interesting new area of research in economics.

CHAPTER SUMMARY

- Most markets in modern economies are neither perfectly competitive nor monopolistic. Usually, the seller has some control over price and other characteristics such as the level of customer service accompanying a sale. However, most firms are constrained by competition from sellers of similar, if not identical items.

- Most goods sold exhibit *product differentiation.* Goods are distinguished on the basis of brand names and variations in their attributes. Different brands of toothpaste, for example, are not identical, but are easily recognized as different qualities of the same basic good.

- Goods are differentiated because of 1) differences in preferences among consumers, 2) differences in demand produced by differences in income, and 3) product differentiation is the cheapest way to provide consumers with valuable information about the product.

- Brand names are a way of creating and enforcing property rights in information consumers desire. Many attributes of goods are difficult to determine, such as reliability and improvements. Brand names provide a mechanism which allows a firm to capture the benefits of producing a better but more costly product.

- If an industry contains only a few firms, they might be able to organize a *cartel,* in which the individual firms agree to act in concert (collude) to emulate the actions of a monopolist. That is, the firms might all agree to reduce output, thereby raising the price received by each firm.

- Although cartels are potentially profitable, they are difficult to maintain. Because the price exceeds each firm's marginal cost of production, each firm has a tremendous incentive to cheat on the arrangement and increase output. However, if all firms expand output, the cartel disappears. A successful cartel must find a mechanism for discovering cheating and imposing penalties on it.

- The most famous cartel of our times, OPEC, has, almost since its inception, been largely unable to enforce reductions in output by its members. A further hindrance to cartels is that they are illegal under most countries' antitrust laws.

- There are three major antitrust statutes in the United States: the Sherman Act (1890), the Clayton Act (1914) and the Robinson Patman Act (1936). The antitrust laws are enforced by the Justice Department and the Federal Trade Commission.

- These antitrust laws restrict collusion, mergers and discriminatory pricing. Unfortunately, the laws are not easy to apply to actual business practices, and the various Supreme Court rulings, which have for the most part defined the reach of the laws, are often inconsistent with each other.

- Certain actions, for example, a tie-in sale that forces a customer to purchase a less desired good along with another purchase, are generally considered to be illegal *per se,* though it also must be proven that it substantially lessens competition (which makes it something of a *rule of reason.* In other cases, the courts examine the merits of some alleged monopolistic actions to see if they are truly monopolistic, and, if so, whether there is sufficient injury to consumers to ban the activity.

- The combining of firms selling a similar product is called a *horizontal* merger, and these combinations are usually regarded with suspicion by the Justice Department and/or the Federal Trade Commission. *Vertical* mergers are when firms engaging in different stages of production combine, such as a manufacturer acquiring a formerly independent retail outlet. These are usually regarded with less misgiving by the government.

- Recently, economists have taken a new look at various practices originally thought to be monopolistic, such as fullline forcing and vertical integration. These actions seem consistent with attempts to save resources by avoiding costly duplication of effort in the production of information about a product's quality or price. In that case, they serve to increase efficiency.

REVIEW QUESTIONS

1. What is a monopolistically competitive firm? Is it more like a competitive firm or a monopolist?
2. Why does product differentiation cause us to depart from the model of perfectly competitive firms?
3. What are the three primary reasons for product differentiation? How does the size of the market affect product differentiation?
4. What is a contestable market?
5. why is it easier to form a cartel than to actually act like one? Give an example using OPEC.
6. What are the major antitrust statutes in the United States?
7. What is a *rule of reason* and how does it differ from a *per se* rule?
8. What is the Herfindahl-Hirschman (HH) index? How is it calculated and what does it measure?

PROBLEMS

1. Monopolistically competitive firms face downward sloping demand curves, and thus can charge a price higher than marginal cost. Yet unlike monopolists, these firms are expected to derive no rents from their monopoly position. How can this be?
2. Even if firms in monopolistic competition derive zero profits, is there an area of "deadweight loss" created by selling less output than the level where marginal cost equals price?
3. What are some of the reasons for product differentiation? Many people regard the variety of, say, breakfast cereals or toothpaste as wasteful, since, for example, resources are spent advertising differences between goods that consumers hardly care about, such as the color of soap. Comment. How would you distinguish "wasteful" advertising from "informative" advertising?

4. Many people, when they find the car they have purchased is a "lemon," trade the car in for a new one.

   a. How do we describe the problem consumers have in evaluating whether a used car is actually a lemon?
   b. How does this affect the proportion of used lemons for sale versus the proportion of all cars that are lemons?
   c. How does this affect the price of used cars?
   d. What steps do sellers of used cars that are not lemons take to overcome this problem?
   e. What steps can private owners who wish to sell their car because they are moving across the country take to get a price more reflective of the true value of their car?

5. What problems might perfectly competitive firms face with regard to the development of new products? How does the use of brand names affect this decision?

6. Consider the duopoly problem analyzed in the text. Suppose you knew for certain that the other firm would always sell 50 units at $200 each, and that you could cheat on the arrangement with impunity. How many units would you sell, and at what price? What monopoly rent would you receive?

7. Is OPEC a successful cartel? How can you tell? How do the incentives for maintaining a high price differ for large producers like Saudi Arabia versus some of the smaller states in the middle east? How are their incentives affected by the political stability of their regimes?

8. Suppose you find that several different stores sell certain goods at the exact same price. Is this evidence of perfect competition or of cartel behavior? Likewise, suppose the price of certain goods in several stores increases by the same amount. Is this evidence of perfect competition or of cartel behavior?

9. Suppose the government gives you and one other airline owner the exclusive rights to offer scheduled passenger service between St. Louis and Kansas City. They set a price above what would prevail under competition. Will you and the other airline earn greater than normal profits? What arrangements have to be made in order for that to be true?

10. When the airlines were regulated by the Civil Aeronautics Board (CAB), prices were kept above the competitive level, and entry was limited to a very few carriers over most routes. Fliers were treated extremely courteously, planes were rarely crowded, and the food was at least better than it is now. Since deregulation, most people find the qualities of these amenities have deteriorated. Explain why these amenities would be greater under regulation.

11. Distinguish between horizontal and vertical mergers. What kind most provoked the original antitrust legislation? Give examples of firms considered horizontally and vertically integrated. Are your examples monopolists or oligopolists?

12. What reasons other than collusion or attempts to form monopolies are there for firms to merge, either horizontally or vertically?

13. How does one determine what the market is for a firm's product? That is, How does one take into account of closely related goods?

14. In the American West of the 19th century, wide areas were often served by one country store. Did those stores have monopoly power over their customers?

15. Suppose you own a string of hardware stores and a new competitor opens in one of your market areas. You decide to force her out of business through predatory pricing. What costs will this impose on you and your competitor, and whose costs are apt to be larger? If a gain is to be had from monopolizing this business, how does the present value of those future monopoly profits compare with the present value of the competitor's profits? What lower cost strategy for achieving a monopoly does this suggest?

16. Suppose the amounts consumers are willing to pay for "GWTW" and "Gertie" are as follows:

	GWTW	GERTIE
High Brows	\$7,000	\$3,000
Low Brows	\$4,000	\$2,000

In this table, the highbrows still favor GWTW more than "Gertie", but now only *relatively* so. Is block booking still a feasible method for extracting monopoly profits?

17. Many industries seem quite concentrated, e.g., breakfast cereals and detergents, in which the top four firms produce virtually all the output. Are these firms thereby able to exert monopoly power? What factors are important in determining the extent of potential monopolistic behavior?

18. What are *per se* rules and "rules of reason?" what are the advantages and disadvantages of such rules? Sometimes a certain practice, e.g., a tie-in sale, is considered illegal *per se,* but only if it injures competition. what kind of rule is that?

19. Some famous antitrust cases not discussed in this text are *Arizona v. Maricopa County Medical Society, Morton Salt* and *Utah Pie.* Familiarize yourself with these cases and contemplate the practical difficulties of achieving useful antitrust policy.

20. Explain the problem of duplication in measurement. What market mechanisms have been developed to avoid this dissipation of rents? Are these methods easily distinguished from cartel or monopolistic behavior?

QUESTIONS FOR DISCUSSION

1. What do you think the proper purpose of antitrust laws should be, for example, protection of the consumer or protection of one firm against another? How have the antitrust laws been applied in these regards?

2. Do you think Microsoft is a monopoly? What should the proper concept of the market for Windows be—personal computers only, or should we also include computers used by small and large businesses?

3. Not too many years ago, AT&T held a monopoly in both long distance and local telephone calls. The long distance market was opened up to competi-

tion during the 1980s. Do you think this has been a good thing? How has it affected local rates, and can we, or should we allow any phone company to provide local service?

SOURCES

Below are all the citations for the antitrust cases in Chapter 12.

Arizona v. Maricopa County Medical Society, 457 U.S. 332 (1982)

Brown Shoe v. United States, 370 U.S. 294

Standard Oil Co.of New Jersey v. U.S., 221 U.S. 1 (1911)

FTC v. Morton Salt Co., 334 U.S. 37 (1948)

United States v. American Tobacco Co., 221 U.S. 106 (1911)

United States v. Addyston Pipe & steel, 85 Fed. 271 (6th Cir. 1898)

United States v. Aluminum Co. of America (ALCOA) 148 F. 2nd 416 (2nd Cir. 1945) U.S. 271

United States v. Knight Co., E.C., 156 U.S. 1 (1895)

United States v. Loew's, Inc. et. al.,. 371 U.S. 38, 52 (1962)

United States v. United States Steel Corp., 251 U.S. 417 (1920)

United States v. DuPont de Nemours & Co., E.I., 351 U.S. 377 (1957)

United States v. Paramount Pictures Inc., 334 U.S. 131 (1948)

Utah Pie Co. v. Continental Baking Co.386 U.S. 685 (1967)

CHAPTER 13

Labor Markets

In the United States, there is considerable variation in the average incomes of various ethnic and gender groups. Black families' incomes are only about two thirds that of whites, though the gap has been closing in recent years; Asians and Jews have higher than average incomes; men have higher earnings than women on average. Some commentators attribute all this to societal and labor market discrimination, but that would clearly fail to explain the relatively high earnings for Asians and Jews, two groups that have certainly faced discrimination in the past. How much of these differences can we attribute to factors other than discrimination, such as differences in age, education and the types of education? We know that young people earn less than people in their forties. Because of their relatively high birth rates, black earners are on average younger than others; this alone accounts for some part of that earnings differential. The field of labor economics attempts to sort out these and other interesting aspects of the value of human labor.

13.1 The Supply of Labor

Some of the most important decisions we make concern the time and effort we put into producing income. In modern societies, income most often is produced by participation in the labor market. The decisions we make concerning when, if at all, to begin regular work (for example, right after high school versus after college or graduate/professional training) have life long consequences. If you're reading this text, you've probably decided not to enter the labor force right after high school, at least not on a full time basis. Attending college is an *investment* activity. One sacrifices income (the ability to consume) for four or more years in order to be able to enjoy greater income for the remainder of one's life. This greater income is likely to be of a pecuniary nature, in the form of higher wages, but it could also be all or partially in the form of a more enjoyable job or more favorable working conditions.

Some people, on the other hand, choose not to participate in the organized labor market at all. The most common instances of this are homemakers who stay home to tend to children and maintain a household. One of the most dramatic changes in this regard in recent generations is the increase in labor force participation of women, especially married women. Prior to World War II and continuing to the early 1960s, the stereotypical behavior for women was to work briefly prior to marriage (which occurred, on average, at age 20), then to leave the labor force to raise a family, and then possibly to reenter the labor force in their forties after the children were grown. In 1960, less than thirty percent of married women aged 25–34 worked outside the home. By 1998, the figure had risen to over *seventy* percent! A change so dramatic demands an explanation. It means that large numbers of people are systematically making choices different from those made by their parents and grandparents. It is reflective of one of the important societal changes in recent years. It is one of the topics economists who specialize in the field of labor markets study.

The primary source of income for most people in their adult years is their participation in the labor market. We refer to this as *wage income* to denote that this income is produced by working at some wage rate. People also receive *non-wage* income, that is, income from some source other than participation in the marketplace. This can take the form of allowances from parents, interest or dividend payments on investments, welfare payments from the state, annual payments from winning the state lottery.[1] The decision about how many hours per day (or per week, month, year or lifetime) to work is called the **labor-leisure choice**. For convenience, we combine all the items such as food, clothing, shelter, recreational goods such as stereo equipment, etc., which can be consumed only if a person has money income, into a single good, called, appropriately, "income." We measure it in dollars or some other currency.[2] The other good we consume is "leisure." We consume leisure by not working, that is, not producing income. We assume that all individuals desire more of both income and leisure. However, the production of income necessarily entails a loss of time to enjoy leisure, since income production always takes time. Therefore, individuals have to choose between these two desirable goods, that is, we have to make trade-offs between more income versus more leisure.

Let us assume initially that some person earns $10 per hour, and he or she (let's say, she) can decide for herself how many hours she wishes to work. Then if this person works 40 hours per week for 52 weeks, her annual income is 2,080 hours times $10 per hour, or $20,800. If she were to take two weeks of unpaid vacation, her income would fall by 80 hours times $10, or $800. The cost of leisure to a wage earner is thus the foregone income associated with each hour of leisure consumed. A person's wage represents the price he or she has to pay in order to consume an additional hour of leisure. At the margin, therefore, when a person has adjusted his or her hours to the level most desired, their marginal value of leisure must equal this opportunity cost. Thus the marginal value of leisure is a person's market wage. The analysis is identical to the theory of demand we presented earlier in Chapter 2 for ordinary goods and services.

Recall that in Chapter 4 we discussed the case where a person had some endowment of a good he or she also wished to consume. The supply curve was simply the entire endowment less the quantity the person wished to personally consume at various hypothetical prices. We use this same analysis to derive a person's supply of labor. Each day, a person is endowed with 24 hours of potential leisure. We make various decisions as to allocate that time within each day. Each day we decide how many of those hours to *sell* to an employer. The decision about how many leisure hours to consume (demand) is equivalent to a choice of how many hours to sell to an employer in return for income. Thus the supply of labor is determined from the quantity of leisure demanded at given market wages. If, for example, at a wage of $10 the quantity of leisure demanded is 16 hours, it means the *quantity supplied of labor* is 8 hours at that wage and income. Hypothetically, as the wage is changes, we can draw a schedule of hours of leisure demanded and thus an equivalent schedule of hours of labor supplied. This schedule is a person's supply curve of labor.

A hypothetical supply of labor schedule is depicted in Fig. 13-1. Note its somewhat unusual shape. This curve is described as "backward bending." For wages between 0 and $10, *no* labor is supplied. The person consumes 24 hours per day on either leisure or other activities around the home. At the wage $10,

1. This nonwage "income" can also include *negative* amounts, such as monthly credit-card debts, home mortgages and any other obligation that is independent of a person's wage rate or the degree to which the person now participates in the labor market.

2. Usually we do not consider income as a "good;" rather, it is something which enables us to purchase goods. In this framework, however, treating money income as something directly consumed enables us to abstract from the choices that are not particularly relevant here, such as the mix of goods to be consumed.

Figure 13-1 *Backward Bending Supply Curve of Labor*

The supply curve of labor generally consists of three parts. At wages up to some point (here it's $10 per hour) it is zero. No labor is supplied. Beyond this wage, the supply curve is upward sloping. However, the amount of hours supplied reaches a maximum of 12 hour, at a wage of $25 per hour. At still higher wages, the amount of labor supplied actually *decreases,* as the income effect of the higher wage more than offsets the substitution effect of higher-priced leisure.

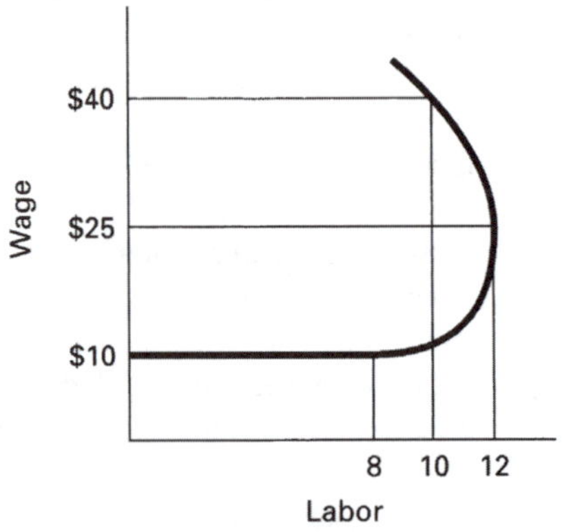

the supply of labor jumps discontinuously to the 8 hours per day. As the wage increases, the amount of labor offered increases. At a wage of $25 per hour, the amount of labor offered is 12 hours per day. Along this section the supply curve is upward sloping in the usual manner of supply curves. Along this segment, as the wage offered a person increases, the quantity of labor offered also increases. However, at wages above $25 per hour, when the wage is further raised, the quantity of labor offered actually *decreases.* At $40 per hour, the quantity of labor supplied is 10 hours per day, less than the quantity supplied is the lower wage of $25. What would account for this?

The reason why this curve may turn back on itself is that a change in the wage rate changes the person's *income* as well as the price of leisure. Wage rate changes produce *two* separate effects on a person's labor-leisure choice, and these effects are expected to have opposite influences. Whenever the price of something we purchase changes, there are two conceptually different things we do in response. If the price decreases, for example, we *substitute* in the direction of that good. This tendency is called the **substitution effect**. However, a decrease in price means that with our same budget we can purchase more goods. For example, if the price of gasoline decreases by 10¢ per gallon and a person consumes 10 gallons per week, this represents an increase in money income of $1.00 per week. Thus in addition to the tendency to substitute towards a good whose price has decreased, we can spend an additional amount on all goods because of the effective increase in income generated by the price decrease. This part of the total change in consumption induced by a price change is called the **income effect**. Because we spend our money on many goods, this increase in income caused by a price decrease is spread out over many goods. Its impact on any single good is therefore very small. It is so small that in the rest of this text we have ignored it altogether.[3]

3. Using more advanced mathematical techniques, it is possible to show that under very reasonable assumptions about consumers' preferences, the substitution effect is always in the opposite direction to price change. An increase in price induces *less* consumption; a decrease in price induces *more* consumption, even if the consequent change in income is adjusted to leave the consumer no better off than before the price changed. This is the fundamental basis of the law of demand. Using the example above, even if the government were to tax away the extra dollar of income created by the decrease in the price of gasoline by 10¢, the consumer would still consume more than 10 gallons at the new lower price. Of course, a similar analysis holds for price increases.

An income effect is the impact on consumption caused by a change in income *without any change in relative prices.* In the labor-leisure choice, a change in *nonwage* income, for example, a change in a person's allowance or some government transfer such as a welfare payment, would produce a pure income effect, since the price of leisure, the wage rate, would not be affected. Unlike the substitution effect, the income effect is theoretically of an indeterminate nature. We usually think of goods as "normal" in the sense that we consume more of them as income increases, but there are goods that are "inferior" in the sense that we consume *less* of them as our income increases. (See the discussion of this issue in Chapter 5.) Thus the extra weekly income of $1 in the preceding example might induce us to spend more on some goods and actually less on others. However, in the empirically important cases where the good whose price has changed, say gasoline, is a normal good, then the income effect of the price change *reinforces* the substitution effect. The lower price of gasoline makes people substitute towards gasoline; in addition, the extra income created by the price decrease also induces consumers to purchase more gasoline, because gasoline is a normal (noninferior) good. Again, because this dollar is spread over so many goods, we have typically ignored the induced effects of the income change as insubstantial.

In the case of the labor-leisure choice, however, the income effect of a change in wages is reasonably *not* insubstantial and therefore cannot be ignored. Moreover, since the individual is *selling* a good—leisure—not buying a good, the income effect is in the opposite direction of the substitution effect. Suppose a person receives a pay increase from $10 per hour to $11 per hour. The substitution effect of this pay increase is unambiguous. The higher wage is an increase in the price of leisure. Leaving work an hour earlier now costs the worker $11 of consumable goods instead of $10. Therefore, this person will substitute *away* from leisure, *increasing* the amount of hours worked. However, the pay increase also produces an income effect. With full time work of 2,080 hours per year, the individual's annual income increases by $2,080. This increase in income is spent on both more consumable goods and possibly on more leisure. We expect a pure increase in income to cause individuals to consume *more* leisure; that is, we expect leisure to be a normal (noninferior) good. We base this conclusion on the empirical observations of persons who receive pure income increases, such as winners of state lotteries. These individuals invariably work fewer hours (often zero hours) after they win the lottery. Therefore, if a person's wage increases, the substitution effect makes people choose more work, but the income effect induces people to choose less work. In contrast to the case where we *buy* noninferior goods, in which the income and substitution effects reinforce one another, in the labor-leisure choice, the two effects always oppose one another, because the person is *selling* one of the goods—leisure. As a result of these two opposite effects, we can't be sure that the supply curve of labor is upward sloping. It is an empirical matter, to be determined by investigation of the facts.

Participation in the labor force seems to involve two separate decisions. A person first decides whether or not to participate at all. Then, if the decision is made to participate, the person decides how many hours per week to work. The first decision is "all-or-nothing:" a person either participates or doesn't participate in the labor market. The second decision allows a marginal response to change in wage rates. If the wage rate increases by a small amount, the individual adjusts the number of hours worked by some appropriate amount.

Both of these participation decisions depend on individuals' tastes for income versus leisure, and their endowments of nonwage income. If a person has no source of income other than that received from working, then even at a very low wage, that person will probably choose to participate in the labor force, and work many hours per week in order not to starve to death. An increase in the wage rate will surely not induce the person to leave the labor force, but the effect on the hours worked is indeterminate. As the wage available increases, the person might very well spend the extra income on leisure, by working fewer hours. Alternatively, the person might find it worthwhile to take further advantage of the higher wage by working more hours per week.

On the other hand, suppose this person had available some nonwage income from a trust fund set up by a wealthy relative, or from a government transfer payment, say, welfare payments or unemployment compensation. In that case, a low wage might not induce the person to work at all (even if the level of welfare payments were unaffected). The postulate of diminishing marginal values implies that the marginal value (relative to leisure) of the increase in income gained by working a greater number of hours is relatively less with an endowment of nonwage income. A low wage may therefore be insufficient to induce this person to give up the requisite leisure. The choice to participate in the labor force might not occur until the wage rate was sufficient to provide a substantial increase in income over the nonwage source, so as to compensate for the loss of leisure.

Many important policy issues hinge on the empirical realities of the labor-leisure choice. For example, in the 1980s, federal income tax rates were dramatically lowered. Previously, up to 70% of a person's income over a certain amount could be taxed away. This was reduced to 50% and then to 28%. In recent years the marginal tax rate on high incomes has again been increased, to about 41% in 1993. Throughout these years a debate has raged as to the impact of these changes on work effort. Some have argued that raising these tax rates is harmful to the economy because it discourages people from working. A decrease in the income tax rate is an increase in the effective wage rate, in terms of after-tax income. Thus a change in tax rates should produce changes in the labor-leisure choice in the same fashion as an opposite change in wage rates. But we have seen that no clear answer is available from theory alone. We can be fairly certain that as tax rates approach 100%, so that a person would keep none of the income he or she produces, the quantity of labor supplied would fall to zero. People will rarely work for nothing. But what is the actual impact of these changes in tax rates?

Recent research provides some clues to the empirical reality of labor supply. It seems clear that *over time,* as real wages and thus incomes have risen, the amount of leisure consumed has also risen. (This is referred to as *times series* data.) In the early part of the twentieth century and earlier, men commonly worked 12 hours per day or longer. Over time, the increase in real wages produced by technological change and economic growth has been accompanied by a *decrease* in the hours men have worked in the labor market. These data indicate that the income effect dominates the substitution effect of more expensive leisure, at least in the long run. However, some highly paid individuals are observed to work more than the average number of hours per week. For example, lawyers in prestigious firms or practices, whose billing rates are well over $100 per hour (often over $200 per hour) work 50 to 60 hours per week.[4] (The same is true for physicians.) Studies indicate, however, that on average, as the wage rate increases, more people decide to participate, while the effect on hours worked by those already in the labor market is small, but probably negative. The total effect of an increase in real wages seems to be an *increase* in the amount of labor offered, but it derives mainly from in increase in the participation rate in the labor force.[5]

However, rising real labor market wages for women over time have been accompanied not only by increasing labor force participation of women, but increasing amounts of hours worked per person. Economists also investigate the slope of the labor supply curve in a given year, using data for different individuals at differing wages. (This kind of data is called *cross section* data.) In the case of married women, the decision to participate appears at a higher wage relative to single women. This occurs because a spouse's income is an endowment of nonwage income to an individual, just like some government transfer. The labor-leisure decisions of husbands and wives depend on the other spouse's decisions. A person with a high-wage spouse is less likely to work in the labor market than one whose spouse has low wages. Since more married women have husbands in the labor force than vice versa, and men have typically earned more than women, married women on average have a higher endowment of nonwage income than married men. We would therefore expect women to enter the labor force at a relatively higher market wage than men. However, the elasticities of supply for women already working also appear to be very small, indicating little responsiveness to changes in wages.[6]

Finally, as with any good or resource, the actual shape and location of a labor supply curve depends on the availability and ease of replicability of the labor in question. There is some type of labor, particularly relatively unskilled labor such as farm workers, which is in relatively abundant supply. Many of these workers and their families migrate to where the work is more plentiful. The supply curve of such workers is practically flat, that is, nearly perfectly elastic at the market wage. On the other hand, the supply curves of skilled craftspersons and professionals are likely relatively inelastic. It is not easy to acquire the skills needed for these occupations, and thus the ability to replicate these workers is limited, at least in the short run. There are very few people with the skills to be a quarterback in the National Football League. They need to be able, while running to one side, to throw the ball and have it arrive at the exact spot where someone else is running along a diagonal or zig-zag path. They seem to solve a very complicated differential equation in their minds. The supply curve of quarterbacks is likely fairly steep. It rises for the same reason that, say, the supply curve of land used to grow wheat rises. A few individuals

---

4. Of course, by using the number of hours *billed,* the sacrifice of leisure would be even more pronounced.

5. See, for example, "Household Behavior and Tax Reform," by Jerry A. Hausman and James M. Poterba, in *The Journal of Economic Perspectives,* Vol. 1, No. 1, Summer 1987, 10119.

6. See *The Journal of Labor Economics,* January , 1985, Part 2, which is entirely devoted to female labor force participation. The issue contains some interesting inter-country comparisons. See also, "The Sensitivity of An Empirical Model of Married Women's Hours of Work to Economic and Statistical Assumptions," *Econometrica,* Vol. 55, July 1987, 76599, and *Labor Supply* by Mark Killingsworth, Cambridge Surveys of Economic Literature (Cambridge: Cambridge University Press, 1983).

have tremendous skills, based on natural gifts (and a lot of past hard work); they are the most efficient producers of the service. As team owners recruit additional quarterbacks, the cost of providing the same level of play increases, because the new quarterbacks are not as efficient at producing touchdown plays, etc., as the initial units. The most efficient players stand to receive the greatest rents, based on the differences between their skills and those players "at the margin," who just barely qualify to play in the league. The same is true to one degree or another in all fields.

13.2 Families: The New Home Economics

In the preceding section we have characterized the labor leisure choice as a decision between staying "home" and not working, versus participating in the organized labor market. More realistically, there are *three* options: in addition to leisure and labor market participation there is production of income *in the household.* Many of the things we do at home are not really leisure. A famous old story concerns a man who hires a maid (it could just as easily be a woman who hires a butler) to cook and clean the house for him. He pays her $15,000 per year for these services, duly filling out the requisite government forms, withholding income and social security taxes and issuing her a W-2 statement at the end of the year. Her income becomes part of the "national income accounts," that is, part of the "gross domestic product" of the nation. She pays various income taxes on the money she earns. Then, the two decide to marry. She still does the same work, but now he no longer makes cash payments to her. Her *reported* income legally falls to zero. But clearly, she still is producing the same income as previously. It's just not being recorded anywhere (and, what's more, it is no longer taxable).

Thus, when we go shopping, cook a meal, do the laundry, we are producing income for ourselves (and perhaps others). It takes some time and effort to get a cooked meal onto the table. When we go to a restaurant, we hire others to do the shopping, cooking and cleaning up for us. The bill for the meal exceeds the cost of the raw food several-fold; this represents the cost of labor and other inputs the restaurant uses. If we cook that same meal at home, we "hire" ourselves to do the work. But our cooking and related activities are surely not "leisure," even if we derive some pleasure in the activity, any more than are the efforts of the hired cooks and waiters at the restaurants. Rather, we are producing household income.

We can analyze the decision to hire ourselves in the household instead of others using the laws of demand and supply. Production of income in the home requires time. The allocation of time between household production versus income production in the labor market depends in part on a person's market wage and their implicit household "wage," that is, the amount they actually produce in the home per hour. The relationship between these two wages and the wages of others who we might otherwise hire to do household work for us are key ingredients in these decisions.

Consider initially a single person household, in which the individual works at some market wage w. Assume he or she (let's settle on she) can adjust her working hours enough so that the decision to stop her market work truly carries with it the opportunity cost of $\$w$ per hour. In order to derive the maximum benefits from her 24 hour day, the marginal value of her time in the various activities should all be equal to this marginal opportunity cost. That is, if she can work as many hours as she wants at a constant hourly wage, she allocates household time to household production and to leisure activities until the marginal values of these activities falls to her market wage. Like all other productive processes, household production is subject to the law of diminishing marginal product. Likewise, the marginal value of leisure, like other consumer goods, also diminishes. If the marginal value of either working, working at home or leisure is, say, greater than *w*, then if that activity is increased, it produces a benefit in excess of its cost. Likewise, if the marginal value of one of these activities is less than *w*, she receives benefits by curtailing that activity. The gains from reallocation are exhausted when the marginal values of all these activities are equal, and equal to their common marginal opportunity cost. If the hours of labor market work are not adjustable, as is common at least in the short run, then the greatest benefits still are realized when the marginal values of the other activities are all equal to each other, but not necessarily to *w*.

Consider now the effect of an increase in a person's market wage. This raises the opportunity cost of all home activities. In addition to adjusting the number of hours in the labor market, people adjust the times spent in household tasks and also the way in which that time is used. As we discussed previously, an increase in the market wage is an increase in the price of leisure, but since the income effect might dominate the pure substitution effect, the effect on the number of hours spent in leisure activities is ambiguous. Let us now assume for the moment that the production of income in the home is independent of other activities.[7] This activity now takes place until the person's marginal product in this work equals the now higher wage. With diminishing marginal product of home production, this implies that if no other adjustments are made, less time will be spent in production of income in the home.

However, a person can increase the marginal product of household production in ways other than by merely decreasing the number of hours spent on it. Microwave ovens and ready-to-eat (or ready to microwave) foods are two examples of "capital" that increases the marginal productivity of a person's labor in the home. Data on food consumption from the U.S. Department of Agriculture indicate, for example, that whereas consumption of potatoes increases roughly in proportion to income (the income elasticity of potatoes is about unity), consumption of frozen French fried potatoes increases much more rapidly with increases in income (the income elasticity of frozen, semi-prepared potatoes is much larger than unity). Frozen foods, and especially frozen ready-to-cook meals generally require less time to prepare than preparing fresh foods from scratch. These foods permit a person to economize on time used in household production. Thus these foods are consumed in relatively greater amounts by high-wage earners. When the opportunity cost of a person's leisure time is low, it does not pay to invest in these productivity-increasing commodities. However, with a higher opportunity cost of time, these devices become cheaper relative to labor. Thus an increase in market wage rates induces people to spend money on capital that makes their time spent in household production more productive.

---

7. Strictly speaking, an increase in the market wage causes a change in *two* relative prices simultaneously: the price of leisure relative to market work and the price of home production relative to market work (or to leisure). Thus the law of demand, which pertains only to changes in a single relative price cannot easily be invoked. However, we abstract from these considerations by assuming that the activities are all independently produced and consumed.

Other examples are easy to cite. Cellular phones, a fairly new innovation, permit people to use time otherwise wasted commuting in a productive way. Although these phones are becoming cheaper, cell-phone calls are still fairly expensive relative to phones in the home. For people earning "moderate" wages, it is cheaper to wait until you get home or to the office to make calls. For high wage earners, however, these calls are cheap relative to the opportunity cost of their time. In a similar fashion, electronic pagers increase the productivity of time spent away from a central place of employment.[8] Home computers can increase the productivity of household labor. In some instances, computers are altering our concept of "household" production. For example, many people for whom writing is a significant job component are able to work just as well at home or on public transit.

Shopping is a generally time-intensive activity. We expect it to decrease as a person's market labor wage increases. Some supermarkets, for example, hire less checkout help than other outlets, and use the savings to charge relatively low prices for the food items. Other stores have lots of checkers and have their managers watching the counters to make sure the lines don't get very long. They pay for this extra help by charging relatively more for the items they sell. For persons whose value of time is low, shopping at the first type of market produces income (by the dollar amounts saved on food purchases) in excess of the value of time lost by the longer wait. High wage earners are more apt to find the value of time more expensive than the income earned by the low prices, and are therefore more likely to shop at the more expensive supermarket.

The advent in the past generation of "fast food" restaurants, home-delivered pizza and other foods are additional responses to relatively high market wages. These food outlets permit relatively high wage earners to further economize on production in the home by reducing the amount of time spent preparing meals. Supermarkets are in fact evolving into extremely large markets selling a wide variety of goods. Many food stores are now combined with "discount" type stores in one large complex. These stores lower the time cost of shopping by providing a large variety of goods under one roof. Some of this is undoubtedly due to technological change, in particular, the application of computers to inventory and checkout procedures. However, on the demand side, the growing market wage over the past generation has made these time-saving innovations relatively more worthwhile.[9]

Supermarkets frequently issue colored stamps (for example, S&H "green stamps") which consumers can use to purchase goods through a catalogue, and various food manufacturers and the stores themselves print coupons in the newspapers or mailers which provide discounts on the specified items. An interesting explanation of this phenomenon is based on the differing values of time of the stores' customers. Clipping coupons, or pasting green stamps into books consumes part of an individual's leisure time. The consumers produce income by this activity by saving money on food purchases. The amount of money they earn per hour rarely is above the wages paid entry level labor. This activity is

---

8. A good example of an *optimist* is a banjo player with a pager.

9. In the late 1970s through the present, increases in real (adjusted for inflation) wages has been small, though relatively largest for high income groups, who are most likely to use these time saving devices. It may be the case that lower costs of these devices through technological change is the main reason for their prevalence.

therefore most appealing to those individuals with relatively low wages. Doctors and lawyers don't waste their valuable time clipping coupons; assuming they don't *enjoy* clipping out coupons; they can earn much more by staying at the office a bit longer. The effect of this process is that consumers whose incomes are relatively low pay less for food than those with relatively high wages. Trading stamps and coupons thus are actually a subtle form of price discrimination. We should expect to see these marketing strategies relatively more frequently in heterogeneous neighborhoods or cities. If all of the potential customers had similar incomes, either high or low, then stores would more likely use a single profit-maximizing pricing/quality structure. When market wages vary considerably, these price differentiation schemes become more attractive.

Acquiring information, often a part of shopping, is another time consuming activity. Prices usually vary from store to store. For very low priced items the time we would spend seeking the lowest price would rarely exceed the value of the time spent searching. As the items we desire become more expensive, it pays to search relatively more. Thus we shop around more for stereo systems than for sneakers, and still more for cars. At some point, the value of additional search falls to the marginal opportunity cost of time (the market wage) and we make a purchase. For persons with a higher market wage, the opportunity cost of time is greater and thus little or no shopping for lower prices occurs for inexpensive goods and relatively less occurs for more expensive goods than for those whose value of time is lower.

Often, savings are available by shopping at factory outlets. These stores are usually located away from the usual retail centers and often sell "second quality" or slightly blemished merchandise. The inventory usually is less predictable than at a retail store, so there is a greater chance that a trip will be fruitless. This kind of shopping is relatively expensive for high wage earners. As a result, most shoppers at these stores are those with relatively low market wages. Likewise, in many areas, auction houses sell antiques and other used items. It is possible to get a real bargain at these establishments, but the time cost can be very severe. Most high income people thus shop at regular antique stores, or, to further economize on shopping time, hire designers to shop for them.

Marriage

Let us now turn to the analysis of households containing more than one person. The value of time is an important explanatory variable in understanding some of the relationships that occur in these households, in particular the choices about who produces labor market income and who produces the bulk of household income. First, however, note a well-known aspect of joint living. An old saying goes "two can live as cheaply as one." That's not exactly true of course, but there are substantial economies of scale in household production. In the first place, many household items have the characteristics of pure public goods. That is, some goods in the household exhibit an absence of congestion. Consumption of the dwelling by one person may interfere little with another. Two can watch the same television program and listen to the same music at the same time. A person can shop for two people almost as easily as shopping for one. Secondly, some food and other items are more economically purchased in amounts greater than what a single person consumes alone. According to the *Survey of Consumer Expenditures,* published by the Bureau of Labor Statistics each year, housing and house furnishings and other jointly consumed goods typically account for only about 50 percent of a person's budget, the rest goes for goods that cannot be shared with others. Even with some economies of scale, two can't really live as cheaply as one, but they can save perhaps one quarter of their budget by rooming with another person.

The above remarks apply to persons of either gender who live in the same household. The savings due to joint consumption are available to roommates as well as married couples. However, there are some costs of cohabitation. You have to reasonably like the other person or persons. Joint consumption or production requires cooperation. If musical tastes differ, the stereo system can become more of an instrument of torture rather than a jointly consumed public good. People have to be considerate of others in the household by doing their share of cleaning up, not leaving the bathroom messy for others. Thus it is easier to cohabit when you are fond of the other person. Some formerly popular communal arrangements such as those which "flowered" in the late 1960s and 1970s notwithstanding, living together seems most easy when two adults who love each other live together, possibly with their children. This has traditionally occurred in the framework of marriage, though new living arrangements are becoming more common.

Marriage is a contract between a husband and wife.[10] It is an agreement backed by an extensive legal history in both common and statutory law. Unless otherwise specified, the couple agrees to share to some degree the market income produced by either person, to cooperate to some extent in the production of household income and in particular in the raising of children. For reasons we shall specify in a moment, there are abundant occasions in these arrangements for "opportunistic" behavior on the part of either spouse. The husband and wife can derive the largest benefits if they agree to not take short-run advantage of the other. If both act in this way, they wind up in the noncooperative outcome we described in the "prisoner's dilemma" model of Chapter 9. Some form of marriage has existed in virtually all known human societies. It is obvious that this institution has served some fundamental purpose, that is, it must be extremely convenient and productive to have this arrangement, and extremely inconvenient to not have it. It demands an explanation.

The principal occasion for marriage most likely has been the raising of children. Children require market income and substantial amounts of household income. Having two people raise children allows for greater gains through specialization and division of labor. The question is, what arrangement provides the greatest amount of *total* family income, including the household component? What considerations explain the historically traditional marital arrangement in which men were the principal providers of market income and women were the main providers of household income?

We have already discussed briefly, in Chapter 3, that human reproduction has a much greater impact on women than on men. For males, reproduction is completed with the sex act. Human females, however, must spend nine months in pregnancy, during which time they become progressively less able to engage in market labor. Before recent generations, when most market labor involved

10. Most of what follows also applies to homosexual "marriages" as well, but we ignore that topic for expositional ease. It is an interesting exercise to see what changes and what can be used in analyzing these newer relationships.

substantial physical effort, the physical aspects of pregnancy led most women to very quickly drop out of the labor force completely. Infant formula and other modern conveniences were not available. Thus until recently, children required almost full time attention of the mother until they reached age 2 to 3. Therefore, a sensible strategy for a woman contemplating children has been to anticipate their separation from the labor market and to consider carefully the ability and willingness of her mate to provide for her during this time. Moreover, since the process begins anew with each pregnancy, a woman contemplating several children would have to plan for an extended period of time during which little labor market income would be earned by herself.[11]

We tend to forget that modern conveniences such as gas and electricity, indoor plumbing and running water, central heating, have not always been with us. There are still many people living in America today who remember not having these amenities in their youth. Moreover, these amenities are often still not available in many parts of the world. Think for a moment about raising children and maintaining a household without electricity and running water. A corny but true old saying went "Man works from sun to sun, but a woman's work is never done." Women had to plan and prepare for dinner almost as soon as breakfast was done. There was endless laundry and clothing repair. Water had to be brought in from a well. Homemaking was a full time job. Even with household help in the form of nannies and maids, having a career along side was for the most part out of the question.

Moreover, most jobs, including household work have some component of "on-the-job" learning, that is, acquisition of human capital through working. However, it is often the case that this human capital is useful mainly in one occupation, or even in one job. We call this **specific human capital**, in contrast with **general human capital**, which is readily transferable to other jobs or careers. As we specialize and develop skills in a particular line of work, we become more productive and thus more attractive to employers. These productivity increases usually come at the expense of not acquiring skills in other fields, and perhaps even forgetting previously acquired but unrelated skills. Thus, journey electricians and carpenters usually know little about each other's skills; and likewise for lawyers and doctors, economics professors and chemistry professors. This is why switching careers even once in a lifetime is so costly almost nobody does it. One would lose the specific skills that may be very valuable in one occupation, but which may be practically worthless in another.

The same analysis applies to specialization in household versus labor market employment. The skills we acquire increase over time in both occupations, but the transferability between the two career paths usually is extremely limited. It would therefore be extremely costly in most marital situations for women in previous generations to have attempted to specialize in the production of labor market income, with the man producing the household income. The interruptions childbearing and nurturing would cause would have led these women to

11. It should be noted, however, that the stereotypical specialization within the family is really a creature of *urban* societies, where work takes place away from the home. In older, or even present day agricultural societies, women have worked alongside men in often strenuous tasks, taking little time out for either pregnancy or infant nurturing. It is the inconvenience that urban work away from the home imposes that bears most heavily on female participation in the labor force during childbearing years.

acquire lower amounts of human capital with consequently lower market income than if men with the same talents pursued those jobs. Thus, given the biological necessity of having the mothers perform the essential nurturing tasks for small children, it is not surprising that historically, specialization took the form of females staying at home and providing most of the household income, and men providing the bulk of the labor market income. The gains from this traditional division of labor are so great that it is difficult to find an example of any society in which this has not been the dominant arrangement.

For all these reasons, women who spend their early adulthood specializing in household income find, when they attempt to enter the labor force after their children are independent, that their household skills are not highly valued in the competitive labor market. Unless these women have prior training is some profession, they often return to the same jobs they had when they left school at entry level wages. Proceeding up a career ladder is usually very difficult at that stage. Thus a sensible strategy for girls was to plan for a career for which *reentry* into the labor force was relatively easy. There are certain jobs for which this has been true, at least in the past, for example, teaching, nursing, waitressing, typing and related office work. It is significantly for this reason that women were and still are overrepresented (in terms of their proportion of the population) in these professions.

Divorce

In previous generations and in older European and Asian societies, marriage really meant a lifetime commitment. Divorce was and still is forbidden by the Catholic Church; in countries in which this was the dominant religion, divorce was impossible. Even though tolerated in Protestant and Jewish societies, divorce was always considered something of a last resort, to be utilized only in extreme situations. Moreover, until recent generations, birth control was largely unavailable. A significant part of the reason for this societal disdain for divorce is rooted in the consequences of the division of labor between husbands and wives, and the consequences of removing the person producing market income from the household. When marriage was assumed to be lifelong, women usually didn't bother to acquire labor market skills. Women took it for granted that their husbands would provide the market income for the family. (Men similarly were often totally ignorant about household tasks, though this was usually of less consequence). As a result, women became dependent on their husbands for market income, and had little prospect for generating it themselves after their children were born.

Economists tend to regard laws and customs limiting divorce and providing alimony to the women and support payments to children as a means of enforcing the marriage contract. Although it now has a distinctly paternalistic ring, divorce laws seem to have been enacted at least in part in recognition of the vulnerability of married women to opportunistic separation by their husbands. After a couple has been married for some time and children are present, the man earns income which, being in the form of money, can be spent in a variety of ways. His income is "liquid." The wife's income, however, is highly illiquid; it can only be "spent" in the home. The wife has little ability to take her income elsewhere. Thus historically, marriage, and particularly having children was a much riskier contract for women than for men. In the absence of divorce laws, men could simply leave if they were unhappy with the way things were turning out. Women, too, could in principle have abandoned their children and husbands, but having specialized in household tasks for most of their adulthood and therefore having few marketable skills, they would be faced with lower incomes than that available to their husbands. They were thus much less likely to separate from their husbands than the reverse.

Because of these considerations, it would have been foolhardy for a woman to agree to marriage and childbearing in the absence of a contract that would protect her when she was unable to earn market income sufficient to support herself and her children. Since in the absence of such guarantees men would find few women willing to become their wives and have their children, a legal structure was created in which divorce was if not impossible, at least difficult, and accompanied by the anticipation of alimony and child support should the marriage end. Thus ultimately it was in the interest of men as well as women to have a strong, enforceable marriage contract. These laws were backed up by the promotion of social norms that stressed marital fidelity. These norms served to lower the transactions costs associated with raising children.

In modern times, these constraints have undergone significant modification. The technology of household production changed enormously in the twentieth century. Modern household conveniences have dramatically reduced the time necessary for virtually all household tasks. It is now possible to have a full time career *and* raise a family, with, perhaps some form of outside assistance such as daycare and house cleaning help. Women are no longer tied to the house, even if they have children, and as a result, many more women are choosing careers in the labor market than in previous generations. Secondly, the percentage of jobs where physical strength is important is now much smaller than in previous generations. The economy is now service oriented, with heavy manufacturing becoming a smaller and smaller part, evidenced by a dramatic reduction in the wages of less educated men relative to wages of more highly educated males. Thus the comparative advantage some men enjoyed because of greater strength is diminishing in importance, though there are still many jobs, for example, in heavy construction, which are predominantly male because of this consideration.

Lastly, and perhaps most significantly of all, accompanying these changes has been a dramatic shift in divorce laws. Prior to the early 1970s, divorce in the United States required the consent of *both* parties. Even then, it was only granted for "cause," such as adultery and "mental cruelty." One party had to be found "at fault." If, say, the wife did not want to divorce, there was little the husband could do about it, unless he was able to prove "grounds." In the early 1970s, most states enacted no fault divorce laws. Not only was fault removed from the action, but *only one person had to want the divorce.* If either the husband or the wife chose to divorce, the other party was powerless to prevent it. Courts now divide the marital community's assets, set child support payments and provide alimony to some generally limited degree.[12] The divorce itself, however, cannot be stopped by an unwilling spouse.

The dramatic increase in labor force participation amongst married women in the last generation is partially in response to this important change in the

12. This, and all other aspects of marriage and divorce are covered by *State* laws in the United States and Provincial law in Canada. The details therefore vary from state to state and province to province.

guaranties associated with marriage, as well as the greater efficiency of household technology. Unilateral (no fault) divorce has made specialization in household income much riskier than in previous generations. It is thus now relatively more prudent to acquire some labor market skills before entering into a marriage, and perhaps even to continue that labor market experience even when children are present. This strategy is an insurance policy against the prospect of divorce with limited alimony and perhaps uncertain child support payments. As a result, we see later marriages than in previous generations.

13.3 The Demand for Labor

The demand for labor is based on the usefulness of labor in the production of goods useful to humans. Some goods are produced for direct consumption—food and cars—while other goods, which we call *capital,* are produced because they lead to greater or more efficient production of other goods. Firms producing either consumer goods or capital have demand curves for labor and for the other inputs in production. We say that the demand for labor (and for capital also) is a *derived demand,* because productive inputs are not desired for their own sake, but rather for the useful goods they produce. We discussed these concepts in Chapter 7 and won't repeat them in detail here. But recall that the demand for labor is a downward sloping curve because of the law of diminishing marginal product. The amount a firm is willing to pay for an additional unit of labor is the value of that labor's marginal product, that is, the additional physical output created by that labor times the price of the product. If the value of this marginal product is greater than the wage of the person, firms will seek to hire more of that labor. The decision to cease additional hiring of labor occurs when the value of the marginal product of labor falls to the market wage.

The marginal product of a worker is greater when that person brings skills to the job. An experienced journey electrician is more valuable to an employer than a handyman. The skilled electrician's wage is higher because in the same period of time, the skilled person accomplishes more of value to the employer (and thus ultimately to consumers) than the less skilled person. Skills, or more appropriately, **human capital**, comes in many forms. For electricians, for example, it can mean specific knowledge about how to efficiently and safely connect electrical wiring to some facility. Individuals may have acquired a large part of that human capital in some sort of apprenticeship program or school. However, a large component seems to come from general education. Reading and writing abilities are to some extent important in most present day jobs; we usually acquire these skills in elementary and high school. People who drop out before graduating from high school are less likely to be able to acquire human capital that is highly valued in the marketplace. At the other extreme, individuals who obtain professional training, such as in law, medicine and computer science have capital that is often extremely highly valued. These persons sometimes command wage rates of one to several hundreds of dollars per hour.

Table 13-1 presents statistics on the average annual earnings in 1991 of males employed full time, based on educational attainment. As is apparent, those with more education earn more, on average.

The sources of some of these differences in earnings is the subject of some debate. To some extent, the higher incomes of more educated individuals reflect

Table 13-1 *Average Earnings of Males, Full Time Workers, 1997*[13]

Educational Attainment	Annual Income
Less than 9th Grade	$ 22,746
High School, No Diploma	$ 27,638
High School Graduate	$ 32,611
Associate (2 year) Degree	$ 40,465
Bachelor's Degree	$ 55,832
Master's Degree	$ 71,225
Doctorate Degree	$ 93,106
Professional Degree	$120,052

the skills acquired in school. This is most apparent for specific occupations, such as engineers, where the education is of a more directly vocational nature than, say, a degree in history. Even with liberal arts education, however, the skills involved in being able to read and digest articles or books and to write coherent sentences expressing an opinion about the material should not be taken lightly. These skills help a person make executive types of decisions, and are likely an important part of upward mobility in a career and therefore higher income. However, it also seems apparent that those who acquire relatively more education are on average the more gifted and intelligent part of the population. We would expect these individuals to accomplish more even with the same education as those less capable. Some part, therefore, of these earnings differences are due to the innately higher skills possessed by the people who get more education. This issue is the subject of ongoing research.[14]

Additional evidence of the role of human capital in earnings is discernible from data on earnings over a person's working life, called an *age-earnings profile.* In Fig. 13-2 the earnings of male high school dropouts, high school graduates and college graduates are plotted by five-year age intervals. Notice that in each case earnings start quite low, but then rise as people get older. Eventually, as people reach their fifties, earnings start to fall off. It seems likely that the human capital acquired during employment is a major component of this pattern. When people first enter the labor force, they invariably find they have a lot to learn. It takes time to learn how an organization operates and what skills are especially important. With repeated application and perhaps greater specialization over time, our skills improve and we are able to accomplish things in less time. These increases in productivity are part of the explanation of the age-earnings cycle. In addition, over time, as a person masters the more elementary tasks, employers assign him or her to jobs with greater responsibility. These jobs often require knowledge of the firm and its relation to the industry, the ability to make longer

13. *Source: Money Income of Households, Families and Persons in the United States: 1997,* U.S. Department of Commerce, Bureau of the Census, Series P-60, No. 200.

14. A further theory suggests that a liberal arts education may have little market value in itself, but the fact that a person has completed four years of demanding college coursework acts as a *signal* to employers that the person is intelligent, hardworking and diligent. It is these personal habits, the theory asserts, that are valuable, and graduation from college is a way for workers to reveal to prospective employers that they have these attributes. The theory has been criticized because it seems an expensive way to produce this information. Other means, such as examinations and on the job experience seem much less expensive than four years of tuition and lost earnings.

Figure 13-2 *Age-Earnings Profiles*

The earnings of male high school dropouts, graduates, and college graduates are plotted by age. For all groups, incomes increase with age, but the earnings are higher for those with more education.

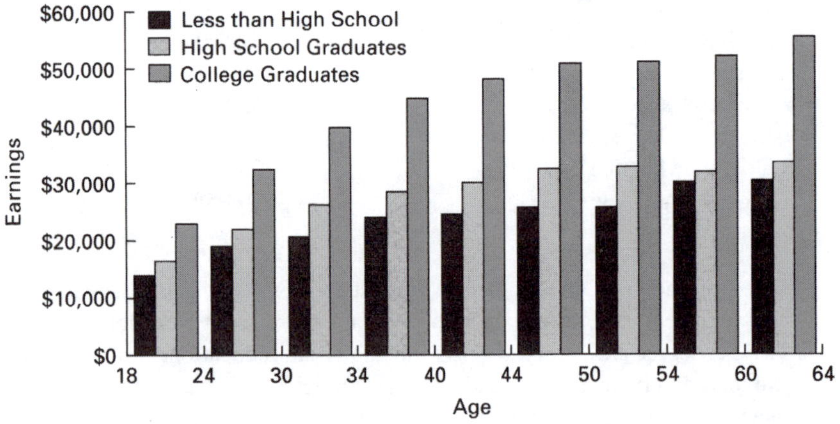

range plans, and judgment regarding current operations. New hires rarely possess these skills. In time individuals acquire more sophistication about how decisions are made and implemented, and what their effects are. Often a company stands to gain a great deal if these managerial decisions are made correctly, and they stand to lose a lot if they are done badly. A person who can make beneficial decisions is therefore often a very valuable employee. Thus we expect wages to increase with experience in the labor force and especially in a particular job.[15]

The steepness of the slope of the age-earnings profile depends in an important way on the type of human capital a person acquires during his or her employment, especially in the early years. Some skills are of a *general* nature, being useful in many jobs and employers. Other skills are more *specific* to a given job or employer. Examples of general skills are, for example, word processing, computer programming, computer repair, mechanical skills and the like. If these skills are acquired on the job, wages will be low during the time of learning. The employer is unlikely to be willing to pay for training that the employee can easily abscond with to some other employer. Moreover, employees are willing to accept the lower wages because they realize they are receiving valuable training. Thus employees typically "pay" for this training by accepting a relatively low wage that reflects these costs. Once these skills are mastered, wages rise to reflect the employee's greater productivity.

Some human capital, on the other hand, may be specific to a given firm. The ability to manage a business and make executive decisions usually involves knowledge about the firm's particular mode of operations, where specific resources and people are located, what particular individuals have certain specialized skills and where they are located. It takes time to acquire this kind of human capital, but the manager is in a sense a captive of the firm, since he or she

15. The decrease in wages after middle age may be due to a decrease or obsolescence in a person's human capital, but it also may be due to reduced effort. As a person gets older, the demands on their income often become less, for example, the children have moved out of the house and they no longer have the responsibilities they once had.

may be worth a lot more to the current firm than to any other firm. In this kind of situation, the firms and employees typically enter into some type of long term commitment, which enables them to share the cost of training. Thus in a sense the employee is "overpaid" in his or her early years with a firm, and "underpaid" in later years, when the human capital they have is worth more to their present employer than to any alternative employer.

The other important influence on wages from the demand side is the amount of nonhuman capital available to the worker. The effect of technology on a person's marginal product depends on whether that technology is *complementary* to a person's labor, or whether it is a *substitute* for that labor. In modern offices, for example, employers provide workers with word processors, telephones, fax machines, and other computing facilities. Reports and memoranda can be written and rewritten without time-consuming retyping. Complicated diagrams can now quickly be drawn by computers for engineering and architectural use that would have taken weeks to do only a decade ago. This technology is complementary to labor; its availability enhances the productivity of individuals who master it. On the other hand, consider that the electronic revolution has decreased the demand for many individuals who were formerly engaged in making precision mechanical devices. To make a quality mechanical wristwatch, cash register or typewriter involves crafting metal to very precise tolerances. Setting movable type for a newspaper or book meant fitting different sized letters and spaces into printing frames so as to make the columns come out justified on both margins. These were difficult tasks, and wages in these occupations were among the highest in the blue collar trades, because relatively few craftspersons were able to master them. These older machines and skills have to a large extent been replaced by electronic devices with few moving parts. The demand curve for persons with these older skills has therefore shifted to the left, or down, reducing the wages of these individuals. It is not a new story: when the wheel was invented, it must have decreased the demand for individuals who had a comparative advantage in hauling things by brute strength.

13.4 The Market for Labor

As with other goods and services in an exchange economy, the services of labor are transacted in a market, called—the labor market. This market consists of the interactions of those individuals who *supply* labor and others who have a *demand* for it. We use the same basic concepts and tools of supply and demand curves we used elsewhere in this text to analyze labor markets. However, markets for labor often have institutional features not present in other markets. To cite an obvious example, whereas most goods can be purchased outright, a person's labor can only be *rented.* Since the abolition of human slavery, it is not possible to completely own the labor of another person. We can purchase a computer outright, because the computer has no "inalienable rights" created or enforced by the state. A computer can't decide to back out of a deal. A person, on the other hand, can decide to sever an employment situation at any time; he or she is distinguished from a slave by being "free to leave."[16]

16. However, if a person has contracted with an employer to do some work and the employer undertakes certain costs in preparation, and then the worker backs out, the worker can be sued for damages the employer sustains due to the breach of contract. Hollywood movie stars have been successfully sued for such breaches.

The supply of labor is based on the distribution of skills in the workforce and on individual labor-leisure choices. As we indicated previously, the decision to forego leisure or household production depends on the relative values of one's market wage, household wage and value of leisure. As in the case of ordinary market goods, the *market* demands and supplies for labor are simply the aggregates of the individual supply and demand curves. We assume, however, that increases in market wages lead to sufficient additional entry into the labor force so that market labor supply curves are upward sloping, even though a particular individual's response to a higher wage may be to supply less labor. A typical labor market diagram thus appears as other markets (see Fig. 13-3). On the horizontal axis is the quantity of labor; the price of labor, that is, the wage rate, is plotted vertically.

At wage rate *w* the quantity of labor demanded equals the quantity of labor supplied, exhausting the mutual benefits from exchange in this market. The markets in which labor is transacted are distinguished by high degrees of regulation, because the participants are humans with individual rights. We therefore sometimes have to modify the analyses to account for these constraints. These characteristics are part of what makes labor markets particularly interesting to study.

The price of any good or service is determined by both the supply and demand for that item. It cannot be attributed to only supply or only demand. Recall the diamond-water analysis in which water, a necessity of life, is generally inexpensive because it is relatively plentiful (usually), whereas diamonds, which are pleasant frivolities are expensive because they are relatively rare. Other things equal, a person's wage will be high relative to others if the labor service that person provides is relatively highly valued by employers. This can happen because the person directly produces a good for consumers that is highly valued (or because the person provides a service that is highly valued to someone else who sells something to consumers) or because the type of labor supplied by the person is relatively uncommon. Ultimately, the person's labor must be useful in producing a good or service that results in satisfying the demands of consumers.

The wage employers pay in a given job reflects the various working conditions attached to the job. Computers may not care whether the place of employment is pleasant, has a good view, doesn't smell bad, but human employees do

Figure 13-3 *The Market for Labor*

Like other markets, the market for labor consists of the supply and demand for labor. The demand for labor is based on the marginal product of labor in some eandeavor; the supply of labor is based on the willingness of humans to trade off leisure for market income.

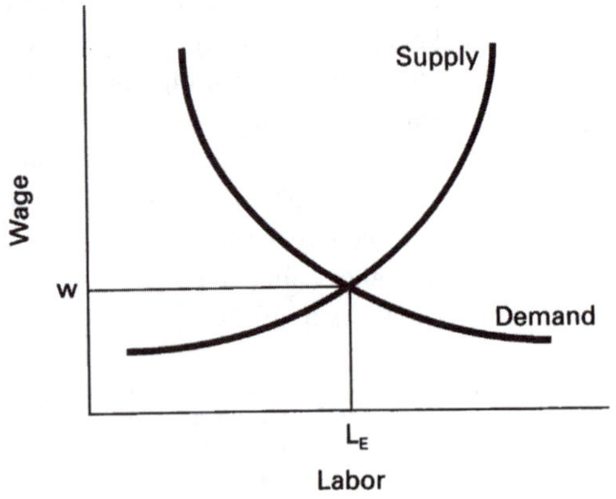

care about these things. If a place of employment is unpleasant, fewer employees will be willing to work than if the unpleasant aspects of the job were reduced. We say that wages reflect a **compensating differential** for the nonpecuniary aspects of a job. Jobs that are dangerous pay more than a job requiring the same skills but which is safer for employees. Garbage collectors earn wages similar to teachers because their work is unpleasant to most people. In order to induce people to apply for those jobs, employers must compensate employees with a higher wage. Recall that in Chapter 2 we showed how economists estimate the value of life using wages for similar jobs but which have differing probabilities of death on the job. People do in fact agree to work at dangerous jobs, but only if they get a wage premium.

As with all other goods and resources, anything that causes a decrease in supply, that is, a leftward shift in the supply curve will increase the price of the resource, in this case the wage of labor (other things remaining the same). Increases in supply similarly lower the wage rate. Workers have therefore sought over the centuries to shift the supply of workers to the left by reducing the availability of substitute workers. These efforts are of course always opposed by employers who stand to receive higher rents on the specific factors of production they own such as land, specific capital already in place and entrepreneurial skill, when other costs are lowered. There are several outstanding ways in which workers have tried to reduce the supply of their type of labor. One of the most important is the creation of labor unions. We discuss this important topic in the following section.

A sure-fire way of eliminating competition is to make it illegal for certain other persons to work. In the United States, foreigners cannot work unless they have a "green card." Under terms of the immigration law passed in the late 1980s, employers are liable for a $10,000 fine for each occurrence of hiring an illegal alien. The law was directed mainly at the hiring of Mexican farm workers in California. (This law is the reason why employers carefully check your social security card and other documents are carefully checked when you seek employment.) By restricting the supply of foreign workers, the supply of farm workers (mostly, but not exclusively Hispanic Americans) is shifted to the left, increasing wages to some degree. The quantitative effect of this is an empirical matter still under investigation. One suspects, in this particular case, that due to the highly elastic nature of the supply of this type of labor (and, apparently, large scale counterfeiting of green cards) that the resulting increase in wages is likely not large.

Occupational licensure is another way in which competition from other workers is reduced. These laws require a person or business to have government (usually a state government) license in order to practice some field. Lawyers and doctors, for example, cannot ply their trade unless they have passed various exams and are certified by some state governing body. These laws have a dual purpose. By setting minimum professional standards, they create information about a practitioner's competence. Consumers are relieved of at least some of the burden of checking the credentials of these individuals. Also, since unqualified doctors, for example, have the potential of creating harm that might be very costly to undo, these laws may actually save resources. However, they also serve to restrict entry into these fields of possibly qualified individuals, which has the effect of raising the price of the service.

Although law and medicine are perhaps the most prominent and economically most easily justified services requiring licensure, other cases seem to lend support to the restriction of competition hypothesis. Most states, for example, license hair stylists, often requiring 2,000 hours of beauty school. This had an impact on a shop in Washington D.C. whose owner only *braided* hair, mostly of African Americans. She performed no other service. The licensing board sought to close the shop because the owner did not have the requisite beauty training and license. Other frequently licensed occupations include dog grooming, taxis, morticians, radio and TV stations and real estate agents. That these licenses were meant mainly to protect consumers from "quacks" varies in plausibility from one field to another.

Minimum Wage Laws

Minimum wage laws are another way the terms by which labor is transacted is affected by law. These laws set a minimum amount that can be paid for labor. The first minimum wage law in the United States was passed in 1937 and set a minimum of 25¢ per hour, about 40 to 50 percent of the average wage in the country at that time. It covered about 43 percent of all workers in the economy. The Supreme Court at first declared the law unconstitutional, ruling that labor did not represent interstate commerce. Under strenuous prodding from the Roosevelt administration, the Court reversed itself the following year. The federal minimum wage was raised as inflation raised price levels and stood at $4.25 per hour in 1993 and now covers about 87 percent of all workers.

We can show the effects of this law with a supply and demand diagram. In Fig 13-4, a minimum wage of $5 per hour is imposed on a market which would otherwise produce the lower wage of $4. For some hypothetical firm depicted here, 100 workers would voluntarily show up for work at $4 per hour. The diagram makes clear that the analysis is the same as for any other price floor, such as occurs frequently for agricultural products. The price floor, in this case the legal minimum wage creates a *surplus* in the good being transacted. Raising the price of labor above $4 has two consequences. The quantity of labor demanded falls from 100 to 75 workers in response to the law of demand. This can take the form of a loss of jobs outright, or cutting back on the hours offered for employment or some combination of both. For example, a fast food restaurant faced

Figure 13-4 *Effect of Minimum Wage Law*

When government imposes a minimum wage law on a market, the quantity of labor demanded decreases, while the quantity of labor supplied increases. This creates a *surplus* of labor, creating unemployment in this market.

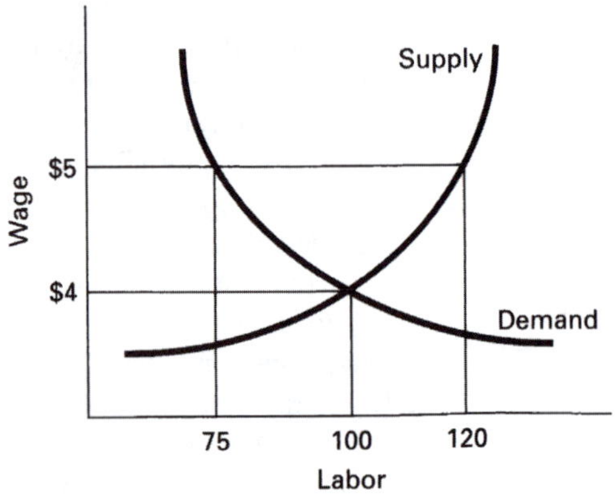

with an increase in the minimum wage for its teenage employees may decide to not stay open as late, when customers are few, thus reducing the hours worked. They may also lay off some part time workers for those slack times. Similarly, the quantity of labor supplied to this market, that is, offered to employers by individuals seeking work, *rises* from 100 to 120. The minimum wage creates a permanent excess supply of 45 workers, in the same manner as agricultural price supports create permanent surpluses of the affected foodstuffs. In the case of agriculture, the government purchases and stores the excess of food supplied over that demanded. In the labor market, *no one* purchases the excess labor supplied. The surplus workers either become unemployed, or hours of employment are reduced by 45, so that the combined amount of labor demanded falls to 75. Some workers receive a windfall increase in wages from $4 per hour to $5 per hour. Forty-five additional units of labor are offered but not hired.

The minimum wage laws do not cover all jobs. Some 13% of all workers, mainly household workers and employees of small retail establishments are not covered by the law at present.[17] An additional impact of the minimum wage law is therefore to shift some of the excess supply of labor into the uncovered sector. This is a shift to the right of the supply of labor in those markets, resulting in a decrease in the wages paid those jobs and an increase in the amount of labor hired there.

Since the legal minimum wage of, say, $4.25 per hour in the early 1990s is what is paid to only relatively unskilled, entry level workers, it is clear that Fig. 13-4 would not apply to, say skilled electricians. The people who earn close to the minimum wage are usually unskilled, entry level workers. Most of these individuals are teenagers and other younger workers and also some handicapped persons. Also, most of the jobs in which these workers are employed are less than full time. The minimum wage benefits those who remain employed and harms those who either lose their jobs or whose hours are reduced. However, the workers who lose their jobs are not likely a random cross section of these workers. The least capable workers are the ones most likely to be let go. At the higher wage, more qualified workers apply for work, and are the ones that will be most desired by employers.

Minimum wage laws are passed ostensibly "to help the poor." However, recent research indicates that only about 20% of the minimum wage workers are actually from households living in poverty; most of these workers are secondary earners such as teenagers and spouses supplementing family income. It is clear that these laws are at best a mixed blessing. These laws are pushed most vigorously by organized labor. However, there are virtually no union workers who earn wages near the legal minimum. Why would the AFL-CIO be so interested in passing minimum wage laws? Their interest almost certainly has something to do with minimum wage workers being substitutes for higher priced union labor. Recall from Chapter 5 that when the price of a substitute good increases, it shifts the demand curve for substitute goods to the right. In Fig. 13-5 the demand for skilled labor that is a substitute for unskilled labor shifts from D to D'. This raises the wage of this group of workers from w to w' and increases the amount employed form L to L'. Thus as a group, these workers benefit from passage of minimum wage laws.

---

17. Neither are executives and professionals, but it seems unlikely that the law impinges on them at all.

Figure 13-5 *Effect of an Increase in the Minimum Wage on Skilled Labor*

Since unskilled labor is often a substitute for more skilled workers, an increase in the price of unskilled labor shifts the demand for skilled labor to the right. This increases the wages and hours worked for the more skilled workers.

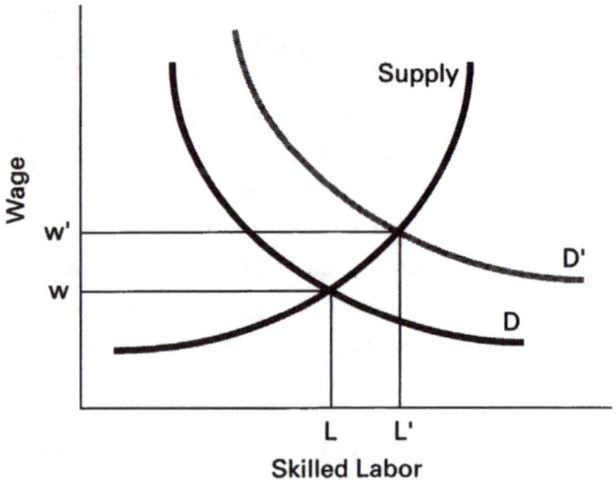

A great deal of empirical research has been done on the effects of minimum wage laws. The implication that some workers are harmed by these laws is often greeted with some hostility. Since these laws remain perennially popular, it is important to determine the actual quantitative outcomes. Does employment fall by a lot or a little when the minimum wage is increased? The empirical research does confirm the theory that minimum wages cause a decrease in employment, and that this decrease is most pronounced amongst teenagers. Most researchers have found a decrease in employment of 1 to 3 percent per 10 percent rise in the minimum wage, that is, a demand elasticity of –.1 to –.3. Also, firms do tend to shorten hours as predicted by the theory. The incomes of the adults in this labor pool seem to increase, especially for women, but the incomes of teenagers probably falls. Most of the teenagers who lose their jobs do not remain unemployed; rather, they drop out of the labor force entirely and stay in school. Perhaps most importantly, though this is the subject of partisan debate, minimum wage laws make it more difficult for teenagers to get that "first job," which may be of greater significance than the income earned.[18]

13.5 Labor Unions

Beginning with the European *guilds* in the middle ages or earlier, craftspersons organized their profession into associations that sought to increase wages by restricting entry into their occupation. The guilds set high standards of craftsmanship for certification, and individuals were forbidden to practice a trade such as carpentry, leather working and blacksmithing unless they were members of the guild. These organizations reduced the number of people who could work in the controlled occupations. The guilds argued that they were protecting the public from shoddy workmanship. They probably did accomplish that to some

18. Discussions of these findings are presented in two excellent texts on labor economics, *The Economics of Labor Markets,* by Bruce E. Kaufman (Dryden) and *Modern Labor Economics,* by Ronald G. Ehrenberg and Robert S. Smith (Harper Collins).

degree. However, sometimes a task is elementary and people don't want to hire a superb craftsperson; a lower skilled, lower wage handyman often will do. By requiring work to be done only by journeymen, the guilds effectively shifted the supply of workers to the left, raising wages.

As the modern era dawned and population and commerce in Europe increased, the power of the guilds weakened and those organizations disappeared. With the coming of industrialization and factories employing large numbers of workers, workers again began to organize into associations, called unions, to raise wages and improve working conditions. Around 1900, only a very small fraction of the American labor force was unionized, about 2 to 3 percent. By 1930, it had risen to 6.8 percent, 11.6 percent of the nonagricultural labor force. These percentages peaked in the 1950s; in 1954, unions represented 25.4 percent of all workers, and 33.7 percent of the nonagricultural labor force. Union membership has since fallen dramatically in the private sector, to only 18 percent in 1990s.[19] The major growth area has been in the public sector, for example, teachers. The overall fraction of the labor force that is currently unionized is approximately 20 percent. Most labor unions are affiliated with the AFL-CIO, a merger of the old American Federation of Labor and the Congress of Industrial Organization. The Teamsters Union, originally a union of transport workers, remains outside of this federation.

In the very early part of the twentieth century, the legal climate was not favorable to unions. The Sherman Antitrust Act, passed in 1890, was used to prosecute unions for restraint of trade. The Clayton Act of 1914 exempted unions from the antitrust laws, but employers could, for example, force workers to sign a contract, called a *yellow dog contract,* to not join a union if employed. In the Great Depression of the 1930s, the law became much more favorable to unions. The Norris-Laguardia Act of 1932 prohibited yellow dog contracts and many other anti-union activities of employers. The National Labor Relations (Wagner) Act of 1935 required employers to bargain "in good faith" with unions and forbade employer interference with union organizing. It set up the National Labor Relations Board to monitor employer and union activities and unionization elections, and to investigate alleged "unfair labor practices." In 1947 the pendulum swung back with the passage of the Taft-Hartley Act. This law prohibits *closed shops* in which prior union membership is a condition of employment and allows states to pass *right-to-work* laws which prohibit *union shops,* which mandate union membership once employed. The Landrum Griffin Act of 1959 provides for periodic reporting of union finances and greater disclosure of the activities of union leaders to the general membership.

Unions bargain *collectively* with one or more employers and set minimum wage and fringe benefit levels for all workers in the bargaining unit. The unions can seek to raise wages above their competitive levels by threatening to *strike.* If only one person leaves a job in protest over wages, say, that person is easily replaced. If most or all of a firm's workers leave simultaneously, firms can rarely replace them all. Strikes impose costs on firms, but they also impose costs on the workers in terms of foregone wages. The benefits from joining a union are greatest when the firm has a relatively inelastic demand for the workers, so that wage

19. See annual issues of U.S. Department of Labor *Handbook of Labor Statistics,* (Washington, D.C.)

increases lead to only small reductions in the workforce. It certainly must be the case that the workers cannot be easily replaced. These conditions seem to have been met in the large concentrated manufacturing and mining industries of past generations. These favorable circumstances for union organizing are much less present in the highly competitive service industries that have emerged in recent years. These firms are relatively small, so that an entire workforce could be replaced (albeit at some cost). The demand for the firm's services is likely elastic, so that the firm's demand for labor is elastic also.

Consider also that forming a union always involves costs, even in the absence of an actual strike. The workers who are most apt to gain from a union are therefore those with a long term interest in the job. Historically, for example, women tended to have relatively short term employment. It is thus not surprising that in the past, firms with mainly female workers were less frequently unionized than firms with male workers.

Deregulation of the transportation industry has had a substantial impact on the unions representing those workers. Formerly, the airlines derived rents from the monopoly or near monopoly rights they held over various routes. The labor unions were able to capture some of these rents through their monopoly power in the labor market. When the airlines were deregulated, their rents disappeared as new airlines served those routes. As a result, wages in the airline industry were stagnant or falling through most of the 1980s. In the trucking industry, workers were represented almost exclusively by the Teamsters Union. Again, firms derived rents from monopoly rights issued by the Interstate Commerce Commission (ICC). When these routes became available to competitors, many truckers bought or leased their own rigs and became independent truckers. As a result, membership in the Teamsters Union has fallen dramatically in that industry.

Although we can use supply and demand curves to depict some of the overall effects of certain union activities, labor unions are in fact complex organizations, whose behavior depends to some extent on their internal politics. Unions establish *property rights* in jobs. Protection against layoffs are stated in terms of a member's *seniority* in the union. Seniority is a valuable property right because it gives a worker priority over others in employment. This sometimes gives the older, more established members a different interest than the new, younger members. The older members are more insured against changes in the size of the labor force due to wage increases (due to the law of demand), because their seniority often protects them against layoffs. They are thus more apt to be in favor of wage increases rather than employment expansion. Also, as economists Orley Ashenfelter and George Johnson have argued, the leaders of a union are more apt to be informed about an employer's true financial position than their members. The union leadership might know that the company is ailing and that only a small wage increase is available. However, if this view is not shared by the membership, the leaders can lose their jobs in the union. It might be better from the leadership's point of view to first have a protracted strike and then settle for the low wage increase to protect their positions.[20]

20. See Orley Ashenfelter and George Johnson, "Bargaining theory, Trade Unions, and Industrial Strike Activity," *American Economic Review,* 59, March 1969, 35–49. Also see the extension and additional confirmation of Michael Farber, "Bargaining Theory, Wage Outcomes and the Occurrence of Strikes," *American Economic Review,* 68, June 1978, 262–71.

It is not easy to evaluate the actual impact unions have had on workers' earnings. Union workers on average make more than nonunion workers, but that is partly due to the relatively higher skill levels possessed by union workers, even in the same craft. Also, accompanying the leftward shift in the supply of union workers is a *rightward* shift in the supply of labor in the nonunionized sector, as workers not able to find the higher-paying union jobs seek work elsewhere. This has the effect of lowering wages and increasing employment in the nonunion sector of the labor market. The effect of unionization on wages is not the same for all industries. For example, many classical orchestras are unionized, but almost all the costs of orchestras are salaries, and these organizations are perpetually dependent on wealthy donors. It seems unlikely that a union could substantially increase overall wages by threatening to withhold services. On the other hand, it is easy to imagine that a craft union that successfully restricted entry could raise the wages of its members.

The empirical impact of unions has been analyzed by a number of economists, using different data sets and techniques. A famous early study by H. Gregg Lewis suggested that in the 1960s and earlier, the wage premium for unionization was on the order of 10 to 15 percent. Economists Richard Freeman and James Medoff studied *cross section* data in the 1970s and concluded that the wage differential averaged about 25 percent.[21] The data used were different jobs in the same year, some unionized and some not. However, some researchers felt this unusually high differential was due to unmeasured productivity differences and to compensating differential pay for the union jobs. Freeman and Medoff later studied longitudinal data, in which the same workers are observed over time. They analyzed the effects of workers who joined unions or who left unions. They then found wage differentials in the more traditional range of 10 to 15 percent. They and other economists have studied the effects of unions broken down by race, sex, age and education. The evidence suggests that unions raise wages relatively more for men than for women, for the relatively less educated, for whites more than for blacks and for blue collar occupations as opposed to white collar occupations. These questions and estimates are all the subject of ongoing research.

13.6 Labor Market Discrimination

In the nineteenth and early part of the twentieth centuries, some employers in America hung signs in front of their establishments saying "No Irish need apply." In our lifetimes some employers have turned away or passed over qualified individuals of virtually every ethnic group, preferred men over women, women over men, young over old, old over young, and combinations thereof. Discrimination against African Americans and other ethnic minorities is a widely condemned but seemingly durable institution. Many observers attribute these actions to mindless prejudice, that is, peculiar tastes, but economists are unsatisfied with that simplistic observation. Actions are based on constraints as

21. H. Gregg Lewis, *Unions and Relative Wages in the United States,* Chicago, University of Chicago Press, 1963, and Richard B. Freeman and James L. Medoff, *What Do Unions Do?,* New York: Basic Books, 1984. See also Lewis' "Union Relative Wage Effects: A Survey of Macro Estimates," *Journal Of Labor Economics,* 1, No. 1, January 1983, 1–27.

well as tastes. Employers are constrained by competition from other firms and can ill afford to make capricious employment decisions. Two theoretical questions are pertinent:

- Assuming employers have a taste for discrimination against some identifiable ethnic or gender group, what affects their willingness to *act* on that taste? Does a taste for prejudice imply that employers will indeed discriminate?

- Is actual discrimination in hiring or employment only the result of a taste for discrimination on the part of employers? That is, are there circumstances where an employer who had no prejudice against any group would none-the-less discriminate as a matter of wealth-maximizing self interest?

Lastly, an important empirical question remains. We know that differences in earnings exist between ethnic and gender groups. For example, according to Census figures in the United States, for males over 25 years of age, Black Americans on average earn only 70% of what Whites earn. As a group, women earn only about 70% of what men earn.[22] However, not all of these differences are due to current labor market discrimination. For example, men are relatively much more frequently in higher earning professions such as engineering, medicine and the skilled crafts than women; women are relatively much more frequently in low paying jobs such as clerical work (though it is possible that some part of this pattern is due to labor market discrimination in the past). Thus the comparison of current earnings differentials of men and women is to some extent a comparison of the earnings of, for instance, engineers versus secretaries. Even with no prejudice or discrimination, earnings differences will appear between men and women until men and women have the same jobs. Similarly, comparisons of earnings by race show that the numbers change if, say education and experience are equalized. Black males with a Master's degree earn about 80% of what white males earn with that degree, and new black Ph.D.s earn the same or more than new white Ph.D.s. Lastly, some differences may be due to prior discrimination in the opportunities available, such as education, *before* people reach the labor market. Thus, perhaps the most important question is: To what extent are observed earnings differences between ethnic and gender groups due to actual labor market discrimination?

In these few pages we can only briefly discuss these issues, which some economists spend their entire careers investigating. Let us turn first to the first question, which Nobel Laureate Gary Becker analyzed. An employer with a taste for discrimination is willing to pay more for an employee of a favored group than one from a less favored group. We presented Becker's argument in Chapter 3: this type of discrimination is penalized by the market. Imagine an employer who had a preference for blue-eyed blonde women, so that he wanted his entire labor force of 100 employees to consist of workers with this characteristic. This firm's labor costs will exceed those of firms whose owners do not act on such tastes. The employer will have to search wider and longer to find quali-

22. Bruce E. Kaufman points out that the 60% measure for women is older than one might guess. In the Old Testament, the measure of compensation for injured persons was based on their probable productivities in the following way: "And the Lord spake unto Moses saying, and thy estimation shall be of the male . . . fifty shekels of silver. . . . And if it be female, . . . thirty shekels." (Leviticus 27:3–4)

fied employees with these characteristics than employers who consider only productivity. If the firm is part of a highly competitive labor market, it risks bankruptcy. Even if the market is monopolistic to some degree, discrimination of this sort means the owner gives up the present value of the difference between the annual profits he could realize in the absence of discrimination and his current level. With a large labor force, this could be a substantial sum. The owner could endure this loss, but this amount also represents what another entrepreneur would be willing to pay for this business, because by running it without discriminating, it would earn that much more in present value. Thus we would expect that over time firms that discriminate because of the preferences of the owner would tend to disappear partly from bankruptcy and partly by passing into the hands of employers without such costly preferences.

Becker tested this theory by investigating differences in earnings and job advancement of blacks and whites in industries with government protected monopolies such as the railroads and public utilities in comparison with private firms.[23] The data were from prior to the passage of the civil rights laws of the 1960s. Becker found greater levels of discrimination in the protected monopolies than in private firms, supporting his theory.

A related theory of discrimination is based on the preferences of the workers within a firm. If workers from different groups cannot get along with each other, firms will have an incentive to segregate the workforce. In that case, wage differentials would not appear, unless there were insufficient workers in one group with certain skills to allow complete segregation. Some factories in the South in previous generations seem to provide some confirmation of this theory.[24] Also, discrimination can occur because of the preferences of consumers. Consumers have sometimes not wanted to be served by people of various groups. In that case, wealth maximizing employers will discriminate against that group. Segregation in housing probably has occurred because of this phenomenon. Why would it have paid for a property owner to exclude Blacks, say, from an apartment complex. After all, some African Americans might be the high bidders for some apartments. Why exclude a group of potential customers? This type of discrimination is most easily explained as the property owner enforcing a contract in behalf of the *tenants* to exclude people the tenants didn't like. If the tenants don't wish to live near members of some ethnic group, the apartment house will have the highest value if all of its tenants are of the same group, because the tenants are willing to pay more for such living arrangements.

Consider now question 2. Why would employers in times gone by refuse to hire, for example, Irish workers? Why would employers systematically exclude women, blacks or any other group from consideration? Surely they must know that they risk overlooking qualified workers who would be good employees by such tactics. One possible reason is that employers rarely are able to tell what kind of employee a prospect is going to be, on the basis of interviews and resumes. Information is costly and imperfect. Therefore, it pays to economize on information gathering. Employers have experiences hiring from different

23. Gary Becker, *The Economics of Discrimination,* 1956, 2nd ed. 1971, (Chicago: University of Chicago Press)

24. See, for example, *Labor in the South,* by Ray Marshall (Cambridge, Mass.: Harvard University Press, 1967)

groups, and draw conclusions based on their experiences. For example, in previous generations, most women left the labor force in their twenties to have children. Employers were generally loathe to invest their resources training such employees for career jobs in their firms, only to have the effort largely wasted when the young women quit. Of course, not *all* women left to have children, but employers couldn't tell who would and who wouldn't. As a result, employers frequently discriminated against women in hiring and promotion in career type jobs, because of what they considered "good business practices," not because of prejudice, that is, a taste for discrimination. For similar reasons, college students often have trouble finding anything better than menial type jobs (for example, "hamburger flipping") during summer vacations. Employers are wary of their intentions even if they swear they have quit school and are seeking permanent employment. Employers use the best information they have, sometimes based on the group association of the applicant.[25] In the nineteenth century, the Irish were an often despised minority, perceived by many to engage in more than the usual amount of drunkenness and brawling.[26] They were therefore often not regarded highly as employment prospects.

Because this type of discrimination is based on perceptions of group averages, economists refer to it as **statistical discrimination**. It is not an outcome of employer, employee or customer prejudice, but rather a wealth maximizing decision for firms. Similar phenomena are the fabled "old boy" networks in which information is traded. Employers often call their friends in other businesses and old associates to solicit information about prospective employees. Though widely regarded as discriminatory in intent, this practice seems most likely a case of economizing on information. People who have regular dealings with a firm are more likely to give honest appraisals than someone who rarely if ever has such occasions. Their word is more highly valued and therefore sought out.

We should mention one last source of discrimination. Around the time the major civil rights bills were passed in the United States (1964) and for quite a few years thereafter, the number of blacks, women and other minorities in the craft unions (electricians, plumbers, etc.,) was approximately *zero*. Although many attributed this to racism, and although we cannot disprove that contention, this outcome seems driven mainly by efforts of these unions to raise wages by limiting the supply of qualified workers. In manufacturing, where thousands of workers may be employed, unions such as the United Auto Workers use the threat of a strike to raise wages, since employers cannot replace thousands of strikers easily. Construction jobs, on the other hand, are relatively small, employing few workers. A strike would likely not be successful. The craft unions have therefore opted to raise wages by placing severe limits on entry into the union. These unions rarely admitted other than males who were close relatives of existing members. When these unions were founded, there were few if any minority journeymen,

---

25. Some groups may even be beneficiaries of favorable discrimination. Japanese Americans are widely perceived to have strong "middle class values" and may find it easier to obtain employment and housing than European-descendants. The author recalls an article in the *Seattle Times* about the experience of a man recently released from a World War II detention camp for Japanese Americans. He recalled poking through a furniture store, penniless. To his shock, the owner told him he could buy anything he wanted on credit. The owner explained, "The Japanese always pay their bills."

26. The term *paddy wagon* which came into use in the late nineteenth century describing a vehicle the police use to round up street drunks, derives from the colloquial word "paddy" for young Irish man.

and hence this practice effectively excluded future minorities. These practices were outlawed under the civil rights laws as discriminatory.[27]

Lastly, there is the important question of measuring the extent of discrimination in the labor market. This is a very difficult task and the subject of much ongoing research. Gross comparisons of earnings between ethnic or gender groups are rarely to the point. One must be careful not to compare apples with oranges. About half of the earnings disparities between blacks and whites disappears if one corrects for experience and years of schooling. But "schooling" is itself a very broad measure. It matters if a person has majored in engineering versus sociology. One therefore also has to correct for the particular kind of schooling, and the quality of the schools themselves. In previous generations, many blacks attended fewer hours in secondary schools than whites in the segregated South, and attended inferior colleges due to discriminatory entrance policies. Resulting disparities in earnings were then due in some large part to premarket conditions rather than labor market discrimination. If all objective measurable influences on productivity are considered, and earnings differences still emerge, the hypothesis of discrimination is given some weight. However, it is always possible that the underlying "objective" measures are only faulty measures of productivity, leading to spurious tests. We leave this important topic to more advanced classes.

CHAPTER SUMMARY

- The primary source of income for adults is their participation in the labor market. The decision to work outside the home is called the *labor-leisure* choice.
- The market wage available to a person is the opportunity cost of leisure. When a person decides to leave work, he or she gives up income. When an individual can choose the number of hours worked per day, the marginal value of leisure is his or her market wage.
- As the wage available to a person increases, it becomes more likely that he or she will choose to participate in the labor force. However, once working, increases in the wage rate have two opposing effects. The opportunity cost of leisure increases causing the person to *substitute* towards less leisure and thus more work. However, the resulting higher income tends to increase the consumption of leisure and thus reduce the hours worked. These *substitution* and *income* effects oppose each other in the labor leisure choice.
- People produce income in the home as well as consume leisure. The duties of a homemaker in a family represent income, as evidenced by the cost of replacing those services with hired help.
- As their market wages increase, people economize on time in the home. Higher income individuals purchase more "ready to eat" and microwavable foods, shop at stores featuring fast service, and spend less time shopping for bargains than those with lower opportunity costs of their time.

27. This argument is due to Orley Ashenfelter. See his "Racial Discrimination and Trade Unionism," *Journal of Political Economy,* 80, No.3, part 1, (May/June 1972), 435–64.

- Marriages are a pervasive institution in all societies. It must serve an important purpose. It lowers the transactions costs of bearing and raising children, and protects parents, and historically, women in particular, from opportunistic shirking of duties by the spouse.
- Women who specialized in rearing children and homemaking had skills that were worth very little when the children were grown. Men, on the other hand, who had specialized in labor market activities during the years of childraising, had relatively more valuable market skills. Laws restricting divorce made childbearing less risky for women by providing insurance for women against abandonment.
- The demand for labor is based on a person's productivity. Education seems to increase productivity, especially in the relatively "vocational" areas such as engineering and business. However, some argue that the higher earnings of educated individuals is due to their inherent greater talents, with college degrees serving mainly as a "signal."
- Various laws and institutions attempt to raise wages of some individuals by restricting access to labor markets. Restrictions on immigration, restrictions into a union, and minimum wage laws all serve this purpose.
- Market wages reflect the amenities of jobs such as working conditions, location and risk of injury, in addition to worker productivity. Economists have used these *compensating differentials* to estimate the amounts by which wages must increase in order to attract workers to less desirable jobs.
- Some labor market discrimination occurs because of tastes ("prejudice"). Decisions to *act* on discriminatory tastes are constrained by the market. Employers who decide to exclude some ethnic or gender group because of their own tastes likely raise the cost of acquiring capable workers. This would tend to discourage such discrimination.
- Labor market discrimination can also occur because of scarce information about employees. Employers have imperfect information about employee productivity. Some employers have had more favorable experiences with some ethnic or gender groups than others. This has sometimes led them to favor one group over another in employment, even in the absence of personal tastes for discrimination.
- Empirical testing for discrimination in the labor market is a difficult process. Not all group differences in earnings are due to discrimination. One must take into account differences in education and training, experience, language skills and the like.

REVIEW QUESTIONS

1. Why does a person's wage measure his or her marginal value of leisure?
2. What are income and substitution effects and how do they relate to the supply of labor?

3. What do we mean by income produced in the household? How would one measure it?
4. What are some economic reasons why women have historically had lower wage than men, apart from any labor market discrimination?
5. How have no fault divorces divorce laws affected many women's decisions on participating in the labor market?
6. What is statistical discrimination in the labor market, and how does it differ from discrimination based on tastes? Which is more likely to persist in highly competitive markets?
7. What do the following terms, associated with labor unions mean: closed shop, union shop, right to work law, yellow dog contract?

PROBLEMS

1. Suppose the federal income tax schedule is changed from one which is relatively *proportional,* that is, taxes increase roughly in the exact proportion as increases in income, to one which is highly *progressive,* so that taxes increase in much greater proportion than the increases in income. What effects would this change have on:
   a. choosing a risky occupation where there is some small chance of an extremely high income
   b. choosing entrepreneurial occupations where income is apt to vary substantially from year to year
   c. the amount of schooling a person a person might choose?
2. Some empirical studies of female labor supply indicate that the elasticity of supply is greater for working women than for working men. Consider that traditionally, women produce most household income, and are therefore likely better at it than men, because of the gains from specialization. Use this information to explain why responses to changes in market wages might be different for women than for men.
3. In the last 50 years, real wages have increase considerably, yet the number of hours worked per week has declined. This show that the long run demand for labor is downwars sloping. Comment.
4. Lazy people will tend to earn relatively high salaries, because they have to be paid more to overcome their higher opportunity cost of working. Do you agree? Explain.
5. Most people must be paid "time and a half" for overtime work, that is, time exceeding 8 hours per day. How does this affect the amount of overtime people are willing to engage in? How does it differ from simply paying people a higher average wage, for all hours including overtime?
6. Some municipalities, for example, New York City levy taxes on the income of professionals such as doctors, lawyers, etc. Who pays these taxes in the short and long runs—the professionals themselves or their clients?

7. Recently passed immigration law assesses very high penalties on employers for hiring undocumented aliens ($10,000 per illegal hire). It would seem that this supply restriction would have increased the incomes of these workers, mostly farmworkers from Mexico, but seems to have had little effect. Can you explain why this would be expected?

8. Suppose there are two industries. Industry 1 produces milk and industry 2 produces honey. All workers in the economy are employed in these two industries, and receive the say pay regardless of industry. Suppose now women are restricted from working in the honey industry. How would this affect the allocation of workers and wage rates in these industries? Will women necessarily receive lower wages as a result?

9. One often hears someone say that they "love their job." Does this mean that they would pay their employer for the right to work there? If not, what does it mean?

10. Suppose it is found that reducing the speed limit from 70 mph to 55 has saved 10,000 lives per year, but that the public is adamantly opposed to any further reductions in the speed limit. How would you use this data to derive a market value of life?

11. Explain why the supply of labor is backward bending. What is the distinguishing feature of labor which causes the supply curve to bend back on itself?

12. Why have income effects safely been ignored in the rest of this text, whereas we choose not to ignore them in the context of labor markets?

13. What is the meaning of your "reservation wage?" How is it affected by such things as the financial support you receive from your family, your level of education, the presence of a spouse, the presence of children?

14. It seems that the reservation wage is higher for married women than for single women. Why? Is this a good reason to get married?

15. The historical specialization that has taken place within the family has been for the man to specialize in market income and for the woman to specialize in household income. Why has this been the case? What assumptions does this outcome rely on, and how are these conditions changing at present? Do you think it will ever come to pass that men will be the predominant providers of household income?

16. How has the introduction of no-fault divorce likely affected female particiapation in the labor force? Why? How would it affect the age of first marriage for women?

17. Do minimum wage laws help the poor? What effect would they have on diabled workers?

18. Why do labor unions support minimum wage legislation, even though very few if any union workers earn the minimum wage?

19. In the 1980s, income tax rates were lowered, in part because it was felt that with a higher after-tax wage, people would have a greater incentive to work. Recently, tax rates have been raised. Is it possible to argue on theoretical

grounds that lower tax rates on wage income will increase the amount of time people work per week?

20. Although labor market income is taxed, income produced in the home is tax free. Suppose household income were taxed like labor market income, with tax rates adjusted so as to keep total tax revenues collected by the government the same. What effect would this have on female participation in the labor market?

21. The percentage of Americans who belong to unions has been steadily declining since the 1930s. How might this be related to the concommitant decline in manufacturing in the U.S. economy and the rise of the service sector?

22. Many people have argued that the rise in the standard of living of American and Canadian workers is due principally to the formation of labor unions in this century. What do you think of this argument? Can cartels raise average incomes in the economy?

23. Is actual discrimination in hiring or employment only the result of a taste for discrimination on the part of employers? Would an employer who had no prejudice against any group would nevertheless discriminate as a matter of wealth-maximizing self interest? What effects on a firm's wealth would discrimination based on these different motives produce?

QUESTIONS FOR DISCUSSION

1. Faculty at some universities have attempted to form a union which would represent the faculty and bargain collectively with the administration. What affect would this have on universities? Would it make it more likely or less likely that you would attend that university, and why?

2. Do you favor minimum wage laws? How do they affect your prospects for entry level work and the total compensation you might receive? Is it a good way to help disadvantaged youth who have poor job skills?

3. Do you favor strong unions for public employees, such as teachers, civil servants and fire and police officers? Should their right to strike be restricted in any way?

Hints and Answers for Problems

Chapter 1. But Will it Work in Theory?

1., 2. This text is largely about these two questions; we will have much to say about them. The answers have to do with the coordination of mutual gains through the price system.

4. "Scientific" is not the same as "true." Science consists of positive statements, statements that are either true or false. Sometimes the scientific method produces false answers.

5. Propositions that could be wrong but which are confirmed by the facts are the most interesting.

7. No. A theory cannot be good in theory but lousy in practice because by definition a good theory is one that is good in practice. If a theory is lousy in practice it means it is a lousy theory.

10. No. What do you suppose the price of water is in the Northwest, where it is plentiful, relative to the Southwest, where it is relatively scarce? How would this likely affect consumption?

11. Are cockroaches, which are in limited supply, thereby scarce?

12. Unfortunately, the fundamental reason for the existence of competition is scarcity, not because of any lack of love or respect. Even if all people were angelic, scarcity would force us to choose some rules for competing for scarce goods.

14. The cost to an individual of going to college includes the cost of the opportunities foregone by going to college, in particular, the income one could make if one entered the labor market instead and the value of leisure foregone because of time spent studying.

15. This is going to increase the value of women specifically as females, that is, as wives and mothers. We should expect traditional marriage patterns to be reinforced by this process.

17. Yes. Are there some foods you would not eat, even if they were free to you?

19. Free enterprise does not mean one is free to do anything one wishes. "Free-enterprise" means individuals can own resources and direct those resources to the uses they choose. Even so, individuals are constrained by laws, such as environmental rules, zoning and the like.

20. The proposition "there is no such thing as a free lunch" is a statement about only one aspect of economics that of opportunity cost. It does not really provide a good definition for economics. Instead, economics is defined most precisely as the study of how scarce resources are allocated amongst competing ends. It is the study of how people respond to changes in the constraints that scarcity imposes.

21. It could only be white.

Chapter 2. The Theory of Consumer Behavior

1. The important criterion is whether these postulates enable us to reliably explain and predict behavior. The behavioral postulates are assertions about observed behavior, not necessarily conscious calculations. We may not actively consider Newton's laws when driving, but this does not mean they are irrelevant to science.

2. The law of demand is about rates of consumption. Does the rate change when the price changes, even if no immediate change is apparent?

3. Addictive drugs like crack cocaine are obviously goods to the people who consume them. They must therefore be subject to the behavioral postulates. Can you find evidence of the substitution postulate and diminishing marginal values?

4. What are the trade-offs individuals make when they choose to purchase a new, safe, car? Is safety a good that people value above everything else?

7. Who receives the benefits of the gift? Does the giver of a food processor have an ulterior motive?

8. This is the diamond water paradox in another guise. These wages reflect only the marginal values of these workers, not their total values to consumers.

10. The child demonstrates he or she has preferences. He or she is willing to substitute (Postulate 3) less broccoli for more dessert. How do you suppose the size of the bribe will change for each successive amount of broccoli?

11. This example shows that goods and services that some observers insist are comparable are not comparable to many consumers.

14. The "total value" referred to in these calculations are not the total values as we have defined them. This argument ignores the consumer's surplus people receive from these goods.

15.a,b. The consumer purchases 5 steaks and 5 pizzas, where the marginal value of each falls to \$5. Therefore total expenditure on each is \$25, but does this mean the consumer values each the same? What, if anything, does the coincidence of total expenditures on each good tells us about which good yields the greater consumer's surplus?

c. The consumer would be willing to pay the increase in the consumer's surplus for the right to purchase steaks at \$3.00 rather than \$5. This difference is \$21—\$10 = \$11.

16. a. Aron eats where he gets the greatest consumer's surplus. He eats 4 burgers and 6 fries per week at Joe's.

b. The amount Aron would be willing to tip the waitperson is the difference between the consumer's surplus before the new pricing policy and under the old pricing policy. Aron would be willing to tip the waitperson \$1 per week in order to be able to buy burgers and fries separately.

17. Another diamond-water paradox question. How, if at all, do these wages reflect the total values of these services?

19 a. Clearly wrong.

b. This ignores the downward slope of the demand curve. What is the gain in consumer's surplus?

c. If the demand curve is linear, the area of the trapezoid representing the gain in consumer's surplus is $\$2 \times (40 + 50)/2 = \$90$. If you're not into geometry, assume that at \$9, Rachel purchases 45 units. Calculate the resulting change in total values of the purchases and evaluate the gain in consumer's surplus. This procedure yields \$85.

20. The classical explanation just relabels the puzzle.

21. Individuals trade off the convenience of getting somewhere more quickly against the decreased probability of death on the highway. How does the marginal value of additional safety change as the speed limit decreases?

22. The remarks of Senator Kennedy show that "needs" is a subjective term. With the improvement in the standard of living in the past one hundred years, we no longer accept certain degrees of privation, and thus redefine needs to fit today's values.

24. a. Without food stamps Charlotte will buy five units of food at a price of 6 dollars spending a total of \$30 and receiving \$10 consumer's surplus. When food stamps are available and neither food nor food stamps can be traded, the price of food essentially is cut in half, as long as Charlotte doesn't run out of food stamps. The effective price Charlotte faces is \$3 rather than \$6. According to Charlotte's demand curve, she will then purchase 8 units of food. She purchases \$48 of food for \$24.

b. The gain to Charlotte of being able to purchase the food stamps is the consumer surplus from being able to purchase 8 units of food. She spends \$24 to obtain food whose total value is \$52; her gain (consumer's surplus) is \$28, \$18 more than with no food stamps.

c. The effective price facing Charlotte is no longer \$3. Her consumer surplus is \$40 – \$25 = \$15.

d. Assuming food stamps can be resold Charlotte will treat her food stamps as if they were real dollars. The opportunity cost of one food stamp is \$1 since they can be traded. Her gain is \$40.

25. Sam buys 3 green eggs and 3 slices of ham.

b. His gets greater net benefits from ham. His consumer's surplus is \$12 for ham and only \$6 for eggs. If the price of eggs was \$6, his net benefits would be the same.

c. He'd pay \$12.

26. Assuming a linear demand curve, the consumer's surplus when the ticket price is \$10 is \$160 million per season. The fans would pay up to this amount per season. In Chapter 10 we discuss how to compress this future stream of benefits to a present value now. At \$30, fans would pay much less, \$40 million per season but they would make more on the ticket sales. If the owner could capture these net benefits, he would do better with the lower price.

Chapter 3. Aspects of Demand Theory

1. No, it has much more than halved. This comparison ignores the changes in the general price level and the enormous quality differences between today's PCs and the original IBM PC.

3. a. Consumers mitigate the adverse effect of the price increase by shifting their consumption away from the now relatively more expensive good to a cheaper substitute.

b. The calculated increase in the CPI therefore overstates the true impact of this price. Why?

4. See question 1.

5. At a price of \$8, if price increases by \$1 to \$9, this is a 12.5% increase. When the price rises from \$8 to \$9, quantity demanded decreases from 3 to 2, a 33.3% decrease. Hence, the elasticity of demand at the price of $\$8 = (-33.3\%)/(12.5\%) = -2.67$. Alternatively, $\epsilon = (p/q)(\Delta q/\Delta(p) = (8/3)(-1) = -2.67$. Proceeding in a similar manner, at $p = \$5$, $\eta = -0.835$; at $p = \$3$, $\eta = -0.375$.

6. This is one more confusion between total expenditure (or total revenue received by farmers) and total value.

Consumers moved up an inelastic demand curve. The claim made that there was no harm to consumers is incorrect.

9. This does not imply that rich people are less fond of children than poor people. This has occurred mainly because American society has changed from one predominantly rural to one predominantly urban over the past two centuries. Also, better market opportunities for women raise the cost of rearing children.
10. No, this only indicates the employers believe and anticipate, based on the historic trend, that the women hired in their early 20's will most likely leave to have children in the future. In that case, the costs of training these women would be lost. Because employers cannot distinguish women who will really stay on the job and those who won't, women, as a group, were less attractive prospects in career jobs than men. It does not necessarily indicate a belief by employers that women were incapable in the jobs from which they were restricted. Some employers preferred, for rational business reasons, men to women in career jobs. Historically, women more easily obtained jobs involving little employer-paid training costs.
11. New York.
12. If the tuition is the same for credits over 12 per quarter or semester, the price to students for those marginal credits drops to zero. What does the law of diminishing marginal values imply?
14. The price of steak has increased by 33.3 percent, more than the 20 percent increase in the price of potatoes. Thus?
15. In this case, the answer is ambiguous because more than one relative price has changed.
16. a. No, an observation of changes in behavioral patterns does not necessarily imply changes in tastes. It could be a change in constraints.
    b. Young people.
    c. The wage a person could earn in the labor market is the opportunity cost of participating in political or idealistic activities.
    d. Typically as one ages, one's wage increases (Why?). Therefore, we observe a larger number of younger people active in idealistic activities than older people.
    e. The post World War II baby boom increased the supply of young workers in the 1960s and 1970s.
18. The cost of closely measuring the good is relatively least when the good is relatively higher priced. Thus more measuring takes place when the good is out of season, and for relatively higher quality goods.
19. 4,211,200,000 lbs.
20. Whether a good is elastic or inelastic depends on the availability of substitutes. Elastic goods are goods with numerous available substitutes, whereas, inelastic goods have few or no available substitutes. A generic cup of regular coffee probably has the fewest number of substitutes. Hence, the demand for a cup of regular coffee is expected to be inelastic which is what has been observed, see Table 3-2. The demand for decaf coffee should be about the same. A latte, being a more specialized good, probably has a greater elasticity than regular coffee. A particular brand will have the most elastic demand because competing brands are likely close substitutes. If there are many competing brands, the demand for any one brand is likely to be elastic.
22. Not in real life. As the price increases, a greater and greater amount would be spent on such a good. Eventually, it would exceed people's incomes.
23. For the same kinds of reasons, no.
24. Individuals in these poor countries find that the benefits of more mouths to feed outweigh the costs. Although there are more mouths to feed, every mouth has two hands; family incomes increase as there are more family members to work either within the household or outside. Parents also get someone to look over them later in life.
26. a. Another example of the confusion of total value and total expenditure. The demand for apples is apparently inelastic.
    b. Adding a fixed transportation charge makes the better apples relatively cheaper.
27. The Bus company must consider the elasticity of demand. They might lose money by raising the fares.

Chapter 4. Exchange and Supply

1. No, this is a common fallacy. Trade occurs because individuals value a good differently at the margin.
2. a. The individual is endowed with seven hamburgers. For the individual to give up one hamburger (supply one hamburger), the individual must be paid at least the marginal value of this seventh burger ($1). We assume she consumes 7 hamburgers when the price is $1, so she supplies none at that price. When the price rises to $2, she consumes 6 and supplies 1, etc.
   b. If the person started out with only five hamburgers, she would supply 1 hamburger when the price rose to $4, 2 hamburgers when the price is $5, etc.
3. a. Another individual enters the hamburger scene. Since this person initially values hamburgers more than the person of question 2, he purchases hamburgers from her. Their marginal values become equal when he purchases 4 hamburgers from her. He now has 8; his marginal value is $5. She consumes 3, where her marginal value is also $5. The total gain from trade is the sum of the differences in their marginal values for

the items traded: $20 = (9 – 1) + (8 – 2) + (7 – 3) + (6 – 4)

b. With an endowment of 13, this person's marginal value of hamburgers is zero. He will sell hamburgers to the other person, if her endowment is less than 7, so that her marginal value exceeds his.

4. Exchange is voluntary. Exchange, therefore, does not pit seller against buyer. Sellers compete with other sellers, and buyers compete with other buyers.
5. The warehouse stores have not eliminated middlemen; they have discovered they can lower costs further on standard items by bulk packaging and offering minimal retail service. For many items, this is just what many consumers desire.
7. Uniform prices are a low cost way to bring buyers and sellers together.
9. Whether this is a good idea or not is of course a value judgment. Prohibiting the restriction of the free flow of people and goods across state lines or across national borders allows a more efficient allocation of resources. Resources will tend toward their highest valued use if they are free to do so. The gains from trade are larger because of the commerce clause, but some individuals have been made worse by competition from buyers or sellers in other states. Do you think the argument is the same for California and Arizona versus California and Mexico?
11. The former Soviet Union was a command economy. The state paid farmers less than what they could earn by direct sale to consumers. However, there was no legal mechanism in which wholesalers and retailer could operate. Those activities were illegal. Thus, farmers undertook the task of wholesaling and retailing themselves.
12. Damage deposits occur because information about tenants is costly. Restricting them causes damage to be incorporated into the rent. Such restrictions will make apartment owners worse off, college students possible worse off, people with alternative lifestyles probably worse off, yuppy couple better off, working couples with children probably worse off.
14. The famous problem of "Athenian democracy" in which all citizens vote is the "tyranny of the majority." When votes can be traded in the legislature (and they will be when marginal valuations of legislators differ), the majority no longer has the ability to run roughshod over the rights of the minority. Through trade, enough majority legislators will find it in their own self-interest not to vote against the minority in given instances because their vote may be needed in the future on an entirely different issue.
16. a. The road out to C's house will not be paved.
    b. If this electorate votes on many issues in a given year, individual C might be able to induce individuals A and B to vote for the road by promising to vote for bills they desire .
    c. With 1,000 voters each of type A, B, and C, vote trading is not likely to occur.
    d. The above analysis suggests that a republican form of democracy will be preferable to a pure democracy because there is a likelihood that greater mutual benefits will occur.
17. a. Average.
    b. Marginal.
    c. Marginal, as usual.
    d. "Citizen's duty" or "social responsibility" could not explain these variations.
    e. The anticipated closeness of the election increases voter turnout of the vote.

Chapter 5. Supply and Demand

1. This is a confusion of movements along a demand curve and shifts in the curve. Straighten it out!
3. Goods x and z are substitutes. In the second scenario, x and z are complements. Examples?
5. CD players and tape decks are substitute means of listening to music. Only if the desired end is taping CDs would the two be complements. TVs and VCRs are complements, they are used together. A VCR is useless without a TV. Hot dogs and beans may be either substitutes or complements depending on one's income. At low levels of income hot dogs and beans will be substitutes and at higher income levels they will be complements.
6. As the rich become less rich, they demand more of goods they find inferior, for example, peanut butter, while the poor, who are becoming richer demand more peanut butter, because that good is not inferior to them.
8. The effect is ambiguous.
9. What do you suppose is the principle cause of road congestion? What price is charged for the use of roads?
12. Analysis of these kinds of problems has to become second nature.
    a. The price of coffee rises.
    b. The demand curve shifts to the left. Perhaps the American Medical Association has reported that drinking coffee causes cancer.
    c. This is a decrease (leftward shift) in the supply of coffee. The coffee trees froze?
    d. The supply of coffee decreases (shifts to the left), maybe due to poor weather conditions, and the demand for coffee increases (shifts to the right), by the same amount, perhaps if the National Institute of Health finds that drinking coffee can reduce the risk of cancer.
13. *Roe v. Wade* lifted the legal restrictions on abortions. This ruling caused an increase in the supply (shift in the supply curve to the right) of abortions. This

resulted in a decrease in market price and an increase quantity of abortions performed.

b. If the demand curve had shifted to the right, then although the quantity would have increased, the price would have increased also, contrary to observation.

c. All licensed doctors can perform abortions. With the legalization of abortions, doctors are performing more abortions, and therefore they supply less of other medical services. This is a leftward shift in the supply of these other services. As a result, the quantity of other medical services doctors perform decreases and the price for these other medical services increases.

d. Roe vs. Wade, by legalizing abortion decreased the number of unwanted pregnancies. This decrease in unwanted pregnancies decreases the supply of babies available for adoption. Those babies offered for adoption will therefore command a higher price.

e. If the laws regarding adoptions were made much clearer, this constitutes a reduction in the transaction cost of adopting. From our earlier discussion of middlemen, we know to expect the number of adoptions to increase because they will be cheaper, no fear of legal entanglement; the price received by the biological mother will increase; and the amount paid by the adoptive parents falls.

15. In general, the cost of these benefits are shared by buyers and sellers of labor. However, these benefits are a substitute for cash. If they are a perfect substitute, then no change in total compensation occurs.

17. With electric cars as a viable, competing alternative, we expect consumers to shift from gasoline powered cars to those powered by electricity. We expect a decrease in the demand for petroleum. This shift in the demand for petroleum leads to a decrease in the quantity and price of petroleum. Since the new batteries essentially make it possible to use coal for cars, by generating electricity, the demand for coal shifts to the right, increasing its price and quantity sold.

b. Relaxing environmental laws regarding the burning of coal lowers the cost of using this fuel. This is a shift to the right of the supply of coal. This will decrease the price and increase the quantity demanded of coal. The lower price of coal shifts the demand for petroleum to the left, lowering both the price and the quantity sold.

18. No. The relative elasticities of labor supply and demand will determine their respective shares, with the more inelastic curve bearing more of the tax.

19. There is no contradiction. This happens if and only if price is maintained above the price that would prevail in the market.

20. b. The price of corn falls to the market clearing level. Consumers increase their quantity demanded for corn due to the fall in corn price. In the wheat market, the surplus remains. If in fact consumers view corn and wheat as substitutes, then consumers may switch from consuming the higher priced wheat to consuming the cheaper corn, increasing the wheat surplus. Furthermore, over time, some farmers will have an incentive to switch from corn production to wheat production, further exacerbating the wheat surplus.

22. The long waiting-lines for gasoline and other petroleum products during the oil crisis of 1973–74 were caused entirely by price controls imposed by the government. Without price competition, competition occurred through nonprice means, such as waiting in lines, and occasionally, violence. Because price was allowed to adjust in 1990 to equate the quantity supplied and the quantity demanded, no shortage and or other memorable economic events ensued.

23. b. Rent controls, because they induce shortages of housing, create waiting lists of prospective tenants. This allows landlords to select tenants on the basis on nonprice characteristics without the cost of possibly losing good tenants.

c. If rent controls are imposed in cities with many single-family houses, houses that were formerly rented will be sold. this will decrease the supply of rental housing, increasing the shortage (excess demand).

24. a. The shortage is due to the failure to adjust the price in the face of a leftward shift in the supply of water.

c. Consumers' demand for garden plants falls in either scenario. The quantity of garden plants sold decreases, and the price decreases as well.

25. a. The surplus created by the minimum wage (a form of price support) in the labor market is called unemployment.

b. The marginal workers, the workers currently being paid the minimum wage, such as teenagers, the less skilled, handicapped workers, will be most affected by the minimum wage law.

c. These laws raise the price of a substitute form of labor. Raising the price of substitutes shifts the demand for some union labor to the right, raising union wage rates as well.

26. A person earning the average wage and who waited two hours for a fill-up, would be revealing a willingness to pay of approximately \$8.00 + \$4.00 = \$12.00 for ten gallons or \$1.20 per gallon.

Chapter 6. Costs and Production

1. It is probably true that virtually anything produced can be purchased in New York City. Because of the very large concentration of people there, NYC has highly developed and extensive markets for goods, highly developed transportation and communication networks, and an extensive degree of specialization. This degree of division of labor occurs only when markets are very large.
2. a. Given that they each consume 2 fish each, Mutt can consume 3 rabbits; Jeff can consume 1 rabbit.
   b. For Mutt: the marginal cost of an additional fish is 3 rabbits; the marginal cost of an additional rabbit is 1/3 of a fish. For Jeff: the marginal cost of an additional fish is 1/2 of a rabbit; the marginal cost of an additional rabbit is 2 fish.
   c. If Mutt specializes in rabbit hunting and Jeff specializes in fishing, the total amount available for consumption will be 9 rabbits and 4 fish. If both Mutt and Jeff consume 2 fish each. However, there are now 5 rabbits left which can be divided among the two individuals. The gains from specialization and trade are the five rabbits.
4. Even if individuals choose occupations randomly, specialization will eventually produce comparative advantages because over time individuals will become more skilled in the activities they pursue, and develop specialized machinery for those tasks. So even with no initial comparative advantages, specialized production and trade is likely to occur eventually.
5. Comparative advantages determine trade, not absolute advantages. How much clothing would Bangladesh have to give up in order to build a jet airplane?
6. A shift in consumer demand will cause a change in output and price of the good in question, causing resources to be either allocated toward or away from production of this good depending on whether demand increases or decreases.
8. The lower wages in Mexico reflect lower worker productivity there. American workers had a comparative advantage in the more skilled tasks use in higher quality garments.
9. Same output in each factory with either strategy. In either case, the rule is to set the marginal costs equal to each other at the desired output.
10. The fundamental reason for the existence of rents is the inability of humans to completely replicate resources.
11. This payment is of course a cost to the individual making it. In the short run, when the apartment exists in any case, the payment is an economic rent. However, such payments are really quasi-rents because if they are not made, no apartments will be built.
13. The auction system will produce gold at a lower resource cost to society.
14. a. No, the existence of imports does not indicate energy "dependence." It most likely indicates the existence of comparative advantages.
    b. See question 5.
    c. Foreign energy imports encourage domestic energy conservation.
15. Consumers now value this land more than previously.
17. Sunk costs are irretrievably sunk. They don't affect current prices.
18. These subsidies come at cost to the Mexican economy. In some way, Mexicans have to reduce their consumption of other goods so as to produce the greater amount of food. Subsidies move the economy to a point where the marginal cost of producing food exceeds consumers' marginal values of food, causing welfare losses.
20. Comparative advantage means that the person who can produce a good at the least cost, that is, with the lowest opportunity cost of producing a good, will be the most efficient and hence would be the one to produce the good.
21. a. Firm A produces 10 tons, B produces 20.
    b. Same as in part a.
    c. The $2 per ton of pollution costs is an added cost of production. So the Marginal cost schedules are both shifted up by $1. The economically most efficient way is to set the *MC*s (including the pollution costs) of the two firms equal, as before. A produces 8 and B produces 16.
    d. Would the *MC*s of the two firms still be equal?
22. This is an application of problem 21. Yes they would trade, and it would improve efficiency.
23. They take 20/9 hours to do the job.

Chapter 7. The Law of Diminishing Returns

1. The Reverend Thomas Malthus' prophesy failed to come true because he did not anticipate the increases in other factors of production besides land. These include improvements in productivity such as new fertilizers, hybrid crops and new agricultural techniques.
2. a. Common property leads to too much fishing because individuals do not pay the full cost of their actions. Seven individuals will fish in this example. For any number of individuals over four, there will be a net loss of gains to society. For instance, when the sixth individual joins the scene, she or he produces $80 worth of fish, but at an alternative cost to society of $100 of other goods. With seven fishermen, $700 worth of fish are produced, but at a cost to society of $700 worth of other goods. Rents are completely dissipated.

b. If the lake were privately owned, the lake owner's private cost of allowing individuals fish and society's alternative cost of employing these individuals in the next best alternative are equal: $100. A private owner will allow only four individuals to fish. Rents, the gain in the value of resources created by using workers in this endeavor is greatest when four people fish.
c. If the fish are being depleted by fishing even at the static efficient level of four fishers, it means that fishing costs more than the $100 labor cost. The additional cost is the lost fish, or increased difficulty of fishing in the future. At this higher cost of fishing, the amount of people an owner will employ decreases. For example, if the cost of fishing is now perceived to be $110, only three people will fish.

4. Profits per square foot of store space is an average product measure. Owners base decisions on marginal product.
6. a. You should allocate your campaign time in each state such that the marginal product per dollar spent on your campaign in each state is the same across all states. Your marginal product of campaigning is greatest in states most likely to be swayed.
   b. With straight majority voting, campaigning in closely contested states will diminish.
   c. The strategy is the same whether you are a Republican or a Democrat.
7. Compelling as it is, this testimony frequently ignores the constraint imposed by scarcity. By subsidizing research in some diseases but not others, we reduce the chance that the marginal product of research will be the same for all diseases.
8. Police departments don't allocate all of their resources to only major crimes for the same reasons as in the previous question about orphan drugs. After some point, the marginal product of adding another police officer to some investigation may be less in terms of producing services citizens desire than engaging in some other activity.
9. a. With less labor input, we get a lower output, assuming the marginal product of labor is positive. The stock of money did not change, assuming the plague victims weren't buried with their savings of metal coin.
   b. Total output fell but the stock of money stayed the same. By the fundamental postulate of behavior, the marginal value of money relative to goods must have fallen.
   c. Since the plague affected only labor inputs, after the plague there was a smaller amount of labor applied to the same amount of other inputs (principally land). Apply the law of diminishing marginal product.
11. a. If less plastic is available, its price will rise. In response, each firm using plastic will reduce its use of that input. However, it is extremely unlikely that each firm would contract its use of plastic by the same amount. If a requirement for equal reduction across firms were imposed on these firms, the decrease in the aggregate value of output will be greater than if firms can adjust input levels efficiently.
13. a. Capital such as equipment and machinery does indeed produce value. With the use of machines individuals can increase production beyond levels when machinery is not employed.
    b. How would this affect the incentives to produce new capital, and, ultimately, the wages of labor?
14. a. Yes, it's possible.
    b. No you wouldn't reduce one or the other on the basis of this data alone.
    c. Yes, you would still sell some specialty items like Kasha. It's the same reasoning as the slot machine example in the text.
15. No you wouldn't. Have to pay attention to diminishing marginal products.
16. Another variation of the diamond-water paradox. Professors get paid differently because of the different demands for them and because of the ease of supplying these services to students.

Chapter 8. Supply in Competitive Markets

2.

L	TP	MP	TC	MC	AC	TR	Rents
1	13	13	$100.00	**$ 7.69**	$ 7.69	$130.00	$30.00
2	25	12	200.00	**8.33**	8.00	250.00	50.00
3	36	11	300.00	**9.09**	8.33	360.00	60.00
4	46	10	400.00	**10.00**	8.70	460.00	60.00
5	55	9	500.00	**11.11**	9.09	550.00	50.00
6	63	8	600.00	**12.50**	9.52	630.00	30.00
7	70	7	700.00	**14.29**	10.00	700.00	0.00
8	76	6	800.00	**16.67**	10.53	760.00	–40.00

The marginal cost schedule increases because as the firm hires more laborers, the marginal product of labor diminishes. As the marginal product decreases, the marginal cost of output rises. The rents of the firm are maximized ($60.00) at an output of 46 units, when the price, $10.00, equals marginal cost. The "immobile" or specific factors of production are the source of rents.

4. a., b. With common property, 8 workers work on this farm; with private property, 5 workers work. The marginal product of the eighth worker is in fact zero on the farm, and thus society loses the entire amount he or she could have produced elsewhere.
   f. Yes the farmer would use both farms, to the point where $MC = \$10$, the price of popcorn.
5. The firm's combined marginal cost curve is the lateral (horizontal) sum of the two marginal cost curves, in the same manner that an industry supply curve is the lateral sum of each firm's supply curve.
7. Labor and capital used by the firm still exhibit the law of diminishing marginal product. Economies of scale occur when all inputs can change.
8. The demand curve for spinach shifts to the left. As a result, the price of spinach will decrease. The decrease in spinach price will discourage production of spinach (movement down the supply curve), decreasing the output of spinach. In the short run, the quantity of spinach decreases, the price of spinach decreases, the quantity of labor employed decreases, rents to landowners decrease. Wages of farm workers may decrease if the decrease in industry output is sufficiently great that workers of greater efficiency can be used. In the long run, lower rents induce current spinach producers to leave the industry. The long run price rises above the short run decrease as the supply of spinach decreases. Rents to landowners are less than without the decrease in demand, but more than in the short run. Wages are assumed constant, equal to that which could be earned in the next best alternative employment.
10. I don't think so.
11. Almost all the commercial traffic is downstream. Which rates do you suppose are lower, upstream or downstream? Is it possible to schedule only downstream trips?
13. The fixed costs incurred are sunk, and irrelevant. It doesn't pay to scrap older equipment unless the marginal cost of producing even a small amount of service is greater than the price. Thus, airlines continue to use the older 727s, even though the average variable cost of using the newer planes may be less.
14. You do if you want to reflect the true opportunity cost of the oranges you have in stock. Sometimes, however, groceries seem not to do this, apparently because they are afraid their customers will regard it as price gouging.
15. It is definitely not a very reliable claim that many jewelry stores will sell you diamonds at wholesale prices. Retailers incur costs of selling that wholesalers do not incur, such as hiring salespeople to explain the gems to consumers, and displaying the diamonds in an attractive store. There is no free lunch.
16. It will raise it. the opportunity cost of land has increased.
17. a., b. The service of being checked out is a common property; groceries never charge for it explicitly. Eventually, checkout times will equalize, but then Joe's will have to charge higher prices to cover the costs of the extra checkers.
    c. Smaller at Joe's. Use the "shipping the good apples out" argument.
    d. Hard to say, really.
    e. The cost of time (What is this cost?) is higher for rich people; they will tend to shop at Joe's.

Chapter 9. Transactions Costs and Property Rights

1. The extensive relief provided by the federal government after Hurricane Andrew struck southern Florida reduces the incentives for individuals to prepare for the next storm because individuals will expect the federal government to come to the rescue once again.
2. a. The land near the airport can be used either for housing or as a repository for noise.
   b. In this case there may be too much noise pollution. The airlines have no incentive to reduce noise at especially inconvenient times. Passengers will benefit from the greater frequency of flights but residents will undoubtedly lose.
   c. If transaction costs were zero between the airport and home owners, the land would be used efficiently, even if the airport was not liable for its noise pollution.
   d. When the airport is liable for the damages from noise pollution, homeowners have no incentive to mitigate the damages from noise pollution. They will overbuild in locations near the airport.
   e. One solution would be for the airport to purchase the land near the airport.
4. a. Ten cars. How much time does this driver save, and how much time does he impose on others by taking the freeway?
   c. When the road is privately owned, the owner "owns" not only the rents generated, but also all the damages inflicted on other drivers as congestion increases. The private owner will charge a toll of $2.20 to induce the efficient five cars to use the freeway.
5. Under the new assumptions a, b, and c, ignoring the new constraint that side streets become more congested as people avoid the freeway for now, if access to

the freeway is unrestricted, 15 cars will enter the freeway. If access is restricted, the efficient number of cars entering the freeway is eight. A private owner of the freeway will charge a $7.00 toll for use of the freeway.

6. When freeways and other public access facilities are sometimes congested and sometimes not, an efficient structure of tolls would be one that discourages use during congested times which would imply not collecting the same toll at each hour of the day. An uncrowded freeway, for example, late at night, is a pure public good. The marginal cost of a person using it is zero. Therefore, the efficient toll for its use is zero. However, during rush hour, a rather substantial toll will be needed to induce an efficient use of the freeway.
9. The cost of collecting tolls may be small compared with the cost of added congestion at the mall. Is this a plausible explanation?
11. If two people share a stereo system and their music tastes differ, there will be congestion so that the stereo is no longer a public good.
13. This is a complicated issue deserving more space than what is available here. Marriage is now a more risky contract for women. No fault divorce has created an incentive for women to be economically independent. As such, it has probably decreased the incentives to marry.
14. a. On a straight wage contract, the owner will hire 5 workers.
    b. The owner's share will be $150/$400 = 37.5%.
    d. The landowner is more likely to offer a straight wage contract.
    e. The lower share cap induces workers to move from the industrial sector of the economy to the farms. As more workers are hired, the value of their marginal product falls. These extra workers are coming from the next best alternative where they were earning $50/day. This is a movement towards the common property solution.
15. If transaction costs were zero, teams would select players with the greatest market value. Why?

Chapter 10. Interest Rates and Capital Values

1. This answer depends on knowledge of continuous compounding. If interest is compounded daily, the future value of some amount P in n years, at interest rate r is Pe^{gt}.
2. If the first payment of the lottery is received immediately as opposed to at the end of the year, the present value of the lottery is one payment of $40,000 in the present plus an annuity of 24 additional payments. Using Table 10-3, PV = $421,160. Thus the value of the lottery is $461,160.
3. a. The present value of the Publisher's Clearinghouse Sweepstakes is $500,000 + a 29 year annuity of $250,000 paid at the end of the year + the present value of $2.5 million in 30 years. At 7% interest, PV = $3,896,919. At 10% interest, PV = $2,984,901.
    b. The present value of the American Family Sweepstakes is a simple 30-year annuity; in this case, a payment now plus a 29-year annuity of payments received at the end of the year. At 7% interest, PV = $4,425,000. At 10% interest, PV = $3,456,666.
    c. Only at extremely high interest rates would the Publisher's Clearinghouse prize be worth more.
4. a. Using Table 10-3, at 8% interest for four years, the present value of this loan is 3.312 × $10,000 = $33,120.
    b. Your repayments consist of five payments of $12,166.
    c. If the government calculates this loan at 5% interest, the present value would be 3.546 × $10,000 = $35,460. Your repayments are now $10,452. You save ($12,166 – $10,452) = $1,711 per year. Since the market interest rate is really 8%, the value of this annuity at the beginning of year 6, (end of year 5) is $1,711 × 3.993 = $6,832. Bringing this sum back to the present, the present value of the savings, which is the amount of the gift to the student is $6,832 × 0.681 = $4,652.
5. With fixed monthly payments, inflation causes the real value of these payments to decrease over time. Since with greater inflation the real value of future payments diminish, the value of the payments in the near time must increase to offset the lower future payments. With greater anticipated inflation, the nominal rate of interest increases. In the near term, this raises the real amount of the payment, but inflation eventually erodes its value to an amount lower than what would prevail if there was no inflation.
7. The exact amount of the subsidy will depend on the market rate of interest. For a market rate of interest, i, the subsidy is the difference between $2,000 and present value of the four annual payments of $500. If, for example, i = 8%, the value of the subsidy is $344.
10. This question applies the Fisher separation theorem. If the person is indifferent to these professions, the present value of her consumption is greatest if she first maximizes wealth and then rearranges her consumption by borrowing and lending in the capital market.
    a. True. c. True. e. False.
11. a. An increase in the Fisherian premium for earlier availability funds (the real interest rate) reduces the value of any future nominal amount. Therefore, the prices of both your stocks and your bonds decrease when the real interest rate rises.

b. If greater anticipated inflation raises the nominal rate of interest (and we assume the inflation is correctly assessed), the value of previously issued bonds falls. There should be no effect on real profits and thus the price of the stocks of this company. However, since the value of the bonds the firm has issued has fallen, its liabilities have decreased, and on that account, it is wealthier. For that reason, the price of the stocks should rise.

c. When the new trees reach maturity, the supply curve of fruit will shift to the right, decreasing the price of fruit. If this firm owns none of the new hybrid trees, its wealth will be lower, and thus the price of the firm's stock will fall immediately, reflecting this outcome. The answer is not so clear if the firm purchases the new trees as they become available.

12. a. Under the maximization of the total value of trees harvested each year, 26 years. This harvesting plan, however, is economically inefficient. How much could the funds produce in some other endeavor?

b. Under the maximization of the average sustained yield harvesting plan, 25 years. This is also inefficient.

c. Under the maximization of the net present value of the trees, the trees are harvested after the 23rd year, where the growth rate of the investment equals the expected interest yields on like investments, 15%. This rule is known as the Fisherian solution. This harvest plan is economically efficient.

13. a. The supply of coffee decreases, raising the price of the coffee and lowering the equilibrium quantity. Because tea is a close substitute for coffee, when the price of coffee rises, the demand for tea increases, thereby raising both the equilibrium price and quantity of tea.

b. When hearing the news, "speculators" (and homemakers) purchase current stocks of coffee and hold them inventory, or for future sale. This reduces the supply below what it would otherwise be.

c. This "speculation" reduces the current supply and raises the price of coffee in the immediate present. It usually gets a lot of bad press. What is ignored, is that this coffee is ultimately sold, and then the supply of coffee is greater than what it would otherwise be, lowering the price at that time. Speculators therefore even out the flow of coffee for consumers.

d. The speculators lose wealth if they forecast these events incorrectly. If there really is no frost, and speculators have withheld coffee beans from the market, they will have created an uneven flow out of an even flow, something consumers value less highly.

14. Trucking Regulation

a. The value of the licenses to operate on certain routes represents the present value of the anticipated future rents from trucking. These rents are created by the restrictions on entry into the industry, either in total or over certain designated routes.

c. If the real interest rate rises, the present value of the future rents from using the license falls. Therefore the value of the license falls.

e. When the supply of truckers increases in six years, trucking rates will decrease. This will lower rents received in this business beginning in year six. However, with this expected increase in the supply of trucking licenses, the license price will immediately decrease.

16. a. This will decrease the value of your bonds. On the simplest level, there will be no effect on the value of your stocks since profits will rise with inflation. However, inflation has real effects on corporate profits because accounting costs are not indexed to inflation. The IRS insists that firms use historical costs. When inflation occurs, profits are therefore overstated, and corporate tax liabilities increase.

b. This will probably increase firm profits, at least in the short run. As a result the value of your stocks will increase. There will be no change in the value of your bonds since the interest rate does not change. The new environmental law will probably not have a significant effect on the risk investors perceive in these bonds. The value of your wealth will thus increase.

c. The value of both your stocks and your bonds decreases.

17. This question is a rerun of the trucking question.

18. If half the complex burns, this provides fewer consumption possibilities than if the interest rate doubles. Only if you expected to die in the near future, without heirs, would you be indifferent between the two events.

19. Prohibiting borrowing and lending does not eliminate the reasons why individuals want to borrow and lend.

20. This argument is nonsense. You never help someone by destroying their capital. The Germans and Japanese were not happy about our destroying their factories. The critical reason for the postwar recovery of the axis powers was that although the physical capital was destroyed during the war, their human capital was left largely intact.

21. b. Both you and your friend have errors in your reasoning. You are both failing to calculate the present values of these options.

22. a. The prices paid for TV shows will drop if Congress were to pass a law limiting the number of times TV shows can be rerun. The future stream of income generated from a particular TV show will be truncated, thus lowering the present value of the show.
    b. The incomes of TV stars will undoubtedly fall as the price for TV shows drop.
    c. The incomes of actors who obtain jobs through "central casting" will probably increase.
    d. Avid soap opera viewers may be slightly better off with such legislation, but will probably be largely unaffected.
    e. Avid viewers of expensive prime time shows will be worse off with this legislation.
23. Large corporations are not immune to changes in interest rates, John Kenneth Galbraith notwithstanding. If the market rate exceeds the rate of return a firm would get if invests its funds in itself, it loses wealth. It would be better for the firm to simply invest elsewhere. If the rate it could get by investing internally is greater than the market rate, it should invest until the marginal rate of return falls to the market rate. In either case, the firm's decisions depend on the market rate.
24. Speculators cannot drive up prices. Consumers can drive up prices, and supply interruptions drive up prices.
25. Diamond merchants are not known for their altruism. If such events are anticipated, the present price of diamonds, a durable product, reflects this information. This slogan is not credible.
26. With higher real interest rates, the demand for the durability of goods will decrease. The answers perhaps become clearer if one views the increase in the interest rate as caused by increased risk, for example, an increased threat of war.
27. Over the long term this might be true, but there is also a greater risk they will do badly in a given year, or even go under entirely.
28. The interest yields these bonds pay reflect the fact that taxpayers won't have to pay taxes on the interest they earn. the marginal buyers are high income earners and corporations; for most people, these bonds are not a good investment.
29. a., b. The higher wages induce a surplus (excess supply) of workers looking for these union jobs. The union has to find some device for choosing who to admit into the union.
    c. How does $1 per hour translate into an annual increase in income. The amount a young person would pay to get into the union is the present value of this amount, usefully approximated with the perpetuity formula. The interest rate should reflect, among other things, the probability that the worker might not spend his or her entire career with this union.
    d. Since wages can be expected to rise with inflation, inflation should not affect anything here. An increase in the real rate will lower the initiation fee, but not current or future wages.

Chapter 11. Monopoly

2. No supply curve exists for a monopolist because a monopolist simultaneously chooses output and price. The question "How much would the monopolist supply if the price were such and such?" makes sense only if the price is determined by forces beyond the monopolist's control.
3. Maximum revenue is not the same thing as maximum profits. Firms don't ignore costs of production. Only if there were no costs would firms maximize revenue.
5. Society faces a trade-off of possible deadweight losses due to monopoly versus greater technological change and greater output. Economists generally defend patents and copyrights on efficiency grounds because we fear that in their absence, many of the patented or copyrighted products might not exist at all.
8. A monopolistic firm that operates two plants with marginal cost curves MC_1 and MC_2 minimizes costs by allocating resources between production at the two plants until the marginal cost of production in both markets are equal. A monopolist maximizes profits by choosing output where $MR = MC$. The monopolistic firm thus maximizes profits by producing where $MR = MC_1 = MC_2$.
9. No simple rule can be stated about the effects of market structure on product durability. However, a firm stands to make the greatest rents from its monopoly position by producing light at the lowest cost. This is determined by the technology of light bulbs, in particular, the trade-offs of greater durability versus output of light, per amount of electricity used. If the technologically efficient bulb doesn't depend on the quantity of bulbs produced, then the monopolist and the competitor will produce products of the same durability. Otherwise, the relation could go either way.
10. Under what conditions would price-discrimination occur? What characterizes the market with the higher price?
11. Which service is more likely to be retraded?
12. b. A percentage tax on the monopolists profits will not affect either output or the amount of pollution produced.

c. One solution is to try to tax the pollution itself. In particular, if a tax can be assessed on the pollution in the amount of the marginal damages the pollution causes, then this is equivalent to making the firm pay for all of its costs, including the pollution. This could lead to an efficient allocation of resources.

13. In the case of simple, or third degree price discrimination, the effect on economic efficiency is ambiguous. It might be the case that price discrimination increases output enough to reduce the deadweight loss.
15. This pricing scheme by movie theaters might be price discrimination. There may, however, be competing explanations. It may be that the theaters are engaging in "peak-load" pricing. One might expect the price of movies to be lower during the day than during the evening. The theater pricing policy encourages children and retired adults, who often have lower incomes than working adults, to attend when the rent for using the theater is effectively less.

Chapter 12. Imperfect Competition

1. Monopolistically competitive firms face potential entry of new firms. Their markets are always contestable.
2. Applying the traditional monopoly diagram (Figure 11-3.) to firms in these differentiated industries, even with zero profits, the price charged to consumers exceeds the marginal cost of production at the output produced.
4. a. The problem that consumers have in evaluating whether a used car is actually a lemon is one of asymmetric information. The seller often has more information than the consumer about the used car.
   b. Because consumers have difficulty determining which used cars were lemons, the price of good used cars is less than their true worth. However, this discourages some sellers of "good" used cars from engaging in mutually beneficial trade with buyers who would prefer those cars to the more expensive ones. Therefore the proportion of used lemons for sale is greater than the proportion of all cars that are lemons.
   c. The price of used cars consequently falls, reflecting their disproportionate mix of lemons.
   d. Sellers of used cars that are not lemons, can try to signal to buyers the high quality of the car by offering a partial warranty or offering to get the car checked by an independent mechanic.
   e. Private owners can offer to have their car appraised by an independent mechanic in order to receive a price more reflective of the true value of their car. A private owner obviously cannot offer potential buyers guarantees because they are moving across the country.
5. Perfectly competitive firms face the problem of capturing the gains from research and development (R&D). How does the establishment of brand names encourage innovation?
6. You sell 75 units at a price of 175.
7. OPEC, although a very famous cartel, is not really successful. Almost since its inception it has been largely unable to enforce reductions in output by its members. Watch for new meetings where they struggle with that issue.
8. It would be very unusual to find actual competitors selling goods at the exact same price. All stores and vendors have differences in costs and levels of services offered.
10. Under regulation by the Civil Aeronautics Board (CAB), air carriers to competed among each other for passengers by providing better amenities. By differentiating themselves by the quality and quantity of amenities offered airlines were competing in the only way they legally could. When these regulations were lifted, airlines resorted more to competition by price in order to attract passengers.
13. It's not easy. Are all computers part of the same market? Are PCs the same as minicomputers? Are electronic typewriters, which have some memory capabilities part of the computer market?
14. If general stores charged monopoly prices, they faced entry by other stores. Why was there commonly only one store?
15. Predatory pricing is an expensive way to gain a monopoly. For whom is it more expensive, small or large firms? Who is generally the predator?
16. No more rents can be extracted by block-booking than by individually pricing the movies.
17. Determining the extent of monopolistic behavior is a quite difficult undertaking. These firms face potential competition, as the number of smaller fringe firms attests. If the prices the larger firms set exceed the marginal costs of the small firms, these smaller firms can become large firms. Can you think of any examples?
20. The problem of duplication of measurement is that oftentimes sellers expend costly effort producing information which is not apparent to the buyer. The buyer wants to confirm the representations of the seller. Various practices originally thought to be monopolistic, such as full-line forcing and vertical integration, are often consistent with attempts to save resources by avoiding costly duplication of effort in the production of information about a product's quality or price. These methods, however, are sometimes not easily distinguished from cartel or monopolistic behavior.

Chapter 13. Labor Markets

1. Progressive taxes penalize risky activities relatively more than careers with steady income streams. This

would include entrepreneurial activities. Going to college means having low incomes in the present in return for hopefully higher incomes in the future. Those higher college incomes may be relatively more secure, but perhaps not. How do these assumptions affect your answer?

2. With relatively higher earning potential in the home, women are more likely to switch to household income when their market wage falls.
3. The price and quantity of labor transacted in the market is determined by the intersection of supply and demand curves for labor. The long run trend might reflect either supply or demand factors. How would the higher real wages affect the quantity of labor supplied?
5. The overtime wage raises the opportunity cost of leisure at the margin more than does a higher average wage. Therefore?
6. This question reviews the analysis presented in chapter 5. In the short run, the supply of these services is largely fixed. In the long run, however, the supply of these services in high tax localities will diminish. How does this affect the fees patients pay in the short and long runs?
7. There are two separate issues. Are these workers in elastic or inelastic supply? Is the law enforceable?
8. If women are restricted from working in the honey industry all women will be employed in the milk industry and none in the honey industry. Under what conditions would the wages of women fall?
10. This kind of trade-off allows a marginal assessment of the value of life. Raising the speed limit to 70 mph would create extra income in terms of the time individuals save. Suppose, for example, the higher speed limit saves 50 million people 100 hours per year. Suppose their alternative wage, on average, is $10 per hour. What is the resulting gain, per life lost?
12. Income effects have safely been ignored in the rest of the text because they are generally very small, and they usually reinforce the substitution effect. Why are these assumptions suspect in the analysis of labor leisure choice?
13. Your reservation wage is the minimum wage that must be offered for you to accept an offer for employment. The threat of starvation is a powerful inducement to work. How is you reservation wage affected by your responsibilities to others?
16. The introduction of no-fault divorce is likely to increase female participation in the labor force. Women are now more likely to be able to support themselves, that is, not rely on their spouse's income. The introduction of no-fault divorce will raise the age of first marriage on average for women because more women will attempt to gain valuable human capital in case of divorce later on.
17. Minimum wage laws are at best a mixed blessing. Only about 20% of minimum wage workers are from households living in poverty. Raising the minimum wage causes employers to reduce the employment of low wage workers. Disabled workers are among the low wage workers, due to their disabilities. These workers may be among the least employable in the economy, and therefore most adversely affected by increases in the minimum wage.
18. Are minimum wage workers substitutes or complements to skilled union labor?
19. It is not possible to conclude on theoretical grounds that lower tax rates on wage income will increase the amount of time people work per week. That outcome depends on the empirical question of whether the substitution effect of the higher after-tax wage rate outweighs the income effect of the tax break. The issue is still under investigation.
20. It would likely increase the labor market participation rate for female workers.
21. For what type of employment, large manufacturing concerns with many workers performing similar tasks, or small service oriented firms, whose employees perform individualistic services, would unions likely be more successful? Why? Which sector has been declining?
22. Cartels of labor can raise average incomes of the laborers within the cartel by restricting the supply of that particular labor. However, the creation of monopolies results in deadweight losses. The rise in the standard of living is due to the increased productivity of labor and other resources. It is now possible for the same number of humans to produce vastly greater output than in previous generations.
23. Not necessarily. Statistical discrimination occurs because of rational business decisions.

Glossary

Absolute advantage When one producer can produce more of all goods, for given levels of inputs, than other producers.

Absolute price The price of a good in money terms; the monetary valuation of a good without reference to the general price level.

Ad hoc Explaining only one event or being useful for only one occasion.

Affirmative action Government policy giveing preference to selected minority groups, particularly in hiring.

Affirming the consequent The fallacy of concluding that event A must be true because event B is true, from a theory that states that event A implies event B.

AFL-CIO The resulting labor union from the merger of the old American Federation of Labor and the Congress of Industrial Organization.

Age-earnings profile The relationship between an individual's age and their earnings or income over their lifetime.

Agency problem or principal-agent problem The problem one party, the principal, faces, when he or she delegates tasks to another party, the agent. How does the principal create incentives for the agent to do what the principal wants, rather than what the agent wants?

Aggregate demand In macroeconomics, the total amount of goods and services demanded by consumers, businesses, and the government in an economy. In microeconomics, the sum of individual demand curves into a market demand curve.

Allocative efficiency When the distribution of resources among competing ends leads to the exhaustion of mutual gains.

Allocative inefficiency When the distribution of resources among competing ends leaves mutual benefits unclaimed.

Alternative cost or opportunity cost The highest valued option which is foregone when an action or decision is undertaken.

American Federation of Labor or AFL A union of skilled laborers founded in 1881, now merged with the Congress of Industrial Organization (CIO).

Annuity A contract to pay or receive a series of uniform payments occurring at regular intervals for a stated number of years.

Antitrust legislation or antitrust statutes Laws or statutes which discourage monopoly and collusive practices and encourage increased competition.

Arc elasticity The percentage change in quantity divided by the percentage change in price calculated by using the midpoint of two points along a demand or supply curve of as the point of reference.

Assertions The universal postulates of a theory. See, in contrast, Assumptions.

Asset An item owned by an individual, firm, or the government that generates income.

Assistance in kind Support from the government in the form of goods and services rather than monetary outlays.

Assumptions Simplifications made to make a theory more tractable, or usable. See in contrast, Assertions.

Asymmetry of information or asymmetric information When a party to a transaction has more or at least different information than the other party or any of the other parties involved. Usually, the case where the seller has more information than the buyer.

At the margin (figuratively speaking) Where the decision one makes concerns incremental units of a good.

Athenian democracy A form of government where all citizens vote on all issues, as in ancient Athens.

Average costs or AC Total costs divided by the total quantity of output produced.

Average cost curve or average total cost curve A "u" shaped curve (because of scale economies at low levels of output) which graphically represents the average level of costs at each level of output produced.

Average fixed costs or AFC Total fixed costs divided by total quantity output produced.

Average fixed cost curve A declining or negatively sloped (asymptotic to the origin) curve which graphically represents the level of average fixed costs at each level of output produced. This curve is always a rectangular hyperbola.

Average product (of an input) or AP The total product of particular input divided by the quantity of the inputs used.

Average rate of consumption Total consumption divided by the relevant duration of time.

Average revenue or AR Total revenue divided by the total quantity of output produced. This always equals the unit price of the good.

Average total costs or ATC Total costs divided by the total quantity of output produced. Equivalently, the sum of average fixed plus average variable costs.

Average total cost curve or average cost curve A "u-shaped" curve (because of scale economies at low levels of output) which graphically represents the level of average total costs at each level of output produced.

Average variable costs Total variable costs divided by the total quantity of output produced.

Average variable cost curve A "u" shaped curve which graphically represents the level of average variable costs for each level of output produced.

Bad or economic bad An undesirable entity, something individuals would pay to have less of.

Bankrupt When an individual, firm, or organization legally declares that they are unable to pay their debts.

Barrier to entry Restrictions on the abilities of other firms to go into business in a monopolistic industry, where existing firms are earning positive profits; examples of barriers range from patents, to actions of governments or government agencies such as licensing arrangements, or huge start-up costs, where the underlying technology may result in a single firm being the least cost method of producing the good.

Barter The direct exchange of goods and services for other goods and services without the use of money.

Basing point pricing Establishes prices of delivered goods including an amount for transportation from a given production locale, whether or not the producer is located there.

Bilateral trade Exchange between two parties.

Black market or underground economy Exchanges of either illegal goods or those goods in violation of government regulations such as tax laws, price controls.

Block booking A tie-in-sale where movies are sold as a bundle without allowing the possibility of theaters to select only those they wish to show.

Bonds Legal obligations of corporations and governments to pay periodic fixed sums for a specified number of years, plus the faced value of the bond, the principal, at maturity.

CAFE standards or Corporate Average Fleet Equivalency Regulations which force car companies to produce cars so that the average miles per gallon for the fleet of cars produced by each company meets some government standard .

Capital Any resource or produced good that produces income in the future.

Capital gain The increase in the market value of an asset between the time at which the asset is bought and subsequently sold.

Capitalism The economic system wherein the means of production, capital and land, are privately owned and operated in the pursuit of individual gain.

Capitalized value The present value of an expected future income stream.

Capital market Markets in which borrowing and lending take place. Households and firms and the government lend or supply their savings for claims to future profits or for interest to other individuals, firms or governments who borrow to increase present consumption or to finance the production of capital goods .

Cartel A group of producers who agree to set price and output collectively so as to increase joint profits by achieving a monopoly position in the market.

Cash balances Money held by an individual.

Centrally planned economies Economies in which resource allocations and production decisions are made by a central planner, the central government.

Ceteris paribus All else being equal; holding all other variables fixed so as to investigate the effect of a change in one variable on one other variable.

Change in demand A shift in the entire demand curve for a good. This occurs when anything other than the price of the good changes, such as income, the price of a substitute or complementary good, information about the good. The amount an individual is willing to purchase of a certain good changes at each level of price.

Change in quantity demanded The change in the amount of a good a consumer is willing to purchase caused by a change in the price of the good. This is a movement along the demand curve.

Change in quantity supplied The change in the amount of a good a producer is willing to offer for sale prompted by a change in the price of the good. This is a movement along the supply curve.

Change in supply A shift in the entire supply curve. This occurs when something other than the price of the good changes, such as new technology, weather or natural disasters.

Clayton Act of 1914 Antitrust law that outlawed certain monopoly practices such as price discrimination, tying contracts and unlimited mergers, in addition to clarifying the "rule of reason."

Closed shop Where prior union membership is a condition of employment.

Coase Theorem The proposition that in the absence of transaction costs, that is, with clearly delineated property rights, the assignment of liability to damages created by one individual will not prevent the exhaustion of mutual benefits, though the incomes of the parties involved will be affected.

Collective bargaining The process by which union representative and managers of a firm negotiate labor contracts, that is, conditions and terms of employment.

Collusion The coordination in secret of producers to raise price and reduce output, that is, set a monopolistic price and quantity, in order to maximize joint profits; generally illegal.

Confirmed Consistent with the theory. Not to be confused with proven.

Command economies Economies wherein the government determines by fiat the allocation of resources and all production decisions, the quantity to be produced, the price charged, and the means of distribution.

Commodity Any item which is bought and sold.

Commodity money Any item which is used as a medium of exchange that also has an alternative nonmonetary use, for example, gold.

Common law The unwritten law of a country based on custom, tradition, and precedents of court rulings.

Common property or public domain A resource for which there is no owner. No individual has the right to exclude any others from its use.

Comparable worth The policy which requires jobs with similar characteristics to pay similar wages.

Comparative advantage When a producer can produce a good with a lower opportunity cost of production than another.

Compensating (wage) differentials The difference between wages accounted for by the differences in working conditions or nonpecuniary aspects of a job; an addition to a wage in order to attract workers to unpleasant jobs.

Competition The efforts of parties to secure rights to scarce goods.

Competitive equilibrium The price and quantity determined by the intersection of the supply and demand curves for goods, where the quantity demanded equals the quantity supplied.

Competitive firm A firm which takes price as given and produces where its marginal cost equals the market price.

Complementary goods (or inputs) or complements Goods which are used jointly in production or consumed jointly, for example a hammer and nail. Two goods are complements if a rise in the price of one good leads to a decrease in demand for the other, holding everything else constant.

Compound interest Money paid or received for the use of money which based on the accumulated principal, that is, the original principal and the accumulated interest, not just on the original amount.

Concentrated industry An industry with HH, a Herfindahl-Hirschman index, greater than 1,800.

Condercet's paradox, or voting paradox The possibility that a changing majority might always prefer a different outcome, no matter what choice is made.

Congestion Crowding on a resource so that the actions of one person affects the costs or productivity of others using that resource.

Congress of Industrial Organization or CIO Founded in 1935, the first union organizing semi-skilled laborers in mass production industries.

Constant returns to scale The property that when all factor inputs change in the same proportion, output changes in exactly the same proportion.

Constraints All things which impinge on behavior and are in principle capable of being measured, in contrast to preferences. In the theory of the consumer, prominent constraints are income, prices, time, technology, education and laws.

Consumer Price Index, or CPI The most widely used measure of the average price level in the economy. It is calculated using the cost of a market basket of goods consumed by households, reported every month by the Bureau of Labor Statistics.

Consumer's surplus The difference between what a consumer would be willing to pay for the units purchased, total value, and what the consumer actually pays, total expenditure. Graphically, the triangular area under the demand curve and above the market price.

Consumption S pending by households on final goods.

Contestable market A market with no significant barriers to entry by new firms.

Cooperative An organization for the production of goods owned collectively by all members who share in the rents.

Copyright The exclusive right to the publication or production of a form of literary or artistic work granted by law for the rest of one's life plus 28 years (U.S.).

Corporation A firm owned by stockholders whose liability is limited to the value of the assets of the firm. The private assets of the stockholders are beyond the reach of creditors.

Correlation When a change in one variable is regularly associated with a change in another variable.

Cost or economic cost In economics, synonymous with alternative, or opportunity cost. The highest valued option which is foregone when an action or decision is undertaken.

Craft union A labor union where only individuals involved in a certain same craft or trade belong.

Credit market A market where funds are loaned to borrowers.

Creditor A n individual to whom another or others are indebted.

Cross elasticity of demand A measure of the responsiveness in quantity demanded of one good to the change in price of another good. The percent change in the quantity demanded of one good divided by the percentage change in price of another good. It is positive for substitute goods and negative for complementary goods.

Cross section data Observations on any number of economic units at a given point in time, in contrast with time series data.

Currency Paper money and coins.

Current price or current dollar terms The price consumers actually faced or the number of dollars actually paid in the designated year.

Dead weight loss The lost mutual benefits from trade when output is reduced below its efficient level, that is, where price equals marginal cost.

Debtor One who owes something to another or others.

Decreasing average cost industry An industry where average total costs decrease as a firm's output increases, so that the lowest average costs occur when the industry consists of only one firm.

Decreasing returns to scale A production process where proportional increases in all factor inputs leads to an increase in output in a smaller proportion. See, by contrast, constant returns to scale, and increasing returns to scale.

Deflation A fall in the general level of prices.

Demand curve A curve which graphically represents the quantity of a particular good a consumer is willing to purchase at each level of price. The fundamental law of demand states that this curve is downward sloping.

Demand deposit Funds deposited in a bank which is transferable by check, that is, withdrawn on demand.

Demand curve for labor The curve depicting the amount of labor firms desire at various wage rates. It is a derived demand because labor inputs are not desired for their own sake, but rather for the useful goods they produce. It is downward sloping curve because of the law of diminishing marginal product.

Demand curve for money The curve depicting the negative relationship between the amount of real money balances desired by individuals at any given nominal rate of interest, the price of holding money.

Demand schedule A table displaying the quantity demanded of a good for selected prices. A discrete form of the demand curve.

Depreciation The amount by which the value of capital is reduced by wear and tear or used up over a given period of time.

Depression A severe or prolonged economic recession, marked by substantial unemployment and reduced aggregate output.

Deregulation The revoking of government regulations to allow the market to function more freely.

Derived demand The demand which results not from the desire for the good (input) itself but from the goods or services the good (input) produces, for example, the demand for labor.

Diamond-water paradox The puzzling observation that water, a necessity of life, is relatively very cheap, whereas diamonds, which are pleasant frivolities are relatively expensive.

Differentiated industry An industry where firms sell nonhomogeneous products, and face demand curves that are downward sloping to some degree.

Differentiated products Goods which are very similar but not viewed as perfect substitutes by consumers, such as different brands of the same good.

Diminishing returns An imprecise term; in economics, meaning one of the two following alternatives.

Diminishing returns at the extensive margin The phenomenon that when industries expand, eventually the ability to replicate the productive process decreases, as firms must use inputs that are less and less efficient.

Diminishing returns at the intensive margin When more of identical units of a productive input are added to a fixed amount of other factors of production, the amount by which the input increases output becomes smaller and smaller.

Discouraged workers Those workers who have dropped out of the labor force because they have been discouraged, that is, unable to find employment.

Discrimination In the labor market, the use by firms of factors unrelated to marginal productivity in employment. More generally, the use of variables unrelated to merit in decisions affecting people.

Dissipation of rents The loss of mutual benefits, especially due to lack of clear property rights.

Distortionary taxes Taxes which cause prices to deviate from marginal costs, creating deadweight losses.

Dividends A share of a firm's profits which are paid to shareholders.

Division of labor Breaking up a given task into smaller and more specialized tasks.

Double coincidence of wants The condition of successful barter; individual A has what individual B wants and individual B has what A wants.

Duplication of measurement The problem caused by imperfect information, where both the buyer and the seller expend resources to evaluate some good.

Durable good Consumer goods which provide a service over a relatively long period of time.

Dynamic consistency The property that the marginal value of consumption in any period, in terms of foregone future consumption, is independent of the date of that choice.

Economic bad or bad An undesirable good, anything which individuals would pay to have less of.

Economic behavior or maximizing behavior When individuals strive to mitigate adverse consequences and exploit beneficial consequences of the changes in constraints they face.

Economic cost or cost See alternative, or opportunity cost.

Economic efficiency The exhaustion of mutual benefits. When it is impossible to make anyone better off without making someone worse off.

Economic explanation An explanation based on responses to changes in constraints, using the postulates of economics, such as the behavioral postulates and the law of diminishing marginal product.

Economic good or good Any item which is scarce, that is limited and desirable.

Economic growth An increase in the real (inflation-adjusted) gross national product of an economy.

Economic model For some. a simplified economic theory; for others, the logical or mathematical framework of an economic theory.

Economic paradigm The framework of using economic explanations to analyze social events.

Economic problem There are not enough of the items humans find desirable to satisfy their unlimited wants, so that every society must make decisions about the production and allocation of resources and goods.

Economic profit The difference between total revenues and total costs where opportunity costs of production are included in total costs. These profits must always be identified with some specific, nonreplicable resource.

Economic rent The payment to a factor of production over and beyond the minimum amount which is required to keep the factor in its present use.

Economics The study of how scarce resources, that have alternative uses, are allocated amongst competing ends. More generally, the study of human behavior using the economic paradigm.

Economies of scale When the average cost of production decreases as output expands and factors of production are variable; for example, when inputs increase by some fixed proportion and output increases by some greater proportion.

Elastic demand When the percentage change in quantity demanded exceeds the percentage change in price. The demand for a good will be elastic when numerous substitutes are available.

Elasticity of demand, price The responsiveness of the quantity demanded of a good to a change its price, measured by the ratio of the percentage change in the quantity demanded of a good to the percentage change in price.

Elasticity of demand, income The responsiveness of the quantity demanded of a good to a change in consumer's income, measured by the ratio of the percentage change in the quantity demanded of a good to the percentage change in income.

Empirical Based on observations of individual cases or experiments.

Endogenous Determined within the particular framework.

Endowment The assets a person possesses prior to some event.

Engel's law The empirical observation that as income increases individuals spend a smaller proportion of their income on food and other "primary" goods.

Entrepreneurial skill The particular talent of being able to recognize a profitable situation and to organize factors of production for the purpose of production.

Equilibrium The price and quantity where the quantity demanded of a good equals the quantity supplied; a point from which producers and consumers have no incentive to deviate.

Equilibrium price The price which equates the quantity demanded and quantity supplied.

Equilibrium quantity The quantity at which the quantity demanded and quantity supplied are the same.

Equitable Fair or just.

Equity capital Funds owners or stockholders use at their own risk for investment and production by firms.

Excess demand The condition where the quantity demanded exceeds the quantity supplied at the given price.

Excess supply The condition where the quantity supplied exceeds the quantity demanded at the given price.

Exchange The mechanism whereby one good is voluntarily given or taken for another.

Excise tax A tax on the manufacture, sale, or consumption of a particular good.

Exclusivity One of the three conditions for a good to be private; the right to exclude others from use of the good or property.

Exogenous Determined outside the particular framework; taken as given within the confines of the relevant framework.

Export To sell domestically produced goods abroad.

Exports or export goods Domestically produced goods which are sold abroad.

Extensive margin The margin for decision making at the level of the industry, that is, the margin external to individual firms.

External cost A cost that is not taken into account by the firm which imposes it.

Externality Damage (negative externality) or benefit (positive externality) to a third party, external to an activity or transaction, that is not taken into account by the firm or individual which generates it.

Factor demand The amount of an input desired by a firm at the given input and output prices.

Factor of production Any input that contributes to production, typically, land, labor, and capital.

Fair-traded A situation where retailers could not sell a good below the retail price fixed by the manufacturer.

Fault divorce The ruling where one party could not leave the marriage without the approval of the other, usually, where a divorce is granted upon the establishment of wrongdoing or fault of one of the parties.

Federal Trade Commission or FTC Created by Congress in 1914 to enforce the provisions of the Sherman and Clayton Acts; to investigate and regulate firms engaging in unfair business practices in interstate commerce.

FTC Act The 1914 law that established the Federal Trade Commission.

Firm An organization or entity involved in the production of goods and services in an economy.

Fiat money A medium of exchange which has no value as a commodity but which is used because of the common experience that other people will always accept it as payment for goods and services.

Final good or service A good or service that is purchased by a final consumer, as opposed to goods purchased for resale to other firms.

First degree, or perfect price discrimination When a monopolist can charge each consumer their maximum willingness to pay for each unit of a particular good.

Fisher equation The relation expressing the nominal interest rate as the sum of the real interest rate and the anticipated inflation rate. More generally, the relation includes the relevant risk premium.

Fisher Separation Theorem In the presence of well developed capital markets, consumers derive their most preferred consumption plan by first choosing that income stream that maximizes wealth, and then rearranging consumption through borrowing and lending so as to achieve the particular stream of consumption they desire.

Fixed costs Costs which occur independently of how much a firm produces or whether it produces at all, and which therefore have no effect on marginal costs.

Fixed factor A factor whose level of use is not variable in some relevant time period. Typically, the physical plant of a firm and other items of capital.

Flow Income or good or service per unit time derived from a stock.

Food stamps Coupons which are redeemable toward the purchase of food.

Free good A good such that at a price of zero the amount available exceeds the amount people would want.

Free market When the sale and purchase of goods and services is for the most part unhindered by the government.

Free rider An individual who does not pay for the benefits received from a good, typically in the provision of public goods because individuals can receive the benefits of the good without having to contribute to its cost.

Frictional unemployment The unemployment that results when participants in the labor market change jobs.

Fringe benefits Payments made to workers in kind, principally pensions and medical coverage.

Full-line forcing contracts Where buyers must purchase some packaged group of the seller's commodities, rather than be able to pick and choose among the various goods offered for sale.

Fundamental postulates or postulates of behavior The four propositions which characterize the behavior of individuals: 1. People have preferences; 2. More is preferred to less; 3. People are willing to substitute one good for another; 4. For all individuals and goods, the marginal value of goods decreases, as more of that good is consumed, holding other things constant.

Future value The value to you sometime in the future of an investment made today.

Game theory A relatively new branch of economics originating in mathematics, where strategies of individuals are specifically incorporated into the decisions of others.

General human capital Human capital which is readily transferable to other jobs or careers.

General skills Abilities that are useful in many jobs, that is, word processing, computer programming, mechanical skills, etc.

Geoduck A hideously large clam, whose body extends several feet, considered a delicacy by some who violate the economic postulates; found in the Pacific Northwest. Pronounced "gooeyduck."

Geometric series A sum of terms where the ratio of each term to the preceding is the same.

Gold standard The monetary arrangement where a country's paper money is redeemable either wholly or fractionally by gold.

Good or economic good Any item which is scarce, that is, limited and desirable.

Goodwill The value of a business over and above the value of its material assets.

Government budget deficit When government expenditures and transfer payments exceed government tax revenues.

Government budget surplus When government tax revenues exceed government expenditures and transfer payments.

Government debt The total amount of outstanding securities held by the public for which the government is liable.

Government expenditure or government spending Outlays or payments made by agencies of local, state, and federal governments for goods and services.

Government licensure A practice whereby individuals or firms must have explicit permission granted by the government to exist or remain in operation, such as licenses to practice medicine or to operate some local utility.

Government transfers Payments made by the government to some individuals from others, for example, veterans and welfare benefits, social security.

Greenbelt legislation Laws to preserve open spaces in suburban areas by restricting the construction of housing developments.

Gross domestic product or GDP The total value of all final goods produced in the domestic economy in one year's time, including those goods produced by foreign owned factors of production.

Gross national product or GNP The total value of all final goods and services produced by a nation's factors of production in one year's time, including those goods produced by domestic factors abroad.

Guild A medieval union of individuals involved in the same trade and upholding the same ideals.

Herfindahl-Hirschman index or HH Measures the degree of concentration in an industry; by calculating the percentage share of the market for each firm, squaring those percentages, and summing them. HH has a maximum value of 10,000 for a monopolistic industry and approaches zero as the number of firms increases.

High-powered money or the monetary base The sum of currency and bank reserves.

Historical cost The price actually paid for an item.

Horizontal merger When firms selling a similar product combine into a single firm.

Household income The implicit earnings from the performance of household tasks.

Household wage The implicit amount one actually produces in the home per hour.

Households The suppliers of labor and the consumers of an economy's goods and services.

Human capital A form of intangible capital encompassing knowledge, skills, education, training, and anything else which increases the productivity of workers.

Hyperinflation Extremely high inflation.

Impatience An expression of time preference, for example, a given level of income generates less satisfaction, or utility, if it is consumed in the future rather than in the present.

Imperfect competition Competition among firms facing downward sloping demand curves for closely related products.

Imperfect information When all facts relevant for making a decision are not common knowledge.

Implicit cost The value of using factors in production for which no actual payment is made, such as the salary of the owner of a small business.

Import The domestic purchase of foreign produced goods.

Incentive A reward intended to encourage some particular action.

Incidence of a tax The share of a tax is borne by a particular person.

Income M oney or payment received by an individual in return for labor or service or those payments accruing to assets.

Income effect The change in the amount of a good demanded when the price of the good rises due solely to the decreased purchasing power the consumer experiences, that is, the lower real income of the consumer.

Income elastic When quantity of a good consumed increases in greater proportion than the increase in income; the value of the income elasticity of demand is greater than one.

Income elasticity of demand The responsiveness of the quantity demanded of a good to a change in income; measured by the ratio of the percentage change in quantity demanded of a good to the percentage change in income. The income elasticity of demand is positive for normal goods and negative for inferior goods.

Income inelastic When quantity of a good consumed increases in smaller proportion than the increase in income; the value of the income elasticity of demand is less than one.

Increasing returns to scale A production process where proportional increases in all factor inputs leads to an increase in output in a greater proportion. See, by contrast, constant returns to scale, and decreasing returns to scale.

Increasing average cost industry or diseconomies of scale An industry where average total costs decrease as industry output increases.

Indexation Linking payments to the price level. Social Security payments and many union wages are linked to the general price level in this fashion.

Industry marginal cost curve The lateral sum of each firm's marginal cost curve.

Inefficient When mutual gains are not completely exhausted; when it is possible to make some people better off and no one worse off by reallocating resources.

Inelastic demand When the percentage change in quantity demanded is less than the percentage change in price; the elasticity of demand is between zero and minus one. The demand for a good will be inelastic when there are few available substitutes.

Inferior good A good for which the demand falls as income rises or the demand rises as income falls, holding prices constant.

Inflation An increase in the general price level; serves as a tax on all holders of nominally denominated assets.

Innovation A new idea introduced and put into practice such as a new process, method, or device.

Input Something used in the production process.

Inside information Facts known only to a small number of individuals within a firm; knowledge that is not public. Buying and selling corporate stocks on the basis of inside information is illegal.

Insider trading Exchange which is prompted by individuals having inside information. Can land you in jail.

Intellectual property Valuable contributions of the intellect that can be employed for specific purposes.

Intellectual property rights Legal ownership to intellectual property which serves to protect against theft or imitation and serves as an incentive for further generation of intellectual property.

Intensive margin The relevant margin for decision making at the level of the firm, that is, the margin internal to individual firms.

Interest rate The premium for the earlier availability of funds; the premium borrowers pay to lenders for the use of money.

Intermediary or middleman A facilitator of trade between producers and consumers, or between two producers in the chain of production.

Intermediate goods Goods such as components of a TV or computer that are desired not for their own use, but because they are useful inputs in the production of some other good; goods which are not for final consumption.

Internalizing an externality The process by which a firm or individual takes into account either damages or benefits to third parties of their action or production to arrive at a socially efficient level of action or production undertaken.

International trade Exchange of goods between countries.

Interstate commerce The buying and selling of goods which occurs between states.

Interstate Commerce Commission or ICC Established in 1887, due in large part to public concern over monopolistic practices of the railroads, to regulate trade between firm engaging transporting goods over state lines.

Intertemporal Over time.

Intramarginal A event not affecting decisions to produce or consume an additional unit.

Intrastate commerce They buying and selling of goods and services within a state.

Intrinsic value The supposed worth of a good without reference to the value humans place on it. Inconsistent with the behavioral postulates.

Inversely related Two variables are inversely related if they move in opposite directions, that is, as one increases the other decreases.

Investment Expenditure on capital goods to be used in the production process.

Invisible hand A phrase coined by Adam Smith to describe the functioning of markets by the actions of individuals motivated by self-interest.

Justice Department Presidential cabinet level agency involved in the enforcement of federal laws, both criminal and civil, e.g., antitrust statutes.

Labor Both the physical and intellectual services of individuals used in production.

Labor force All individuals either currently employed or actively looking for work.

Labor-leisure choice The decision about how many hours to work per day.

Labor market The market in which households supply labor to firms that demand labor, and which establishes a price, called the wage, of that labor.

Labor market discrimination See discrimination.

Labor union See union.

Land All natural resources such as minerals, water, forests, etc. Actually pat of the more general category of capital goods.

Landrum Griffen Act of 1959 Federal law providing for periodic reporting of union finances and greater disclosure of the activities of union leaders to the general membership.

Lateral sum The aggregation of curves, for example demand curves, sideways or across horizontally. A peculiarity in economics of plotting the dependent variable, quantity, along the horizontal axis.

Law of demand The quantity demanded of any good, or the level of any activity pursued varies inversely with the price of that good or activity, *ceteris paribus*. The fundamental behavioral assertion of economics.

Law of diminishing marginal product, or law of diminishing returns As one input of production is added to a fixed amount of other inputs, after some point, the marginal product of the variable input continually declines.

Law of diminishing marginal values For all individuals and goods, the marginal value of goods decreases, as more of that good is consumed, *ceteris paribus*.

Law of factor demand If the wage of any factor decreases, the firm will choose to hire additional units (and vice-versa), *ceteris paribus*.

Law of one price If the costs of transportation are negligible then the price of a good will be the same in different locations.

Layoff When a laborer is put out of work, usually in the context of a reduction in the demand for the firm's product.

Learning-by-doing The increase in productivity that results from performing a particular task often.

Leisure An activity an individual does not consider as work; something a person will do without compensation.

Lender One who provides funds to another at some rate of interest.

Liability Amounts firms or individuals owe to others.

License fee Payment to the government for the right to engage in a certain activity or production.

Life-cycle hypothesis The proposition that households base their consumption decisions on their expected income to be accrued over their lifetime.

Liquidity The ease with which an asset can be converted to cash (sold).

Logrolling The exchange of votes in legislatures in order to gain support for legislation.

Longitudinal data Data where the same subjects are observed over time.

Long run The period of time when all factors of production are variable.

Long run average total cost curve The graphical representation of the locus of lowest per unit costs of production for each level of output a firm can produce.

Long run competitive equilibrium Where there are zero economic profits and hence no entrance or exit of firms into the industry; production is at the level of minimum long run average cost.

Long run industry supply curve The graphical representation of the level of output producers are willing to supply at every level of price when all inputs are variable and there is no entry or exit of firms in the industry.

Long run supply curve The graphical representation of the level of output a firm is willing to supply at every level of price when all factors of production are variable.

Lump sum tax A tax independent of the amount individuals or firms buy or sell.

Lump sum transfer A payment to an individual, the amount of which is independent of any variable the individual can choose.

Luxury goods Subjective, or normative term. Some define such goods as those for which income elasticity of demand is greater than one.

M1 The amount of money in the form of cash and cash substitutes plus checking accounts or demand deposits held in banks in the economy.

M2 M1 plus near money, money that can be easily converted into cash or cash substitutes such as money market funds.

M3 M2 plus large time deposits.

Macroeconomics The study of why the aggregate rate of utilization of resources in the economy varies over time.

Macroeconomy The economy as a whole.

Marginal analysis The weighing of the additional benefits of a some action against the additional costs.

Marginal cost The cost of producing an additional unit of output; the cost of an additional unit of activity.

Marginal cost curve The graphical representation of the costs of producing an additional unit of output at every level of output

Marginal cost pricing When price is set such that it equals marginal cost; leads to an efficient level of output produced, where all mutual benefits are exhausted.

Marginal firm The firm which is just indifferent to remaining in business or shutting down.

Marginal private cost The costs to private producers of producing an additional unit of output that does not take into account damages to third parties. See, in contrast, marginal social cost.

Marginal product The increase in output that occurs when an additional input is added to a fixed amount of other factors.

Marginal product of capital The increase in output that occurs when an additional unit of capital is added to a fixed amount of labor and other factors of production.

Marginal product of labor The increase in output that occurs when an additional unit of labor is added to a fixed amount of capital and other factors of production.

Marginal revenue The additional revenue a firm or producer receives from selling one more unit of output.

Marginal social cost The marginal cost to society of producing an additional unit of output; takes into account marginal private costs and the damages production imposes on third parties.

Marginal utility The extra satisfaction or utility that an individual derives from consuming an additional unit of a good. Not taken by economists to be a numerically measurable quantity.

Marginal value The extra benefit that an individual places on the consumption of an additional unit of a good, measured by the sacrifice of some other good a person is willing to make in order to consume the good.

Marginal value of leisure The extra benefit, usually measured in terms of foregone income that an individual derives from the consumption of an additional unit of leisure.

Marginal value of present consumption The amount of future consumption that an individual is willing to forego in order to have an extra unit of present consumption.

Marginal value product or value of marginal product The value of the increase in output that results from adding an additional unit of a factor to a fixed amount of other factors.

Market basket An average bundle of goods consumed by a typical family; used in the calculation of the Consumer Price Index.

Market clearing When the quantity supplied equals the quantity demanded such that there is neither excess demand nor excess supply.

Market demand curve The curve showing the relationship between price and the total amount of a good or service demanded by all consumers in the market. The lateral sum of individual demand curves.

Market supply curve The curve showing the relationship between price and the total amount of a good or service supplied by all producers in the market; the lateral sum of individual firm's supply curves.

Market economy An economy whereby resources are allocated by the interactions of households and firms in markets, as opposed to resource allocation by central planning and command.

Market equilibrium The price and quantity at which the quantity demanded of a good by all consumers in the economy equals the quantity supplied by all producers in the economy.

Market value of life The value of human life measured by the amounts people accept in compensation for a higher probability of death.

Market wage The wage that people actually pay or receive for services they perform.

Maximizing or economic behavior When individuals strive to mitigate adverse consequences and exploit beneficial consequences of changes in the constraints they face.

Median voter The voter whose preferences are in the middle of the political spectrum.

Merger The combining of several firms, in either a vertical or horizontal way.

Microeconomics The field in economics which deals with individual decision makers, particularly consumers and firms and their responses to changes in laws, the invention of new technologies, changes in the availability of resources and the like.

Middleman or intermediary The go-between consumer and producer.

Minimum wage A wage set by legislation, usually above the market wage for some generally less skilled workers.

Mixed economy An economy that allocates resources by some combination of government decree and market mechanism.

Model See economic model.

Moderately concentrated industry Industries with a Herfindahl-Hirschman index (HH) above 1,000 but below 1,800.

Money Anything which serves as a medium of exchange, store of wealth, and unit of account.

Money demand The amount of money consumers in the economy desire to hold. The demand for money is inversely related to the nominal rate of interest (the opportunity cost of holding money) and directly related to an individual's income.

Money market mutual fund Funds composed of hundreds or thousands of short-term bonds and high-grade (low risk) commercial paper (essentially, privately issued bonds of short duration); these accounts offer interest and limited check writing privileges.

Monopolistic behavior Charging a price that exceeds marginal cost, producing a level of output that is less than the amount which exhausts the gains from trade.

Monopolistic competition A type of imperfect competition where there are many firms competing in an industry with similar but differentiated products and where each firm faces a downward-sloping demand curve for their product, and exit and entry in the industry is unrestricted.

Monopoly A market where there is only one supplier of a particular good. The sole supplier that decides what price to set based on the demand curve it faces and its marginal cost curve.

Monopoly power The ability to set a prices above marginal cost.

Monopoly pricing Setting price by the demand curve above the intersection of marginal revenue and marginal cost.

Monopoly rents The rents that accrue to a firm due to its monopoly position in a market.

Monopolist The sole supplier of a good.

Monopsonist A firm that is sufficiently large so that its decisions as to how much to buy affect the price of items purchased.

Movement along the demand curve A change in the quantity demanded of a good due to a change in the price of the good, *ceteris paribus.*

Movement along the supply curve A change in the quantity supplied of a good due to a change in the price of the good, *ceteris paribus.*

Mutual fund Funds composed of hundreds or thousands of corporate stocks. By purchasing shares of such funds, individuals diversify the risks of purchasing individual stocks.

National income or NI Measures the aggregate incomes of individuals and corporations in the economy; net national product less business taxes and plus subsidies.

National income accounting The procedure for the measurement of important statistics of the economy's performance over a given year.

National Income Accounts The statistics that comprise the measurement of the gross national product.

National Labor Relations Act or Wagner Act of 1935 Required employers to bargain "in good faith" with unions and forbade employer interference with union organizing.

National Labor Relations Board Set up by the National Labor Relations (Wagner) Act to monitor employer and union activities and unionization elections, and to investigate alleged "unfair labor practices."

National saving That part of national income that is not consumed; the combined savings of the individuals in a nation.

Natural rate of unemployment or full employment That level of unemployment which the economy tends to in the long run, consisting of only frictional and structural components.

Near money Funds such as savings accounts and money market funds that are close substitutes for cash, that is, they can be easily converted into cash.

Need That which does not present an alternative to an individual other than death.

Negative slope When the ratio of the change in price to change in quantity is negative, that is, the changes are in the opposite direction.

Neoclassical economics The school of thought in economics that first incorporated marginal analysis. Its principal early architect was English economist Alfred Marshall, who first published his *Principles of Economics* in 1890.

Net national product or NNP Gross national product less capital consumption (depreciation) allowance.

Net worth The difference between assets and liabilities.

Neutral inflation When all prices including wages rise by the same proportion, so that no relative price changes.

New Keynesian economics The school of thought in economics built on the Keynesian tradition focusing on the failure of wages and prices to adjust to clear the labor market.

No fault divorce The situation where either spouse can terminate the marriage contract unilaterally, without the agreement of the other or establishment of any party's wrongdoing.

Nominal Not adjusted for inflation or changes in the general price level, for example, nominal price, nominal wage, nominal interest rate.

Nominal interest rate The return to saving or the cost of borrowing without any adjustment for inflation; by the Fisher equation, the nominal interest rate equals the sum of the real interest rate and the anticipated rate of inflation.

Noncooperative outcome The result when individuals take only their self-interest into account and behave opportunistically, not collaborating with other individuals.

Non-economic behavior Behavior that violates the behavioral postulates.

Noninferior or normal good A good for which the demand increases as income increases and vice-versa.

Non-pecuniary Not involving money.

Nonprice competition Competition on the basis of something other than price, such as quality of service.

Nonprice rationing The allocation of a fixed amount of goods or services to individuals by some means other than charging a price, for example, a lottery, waiting in line.

Nonrenewable resources Resources that once used up cannot be replaced, such as coal and oil.

Nonreplicable resources Resources that cannot be reproduced with new units of the same efficiency.

Nonrival in consumption A characteristic of a public good that one individual's consumption of the good does not detract from anyone else's consumption of the good. Prominent examples are national defense and uncrowded freeways.

Nonwage income Earnings that are received from an activity other than participation in the labor force, typically, from working in the home.

Non-zero sum game A game where the sum of the payoffs does not equal zero, that is, where mutual benefits and losses are possible.

Normal or noninferior good A good for which the demand increases as income increases and vice-versa.

Normal profit The zero economic profit that accrues to firms in a competitive market.

Normative statement A statement of what ought to be; a value judgment.

Norris-Laguardia Act of 1932 Federal law which prohibited yellow dog contracts and other anti-union activities of employers.

Occupational licensure Laws requiring a person or business to have a government granted (usually state government) license in order to practice some business, for example law and medicine.

Oligopoly A form of imperfect competition where there are only a few firms in the industry, some or all of which can influence the market price.

Open Market Committee see Federal Open Market Committee.

Open market operation The purchase or sale of U.S. Treasury Bonds by the Fed in order to change the money supply.

Operational significance An interpretation of a phenomenon in terms of some observable action.

Opportunistic behavior Acting so as to make a short run gain, ignoring possible long term benefits of cooperation with others.

Opportunity cost or alternative cost Synonymous with cost. The highest valued option which is foregone when an action or decision is undertaken.

Organization of Petroleum Exporting Countries or OPEC The most famous cartel of recent times, composed mainly of Middle Eastern countries and Venezuela.

Output The new good resulting from the combined actions of inputs; goods and services which are more useful, that is, more highly valued to consumers than the total of the input values in their raw state.

Ownership of income A condition for a good to be private: individuals may keep the income produced by the property.

Pareto efficient or Pareto optimal When all mutual benefits are exhausted; the situation where it is impossible to make someone better off without making someone worse off.

Pareto superior An allocation where at least one person is better off and no one is worse off, in comparison to some other allocation.

partnership A business organization having two or more owners who share the firm's profits and are legally responsible for the firm's debts.

Patent A legal grant of exclusive rights to the production, sale, or profits of a process or invention.

Payoff matrix A tabular representation of the payoffs, or rewards for certain actions in a game.

Payroll tax A tax on wages to finance Social Security, Medicare and other government programs.

Pecuniary Involving money.

Pension Regular payment to an individual who has reached a certain age or fulfilled certain requirements of service.

***Per se* rule** Declares that actions that are construed as anticompetitive without a showing of actual harm.

Per unit tax A tax on each unit of a good or output.

Perfect competition The market structure where there are many buyers and sellers, information is perfect, sellers sell identical goods, and exit and entry into the market is costless. Each buyer and seller takes price as given.

Perfect or first degree price discrimination When a monopolist charges each consumer their maximum willingness to pay for each unit of a particular good.

Perfectly competitive firm A firm which takes price as given.

Perfectly competitive industry An industry characterized by perfect competition.

Perfectly elastic demand The same as infinite price elasticity. The demand curve is horizontal, as perfectly competitive firms face. When price increases just slightly quantity demanded drops to zero.

Perfectly inelastic demand Zero price elasticity. The demand curve is vertical, so that no change in consumption occurs when the price changes.

Permanent income The expected long run income of an individual.

Permanent income hypothesis Individuals base their current consumption decisions on their permanent income as opposed to current income.

Perpetuity An annuity that lasts forever; a promise to receive a sum of money each year for the indefinite future.

Piece rate contracts Payments made contingent on some numerical specification of output.

Pooled data The combination of time series data and cross section data.

Positive statement A statement that is either true or false, as opposed to a normative statement, which expresses a person's value judgment.

Postulates of behavior or fundamental postulates The four propositions which characterize the behavior of individuals: 1. People have preferences; 2. More is preferred to less; 3. People are willing to substitute one good for another; 4. For all individuals and goods, the marginal value of goods decreases, as more of that good is consumed, holding other things constant.

Predatory pricing Attempts by a firm to drive its competitors out of business by selling below cost. Supposedly, once the other firms have gone bankrupt, the predator firm can purchase the victims' assets cheaply and enjoy monopoly profits.

Preferred In the scientific sense, a person is better off according to their own preferences.

Preferences Tastes; unmeasurable influences on the choices consumers make.

Prejudice An inclination or taste for discrimination.

Premium An additional amount paid or charged, typically in compensation for added risk.

Present value The value today of some amount to be paid or received in the future, including the interest that can be earned in the interval.

Price ceiling A maximum price set by the government above which prices are not legally allowed to rise. The most common examples are rent controls and usury limits on interest rates, though the most famous in recent times was the price controls on petroleum products in the early 1970s.

Price control Same as price ceiling.

Price discrimination Charging different amounts to either the same consumer, or between consumers for identical units of the same good in an attempt to increase rents to the seller.

Price-earnings (P/E) ratio The ratio of the price of publicly traded corporate stocks to current earnings; typical numbers are 8 to 15, 5 is considered low and 20 is high.

Price floor A minimum price set by the government below which prices are not legally allowed to fall. The most common examples are in agriculture, where the government agrees to purchase all wheat, for example, that farmers cannot sell to consumers at the minimum price.

Price level The weighted average of the prices of goods and services in an economy.

Price maker A firm (monopolist) that can influence the market price.

Price taker A firm (perfectly competitive) that takes price as given, that cannot influence the price.

Principal-agent problem or agency problem The problem one party, the principal, faces, when he or she delegates tasks to another party, the agent. How does the principal create incentives for the agent to do what the principal wants, rather than what the agent wants?

Prisoner's dilemma The classic statement of the nonzero sum game, where two prisoners are interrogated separately by the police. Each has an incentive to cheat on the other, even though both would be better off by stonewalling.

Private cost A cost that is incurred only by a private individual or firm and not society as a whole.

Private good A good which satisfies exclusivity, ownership of income, and transferability.

Private property Property that is a private good, that is, owned by a private individual who receives its rents and has the right to exclude others from consumption and to sell the property.

Producer tax burden That portion of a tax that a producer winds up paying.

Producer's rents or producer surplus The difference between the minimum total amount a producer must be paid in order for them to voluntarily offer a given quantity of a good for sale and what the consumer actually pays for this quantity; graphically, the triangular area above the supply curve and below the market price.

Production The process of combining inputs to yield goods and services of greater value as outputs.

Production function The quantitative or mathematical relationship between inputs used in production and the level of output forthcoming.

Production possibilities frontier The graphical representation of the possible combinations of goods that can be produced using a limited number of inputs.

Profit or rent maximization The production of goods such that a firm generates the largest rents or profits.

Profits In an accounting sense, the excess of total revenues over total costs; in economics, a return to some specific factor of production or to an owner bearing risk.

Property rights One's ability to exercise a choice concerning some resource freely.

Public domain or common property A resource for which there is no owner. No individual has the right to exclude any others from its use.

Public good A good jointly consumed by many individuals at one time, goods for which there is no congestion.

Purchasing power The quantity of goods and services a given amount of income can buy.

Pure economic rent The return to any factor that is in fixed supply.

Quantity demanded The amount of a good a consumer or household buys at a given price.

Quantity supplied The amount of a good a producer supplies at a given price.

Quantity equation of money $MV = PY$; the money supply times the velocity of money equals total nominal output (income) of the economy.

Quantity theory of money The theory based on the quantity equation of money and the assumption that the velocity of money is relatively constant, so that changes in the money supply lead to a proportionate change in total nominal output of the economy.

Quasi-rent Rents that exist only because of past investments. Rents, which if taxed, will gradually disappear over time.

Quota A legal limit on the quantity, typically, of imports.

Rate of interest See interest rate.

Rate of unemployment See unemployment rate.

Rational expectations Expectations of the future course of the economy based on all information available to the individual.

Rational expectations theory The theory that asserts that individuals use all the information about the macroeconomy and government policy at their disposal in forming expectations of the future course of the economy. The theory precludes systematic error over time.

Ration coupon The right to purchase a unit of a good at a given price, an attempt to establish property rights in the nonexclusive income produced by a price control, and thereby to avoid the dissipation of rents associated with nonprice competition.

Real Used in economics to mean adjusted for inflation, as opposed to nominal. Thus, for example, the real price of a good is its price relative to other goods. If literally all prices increase by 10 percent due to inflation, real prices are unaffected.

Real effects Effects on inflation adjusted variables in the economy.

Real interest rate The premium for earlier availability of income; the nominal interest rate less anticipated inflation and the relevant risk premium.

Recession A period of sustained falling real national product, usually marked by higher than normal unemployment.

Refutable proposition A statement that could in principle be wrong and is subject to empirical testing.

Regulation Laws or orders restricting activity.

Relative price The price of one good in terms of a quantity of another good. Synonymous with real price.

Rent Payment to some resource over and above the minimum needed to call forth production.

Rent or profit maximization See profit maximization.

Rental rate The amount paid per unit time for the use of capital.

Required reserves The percentage of deposits or cash that a bank must keep either on hand or with the Federal Reserve.

Reservation price The price at which a consumer first decides to consume some good.

Reservation wage The minimum wage that employers must offer in order to entice a worker to accept a job or remain in employment.

Reserve requirement The regulation imposed by the central bank which requires banks to retain some minimum amount of their deposits either on hand or on deposit with the central bank.

Reserve ratio The ratio of a bank's reserves to total deposits.

Residual claimant The one with a legal right for any amounts received in excess of the legally contracted debts or liabilities. This person also is liable for deficiencies in amounts received. Typically, the owners of firms.

Resources Everything of value, but most commonly restricted to items which are not final goods for consumption.

Returns to scale See either increasing, constant, or decreasing returns to scale.

Reverse discrimination Discrimination against the majority in the conscious effort to counter past discrimination or bias against a minority.

Ricardian equivalence The proposition that it makes no difference how the government finances its deficit; debt financing is equivalent to raising taxes because rational individuals save to offset future taxes.

Right-to-work laws Laws which prohibit the mandate of union membership once employed, that is, union shops.

Risk The degree of probability of loss.

Risk premium The extra return investors require to offset the probability of loss.

Robinson-Patman Act A controversial antitrust law enacted in 1936 that seeks to outlaw price discrimination by forcing firms to prove that their lower prices are not an attempt to monopolize the market.

Rule of reason A rule sometimes adopted by the courts in antitrust cases which requires plaintiffs to prove that an action is monopolistic, as opposed to a *per se* rule.

Rule of 72 The number of years it takes for a principal to double is 72 divided by the annual growth rate of the principal.

Sales tax A tax imposed on the purchase of certain goods.

Savings The amount of personal income that remains after taxes and consumption.

Scale economies See economies of scale.

Scarce The characteristic that there is not enough of the item to satisfy everyone's desires when the price of the good is zero; for a good to be scarce it must be limited in supply and desirable.

Scarcity The pervasive situation where the available amount of goods at a price of zero cannot satisfy the unlimited wants of individuals.

Search costs Costs that are incurred in pursuit information, for example, in looking for a job.

Second law of demand With the passage of time, the response to a change in price becomes absolutely greater, or the absolute value of elasticity of demand increases over time.

Self-select To unwittingly categorize oneself merely by one's actions or choices.

Seller's surplus See producer surplus or producer's rent.

Seniority A valuable property right, which gives older, more established workers priority over others in employment. Virtually universal in labor union contracts.

Service An activity which others value other than the production of some tangible good, for example, examinations by a doctor, creation of music at a concert.

Share contract An agreement between a tenant and landowner whereby the tenant is granted the use of a parcel of the landowner's land in return for which the landowner receives a share of the output tenants produce on the parcel.

Sharecropping The practice where landowners grant parcels of their land to tenants in return for some share of the output the tenants realize.

Sherman Act of 1890 First major antitrust law in the United States. Declares illegal restraints of trade and attempts to monopolize.

Shift in demand See change in demand.

Shift in supply See change in supply.

Shirk To engage in less effort than that which is agreed upon.

Shortage Continuing situation of excess demand, that is, where the quantity demanded exceeds the quantity supplied. Shortages occur only when the government maintains a price control on some good.

Short run A period of time during which not all factors of production are variable; that is, during which there is at least one fixed, nonvariable, factor of production.

Short run marginal cost curve The graphical representation of the costs of producing an additional unit of output at every level of output, when there is at least one fixed factor of production.

Short run supply curve The supply curve when there is at least one fixed factor of production; the marginal cost curve above the level of average variable costs.

Signal A way of economizing on costly information; a gesture or action conveying information.

Site value of land The value of a piece of land derived from its convenience of location, for example, for its proximity to other commercial activity or for an exceptional view.

Skilled worker A laborer having a special ability or training.

Slope The rate of change along some curve of the variable plotted on the vertical axis in relation to the variable plotted on the horizontal axis.

Social cost The private and external costs of an activity.

Socialism The economic system wherein the factors of production are not owned privately, but rather government central planners direct production and the distribution of goods and resources.

Socialist cooperative A type of firm in which the laborers in the firm collectively decide the activities of the firm, as opposed to an individual owner.

Social science The study of human behavior.

Sole proprietorship A firm owned by a single individual who is the only recipient of the profits and the only one responsible for the liabilities of the firm.

Specialization When individuals engage in a specific or limited aspect of an endeavor.

Specific human capital Human capital that is useful mainly in one occupation, or even in one job.

Standard of living A subjective evaluation of the quality of one's daily life.

Statistical discrimination Discrimination based on perception of group averages.

Stock A physical item, typically capital, as opposed to a the flow of services the stock creates.

Stocks, corporate Shares of ownership in a corporation.

Strike Collective cessation of work by employees of a given firm, in order to secure some advantages to the workers.

Structural unemployment Unemployment of an enduring nature due to changes in the economy, necessitating the retraining, education, or other costly and time- and consuming investments by workers.

Subcontracting Contracting parts of contracts to others; by so doing, firms avoid the costly development of expertise in specialized areas.

Subsidy Payments made, generally by the government, to offset costs so as to encourage production or consumption.

Substitute goods Goods that are similar in use. Two goods are substitutes if a rise in the price of one good leads to an increase in demand for the other, holding everything else constant.

Substitution effect The reduction in the amount of a good demanded when the price of the good rises, compensating for changes in real income the price change creates, and similarly, for price decreases.

Substitution postulate Universal postulate of behavior which asserts that individuals will substitute one good for another, that is, make trade-offs between goods.

Sunk cost A cost which is irretrievable and therefore irrelevant to the production decision.

Supply The amount of a good offered for sale.

Supply curve The graphical representation of the amount of a good sellers offer for sale at each level of price.

Supply curve of labor The graphical representation of the quantity of labor individuals will offer at each wage rate. It is backward bending because at some level of wages, the greater demand for leisure a higher wage creates more than offsets the greater substitution of income for leisure.

Supply schedule A table displaying the quantity supplied of a good at selected prices.

Supply of money The amount of money in the economy created by the central bank, for example, the Federal Reserve System in the United States.

Supply shock Something which causes the supply curve to shift rightward (beneficial) or leftward (adverse).

Surplus Enduring situation of excess supply, that is, where the quantity supplied of a particular good exceeds the quantity demanded of the good. Surpluses exist only because the government maintains a price floor on some good, typically, agricultural products such as wheat.

Taft-Hartley Act of 1947 Federal law which prohibits closed shops and allows states to pass right-to-work laws which prohibit union shops.

Take-over A change in control or management of a firm, typically by an outside party.

Tariff A tax on imported goods.

Tax A charge the government imposes on the consumption and/or production of a good.

Tax burden The amount or fraction of a tax that must be paid by specified individuals.

Technology In a general way, the "state of the arts." A metaphor for the way resources are combined in production.

Teamsters Union A labor union composed originally of people in the transportation industry, particularly trucking.

Tenant An individual who pays for the use or the occupation of land, for example an apartment, but also for the use of agricultural land.

Terms of trade The prices at which goods are exchanged

Theory Assertions or propositions considered to be universally true to explain events and to predict future events under certain observable test conditions.

Third party An individual not involved in a particular contract or agreement.

Tie-in-sale A purchase where one good can be bought only if another good is also bought.

Time deposits An interest bearing account at a bank that matures at some contracted date, often with a penalty for the early withdrawal of funds.

Time series data Observations over time.

Tit-for-tat A strategy in game theory where the action of one player is reciprocated by the same action of the other player.

Total cost The sum of total variable costs and total fixed costs. More generally, the same as cost.

Total expenditure The total amount actually spent to purchase a given quantity of a good; calculated as the price of the good multiplied by the quantity of the good purchased.

Total fixed costs The sum of the costs which occur independently of how much a firm produces or whether it produces at all.

Total net benefits The sum of producer's rent and consumer surplus.

Total product The amount of output that factors of production create.

Total revenue The sum of receipts a firm receives from the sale of output. The same as total expenditure, the amount consumer spend.

Trade Exchange; buying and selling; secondarily, an occupation.

Trade-off Giving up one good or activity for another good or activity.

Tragedy of the commons The inefficient allocation that occurs because common ownership does not provide adequate incentives for individuals to bear the full costs of their decisions.

Transaction Any exchange; a business deal or agreement.

Transactions costs The costs that are incurred establishing property rights over goods.

Transferability One of the three conditions which must be met for a good to be private, namely, that individuals can transfer the property to others at a mutually agreed upon price.

Transportation costs The costs that are incurred in the movement of goods.

Transfer payment Payments made by the government to individuals who do not exchange current goods or services in return.

Treasury Bill A bond issued by the United States government whose term is less than a year.

Treasury Bond A bond issued by the United States government.

Trough In economics, the low point real national product reaches over the course of the business cycle.

Truck farmer Farmers who bring their own produce to urban centers for direct sale to consumers. From the French verb *troquer,* to exchange.

Trusts In commerce, old fashioned term for elaborate and sometimes illegal business combinations.

Tying See tie-in sale.

Tyranny of the majority The tendency of a majority to ignore the wishes of the minority in majority rule voting.

Unconcentrated industry An industry with a Herfindahl-Hirschman index (HH) below 1,000.

Underground economy or black market Exchanges of either illegal goods or those goods in violation of government regulations such as tax laws, price controls.

Unemployment An excess supply of labor, that is, when the quantity of labor supplied exceeds the quantity of labor demanded by firms at a given wage rate. In order to be counted as unemployed in the United States, a person must be actively seeking work.

Unemployment rate The percentage of the labor force that is unemployed; The ratio of the number of unemployed workers to the number of workers in the labor force, the sum of employed and unemployed workers.

Union shop Unionized firms which mandate union membership once an individual is employed.

Unit of account The measure which all prices are quoted; a function of money.

Unitary elastic demand When the percentage change in quantity demanded equals the (negative) percentage change in price.

United States Treasury Department Agency responsible for issuing government Treasury bonds, minting coins, collecting taxes and other related functions.

Unskilled worker A laborer having no special ability or training.

User fee A charge for the service of a good provided by the government.

Utility An ordinal measure or index of the satisfaction consumers derive from a consumption of goods and services. Not discussed in this text.

Utility maximization Choosing so as to gain the greatest degree of satisfaction. Not discussed in this text.

Value In economics, the amount of other goods one is willing to give up in order to obtain some good or engage in some activity.

Value-added The difference between the value of a final good and the value of the intermediate goods used in the production of the good.

Value-added tax A sales tax which is collected at every stage of production where intermediate goods are sold, in addition to when the final good is sold. The tax is levied only on the value added at each stage.

Value judgments Statements about one's own assessment of the desirability of some policy.

Variable costs Those costs that arise due to production and change as the level of output produced changes.

Velocity of money The measure of the number of times a the stock of money changes hands in a given time, typically a year.

Vertically integrated A firm resulting from a vertical merger.

Vertical merger A merger of firms engaging in successive stages of production of some final good.

Village economies Local production in small villages in underdeveloped countries of almost all the goods and services consumed by the local population.

Voting with dollars An imprecise and faulty way of describing market exchange.

Voting paradox or Condercet's paradox The possibility that a changing majority might always prefer a different outcome, no matter what choice is made.

Wage The price, or payment for the service of labor; often, the opportunity cost of leisure.

Wage equation An equation that attempts to predict the wage of a given job on the basis of 1. Personal characteristics of the employee such as age, education and training, union status, 2. Job characteristics, such as job security, the pace of work, availability of training, and, sometimes, 3. A measure of the risk involved in the job.

Wagner Act or National Labor Relations Act of 1935 Required employers to bargain "in good faith" with unions and forbade employer interference with union organizing.

Waste In economics, dissipation of rents, such as that created by unclear delineation of property rights. Also called deadweight losses.

Wealth The net present value of a person's assets (capital) less liabilities.

Welfare A government program to assist poor, unemployed or impaired individuals.

Welfare payment A transfer from the government to poor and/or unemployed and/or impaired individuals.

Windfall An unexpected financial gain.

Workforce See labor force.

Yellow dog contract A contract to not join a union if employed.

Yield The interest return on an investment; the amount produced.

Index